Wooden Dreadnaught
The Biography of the USS YMS 183

by

John Dixon Davis

authorHOUSE

1663 Liberty Drive, Suite 200
Bloomington, Indiana 47403
(800) 839-8640
www.authorhouse.com

© 2004 John Dixon Davis
All Rights Reserved.

No part of this book may be reproduced, stored in a retrieval system, or transmitted by any means without the written permission of the author.

First published by AuthorHouse 06/17/04

ISBN: 1-4184-1244-9 (e)
ISBN: 1-4184-1245-7 (sc)

Library of Congress Control Number: 2004093053

Printed in the United States of America
Bloomington, Indiana

This book is printed on acid-free paper.

Table of Contents

Foreword vii
Acknowledgments xi
Introduction xiii

Chapter 1
The Keel Is Laid 1

Chapter 2
The Launching 11

Chapter 3
Fitting Out and Finishing The Ship 15

Chapter 4
Commissioning, Shakedown and Training 19

Chapter 5
Shakedown 51

Chapter 6
A New C.O. Takes Command 65

Chapter 7
Underway for Assignment to the 3rd Fleet in the South Pacific 75

Chapter 8
Into The Pacific Theater 89

Chapter 9
First Assignment - Tutuila 101

Chapter 10
The Third CO Takes Command 133

Chapter 11
The Fourth CO Takes Command 151

Chapter 12
Preparation For The Invasion Of Japan 225

Chapter 13
On To The Mine Fields of Japan
(The War Is Over, But Not for Mine Craft) 241

Chapter 14
Fifth CO Takes Command 271

Chapter 15
Break Out The Homeward Bound Pennant 289

Chapter 16
California Here We come 301

Chapter 17
Sixth CO Takes Command and Decommissioning 321

Chapter 18
Epilog 329

Appendix A
"Newspaper Articles from The Suffolk Times, of Mattituck, NY" 333

Appendix B
"YMSes, Their Builders and Their Post War Dispositions" 337
War Losses of US YMSes 359

Appendix C
Primer on WWII era Mines and Minesweeping 363

Appendix D
Misc. Items Not In Text of the Book 373

Appendix E
Muster Roll of The Crew of YMS 183" 381

Foreword

When the WWII 50th anniversary retrospectives and celebrations began on December 7, 1991, I realized that what I had always felt I wanted to do when that time came, I would do: that is, I would write down, for my family at least, some sort of record of my part in that war. Even though the 50th anniversary of my direct involvement in WWII would not begin until November of 1992 (I enlisted in the Navy's V-7 program in November, 1942, just eleven months after the sneak attack on Pearl Harbor), I began seriously to gather pictures, souvenirs, personal military papers, maps, charts, flags, empty shell cases for 30, 50 caliber, and 20 mm guns, even one shell case from the 3 inch 50 caliber dual purpose "cannon" that reigned supreme on our forecastle deck. These items were gathered together from various places like desk drawers, boxes (corrugated and cigar), sea bags, shelves in the basement and my workshop.

My wife often mentioned that I had a lot of "stuff" and now that she had seen it and heard stories about many of the items she asked what I was going to do with it. I will not pursue the matter of her concern any further. May it be enough to say that I did have plans for this "stuff".

During this period of looking back to those days, I often talked with close friends who were also involved in WWII. I asked about their writing the memories of their itineraries and in whatever else they were involved. It didn't matter if it was "hot action" (that a relative few were thrust into) or the seemingly unending boredom that most of the rest of us were heir to. Remember, the saying still in vogue today, "double time to get in line and wait," was not the product of fantasy but of grim reality.

I am saddened to report that very few of these close friends had any interest in writing their memoirs. They would say, "I didn't do anything in WWII that anyone would have the slightest interest in," or, "I did write down a few experiences in an effort to write a novel, but those pages (my perception was that there may have been several hundred) shall never see the light of day." I protested that I would enjoy reading them, but to no avail. Others said they did plan to write something so their children and grandchildren would know of their part in WWII, even though it was minuscule and insignificant, and they planned to start on it very soon. I can count on my fingers and toes the friends who said this in all sincerity, but who died before they ever wrote the first word. It saddens me that in all probability, 98 percent of those in uniform in WWII never wrote the first word or even mentioned anything that happened to them during that conflict. There are many reasons for this, some of them I judge to be legitimate. For example when the memories of unearthly horrible experiences are much too difficult to recall, they are much more difficult to write about. Even though fifty years have passed since these events took place, they still leave deep impressions that sometimes cannot be erased even when written about.

I think some of their reticence may result from feeling that since they were not a Sgt. York, or Audie Murphy or "Pappy" Boyington, their involvement was somehow of little worth. What a shame. It was a worthy enterprise to be one of the seven it took to keep one combatant on the firing line in WWII. Where would York or Murphy or Boyington have been without the seven backing them up? Stories many of these "seven" supporters tell would add immeasurably to our body of knowledge and without them we and our children's children will be all the poorer.

Many civilians gave solid support to the country in its time of great need. Most of them were not involved in the black market, or cheated on the sugar ration or claimed a need for extra gasoline where none existed. Many have written about life at home in those years when sons and daughters were scattered, literally, all over this globe. More of them need to do this before they are all gone.

Last, but not least, we need to hear from the civilians who built the ships (you'll learn about some of them later in this book), the tanks and planes. They are desperately needed to tell what was going on where they worked. They are the ones who really made all of the pieces fit, men and women working together, "Rosie the riveter" and her male counterparts. We need to know more about what they did, for it was tough, boring, and fatigueing but excellent.

It occurred to me, as I began to make a mental outline of what I would write in my own memoirs, that few people in the general public have the slightest notion of what I did during WWII. I came to this conclusion after years of explaining that I served on a YMS. "What's was that? I've never heard of those things. What did you do?" Even during the war in the 1940's, a great many Naval personnel did not know what a YMS was, much less what its purpose was. This lack of knowledge was exhibited by commissioned as well as enlisted personnel. My brother, Tom I. Davis, "skipper" of the YMS 362, related the following incident at the close of the war. His ship was one of those assigned to be present in Tokyo Bay for the Japanese surrender. A small vessel, the 362 was ordered to go alongside a battleship (she shall remain nameless) to receive fresh water and food supplies. While climbing the gangway of the battleship to pay his respects to the Captain, he could hear the battleship sailors calling down to the YMS crew "What kind of 'boat' is that? What ship brought you all out here?"

This wasn't too hard to understand, but when the Officer of the deck logged my brother aboard, he said to my brother, "I hate to admit my ignorance, but what is a YMS and how did you make it to Japan in that little vessel?"

These incidents led me to believe that I needed not only to write my memoirs for family members, but to do something to acquaint more of the population with the YMS in WWII and the men who sailed on them. The YMS didn't win the war, but the war could not have been won without them and other somewhat larger vessels of the same type and purpose. The YMS or Yard Mine Sweeper and others, cleared ship channels, harbors, bays and oceans of mines - those of the enemy and our own when they had served their purpose. I do not know of any invasion of enemy territory by sea that was not preceded by mine sweepers clearing the ocean approaches and the shallow waters leading to the beaches.

So my purpose for writing this book is to leave a record for my family of my humble part in WWII. Also to acquaint survivors of the WWII era and those who have come on the scene since with the key part the mine sweepers played in that war.

Last, but not least, this will help to memorialize the crew members, now deceased, and honor those still living, who served at one time or another on that gallant little ship. I have chosen the story of the USS YMS 183 to accomplish this. She was the ship I served on and came to know from the time her keel was laid until she was decommissioned at the war's end and finally destroyed by fire, because she was no longer of use to anyone.

This brings me to the title of this book, Wooden Dreadnaught, The Biography of the USS YMS 183.

There are several meanings of the word dreadnaught. Perhaps the one most people relate to has to do with the British Navy's 17,000 ton battleship built in 1906-07 and armed with ten 12 inch guns and thus having "no fear" of any naval adversary. The other meaning which relates to the one above, but with a more specific reference, according to *Webster's Collegiate Dictionary, Fifth Edition*, is "a fearless person". *(See End Note No..1)*

Now, to be sure, the YMS was no battleship. But she was fearless in the sense that she took her crews into all of the oceans of the world. They cleared the way for invading troops, made the shipping lanes safe from the mines the Allies laid, and those sown by the enemy. These ships, so-called "small boys," were built of wood.

Arnold S. Lott, Lt. Commander, US Navy, has written an excellent history of mine warfare in his book *Most Dangerous Sea,* published in 1959. In the Dedication he writes,

"Mine warfare is a dreary business: always dull, sometimes dangerous, and at times deadly... In mine warfare, men did their duty, men dared danger, men died-but who they all were, no one will ever know. They were the anonymous crews, the impersonal personnel, the faceless statistics-the men without names. To them-the faceless, the nameless, the unknown-this book (*Most Dangerous Sea)* is dedicated." (See End Note No.**2**).

Commander Lott deals with the total sweep of mine craft activity in WWII and Korea and thus did not have the space or time to deal with individual people or ships in any detail. This, however, is not the case with this book, *Wooden Dreadnaught, The Biography of the USS YMS 183.* We will tell the story of this one ship - where she was built, where she went, and what she did under the direction of her officers and crew.

Acknowledgments

The events leading to the production of this book make an interesting story in their own right. As mentioned in the Foreword, I had an interest in this for some time and I began to gather whatever information I could.

I remembered that a brass plaque was fastened to the bulkhead in the wardroom next to the inclinometer. The plaque seemed to proudly declare the following: USS YMS 183, Built by The Greenport Basin and Construction Co., 1942, Greenport, L.I., New York. Two interesting bits of "scuttlebutt" that I heard when I came aboard, in February of 1945, also gave me some impetus and direction as I began to map out my plan. The first hearsay item was that the 183 was the first of a new design or class of YMSes to be constructed and commissioned. The most noticeable external characteristic of the new class was that it had a single smokestack. The older class vessels had two smokestacks. (Many other changes and upgrades in design and equipment will be mentioned later).

The second item had to do with "christening" and launching of the hull. It was alleged that none other than Kate Smith, of radio and music fame had been present, made a dedication speech, and broke the champagne bottle on the bow. (Note: For those not old enough to remember, Kate Smith was the vocalist and radio personality who made the song "God Bless America", by Irving Berlin, the patriotic rallying cry of the World War II era and the years following).

I began with an effort to find someone or some institution in the Greenport, NY area which might have information about those early war years and perhaps about the place where the 183 was built. I found addresses for a museum and a newspaper in the area through the North Fork Promotion Council, Inc. of Southold, NY.

The East End Seaport Museum and Marine Foundation of Greenport provided the document which substantiated the "scuttlebutt" that Kate Smith had indeed launched the USS YMS 183 in late June of 1942. *The Bowline*, a bi-weekly newsletter published by the Greenport Basin and Construction Co., gave its whole issue of July 3, 1942 to the events of the previous week when Kate Smith was present to do the "honors." *(See End Note No.3)*.

I made contact with Tim Wacker, a reporter for *The Suffolk Times*, Greenport's newspaper. After discussing my plan to do a history of the 183, he and his editor decided to give my search two stories, one in late June and another in early July of 1999. The paper's archives produced an article, dated June 18, 1942, announcing plans for the appearance of Kate Smith for the following week. (These articles are printed in their entirety in Appendix A).

The response from local residents was gratifying. Several, now senior citizens, actually worked at the shipyard and helped to build the 183. Others, now in their middle years, were children, and remembered their fathers' working at the yard and some remembered fondly Kate Smith's visit. A number of photographs and narratives were shared.

I want to thank my wife Bettye C. Davis for her long-suffering support, proofreading and suggestions. Other proofreaders include Carolyn Davis, Jim Aycock, Edwin G. Wilson, John G. Barrett, Fred Scripture, Allan McCartney, and from the YMS 183 family, Pete and Charlotte Dill, Walter Weltzien, Bob Clayton, Ken Storey, George Beck, and A.J Richard. Several friends who gave timely suggestions, moral support and answered vexing questions of fact include John J. Baker, Allie Ryan, Joe Schreiber, Jr., Patrick Clancey, Tom I. Davis, George Schneider, Irwin Daniels, Marcel B. Humber, Tom Nye, Lib Orsini, Andy Price, Robert B. Rice, Chuck McKeown, Elmer Renner. Ed Pond, Patrick Griffiths and Art Kosar. A special thanks goes to Barry Webb for proofreading and his interviews with his Uncle "Mo" Burt and his friend Sherrill "Rip" Pemberton in Greenport, NY. A special thanks to Don Yost for his interview with Emery Hanson, and to Emery Hanson himself, the last owner of YMS 183, in Coos Bay, Oregon. Thanks also to Susan Chambers and Jane Gigler of Coos Bay. In Greenport my thanks to Walter Millis, Lisa Richland, Merle Wiggin, Peter Coleman, Steve Clarke, Donald Frederick and his daughter Kathy Geehreng in Maryland, Stewart Dewars, Edward Lademan, Jr. and Mrs. Ida Webb. Thanks to Latitia Upton for information and a picture of her late father, King Upton; to Mrs. Robert Seaver for information on her late husband Robert Seaver, and to Mrs. Rhea Klein for the picture and information on her late husband, Stanley C. Klein, and photos from his collection.

Introduction

"In July 1940, at Roosevelt's recommendation, Congress voted funds to enlarge the navy by more than a million tons of new construction. A month later, the U.S. Maritime Commission was given approval to contract for two hundred new merchant vessels." *(See End Note No. 4)*.

There are a few of us whose memory of those days is still quite vivid. Poland had been invaded by Germany and The Soviet Union on September 1, 1939. France, Holland and Belgium fell in early May, 1940 and the full force of Hitler's military might was directed against the British Isles. German U-boats were sinking merchant ships in record numbers and it appeared that Britain might be successfully invaded and occupied. Britain stood alone while the United States, obsessed with a "head in the sand" isolationism, refused to go to Britain's aid and the U.S. Congress declared, in effect, that this was not "our fight" and "we should stay out of it."

President Roosevelt, however, realizing that it would eventually be our fight indeed, though he could not for obvious reasons say so at this time, persuaded the Congress to authorize the strengthening of our Navy and Merchant Marine, as noted above. A very interesting account of the events of May 10, 1940 and following, which involved President Roosevelt, his Cabinet and others can be found in Doris Kearns Goodwin's *No Ordinary Time*. *(See End Note No.5)*.

In the October, 1942 issue of *Yachting* Magazine, Herbert L. Stone wrote, "With an exposed coast line of some eight thousand miles, containing many harbors and bays into and out of which pours the seaborne commerce so vital to the United States, it was natural that one of the largest (in point of numbers) and most important of the Navy's building programs was that for new mine sweepers, or "sweeps" as they were generally called in the service." *(See End Note No. 6)*.

This building program included several types and classes of mine sweepers, the 98' AMc (Auxiliary Mine Sweeper, coastal) and the 136' YMS (Yard Mine Sweeper) both built of wood. Three classes of steel hull sweeps, designed to operate with the fleet for longer periods, in deeper water and at relatively high speeds included the 180' AM, the 220' AM (Auxiliary Minesweeper) and the Destroyer Mine Sweeper (regular Destroyer fleet types fitted with high speed sweep gear). The histories of the various mine sweepers are important and some of their stories have been written, but our purpose in this book is to tell the general story of the wooden hull Yard Mine Sweeper and the USS YMS 183, in particular.

Sooner or later the reader will ask why the YMS, a Commissioned ship, was not given a name and all other commissioned mine craft were given names. Even the "lowly" 97' AMc, which early in the war was not commissioned, was given a name. What was going on here? To say that YMS personnel were troubled by this oddity is only half of our frustration. One answer that was particularly onerous was that there were so many YMSes (481 to be exact) that it was too much trouble to find names for them all, so a number would have to do. Closer to the truth, however, was the cynical answer that it was a "typical" Navy "snafu". According to Franklyn K. Zinn, former member of Experimental Minesweeping Group One in 1941-42, there is credence in this answer. He writes in U.S. Naval Institute *Proceedings* issue of October 1999, "Never in all my years in mine warfare did I ever hear anyone ask why the sleeker, longer, more seaworthy minesweepers were named yard mine sweepers or YMSs (no names, just numbers), but the shorter, less seaworthy, homelier AMCs or coastal mine sweepers all had names. Of course, the prefix 'A' also was used for Aps, Ads, Ars, and even Ams, to indicate auxiliary ships. For those of you who may have wondered about this all these years, let me elucidate. In 1941 and 1942, I was faced with this question, and being part of Experimental Minesweeping Group One some of this time, I asked the group commander, Nathan W. Bard, why this was so. He told me that in the rush to build sweepers right before and right after we got into World War II, someone in the Bureau of Ships mistakenly had wrapped the specifications for YMSs in an envelope marked 'Specifications for AMCs' and vice-versa. When the error was discovered, it was too late to change this, as they had to get the new ships out to sea. So the error was allowed to stand, lo these many years." *(See End Note No. 7).*

Looking back to 1940 from a perspective of sixty years, it is still "mind boggling" to be aware of the size and complexity of the building program for the YMSes. This does not include those programs for the other classes of 'sweeps,' and there is yet to come, in 1941 and beyond, the gigantic explosion of factories, shipyards, foundries the likes of which the world had never seen before and, hopefully, will never have to see again.

George W. Sutton, Jr., in an article in *Motor Boating* magazine in October 1942 wrote, " After the war I hope somebody will produce an authentic, illustrated book telling the story of the motor boat industry's part in World War II. It will be a massive and exciting volume, entailing much hard study and labor. It was not done last time (for World War I) and that is a pity. Then, however, there was not that much to tell. This time there is a whale of a story and I hope some day to read it." *(See End Note No.8).*

A number of fine volumes have been written about the various industries producing the many artifacts of war since WWII, but I am not aware of a volume that would speak to Mr. Sutton's hope. Also, this story of the USS YMS 183 does not purport to fulfill his hope. This is the story of one ship with some information on the *milieu* out of which she came.

Mr. Sutton goes on to say of his article, "These lines are intended only to give a quick, sketchy picture of the most important part of the minesweeper program, the building of the 136-foot Navy YMS minesweepers, and even concerning these the information can be but fragmentary." He continues, "The YMS minesweeper is the brain child of George F. Crouch, our greatest designer of speed boats, including such history-making champions as Rainbow IV, Baby Bootlegger, Miss Columbia, Miss Syndicate, Sister Syn, the Delphines I to IX, Miss Massachusetts and scores of other notable racing craft. He did not, however, get his experience for designing heavy Navy sweepers from creating speed boats but from his early education in deep sea naval architecture and his 18 years as head of the faculty of the Webb Institute of Naval Architecture…For the past several years Crouch has been with the Henry B. Nevins shipyard, where recently he has been heavily engaged in the building of some of the YMS boats of his own design and for which the Nevins company was for some time the YMS design agent for the Navy. " *(See End Note No. 9).*

One of the real rewards of being in the ship's company on a YMS was the beauty of the "ride." She was really seaworthy, and even in rough weather she rode the waves like she was a part of the ocean. There was no skidding around, or "plunking" into a trough like the amphibious ships were wont to do. Even with the seas coming directly on the beam, her roll was "playful" and relaxed. Most other ships, with narrower widths relative to their length, rolled in a "frantic" way, more like a "whip-lash". The YMS met the next roller head on with a gentle ride up to the crest as if to say, "hey, that wasn't at all bad." Except in really distressed and stormy seas where even the waves did not seem to know from whence they came and where they were going, the YMS rarely buried her bow. I remember only one occasion, in a typhoon off Okinawa, that the 183 took "green water" over the bow. Even those perilous hours were exhilarating, for she seemed to be saying to the sea "You will not make me plow through you for I can scale your crest." And as she did reach the crest and the bow began to drop into the next trough, for a few seconds I was aware that she was perched in a delicate balancing act on the crest of the wave. The bow was momentarily out of the water, and the stern was out of the water. She was literally "sitting" on the middle of her keel. I knew this because the diesel engines suddenly revved up excessively for a few seconds until the ship started "down hill" as if she was a 136' surfboard, and the screws bit into water again. Most other ships would have had to plow through, lose steerageway and fall off to port or starboard and risk capsizing.

Don't get me wrong, there were things to gripe about aplenty (I'll mention some of them later), but the YMS was a Ship and she rode like one and while I didn't know it then, it was due mainly to George F. Crouch and to Henry B. Nevins and to the U.S. Navy for having the good sense to involve these two great ship builders in the design and planning stages of the YMS. *(See End Note No.10).*

The gigantic building program for the Yard Mine Sweeper began in April 1941 and ended in 1945. During that time 481 ships of this type were launched. There were three "classes" or configurations. YMS 1 through 134 had two stacks, YMS 135 through 445 as well as YMS 480 and 481 had one stack, while YMS 446 through YMS 479 had no stack. The engine exhausts of 446 - 479 were discharged through "smoke stacks" in the hull at the waterline. This made them very unpopular when tied up alongside other ships, for the choking fumes could not be blown away as was the case with a smoke stack extending above deck. *(See End Note No.11).*

One of the oddities of this program, and it is probably true of others, is that these ships were not built in the chronological order of their assigned numbers. In point of fact YMS 20 was launched Nov.1, 1941 by Greenport Basin & Construction Co. of Greenport, NY and YMS 1 was launched Jan. 10, 1942 by Henry B. Nevins, Inc. in City Island, NY. *(See End Note No.12).* The most logical explanation of this anomaly is that there were many shipyards, all over the nation, which were given contracts for specifically numbered ships. The point in time the ship was launched had nothing to do with its number, but when the contract was let and the ship completed. [Some yards took longer to build a ship than others]. For example, the first 134 YMSes had two stacks. You would assume that the first of the "one stackers" to be built would be YMS 135. The 135 did have only one stack, but she was not the first "one stacker" to be built, YMS 183 was. *(See End Note No.13).*

This vast building program of YMSes took place all over the nation. There were 481 YMSes built in 33 shipyards from Maine, down the east coast, to the Gulf coast, up the Mississippi River, in the Great Lakes, to the full length of the west coast. The names of these builders, and the YMSes they built are listed in Appendix B. Also listed are YMSes built by U.S. yards under direct contract from our Allies.

Of course, the prime purpose of a minesweeper, is to sweep mines. However, any idea that this was all they did would be to miss their total contribution to the war effort. They did escort duty in between minesweeping assignments. They used their sonar (echo sounding equipment) to detect enemy submarines and when a potential submarine target was located they dropped depth charges until there was evidence that the submarine was incapacitated, sunk or had escaped. They supplemented anti-aircraft batteries on the ships they were escorting in case of enemy air attack and they were available to assist their "wards" in case of problems of any kind, especially in case of damage or possible sinking. Saving survivors from sinking ships was a very important responsibility.

The ships escorted by YMSes included landing craft of all kinds, loaded with the men and materiel for an invasion or back to a rear area after the invasion had been completed. Freighters of all kinds were often shepherded by mine craft. It was not uncommon for YMSes to be used to deliver supplies, mail or personnel in situations where larger ships were not needed or unable to negotiate shallow harbors, or where the distances were not too great. It wasn't unusual for a YMS to tow another vessel that was disabled or to escort the tug towing a disabled ship.

The specifications for the YMS, while very similar, were not always exactly the same from one ship to another. As Fred Scripture writes, "...the design specifications are not universal to all ships built, (as) changes were made to accommodate special requirements and assignments." *(See End Note No.14)*. In general the average of the various specifications that one might find in different publications are those I remember from the YMS 183: Overall length 136'; Beam 24'; Displacement 300 plus tons; Maximum draft 8'; Crew: 4 Officers & 29-30 Enlisted men; Armament: one 3'-50 cal. dual purpose gun on the forecastle deck, two 20 mm anti-aircraft guns, two depth charge racks on each side of the stern and a "K" gun (for throwing a depth charge well away from the side of the ship) on each side mid-ship; Designed Speed: 12 knots (speed was also a function of how much marine growth was attached to the bottom of the ship-the longer we went without scraping the bottom, the slower we were); Minesweeping speed: 9 knots; Engines: 2 GM 500 hp diesels with reduction gears and transmission for remote control of engines; two screws [propellers]; minesweeping generator: 1 GM Diesel 500 hp. The wood hull of the YMS significantly reduced the inherent magnetic field of the ship (as opposed to a steel hull) and made it possible for the YMS to sweep magnetic mines in shallow waters less dangerously than for the larger steel hull sweeps. The YMS (short for Yard Mine Sweeper) was designed to operate out of a Navy Base or Navy Yard; thus the name Yard Mine Sweeper. With a fuel capacity for approximately 1500 nautical miles, food storage for several days for four officers and thirty men, and fairly cramped quarters for all personnel the YMS was designed to operate for several days at sea and then return to base for refueling, etc. before returning to sea again. As it turned out, the war went from our own coast to the far reaches of the world very quickly and we had to use what we had on hand and/or under construction. The YMS went everywhere any other ship went; in fact, a popular motto of all minecraft in general was and is "Where The Fleet Goes, We've Been".

However, the YMS and little sister, the AMc, had to be in the company of larger vessels capable of supplying them with fuel and food on the long voyages across the various oceans. In effect their home base went along with them and they did the job. After the Korean War a vessel similar to the YMS, but considerably larger, the 178 foot MSO, with greater fuel and food capacity, and still made of wood was added to the fleet.

The YMS carried out the four major types of minesweeping of the WWII era:

for moored (contact) mines;

for acoustic mines;

for magnetic mines; and

for pressure mines. Descriptions of these four operations, written with the layman in mind, (the "old salt" will already know about them) will be found in Appendix C.

Chapter 1
The Keel Is Laid

The 28th of March 1942 started out like every other day at the Greenport Basin & Construction Co. of Greenport, Long Island, New York. And yet it was not like any other day, for on this day the first of a new class of Yard Mine Sweeper would be laid down in the framing building. Her keel, like those of the earlier class, would be fashioned from green white oak timbers and secured together by galvanized steel bolts, washers and nuts. The keel of the YMS 31, the last of the 12 "two stackers" built at GBC (YMSes 20-31), was laid on March 16, just twelve days before. Work was well underway on the keel and framing on the 31 when the keel of the 183 was begun alongside of 31. (See Appendix B) This arrangement made it possible to work on two ships at the same time, although one of them was two weeks or so ahead of the other. When the older hull was ready to launch it was moved out to the ways and the one still in progress was moved over on skids in the now empty space and a new ship's keel could be begun. This system made it possible to have two ships in progress in the framing building at the same time. The key was launching the hull as soon as it was completed (caulked and painted and the deck installed). After christening and launching the hull took its turn in receiving the engines, tanks for water, fuel, lube oil, etc., for bulkheads, cabins, pilothouse, and other prefabricated parts. This assembly-line system shuttles the individual vessel around to the various installation points in the basin until it "finally reaches the main dock ready for dock trials, builder's trials and the final acceptance run before delivery to the Navy." *(See End Note No. 15)*

The construction program for the Yard Mine Sweeper exhibited several interesting phenomena. First, there were three distinct "classes" or configurations of these ships. Page xi of the Introduction lists the three classes. Therefore, across the classes there were some interesting differences (even though at a distance they all looked similar). YMS 1-134 had two stacks; YMS 135 through the 400's, except for a few as noted on page xi, had only one stack. There were other differences. Some of these differences were occasioned by redesign as a result of actual experience at sea and some changes were required because of the shortage of certain materials. *(See End Note No. 16)*.

Figure 1 - YMS Construction -Grebe-Chicago – Countesy of Art Kosar

The two stackers generally had a rounded pilothouse and flying bridge. In some earlier productions, as I recall, the pilothouse was covered with steel and the fence around the base of the 3 inch 50 cal. gun on the forecastle was sheet steel. My recollection is that this much metal well above the center of gravity made these earlier sweeps too top-heavy and they often were slow recovering from severe rolls.

The forecastle deck from the bow aft to the chart house was narrower on the two stackers. This area was broadened on the one stackers, which gave considerably more room in the galley and crew's quarters and also much better fairing at the bow. Performance in heavy seas was much safer as the wider bow turned the water away rather than letting it come up over the forecastle as easily. Thus the two stackers were subject to taking more green water over the bow than were the one stackers.

Although I cannot document it, I remember that some of the earlier YMSes had their engines and shafts directly connected. This meant that when the screw, for example, of the starboard engine needed to be put into reverse the starboard engine had to be stopped and started again, this time, in reverse. Apparently later versions of the two stackers had reduction gears and a transmission so that the screws could be stopped by putting the gears into neutral and then reversed without stopping the engines. I observed, on several occasions, a low numbered two stacker coming in for a landing at a pier or alongside another ship, stop its engines and then start them up in reverse so that they were slowed down and could make the landing as "softly" as possible. Every now and then, however, when they tried to start the engines in reverse, they did not start immediately and the YMS did not have, to say the least, a soft landing. Sometimes damage was done to both parties.

Figure 2 - YMS Construction -Grebe-Chicago – Courtesy of Art Kosar

The April, 1944 issue of *Motor Boating*, carries a story by David N. Lott, Lieut., USNR entitled "Canoe-Club Navy," in which he reminisces on his naval career. One of his experiences had to do with his first landing at the con of his YMS. He writes, "Matter of fact, you feel like an old sea-dog by the time you head into pier 41, in Seattle, to make your first landing. Nothing to it, you reassure yourself. Watch me make a one bell cowboy landing! But-between the cross tide and your port engine failing to catch when you call for full astern-if the dock hadn't been there, you'd probably be going yet."
The port engine failed "to catch" because it obviously had been stopped to be started again in reverse. No transmission, no shifting of gears. *(See End Note No. 17)*.

In many respects the 561 YMSes were built similar at the thirty-three yards where those to be delivered to the US Navy were constructed and the three yards where a smaller number were built specifically for Lend-Lease (BYMSes contracted directly by Britain to American Yards and having no connection with the US Navy). (See Appendix B). They were similar according to specifications for each of the three separate classes as noted earlier. However, while the finished products were similar, the procedures, facilities, and materials varied from yard to yard and in a number of cases they varied widely. There were many reasons for the wide variations. Some of them relate to the location of the yard and its launching facilities, the availability of certain key materials, the building facilities at the yard (whether or not ships could be built under cover from the weather or had to be built outside), the traditional building practices for wooden vessels at the different yards, and the availability of an adequate work force

YMSes, including the 183, built at Greenport Basin were launched when the hull and decking had been finished. This included painting, and according to Monroe Burt, of Greenport, a retired engineer of the work force during the war years, the screw (propeller) shafts were also installed before launching. The degaussing coil to reduce or nullify the ship's magnetic field was installed around the inside of the hull planking and secured to the hull's frames after launching. *(See End note No. 18)*.

Emery Hanson of Coos Bay, Oregon was the last owner of the former YMS 183. He cut the wooden hull into small sections using a chain saw. The small sections were burned as the most efficient way to get rid of the hull. This part of the story will be told in detail in the Epilog. It is mentioned now, because something Hanson discovered in cutting her apart relates directly to her construction. He relates that he found a heavy canvas-like material covering the first layer of planking. This planking was bolted directly to the frames. This canvas-like material was impregnated with and covered with a heavy, white paste-like substance. The external planking was fastened to the hull over this material. Mr. Hanson surmised that the canvas and paste-like application may have had two purposes. One was to give an extra measure of caulking for water tightness, and second, that perhaps the paste-like material may have had a "poison" or chemical deterrent for protection against the teredo worm which infests wooden hulls that are not protected with a copper covering or sheathing. As Mr. Hanson put it, "A teredo worm would wear out his teeth before chewing through that." *(See End Note No. 19)*. In any event, the 183 had this "middle layer" as a part of her hull planking. The teredo worm might bore into the outer planking, but met an effective barrier before it could bore into the inner hull planking.

Figure 3 - YMS 12 - Rice Brothers, East Boothbay, Maine. Courtesy, Robert B. Rice

Donald Frederick, a former carpenter at Greenport Basin and Construction, said that there were 1700 men working at the yard. There were two 11-hour shifts every 24 hours. (He writes later, in a letter to the author, that the eleven-hour shift included a one hour lunch period with a short break approximately 2 & 1/2 hours before and after lunch. In Mr. Frederick's case, who always worked the night shift from 7 PM to 6 AM, his lunch time was from midnight to 1 AM. The workers came from Patchogue, Moriches and from distant East Hampton. Hourly wages, depending upon one's skill, ranged from 72 cents, 92 cents or $1.02. "You had all kinds of broad ax and adz work…there was a lot of hand work. It brought out a lot of boat builders and ship builders. Many of the old fellows, they broke in us young fellows." Speaking of the YMSes he helped to build, he said, "They were top-notch, almost yacht-style. They were sound." (See Appendix A, pp. 3-4).

In Feb., 2001, Mr. Frederick, sent an audiotape to me on which he answered a number of questions concerning his personal activities in the construction. He reports, "I did not directly work on the hull strapping itself, but as I recall it did form several Xes for about the middle half of the length of the hull from the deck to about the waterline on both sides of the ship." (Note: the strapping, was made of a special bronze, approximately four inches wide, ¼ of an inch thick, and 8 to ten feet long. As in a house on land, the strapping was fastened diagonally to the frames before the planking was installed.

This gave tremendous stability to the frames both fore and aft and held the hull together as a unit. Emery Hanson of Coos Bay said, "You could take the finished hull of the YMS without the pilot house, etc. and roll it down a hill, and it would remain intact. They were really built to hold together." [Yost audiotape of Emery Hanson]. Later on when bronze became scarce, galvanized steel strapping may have been used. With regard to the installation of the degaussing coil, Mr. Frederick confirms Monroe Burt's memory that it was installed around the inside of the hull just under the decking after launching.

Figure 4 - "Brand Spanking New" Courtesy, Stewart Dewars

Mr. Frederick reports that the yard had three sets of railways. The largest was approximately 150 feet long (the YMS was 136 feet long). The heavy cross timbers, on which the keels rested, were on wooden tracks which extended well out into the harbor. The largest set of ways was floored over and a large steel building was built right over the top of everything. This was the ways on which the hull of 183 was built before launching. The other ships were built in a building adjacent to the carpenter's shop. Two ships were built side by side in this building and were then moved out on greased timbers and then sideways onto one of the other railways for launching. Steam powered the engines, which lowered the ships into or pulled them out of the water as the situation at any given time required. When they were in full production there were three hulls under construction at any given time.

Mr. Frederick continues, "Timbers were sawed out and planed by the day crew. My job on the night crew, which incidentally did all of the bending of the frames, was to select the lengths, and cut the bevels on the bottom ends so they would fit the keel properly. Once, so prepared, I selected four pieces per frame, numbered them and placed them in the steam box for a minimum of 2 ½ to 3 hours. The rule I followed was to steam for one hour per inch of thickness. The timbers were approximately 2 ½ inches thick by 4 inches wide. (The length of each timber was sufficient to make a frame that would reach from the keel to the deck after being bent). The steam came from the same two boilers that powered the ways, the crane, gave heat in winter and powered other machinery. The boiler room was working 24 hours a day. The two boilers were manifolded together, so that they could be run together or separately as when the power needs were less or when one had to be shut down to be maintained or repaired. The steam box was made of wood 3 feet square and approximately 26 feet long. One end was open to receive the timbers; the other end was solid with a pipe to introduce the steam. When the timbers were placed in the box the open end was closed with a plywood door and the steaming process began."

In order to prepare the oak timbers for bending into frames so that they conformed to the Naval architect's blueprint for the ship, there were four things necessary: 1. there were the oak timbers of the right dimensions steamed to become pliable; 2. a mold or template or form of the correct shape against which the pliable timber could be forced so that it conformed to that shape; 3. The power to force the pliable timber against the mold: and 4. Ability to lock the timbers in their new shape, hold them in that shape with braces until they dried and were placed on and fastened to the keel where they became an integral part of the ship's hull. A summary of these steps, as described by Mr. Frederick, is listed here.

Step 1, after the timbers were steamed for the proper time they were removed from the box, taken to the framing building and painted with Cuprinol (a wood preservative).

Step 2 required that the form on which the timbers would be bent was ready to receive the pliable timbers. The form was created by bolting wood blocks to a track fastened to the building floor. The blocks, with space between them, were bolted down tightly, so they could not move, along the curved line drawn on the floor. Therefore, a timber would end up having the same curvature as the blocks along the line. Two timbers, each 2-½ inches thick and 4 inches wide, were placed side by side against the first block. This made the frame to be bent 5 inches thick and 4 inches wide, but since the 5 inch thickness was actually two 2 ½ inch pieces, it was easier to bend than one 5 inch piece. The two 2 ½ inch pieces were bent together, and even though they were side by side they bent as separate elements since they were not yet fastened together. Later they would be fastened together with locust dowels. Their beveled ends, to match the keel, rested against the first block. This end was secured with a chain to hold it in place when the bending process began. An iron strap was placed on the outside of and against the timber, and it ran from the beveled end to the top end of the timber. At the top, a chain was fastened to a block and tackle, which was used to pull the top end of the timber up to the wooden block, which represented the deck level of the hull.

Step 3 involved the block and tackle arrangement for pulling the timbers up against the blocks. This was done slowly so as not to splinter or crack the doubled timber as it was being forced into its new shape. Mr. Frederick says, "We never allowed a splintered or cracked timber to be used in a frame. In fact", he continues, "we only had one to splinter, and only a few to crack. The cracked ones were the result of bending too quickly. I always had several spare timbers steamed and ready to use in case they were needed."

Step 4 had to do with the procedure for keeping the doubled timber in its new shape. As the timber was pulled (the power coming from the block and tackle at the top of the frame) snugly up to each wooden block bolted to the floor track, the timber was immediately clamped to that block. This prevented any further movement of the timber from the clamp down to the beveled end at the keel position. The clamping continued as the timber was drawn against each block, in turn, until the top end of the timber was clamped to the top block. After the clamps were all in place, a half inch hole was drilled through the two timbers, every four to five feet, and a half inch locust dowel was driven into the hole until the end was flush with the other side. Each end of the dowel was then split and a wedge driven in to lock the dowel into place. This prevented any creeping or separation of the dowels backing out. The two 2 ½ inch timbers became one timber in every sense of the word and more so as they dry and shrink, drawing more tightly together.

When the first side of the frame was bent, clamped to the wooden blocks, and locked with the locust dowels, the same process was repeated on the other side. When this side was bent and finished, a complete frame was done except for adding bracing to hold both sides together. The bracing was made of stout timber, probably like the 2 ½ x 4 inch stock used in the frames. The top brace ran from one side to the other at the point, which would be the deck level when the frame was positioned on the keel. This piece had to be at least 24 feet in length, as this was the approximate width of the hull at deck level. After this piece was lag bolted to the frame at each end, another timber of approximately the same length was placed across the frame, from one side to the other, at the level of the waterline and lag bolted to the frame. Two more timbers were placed diagonally from near the middle of the "deck line timber" to either side of the frame. They were lag bolted to the frame between the keel bevels and the horizontal water line brace. The diagonal braces were then lag bolted to each other where they crossed each other and to the water line brace.

This made for an absolutely rigid frame, which could not be moved out of shape. At this point the clamps, block and tackle, chains, iron strap, etc. were removed and the wooden guide blocks unbolted and disengaged from the frame. The entire frame was then lifted up and moved to the hull of the ship under construction and set in place on the keel. Mr. Frederick says, "This process (after the timbers were steamed and ready for bending) rarely took more than ½ to ¾ of an hour, when everybody cooperated. When one completed frame was moved away, the guide blocks were reset and a new frame was begun."

I had asked Mr. Frederick about other aspects of the work on the hulls of the YMSes, including planking and painting before launching. He said, "I did not have anything to do with the actual planking itself. It was done by several gangs, usually a pair to a gang. On the night shift we had two, two man gangs which did practically nothing but planking. I don't know how many on the day crew worked on planking, but there were probably several gangs as they had many more men than we did. The planking was done from the deck down and the keel up meeting about at the waterline. The last plank applied, of course, was called the "shutter." The planking was double. The inner layer was a full one-inch thick fir fastened with 3 inch ringed Monel (a special metal similar to nickel) fastenings similar to large nails. The outer plank, a full two-inch thick fir, was applied so that the seam centered on the center of the inner plank so that there were no seams on top of seams, but were staggered. The outer planking was fastened to the oak frames with galvanized 3/8 inch diameter bolts, the holes for which were drilled through the two layers of planking (3 inches) and the frame (5 inches). The bolts were as long as they needed to be, but probably averaged 9 inches in length. They were secured on the inside of the frame with galvanized washers and nuts. The planking, both inner and outer, was all clear fir. Usually two planking crews prepared the planking and the less experienced men did the hanging (nailing and bolting) of the planks. It was a continuous process, going all the time, like an assembly line. The inner planking was brought together tight and only the outer planking and the deck had to be caulked. For caulking they ran one thread of cotton plus one layer of oakum outside of the cotton. Then the seams were painted with red lead and puttied making a smooth surface. The painting was all done on the hulls before launching, mostly sprayed on. It was fast drying, probably prepared with alcohol rather than turpentine. Copper paint was used on the bottom." (See Appendix D for other comments by Mr. Frederick).

Now the ship, still very much unfinished, was ready for christening and launching. In the case of the 183, her keel was laid on March 28, 1942. The hull was ready for christening and launching on June 25, 1942. The ship was completed and handed over to the Navy for commissioning January 14, 1943. This is roughly nine plus months, from start to finish (including sea trials, etc.) The USS YMS 183 was commissioned January 15, 1943. (See Appendix B).

One of the important differences in some of the other yards was the virtual completion of the ship before launching. This in all probability resulted in a longer net construction time since any incidental delay in getting parts, etc. stopped work on the whole ship. It is interesting to note the differences in total construction time per ship in the different yards. They range from five months, in the case of YMS 10, built by Henry B. Nevins, City Island, NY, to near eighteen months in the case of YMS 15, built by Rice Brothers Corporation, East Boothbay, Maine. It should be noted that not all the YMSes built by Nevins were completed and commissioned in five months, nor did it take eighteen months to complete all of the vessels built by Rice Brothers. (Note: anyone interested in compiling the list of construction times for any and/or all of the YMSes can easily do so using the list from the *Dictionary Of American Fighting Ships, Vol. V* which can be found in Appendix B). Peter Elliott observes that fast building times were, more often than not, dependent "on the achievements of individual yards, rather than on mass-production assembly lines, when building this specialized type of vessel. The whole programme was carried out under great pressure, and the results by any standards were most remarkable." *(See End Note No. 20)*.

Other interesting variations between the practices of the many yards constructing YMSes have to do with launching the hull and/or the nearly completed vessel or the completed ship. Different yards had completely different schedules. Many of the yards in the Great Lakes Area launched their YMSes sideways. Perhaps most of the yards across the nation launched their "progeny" stern first on a boat ways. C. Sherman Hoyt, Lt. Commander, USN, in an article he wrote for *YACHTING,* in June, 1942, describes "the rough-looking but normal lake practice of introducing a ship to her natural element by dunking her in sidewise with a hell of a drop, list and splash. I have never gotten quite used to it but it works well, it is cheaper and, if generally adopted, budding naval architects would be spared many weary hours in working out all the intricacies of the necessary launching calculations." *(See End Note No.21)*. Another factor to be considered where the vessel was launched into fresh water, as around the Great Lakes and the upper reaches of the Mississippi and other rivers, was the freezing of the water for varying periods of time during the winter months. This "stoppage" had to be factored in where delivery schedules and sea trials had to be reckoned with.

Regarding ships built and launched on fresh water, the author remembers hearing a tale of woe from another sea dog whose ship was built on one of the Great Lakes. It seems that all of the tests, etc. had been passed with flying colors during the months of builder's trials, sea trials and Navy trials. The ship was commissioned and began her journey through Chicago, into and down the Mississippi to the Gulf of Mexico and to wherever. It didn't occur to anyone that they never needed to fill their fresh water tanks when stopping along the way for diesel fuel and other supplies. The "light bulb" came on as they first came into brackish water and then pure salt water. A quick check by the engineers revealed that the fresh water tank intakes had been bypassed and the water the vessel was floating in at any given moment (plus their own sewage) was pumped in and distributed to the galley, drinking fountains, lavatories etc. Needless to say the Navy and the builder (whom I do not know) heard tell of this.

Among the various launching methods employed by different yards, sidewise, and stern first, is yet another employed by Associated Shipbuilders of Seattle. Sutton reports, "They build the sweeps on a level pier, and when the hull is complete, skid them onto a floating dry-dock and launch them by sinking the dry-dock." *(See End Note No.22)*.

The availability and type of materials needed for the construction of the YMS resulted in certain variations. For example, there were large forests of white oak in the eastern part of the country; consequently, many of the sweeps built in this area had a reasonable supply of this excellent wood for wooden ship construction of keels, frames and inner hull planking. This was not the case on the west coast. However, as George W. Sutton, Jr. reports, "...Pacific Coast builders are extremely fortunate. This is in having available a great supply of fine timber in long lengths. At the Astoria Marine Construction Company (Astoria, Oregon), for example, the keels are full length fir, worked from 12 by 24 inch timbers 110 feet long…From its first YMS keel, which was cut from the 120-foot spar log, it managed to save…" *(See End Note No.23)*. Regarding the YMS construction at Astoria Marine, Sutton writes, "The vessels are about 98 percent complete (all the work having been done while under a building

Figure 5 - Shakedown

shed) when launched and require only the installation of rigging and final aligning of engines before trials, which are held within two weeks of launching." *(See End Note No.24)*.

The foregoing gives a picture of the variety of construction, launching, etc., practices employed from yard to yard. The ultimate result was a product that was so similar as to be almost indistinguishable to the untrained eye.

Employment practices, relations with local Draft Boards, availability of trained or skilled labor, or the necessity to establish training schools for the untrained, housing for workers, etc. all were involved in different ways from yard to yard. Our ultimate purpose does not allow going into these matters in any detail. However, many of the yards, if not all, incorporated a number of activities designed to give positive diversions to their employees. This was particularly true of Greenport Basin and Construction.

Avery W. Smith, of Public Relations at Greenport Basin, writes in an article in *Motor Boating*, "In many…ways the company is showing consideration for the well-being and morale of its biggest asset, the workmen. The men get a great deal of pleasure from the company paper, *The Bowline*, which is edited by the company Public Relations office with the aid of the men who contribute their thoughts and ideas. The paper is given out to the men in the yard twice a month. In addition to this," Mr. Smith continues, "the company also sponsors a 35 piece military band, a baseball team, a softball league, and plans this winter (1942-43) to sponsor a yard bowling league of about sixteen teams. Members of the night shift, who rarely are able to see a show, were recently entertained by a Broadway Preview during their lunch hour." [Note: according to Donald Frederick his lunch hour was from midnight until 1 AM]. *(See End Note No.25)*.

Sherrill "Rip" Pemberton was the sign painter at GBC, Art Editor and Cartoonist for *The Bowline*. He reported to Barry Webb, nephew of Monroe Burt, in a taped interview in August 2000, that the band at GBC had a professional conductor. Sherrill said, "I believe this band was the best one Greenport ever had. Membership in the band was not restricted to GBC employees and we played for launchings and at other occasions." Pemberton played snare drum in the band and was also a talented pianist. He fondly remembers playing piano at Mr. Tulloch's house at the cocktail parties following every launch. Mr. Tulloch was Sec.-Treasurer of GBC. Sherrill did his cartoons for *The Bowline* working evenings, and while browsing in an old copy of *The Bowline* he was critical of some of his own work, saying, "I didn't put in enough detail in some of them. I was just too busy in those days and didn't have the time." *(See End Note No.26)*.

Looking back on those years it is difficult to remember that this nation was in a fight to the finish with the Axis powers. Literally, to have lost World War II would have changed the history of the world in ways we cannot even imagine. The Monroe Burts, Sherrill Pembertons, Donald Fredericks and, yes, the Ida Webbs of Greenport are representative of the millions across this nation who gave us the tools to do the job. It was my honor and privilege to serve on a stout ship built at Greenport Basin and Construction Co. The USS YMS 183. A Wooden Dreadnaught. When we were finished, she brought us home.

John Dixon Davis

Chapter 2
The Launching

"I christen you YMS 183 and I pray to God that you may always float, that you have a good crew and that you will always bring your crew back to shore safely." This was the prayer Kate Smith, the "Songbird" of the South, as she was known to millions, offered just before she smashed the champagne bottle on the stem of the hull of the YMS 183. Avery W. Smith, Editor of *The Bowline*, the official newsletter of the GBC, writes, "Kate smashed the bottle and we do mean smashed. She swung the bottle just like a baseball bat and when it shattered she got a fine champagne bath." *(See End Note No. 27)*. Sherrill Pemberton, Art Editor and cartoonist, whose "pen name was RIP", caught the "vigor of the moment" in his cartoon in that issue. (The cartoon appears below and is used with Mr. Pemberton's permission). *(See End Note No.28)*. Although it is not stated specifically, it can be presumed that the just christened hull of the YMS 183 rolled down the ways, stern first into the water, to begin the months-long process of completion.

Figure 6 - Kate Smith with Greenport B&CC Officials, ready to smash Champaign on bow of YMS 183 - Courtesy, Stewart Dewars

Edward A. Lademan, Jr., now deceased, was a resident of Southold, NY. His father, Edward A. Lademan, was in charge of the electrical work on a number of the minesweepers including YMSes. Edward, Jr. often visited his father at the shipyard and especially on the days when there was to be a launching. In a fascinating letter to the author in which he reminisces about the activities of his early teens, he writes, "My biggest thrill was when the YMS 183 was sponsored by our most famous singer, Kate Smith. I was on it when it was launched and rode the railway into the water. After the launching I was brought up to see Kate Smith and received her autograph and she sang a few lines of "God Bless America" for me. There was never or will there ever be a singer who can sing that song like she did. This was a special occasion which I have never forgotten and will always remember." (See Lademan letter in Appendix D).

The date for the launching was Thursday, June 25, 1942, in the afternoon. The ship would not be ready for commissioning until January 14, 1943.

Figure 7 - Kate Christens 183 - Courtesy, *The Bowline*

It was a festive day. *The Suffolk Times* in its June 19, 1942, issue had announced that it was originally planned for Kate Smith to have her regular noonday broadcast, "Kate Smith Speaks," made from the shipyard. Her program was regularly heard over 93 stations nationwide, on the Columbia Broadcasting System. However, "circumstances" would not allow this to be done from the shipyard; so the broadcast was to be made from New York City and then Kate and her party would travel to Greenport for the launching. The article in *The Suffolk Times* urged all of the people of the area to listen on the radio to Miss Smith's broadcast on the 25th. (See Appendix A).

In all probability the Navy, or some other agency of the wartime government, would not allow this to be done for security reasons. Radio signals could be picked up by German submarines or other enemy agents, and even the remote possibility of something happening at an affair of this kind was reason enough to disallow the live broadcast from Greenport and the Greenport Basin and Construction Co. In fact, Avery Smith, Editor of *The Bowline*, wrote in the July 3, 1942, issue, "Most of you, I hope, heard her (Kate Smith's) broadcast at noon on Thursday. In this broadcast she mentioned the fact that she was coming to Greenport to sponsor a ship but did not say what yard or the name of the boat." *(See End Note 29).*

Figure 8 - Cartoon by "Rip" Pemberton say it all.
- Courtesy, Sherrill "Rip" Pemberton

Mrs. Ida Webb, of Greenport, who is Monroe Burt's sister, has written a number of letters to the author. In her first letters she recalled the capture of German spies and saboteurs on the shores of Long Island not many months before December 7, 1941, and not terribly distant from Greenport. She wondered if there were others, put ashore from German submarines, who were not captured. (And there may well have been). Security measures that today seem almost ridiculous were very necessary in those war years. She also put the author in touch with her brother, Monroe Burt, and with Sherrill Pemberton, both of whom worked on the YMSes at Greenport Basin and Construction Co. *(See End Note No.30).*

Avery Smith's account of the day's events continues. "Following the conclusion of the broadcast Miss Smith and her manager, Ted Collins, boarded the convoy for Greenport and started out. There were five cars in the convoy, headed by the car with Kate, Ted Collins and ye *(Sic)* editor. In the other cars were Navy men, newspapermen and a car for the Paramount News men. At the western Suffolk County line we picked up a police escort which brought us right through the rest of the way to Greenport. We were met at the school by the band, several of the village of Greenport trustees, a guard of honor from THE YARD POLICE *(Sic)*, a color guard and a great many interested townspeople. A line of march was formed which proceeded down Front St. and directly to the yard. The street was lined with interested onlookers who were eager for a sight of their favorite singer of songs and Kate responded very generously to their cheers and waves." *(See End Note 31).*

These events took place on Thursday prior to the launching of the YMS 183. Kate picks up the story by giving a description in her Friday broadcast over the CBS network. "And now", she said, "I'd like to devote just a minute to thanking the good people of Greenport who, young and old, turned out yesterday to greet our party when we went up to officiate at a launching... I went out there on Long Island to christen, as I told you yesterday, a "wooden ship for iron men"... the men of our U.S. Navy ... and it was truly an inspiring and thrilling occasion. On our arrival at the outskirts of the village, we were met by State Troopers forming a guard of honor ...the Greenport Basin & Construction Company Band also turned out in full force, filling the summer air with the sweet music of "Anchors Aweigh", and "Remember Pearl Harbor" ... we were driven through the streets of the lovely little town in an open car ... and on the steps of the High School, hundreds of school-children waved flags and called out a welcome to us. I can't go too much in detail about all this for obvious reasons ... but I can tell you this - that all the officials and the workmen who helped build the ship launched yesterday were present for the stirring occasion." She continues, "The village of Greenport itself is old, serene, and beautiful. It was founded in the middle 1600's as a small fishing village, with a fine harbor. More than a hundred years ago (in 1837) the firm of Smith & Terry formed a shipbuilding company on the same site now used by the Greenport Basin and Construction Company. Many ships have been built there through the years ... and in the past nine months the company has increased its personnel considerably. Some forty men there have been with the company for 25 years or more ... some of them started as far back as 1896 ... most of the old timers are carpenters or caulkers ... and I can tell you they were very, very much interested in yesterday's proceedings ... yes, it was a great event for Greenport yesterday ... the old shipbuilding town had a big time ... and so did I." And then she spoke her famous lines, "And now, Ted, what's new?" *(See End Note No.32).*

After the dignitaries arrived at the shipyard on Thursday afternoon, and just prior to the launching of the YMS 183, Kate and others took a short trip on the YMS 27. During the trip she toured the entire ship and also handled the controls under the expert guidance of Captain Jim Hardy (a civilian and GBC skipper). *(See End Note No.33).* It is interesting to note that the YMS 27 was commissioned on June 30, 1942 and Kate's "boat ride" on it took place just five days prior. The YMS 27 was obviously fully completed, had passed all her dock and builder's trials and perhaps only waited for the final Navy acceptance inspection which would undoubtedly come in the next three days. It took one day for Captain Jim Hardy and his GBC crew to deliver the ship to the Navy at the New York Navy Yard where she was commissioned the next day, June 30, 1942. (See Appendix B, No. 27 ; No. 183).

Donald Frederick gives his own view of the Kate Smith launching and the events attendant to it. He says, "I attended the launching and we stayed on the dock, alongside the ways where the ship came out. As it entered the water it was not much further than an arm's length away. After the launching Kate Smith and the party and the "big wheels" from the shipyard were driven around town in a borrowed "flower car". The flower car was borrowed from the local undertaker. After that they were taken for cocktails and dinner at a local restaurant. The night crew came in as usual at seven PM and they were treated to a half barrel of beer which we couldn't tap until four AM at which time the stocks were set up and the next keel was in place on the ways ready to be built onto."

Thus this stellar day ended the first major step in the voyage of our "Wooden Dreadnaught". It would be just over 6 months before the YMS 183 would be awarded her Commissioning Pennant, on January 15, 1943, and her real voyage would begin.

John Dixon Davis

Chapter 3

Fitting Out and Finishing The Ship

After the launching the YMS 183 was hauled around into the "wet basin" where she would receive, in an orderly sequence, all of the rest of her parts. She was hauled, (pulled), probably by manpower, to the first stop, and then the second and so on until she was completed.

The wet basin was simply a rounded dock, almost in the shape of a large "C". It was of sufficient size to allow for the mooring of up to six YMSes, bow to stern, at one time, each one receiving the unit or part that it needed at that place. This is called the fitting out process. At the first stop, the hull was secured by ropes to that section of the dock. At this point, whatever part of the ship that was to be added first was added. After this was done, the hull was moved down the dock to the next location, etc.

While the hull was being built in the shed connected to the ways for launching, in other sheds adjacent to the wet basin various parts were prefabricated. These prefabricated items would be ready for placement in or on the newly launched hull at the proper time. This assembly line method proved to be a great time saver for the yards, which used it, enabling them to work on many parts of the ship away from the hull.

At Greenport Basin and Construction as many of the parts of the completed ship were prefabricated as was possible. This reduced reliance on subcontractors to a minimum which was a tremendous boost during this time when many yards were literally competing with each other for the material to finish their contracts with the Navy.

Avery W. Smith writes, "Among the prefabrication jobs which are done here are pilot and deck houses, bulkheads, engine beds, tanks, and other miscellaneous parts...One of the largest single operations, exclusive of the hull, is the construction of the forecastle deck and the pilot houses, made of Weldwood. These are built in a separate building where a reproduction of the deck is set up. These houses are completed indoors and then, when the ship is ready for the installation of the houses, they are set in place with a large crane and bolted fast. Engine beds, tanks and bulkheads are also finished and put into place in the same manner when the ship is ready for them to be installed." (See End Note No. **34**).

Monroe Burt had been a busy man even before the keel of the YMS 183 was laid, for his main job was to make all the tanks for water, fuel oil, etc. from scratch. Using sheets of mild steel he cut the pieces, almost like a jigsaw puzzle, in just the right shape and size so when the pieces were welded together they would make a tank that would hold the water or fuel and not leak. It also had to fit into its own special place. No two tanks were exactly alike, on the same ship. They were not square "boxes" but rather odd shapes, wider at the bottom than at the top, or narrower at one end than at the other, and/ or curved to conform to the side or bottom of the hull. Each tank was especially made to fit in one place. It had to be done exactly right. Monroe Burt says that he got into the tank-building specialty when the person in charge of this responsibility got behind in the production of these tanks and a number of those he had finished leaked. One had 120 leaks, by count. Monroe was a natural born "trouble shooter", and he was moved from his engineer job to the tank-welding shed. He took his co-worker "Old Man Hansen," with him.. [During the time he was an engineer he was in charge of the engine rooms on a number of the small sweepers, AMc's, when they were delivered by GBC to the Navy in New York City. He said it took about 11 to 12 hours to make the voyage from Greenport to the city. After the delivery, the six man civilian crew was either picked up by car or took the train back to Greenport].

Monroe (often called "Mo") and Hansen caught up with the production quota of tanks and actually exceeded it. So now, they not only had the tanks ready (without leaks) but they were ready ahead of time. This was a great time saver, for certain bulkheads and other items could not be put in place until certain tanks had been positioned and secured first.

Some people in the former crew were let go and "Mo" began a recruitment and training program for apprentices from the Cleanup Crew and developed them into welders. Electric welding was in its infancy and the yard that could not train its own sometimes did not have capable welders. "Mo" apparently put Greenport Basin on an excellent footing in this matter.

Inspectors from the Navy, the yard itself and the various divisions were constantly checking, testing, and re-testing all components to be sure they were right. This was also true of the tanks. The tanks were welded together from the inside as well as the outside. They were obviously big, capable of holding thousands of gallons. They had baffles inside to prevent the "free-surface effect". This effect is devastating on a ship, which is rolling and pitching constantly. The layman learns of the "free-surface effect" when he tries to put an ice tray filled with water, but without the ice cube dividers, into the freezer. Almost every time half or more of the water will slop out one end or the other. That's the "free surface effect" and on a ship at sea it is like having a loose cannon rolling around in the bilges.

"Mo" remembers the day an inspector from the Navy was checking welds inside a tank. The inspector, for some reason, became ensnared while crawling through the hole in a baffle. He couldn't get loose and began to panic. "Mo", who did this all the time, chuckled as he recalled how they calmed him down and got him loose. This was no job for claustrophobics.

When it was time to install a certain tank, a crane on the dock picked it up, lowered it into the hull and the workmen then secured it in its own place. *(See End Note No.35)*.

The other components of the ship's fixed equipment were positioned and secured at the proper time. These included the engine beds, the two main propulsion diesels, the magnetic sweep generator and diesel engine with a 2 ton flywheel to drive it, the water- tight bulkheads, ship's service generators, gyrocompass, etc.

Sherrill Pemberton, known to all as "Rip", a drummer in the Company Band, pianist, Art Editor and Cartoonist for *The Bowline,* was also the sign painter for the GBC. He had the responsibility of painting the numbers (and names, if a ship had a name, the YMSes did not) on the various ships. He had brass templates, which he used to trace the outlines of the numbers and letters and then he filled in with white paint. Most of this work was done after the vessel was put in the wet basin. This necessitated doing the outside painting on the hull from a barge alongside the ship. He remembers that the draft markings on each side of the stem were difficult to do. After tracing the number, using the brass template, he chiseled out the shape and filled it with paint also. He says that the YMSes had 110 control boxes and he had to hand letter them all. The use of brass plates for this kind of use was avoided (probably because brass was in short supply). "Rip" recalled that all of the ship's furniture, tables, chairs, cushions, bunks, desks, etc. were manufactured by the shipyard. *(See End Note No.36)*.

The fitting out process continued in its very deliberate pace. Engine beds, engines, etc. were placed and tested. A large crane lowered the forecastle deck (made of 7 ply, Weldwood plywood) to its place after the main deckhouse was lowered into position. These components were built separately on a "mock up" of the main deck. The deckhouse on the main deck housed the officers' wardroom, (with table space for four). There were two staterooms, one with two bunks and one desk and in the Captain's stateroom one bunk and desk. (When the YMS was first designed it was planned for it to carry three officers who would operate the ship out of a Naval base or a Navy Yard for two or three days and then return to base to refuel, etc. It was soon apparent that the YMS would have to travel long distances across the oceans of the world. This unplanned for activity required the assignment of a fourth officer.

A metal swing out bunk was installed above the Captain's bunk). The officer's head (toilet) with shower stall and lavatory was also in the wardroom area. Each stateroom and the wardroom had benches with cushions and storage space underneath the seat and there were very small closets in the staterooms.

Forward of "officers' country" and on the main deck were the galley and mess for the crew, space for tables for eating and recreation, etc. Forward of the galley were the crew's lavatory with shower stall and head. The crew's sleeping quarters were on the deck below the galley and was entered by descending a ladder from the galley. The pilothouse, flying bridge, and the chart house (which housed the ship's office, radio, radar, and sonar spaces) were built of the 7 ply Weldwood. They were finished on the "mock up" of the forecastle deck and lowered into place by the large crane and bolted to the ship.

From time to time, probably three or four times, the hull now closer to completion was hauled out of the water for the addition of and adjustment of various external components like the screws, rudders, etc.

As the weeks moved on and the 183 became more and more like what she was designed to be, another element, and the most important one, began to appear. Personnel assigned to the ship by the U.S. Navy began to arrive. The first to report for duty was J. Madison "Pete" Dill, of Murfreesboro, Tennessee, and date of birth 11-11-17. Pete was a June 1940 Music Major graduate of Middle Tennessee State University. He had enlisted in the Navy V-7 program in the summer of 1941 and was called to

Figure 9 - Builder's Trials - Courtesy, Stewart Dewars

active duty on January 2, 1942. His assignment was Midshipman's School at Abbott Hall, Northwestern University, and Chicago, Illinois. He was commissioned an Ensign in the U.S. Naval Reserve in early May 1942. He then was assigned to the Naval Mine Warfare School, Yorktown, Virginia, in the middle of May and finished that period of training, August 1, 1942. He then received orders to report to Greenport Basin and Construction Co. for service on the YMS 183. (Ordinarily, one would expect that the story would now move on to the second and third, etc. arrivals and a brief resume of each, but this will not be done, because it cannot be done, and there are two reasons for this. The first is, that we do not know who was second or third because so many have passed away from that first crew and many of those few still living are unknown. The second reason has to do with the absence of written records. The ship was yet to be commissioned; therefore, there was no log book recording this information. We do, of course, know the names of all of those who served on the 183 when she was commissioned and until she was decommissioned. These names can be found in Appendix E. Therefore, Ensign Dill is the only one we know of who was involved with the 183 before she was commissioned. He and his wife provided us with important information regarding Greenport, the town, and some of the events of those days.

Pete Dill was in the last few weeks of mine warfare training at Yorktown, Virginia, when he was given five days' leave to go back to Murfreesboro to marry Charlotte Ezell.

Figure 10 - Newlyweds "Pete" and Charlotte Dill- Courtesy, Charlotte Dill

He had written to the author about these early days before his last illness. (Regrettably, he passed away in late 2000). The uncertainties about assignments and timing (a very common problem for servicemen and their brides-to-be in WWII) convinced him that he had one chance to get a few days off. Even though it had already been announced that no leaves would be granted after completing Mine Warfare School, Pete believed that if he could get a tennis game with the Executive Officer of The School he might get permission. As Pete wrote, "I remember playing tennis with the Executive Officer and thinking it would be easier to ask for time off on the court…and it worked."

Charlotte Dill picks up the story here. "After our wedding on July 18, 1942, Pete had two more weeks of duty at the Mine Warfare School in Yorktown. We stayed at the Williamsburg Inn, which had been taken over by the Navy. Upon completion of his training, he received orders to the Greenport Basin and Construction Company where his ship was under construction.

Pete writes, "I presumed I would report to the ship and depart shortly for overseas duty. We had a hard time deciding whether Charlotte should go with me or not, and finally decided to take a chance on having some time together before going overseas. Imagine our surprise that our ship had only recently been launched and I was the first person assigned to go aboard. We were pleased to find that it would be several months before the ship would be outfitted and ready for service."

Charlotte remembers, "When we arrived, we found a very small village with limited accommodations. We registered at the Wyandank Hotel (a summer hotel) owned by Mr. and Mrs. Ansel Young. It has since been torn down as we discovered on a visit there a few years ago. When Pete reported to the construction company, he found that no other men of the crew had arrived. He only reported every day to check the mail! This being a patriotic war, he applied for temporary duty at the communications center, 90 Church Street, in New York City."

She continues, "Our social life (in Greenport) consisted of launchings of more ships in Greenport with a gala dinner at the only large restaurant, Mitchell's, and a few bridge games with Lou and Avery Smith. He was an employee of the construction company. Mr. and Mrs. Snyder were very dear to us newlyweds and we spent some pleasant times with them. He was an officer of the construction company…we were back in Greenport in November, and as the Wyandank was a summer hotel, we were very uncomfortable. So we found a cottage on Long Island Sound, which we rented by the month. Lou, and Avery Smith invited us to spend Christmas with his parents in Southampton and we really appreciated being included. We southerners never felt a lack of hospitality anywhere in our seven years in the Navy." *(See End Note No.37).*

On January 14, 1942, the YMS 183 was delivered, under her own power, by the civilian crew of GBC to the Navy Yard at New York.

Chapter 4

Commissioning, Shakedown and Training

Log of the USS YMS 183.

January 15, 1943

Wnd NW, 2. Or.cast-cumulus. Sea-smooth

1520 - USS YMS-183 Commissioned by Commander H.F Sarre, USN, Assistant Captain of the Navy Yard New York, at berth 18, Pier K, Navy Yard, New York. In accordance with BuPers order 37565, King Upton, Lt.jg, USNR assumed command. Lt.jg Adrian W. Doherty, USNR reported for duty, BuPers order 5775, and Ens. Jesse M. Dill, USNR reported for duty, BuPers order 5729. (The list of enlisted personnel reporting aboard on this date is to be found in Appendix E). (Biographical note: Lt.jg King Upton, the first skipper of the 183, was born Nov. 18, 1909 in Salem, MA. He graduated from Harvard College, Cum Laude, in 1933. He was commissioned an Ensign, Jan. 18, 1941 and underwent training on an LSD in Charlestown for 12 weeks, after which he was Executive Officer and then C.O. of USS Acme, AMc-61, minesweeping out of New London, Conn. During this time he was promoted to Lt.jg, and as noted in the log entry above, became C.O. of the 183. Following his "hitch" on the 183 he continued to have a distinguished Naval career. (No biographical information is available on Lt.jg Adrian Doherty).

1551 - Engines tested - 1/3 ahead on starboard - 1/3 astern on port

1554 - All bridge Tests completed and standing by

1604 - U.S. Navy Tug Tavibo moored alongside; dock lines cast off

1605 - Tug Tavibo + USS YMS 183 underway from slip to East River. 1606 - Clear. 1610 - Midstream; cast off from tug - all engines 1/3 ahead, down East River and proceeding to Marine Basin, Gravesend Bay in accordance with verbal orders of Commander H.F. Sarre, Assist. Captain Navy Yard NY.

1613 - Passing underneath Brooklyn Bridge (Note: slightly more than three years later in March, 1946, the 183 passed under the Golden Gate Bridge on her way to decommissioning in Seattle.)

1615 - Various courses down East River to Butter Milk Channel and various speeds

1631 - Starboard Strut bearing reported to be making unusual amount of noise. Slowed on starboard engine to 1/3

1645 - Abeam of Buoy 7. CC (changed course) to 215° T (True).(True readings are only possible with a gyro-compass. With the ancient magnetic compass the navigator had to compensate for the earth's magnetic field in that locality in order to get a correct course. It was not always reliable, but all Naval vessels had a magnetic compass in the binnacle, just in case the gyrocompass failed).

1658 - Starboard Strut housing noise disappeared - increased speed to 2/3 on Starboard and then to standard - no noise

1714 - CC to 145° T

1719 - All engines 2/3 ahead, approaching Marine Basin

1720 - Num 2 (Yard Craft?) close aboard to Starboard. All engines 1/3 ahead

Figure 11 - 1st CO, Lt. King Upton - Courtesy, Letitia Upton

1740 - In Basin; lines out - Yard Craft swinging vessel starboard side to pier - Stopped

1743 - Secured Engine Room, Bridge, and gyro

1815 - Taking light and power from Pier. Gangway watch set. (Signed: King Upton, Lt.jg, USNR, Commanding). [See Appendix D for instructions for the writing of a proper log]. *(See End Note No. 38).*

January 16, 1943

0000 - Moored Starboard side to, Marine Basin Pier (Gravesend Bay) taking light and power from pier. (Frequently, when a YMS or other small craft was moored to a pier or other vessel capable of supplying electric power this was done to save fuel, wear and tear, etc. on the ship's generators and sometimes so that the crew of the receiving ship could reduce their watch personnel for that period of time. Lines to the pier or adjacent vessel still had to be checked periodically and a gangway watch maintained, but the generator watch could be reduced).

0800 - All hands accounted for and ship's routine in force -

0900 - Workmen from outfitting yard on board, carrying out work planned by Lt. Grim, USNR, Naval Planning Officer at the Marine Basin. (The log does not describe what work is being done, but since this is only the second day of her life as a U.S. Naval Ship there are innumerable details to attend to in finishing the fitting out process. This involves minor, auxiliary, not considered vital, but nevertheless important parts of the finally properly functioning vessel).

1248 - Lt. Comdr. Wright & Lt. Larrymore came on board to see C.O. (Reason for the visit is not revealed).

1300 - Lt. Comdr. Wright & Lt. Livermore left ship

1340 - Received aboard 12 drums of lubricating oil from the Navy Yard New York, weighing 465 lbs. each. (This lubricating oil is for the three 500 hp diesel engines)

1600 - Smith, Sea1/c *(Sic)*, 201-08-87 and Verity, H Sea2/c *(Sic)*, 642-72-30 reported aboard for duty in conformity with orders. (Signed: King Upton, Lt.jg,. USNR, Commanding). (Two things regarding the matter of careful log keeping are noted here: first, the first name of Smith is left out although there is space for it, and second, the rate of each man, Seaman First Class or Seaman Second Class is normally abbreviated S1/c or S2/c rather than Sea 1/c or Sea 2/c as written. Picky, yes, but the entries are not correct. However, the names and rates are correctly recorded on the Muster Roll in Appendix E).

January 17, 1943

0000 - Moored starboard side to Marine Basin Pier - taking light and power from pier & maintaining security watch; Depth - Forward Aft. (If the security watch checked the depth numbers at the bow and stern, which numbers were painted by hand of Rip Sherrill, they didn't enter them in the log. These numbers can be very important. They obviously tell the watch if the hull is taking on water and are an indication of a leaky hull. Picky, yes, but the numbers should have been entered in the log.).

0800 - All hands present & accounted for - Sunday routine in force. Workmen aboard from Marine Basin, work planned by Navy Planning Officer at Marine Basin Lt. Grosen, USNR.

1140 - Ensign Roen and Ensign Underwood came aboard to see Lt.jg Doherty.

1345 - Ensign Roen and Ensign Underwood left ship.

1800 - Checked lines & secured ship for the night. (Signed by King Upton, Ltjg. USNR Commanding).

January 18, 1943

0000 - Moored starboard side to Marine Basin Pier. Taking light and power from pier & maintaining security watch.

0800 - All liberty party aboard, no absentees. Working party from Marine Basin came onboard under direction of Navy Planning Officer, Lt. Grosen, USNR in charge.

1600 - Verity, H.W., Sea1/c [sic] (6427230) and Smith, R.R, Sea1/c [sic] (2010887) reported aboard this ship for duty. Assisted by two Navy Tugs, this ship shifted berth to inboard end of pier. (It is interesting to note that both Verity and Smith were logged in reporting for duty at 1600 on January 16, 1943. Smith had moved up in rate from S2/c to S1/c. Errors of this kind are prevalent even when there is a rated Yeoman in the ship's company). (Signed: King Upton, Lt.jg, USNR).

January 19, 1943

0000 - Moored starboard side to Marine Basin Pier, taking light and power from pier and maintaining security watch.

1800 - All liberty party aboard and accounted for. Working party aboard from Marine Basin under direction of Navy Planning officer, Lt. Grosen, USNR.1235 - Ensign Dill came aboard with Armed Guard escort and Confidential publications from Communications Office 90 Church Street. Publications stowed in Safe. (The YMS was way down the list of Navy ships in the matter of sending and receiving encoded messages. They were in possession of and expected to use, when needed, certain lower order codes. Lower order or not, they were still highly confidential & had to be kept in a locked safe in the Officer's Wardroom. Only the C.O. and the Communications Officer had the combination. Also, when there was the need to encode or decode a message it had to be done in the Ward Room under tight security. Fortunately, being a small craft, and almost always in company with larger vessels it was relatively rare for an encoded radio signal to be sent to a single YMS as the principal addressee. The larger vessels with more personnel and better facilities for encoding and decoding usually volunteered to pass this sort of traffic on to the YMS in such a way that they would get the message in plain language without compromising the code. Perhaps the most important task the Communications Officer had in regard to these Confidential Publications was his responsibility to destroy them if there was any danger at all of their falling into the hands of the enemy. If there was time, they would be destroyed by burning. If there was little time to do this and the water was at least several fathoms deep, the publication bag was thrown overboard. In Navy parlance this is giving it the "deep six". The bag, containing the publications, was always stored and locked in the safe. The bag was especially made, not only to hold the publications, but to sink quickly. It had many ½ inch grommets throughout the canvas which allowed water to fill the bag. The speed of sinking was augmented by a 40 lb. Lead weight fastened to the inside of the bag at its bottom. In addition, the destruction in the water was hastened because the printed matter was water soluble and in a matter of seconds it could be washed away. We never had beverages close by when working with these publications, for obvious reasons. From time to time, certain of the publications would be superseded by new editions. In this case, the outdated publications would be burned and the ashes pulverized and given the "deep six".In the event that the bag was to be thrown over the side the Communications Officer was expected to offer life or limb to see that this was accomplished).

1625 - Food and Supplies on board, ordered by Ensign Dill.

1645 - Tested fire hose and fire and bilge pumps. All in good order. (Signed: King Upton, Lt.jg, USNR, Commanding).

John Dixon Davis

January 20, 1943

0000 - Moored starboard side to Marine Basin dock, taking light and power from dock and maintaining security watch.

0800 - All hands aboard.

1100 - USS YP 249 got underway from along our port side.

1345 - Lt. Upton left ship. (Whenever the Commanding Officer was absent from the ship a signal flag, the third repeater, was flown from the inboard halyard. When he returned aboard the third repeater was lowered and returned to the flag bag. An interested party could tell at a glance when the skipper was on board).

1600 - Liberty began

2400 - All lines secure. (Signed: King Upton, Ltjg, USNR, Commanding).

January 21, 1943

0000 - 0400 - All lines observed and checked at regular intervals. All secure. Moored as on Jan. 20.

0400 - 0800 - All lines observed and checked at regular intervals. All secure.

0800 - 1200 - Regular yard workmen came aboard. Received magnetic cable aboard. (Here is another case when we would like for the log to tell us more, for receiving the magnetic cable is an extremely important event. Fully one quarter of the value of this ship in the war effort is related to this magnetic cable. It would be of interest to know if the cable, already wound on its reel, was lifted by crane from the pier and set into the well prepared for it, or if the reel was already in place and the cable wound on it. This cable, as described in Appendix C, made the sweeping of magnetic mines possible).

1200 - 1600 - Lines secure

1600 - 1800 - Liberty announced, Liberty party went ashore.

2000 - 2400 - Lines secure. (Signed: King Upton, Ltjg, USNR, Commanding).

January 22, 1943

0000 - Moored as before, Marine Basin Pier, taking light and power from pier & maintaining a security watch - starboard to. (Note: Starboard to or starboard side to means that the starboard side of the ship was against the pier or an other vessel to which it was moored. In port side to it was the port side moored to the pier or other vessel) 0800 - All hands present and accounted for - regular ship's routine in force; workmen aboard; work planned and supervised by Lt. Grosen, USNR, Naval Planning officer, Marine Basin.

1600 - Liberty Party ashore. (Time off from the work and routine of shipboard life -liberty - was very important. Usually a ship's company was divided into three groups according to the work they did: the bridge personnel included helmsmen, signalmen, quartermasters who kept charts up to date, manned radios, radar, etc.; the deck crew (popularly known as deck apes by the other rates), headed by the Chief Boatswain kept the ship clean, in good repair, had oversight of the minesweeping gear, ordnance, etc.; the electricians and machinists (popularly known as the "black gang" by the other rates) had charge of the engines, generators for ship's service and minesweeping and main propulsion. In port each group did the routine work required by that group. While tied up at a pier fewer people were needed for routine watches, therefore more people had time for themselves and this included time away from the ship for a few hours for rest and recreation after the day's work was done. Normally, the personnel of the ship was divided into two major groups. One was referred to as the "port watch" and the other as the "starboard watch". These became the "port liberty group" and the "starboard liberty group" and when in port or an area where the ship would be tied up and liberty was possible you had the "watch" or duty every other day. If an individual had no infractions on his record he might have liberty every other day. Each major group could let a portion of its total number go ashore at any given time. Usually liberty ended at 0800 the following morning. If someone did not report present at 0800 roll call they faced possible disciplinary action for not reporting on time. The next time liberty was possible a different portion of the larger group was given liberty, and so on until all had had liberty. Then the cycle would begin again when liberty was possible. Liberty is not leave. Leave involves permission to be absent from the ship for varying lengths of time and is usually granted to the crew on an individual basis. When a member of the crew fails to return when he should he is said to be "absent without leave" or is AWOL. Liberty and/ or leave was granted by the Commanding Officer whenever he saw fit to do so.

1630 - Taking stores aboard. (Food, etc. for the galley, spare parts, etc. for engine rooms, rope, paint, caulking and anything else that might possibly be needed in the days to come).

1800 - Secured ship for night. (Signed: King Upton, Ltjg, USNR, Commanding).

January 23, 1943

0000 - Moored as before taking light and power from pier, starboard side to.

0800 - All hands present & accounted for; regular ship routine in force - workmen aboard executing work supervised by Lt. Grosen, USNR, Navy Planning Officer, Marine Basin

1630 - Liberty party ashore; Smith, S1/c, 201-08-67 detached.

1930 - Shifted berths, towed by Yard Craft of Marine Basin. (Signed: King Upton, Ltjg USNR, Commanding).

January 24, 1943

0000 - Moored as before, port side to, Marine Basin, taking light and power from pier.

0730 - Testing engines.

0755 - All Bridge tests completed and satisfactory; engine test completed. (Note: When preparing to get underway the testing of engines, etc was initiated by the order to "set the special sea detail."

0800 - All hands present and accounted for.

0802 - Underway for Bayonne Degaussing Terminal; verbal orders of Ensign Russell of Degaussing Section, Navy Yard New York and Lt. Comdr. Giradiet, Naval Inspector & Supervisor at Marine Basin.

0803 - Cleared Basin; course 280° T; 1/3 speed.

0810 - CC to 318° T, various courses and speeds to Narrows.

0811 - Held fire drill and pressure on fire mains and hose.

0836 - Passed Buoy 22 abeam 50 yds to port and changed course for channel to Bayonne Terminal

0846 - Entering Bayonne Terminal Channel

0909 - Approaching Degaussing Terminal at Bayonne

0912 - Backing into slip, and moored in Degaussing slip

0917 - Secured Bridge & engine room.

1015 - Degaussing crew passing cable around vessel for Degaussing. (Note: Degaussing is the process in which the ship's own magnetic field is measured and evaluated and a wire or coil carrying the proper amount of electricity so as to nulify the ship's field is placed around the inside of the hull. The ship's field is tested with the ship in various headings so that the optimum benefit can be attained in the protection of the ship from setting off a magnetic mine. Before the process begins all clocks, watches, magnetic compass, etc. must be removed to prevent damage from the Degaussing currents during the test and to prevent changes to magnetic signature of the ship. See Appendix C).

1400 - Lowered Acoustic Boom into horizontal position so cables could be placed around it. (Signed: King Upton, Ltjg, USNR, Commanding).

January 25, 1943

0000 - 0400 - Moored in Degaussing slip at Bayonne, heading 000° M (Magnetic Compass). All lines secure.

0400 - 0800 - Ship Secure.

0800 - 1200 - Shifted ship's position for degaussing purposes. Heading 090° M. Held following drills: fire, Gen'l Quarters, collision, abandon ship. (General Quarters is the drill when there is danger of being attacked by the enemy and/or the ship is standing by to attack the enemy. In this drill each person has a specific station to man and job to do. Many of the crew are assigned to certain guns including the 3" 50 caliber on the forecastle which requires six to eight men to man. There are two 20mm anti-aircraft guns, one on each side of the ship, there are the depth charge racks, and K guns for submarine attack. Special assignments on the bridge and in the engine rooms and sound powered phone operators in various parts of the ship. General Quarters is sounded by the "blowing" of a very loud electric horn, located in various places on the ship where everybody can hear it. When sounded all personel must stop whatever they are doing, wait to be relieved by another if this is required, then run to their General Quarters station. They don steel helmets, life jackets, phones, and any other items required for their job. A designated phone operator in that area reports, when asked by the Commanding Officer's phone operator, that their position is manned and ready. At this point all hands are ready for whatever commands may come down from the Bridge, which is the Commanding Officer's GQ station. The GQ horn has been said by Naval personnel through the years to be able to wake the dead. No one I have ever known disputed this).

1200-1600 - Shifted ship to heading of 270° (M). Later swung again into slip, heading 000° (M), mooring as before.

1600 - 2400 - Took 800 gals of (fresh) water. Ship secure. (Signed: King Upton, Ltjg, USNR, Commanding).

January 26, 1943

0000 - Moored in Degaussing slip Bayonne Terminal, NJ on 000° (M) heading.

0800 - All hands present and accounted for. Regular ship routine in force.

0807 - Warmed up. Special Service Examination, in order that Degaussing Personnel could conduct tests. (This apparently included the magnetic sweep generator).

0952 - Secured sweep generator from tests.

1000 - Made all bridge tests for getting under way - satisfactory.

1010 - Underway from slip to dock at Bayonne Terminal, to wait for supplies from Naval Supply Depot.

1022 - Moored starboard side to

1119 - Receiving aboard supplies

1120 - Preparations made for getting underway

1125 - Underway for Marine Basin Company, verbal orders of Ensign Lees of Degaussing Pier. Advised Lt. Cmdr. Giradiet of our intention to return to Marine Basin. Various courses and speeds to Marine Basin.

1220 - Man overboard drill held

1230 - Entering Channel to Marine Basin; CC 095° T - taking docking stations (preparing to pass mooring lines over to the pier to secure the ship).

1235 - Approaching Marine Basin - stopped all engines
1240 - Moored Port side to Marine Basin, taking light and power from pier
1255 - Swung ship starboard side to by means of Yard Craft. All lines secured.
1410 - Workmen aboard; Supplies coming aboard
1800 - Secured ship for night. (Signed: King Upton, Ltjg, USNR, Commanding).

January 27, 1943

0000 - Moored starboard side to, Marine Basin Pier - maintaining security watch & taking power and light from shore.
0800 - All hands Present and accounted for. Regular ship's routine in force. Workmen aboard executing work planned by Lt. Grosen, USNR, Naval Planning Officer at Marine Basin.
1630 - Commissary Supplies aboard
1800 - Secured ship for night. (Signed: King Upton, Ltjg, USNR, Commanding).

January 28, 1943

0000 - Moored starboard side to Marine Basin Pier - Taking light and power from pier and maintaining security watch.
0800 - All hands present and accounted for - Regular routine of ship in force - workmen from Marine Basin aboard - work planned by Lt. Grosen, Navy Planning Officer at Marine Basin.
2210 - Commissary supplies came aboard. Ship secured. (Signed: King Upton, Ltjg, USNR, Commanding).

January 29, 1943

0000 - Moored starboard side to Marine Pier, taking light and power from pier. Maintaining Security watch.
0800 - All hands present and accounted for - Regular ship routine in force.
0930 - De-energised "Mike" coil - Degaussing personnel from Marine Basin making alteration on control panel. (The recent days spent at the Degaussing Terminal were for the purpose of reducing the inherent or natural magnetic field of the YMS Once its natural magnetic "signature" had been determined, the degaussing experts determined how much current and in which coils this current was constantly needed to reduce the magnetic field of the 183 to its minimum. This, of course, was absolutely necessary for protection from magnetic mines. The degaussing coil was installed in the hull when the ship was under construction. Even though YMSes were very similar, it is doubtful that any two had the same magnetic "signature". Therefore, each one had to be tested to find its own unique "signature" and have its own prescription determined for reducing that signature to a minimum) (See 1015 hours above).
1130 - Members of Trial Board and representatives of Greenport Basin and Const. Co. on board. Last members of Trial Board left ship after inspection..(Acceptance trials are required by law so that it can be determined whether or not the contractor, here, Greenport Basin and Construction Co., has fulfilled the contract with the Navy and produced a ship that is acceptable in all respects. The trials are conducted so that any "weaknesses, defect, failure, breaking down, or deterioration, other than that due to fair wear and tear, through fault of the contractors, and which have not been corrected and made good by them," may be revealed. This is "for the purpose of furnishing accurate information for use in determining final settlement with the contractors for the cost of the vessel.") *(See End Note No.39)*.
1815 - Commissary stores brought on board. (Signed: King Upton, Ltjg, USNR, Commanding).

John Dixon Davis

January 30, 1943

0000 - Moored starboard side to pier at Marine Basin, taking power from pier. Maintaining security watch.
0800 - All hands present - regular routine - Marine Basin workmen aboard.
1240 - Started general drills - Fire and General Quarters.
1251 - Secured from drills
1600 - Supplies brought aboard. (Signed: King Upton, Ltjg, USNR, Commanding).

January 31, 1943

0000 - Moored starboard side to - Marine Basin Pier - taking light and power from pier and maintaining Security watch.
0800 - All hands present and accounted for. Regular Sunday routine in force.
1600 - Fueling - 2400 gals of Diesel oil taken aboard.
1800 - Secured ship for night and checked all lines.
1815 - McDaniels, C.F., MM2/c, detached: authority form G, to Brooklyn Naval Hospital. (Signed: King Upton, Ltjg, USNR).

February 1, 1943

0000 - Moored starboard to, Marine Basin Pier - taking light & power from Pier & maintaining a Security watch.
0800 - All hands present and accounted for. Working party aboard from Marine Basin, work supervised by Lt.jg Grosen, USNR, Navy Planning Officer at Marine Basin.
1603 - Supplies coming aboard - Commissary
1800 - Secured ship for the night. (Signed: King Upton, Ltjg, USNR, Commanding).

February 2, 1943

0000 - Moored starboard side to - Marine Basin Pier - Taking light and power from pier - Maintaining Security Watch.
0800 - All hands present & accounted for. Ship's routine in force - Workmen on board from Marine Basin executing work supervised by Ltjg Grosen, Navy Planning Officer at Marine Basin.
1530 - Received aboard contents of NY Ny Yd (New York Navy Yard) movies 609202 & 609203.
1600 - Degaussing Tests completed. Mike Coil energized at 13 amps. - Instructed to keep current on coil at 13 amps at all times by Personnel from Degaussing Section Ny Yd NY. (Apparently the bulk of iron and/or steel items, guns, engines, sweep gear, etc. all items that would affect the magnetic signature of the 183 have been in place since the degaussing procedures began. In order for the signature (sometimes called the magnetic profile) to be maintained at its minimum level, the degaussing coil must have 13 amps of direct current coursing through it at all times. If this is not done the magnetic profile of the 183 will be such as to put her in greater danger of triggering a magnetic mine close to or under the ship. The Electrician's Mate is charged with maintaining the proper amperage and checking same every four hours, everyday for as long as the ship is a U.S. Navy minesweeper).
1800 - Made ship secure for night. (Signed: King Upton, Ltjg, USNR, Commanding).

February 3, 1943

0000 - Moored starboard side to Marine Basin Pier; taking light and power from pier; maintaining a security watch.

0800 - (Two men reported absent without leave. One of them returned to ship 53 minutes over leave. The names of crew members charged with offenses will not be revealed in this book).

1700 - Received commissary stores aboard. Present work at Marine Basin by workers finished, plans made to get under way for Tom Kinsville on Feb. 4. (The Marine Basin was in Brooklyn and probably a part of the Brooklyn Navy Yard. Tom Kinsville, the Navy Section Base for this area, was located on the western side of the Staten Island Ferry Landing on Staten Island. The 183 would be based here for minesweeping trials).

1800 - Ship made ready for night. (Signed: King Upton, Ltjg, USNR, Commanding).

February 4, 1943

0000 - Moored starboard side to Marine Pier, taking light and power from pier. Maintaining a security watch.

0745 - Prepared to get underway for Tompkinsville, in accordance with verbal orders of Comdr. Meggs.

0800 - Underway, draft 8' 6" aft - 7' 9" forward.

0857 - Received flashing message (blinker light using Morse code was a rapid means of communication between ship and ship and in this case between shore and ship) from Section Base to moor at Pier 6, North, Berth 4.

1330 - Bridge tests made in preparation for getting underway for Fort Lafayette for ammunition.

1340 - Got underway, Visibility ¾ mile, foggy.

1420 - Tied up at Fort Lafayette, alongside Navy Dock Barge, on Southeast side, portside to.

1433 - Started taking ammunition. One depth charge dropped accidentally. Reported incident to Warrant Gunner in charge. Subject (depth) charge had no extender, booster, or ku pistol unit. Incident also reported to Chief Gunner in charge of working party. Advised no further report necessary. (The depth charges received from the ammunition barge were essentially a steel barrel filled with 300 lbs. of explosive, probably TNT. The depth charge was popularly called an ash can. The barrels were approximately 36" long and 20" in diameter (not sure of dimensions) A round, empty cylinder, about 5" in diameter extended into one end of the barrel for 18 inches. After the charges are placed in their racks on the port and starboard sides of the fantail or stern they were prepared for use against submarines. So the dropped charge was not really a danger. TNT is very stable and can stand a lot of bumping around without exploding. Once the ash cans are in place, the Gunner's Mate inserts the detonator in the cylinder. When activated, the detonator actually causes the TNT to explode. Until the detonator is activated, the main charge is relatively benign. In order to activate the detonator, causing the whole charge to explode, the Gunner's Mate must insert the booster, which is sensitive to water pressure and can be set to activate the detonator at a pre-selected water depth. For example, if the pre-set depth is 50', the depth charge must sink to 50' below the surface before the detonator is activated and the charge explodes. If the bottom of the ocean in this example is only 40' deep and the depth charge comes to rest on the bottom at 40' it will not explode, because the detonator was set to activate at 50'. When the depth charge is sitting in the rack on which it rolls off the stern of the ship into the water, it cannot explode unless it is set for a certain depth and the locking pin is removed. No matter what happens, if the locking pin is not removed it is impossible for water pressure or anything else to cause it to explode. The locking pin is never removed until the depth charge is to be dropped immediately. If there is a delay, the pin is placed in lock position. This protects the ship and crew from being blown up in case the ship is sinking. If the locking pin is in place, the depth charge cannot explode. In addition to rolling the depth charges off the stern to sink a submarine a depth charge could be hurled off either side of the ship by means of a K Gun. The same settings are needed to be made and if the locking pin was not removed the depth charge could not explode).

1725 - Underway for Tompkinsville

1815 - Docked port sided to Pier 6, Berth 4, Tompkinsville. Ship secured for night. (Signed: King Upton, Ltjg, USNR, Commanding).

February 5, 1943

0000 - Moored as before, Port side to, Pier 6, USN Section Base, Tom Kinsville.

0400 - (One man) reported on board, 44 hours over leave.

0845 - Tested engines & made Bridge tests. (A YMS could get under way in a relatively short time if the main engines were already heated up. Usually it took about 30 minutes to warm them up sufficiently to run well without the danger of them not responding to a call for full speed by choking down. When the engines were warmed up and just prior to getting under way, the remote controls for the engines were tested. On the 183 these controls were on the (port) left side of the helm (steering wheel) at the front of the pilot house. They consisted of two brass cabinets, side by side and bolted to the deck. The remote control cabinet on the left was for the port engine and the cabinet next to it to the right of it was for the starboard engine. There were two levers on each cabinet: the lever on the left side controlled the gears to the shaft and screws, stopping the screws when the lever was in neutral, putting the screws in reverse when the lever was moved to reverse or going from neutral to forward by moving the lever to that position. Therefore each engine could be operated separately, going forward or reverse, or screw not turning. The engine continued to run at whatever speed was called for by the position of the lever on the right side of the cabinet. This remote control facility made it possible to control the engines while sweeping mines with only two people in the pilot house. All other crew members, including engine room personnel, could now be on deck without anything over their heads like an overhead (ceiling). If the ship hit a mine, a person standing under the overhead could be killed simply by the force of the explosion driving him upward and crushing his skull or breaking his neck. It was even possible to set the engine controls from the wing of the bridge by leaning in long enough to make the proper adjustment of levers and then moving outside again. In this case only the helmsman is under the overhead and it is possible to give him some cushion by securing mattresses to the overhead over the helm. Another, though less vital product of the remote control system, was the ability it gave the officer at the con to turn the ship around "on a dime". When wind was calm and currents were slack, by putting one engine forward and one in reverse the ship could be turned 360° or 180° degrees or whatever position in between was desired. So when the engines were tested, it was determined if they responded to the remote control levers in a normal manner. The other test was on the helm to be certain that the rudders responded to the turn of the helm to right and left. If there was a problem with the engines or the helm it would be revealed before the mooring lines were cast off.). Underway for Degaussing Range, verbal orders of Lt. Comdr Meggs, indoctrination officer.

0854 - Cleared pier - various courses and speeds to Net (Anti-submarine net across the shipping channel).

0931 - Passing through Nets. (The anti-submarine net was constructed of woven steel cable and resembled a fishing net. It was designed to prevent a submarine or torpedo from entering the shipping channel. Like a fishing net, it had large steel floats to keep the top of the net at the surface. The bottom of the net was weighted to rest on the bottom of the channel. When a vessel needed to pass through, a ship called a Net Tender, pulled open an overlap in the net so the vessel could pass and then the Net Tender immediately closed it).

0945 - Shifted to Remote Control
1000 - Degaussing Personnel coming aboard from launch
1005 - Proceeding with ranging, on North South Magnetic headings, various speeds as necessary
1317 - Completed ranging. (This ranging procedure probably had to do with the checking the effect the Degaussing Coil had on the accuracy of the magnetic compass. The Degaussing coil was designed to reduce the magnetic field of the whole ship by producing its own magnetic field in opposition to that of the ship's field. However, unless the magnetic compass (which was located on the flying bridge) was shielded from the effects of the Degaussing Coil the magnetic compass could not be as accurate as it was designed to be. To counteract or nullify the effects of the Degaussing coil small permanent magnets called Flinders bars were placed in various locations in the brass binnacle. The best way to compensate the magnetic compass with the Flinders bars, was while underway, on various headings and also taking into account the earth's magnetic field. It was a slow task requiring great patience, but was necessary to provide a dependable backup compass for the Gyro-compass, should it fail. The bars were named for an English navigator of the late 18th and early 19th centuries by the name of Nathaniel Flinders.)
1318 - Lowered Acoustic Hammer and running test on it. (See Appendix C).
1425 - All tests completed; shifted control to engine room and returning to Base, various courses and speeds
1445 - General Quarters Drill and rescue drill. (These drills, by now, were not announced to the crew in advance. They know where they are supposed to be and what to do for the various emergencies. The effort now is to get to the proper place as rapidly as possible. In some situations seconds could make a difference. Practice, practice practice was the order of the day, every day. This, of course, would pay rich dividends later).
1519 - Docking stations
1529 - Moored port side to, Pier 6, USN Section Base
1835 - Compass men on board working on Degaussing Compensating coil. (Signed: King Upton, Ltjg, USNR, Commanding).

February 6, 1943

0000 - Moored as before, North side Pier 6, USN Section Base, Tom Kinsville, S.I. (Staten Island) NY.
0800 - All hands present & accounted for.
1805 - Commissary stores aboard and checked for quantity & quality.
0900 - Testing engines & making Bridge Test. Compass compensating Personnel on board. Underway for Compass adjustment, verbal orders of Lt. Comdr. Meggs, Indoctrination Officer. Also on board, Warrant Gunner Martin and Warrant Bo'sn Kuzy.
0928 - Clear of Pier, Various courses to Anti-Sub Net & various speeds.
0952 - Returning to Base, weather too bad to Compensate compass. Various courses and speeds.
1000 - Docking, Port side to Pier 6, US Navy Section Base, Tom Kinsville, S.I., NY.
1800 - Secured ship for night - maintaining security watch. (Signed: King Upton, Ltjg, USNR, Commanding).

February 7, 1943

0000 - Moored as before, Port side to Pier 6, USN Section Base, Tom Kinsville, NY.

0800 - All hands present and accounted for - regular Sunday routine in force & maintaining security watch.

1800 - Checked all lines for night & secured ship for night. (Signed: King Upton, Ltjg, USNR, Commanding).

February 8, 1943

0000 - Moored as before, Port side to, Pier 6, USN Section Base, Tom Kinsville, NY.

0800 - All hands present and accounted for.

0924 - All Bridge and engine tests completed, preparing to get under way, verbal orders of LtComdr Meggs, Indoctrination Officer at Tom Kinsville, for compensating Compass and swinging ship. Compass personnel on board. 0935 - Cleared slip; various courses and speeds to anti-sub net.

1019 - Passing through nets.

1020 - Proceeding on various courses to area Southwest of West Bank Light in Compass adjustment

1055 - Proceeding with Compass adjustment and operating on remote control - Swinging on various headings.

1300 - Completed Compass Compensation - Returning to Sub nets

1322 - Shifted Control of Engines to engine room.

1323 - Abeam of Subnets

1341 - In Gravesend Bay - Maneuvering for man overboard drill and holding same.

1400 - Secured from man overboard drill and proceeding on various courses to Section Base.

1510 - Held General Quarters drill

1530 - Held Fire drill

1533 - Secured from General drills

1800 - Secured ship for night and maintaining security watch. (Signed: King Upton, Ltjg, USNR, Commanding).

February 9, 1943

0000 - Moored as before, Pier 6, Port side to, USN Section Base, Tom Kinsville, NY.

0800 - All hands present and accounted for.

0830 - Testing engines and making Bridge test and preparing to get under way, verbal orders of LtComdr Meggs, Indoctrination Officer Section Base, Tom Kinsville, for gunnery range to test all ordnance equipment. Warrant Bos'n Kuzy and Ensign Adams, USNR on board as observers.

0857 - Clear of slip - Various courses to Subnet

0931 - Shifted to remote control; having completed passing thru nets

0935 - Various courses down Ambrose Channel to Buoy 1, thence to Gednay Buoy, thence to Buoyuturn, [*sic*] George and How.

1100 - Abeam Buoy How. CC to 090° True - on range and proceeding gunnery exercises. Sounded General Quarters stations.

1111 - Fired one (depth) charge Starboard rack. All satisfactory.

1113 - Fired one (depth) charge Port rack. All satisfctory.

1114 - Fired one charge starboard K gun. All satisfactory.

1115 - Fired one charge Port K gun. All satisfactory.

1122 - Checked stations & ship for casualties to gear - all satisfactory. Tested Port and Starboard 20 millimeter (anti-aircraft rapid fire guns) - Cleared guns satisfactorily.

1135 - Structural firing (the firing of this dual purpose gun was to determine if the noise and or vibrations of the gun when fired would cause any structural problems for the ship, rather than to see if the gun crew could hit a target) on 3" 50 cal - 8 shots - 4 common and 4 anti-aircraft. Casualties to gear, minor - Ship's Bell knocked off (it was fastened to the bulkhead on the outside front of the Pilot House) and Compensating Coil on the magnetic compass knocked out of position by vibration.

1205 - Secured from Exercises and General Quarters.

1206 - CC to 325° True

1245 - Ambrose Light Vessel (Lightship) abeam to starboard, 400 yds distant. Proceeding to Sandy Hook Bay by various courses.

1400 - In Sandy Hook Bay and maneuvering - practicing Ship handling and giving instruction on the helm.

1447 - Secured from Instruction and proceeding to Sub-nets via Chapel Hill Channel.

1530 - Passing through Nets - Shifted to manual control.

1533 - Various courses to Pier 6, USN Section Base, Tom Kinsville.

1610 - Docked Port side to Pier 6, outboard of YMS 207. (The 207 was completed by Robert Jacob, Inc. of City Island, NY just 4 days after the 183 was commissioned. The 207 and doubtless others built in the New York area are going through the same exercises and drills).

1800 - Secured Ship for night & maintaining a security Watch. (Signed: King Upton, Ltjg, USNR, Commanding).

February 10, 1943

0000 - Moored to North side Pier 6, Sec. Base, Tom Kinsville. Regular night port watch in force.

0800 - All present and accounted for. Ship's crew at work on stowage and preparing to paint deck. (It is interesting to note that not all YMSes had painted decks. In fact it seemed as the 183 tied up alongside other YMSes during her career through the war that more of them did not have painted decks than did. This, however, is an impression as to the ratio. The fact is that some did paint their decks and some did not. One theory is that a painted deck did not reflect light that could be seen from above by enemy aircraft).

1200 - Stowage work and paint work being carried on.

1800 - Secured ship for night. (Signed: King Upton, Ltjg, USNR, Commanding).

February 11, 1943

0000 - Moored port side to Pier 6, Sec. Base, Tom Kinsville. Regular port routine in force.

0800 - Held Captain's Mast on, one man; charge - over leave 43 hours (Feb. 3-5). Restricted to ship until March 1.

1600 - 1800 - Bula, S.S., 707-94-45, F1/c, USNR reported for duty in compliance with order No. MM/Pib - 4/MM. Gyro compass checked by Navy representative; compass started, but no repairs made as yet. (Signed: King Upton, Ltjg, USNR, Commanding).

February 12, 1943

0000 - 0400 - Moored port side to Pier 6, Section Base, S.I. Maintaining security watch.

0400 - 0800 - Ship secure as above.

0800 - 1200 - Ship inspected by officers of Mine Warfare Dept. Got under way for Sandy Hook Bay to conduct ship tests. Rail on starboard gun deck reported bent by ship moored out outboard of YMS 183. - This was the USS YMS 207. (Apparently this was not serious damage. Also, it was not an uncommon occurrence. Failure to put proper fenders between ships moored side by side would allow rocking of one or both and causing them to bump into each other. In effect a fender is a cushion that keeps two ships from bumping or one ship from bumping a pier. Fenders are made of rope, wood slats, heavy canvas, etc. Failure of the watch on each ship to be alert to proper tension on mooring lines, and sometimes a ship coming along side may be moving too fast and actually hit the receiving vessel too hard).

1200 -1600- Maneuvering in Sandy Hook Bay. Swung ship to check on compass deviation. Conducted various speed trials.

1600 -1800 - Returned to dock at Pier 6, Section Base, Tompkinsville

2000-2400 - Ship secured for night. (Signed: King Upton, Ltjg, USNR Commanding).

February 13, 1943

0000 - 0400 - Moored alongside YMS 83 at Pier 6, Section Base, Tompkinsville. Maintaining security watch. (The 83 was built by Stadium Yacht Basin Co. of Cleveland, Ohio and commissioned in June 1942).

0400 - 0800 - Navy workmen aboard doing repairs. Magazine Temperature Max 51 - Min 50 at 0745. (The magazine, where the ammunition for the 3" gun, the 20 MM AA guns and any other explosive ordnance was kept, had to be kept at a constant moderate temperature. The Gunner's Mate kept tabs on this among his other duties. At a site near each of the guns was an immediate supply of ammunition stored in safe containers called ready boxes. In the event the guns had to be fired at a moment's notice there was enough ammo to start and continue firing for a short time until more rounds could be brought up from the magazine.).

1800 - Secured ship for night and checked lines. (Signed: King Upton, Ltjg, USNR, Commanding).

February 14, 1943

0000 - Moored Port side to, Pier 6, USN Section Base, Tom Kinsville, New York and maintaining security watch.

0800 - Holiday Sunday Port Routine in force - Section Base repair crew working on anchor winch and acoustic air valve. (The anchor winch, driven by an electric motor, hoisted the anchor chain and the anchor aboard the ship. As the chain was hoisted aboard it was deposited in a special space in the fore peak of the ship called the chain locker. Interestingly, the bitter end or end of the chain at the other end from the anchor was not fastened to the ship. This meant that when paying out chain when the anchor was dropped over board, if care was not taken, the whole chain would be on the bottom and for all practical purposes, lost. The reason for not securing the chain to the ship had to do with the possible emergency when the ship would have to get under way more quickly than the anchor could be brought up by the winch, which was quite slow. In such an emergency the chain would be "slipped" or let go, which only took a minute or two and the ship was free to speed away on its emergency. The anchor chain was painted different colors every few fathoms (6' is a fathom) so that as it was paying out at a fairly rapid pace, the Bos'n could tell how much chain was already out and therefore he would know how much was left. Among other things, this enabled him to stop paying out chain before it came to the bitter end and would go over the side. Except in the most dire circumstances the Navy looked upon commanding officers who lost their anchors and chain with grave misgivings). (The acoustic air hammer, as described in Appendix C, was used in sweeping acoustic mines. The riveting hammer was powered by compressed air from the engine room. An air valve controlled the admission of compressed air or shutting it off).

1030 - Liberty up for Port Section. All hands present and accounted for. (The various departments on the ship divided their personnel into two groups for the purposes of rotating liberty or time ashore. One group was designated the Port section and the other the Starboard section).

1100 - Completed all tests & preparation for getting under way.

1107 - Under way for fuel dock, Bayonne River, Bayonne, NJ; Permission of LtComdr. Meggs, indoctrination officer.
1114 - Cleared slip
1116 - Proceeding to fuel dock, around Staten Island, to Bayonne River.
1121 - In Bayonne River
1135 - Swinging right to enter fuel dock (When fueling or handling other hazardous materials the square red signal flag, Baker, was hoisted to the signal yardarm to announce that dangerous activity was in progress. All interested parties should take note, and among other things no smoking was allowed. The smoking lamp was out. After completing the activity, the Baker flag was lowered).
1200 - Temperature of Magazines - 51 Max and 49 Min.
1435 - Completed fueling - took on 3120 gallons
1437 - Completed all preparations for getting under way and returning to Section Base.
1441 - In Bayonne River
1510 - Entering slip at Section Base
1516 - Moored Port Side to YMS 43, Pier 6, USN Section Base, Tom Kinsville, S.I., NY. (The YMS 43 was built by Wheeler SB Corp. of Brooklyn, NY, completed and commissioned in May, 1942).
1800 - Secured ship for night and checked lines.
2015 - Section Base workmen # 385 and # 273 on board working on Acoustic air valve. (Signed: King Upton, Ltjg, USNR, Commanding).

February 15, 1943

0000 - 0400 - Moored alongside YMS 42, YMS 183 being outboard ship. Maintaining regular security watch. All lines secure. (On 14 Feb. at 1516 the 183 was moored to YMS 43. Now a few hours later 183 is moored to YMS 42. Which was it, 42 or 43?).
0400 - 0800 - (No entry in log).
0800 - 1200 - YMS 42 and YMS 82 got underway and in doing so, damaged our port life- raft. YMS 183 was then tied to dock. (On the 13th of Feb. YMS 83 was tied to the dock. Now on the 15th the 83 has become the 82 and joins the 42 in damaging the port life raft of the 183. Who can tell whom it was involved in damaging the life raft? Lt.jg Upton , the CO signed both logs as "examined and being correct". This is an example of at least two things. First, the officers at the con of the vessels getting under way leave something to be desired in their ship handling skills. Secondly, it would seem, that no one has read these logs since they were written on Feb 15, 1943. No one until now).
1200 - Liberty began.
1600 - Ship secured for night

February 16, 1943

0000 - 0400 - Moored port side to Pier 6, Section Base, Tom Kinsville, maintaining security watch. Yard workmen on board welding rail on port gun deck; fire watch posted.
0800 - 1200 - Under way in accordance with verbal orders to test and stream "O" type mine-gear, near Ambrose Lightship area. (See Appendix C).
1200 - 1600 - On way back to Section Base. "O" type gear streamed, tested and found to operate satisfactorily.
1600 - 2000 - Entered harbor and returned to Section Base. Tied up alongside YMS 226. Prepared ship for night. Liberty announced. Ship secure. (Signed: Ltjg King Upton, USNR, Commanding).

(YMS 226 was built by Frank L. Sample, Jr. of Boothbay Harbor, Maine. Completed and commissioned Jan. 16, 1943).

February 17, 1943

0000 - 0400 - Moored to Pier 6, Section Base, Tom Kinsville, maintaining security watch. Periodic inspection of lines.

0400 - 0800 - Periodic inspection of lines. All secure.

0800 - 1200 - All hands present. Trial Board headed by Lt. Comdr. Fluhr aboard to test out magnetic sweeping gear. Under way in accordance with verbal orders of Comdr. Fluhr. Test of gear to be made in vicinity of Ambrose Lightship. 1200 - 1600 - Tests completed, and returning to Base. Mine gear tested satisfactorily. Arrived at base at 1556. Moored alongside AMc 74, North Pier 6.

1600 - 2000 - Liberty commenced. All lines secure.

2000 - 2400 - Lines checked periodically by security watch. All secure. (Signed: King Upton, Ltjg, USNR, Commanding).

February 18, 1943

0000 - 0400 - Moored alongside AMc 74 North Pier 6, Section Base, Tom Kinsville, maintaining security watch. (The AMc, Auxilary Minesweeper Coastal an older, in design, and smaller ship than the YMS, nevertheless did its share of escort and minesweeping work even in the far reaches of the Pacific. There were three lengths, 96', 97' and 98'. They only had a single main propulsion engine and the single magnetic sweep generator. They did acoustic, "O" type and magnetic sweeping. They had to travel in company with other vessels for refueling, water and commissary stores. Some were commissioned and most were not. They had a complement of 3 officers and 12-14 crew. The AMc's had names, and the YMSes did not. The AMc 74, named "Demand" was built by Gibbs Gas Engine of Jacksonville, Florida in early 1941 and placed in service September 5, 1941. She operated out of the 3rd and 6th Naval Districts and was struck from the Naval Register December 5, 1945. She was 97' 1" long, 21' wide and weighed 290 gross tons. I am indebted to Allie Ryan for this detail on the "Demand").

0400 - 0800 - Lines checked periodically. All secure.

0800 - 1200 - Lines checked periodically. Secure.

1200 - 1600 - Crew and Officers received pay. (According to the Bluejackets' Manual of 1943 the following pay grades were in effect per month: Chief Petty Officer (permanent) $138.; (acting) $126.; Petty Officer 1/c $114.; S 1c $66.; S 2/c $54.; Apprentice Seaman $50. *(See End Note 40)*. Enlisted personnel were furnished food and quarters in addition to the above. According to an officer friend, he says he remembers an Ensign was paid $150. and a Lt.(jg) $160 per month. Officers paid for their food and quarters, even when on board ship.

2000 - 2400 - Lines checked periodically. All secure. (Signed: King Upton, Ltjg, USNR Commanding).

February 19, 1943

0000 - 0400 - Moored alongside Pier 6, Section Base Pier, Tom Kinsville, maintaining security watch.

0400 - 0800 - Lt. Upton came aboard, and remaining for about 10 minutes, then left. Regular ship's routine in force. Minor repairs being done, painting by ship's crew. Lines inspected periodically. All secure.

0800 -1200 - Regular routine in force.

1200 - 1600 - Regular routine. Lines checked periodically.

1600 - 2400 - Regular security watch.

February 20, 1943

0000 - 0400 - Moored alongside Pier 6, Section Base, maintaining security watch. Lines checked periodically.

0400 - 0800 - Lines checked periodically.

0800 - 1200 - Regular port routine in effect. 0910 - Under way to Pier 7, for purpose of checking pulsing; by verbal orders of Lt. Comdr. Fluhr. (When sweeping for magnetic mines the big 500 horse power diesel engine turned a 2 ton steel flywheel and an electric generator. The engine would be speeded up to a set number of revolutions per minute and all the while the flywheel is turning at the same speed. The generator is also turning at this speed, but it is not making any electricity. When the proper speed is reached, the field coils of the generator are charged with a designated current which now causes the generator to make electricity for the magnetic cable towed from the stern of the ship. Because the amount of electricity needed to make a strong magnetic field is so great, to call on the generator to make it continuously would be more than the diesel engine, even with the help from the flywheel and its residual inertia, could do and it would grind to a halt. In order to create the proper strength magnetic field and not have to start the diesel engine up repeatedly, the electrical system of the generator was placed on a timer. When the engine loses rpm's to a certain point, before grinding to a stop, the current to the field coil of the generator is turned off, and the generator is no longer generating electricity. This allows the engine to speed up again to the proper rpm's and the field coil is turned on again making the current for the magnetic cable being towed behind the ship. This on again, off again, generation of current is called pulsing. Apparently the electrical panel governing the pulsing needed some refinement. See Appendix C).

2205 - Underway with Tug to return to pier 6. Large fender lost because of Tug. At Pier 6, secured ship for night. (Don't know if they found the fender, They were expensive. If it didn't float it was lost. If it did float and was not picked up, it could foul another vessel's screws at great expense).

February 21, 1943

0000 - Moored alongside Pier 6, Section Base; maintaining security watch.

0400 - 0800 - Regular port routine in force. Lines checked periodically; all secure.

0800 - 1200 - Lines checked periodically.

1200 - 1600 - Took on fresh water.

1600 - 2000 - Secured from taking on fresh water. Liberty began. Ship secured for night.

2000 - 2400 - Security watch - lines inspected periodically.

February 22, 1943

0000 - 0400 - Moored alongside Pier 6, Section Base. Maintaining security watch.

0400 - 0800 - Lines checked periodically. All secure.

0800 - 1200 - Regular port routine in force. Ship moved forward at Pier.

1200 - 1600 - Took on fresh water. YMS 184 came alongside and moored to starboard. (The YMS 184, sister ship of the 183, launched about three weeks after the 183 and christened by Mrs. Inez Robinson, wife of the Commanding Officer of the CL-12, USS Marblehead, Arthur G. Robinson, Captain, USN, now a Rear Admiral. His heroic leadership in bringing the severely damaged cruiser Marblehead back to the U.S. after the battle of the Java Sea is firmly fixed in

John Dixon Davis

Naval history. The 184 was completed at Greenport Basin and Construction Co., Jan. 25, 1943 and commissioned at Brooklyn Navy Yard, Jan. 27, 1943. Now the two sisters are in Naval Service and will remain together for quite some time to come).

1600 - 2000 - Liberty. Ship secured for night.

2000 - 2400 - Workmen examined starboard raft.

February 23, 1943

0000 - Moored as before, Port Side to Pier 6, USN Section Base, Tom Kinsville

0800 - All hands present and accounted for. Regular ship's routine in force, working on hull and gear.

1945 - Secured from taking on fresh water.

2000 - Secured ship for night. Magazine temperature at 1200 maximum 55, minimum 53. (Signed: King Upton, Ltjg, USNR, Commanding).

February 24, 1943

0000 - Moored as before, Port side to Pier 6, USN Section Base, Tom Kinsville, NY.

0800 - All hands present and accounted for - regular ship's routine in force.

1307 - Under way to shift Berth, Pier 7, Berth 8 - North

1330 - Moored Pier 7. Running test on Controller. (Probably has to do with the magnetic control panel).

1800 - Secured ship for night. Magazine temperature maximum 56, minimum 54. (Signed: King Upton, Ltjg, USNR, Commanfing).

February 25, 1943

0000 - Moored as before North Side Pier 7, Port side to, USN Section Base, Tom Kinsville, NY

0800 - All hands present and accounted for

0815 - Under way to sweep with USS YMS 42 and USS YMS 82, verbal orders, Minesweeping Officer indoctrination, Section Base.

0847 - Passed through Nets.

0904 - Shifted to remote controls, various courses down Siwash Channel.

0927 - Vicinity Scotland Buoy - streaming acoustic & magnetic gear.

1019 - Sweeping in tail position (probably refers to being last ship in a line of sweepers) Area, Manasquam - Buoy Dog - Scotland Buoy.

1530 - Recovered gear, Vicinity Scotland Buoy. Proceeded up South Channel..

1630 - Entering Sandy Hook Bay.

1634 - Shifted to Manual Control.

1655 - Docked Port side to YMS 82, Army Pier, Sandy Hook, NJ.

1856 - AMc 76 tied up to starboard side

1900 - Secured Ship for night. (Signed: King Upton, Ltjg, USNR, Commanding).

February 26, 1943

0000 - Moored alongside YMS 82, at Sandy Hook, maintaining security watch.

0705 - Under way for sweeping operations.

0850 - Electric steering motor failed because of blown fuse. [The electric steering motor was activated by the helm (steering wheel). The helmsman turned the wheel and a motor turned the rudders to match the helmsman's turn. It required very little energy on the part of the helmsman. However, when the helm was in mechanical position, or direct drive, the helm was connected by steel cable with the rudders and required a good deal of strength to turn the helm. When the helm was in electric drive it sometimes "went out' for a variety of reasons. When this happened, the helmsman had to be alert and shift the helm to mechanical or direct drive, for when the motor failed the rudders would turn "hard right" on their own, and the ship would start turning hard right and continue to do so making the ship go in a circle unless and until the helmsman could turn the helm hard left to get the ship back on course. Aside from being frustrating it could be dangerous if the ship was in company with others and they were too close to the starboard side. A collision was possible with the ship on the right].

0950 - Started first leg of sweep with magnetic & acoustic gear in operation. Area (of sweep) Fringe of Channel from Buoy "E" to Buoy "A". Abeam of YMS 82.

1330 - Recovering magnetic gear by orders of YMS 82. (When two or more ships were working together, one ship was designated the command ship, usually based on which ship had the senior officer. This was determined by the serial numbers of the various skippers. The lowest number made that CO the group commander. In this case the skipper of the YMS 82 was senior to Lt.jg Upton of the 183).

1422 - Started streaming "Option" type gear in preparation for exploratory sweep of same area as before - "E" to "A" along fringe of channel. Sweeping in No. 2 position to YMS 82. (The writer of this log apparently did not know the name of the type of sweep for moored mines. It is Oropesa or "O" type).

1915 - Option (*Sic*) gear aboard. Proceeding to Section Base by orders of YMS 42 relayed from Mine Warfare Office, Section Base.

2235 - Tied up alongside YMS 184 at Pier 6, Section Base. Ship secured for night. (Signed: King Upton, Ltjg, USNR, Commanding).

February 27, 1943

0000 - Moored alongside YMS 184, maintaining security watch.
1050 - AMc 80 moored outboard of YMS 183.
1321 - Under way for Bayonne to refuel.
1357 - Moored alongside Pier 4, Bayonne, starboard side to.
1450 - Finished taking fuel. Ready to return to Tom Kinsville.
1520 - Tied up alongside AMc 80 at Pier 6, Tom Kinsville.
1605 - Held Captain's Mast for one man; Charge over leave 20 hours - Restricted to ship 'til March 12th.
2000 - Ship secured for night. (Signed: King Upton, Ltjg, USNR, Commanding).

February 28, 1943

0000 - Moored alongside Pier 6, Section Base, Tom Kinsville, maintaining security watch.
0800 - Sunday port routine in force.
1130 - Liberty for one section expired; for other, began.
1945 - Ship secured for night. (Signed: King Upton, Ltjg, USNR, Commanding).

March 1, 1943

0000 - Moored alongside Pier 6, Tom Kinsville.
0630 - Under way for sweep operation in accordance with orders of minesweeping office. Other ships in formation to be YMS 3 and YMS 207.
0705 - Passed anti-submarine nets.
0825 - Held General Quarters drill.
0945 - Streaming magnetic gear.

1043 - Pulsing in tail position of formation.
1540 - Began retrieving magnetic gear. (When magnetic gear is retrieved, the generator is secured and the cable is wound on the reel which is turned by an electric motor).
1639 - Approaching Sandy Hook Point.
1825 - Heaving lines passed and docking completed on west side of Pier at Sandy Hook. (When preparing to go alongside a pier or another ship, the line handlers on the ship making the approach throw a light weight line, with a special rope ball called a monkey's fist, fashioned on the thrown end, to a crew member of the already moored ship. The other end of this heaving line is tied to the regular mooring line of the approaching ship. The receiving line handler pulls the heaving line in until the regular mooring line is on board. He then places the loop on the end of the mooring line over a cleat or bollard on the receiving ship. The slack is taken out of the mooring line and secured on a cleat on the approaching ship. The heaving line is returned to the approaching ship for use again. Generally there are four mooring lines from the ship being moored to the dock or ship. From the bow straight across the line is # 1. One quarter of the distance from the bow aft the line is # 2 and it goes from the moored ship toward the after quarter of the receiving ship. From the after quarter of the approaching ship the line is # 3 and it goes forward to the first quarter of the receiving ship. From the stern of the approaching ship the line is # 4 and it goes straight across to the stern of the receiving ship. Lines # 2 & # 3 are also known as spring lines. With lines # 1 and # 4 taken in the Officer at the Con is able to either spring the bow or stern away from the pier or the other ship which enables him to pull out into the main channel with relative ease. If line # 2 is also taken in, he can back down slowly on line # 3 and the bow will come away from the pier and the ship can now go forward away from the dock and at the same time have line # 3 released from the pier and taken aboard. If on the other hand, the best way to get away from the pier is by backing out into the main channel the Conning Officer will take in all lines except # 2. He will then go forward slowly and spring the stern away from the dock at which point he can put his engines in reverse and back into the channel being sure that line # 2 in now taken aboard). (Signed: King Upton, Ltjg, USNR, Commanding).

March 2, 1934

0000 - Tied to dock at Sandy Hook, maintaining security watch
0300 - Began guarding 2854 KC on radio. [This was the frequency used for "talk between ships" or TBS. The range was not great but allowed ships within 10 or 15 miles to converse regarding Naval matters. Having a short range all but precluded the enemy from picking up the signals and allowed the great convenience and time saving of radio as over against blinker light (completely silent) or semaphore flags. The radio receiver and transmitter combination is really a transceiver. It was located in the pilot house and was "on" all the time. No matter the time of day or night a ship could call another or a shore base, if close enough. Since the radio was on all the time it was said that the frequency was "guarded", listened to. The watch in the pilot house, whether in port, at sea, on Sunday or Christmas heard every transmission and response from every other ship, within range, on this frequency. If the 183 needed to call the YMS 184, or the 207, the Officer of the Deck, or the Radioman would wait until there was no one else on the radio. It was like the CB radio networks among truckers on today's highways. There was a telephone type hand held voice microphone hooked to the speaker box. When the OD picked up the "phone" he pressed and held down a button in the handle. Instantly the 183's receiver was turned off and only the 183's radio signal could be heard. It sounded like a soft but continuous hiss. All the OD had to do was hold the transmitter button and speak his message. When it was

done, he released the button, his transmitter automatically turned off, and his radio receiver was back on to hear the answer. If more information needed to be sent or questions asked the OD on the 183 repeated the same procedure. A typical exchange might be as follows: "Donniker 4, Donniker 4, this is Donniker 3, Come in please. Over". There were only two YMSes in the 180 -189 series that remained with the US Navy for any length of time. Those two were the 183 and 184. However, any of the 180's, had they remained with the US Navy would have had the call sign Donniker followed by the last digit of its number, viz. Donniker 3, or 4. Continuing the example above: The OD on the 183 could hear the transmitter of the 184 come on and then the voice of their OD - "Donniker 3, Donniker 3, this is Donnike 4, over'. "Donniker 4, this is Donniker 3. Could you tell me how many rpms you're turning on your main engines, we seem to be having trouble maintaining good station with you folks. Maybe we can match the turns exactly and see if that will help. Over." "Donniker 3, this is Donniker 4, I'll check with the engine room and get back to you. Wilco and out." Wilco is short for "will comply". "Out" signifies end of transmission]. (When two or more ships were working together in convoy or sweeping each ship had a place, or station relative to all of the others and it was supposed to maintain this position. There were two ways to do this: change speed, or change course).

0700 - Bridge and engine tests made in preparation for sweeping with the YMS 3 and YMS 207.
0701 - Under way for routine sweep.
0824 - Began pulsing. (Magnetic sweep). Course 160° True.
1145 - Reached turning point, Buoy "A"
1512 - Reached beginning point of sweep; Buoy "I"
1848 - All lights reported on by gun captain. Lights in use: minesweeping, running, stern lights by order of commanding officer of YMS 3. (There were probably two things going on here. It is wartime, but the ships are near the coast in a protected area and a test of whether or not the lights worked and could be seen by other ships was needed. The other objective is to test minesweeping techniques at night. The lights were the only way your ship could be seen by others and they by you. This was very necessary for station keeping and avoidance of collision. YMSes did not have surface search radar this early in the war).
1918 - Failure of remote engine control system. (They probably shifted to engine room control until the remote system was fixed).
2000 - Continuing routine sweep. (Signed: King Upton, Lt;jg, USNR, Commanding)

March 3, 1943

0000 - Sweeping routine sweep with YMS 3 and YMS 207; sweep being night sweep of Ambrose Channel. Course from Buoy "A" to Buoy "E" 313° True; from Buoy "E" to Buoy "I" 339° True.
0737 - All lights secured.
0810 - Recovering magnetic gear, to proceed to Base.
1019 - Tied up alongside Pier 6, Tom Kinsville.
1430 - Spare parts for Gunnery and Engineering Depts. Came aboard.
1530 - Commissary stores came aboard.
1600 - Ltjg F. Murphy (D-Vs) reported aboard for temporary duty. Written orders of Commanding Officer, Ambrose Section, Inshore Patrol, 3rd Naval District. Stationed at USN Section Base Tom Kinsville.
2200 - Starboard life-raft damaged by YMS 20 as it came alongside to tie up. (Signed: King Upton, Ltjg, USNR, Commanding). (YMS 183 was assigned 3 Officers when commissioned. Ltjg King Upton, Ltjg Adrian Doherty and Ens. Jesse M. Dill. Now that the 183 is assigned to the Inshore

Patrol and this is going to involve much night sweeping, etc. the need for another Officer was apparent. The CO needed to be relieved of the necessity of standing Bridge watches as he was on call all of the time. The original plan for the YMS complement called for three officers. During this period, YMSes began to have a fourth Officer assigned and this continued for the rest of the war and after).

March 4, 1943

0000 - Tied alongside Pier 6, Tom Kinsville, maintaining security watch.
0800 - Two men absent over leave.
1613 - Returned spare parts in excess to Supervisor of Shipbuilding, Greenport, L.I.
2000 - All lines secure; ship secured for night. (Signed: King Upton, Ltjg, USNR, Commanding).

March 5, 1943

0000 - Moored alongside Pier 6, Tom Kinsville, maintaining security watch.
0430 - Liberty expired. Two men over leave since March 4, 0800.
0930 - Under way for minesweeping operations in conjunction with YMS 43 and 105 in accordance with verbal orders of Mine Warfare Office.
1110 - Began streaming magnetic gear.
1250 - Began pulsing.
1830 - Began operating with YMS 3
1915 - Ordered by YMS 3 to extinguish all white lights. Complied with orders.
2000 - Making routine night sweep. (Signed: King Upton, Ltjg, USNR, Commanding).

March 6, 1943

0000 - Sweeping in formation with YMS 3.
0600 - Visibility closing in rapidly. Snow flurries
0755 - Visibility about 900 yds. Continuing sweep
0910 - Recovering gear by order of YMS 3; cause reduced visibility and snow.
0946 - Proceeding to Ambrose Channel.
1015 - Passed abeam Ambrose Light Vessel.
1117 - Recovered acoustic gear.
1145 - Making preparations to dock alongside Pier 6, Tom Kinsville.
1155 - Tied up alongside Pier.
1545 - Under way for refueling at Bayonne.
1705 - Under way for Pier 6 after refueling.
1720 - Tied up at Pier 6.
2000 - Secured ship for night. (Signed: King Upton, Ltjg, USNR, Commanding).

March 7, 1943

0000 - Moored alongside Pier 6, Tom Kinsville.
0030 - One man returned. Absent Over Leave since 0800 March 4.
0844 - Underway for sweep operation with YMS 3 and YMS 106, by verbal orders Mine Warfare.
0947 - Began streaming magnetic gear and making minor repairs on gear.
1054 - Took station and began sweeping.
1340 - Sighted floating cable; requested permission to attempt recovery of same. Recovered 2 floats; unable to recover more.
2010 - Ordered by YMS 3 to secure Range light. Complied.

March 8, 1943

0000 - Sweeping in formation with YMS 106.
0330 - All running lights, stern & minesweeping lights reported burning.
0511 - Received permission from YMS 106 to return to base. Action taken because of engine trouble.
0753 - Entering Nets.
0841 - Tied alongside Pier 6, North.
1430 - Held Captain's Mast - one man, charge - absent without authority from ship. Punishment - 4 weeks restriction to ship. One man, charge - Absent Over Leave 46 hours. Awarded 4 weeks loss of Liberty. One man, held over for further action.
1831 - Under way with tug for Pier 1 to dispose of depth charges in preparation for going into dry dock for examination of starboard shaft, strut bearing and propeller.
1952 - Again at Pier 6. Ship secured for night. (Signed: King Upton, Ltjg, USNR, Commanding).

March 9, 1943

0000 - Moored to Pier 6, Tom Kinsville, maintaining security watch.
0813 - Tug alongside to tow ship to McWilliams Dry Dock.
1105 - Taking power and light from dock at McWilliams Shipyard. Smoking lamp lit in galley and head. (This means that those who wished to smoke tobacco could do so in the galley or the head. In this case smoking was allowed only in these two areas).
1150 - Inspection of propellers, shafts and underwater fittings made by engineering officer. Results entered in Machinery Log.
1847 - Off drydock and underway for Pier 6.
1916 - Moored to Pier 6, North side. Ship secured for night. (Signed: King Upton, Ltjg, USNR, Commanding).

March 10, 1943

0000 - Moored alongside Pier 6, Tom Kinsville, maintaining security watch.
0715 - Liberty expired. All men present and accounted for.
0837 - Under way for South Pier 7 for picking up depth charges.
0945 - One man reported aboard Absent Over Leave from 0715. (At 0715 this man was reported present).
1020 - Depth charges aboard. Under way for Pier 6.
1200 - Held Captain's Mast for -----SC1/c. Absent Over Leave March 5, 2000 to March 7,
2140 while on restriction. Awarded reduction to next inferior rank, 6 weeks restriction. -----Sea1/c, Absent Over Leave March 10, 1 hour 15 minutes and using unauthorized Liberty Card. Awarded 4 weeks loss of Liberty.-----S2/c held for further action for refusal to obey orders.
2027 - Held fire drill. Satisfactory. Ship secured for night. (Signed: King Upton, Ltjg, USNR, Commanding).

March 11, 1943

0000 - Moored alongside Pier 6, maintaining security watch.
0800 - Muster; one absentee.
1200 - 1400 - Lines checked at intervals, all secure.
1800 - Ship secured for night. (Signed: King Upton, Ltjg, USNR, Commanding).

March 12, 1943

0000 - Moored alongside Pier 6, maintaining security watch.

0655 - One man reported aboard 22 hours, 25 minutes over leave.
0700 - Under way for sweeping operations in conjunction with YMS 83 & YMS 20.
1150 - Electric timer inoperative; pulsing by hand.
1739 - Recovery of gear completed. Proceeding to Base.
2100 - Tied to Pier 7, Tom Kinsville.
2155 - Donelly, A.W., S2/c turned in to Sick Bay.
2245 - Lt. Torck, from Base, in charge of repairing timer. (Signed: King Upton, Ltjg, USNR, Commanding).

March 13, 1943

0000 - Moored North Side Pier 7, Tom Kinsville, maintaining security watch.
1020 - Held Captain's Mast. One man, Absent Over Leave 0800 - 11 March to 0655 - 12 March. Awarded Deck Court. (As we have already noted, there have been several infractions of Navy Regulations, mostly relating to staying Over Leave. In cases of this kind punishment is assigned at a Captain's Mast. This procedure is for inquiring into and punishing only minor offenses. For a single offense, or at any one time, the commanding officer may assign any one of the following punishments: 1. Reduction of any rating established by himself; 2. Confinement not exceeding ten days, unless further confinement be necessary, in the case of a prisoner to be tried by court martial; 3. Solitary confinement, on bread and water not exceeding five days; 4. Solitary confinement not exceeding seven days; 5. Deprivation of liberty on shore; 6. Extra duties. A Deck Court is convened when sufficient punishment, should the defendant be guilty, cannot be awarded at mast, and when the defendant does not object to deck court; otherwise he gets a summary court.). *(See End Note No.41)*.
1400 - Deck Court for one man on charges above. Awarded loss of pay of $16.00 per month for 3 months, and restriction of liberty for 4 weeks.
2055 - Ship secured for night. (Signed: King Upton, Lt., USNR, Commanding, The CO apparently received promotion to full Lt. He says nothing about it, but starts sign- the log as Lt. King Upton).

March 14, 1943

0000 - Moored North Side Pier 7, maintaining security.
0615 - One man over leave.
810 - Under way for sweep operation with YMS 43 and 104; complying with orders of Mine Warfare Office.
1000 - Sweeping in tail position with YMS 43 & 104.
1830 - Using hammer in lieu of parallel pipes. (In sweeping acoustic mines the riveting hammer lowered from the bow of the ship is often used. However, there is another means of making sufficient noise to detonate an acoustic mine and this is a device called parallel pipes. In this rig, two steel pipes are mounted side by side with about an inch of space between them. The ends of the two pipes are welded to a steel plate with one inch diameter holes in them so that a steel cable can be attached to each plate. This cable is a bridle that is pulled behind the ship at a safe distance, so that any mine detonations would be well behind the ship. The noise is created when the pipes, while being pulled though the water, are caused to vibrate against each other because of the Bernoulli effect. This creates a lot of underwater noise, but is not as safe for the sweepers as the acoustic hammer. When conducting an acoustic sweep at the same time a magnetic sweep is conducted, the acoustic hammer must be used because the magnetic tail is being pulled from the stern of the ship).

2025 - Tied up at Sandy Hook pier. Ship secured. Posted security watch.

March 15, 1943

0000 - Moored alongside dock at Sandy Hook maintaining security watch.

0730 - Lines cast off; under way to complete sweep operation with YMS 43 and 104.

0818 - Completed streaming gear. Sweeping. All gear functioning properly.

1530 - Started retrieving gear. On way to Base. (When reading the log for a given day it almost seems that neither the ship nor its crew had much to do. At 0818 the gear is streamed and then at 1530, 7 hours later it is retrieved and 2 hours later they have returned to the pier for the night. Soft job. What the log doesn't say, nor is it required to, is that for seven hours the ship and its crew is engaged in activity that could possibly result in their being sunk by a mine, a collision with another ship, crew members lost over the side, or injured. Add to this that the crew is not just sitting around in the galley sipping hot coffee waiting for the sweep to be over. They are at their minesweeping stations, with life jacket and steel helmet on. Except for the helmsman and the engine's remote control operator in the Pilot House, everyone else is outside, on deck, fair weather or foul, so that in the event a mine detonates under them they have a chance to be blown into the water and not driven through the overhead because they were inside keeping warm and cozy. Sometimes those on the beach looked longingly at the Naval vessel. When his ship was going down under him, the sailor wished fervently for a muddy fox hole - for anything but all this water. The ship's log rarely told the whole story).

1742 - Moored alongside Pier 6, Tom Kinsville.

1905 - One man returned to ship, Absent Over Leave since 0600, 14 March. (Signed: King Upton, Lt., USNR, Commanding).

March 16, 1943

0000 - Moored alongside pier 6, maintaining security watch.

0745 - All men returned from liberty.

0900 - Captain's Mast held for one man. Charge, Absent Over Leave. Selected Deck Court.

1135 - All fire extinguishers inspected.

1335 - Deck Court held for one man. Charge, Absent Over Leave. Pleaded guilty. Sentence - (1) Loss of pay for 3 months of $10. Per month, (2) 4 weeks restriction of liberty, (3) 5 hours extra duty.

1340 - Captain's Mast held for one man; no sentence; and another man, no sentence.

1515 - Held Captain's inspection. (From time to time, the Captain or his designate would inspect the ship, for cleanliness, orderly storage of personal gear, and ship's gear, good maintainence of machinery, etc. The inspection could be announced in advance in which case the crew would get things shipshape immediately. But sometimes the inspection was done without notice and then if the crew had not been doing a good job regularly they would not pass the inspection. The possibility of losing liberty time was a great motivator to keeping gear in order and in its proper place.

1800 - Ship secured for night. (Signed: King Upton, Lt., USNR, Commanding).

March 17, 1943

0000 - Moored alongside Pier 6, maintaining security watch. All in order.

1745 - Removed life-raft to carpenter's shop for repairs.

2230 - Received repaired life-raft. Secured ship for night. (Signed: King Upton, Lt., USNR, Commanding).

John Dixon Davis

March 18, 1943

0000 - Moored alongside Pier 6, maintaining security watch.
0600 - Liberty expired. All present.
0733 - Under way for sweep operations with YMS 184, orders of Mine Warfare Office.
1025 - Completed streaming of gear. On sweep.
1945 - Recovering gear.
2125 - Lines passed. Tied up at Sandy Hook alongside YMS 104. Rail damaged by YMS 184 coming alongside. (Signed: King Upton, Lt., USNR, Commanding). (It would seem, that every time somebody comes alongside the YMS 183, to moor there for a time, they manage to damage her rail, either port or starboard side. Thus far it is like a jinx).

March 19, 1943

0000 - Moored alongside YMS 104 at Sandy Hook Pier, with YMS 184 moored to our port side.
0700 - Under way for continuation of sweep operation with YMS 184..
1140 - Started streaming Option (should be "O" type) gear to search for wreck. (Note: Do not know what was involved here, but it could have been a search for some obstruction on the bottom that was snagging otters and/or depressors when they were sweeping in this area).
1335 - Recovering gear to proceed to Base. Visibility closing rapidly. (The weather report for the day in the log indicates overcast skies with flurries).
1839 - Moored alongside Pier 6, Tom Kinsville. (Signed: King Upton, Lt., USNR,Commanding).

March 20, 1943

0000 - Moored alongside Pier 6, Tom Kinsville. Maintaining security watch. Lines checked hourly.
1000 - Taking on provisions.
1015 - Crew and Officers paid.
1305 - Miller, K.N., Sea 1/c, detached for transfer to Norfolk, Va.
1325 - Under way for Bayonne fuel pier.
1450 - Fueling completed. Under way for Base.
1530 - Moored alongside Pier 6. (Signed: King Upton, Lt., USNR, Commanding).

March 21, 1943

0000 - Moored alongside Pier 6, Tompinsville. Checking lines hourly.
0700 - Reveille; chow served.
1200 - Radio repairman came aboard.
2200 - Ship secured for night. (Signed: King Upton, Lt., USNR, Commanding).

March 22, 1943

0000 - Moored alongside Pier 6, Tom Kinsville.
0733 - Under way verbal orders of Mine Warfare Office for sweep operation with YMS 184.
0904 - Held fire drill. Stations manned in 1 min. 25 sec.
0914 - Streaming magnetic gear. Sweeping assigned area from 1005 - 2000.
2030 - Magnetic gear inboard. Under way for Base.
2225 - Heaving lines passed; tied up to YMS 398. Engines & Bridge secured. (Signed: King Upton, Lt., USNR, Commanding). (The YMS 398, built by Henry B. Nevins, Inc., of City Island , NY was completed and commissioned on/or about March 13, 1943).

March 23, 1943

0000 - Moored alongside Pier 6, Section Base

1140 - YMS 207 tied alongside, breaking starboard station-keeping light.

1200 - Checked lines hourly Yard workmen aboard to repair rail.

1800 - Ship secured for night. (Signed: King Upton, Lt., USNR, Commanding).

March 24, 1943

0000 - Moored alongside Pier 6, maintaining security watch. Lines checked hourly.

0410 - Started taking (fresh) water. Took 500 gallons.

0744 - Muster. No absentees.

0752 - Under way for sweep operations with YMS 208.

0825 - Held fire drill. Stations manned in 55 seconds.

0905 - Held general quarters.

0920 - Held abandon ship drill. Drills satisfactory.

1240 - Began sweeping with option (oropessa or "O" type) gear.

1300 - Tested 30 calibre guns.

1551 - Recovered "O" type gear.

1957 - Proceeding up Sandy Hook Channel.

2015 - Anchored in Sandy Hook Bay; depth of water, 6 fathoms (36'); 35 fathoms of chain out.

2200 - Anchor bearings checked. Anchor watch set. (Signed: King Upton, Lt., USNR, Commanding.).
(Technically the anchor bearings and landmarks, fixed beacons, etc. from which they were taken should have been written in the log. At least three should have been taken and recorded. If the anchor is not dragging, and the ship remains in the same place, the bearing will remain the same. This is the main function of the anchor watch, to be sure the ship stays where she is supposed to be. The YMS carries two 300 lb. danforth anchors and has a chain locker on the port and the starboard side of the fore peak of the ship. Approximately 50 fathoms of 3" chain is stored in each chain locker. The anchors are secured on the forecastle deck on each side of the bow. There is a small davit (a crane like arm) at the bow for hoisting the anchor from its resting place and swinging it out over the side. The chain from the chain locker is already on the windlass (an electrically driven winch especially for the anchor chain). The anchor end of the chain has already been led through the chain stopper and shackled to the shank of the anchor. Normally the anchor is lowered by the davit to the surface of the water. The ship is stopped and when the Captain gives the order, "let go the anchor," the Bos'n releases the anchor by pulling a snatch hook and the anchor falls into the water. It pulls chain with it until it hits bottom. At this point the ship backs down slowly and lets more chain pay out. The amount of chain let out is determined by the depth of the water. In a normal situation, the amount of chain is 6 times the depth in fathoms. In the case above, the water was 6 fathoms (36') and they let out 35 fathoms. The chain stopper ratchet lever is flipped over on the chain and engages the next link and prevents any more chain from paying out. When the anchoring is finished a pelican hook is fastened to the chain and attached to a pad eye [an eye bolt welded to a flat, square piece of ¼" sheet steel which is bolted to the deck]. This takes the strain of anchor and chain off the windlass. If the bottom of the bay has good holding power and the wind is not too strong, the anchor should hold the ship in its desired position. Of course, if the bottom is "not right", or if there is a strong wind and/or current, other tactics may have to be used. We will experience some of these later on in the story of the 183).

John Dixon Davis

March 25, 1943

0000 - Anchored in Sandy Hook Bay; depth of water 6 fathoms; length of chain, 35 fathoms; drift lead out. (In case the bearing points are hard to see or just for added certainty that the ship is not dragging anchor, a lead line, normally used to manually measure the depth of the water, can be lowered to the bottom from the forecastle deck so that the rope is vertical. Then many feet of slack are dropped into the water and the rope secured to the ship's rail. Periodically, a member of the watch will gently pull the rope up and take out the slack. If the line is still vertical to the ship it is a good indication that the ship is not drifting or dragging anchor. Sometimes when the bottom is rocky, or otherwise more coarse than sand a dragging anchor can be felt by touching the anchor chain and/or through the timbers of the ship).

0721 - Proceeding down Sandy Hook Channel. (When it is time to get under way from an anchorage, the engines are warmed up, the order is given "weigh anchor". The pelican hook is removed and stowed and the windlass begins winding in the chain. As it comes over the slotted drum of the windlass, it pays out into the chain pipe and into the chain locker. As the chain comes into the locker a member of the deck crew is there to flake the chain out in the locker so that when it is used again, it will pay out smoothly. Someone has a water hose with pressure on it to wash the chain as it comes aboard and especially the anchor when it clears the water. This is important if the water is dirty or full of trash or seaweed and/or the bottom is muddy. It is not good to bring this aboard and put it in the chain locker. When the chain has been pulled in so that only the anchor is still on the bottom and the chain is vertical, the Bos'n will say to the Bridge, "Chain is straight up and down". When the chain is off the bottom the Bos'n yells to the Bridge, "anchor's aweigh". The chain continues to come in and soon the anchor can be seen and the Bos'n yells to the Bridge, "anchor clear of the water". At this point the Officer at the Conn will put the engines in gear, start the ship moving forward and give the helmsman the course. As the anchor comes up near the level of the forecastle deck, the davit is swung over the side, the hook from the davit is put into the shackle on the anchor, it is washed by the hoseman, hoisted over the rail and lowered into its stowage place on deck and secured).

0912 - Magnetic gear streamed; started pulsing. Acoustic gear functioning properly.

1619 - Stopped sweeping. Retrieving gear. Entering Ambrose Channel.

1840 - Heaving lines passed at Pier 6.

1955 - Fire on pier 5. Quickly under control. Secured ship. (Signed: King Upton, Lt., USNR, Commanding).

March 26, 1943

0000 - Moored alongside Pier 6, maintaining security watch.

0530 - 672 gals. (fresh) water taken aboard.

0743 - Underway for sweep operations with YMS 184 and YMS 208; verbal orders of Mine Warfare Office. (A part of each day during this period is spent getting the ship to the area to be swept, and, of course, returning to the Base after the sweep is done. Just like driving to and from "the job". The regular routine of cleaning the living spaces, the working spaces, etc. was ongoing while traveling to the area to be swept and returning from it. While sweeping, a different routine is in place as has been described earlier. It was not uncommon for the same area to be swept day after day. One never knew when a German submarine might slip into the channel during the night, lay a magnetic mine or two and quietly slip out. Also, a mine laid "last night" might have been set to go off only after it had been activated 12 times by ships passing over it. If no other ships activated it at all, which was unlikely, the minesweeper had to sweep that area 12 times to detonate and therefore sweep the mine. The work was slow, often boring, very routine, but that was minesweeping).

0938 - Magnetic gear streamed, started sweeping assigned area.

1521 - Started recovering gear. Started returning to Base.

1849 - Started taking on fuel at Bayonne. (2348 gallons). (One of the many responsibilities of the engine room department was keeping up with fuel consumption. Each day one of the engineers would "sound the fuel tanks" and report his findings to the Commanding Officer. He used a metal tape on a reel with a weight on one end. The fuel tank cap, which is flush with the deck directly above a given tank, is removed. The weight is allowed to hit bottom. It is wound up immediately and the level of fuel remaining in the tank is noted on the tape. The level of the fuel is translated to gallons, used and needed. Before the refueling takes place, the engineer checks a sample to be sure no water or foreign matter is in the fuel. Water in the fuel tanks was a constant problem and since water will not run a diesel engine, it was absolutely necessary to check frequently for its presence in the tanks. When a certain amount was detected, it had to be pumped out. Water could also seriously damage the fuel injectors on the engines. Most water in the fuel tanks came from the supplier of the fuel. Mostly when taking fuel from another ship while underway at sea. Not only the main engines but the ship's service generators and the magnetic sweep generator used diesel fuel).

2024 - Heaving lines passed. Tied up alongside Pier 6. (Signed: King Upton, Lt., USNR, Commanding).

March 27, 1943

0000 - Moored alongside Pier 6, maintaining security watch; taking power from Pier.

0800 - Muster; all men present. Regular port routine in force.

0915 - 32 gas masks brought aboard. (Each member of the crew would be issued a gas mask for use in case of the use of gas by the enemy. Fortunately, they never had to be used for this purpose).

1432 - Hall, C.D., EM1/c left ship for 3 day leave.

1500 - Enochs, C., MM 1/c, 274-32-94, transferred from ship to Receiving ship, Pier 92, New York. (The Receiving ship was essentially a way station for Naval Personnel who were moving from one assignment to another. Sometimes they joined a pool of men who would be assigned to other ships which needed their expertise, or were waiting for assignment to a school for more training, etc.).

2000 - Security watch posted. Ship secured for night. (Signed: King Upton, Lt., USNR, Commanding).

March 28, 1943

0000 - Moored North side Pier 6, maintaining security watch.

0800 - Muster. All men present.

0805 - Port routine in force.

1400 - Supplies came aboard.

1700 - All hands aboard from leave.

2000 - Ship secured for night. (Signed: King Upton, Lt., USNR, Commanding).

March 29, 1943

0000 - Moored North side Pier 6, maintaining security watch.

0800 - Executed colors. (In port moored or anchored the National Ensign was raised on a pole on the fantail (stern) of the ship. At the same time the Union Jack (Navy blue bunting with 48 white stars was raised on a pole at the stem (bow) of the ship. Today there are 50 stars on the Union Jack. Each star represents a State of the Union. When these two flags are flying it indicates that the ship is moored and not underway. The colors are raised at 0800 and lowered at sunset. At each of these times all hands above deck face the flag and come to attention. If wearing their uniform hats they salute during this brief ceremony. When the ship gets underway the Ensign is lowered from the stern and raised on its own halyard to the end of the gaff attached to the mast near its top. Here it flies, day or night, rain or shine as long the ship is underway. When the ship is moored or anchored in the day time after being underway, the Ensign is moved from the gaff to the flag pole at the stern.The Union Jack flies at the bow only when the Ensign is flying from the stern or Quarter Deck).

0805 - Painters aboard to paint hull of ship.

1520 - Fox, V.P., S 2/c reported aboard for temporary duty on emergency sweep.

1537 - Ready to get underway for emergency sweep operation in compliance with verbal orders of mine warfare office.

1538 - Underway.

1620 - Proceeding down Ambrose Channel.

1720 - Streaming magnetic gear.

1805 - Began sweeping with YMS 104.

2341 - Electric steering mechanism failed. Steering manually.

2345 - Steering gear again functioning. (Signed: King Upton: Lt., USNR, Commanding).

March 30, 1943

0000 - Operating on emergency sweep operation with YMS 104, between points "X"-Ray and Affirm".

1645 - Recovering gear by orders received from Base. (The log doesn't say why this was an emergency operation, but it lasted from 1805 (6:05 PM) on the 29th until 1645 (4:45 PM) on the 30th. That's approximately 23 hours straight sweeping. The brevity of the entries in the log gives no clue to the time spent sweeping unless you do the calculation of time).

1720 - All gear recovered; proceeding to Base.

1830 - Fort Wadsworth abeam to port.

1915 - Heaving lines passed. Moored alongside Pier 6.

2000 - Electric steering gear motor checked by electrician, and found to be satisfactory. (Signed: King Upton, Lt., USNR, Commanding). It would appear that the problem with the electric steering motor was systemic, for it was to breakdown frequently in the months and years to come).

March 31, 1943

0000 - Moored North side Pier 6, maintaining security watch.

0930 - Made preparations for getting underway; Visibility very poor.

1316 - Visibility lifted. Under way. Under way for sweep operation with YMS 184, in compliance with orders from Mine Warfare Office.

1405 - Shifted to remote engine control. Proceeding down Ambrose Channel.

1635 - Streaming magnetic - Acoustic gear; 2 miles, 342° True from Buoy "E". YMS 184 position, starboard beam, using A.C. slave. The two ships are working together electronically so that one vessel tells both ships when to pulse. This ship is the "master". The other ship which only pulses when told to do so by the "master" is the "slave".The signal from one ship to the other is passed through the salt water by an Alternating current. This arrangement insures that the strongest magnetic field possible is created by both ships at the same time.

2000 - Making sweep.
2359 - Sweeping as before. (Signed: King Upton, Lt., USNR, Commanding). (As of April 1, 1943 the Officer Complement and next of kin was as follows: Upton, King, Lieut., USNR reported aboard 1-15-43. (He apparently was romoted from Lt.jg on 3-13-43 to full Lt.). Next of kin, Letitia Upton, c/o Mr. Howard Brown, Topsfield, Mass. Doherty, Adrian W., Lieut., USNR reported aboard 1-15-43. (He apparently also received a promotion from Ltjg., to full Lt. Since 1-15-43). Next of kin, Ann M. Doherty (mother), Jersey City, N.J. Dill, Jesse M., Ensign, USNR reported aboard 1-15-43. Next of kin, Charlotte Ezell Dill, Murfreesboro, Tennessee. Murphy, Frederick S., Lieut.jg, USNR reported aboard 3-3-43. Next of kin Frances C. Murphy, Essex Falls, N.J. (See Appendix E for muster roll of the crew).

April 1, 1943

0000 - Sweeping in formation with YMS 184 with acoustic-magnetic gear; visibility 1 mile.
0210 - Sounding fog signals - estimated visibility 100 yds.
0345 - All gear retrieved; heading for Sandy Hook anchorage.
0640 - Anchored 4 fathoms water with 30 fathoms chain. Approximate position 1 3/4 miles from Scotland buoy. Buoy bearing 309° True.
1107 - Visibility increasing; Underway for return to Base. Course 341° True. Sounding fog signals.
1133 - Passed through anti-sub nets.
1314 - Taking power from dock.
2000 - Lines checked every half hour. Ship secured for night. (Signed: King Upton, Lt., USNR, Commanding).

John Dixon Davis

Chapter 5
Shakedown

April 2, 1943

(Minesweeping trials completed, reported for shakedown 04-02-43 to Com EastSeaFron 022128 Apr. '43).

0000 - Moored North side Pier 6, Berth 4, outboard of YMS 110, US Navy Section Base, Tom Kinsville, Staten Island. Maintaining security watch.
0800 - Executed colors. Held quarters for muster; no absentees.
1400 - Began payment of crew and officers.
2050 - Baron, R.R. (Sea. 2c) 706-97-25, USNR, this date reported on board this vessel for duty. (Signed: King Upton, Lt., USNR, Commanding).

April 3, 1943

0000 - Moored alongside YMS 110, Pier 6, Berth 4, Section Base, Tom Kinsville Staten Island, maintaining security watch.
0749 - Sight muster held. 1 absentee.
0806 - Absentee returned absent over leave from 0700, April 3.
0808 - Underway for minesweeping operation with YMS 184 in obedience to verbal orders of Mine Warfare Office, Captain at Con, executive officer and navigator on bridge standing out of New York Harbor on various courses conforming to channel.
0828 - Fort Wadsworth abeam to starboard.
0839 - Passed through anti-submarine nets, set course down Ambrose Channel, 170° True, set degaussing.
0930 - Streaming acoustic-magnetic gear.
1008 - Began pulsing with YMS 184, 300 yards to starboard. (Note: This was a "master"- "slave" sweep.
1052 - Electric steering control failed, manual control used. Electric gear out only temporarily.
1200 - Pulsing in phase with YMS 184.
1613 - Electric steering gear failed momentarily.
2000 - Sweeping channel with YMS 184. (Signed: King Upton, Lt, USNR, Commanding).

April 4, 1943

0000 - Sweeping in formation with YMS 184; area, main channel, Buoy I to Buoy A. Using A.C. sweep current, 2500 amperes. 0030 - All lights reported burning. Lights used are: sweep lights, running lights, forward range light, stern light. (In most cases during the war, no ships of any kind showed any lights whatever, for obvious reasons. However, there were times when sweeping the entrance channels of a port like New York, the navigational lights had to be shown for several reasons: the safety of the minesweeper by showing its position and direction of travel to other vessels at all times; to warn other ships from running across the minesweeping gear and damaging it and/or the other vessel; and facilitating station keeping for the two minesweepers as they swept. This was no mere exercise, of course. It was deadly serious business, for the channels had to be clear of submarine laid mines at all times. No one knew when the German submarines might lay mines in the approaches to New York Harbor. We had to go on the assumption that it could happen at any time, therefore, our minesweepers had to sweep, literally, around the clock. The running lights are the red light on the port side (left) and the green light on the starboard (right) side. If another ship saw the red light alone he knew the ship was passing from right to left. If the green light was seen alone then the viewer knew the ship was passing from left to right. If red and green were seen at the same time then the vessel is coming straight toward the viewer. The sweep lights are red and located on each end of the yard arm and at the top of the mast. These lights can be seen from any position by a viewer. They warn that the vessel is engaged in sweeping mines. In daylight the three black balls, one on each end of the yardarm and one at the masttop warm that minesweeping is in progress. The forward range light is a white light about halfway up the mast with blinders on each side so that the light can only be seen when the ship is heading in the general direction of the viewer. This light, with the running lights, can give the viewer accurate information about the direction of the vessel being viewed. The stern light is a white light that is only visible from the stern and tells the viewer that the vessel being viewed is going away).

0350 - Electric steering mechanism failed temporarily.
0946 - Abeam Ambrose lightship and started retrieving gear.
1030 - Gear inboard. Returning to Base.
1050 - Passed buoy "2A", entrance to Channel. Proceeding up channel on various courses and speeds.
1136 - Passed through anti-submarine nets.
1221 - Entering fuel dock at Bayonne.
1350 - Docked alongside fuel pier. YMS 184 damaged acoustic boom while attempting to dock (The log has reported numerous difficulties on the part of other ships in coming alongside the YMS 183 to tie up. Minor collisions have caused minor damage on a number of occasions. I think it is fair to say that the ship handlers on many of these YMSes had not had a lot of experience. But it also needs to be pointed out that the wind and tidal conditions in New York Harbor on all occasions make for treacherous situations requiring the greatest skill. On this point, A. J. Richard, former Quartermaster 1/c, when detached from the ship in August, 1945, has written about this problem and paid a fine tribute to his former Skipper. He writes, "King Upton was only on the ship for a short while. He was very good at seamanship. If I remember correctly his background was The Merchant Marine. I can remember when he would return from sweeping the channel in New York. Docking the ship in Staten Island was a chore because of the tough current. He was the only one who could handle the mooring. He was a quiet person, so it was hard to get to know him. However, when I was a Seaman 1/c and trying to become a QM 3/c, he took the time to practice semaphore (signaling with a small flag in each hand) with me. He was a big help to me. Sometime after the war, I ran into him in Boston, and after being certain he was my former Skipper, I approached him, reintroduced myself and we had a great time talking about the "old 183").
1405 - Underway for return to Pier 6, Tom Kinsville.
1428 - Lines passed. Tied up alongside Pier 6. (Signed: King Upton, Lt. USNR, Commanding).

April 5, 1943

0000 - Moored alongside Pier 6, Tom Kinsville, maintaining security. YMS 184 moored along starboard side. Taking electricity from dock.
0700 - Held muster. All men present. Turned to for regular ship's port routine.
1005 - Captain Gill, USN, commanding officer of Section Base, came aboard with inspection party to inspect ship.
1050 - Commanding Officer of Base, and staff, left ship.
1310 - Received food supplies from Supply Officer.

1330 - Auxiliary refrigerator came aboard.

1400 - Navy workmen aboard for repairs to electric steering gear, helping to place auxiliary refrigerator, and water cooler.

2300 - Workmen secured (Signed: King Upton, Lt., USNR, Commanding).

April 6, 1943

0000 - Moored alongside Berth 4, Pier 6, Section Base, maintaining security watch. Taking power from Pier. YMS 184 moored alongside.

0800 - Underway for sweep operation with YMS 184, in accordance with verbal orders from Mine Warfare Office. Proceeding down harbor on various courses and speeds

0832 - Passed through anti-submarine nets. Course 190° True to proceed to Siwash Channel.

1018 - Electric steering failed momentarily.

1050 - Starboard engine broke down. Using port engine at standard speed. Started back to Base. YMS 184 to continue sweep. (This is a good place to mention equipment redundancy. On all ships except the very small craft, there were two of everything. There were two main propulsion engines, two ship's service generators, electric and manual steering, bilge pumps, gyrocompass and magnetic compass. The main reason, of course, was for backup, and the ability to continue to operate until repairs could be made. Also, as in the case on April 6, 1943, the YMS 184 could continue the sweep and not have to tow the 183 back to the pier, which would have been the case if the 183 had had only one main propulsion engine).

1333 - Passed Scotland Buoy abeam to port, 500 yds.

1345 - Anchor detail ready to drop anchor if necessary. (If the port engine had failed then the 183 would have been adrift. This is called "underway with no way on". The only alternative in a harbor, or bay where the water in not too deep is to anchor until help, by way of a tug, or another vessel arrives. If the water is too deep then the ship drifts with the wind, waves and tide. The author has experienced this on a number of occasions in the open ocean. It can be very quiet out there. When a ship is adrift a flag hoist is raised on the signal yardarm indicating this difficulty. At night when lights can be shown a combination of masthead lights indicate this problem. Where lights cannot be shown, the situation will have to be dealt with by the senior officer present in the task force. When the anchor detail stands ready to drop the anchor, they have it hanging by its chain off the bow of the ship, part way down to the water, so that in an instant it can be let go and plunge to the bottom to stop the ship from being adrift).

1603 - Entering harbor.

1713 - Lines passed. Moored starboard side to Pier 6, Tom Kinsville.

1800 - Gouge, Edward Carlton, (F 1/c) 244-60-11, USNR, reported aboard for duty.

1825 - Taking power from dock.

2000 - Ship secure. Lines checked hourly. King Upton, Lt. USNR, Commanding. (Constant checking of the mooring lines was an absolute necessity. If the lines became too tight, as when the tide went out and they were not loosened, then they could break from the weight of the ship or cause the ship to rub destructively against the pier. If the lines became too loose, as when the tide came in since the ship was initially moored, and the slack was not taken out, then the lines could chafe in the fairleads [a hole through the gunwale with a smooth metal liner to prevent chafing].and be worn in two over time. No matter what the situation, the lines had to be checked frequently, and adjusted if necessary, for the safety of the ship).

John Dixon Davis

April 7, 1943

(Note: Beginning with the log entry on this date, the hourly entries will not be copied here unless they add some new insight into the operation of the ship or the activities of the crew or some significant event. By now, the reader will have gotten a real sense of the deadening sameness of life aboard ship from watch to watch and day to day. This sameness was characteristic of life in any branch of the military service as training was practiced over and over until the routine responsibilities could be accomplished without having to stop and ponder what was required. There were breaks in the routine, as when there was engine failure, stormy weather, enemy alert, etc. but these times were in the minority and the deadening routine was in the overwhelming majority. Even though the name of the Commanding Officer will no longer be copied, except in special circumstances, be assured that he did sign every day's entry in the log book).

0753 - Preparations made to get underway for sweeping operations with YMS 184. (Sweeping operations were conducted, and the ship anchored in Sandy Hook Bay atAnchor bearings made and drift lead used and all checked every 30 minutes).

April 8, 1943

0000 - Anchored in Sandy Hook Bay, 35 fathoms of chain out. Bearings on the following lights taken for drift. Sandy Hook Point Light, Old Orchard light, West Bank light and Romer Shoal light. (No degree bearings recorded).

0746 - Underway for magnetic - acoustic sweep with 184.

1400 - Continuing sweep, 2nd part of 24 hour sweep

April 9, 1943

1008 - Sweep completed. All gear inboard, laying to awaiting target vessel for gun firing drill. General Quarters sounded and firing of the 3" 50 cal and anti-aircraft   guns practiced. Returned to Section Base. Secured to Pier 6 for the night.

April 10, 1943

Took on fuel at Pier 7 (2373 gallons) Tied up alongside YMS 110 at Pier 6.

1600 - Captain's Mast held for the following: one man failed muster, punishment, loss of 2 liberties; one man, failed muster, punishment, loss of two liberties; one man transferred to Base for medical treatment.   Took on fresh water.

April 11, 1943

0800 - Left harbor with YMS 184 for magnetic - acoustic effective sweep of upper channel. This sweep continued through the day and evening.

April 12, 1943

1200 - sweep continued, and then gear recovered. (This was a continuous sweep of 28 hours ending near Ambrose Lightship). 1600 - Shepherd, J.H., Sea 1/c, (V-6), USNR, 656-29-41, reported aboard ship for temporary duty

April 13, 1943

0800 - Took on 800 gallons fresh water. Proceeded with YMS 184 down Ambrose Channel. Changed electrode on short tail of magnetic cable. Streamed magnetic and acoustic gear.

2000 – Turned on sweep lights, running lights and forward range light.

April 14, 1943

0000 - Continuing magnetic and acoustic sweep, pulsing at 2500 amperes. YMS 183 is "master" ship and YMS 184 "slave" running alternately "forward and reverse". Burning running lights and forward range light in addition to sweep lights.

0320 - 0520 standing by YMS 184 in vicinity of buoy "A". 184 has engine trouble. Sweep continued at 0520. Sweep of triangle concluded at 1015. Recovered gear and headed for Base. Arrived Base 1200.

April 15, 1943

0800 - 1200 Executed Colors. Captain joined staff of Captain Gill for inspection of YMS 184.

April 16, 1943

0745 - Following men on leave, to return 1000 April 19, 1943: Richard, A.J., Sea 1/c; Mulford, Alex, F 1/c; Shurts, C.E., MoMM 2/c; Wright, W., St M 2/c.

0800 - Underway for exploratory "O" type sweep in Ambrose channel. Streamed 150 fathoms sweep wire, 8 fathoms depressor wire and 10' float pendant. Completed "O" type sweep, recovered gear and streamed magnetic- acoustic gear.

1908 - Port engine failed. Retrieved sweep gear, hoisted breakdown lights and started for Base using starboard engine.

April 17, 1943

0232 - Arrived at Pier 6.

1200 - 1600 Received aboard one gasoline powered "handy billy" pump complete with spare parts. (The "handy billy" pump was a portable water pump. It weighed perhaps 30 lbs. and had couplings for two inch hose connections. Its engine was rated at about 3 horse power, and not unlike the modern grass mower. It was used anywhere it could be taken to pump water for fire protection, to drain the bilges, wash down the decks, etc. Primarily for emergency use as when the bilge pumps failed, or extra water was needed for a fire, etc. it was a very useful item and was guarded with great care by the engineers who kept it in running order. Since it was not bolted to the deck it could be, and sometimes was stolen by crew members from other ships. Another factor relating to the "handy billy" was the fuel it used, gasoline. This highly flammable fuel was used only for the "handy billy" and the outboard motor for the life boat. Therefore the gasoline had to be stored very carefully, so as not to start a fire or contribute to one started by something else. It had to be easily jettisoned if necessary. The answer was a heavy galvanized steel tank about 36 inches long and 12 inches in diameter. It was secured to a steel holder which was fastened between the top of the gunwale [wooden railing around the main deck] and the underside of the forecastle deck just outside the officer's wardroom hatch on both sides of the ship. The holder was canted at an angle, so that when the pelican hook, [a quick release hook] securing the tank in place, was released the tank would roll over and clear the side of the ship and sink into the water out of danger).

April 18, 1943

0400 - Took on 1142 gallons of fresh water.
0800 - Underway for sweep operation with YMS 184.
1152 - Sounded gen'l quarters in vicinity of Buoy "A" on sighting depth-charge explosions of a destroyer on our port beam, [port side] distance, one mile.
1200 - more depth charges dropped by the DD.

1224 secured from gen'l quarters, and continued sweep.

April 19, 1943

0000 - Continued sweep with YMS 184, burning sweep, running, forward range lights.

0732 Port engine failed. Recovered gear and returned to Base. YMS 184 continued sweep. Proceeding to Base on starboard engine.

1200 - Shepherd, J.H., (S 1/c), 656-29-41, V-6, USNR detached from temporary duty.

April 20, 1943

0800 - Held muster, 2 absentees. All lookouts attended "Lookout Lecture and Movie" held at A/S [Anti-Submarine] Training Center. The two absentees returned aboard one hour and fifty five minutes over leave.

1200 - Sound men (Sonar) attended lecture on attack at A/S Center. [Sonar training had to do with locating submarines from the noise they made].

April 21, 1943

0800 - Held muster; executed colors. [Raised the flag]. Made daily inspection of magazines. Max temp 55; Min. temp 54. Ship's Cook returned from over leave. (More often than not, on YMSes, the ship's cook was a volunteer from among the crew. If there was no volunteer then the cook was "appointed". Surprisingly some of the volunteers and/or "appointees" were quite good in the galley. When a capable one was found it was likely that he would hold the job whether he liked it or not. A well fed ship's company helped make for a happy ship. There were other variables, of course, but the galley was a very important one).

April 22, 1943

Regular port work carried on.

April 23, 1943

0900 - Lt. A.W. Doherty, DEV(G), USNR, detached this date in accordance with Bu Pers (Bureau of Personnel) dispatch 210337 April. Captain's Mast held for infractions by several of the crew, one for intoxication and one held over. - All water breakers refilled. (A water breaker was a small wooden barrel holding about 5 gallons of water for emergency use. They were attached to the life rafts and placed at other locations on the ship). - Underway to Sandy Hook Bay to test engines and to repair cable. After repair tied up to Army Dock. Maintained radio watch with YMS 105. [At times ships moored together could conserve energy and alertness by sharing responsibility for certain needed activities. Having someone monitor the TBS radio at all times was required of each ship, but they could arrange to take turns and alert the other of radio contacts of importance. This is what is meant by maintaining radio watch with YMS 105].

April 24, 1943

0800 - Underway with YMS 105 to sweep channel with magnetic and acoustic gear. Magazine temperatures: Max 57, Min. 56.

1200 - Sweeping fringe of channel with YMS 105 because of traffic. (During the average daylight hours there were very many ships of all kinds entering and leaving the Port of New York. At times this created problems for the minesweepers and they were reduced to sweeping the edges of the channel until they could sweep the middle of the channels when traffic was reduced and this was usually at night). Leaking gasket on port engine. Repaired immediately.

April 25, 1943

0000 - Continuing magnetic - acoustic sweep with YMS 105.
0912 - Recovering gear. Proceeding to base. Took on 3600 gallons of fuel oil at Bayonne. Tied up at Pier 6
1214 - Port routine in force.

April 26, 1943

0000 - Regular port routine in progress.

April 27, 1943

0630 - Underway with YMS 184 for magnetic sweep operation down Ambrose Channel.
1035 - YMS 184 reported broken down. YMS 183 continues sweep.
1548 - Recovering gear in vicinity of Ambrose Light vessel.
1728 - Anchored in Sandy Hook Bay.
1830 - Holding all general drills.

April 28, 1943

0649 - Anchor's aweigh. Underway for sweep operation with YMS 184 and YMS 42.
1740 - Pulled out of channel to allow freighter to pass. 2241 - Sweeping Lower Channel.

April 29, 1943

0000 - Continuing sweep with YMS 184 and YMS 42.
1108 - Held collision drill. Satisfactory.
1140 - Tied up alongside Pier 6.
1230 - Lt.(jg) Rosenberg of Ordnance Dept. came aboard as member of 3rd Naval District Inspection Board.
1305 - Underway for inspection with following officers in inspection party: Lt. Neusse, USN; Lt. Robertson; Lt. Smith; and Lt. Hughes.
1351 - Began general drills for inspection party. (These drills included "man-over- board", fire, collision, general quarters, abandon ship, etc. Successful performance of these drills indicated that the ship and its officers and crew were about ready to go to their assignment with the fleet).
1424 - Returning to Base.
1520 - Following men reported aboard for temporary duty: Hadden, G.T. (650-56-MoMM 2/c, USNR; Stohn, W.T. (607-04-07) Cox, USNR; Lewis, A.S(646-30-12) S 1/c, USN.

April 30, 1943

1200 - Tug came alongside to tow YMS 183 to Pier 7 for check on Timer. Hammer (acoustic) struck dock with force.
1830 -Took soundings. [In the bilges] Found estimated rise of 1/3" of water in gyro, generator rooms and magazines since 1600. (It would appear that water from some unknown source was getting into the bilges under the decking of these spaces).

May 1, 1943

0030 - Took soundings in magazine, gyro room and generator room. No noticeablechange in depth of water.
0430 - Rise in sounding: gyro room -5 1/2", magazine 4 ¾", engine room normal, generator room normal.

0730 - Rise in sounding: gyro room - 6 3/4", magazine 4 /34", engine room and generator room normal. [Of course, the water was pumped out after sounding].0900 - Following men granted leave of 72 hours: Anderson, A.H., S 1/c; Kelly, D.P., Cox; Rosbury, C.H., S 1/c; Bula, S.T., F 1/c; Daniels, D.T., QM 3/c.

0930 - Underway for sweeping operation with YMS 110.

May 2, 1943

0000 - Continuing sweep with YMS 110. Checked bilges; slight increase.

0751 - Recovering gear.

1036 - Entering Pier 8 to go alongside fuel barge. Took 2665 gallons.

1224 - Struck PC 1195 glancing blow when caught by current. No damage done.

1240 - Lt. Upton consulted captain of PC 1195 in regards to accident. No official report to be made because of smallness of damage.

May 3, 1943

0600 - Liberty muster, one absentee.

0650 - Underway for sweep operation with YMS 184.

2312 - Continuing magnetic - acoustic sweep.

May 4, 1943

0000 - Continuing sweep with 184. Running lights, sweep lights and mast head light being used.

0827 - Sweep completed, retrieving gear.

1050 - Proceeding to make run over degaussing range.

1200 - Completed run of range. Results satisfactory.

1251 - Tied up at Berth 2, Pier 6.

1255 - Anderson, A.H., S 1/c; Daniels, D.T., QM 3/c; Bula, S.T.; Rosbury, C.H., S 1/c; Kelly, D. P., Cox, back from 72 hour leave.

May 5, 1943

0800 - Held quarters, two men absent over leave. Both men returned at 0841.

0935 - Provisions brought aboard. Inspected as to quality and quantity.

1350 - Yard workmen completed tests on acoustic hammer.

1410 - Hadden, G.T., MoMM 2 /c and Sessions, C. G., MoMM 2 /c detached in accordance with temporary duty orders.

1450 - Base held General Quarters. General Quarters stations of the ship manned.

1815 - Lt.jg E.R. Seaver, 119605, E-V(G) USNR reported this date for duty in accordance with Bu Pers Orders 26529 dated April 23, 1943. (Biographical note:Robert Seaver was born July 15, 1915 at Beloit, Kansas. He graduated from the University of Missouri at Kansas City in 1940 with a Doctor of Jurisprudence (J.D.)degree. He enlisted in the Navy in 1941, was sent to the US Navy Midshipman's School at Annapolis, MD where he was commissioned an Ensign after the 90 day training. His first assignment was to the "Heath Hen", AMc-6, a minesweeper, converted from a tuna fish boat. It was operating out of Norfolk, Va. when Seaver was aboard).

May 6, 1943

0800 - The following men left on 72 hour leave: Souza, J. (204-73-37) S 2/c, USN; Deshler, F. G. (620-19-85), Y 2/c; Morgan, E.L. (375-94-68) MM 2/c.

0921 - Streaming magnetic - acoustic gear with YMS 184 in Siwash Channel.

1200 - YMS 184 returning to Base because of trouble with sweep generator. 183 continues the sweep.
2256 - Secured pulse; began retrieving gear.
2332 - Gear inboard. Laying to near swept channel.

May 7, 1943

0609 - Streaming "O" type gear. Using starboard and port paravanes; 50' float pendant and 150' sweep wire. (There are two interesting things involved in this sweep; 1. The "O" type gear, for moored mines, is streamed from the stern of the ship on both sides at the same time. This means that the ship is sweeping on both sides of the course that is being steered. The ship itself is in unswept water, but since mines near the surface are not expected it is relatively safe. 2. The float pendant, which governs how deep the sweep wire and cutters will sweep mines, is 50' long. Therefore, they are sweeping for mines that are within 50' of the surface. This is a fairly deep sweep, but some cargo ships and large Naval vessels will draw almost this much water, so they must be protected by an exploratory sweep to determine if there are mines at the deeper levels). YMS 184 has joined the formation.
2000 - sweep completed, tied up to US Army dock at Sandy Hook.

May 8, 1943

0655 - Underway with YMS 184 for routine magnetic sweep. 0842 - began pulsing.
1718 - Port engine stopped. Fuel line clogged. 184 continues sweep.
1856 - Port engine repaired. Continuing sweep.

May 9, 1943

0000 - Continuing sweep. 184 on starboard beam.
0923 - Recovering magnetic gear, proceeding to Base. Received 2665 gallons fuel oil at Pier 7.
1330 - Liberty began. Hall B.M. (267-88-33) CBM, USN, left ship on 7 day leave.

May 10, 1943

0800 - Executed colors. One man over leave. He returned to ship over leave 2 hours and 45 minutes.
1200 - Stohn, W.T., Cox and Lewis, Arthur, S 1/c detached this date from ship after 10 day training period.
1400 - Captain's Mast held for two men for fighting.
1620 - Blumenthal, A. (709-50-33) F 1/c, USNR left ship on 72 hour leave.

May 11, 1943

0400 - Underway for acoustic - magnetic sweep with YMS 184
1225 - Recovered gear and proceeded to Sandy Hook dock.

May 12, 1943

0745 - Underway for sweep operation with YMS 184. 0812 - Returning to Sandy hook because of thick fog. Tried several more times during the day to sweep, but the visibility due to fog made it too dangerous.

May 13, 1943

0656 - Underway for sweep operation with YMS 184. Swept all day, & through the evening hours (magnetic - acoustic).

John Dixon Davis

May 14, 1943

0000 - Continuing the sweep.
0206 - Sighted darkened ship crossing from starboard to port. Slowed to 1/3 speed.
0800 - Unable to complete sweep because of heavy traffic. Recovered gear.
1120 - Moored North Pier 6, Berth 3.
1300 - Captain's Mast for two men: one man AOL 2 hrs. & 45 minutes. Awarded 10 days restriction; One man, failure to muster. Awarded 5 days restriction.

May 15, 1943

0800 - Held muster after colors. Mulford, A.L. (647-23-29) F 1/c and Baron, R.R. (706-97-25) S 2/c left ship on special liberty.
1030 - took on 1579 gallons fuel oil.
1300 - Liberty for starboard watch section.
1645 - Received spare parts for air compressor.
2025 - Hall, B.M., CBM returned aboard from leave.

May 16, 1943

0746 - Underway, alone, for sweep operation.
1115 - Retrieving magnetic gear and streaming "O" type gear.
1548 - Recovering "O" type gear.
1637 - Completed streaming magnetic gear.
1820 - Recovered magnetic gear.
1945 - Tied up at US Army Dock at Sandy Hook.

May 17, 1943

0800 - Underway for sweep with YMS 184.
0935 - Streaming magnetic and acoustic gear.
1053 - fog becoming a problem.
1512 - impractical to cross channelso as to sweep the other side due to too much ship traffic in the channel.
1600 - finally crossed channel.
1805 - Retrieving sweep gear and returning to Army dock at Sandy Hook.

May 18, 1943

0645 - Underway for another scheduled acoustic - magnetic sweep with YMS 184. Sweep continues through the day and evening.

May 19, 1943

0000 - Continuing channel sweep with YMS 184.
0929 - Sweep gear recovered, proceeding to Base.
1100 - Tied outboard of SC 1038, North Pier 9.
1105 - Roether, J.T. and Boday, S.J. returned from 72 hour leave.
1426 - Finished taking fuel from barge.
1525 - One man brought aboard by guard from Pier 6. Magazine temperature: Max. 70 degrees; Min. 65 degrees. (As the Spring season and the warming of the water with the longer days proceeds the temperatures in the bowels of the ship get a little warmer).

May 20, 1943

0730 - Anderson, A. H., and Rosbury, C.H. left ship on special liberty. Base workmen on board, making repairs. Payday for officers and crew. All fire extinguishers weighed, one refilled.

May 21, 1943

0500 - Liberty expired. Five men absent over leave.
0849 - Streaming magnetic and acoustic gear.
1635 - Recovering gear due to very poor visibility.
1812 - Visibility better. Streaming gear and continuing sweep.
2201 - YMS 184 has trouble with sweep generator, recovering gear.
2342 - YMS 183 joins YMS 104 in channel sweep.

May 22, 1943

0000 - Sweep with YMS 104 continues.
0850 - Sweep completed, recovering gear. 1059 - entering slip at Pier 6.
1240 - One man reported aboard with guard from Section Base. He had reported to Section Base at 1700 on May 21, AOL.
1315 - Captain's Mast held and the following punishments awarded: One Charged as habitual offender of Absent Over Leave, awarded Reduction to next inferior rating; One Charged with refusal to obey orders, awarded 12 hours extra duty; One Charged, AOL 1 hour, awarded reprimand by Captain; One Charged, AOL 35 minutes, awarded 12 hours extra duty; One Charged AOL, held for further action; One AOL 35 minutes, awarded deck court. (The reader may note that different men are awarded different punishments for the same offense. However, if the men were identified, the reader would note that some of the men were more frequent transgressors than were others. These men were often punished more severely).

May 23, 1943

0345 - Liberty expired. Two men absent over leave, but did report aboard before getting underway for sweep operation. Sweep with YMS 184 lasted until 0850 May 24, 1943.

May 24, 1943

1139 - alongside fuel barge at South Pier 8 taking on fuel. Finished taking on fuel, returned to Pier 7, berth 7.
1313 - One man reported aboard 33 hours over leave.
1600 - General Electric workmen completed installation of Mark VI No. 4 Auxiliary Controller in preparation for series of tests to be made during week of May 24.

May 25, 1943

0630 - Boday, S.J. (205-21-23) F 2/c left ship on 48 hour leave.
0730 - Welch, J.L., (201-62-67) S 1/c left for Naval Hospital.
0800 - Got underway for short sweep and to test installation of GE Mk VI No. 4, Aux. Controller, in company with YMS 184. Began pulsing at Scotland buoy and proceeded to point Manasquam. Tested AC Master and slave operation and DC master and slave operation. Both functioned successfully.
1706 - Recovered gear and returned to Base.
1940 - One man reported aboard over leave since 0600 May 20, 1943. – Richard, A.J. returned from 72 hour leave. – Baron, R.R. (706-97-25) S 2/c left on 72 hour leave.

John Dixon Davis

May 26, 1943

0800 - Ship's force turned to for regular routine. Workmen from Base on board working on GE Aux. Controller.

1125 - Following men from GE Company on board for check of equipment by permission from Bu Pers & Minewarfare Office: George Hupman, George Connolly, J.W. Matthews, and B.R. Shephard. (This is an interesting entry in the log, and was added personally by the skipper, Lt. Upton. These Company men, who probably built the Mk VI controller, were civilians and had to have special clearance to board the ship and work on this equipment. The most secret item on a YMS during this period of WWII was the magnetic minesweeping gear and especially the Auxiliary Controller. Officers and crews of minesweepers who attended The Naval Mine Warfare School at Yorktown, Va. remember all too well the strict regulations governing the Top Secret Manuals relating to minesweeping in general and to magnetic sweeping in particular. From time to time an officer or an enlisted man was expelled from the school because of his failure to handle this material properly and when not in use to lock it in the safe in his quarters).

1140 - Captain's Mast for man who was AOL from May 20 to 25. He pleaded guilty and awarded Summary Court Martial. To be transferred to Base for trial.

1145 - Deck Court for man AOL 12 hours, May 16. Pleaded guilty. Awarded fine of $12. per month for three months. Total loss of pay, $36. Transferred to Brooklyn Naval Hospital, NY for treatment in accordance with Form G this date.

1150 - Deck Court for man AOL 12 hours May 21, 1943. Pleaded guilty. Fined $12. per month for 3 months. Total loss of pay $36.00.

1152 - Deck Court for man AOL 35 minutes, May 21, 1943. Pleaded guilty and fined $16. per month for 3 months. Total loss of pay $48.00 (The reader needs to keep in mind that some of these men were repeat offenders. This accounts for the difference in severity of punishment for the same offense).

May 27, 1943

0515 - Boday, S.T., F 2/c returned from 48 hour leave. Smith, C.P., SM 2/c returned from 48 hour leave.

0730 - Man awaiting Summary Court Martial transferred to Pier.

0800 - Underway to make channel sweep and test GE Auxiliary Controller and make other tests of sweep gear. Following men from the Navy Bu Ships and General Electric Company on board: Lt. G.W. Ashley, Lt. W.B. White; George Hupman, George Connolly, J.W Matthews and B.R. Shephard.

1016 - Started pulsing.

1730 Secured tests. Gear recovered and returning to Base.

2049 - Barron, R.R. (706-97-25) S 2/c left ship on 72 hour leave.

May 28, 1943

0000 - Magazine Temperatures: Max. 69 degrees, Min. 68 degrees.

0800 - Underway, proceeding down channel with same workmen from GE and Bu Ships as yesterday for tests.

0946 - started pulsing. and testing different combinations of control with YMS 184.

1835 - Gear having been recovered, tied up at Pier 7, Berth 2, outboard of AMc-65.

May 29, 1943

0700 - Prepartions for getting underway to continue tests from May 28.

0745 - Roether, J.T. (224-47-48) Cox, left ship for 24 hour liberty.
0752 - Underway for sweep.
1230 - Observed failure of depth-charge of DE 162 to explode.
1707 - Ceased pulsing . Retrieving gear.
1902 - tied up North Pier 7, Berth 8, port side to.

May 30, 1943

0910 - men from GE aboard for dock tests.
1608 - Man in Brig at Pier 6 returned to ship and sent to sick bay under custody of Hall, B.M., CBM.
    1845 secured from tests.

May 31, 1943

0600 - YO 58 alongside to refuel both YMS 183 and 184.
0740 - GE men aboard for tests.
0745 - Man in custody returns to sick bay.
0750 - One man reported AOL 1 hour and 20 minutes.
0800 - Underway for channel and tests.
1600 - Completed tests, returning to Base.
2000 - Man in custody returns from sick bay.
2020 - Following men, A-S, V-1 ROTC, reported aboard for temporary duty from Section Base: Walter, W.F. (404-17-17, Kallman, D.C.; Sweet, R.W. (732-61-18), Thomas, E.H. (732-60-12).

June 1, 1943

0800 - Underway for sweep down Siwash Channel and tests with YMS 184.
1628 - Ceased pulsing and tests and started recovering gear.
2300 - Tested ship to ship radio unsuccessfully with BYMS. [A BYMS was a YMS commissioned in the British Navy. Probably not on the same radio frequency as the YMS].

June 2, 1943

0655 - Underway for sweep operations with AM 80 & AMc-109.
0814 - General Quarters held, results satisfactory in all respects.
1515 - Test firing 30 cal. machine guns.

June 3, 1943

0800 - Payday held for officers and men.
1200 - Liberty announced from 1300 - 0800 June 4.

June 4, 1943

0800 - Yard workmen aboard for repairs.
0935 - One man returned AOL 1 hour and 20 minutes. (Magazine temperatures Max. 80 degrees, Min. 78 degrees).

June 5, 1943

0730 - Verity, H.W., F 2/c left ship on 72 hour leave.
0733 - Underway for sweep assignment.
1813 - recovering gear proceeding to Sandy Hook anchorage.

John Dixon Davis

June 6, 1943

0212 - Underway for sweep operation with YMS 184 and YMS 105.
0639 - Proceeding on zig-zag sweep, alternating on courses 116° true and 027° true.
1845 - Recovering gear, Proceeding back to Sandy Hook.
2223 - Dropped anchor in Sandy Hook Bay.

June 7, 1943

0709 - Anchor aweigh. Proceeding out of Sandy Hook Bay for sweep operation with YMS 184.
2337 - Sweep continued all day and into the evening.

June 8, 1943

0000 - Acoustic - magnetic sweep with YMS 184 continues.
0812 - Completed taking in gear. Proceeding to Base.
0956 - Tied up to Pier 6.
1015 - Kallman, Walker, Sweet and Thomas, all A-S, V-1, USNR detached from temporary duty.
1130 - One man reported aboard, AWOL from June 5, 0645.
1325 - The following, all AS V-1 (NROTC) reported for temporary duty and training: Coggins, R.W. (404-16-89); Cannon, J.D. (732-60-40); Masland, W.S. (404-17-04); Mckenna, R.L. (404-17-00)
2135 - Air alert sounded. General Quarters sounded on ship. AA guns manned. (The log for this date was actually signed by Lt.jg J.M. Dill, USNR Commanding, although he did not in fact become the Commanding Officer until the next day, June 9, 1943. By the time the log for June 8, 1943 was ready for Lt. King Upton's signature, his last day as C.O., he had already left the ship).

Chapter 6
A New C.O. Takes Command

June 9, 1943

0800 - Executed colors. Held muster. No absentees.

0950 - Lt. King Upton, D-V (G) USNR relieved as Commanding Officer of USS YMS 183, and detached in accordance with Bu Pers orders 40652, dated 22 May

1943 - (Reference No. Pers - 3136 - JMZ) - Lt.jg Jesse Madison Dill, D-V (G) assumed command in accordance with Commander Ambrose Section order of June 8, 1943 - Article 824, NR complied with. (Article 824 of Naval Regulations has to do with the responsibilities of the officer about to be relieved to the officer about to assume command. It deals with joint inspections, transferring of books, logs, secret codes, keys, etc. and signed receipts by the officer assuming command, so that the officer being relieved has the proof that he carried out his responsibilities. *(See End Note No.42)*.

1000 - Underway for Pier 9 to refuel.

1140 - Completed taking on 3,652 gallons.

1204 - Underway for return to Pier 6.

1214 - Tied up outboard of YMS 184, Berth 7.

1355, Kelly, D.P. (212-44-94) Cox, left ship on 72-hour leave.

1731 - Workmen from the Base aboard for work on lights.

2200 - Fire watch stationed because of welding.

2310 - Secured fire watch. No further remarks. (Signed: J.M. Dill, Lt.jg USNR, Commanding). (It would appear that the change of command was little more than perfunctory. According to the log it took ten minutes. Immediately after the ceremony, which was probably held in the wardroom, and as soon as Lt. Upton could salute the Quarter-deck and walk the short gangway to the dock, the USS YMS 183 was underway to refuel and then return to Pier 6. Regular ship routine and repair work continued on this first day under the new C.O. There was no celebration. The change of command was expedited because Lt.jg Dill was the Executive Officer for sometime before relieving Lt. Upton. In this capacity, Dill knew everything that Upton knew about the ship and its crew. In some particulars, he may even have known some things Upton didn't know. It is certain that an Executive Officer assuming command from his own CO could be sure that he was being dealt with forthrightly. In some rare instances, it is said, this may not have been the case. So now, Lt.jg "Pete" Dill, the first person assigned to the 183 is her skipper. The keel was laid March 28, 1942, the hull was christened and launched, June 25, 1942, Lt.jg (then Ensign) Dill reported to Greenport Basin and Construction Company for duty on the YMS 183 in early August, 1942. The ship was commissioned January 15, 1943 and now, not quite a year after launching, the 183 is almost finished with fitting out, shakedown, minesweeping training and duty in New York Harbor. Charlotte Dill has written that she and Pete moved out

Figure 12 - 2nd CO, Lt.jg J. Madison "Pete" Dil - Courtesy, Charlotte Dill

John Dixon Davis

of the Wyandank in the fall. It was a summer hotel and had no heat. They rented a cottage on Peconic Bay that had a large fireplace and that was really a big help. She remembers a cold winter night in early January, 1943, before the ship was delivered to the Brooklyn Navy Yard. They were listening to Walter Winchell, the famous radio news reporter, when he warned his listeners of the sighting of a submarine and the possibility of spies coming ashore on Long Island. "With every howl of the wind we were expecting to be invaded." When the ship was taken to the Brooklyn Navy Yard, the Dills moved into an efficiency apartment across from Columbia University. The ship was later moved to Staten Island and stationed at the Tom Kinsville Section Base there while still undergoing training and then having the duty, along with others, sweeping the shipping channel into New York Harbor almost everyday. Charlotte continues, "When we lived on Staten Island…had a room with a Mrs. (sounded like a middle European name). She had a heavy accent, and I'll never forget how suspicious I was of her. She would ask when the Leftenent would be home. I guess she thought this little old Southern girl was the dumbest thing she ever saw because I would answer that I didn't know. After all, there were posters everywhere saying that a "slip of the lip could sink a ship." Then too, two spies were caught on Staten Island not too far from where we lived. Our room had 12-foot ceilings and there was a metal cap in the ceiling. I was sure it was a listening device. So one night when Pete came home, I signaled not to say anything but to put a chair up on the dresser and unscrew that "device" up there. He did and determined that it had been an outlet for a light. It was a declared war and we were very careful, sometimes to a funny degree." *(See End Note No.43)*.

June 10, 1943

0530 - Richard, A. J., and Bula, S.S. left on 72-hour leave. Ship underway with YMS 184 for sweep operation.

0643 - Held General Quarters. Satisfactory.

0823 - Streamed "O" type gear.

1149 - Recovered "O" type and streamed magnetic.

1155 - Recovered magnetic gear. Returning to Base.

1655 - Captain's Mast held: Following punishments awarded: one man AOL 1 hour, 35 minutes awarded 20 hours extra duty; one man AOL 76 hours and 45 minutes, awarded trial by Deck Court.

1950 - Following ROTC men detached from ship: Goggins, R.W.; Masland, W.S.; McKenna, R.L. and Cannon, J.D. (Signed: J.M. Dill, Lt.jg USNR, Commanding).

June 11, 1943

0515 - Lt. Poole reported aboard for temporary duty. (When Lt. Upton was relieved of command, the officer complement of the 183 was short by one. Lt Poole was assigned temporary duty to make up for this shortage until a permanent assignment could be made. It had been decided some time ago that the YMS needed 4 officers permanently assigned instead of just 3 as was initially planned).

0550 - Underway for all day sweep. (Signed: J.M. Dill, Lt.jg, USNR Commanding).

June 12, 1943

0720 - Underway for continued sweep operation. (The signature of the new Commanding Officer will be no longer verified, nor will the hourly entries of the log be copied except in unusual circumstances).

June 13, 1943

0000 - Continuing night sweep operation with YMS 184.

0947 - Returned to Base.

0955 - Richards, A.J., Kelly, D.P., and Bula, S.S. returned aboard from 72 hour leave.

1010 - Lt. Poole left ship to return to Section Base.

1025 - Took aboard stores for general mess.

1145 - Took aboard recreational equipment.

June 14, 1943

1330 - Completed taking on 2516 gallons fuel.

1635 - Deck Court for one man who was charged with being AOL from June 5 to June 8, 1943. Pleaded guilty. Sentenced to 10 days solitary confinement and to lose $10. per month for three months. The prisoner was transferred to the Brig at Pier 6. (Signed: J.M. Dill, Lt.jg, USNR Commanding). (This man was probably the most frequent offender where being AOL was concerned).

June 15, 1943

0615 - Daniels, D.T., QM 2/c, Deshler, F.G., Y 2/c; Blumenthal, A., F 1/c left on 72 hour leave.

0626 - Underway for 3 and ½ sweep operation with YMS 184. 1914 - Tied up at Army Dock at Sandy Hook.

June 16, 1943

0545 - Underway for sweep operation with YMS 184.

1245 - Recovering gear near Scotland Buoy.

1332 - Proceeding to rendezvous with target vessel for firing drill with 3" 50 cal. and 20mm guns.

1400 - Holding ship handling drill while awaiting target.

1456 - Sounded General Quarters. Making rehearsal run on target; course 150° True.

1510 - C/C to 330° True. Started first firing run. 4 rounds fired.

1536 - Making second firing run. 4 rounds expended. Wright, Willie, St M 2/c burned slightly on face and neck by hot shell. (It is difficult for the average citizen of the U.S., nearly 60 years after these events took place, to realize that the only place an African American could serve on a U.S. Naval vessel was as a Steward's Mate in the Officer's Mess. This was his regular job. He also had an assigned station for the various drills. On the YMS 183, and I believe on many of the other YMSes he also had the most dangerous job at General Quarters and this was as "hot shellman" on the 3" 50 cal. gun. When the gun was fired, the spent brass shell casing was instantly ejected during the recoil of the barrel and breech. The spent shell casing was several hundred degrees hot and had to be literally caught in mid-air so it could not damage the ship or ship's personnel. Once caught, the hot shellman threw it over the side or placed it in a container provided for it on the forecastle. The spent shell casing could not be allowed to roll around on the forecastle deck. The gun crew had to have sure footing. The hot shellman wore an asbestos coat with asbestos sleeves, huge asbestos gloves and an asbestos hat with earflaps and visor that almost completely covered his face. Although he was well protected, accidents of various kinds did happen from time to time. If the accident was of sufficient magnitude the hot shellman could be seriously injured or worse. In those days of segregation, on the 183 at least, the Steward's Mate had the most dangerous job at General Quarters. Fortunately, in the incident cited in the log, the injury was not considered severe).

1558 - Making AA run with 3" 50 Cal. 4 rounds fired.

1630 - Holding AA fire drill on 20 MM guns.
1815 - Tied up starboard to dock at Sandy Hook.

June 17, 1943

0730 - Underway for daily sweep.

June 18, 1943

(Magazine temperatures: Max 74 degrees, Min 70 degrees).
0000 - Continuing sweep begun on 17 June.
0721 - Stopped pulsing. Recovering gear.
0750 - Proceeding to Base. 0912 - Tied up to Pier 6, Berth 5.
0955 - Daniels, D.T., QM 2/c and Deshler, F.G., Y 2/c returned from 72 hour leave.
1300 - Officers and men paid at Disbursing Office.

June 19, 1943

0940 - Surprise inspection held of ship and crew by Lt. Comdr. Neusse. Comdr. Neusse left ship.
1147 - Completed taking on 2171 gallons of fuel.
1400 - Welch, J.L. (201-62-67) S 1/c reported aboard for duty.
1930 - Albanese, V.P. (403-03-97) BM 1/c reported aboard for temporary duty.

Figure 13 - Lt.jg Walter Weltzien and Lt. jg George Beck. Courtesy of Walter Weltzien.

June 20, 1943

0615 - Liberty expired, one absentee.
0732 - One man returned aboard, 1 hour and 15 minutes over leave.
0743 - Underway for sweep operation.
0838 - Held General Quarters drill.
1640 - Held Captain's Mast: one man absent from quarters. Punishment - 4 hours extra duty; one man failure to arise at reveille, awarded warning and revocation of 72 hour leave to have started 6-21-43; one man AOL 1 hour and 15 minutes awarded 4 hours extra duty. 2100 - Tied to Army pier at Sandy Hook.

June 21, 1943

0745 - Schutt, C.E., F 1/c left ship on 72-hour leave.
0805 - Underway for sweep operation with YMS 42 and 184.
2300 - Sweep continues.

June 22, 1943

0000 - Proceeding on sweep.
0040 - Visibility closed to 200 yds.

0400 - Gear recovered.
1745 - Tied up at Army Dock, Sandy Hook.

June 23, 1943

0655 - Underway for sweep operation.
1217 - Timer giving trouble.
2327 - Sweep continues.

June 24, 1943

0000 - Proceeding on channel sweep. Running lights, stern light, masthead, range and sweeping lights on.
0943 - Recovering gear, proceeding to Base.
1058 - Tied up at Pier 6, Berth 4.
1200 - Man returned from Brig, having completed serving 10-day sentence.
1215 - Albanese, V.P., BM 1/c detached from temporary duty.
1240 - Rosbury, C.H., Cox left ship on emergency leave.

June 25, 1943

(Magazine temperatures: Max 78, Min 73).
0915 - Took 2728 gallons of fuel.
0915 - Welch, J.L. (201-62-67) S 2/c USN transferred this date to Base for duty and medical treatment.
1400 - Levesque, L.J. (202-31-75) SC 3/c reported aboard for duty.
1445 - Krier, J. SC 3/c reported aboard for temporary duty.

June 26, 1943

0600 - Hall, C.D., EM 1/c, Morgan, E. MM 2/c, Stychiewitz, J.P. SC 3/c, Mulford, A.J., F 1/c, and Craft, W. J., GM 1/c left ship on 72 hour leave.
0606 - Underway for 2 and ½ day sweep operation.
1830 - Tied starboard side to YMS 184 at Army Dock at Sandy Hook.
2135 - Underway from Army Dock because of heavy wind and sea.
2145 - Dropped anchor in 30 fathoms, using 45 fathoms of anchor chain. Maintaining anchor watch to check anchor bearings. (There are times when a ship is far better off at anchor than moored to a pier or alongside another ship. This apparently was such a time. Wind and wave can cause an incessant and destructive pounding of one ship against another or against a dock. Efforts to cushion them with fenders, etc. do no good when they rock and pitch on different sequences. They can literally wreck each other. If there is a proper depth of water and the bottom has good holding capacity anchoring is the best course. If the water is too deep, then the best course is to remain underway and ride out the stormy weather. No question here that Lt.jg Pete Dill made the correct decision).

June 27, 1943

0753 - Underway for sweep.
1212 - Changing course to get in front of convoy coming in.
2026 - Turned on lights. All lights burning. Sweep continuing. (Magazine temperatures: Max 80, Min 78).

June 28, 1943

0000 - Sweep continuing, magnetic and acoustic.
0834 - Recovered gear, proceeding to Base.
1024 tied - up alongside YMS 398, North Pier, Berth 5.

June 29, 1943

1000 - Morgan, E.L., MM2/c; Stychiewitz, J.P. SC 3/c; Mulford, A.G., F1/c; Craft, W.J., GM 1/c; and Hall, C.D., EM 1/c all returned from 72 hour leave.
1255 - Completed taking on 1984 gallons fuel from YO.
1500 - One man transferred from ship to Naval Hospital. Took on 500 gallons fresh water.

Figure 14 - Chief Boatswain Hall and Chief Electrician Hall

June 30, 1943

0530 - Liberty expired. No absentees.
0731 - underway for sweep operation.
1232 - "O" type gear streamed.
1603 - "O" type gear recovered, magnetic streamed.
1830 - All gear in, proceeding to Sandy Hook anchorage.

July 1, 1943

0359 - Underway for sweep operation with YMS 184.
1800 - Recovering magnetic gear.
1918 - Tied up to Army Dock at Sandy Hook.
2135 - Underway for return to Base.
2252 - Tied up to North Pier 6.
2255 - Lt. Perry came aboard for inspection trip with us.

July 2, 1943

0618 - Underway to rendezvous at buoy "I" with YMS 184.
0818 - gear streamed and beginning sweep with YMS 184.
2359 - Sweep continues.

July 3, 1943

0000 - Channel sweep continues.
0806 - (Gear recovered). Proceeding to Base.
0946 - Tied up to North Pier 6.
1236 - Received 14 cases of Coca Cola aboard for Ship's Service. (The Ship's Service Store is provided for by Navy Regulations to make available to the crew a convenient source for the purchase of personal items such as tobacco, toilet articles, candy, soft drinks, writing paper, pens and pencils, etc. The various supplies are ordered from the Supply Dept. of the Navy and they are paid for by the sale of those items to the crew. The prices are quite low and even so a small profit is often realized and can be used to purchase items for use by the entire crew. Needless to say, as with every thing else on the ship, life, limb and property, the Ship's Service Store is the responsibility of the Commanding Officer. On a small vessel like a YMS, one of the junior officers is assigned to oversee the purchases and sales of Ship's Store Items. He keeps the accounts and reports periodically to the CO. Money in excess of that necessary to make change would be kept in the ship's safe until turned in for credit with the Navy Supply people. The store was open on a regular schedule at those times when the crew was not involved in

sweeping, and routine work procedures. The Officer in charge of Ship's Service often designated a member of the crew as his assistant in actually opening the store, inventorying the supplies, receiving the money, making financial reports, etc. The Ship's Service Store was not only a great convenience but a morale booster as well. *(See End Note No.44)*.

1342 - Received 1 gallon rust preventative from Naval Supply Depot, Bayonne, N.J.
1830 - Taking on water.

July 4, 1943

0800 - Executed colors.
2030 - Executed colors. (Apparently just another day of in port routine.

July 5, 1943

0415 - Started master gyro.
0802 - Underway with YMS 184 for sweep operation.
1225 - streaming magnetic gear.
1629 - Degaussing set.
1956 - Held gen'l quarters drill. Set Condition II watch.
2345 - Continuing on magnetic sweep with YMS 184.

July 6, 1943

0000 - Continuing sweep.
1253 - Recovering gear.
1320 - Proceeding to Sandy Hook.
1518 - Tied up to Army Dock at Sandy Hook.

July 7, 1943

0758 - Underway for sweep with AMc- 109.
1900 - Recovering magnetic gear.
1950 - Proceeding to take AMc-109 in tow.
2203 - AMc-109 turned over to tug.
2305 - Proceeding to carry out sweep schedule with AMc-74 as ordered by Base.

July 8, 1943

0100 - Began pulsing.
0912 - Recovering gear. Impractical to sweep channel because of traffic and fog.
0946 - Proceeding to Base.
1140 - Lt. Doherty aboard for visit.
1155 - Taking fresh water aboard.
1345 - Captain's Mast held. Following punishments awarded: one man AOL 10 minutes awarded 4 hours extra police duty; one man AOL 10 minutes, awarded 4 hours extra police duty; one man warned for disrupting orderly standby plan.
1420 - Ensign Mervin Sheketoff, D-V (G) USNR reported aboard for temporary duty.

July 9, 1943

0800 - Executed colors. Held quarters for muster. No absentees.
0810 - Fuel barge came alongside with fuel.
0836 - Took on 2094 gallons.

John Dixon Davis

1110 - Officers from Fort Schgler aboard for inspection.
1850 - Yard workmen aboard to make tests on main fuel tanks. Found 50% of fuel to be water.

July 10, 1943

0000 - Standing by to receive tug alongside.
0050 - YNT 344 alongside to tow ship to fuel barge.
0120 - All secured to fuel barge, South Pier 9. Standing by to take off and refill fuel tanks.
0725 - Tanks drained. Began taking on fuel.
1130 - Completed taking on 4400 gallons.
1351 - Williams, S.G. EM 2/c returned from 7 days leave.

July 11, 1943

0511 - Underway for sweep operation with YMS 184.
0528 - Oil leak on starboard engine. Engine force investigating.
0542 - Returning to Base.
0645 - Tied up port side to North Pier 6, Berth 5.
1230 - Ayer, S 1/c returned from leave. Anderson, S 1/c left on 8 days leave.
1320 - Wright, StM 2/c reported from leave.
1347 - Blumenthal, F. 1/c admitted to sickbay with leg infection. YMS 193 tied up on starboard side.

July 12, 1943

0600 - Donnelly, S 2/c left ship on 7 day leave.
0612 - Underway for sweep operation with YMS 184.
0632 - Coming about for return to Base due to heavy fog.
0709 - Tied up North 6, Berth 5.
1117 - Underway for sweep operation.
1235 - Held general Quarters drill.
1310 - Gear streamed.
1335 - Began pulsing.

July 13, 1943

0000 - Continuing sweep.
0542 - Started acoustic hammer.
0742 - Recovered gear.
0958 - tied up at North Pier 6.

July 14, 1943

0800 - nine seamen left ship for lookout instruction at Base.
1320 - Crew turned to painting ship. (Turned to is another way of saying, "started work on.")

July 15, 1943

0800 - Executed morning colors.
0810 - Underway for sweep with YMS 184.
1035 - One man put on report for failure to answer reveille.
1048 - Magnetic gear recovered.
1110 - "O" type gear streamed.
1425 - "O" type gear recovered.

1443 - Magnetic gear streamed.
1628 - Magnetic gear recovered.
1730 - Entered Sandy Hook channel.
1751 - Tied up at Army Dock, Sandy Hook.

July 16, 1943

0554 - Underway for sweep with 184.
0646 - Magnetic and acoustic gear streamed.
1600 - Magnetic and acoustic gear recovered.
1725 - Tied up to Army Dock at Sandy Hook.

July 17, 1943

0453 - Underway for sweep with YMS 184.
0535 - Acoustic and magnetic gear streamed.
1707 - Commenced fog signal.
1758 - All sweep gear recovered.
2012 - Tied up to Army Dock at Sandy Hook.

July 18, 1943

0357 - Underway to continue sweep operations with YMS 184.
0521 - Hammer and magnetic gear streamed.
0535 - Stern pipes streamed. (This is the first time the log entry describes the use of stern parallel pipes at the same time as the acoustic hammer is operated from the bow of the ship. Parallel pipes have been used before off the stern at the same time as the magnetic sweep, which is always from the stern. It may be that the 183 and 184 were experimenting to see how much acoustic noise could be made at one time. This would obviously increase the area which could be covered for acoustic mines).
0700 - Recovering gear because of low visibility. Fog signals being sounded regularly.
0853 - Tied to Pier 6, Section Base.
0945 - Held inspection of ship; all satisfactory.
1030 - Freeman, M.D., PH.M 2/c, 271-71-07, V-6, USNR reported aboard for duty.
1145 - Shurts, C.E., MM 1/c returned from 7 days leave.
1330 - Levesque, Lionel Joseph, (201-31-75), SC 3/c, USNR reported aboard for duty. (It is interesting to note that another crewman by the name of Laurent Leon Levesque, S 2/c, joined the crew on 25 June '43).

July 19, 1943

0900 - Crew paid.
0925 - Hall, B.M., CBM left for 8 day leave.
1000 - One man's leave expired who has not yet returned.
1235 - Anderson, A.H., S 1/c returned from 8 days leave.
1340 - Received 20 cases Coca Cola from bottling company for ship's service.
1720 - Yard workmen aboard to repair acoustic hammer.
1835 - YMS 200 moored outboard of us.

July 20, 1943

0545 - Kelly, D.P., Cox left on 7 day leave; Bula, S.S. F 1/c, left on 5 day leave.

0600 - Underway for sweep with YMS 184.
0755 - Testing taffrail log. (The taffrail log is a mechanical device for registering the distance actually run by a vessel through the water. It consists of a rotator, a propeller like piece of metal fastened to a special type of rope, which is towed several hundred feet behind the ship. As the ship moves through the water pulling the taffrail log, the rotator turns. The faster the ship goes, the faster the log turns. At the inboard end of the special rope (on the ship) it is hooked to a register. The register, which has a dial face, shows the distance run according to the number of turns of the rotator. The taffrail log is not exactly accurate, as tides, currents, etc. can alter its performance. But its use, along with good piloting and navigational practices can serve as a check of how fast and how far a ship has traveled in a given time period). *(See End Note No. 45)*.
2319 - Sweep continues.

July 21, 1943

0000 - Sweep continues.
0811 - Secured magnetic and acoustic gear.
1035 - Tied up to North Pier 6 at Section Base.
1220 - Refrigerator Repairman aboard.
1243 - Man absent over leave50 hours and 43 minutes returned.
2032 - Repairmen for acoustic hammer aboard.

July 22, 1943

0624 - Underway for sweep with YMS 184.
0753 - Magnetic and acoustic gear streamed.
2341 - Sweep continues.

July 23, 1943

0000 - Sweep continues.
1032 - All sweep gear recovered.
1106 - Tied up North Pier 6.
1240 - Captain's Mast for man AOL 50 hours and 43 minutes. Awarded Deck Court.
1540 - 2790 gallons of fuel taken aboard.

July 24, 1943

0000 - Moored as before.
2400- Bula, S.S., F 1/c returned from 5 day leave.

July 25, 1943

0106 - Underway for sweep with YMS 184.
1235 - Gear recovered.
2225 - Moored to North Pier 6.

July 26, 1943

1055 - Took on 644 gallons of fuel from YO 166.
1300 - Crew paid.
2015 - Two men aboard to repair refrigerator.

Chapter 7

Underway for Assignment to the 3rd Fleet in the South Pacific

July 27, 1943

0000 - Moored as before.

0745 - Hall, B.M., CBM, returned from 8 day leave; Kelly, D.P., Cox, returned early from 7 day leave.

0930 - Put fresh water in all breakers. (Breakers are small wooden barrels with a 5 to 10 gallon capacity for emergency use especially on life rafts).

1245 - Lt. F.S. Murphy, D-V(S) left ship after detachment from temporary duty.

1307 - All lines cast off; ship leaving Base to proceed to Miami, Florida in company with YMS 184.

1443 - Abeam Scotland Buoy, course 181° True.

1517 - Abeam Shrewsbury Buoy.

1827 - Abeam Barnegat Buoy; C/C to 193° True.

1840 - General Quarters, Fire, Abandon Ship Drills held; results satisfactory.

1907 - Abeam 30 Foot Shoals Buoy; C/C to 207° True.

2255 - Abeam Ludlum Beach Light; C/C 216° True.

2326 - Abeam Flashing White Lighted Wreck Buoy. (It is interesting to note that with the detachment of Lt. Murphy at 1245 the YMS 183 has only three officers aboard: Dill, Seaver and Sheketoff. Although the first leg of the journey to Miami is not a long one, Captain Dill will be standing regular Bridge watches). (Charlotte Dill remembers that when Pete's orders came, in August, sending the ship to the Pacific, she went home to mother. Actually, the orders came in late July, and the ship actually sailed to Miami, Florida on July 27. She writes, "Our next door neighbors were fascinated that a music major from Tennessee was the Commanding Officer of a ship going anywhere. He asked Pete to be sure to send him a card 'if he got there'".)

July 28, 1943

Figure 15 - Getting your haircut on board

0000 - Proceeding to Miami in company with YMS 184; course 216° True; speed standard. (Probably in neighborhood of 10 to 12 knots. The ship is staying close in to the coast, in sight of lighthouses and sea buoys marking the entrances to shipping channels. These ships do not have radar yet, so they must use the time honored method of going from buoy to buoy. Until they reach the waters off Cape Hatteras they have the current with them close in. The Labrador current runs from north to south on the east coast and this adds some speed to the vessels close to the shore going south. Off Cape Hatteras, the Labrador Current collides with the Gulf Stream coming up from the south. From Hatteras south the 183 and 184 will not have the extra boast from the Labrador Current and will actually be going against the Gulf Stream to some degree, depending on how far off shore their course is).

0057 - Abeam McCrie Buoy Number Two; C/C to 142° True.

0219 - Abeam Buoy "S-6"; C/C to 195° True.

0841 - Abeam Parramore Banks Buoy "10-P"; C/C to 206° True. (When a ship is Abeam a buoy, lighthouse or other reference point on the chart, the object lies 90 degrees relative from the bow of the ship. If the object in the distance is on the starboard side of the ship it is said to be on the starboard beam. If it is on the port side, it is said to be on the port beam. Since these two vessels are traveling generally to the south all of the reference points on land and probably all of the buoys are on the starboard side when they pass them. Technically the log entry should have been written "Buoy so and so on the starboard beam.").

Figure 16 – The job is finished

1109 - Abeam Cape Charles Buoy "14". (This buoy is probably the "sea buoy" at the entrance to the channel leading into Norfolk and Chesapeake Bay. Don't know how far off shore this buoy is. The log does not mention sighting Cape Charles lighthouse, so they may be too far out to see it. However, they know where they are because of the buoy. Their course has been 206° True for nearly two hours and they continue this course for about 40 minutes more and then begin a slight turn to port to 200° True. If you will consult an adequate chart you will note that continuing the course of 200° True for too long will run them aground on the upper Outer Banks of North Carolina. The coast of the Delmarva Peninsula runs roughly 200° True to about Cape Charles - Cape Henry area. From that point the lower Virginia coast and then the North Carolina Outer Banks run roughly 160° True to the Chicamacomico Coast Guard Station-Wimble Shoals area, then the coast runs roughly 180° True to Cape Hatteras. The ships are making pretty good time. From their departure from the Tom Kinsville Section Base at 1307 (1:07 PM) July 27 until passing Cape Charles Buoy "14" at 1109 (11:09 AM) on July 28, an elapsed time of approximately 22 hours, they have traveled roughly 3 and ½ degrees of Latitude. Each degree of latitude is 60 nautical miles. Do the math: 3.5 x 60 = 210 nautical miles. 210 nautical miles in 22 hours is very close to 10 knots. Remember that a nautical mile (6080 feet) is somewhat longer than a statute mile like we use on the highway (5280 feet). A speed of one knot is one nautical mile per hour. A speed of 10 knots is probably close to 12 miles per hour on land.)

1144 - C/C to 200° True.
1302 - All ships clocks reset to synchronize.
1519 - Abeam Corrituck Beach (Currituck Lighthouse). C/C to 159° True. (Their course of 200° True for the last 3 ½ hours has brought them within sight of the Currituck Lighthouse. To have continued the 200° True course would have put them aground on the Outer Banks in a short time. The course, 159° True will take them parallel with the coast down nearly to Cape Hatteras). (The log of the ship seems rather mundane, routine, devoid of exitement, and frankly rather boring. The reader needs to remind himself that every entry in the log, every sighting of a buoy or a flashing light resulted from the watchful eyes of lookouts made sharper by their binoculars, and the anticipation resulting from the instructions of the Officer of the Deck, who is constantly checking the chart and plotting their course. The ship does not run itself. Every turn of the helm, or change in shaft rpms is the result of the direction of the crew. The interesting thing is the absence of any reference to the sighting of other ships. Of course, it is possible that they haven't sighted any, but that is doubtful).

1817 - Abeam Bache (Bodie) Island Buoy. (As often happened the writer of the log made an educated guess from time to time about the spelling of words, particularly place names. The actual scribe would assume that if his guess about spelling is wrong, the Captain would catch and correct it when he read and certified its accuracy. In this day's entries we have the Captain's signature of certification, but I doubt the Captain ever read what he signed for this day and perhaps on many other days as well. This was true of most C.O.'s of most of the other YMSes and other ships as well. They had passed the Bodie Island Buoy on the starboard beam).

1823 - C/C to 164° True. (After passing Currituck Beach on course 200° True, the course change to 159° True takes them close to Bodie Island Buoy. At this time a course change to 164° True is made. Within 2 hours, 164° True will take them to a point far enough off the coast so that they can clear Diamond Shoals and the outer shoals when they turn to go almost due south at 2026, 178° True, and then, 180° True, at 2338. It is difficult to plot their position with real accuracy after they make the turn out to sea to clear the outer shoals off Hatteras. The reason for this is that the influence of the Gulf Stream begins to make itself felt after the ship moves away from the coast even for the short distance of 20 miles. Prior to this time the Labrador Current has been pushing them along at a good clip and now they are experiencing an equal or stronger force against them. This may have cut their speed possibly down to six or seven knots. They are not so concerned with time elapsed to give them their positions, but still rely on a series of buoys to locate their position when a given buoy was sighted. My chart, Feb. 1943, does not have all of the buoys around Diamond Shoals marked. I'm guessing that the skippers of the YMS 183 and 184 were given especially prepared charts of this area with the special buoys indicated. Another interesting fact about this area at this time is that a defensive mine field laid by the US Navy in 1942 between Cape Hatteras and Ocracoke is being removed by sweeping. This might also be a factor in the crews having special charts to navigate around this area. In any event, they clear Diamond Shoals and make their turn to the southwest as they skirt the lower North Carolina Coast and its famous Cape Lookout and Cape Fear).

2016 - Abeam Buoy "10".

2026 - C/C to 178° True.

2338 - Abeam Buoy "D-5"; C/C to 180° True.

July 29, 1943

0000 - Proceeding as before to Miami in company with YMS 184. Course 180° True; Speed standard. (Standard is Approximately 10 knots. Actually probably much less than standard at this point).

0126 - Abeam obstruction Buoy "Y".

0512 - C/C to 234° True.

0700 - Abeam Cape Lookout Buoy "14". (Cape Lookout Lighthouse is within sight of Beaufort, NC, the author's hometown. The buoy replaced the Lightship in 1933).

1410 - Abeam Frying Pan Shoals Buoy. C/C to 246° True. (Frying Pan Shoals, so named, I have always been told, because their general shape as viewed on the chart looks somewhat like a small skillet or frying pan, handle and all. The shoals and Cape Fear are at the mouth of the Cape Fear River which makes Wilmington, NC an important sea port).

2055 - C/C to 270° True.

2350 - C/C to 265° True.

July 30, 1943

0001 - Proceeding as before enroute to Miami in company with YMS 184: Abeam Cape Romain Buoy "6". (This spit of land jutting into the Atlantic Ocean is between Georgetown, S.C. on its north side and Charleston to the south).
0002 - C/C to 250° True.
0214 - Abeam Buoy "2 BC"; C/C 235° True.
0410 - Abeam Buoy "4K1"; C/C to 228° True.
0737 - Abeam Port Royal Buoy "PR". (The Port Royal Buoy is off the entrance to Beaufort, S.C. the home of Parris Island Marine Base).
0845 - Abeam Savannah Lightship, "Relief". C/C to 204° True. (The Savannah Lightship is off the entrance of the Savannah River and the Port of Savannah, Georgia).
1138 - Abeam Buoy "2S".
1409 - Abeam Saint Simon Buoy "2B" (This Buoy is off the entrance to Brunswick, Georgia).
1755 - Abeam Saint John Lightship; C/C to 170° True. (The lightship is off the entrance to the St. John's River and the Port of Jacksonville, Florida).
2049 - Buoy "2STA" abeam.
2050 - C/C to 180° True.
2123 - General Quarters drill; results satisfactory.
2302 - Abeam Flagler Beach Aero Light; C/C to 157° True.

July 31, 1943

0000 - Steaming as before enroute to Miami, in company with YMS 184; course 157° True.
0130 - Abeam Buoy "2"; C/C to 135° True.
0456 - Abeam Buoy "8"; C/C to 170° True.
0956 - Abeam Bethel shoal Buoy; C/C 182° True. (This buoy is off the coast near Vero Beach, Florida).
1200 - Abeam Buoy "12A"; C/C/ to 200° True.
1522 - Abeam Jupiter Inlet Light.
1932 - Abeam Hillsboro Light.
2255 - Abeam Buoy marking entrance to Miami main channel; proceeding up channel.
2330 - Cast lines to Dock; moored to Pier "3", Miami City Docks. No further remarks.(Signed: J.M. Dill, Lt.jg, Commanding).

August 1, 1943

1118 - Stores taken aboard.
1200 - One man absent over leave.
2303 - Man AOL returned. Over leave 11 hours 3 minutes.

August 2, 1943

0800 - Colors; crew mustered at quarters, no absentees.
0830 - Brooks, Nurse, Sell from Radio material aboard to check sound gear.
0945 - Brooks left ship.
1000 - Taking off ammunition; Nurse and Sell left ship.
1158 - Underway from Pier 3 for Warriner DesRocher Ship Yard.
1220 - Moored port side to YMS 184 at Warriner DesRocher Ship Yard.

August 3, 1943

0000 - Moored as before.

1335 - Deck Court held: One man charged with being AOL from 1000 July 19, 1943 to 1243 July 21, 1943. Sentence: to be confined to the ship for a period of 8 days and loss of pay amounting to $ 7. Per month for a period of 2 months, total of $14.

August 4, 1943

0800 - Colors. Nothing of note to report.

August 5, 1943

1100 - Daniels, Durwood Thomas, (266-37-12) QM 2/c reported aboard for duty (from Receiving Station at NY. He had been detached July 27, just before ship left for Miami).

1300 - Roether, J.T., Cox; Smith. C.P, SM 1/c; Richard, A.J, QM 3/c; Rosbury, C.H., Cox; Verity, H. W., F 1/c; Freeman, M.D., PhM2/c; Boday, S.J., F. 2/c; all left for eleven day leave of absence.

1335 - Deck Court Trial: One man AOL 11 hours, 3 minutes. Confined for 5 days and loss of 5 days pay.

1500 - Hansen, Charles E., S 2/c (810-09-60) V-6 USNR (SV) was transferred from ship to US Navy Receiving Barracks, Miami, Florida, FFT to the Atlantic Fleet.

1800 - McFarland, W.E., GM2/c left ship on eleven day leave.

Figure 17 – Mine detonated by sweep gear – Courtesy of Stanley Klein collection Courtesy of Rhea Kline.

August 6, 1943

0800 - Crew mustered at quarters, no absentees. Nothing of note to report.

August 7, 1943

0800 - Colors. Nothing of note to report.

August 8, 1943

0800 - Colors. Nothing of note to report.

August 9, 1943

0800 - Colors. 1430 - Tug R.L. Hise came alongside to take YMS 183 to Shipbuilding Drydock Marine Railway.

1600 - Secured in drydock.

August 10, 1943

0800 - Colors. Secured as before in drydock.

John Dixon Davis

August 11, 1943

0830 - Detail of 17 men left ship to be inoculated.

0905 - 17 men returned from being inoculated. [Before going over seas, all service men were inoculated against all known diseases of the world for which there was a preventive serum. This covered a wide range of diseases, but there were still some that could only be treated with routine medication, such as malaria. One of the most important for which there was no serum at that time was polio or infantile paralysis. Each service man's record included his medical history and all of the preventive shots he had been given and the date. His record stayed with him in his unit and a copy of his total record, including all his training, various areas of duty, etc. was sent to the Bureau of Naval Personnel in Washington. Usually referred to as BuPers. The service person also had two identification disks, or "dog tags". The dog tags had his name, service number, blood type, branch of service, date Tetanus shot was given and religious preference stamped onto a stainless steel (not quite round) disk about an inch and ½, by an inch and ¼ in "diameter". One of the tags was required to be worn on the person at all times. Usually the two tags were worn on a small chain around the neck. In the event of death and the body was not lost one tag was placed in the mouth of the deceased service person and the other filed by grave registration personnel giving the place of burial when known).

1010 - Captain's Mast held for one man charged with neglect of duty - not having Government revolver in possession while standing Gangway Watch on 7 August, 1943. Restricted to ship for two liberties and to memorize the orders of a sentinel as in *Blue Jackets Manual*. (This is an interesting infraction, but an important one). While moored at anchor or at a pier or alongside another vessel, the ship was required to have an officer and an enlisted man designated as the gangway watch, the gangway being whatever was required to enable personnel to board or leave the ship easily and safely. It could be a gangplank to a dock or another vessel, or a sort of flexible ladder made of wooden sections and rope if the ship was at anchor. On occasion the ship might be underway and personnel from somewhere else needed to come aboard. The rope ladder is placed over the side of the ship and the gangway watch stood by to authorize first, by giving permission and then assisting the boarder to come on board and if needed to escort him to the Captain or whomever he came to consult. The regulations required that the Officer of the Deck or OD, and the enlisted man on gangway watch both be armed with side arms. The Officer wore his own service issued 45 cal automatic pistol and the enlisted man wore a 38 cal revolver which was passed from one watch to another, and when not in use under the custody of the Gunner's Mate. It would seem obvious why this regulation was necessary. In extreme circumstances a person might try to board the ship without permission, or be ejected from the ship against his will, or taken into custody waiting for the Shore Patrol to arrive, or to protect life and property aboard the ship. The hand guns were loaded and remained in their holsters as the symbol of authority, but they were ready for use if the need arose. The OD and the enlisted gangway watch both wore arm bands designating them as the gangway watch. For the enlisted man not to have had his side arm was a violation of the regulations]. (Generally, when anyone came aboard, unless he was a known member of the crew, he requested permission to do so and waited until the Gangway granted permission. Then the person coming aboard turns toward the Quarter Deck and salutes the colors. The members of the watch return the salute and allows the person to come aboard).

August 12, 1943

0000 - Moored as before in drydock.

August 13, 1943

0830 - All hands instructed in use of the gangway gun.

0920 - Paymaster aboard.

0935 - Pay Master left ship. [The log does not tell us what is being done while the 183 is in dry dock. However, the only piece of gear that has not been installed, other than radar is the Sonar or sound gear. This piece of equipment enables the ship's personnel to locate submarines, plot the submarine's course and depth and drop depth charges on them. It has three major parts: 1 - the receiver [located on the bridge], which is manned by a Sonarman who has been trained to operate the equipment; 2 - the shaft which is secured in a vertical position in the lower hull in the forward part of the ship allowing the; 3- sound head to be lowered below the ship's bottom or raised into an enclosure inside the lower hull. To operate, the Sonarman lowers the sound head, which is fastened to the bottom of the shaft, from its container inside the hull in the forward part of the ship. The head can be rotated 360 degrees. When turned on, the head sends a high frequency sound wave through the water, in one second pulses, in whatever direction the head is pointed. If the sound wave hits an object in the water it is reflected back to the head which transmits it to the Sonarman at the receiver. This reflected sound wave is called an echo. In a sound search, the head is turned one degree at a time, toward the suspected area. If no object is hit, there is no reflected return or echo. In this case the head is turned one more degree and so on until there is a return sound wave. If there is no echo the process is continued until the suspected area has been covered. Another area may now be checked, or the original area may be checked again. When the operation is completed, and/or when the ship is entering shallow water, the head is pulled up by the shaft into its container inside the hull for protection. Donald Fredrick, whom we met in the construction phase of YMS 183, has written that with the building of the earlier YMSes they knew nothing about Sonar and all there was was a bunch of wires left hanging in the lower hull. They didn't know what they were for. In the later YMSes (even later than the 183) where the wires were left hanging, a welded steel tank "about the size of a bath tub" was secured in place on the bottom planking and made watertight. Later on, the Sonar gear was installed after cutting an opening through the hull to allow the Sonar head to be lowered and pulled up into its container. (See Appendix D, Donald Frederick's Misc. notes). This was what was going on while the 183 was in dry dock in Miami i.e. the Sonar gear was being installed]. (An interesting note has to do with one very low numbered YMS, to be kept secret, a member of whose crew shared this with me. Their YMS was never outfitted with Sonar, and he laughed as he recounted the very many times when they were on the anti-submarine wing of an escort group, ostensibly searching for submarines and they had no Sonar with which to make the search. From time to time strange things happened).

August 14, 1943

0835 - Commenced leaving Marine Railway.

0920 - Tied up alongside dock - Miami Shipbuilding Corp.

1717 - Left Miami Shipbuilding Docks for Warriner DesRocher Dock.

1738 - Tied up alongside YAG 20.

2235 - Ensign George A Beck, D-V(G) 266672, USNR reported aboard for duty. (A permanent third officer is now aboard).

August 15, 1943

1435 - Verity, H.W. returned from leave.

2000 - Roether, J.F.; Freeman M.D.; returned from leave and Deshler, F.G. returned from 72 hour liberty.

2110 - Rosbury, C.H. and Richard, A.J. returned from leave.

August 16, 1943

0730 - MacFarland, W.E. returned from leave.

1402 - W.F. Weltzien, Ensign, D-V(G) 267798, USNR reported aboard for duty. (A permanent fourth officer is now aboard). (Almost everyone is familiar with the old saying "It's a small world." This is one that both George Beck and Walter Weltzien believe is true, for they both had known each other for some time before they found themselves assigned to the same ship and they reported within a day and ½ of each other. In letters and telephone conversations with them both we learn of the following chain of events that brought them together for more than a year and ½ on the YMS 183. Walter writes, "I reported for duty at the midshipman school in Columbia University in New York City on April 5, 1943. We put in our "90 days" and those of us who weren't washed out were commissioned July 10, I believe. We were asked to make a choice of what type of ship we would like to be assigned to. Being new at this Navy Game, I didn't want to be on a big (battleship) ship, nor on a small (destroyer) ship, so I selected a medium size ship (cruiser) and like many of my classmates, I was sentenced to Mine Warfare and ordered to an AMc in Fort Lauderdale (Florida). I had heard tell of another midshipman down on the seventh deck of Furnald Hall who also was sent to an AMc in Miami. I went down and introduced myself to George Beck. I was from Newburgh and since George and his parents already lived in New York City, he invited me and my parents to have dinner with him and his parents at a restaurant in NY City and they could see us off on the train to Florida. It was a nice send off for both of us, and our parents were glad to meet other parents with similar concerns. George and I became friends on the train and enjoyed our trip until we went our separate ways. I spent 3 or 4 days on an AMc out of Lauderdale, and sailed down to Key West where I received orders to report to the YMS 183 in Miami. I caught a bus to Miami and reported to the deck watch of the 183 in August (the 16th) 1943. The watch sailor ushered me in to the wardroom where I was introduced to George Beck. He had arrived the day before I did (actually two days before on the 14th of August.) It was good to see George again and to feel the comfort of having someone "in the same boat" that I was. George was senior to me because he had arrived two days before me and also because his dog tag number was lower than mine since they were designated alphabetically when we graduated from midshipman school. We were shore bound in Miami for a few weeks while they installed several pieces of equipment (I forget what). I think the 3" 50 was installed then because the crew used to take turns sneaking up at night and training the telescopic sights of the big gun on the Henry Clay Hotel across the river from us which housed several hundred Waves. (Actually the 3" 50 was installed before the ship was commissioned. The main installation in Miami was the Sonar gear). *(See End Note No.46).*

1905 - Boday, S.J. returned aboard from leave.

August 17, 1943

0330 - Hall, C.D. returned from leave.
1615 - Mr. Dill returned from leave.

August 18, 1943

1402 - Captain's Mast for one man, charge, Falsehood. Awarded Bad Conduct Discharge. Transferred to Receiving Barracks, Miami, Fla. Under armed guard.
1545 - Armed guard returned.
1620 - General stores taken aboard.

August 19, 1943

1000 - Underway for Miami Shipbuilding Dry Dock.
1045 - Ship clear of water in dry dock, Miami, Fla.

August 20, 1943

0800 - colors. One man AWOL from 1500 Aug. 19 to 0115, Aug. 20.
1635 - Moved from Miami Shipbuilding, tied up port side to YMS 184 at Warriner Des Rocher.

August 21, 1943

1915 - Boday, S.J., F 2/c, injured fingers of right hand on hatch of generator room. Taken to Sick Bay by Mr. Dill.
2100 - Completed 7 hour dock trial of both engines. All checked satisfactorily.

August 22, 1943

0800 - Colors. No items of note for rest of the day.

August 23, 1943

0800 - No items of note all day.

August 24, 1943

0920 - YMS 184 moved astern of us. We moved next to dock.
1115 - Captain's Mast: one man charged with "late hammock" - Restricted one liberty. One man charged with AWOL for 1500 August 19, 1943 to August 20. 1943. Awarded 125 hours extra duty.

August 25, 1943

0800 - Colors. No items of note for the rest of the day.

August 26, 1943

0700 - Tested main engines.
0822 - Underway for acoustic hammer, magnetic sweep gear tests.
1200 - Commenced recovering gear.
1300 - Maneuvering for azimuth bearings. (This activity has to do with finding the magnetic compass deviation, which must be known at sea should the gyro compass fail. *(See End Note No. 47)*.
1459 - Tied up alongside YMS 184, south side pier 3 Miami.

August 27, 1943

0835 - Paymaster came aboard.
0850 - Paymaster left ship.
1015 - Taking ammunition aboard.
1120 - Taking on 4225 gallons fuel at Belcher Oil Co.

1545 - Linder, L.Y., 634-45-43, SC3/c V-6 USNR reported aboard for duty.

August 28, 1943

1115 - Transferred 20 boxes 20 MM ammunition to Ammunition Depot Ft. Lauderdale
1650 - Took Aboard stores for general mess.
2050 - started gyrocompass.
2115 - Four men placed on report by Mr. Dill.
2135 - Commenced taking aboard fresh water.
2306 - All lines cast off; underway to Key West, Fla.
2358 - Held General Quarters drill.

August 29, 1943

0000 - Steaming as before at standard speed, course 174 True. Ship at General Quarters.
0008 - Secured from General Quarters. By various courses and speeds, the ship proceeds down the Straits of Florida from Miami to Key West.
1250 - Sounded General Quarters.
1301 - Secured from General Quarters.
1304 - Sounded Collision Drill.
1309 - Sounded Abandon Ship Drill.
1314 - Secured from all drills.
1544 - Tied up south side of Craig Docks, Berth # 1, Key West, Florida.
1748 - Two men came aboard to check sound gear.
1840 - Two men left ship. Gear reported in good condition.

August 30, 1943

0753 - Four Officers, eight men left for sound school.
0900 - Man came aboard to check sound gear.
0915 - Sound man left ship.
1000 - Man came aboard to work on radio..
1115 - Radio man left ship.
1301 - Underway to practice with sound gear.
1312 - Steering course 210° True. Degaussing set.
1504 - Completed operations. Sound gear found to be installed backwards. (There are many World War Two-isms, still a part of the language, which describe the discovery that the Sonar is installed backwards and therefore inoperable. The most apt is SNAFU,"Situation Normal, all fouled up.").
1630 - Captain's mast: one man absent from General Quarters Drill, 8-28-43; deprived of ten liberties; one man AOL 17 minutes 8-28-43, loss of 2 liberties; one man absent from General Quarters Drill, 8-28-43, loss of 10 liberties; one man absent from Gen. Quarters drill, 8-28-43, loss of ten liberties; One man absent from General Quarters Drill,8-28-43, loss of ten liberties; one man AOL 40 minutes, 8-28-43, loss of five liberties; one man absent from G.Q Drill 8-28-43, loss of ten liberties; one man absent from G.Q. Drill, 8-28-43, loss of ten liberties.
1825 - Captain's Mast for one man reporting to ship in intoxicated condition 8-28-43, unable to stand watch. absent from G.Q. Awarded trial by Deck Court.

August 31, 1943

0640 - Ens. Walters & Holloway, SoM1/c came aboard to give instruction to officers and crew on use of sound gear.

0701 - Underway to work with sound gear.

0829 - Tied up south side Pier # 2, NOB, Key West. Fla.

1540 - Lael, H.J., 406-65-03 SoM 3/c V-6 USNR reported aboard for duty.

September 1, 1943

1050 - Took on stores.

1300 - 4 officers and 6 men left for sound school.

September 2, 1943

0745 - Yard workman came aboard.

1100 - Work on sound gear completed.

1655 - Underway to test sound gear.

1830 - Completed test of sound gear. Returning to Base.

September 3, 1943

0635 - Ens. Walters and Huff, R.R.. RM 1/c reported aboard for day's operation against submarine.

0815 - 1450 Conducted sound gear instruction for officers and men upon submarine.

1615 - Instruction concluded proceeding to Base.

1646 - Moored outboard of SC 1331.

September 4, 1943

1025 - Bringing stores aboard.

1349 - Underway for swinging ship to check degaussing

1738 - Swing ship completed, moored port side to YMS 184, NOB, Key West.

September 5, 1943

1643 - Navy workmen aboard to check ABK set.

September 6, 1943

0849 - Underway to calibrate magnetic compass.

1120 - Calibration of compass completed.

1143 - Anchored in order to bore sight 3" 50 cal gun.

1232 - Lost starboard anchor when attempting to raise anchor. Anchor was a 295 lb. Danforth anchor. (No mention is made of recovering the anchor or of getting it replaced with a new one. It was probably caught on an old wreck or shelf of coral and the chain broke while trying to raise it. In view of the fact that the 183 is on the verge of leaving the States for the South Pacific, it is inconceivable that she did not get another before leaving. There were undoubtedly some vessels that rarely had occasion to use their anchor, but when one was needed it was needed badly.)

1247 - Proceeding to NOB Key West.

1820 - Commissary stores came aboard.

September 7, 1943

0000 - Moored starboard side to YN 22, Craig Dock, Key West.

0750 - All tests made in preparation for getting underway with YN 22 and YMS 184. (A YN was a net tender).

0756 - Underway in company with YN 22 and YMS 184.

0907 - Cleared main channel of Key West. Took station on starboard quarter of YN 22.

0925 - Sand Key light on starboard beam. C/C to 267° True.

1050 - Cosgrove shoal light on starboard beam. C/C to 225° True.

1200 - Steaming on course 230° True.

1640 - Sighted land bearing 310° degrees relative. (To find the true bearing they could have used the alidade or pelorus on the gyro repeater on the flying bridge to get the true bearing of the land. They apparently didn't so we have to figure what it was on our own. The course is 230° True. In a relative bearing the bow of the ship becomes 000° degrees or 360° degrees relative. The relative bearing of the land is 310° degrees. This is 50° degrees less than 360° degrees. To derive the true bearing of the land subtract 50° from 230°, which is the true course. 230° - 50° = 180° degrees true - the true bearing of the land sighted. It was probably high ground or mountains on the western end of Cuba).

1920 - C/C to 243° True.

2030 - Held General Quarters drill. Fired 3" 50 cal gun accidentally. No casualties.

2245 - C/C to 245° True.

September 8, 1943

0000 - Proceeding on course 245° True in company with YN 22 and YMS 184. Speed III

0515 - C/C to 158° True. (The ship is now on a course that will take it through the Yucatan Channel between Cuba and the Yucatan Peninsula. Although the log does not have an entry for it, Navigator Walter Weltzien would have had the clocks set ahead one hour to Central War Time, which was "Daylight Savings time" all year round during the war. [Speed III is standard speed, approximately 10 knots]. In other words, if it was 0700 when the ship entered the Central Zone, the local time became

0700 - C/C to 155° True.

1045 - C/C/ 140° True, Speed III.

1717 - Held general drills.

September 9, 1943

0000 - Proceeding on course 140° True in company with YN 22 and YMS 184. Speed III.

0200 - Sound gear broken.

0950 - Ship's position 18 degrees 00' N. Lat.; 81 degrees 58' W. Long. by sun sights. (By getting the angle of the sun at apparent noon by using the sextant).

1121 - C/C/ to 157° True.

1712 - Held G.Q drill.

2205 - C/C/ to 166° True.

September 10, 1943

0000 - Proceeding on course 168° True (at 2205 the course was stated to be 166° True. There is no indication as to when it was changed to 168°. That isn't much of an error, if it is an error, but over the long haul it could be significant. The course 168° True continued for nine hours before being changed at 0920).

0920 - C/C to 180° True. (This course is almost a straight shot to Colon on the Atlantic (Caribbean Sea end) of the Panama Canal. It is of interest to note that the Atlantic end is actually north west of the Pacific end and that the canal runs from north west to south east. Most people just assume that the canal runs from east to west).

1135 - C/C to 173° True.
1705 - Held GQ drill.

September 11, 1943

0000 - Proceeding on course 173° True.
0402 - Sighted unidentified ship on horizon, bearing 080° Relative.
0935 - C/C to 140° True.
1033 - C/C to 180° True.
1140 - C/Speed to 5 knots.
1305 Passed outer channel buoy.
1350 - Hove to North of Station Ship awaiting affirmative to proceed to Base.
1429 - Proceeding to Base at Coco Solo.
1528 - Tied up to Pier # 1 E, Coco Solo, Panama.
1535 - Began taking on 2950 gallons Diesel fuel.
1600 - Took on stores for general mess.
2000 - All lines secure.
2400 - All lines secure. (Signed: J.M.Dill, Lt.jg USNR, Commanding).

September 12, 1943

0000 - Tied up as before.
0800 - All lines secure. Set all clocks back one hour. (The Canal Zone is in the Eastern Time Zone and they have crossed back into this time zone after having been in the Central Zone for a day or so.
0942 - Underway from Pier # 1 E to Pier # 4.
0952 - Tied up starboard side to pier # 4.
1030 - Deck court for one man who pleaded guilty to being absent from General Quarters Drill 8-28-43 due to after effects of intoxication. Sentenced to be confined for 20 days and to lose 20 days pay. Total loss of pay amounting to $36. 1545 - Blumenthal, A., F 1/c, 709-50-33, V-6 USNR; and Levesque, L.J., SC 3/c, 202-31-75, USN transferred to Receiving Ship, Coco Solo, Panama for further transfer.

September 13, 1943

0859 - Underway from Pier # 4 to Berth Zebra.
0953 - Tied up at Berth Zebra.
1530 - Took on stores and fuel.

September 14, 1943

1037 - Paymaster came aboard.
1045 - Paymaster left ship.
1700 - Bellyue, P.E., MoMM 1/c, 212-50-44, USN reported aboard in exchange for Morgan, E.L., MoMM 1/c, 375-94-68. (There was liberty in Colon, according to Ensign Weltzien, where rum was a nickel a shot. We "poured" several of the men aboard and the next day we went through the Canal).

John Dixon Davis

September 15, 1943

0538 - Underway from Coco Solo bound for Balboa.

0615 - Took aboard Pilot - Mr. Repper. C/C to 230° True.

0616 - Entering Panama Canal. (Walter Weltzien's narrative continues, "At around 0800 we entered the Gaton locks. The locks were too big to waste on one measly YMS so they fitted us in with a submarine and the YMS 184. Each lock we came to, the ships would get in together and get raised or lowered to the next level and then sail independently to the next lock."). - Any good encyclodedia will tell you that the Gaton locks at the Atlantic end of the canal raise a vessel or vessels in three steps to the level of Gaton Lake which is 85' above the sea. While in the locks the vessels are towed by electric locomotives called mules. When the lake level is reached, the ship or ships proceed independently under their own power for 23 miles through the lake and then the narrow channel called the Gaillard Cut at the southern end of which the next set of locks begin, the Pedro Miguel locks. The vessels enter these locks to begin the return to sea level by being lowered 31' to Miraflores Lake which is 54' above sea level. The mules are reattached and pull the vessels through the lock and they continue independently into and across Miraflores Lake. The next two sets of locks, also named Miraflores Locks lower the vessel 54' to sea level on the Pacific side of Panama. The pilot who directed the vessel through the canal leaves it here as the vessel prepares to continue its voyage into the Pacific Ocean. The Canal is about 40 miles long and takes from 7 to 10 hours, depending on the vessel or vessels making the transit. [I wish to acknowledge the technical information above was found in an Encarta Encyclopedia Article Titled "Panama Canal" on the Internet.]

1315 - Through Panama Canal heading for Pier in Balboa.

1325 - Tied up starboard side to YMS 184, Balboa, Panama.

2400 - Checked lines every half hour since 1330. All secure. (Signed: J.M Dill, Lt.jg USNR, Commanding.) (Ens. Weltzien explains that when the liberty section went on liberty that night the dock was a few feet below the main deck (high tide) and when they returned the dock was about 12 feet above the 183's deck (low tide). The tides run about 12 to 18 feet there and they had to have a special watch loosening or tightening the mooring lines every 15 or 20 minutes. (The tidal difference on the Atlantic side is only one foot).

September 16, 1943

0845 - Took on 471 gallons of fuel oil.

0930 - Proceeding under tow to Pier # 18, Balboa, Panama.

1050 - Tied up outboard of and starboard side to USS Talbot (DD-165). (Actually the writer of the log is in error here concerning USS Talbot. She is USS J. Fred Talbot, DD 156. For sometime in the early part of the war the Talbot was engaged in convoy escort duty in and around the Panama Canal zone. Apparently, on the 16th of September she was just a convenient place to moor for the night).

1820 - One man reported on board under guard.

Chapter 8
Into The Pacific Theater

September 17, 1943

0000 - Tied up as before.

0500 - Workmen brought reduction gear aboard.

1430 - Pilot came aboard.

1433 - All lines cast off. Underway from Balboa. Course 140° True.

1535 - Pilot left. Took departure from Station Vessel. C/C to 180° True.

1545 - Came to formation "D" with AM 131 as guide ship; APc 96 second in column, YMS 183 third in column and YMS 184 fourth in column. (The AM 131 was a 220' auxiliary minesweeper, constructed of steel, named USS Zeal. She carries the Senior Officer Present Afloat in this little flotilla and also enough fuel capacity to refuel the three other vessels at sea. Ensign Weltzien remembers that the ships left Panama not knowing where they were going. Obviously this was to prevent any possible leaks of information. Their sealed orders were not to be opened until they were at least 15 miles at sea. At this distance from land they were well into the Gulf of Panama on course 180° True. The sealed orders revealed that the ultimate destination was American Samoa via Bora Bora and the Galapagos Islands. The APc 96 was a 103' wooden hulled cargo ship, very similar to the wooden hulled AMc, but not equipped to sweep mines. The APc was probably going to some island base in the now "backwater" or rear area of the South Pacific to do station duty in a local area).

1716 - General Quarters Drill held.

1720 - Secured from G Q.

2100 - C/C to 146° True.

September 18, 1943

0000 - Steaming as before. Base course 146° True.

0225 - C/C to 208° True.

1609 - C/C to 243° True.

1609 - C/C 243° True. (This course is essentially the base course for the next four days as the ships proceed toward the Galapagos Islands which are roughly 1000 nautical miles from Panama).

September 19, 1943

(This page of the log is missing. No question, but that the base course is being maintained).

September 20, 1943

0000 - Steaming as before on base course 245° True. (During this day all clocks were wound and reset. Practiced General Quarters drill for firing practice).

1436 - C/C to 240° True.

September 21, 1943

0000 - Steaming as before. Course 240° True.

1115 - Sounded General Quarters, held small arms practice.

1215 - Secured from GQ. Chronometer wound. (It should be noted that there are two types of time keepers aboard the naval ships of that day. The clocks scattered throughout the ship and the personal wrist watches of the personnel kept the local time in the 24 hour day. When the ship crossed a time zone line the watch or clock is set ahead one hour if traveling from west to east or back one hour if traveling from east to west. The other time piece on ship is the chronometer. It resides in a special case and rests in a frame that is set on gimbals. The gimbals allow the chronometer (actually a clock) to float freely, so that the face is always level. The chronometer is never reset. When it is started for the first time it is always set for Greenwich (England) time which is on 0 degrees longitude. The chronometer may gain or lose time, perhaps no two run exactly the same speed. Instead of resetting it when this happens, the amount of gain or loss is recorded and this is added to or subtracted from the reading on the face of the clock when the time at Greenwich is figured in navigation at sea. Greenwich time also tells the navigator what his longitude is, that is, the distance from Greenwich, England, either east of it or west of it. The only thing the navigator, or his designated assistant, usually a trained Quarter Master, is allowed to do is to wind the chronometer so that it continues to run at whatever speed is unique to itself. Normally the chronometer is wound each day at the same time. The navigator can tune his short wave radio to the "time tick" which is broadcast from Greenwich every hour on the hour and thus he can keep track of how far ahead or behind his ship's chronometer actually is. Obviously, the chronometer was an extremely important piece of gear for the navigation of the ship in the open sea where no land references are present and/or visible).

1400 - C/C to 250° True; C/S (changed speed) to 5 knots.
1746 - AM 131 had sound contact.
1747 - Sounded General Quarters.
1748 - Secured from GQ.
1800 - Set clocks back one hour. (Note that the Panama Canal Zone is in the Eastern Standard timed zone under war time daylight savings time. The Galapagos Islands are in the plus 6 or Central Time Zone of the US. The ship has not yet reached the plus 7 time zone but the clocks are set back as if they have. In all probability the Galapagos Islands are viewed as being in the plus 7 time zone by the government of Ecuador. The ship's clocks have to be set according to the official local time).
2315 - C/C course to 228° True.

September 22, 1943

0000 - Steering as before course 210° True. (The log does not record when the course was changed from 228° True to the present course of 210° True).
0638 - C/C to 170° True - Proceeding into anchorage at Seymour Island.
0926 - Anchored at Seymour Island in 15 fathoms of water with 75 fathoms of chain out to starboard anchor. (There are 61 islands in the Galapagos group, 13 of which are main islands and the rest of varying size. Seymour Island is one of the lesser islands where the US Navy had access to an anchorage from the government of Ecuador. In all probability Seymour Island appears only on the US Navy charts the navigator on the 183 and the others were using in 1943).
1200 - Chronometer wound.
1550 - Underway to fuel.
1610 - Started fueling.
1635 - Finished taking on 2160 gallons of fuel.
1640 - Underway for anchorage.
1649 - Anchored at Seymour Island in 8 fathoms of water with 40 fathoms of chain out to starboard anchor. Checked anchor bearings, drift lead every half hour. All secure.
2400 - All secure. (Ensign Weltzien remembers going ashore for 15 or 20 minutes and describes the island as a hot, dry, barren rock). (The log does not mention the time when the equator

was crossed or whether or not the ship observed the time honored ceremony inducting new "Shellbacks" into the "Ancient Order of the Deep").

September 23, 1943

0000 - Anchored as before at Seymour Island. Ships present AM 131 (SOPA), YMS 183, YMS 184, APc 96, SC 1046 (Sub Chaser), a U.S. Merchant Vessel, a U.S. Army Transport, two Army tugs and yard small craft. 0345 - Checked anchor chain and drift lead every half hour. All secure.
0600 - Anchor's aweigh.
0619 - Took position astern APc 96. Course 310° True.
0741 - C/C to 298° True. (It is not recorded in the log which ships are leaving the Galapagos. It is presumed that the four which arrived the day before are still in convoy).
0800 - Steaming as before course 298° True.
1705 - Held GQ drill.
1824 - C/C to 252° True.

September 24, 1943

0000 - Steaming as before course 252° True.
0545 - C/S to 1/3rd. 0915 - Stopped engines - lying to waiting for AM 131.
1051 - 0000 C/S to standard.
1200 - Course 252° True.
1605 - Sounded GQ on sound contact.
1615 - Dropped five charges depth charge pattern.
1624 - Regained sound contact.
1630 - Dropped three depth charges.
1647 - Secured from GQ after losing sound contact. Approximate position of attack was Lat. 000° degrees 40' South; Long. 095° degrees 41' West. (Ens Weltzien remembers that someone from the 183 acquired a monkey in Panama and the pet rode contentedly on the fantail and the after life raft. At one point, Weltzien doesn't remember exactly when, the ship responded to a sound contact and went off on a submarine attack. At what seemed to be the proper time, the K - guns were fired sending a depth charge off each side of the ship and dropped two depth charges off the stern. The monkey was resting next to one of the K-guns when it went off and one flying leap was the last anybody saw of him. Shortly after the "sub attack", several whales were seen spouting off our port quarter).

September 25, 1943

0000 - Steaming as before course 252° True.
1100 - Held GQ drill. Fired six 3" 50 shells.
1143 - Secured from GQ.
1213 - Sounded GQ on sound contact.
1320 - Secured from GQ.
1800 - Set clocks back one hour. (The ship has crossed from the plus 6 time zone into the plus seven time zone which begins with the 97th meridian of west longitude).

September 26, 1943

0000 - Steaming as before, base course 252° True.
1106 - AM 131 (USS Zeal) left formation.
1218 - AM 131 rejoined formation.

1430 - C/C to 180° True to take on fuel from USS Zeal.
1452 - Began fueling.
1523 - Finished fueling. Took on 1500 gallons of fuel.
1540 - C/C to 255° True. (AM 131 and YMS 183 left the formation and both changed course to 180° True because this heading afforded the optimum conditions for receiving fuel. The AM provided a fuel hose which the 183 picked up and placed in the fuel tank. After a check was made on the purity of the fuel the AM began pumping the fuel over to the 183. When the tank was full the hose was disengaged and pulled back aboard the AM. Refueling at sea was often very difficult when the wind and seas were up, for there was always the danger that the two ships might collide. Sometimes the waves would cause the ships to move apart suddenly and the fuel hose would be broken and the whole procedure would have to be begun all over again. Although a ship and its personnel became more adept at refueling after months of experience, there probably never was a perfect refueling experience at sea).

September 27, 1943

0000 - Steaming as before on course 255° True.
1110 - YMS 184 transferred starting motor to us.
1455 - YMS 184 received starting motor (30 KW).
1613 - AM131 left formation to investigate sound contact.
1650 - Sounded GQ for drill purposes.
1704 - Secured from GQ. (As tranquil and pleasant as the South Seas can be much of the time, it is no pleasure cruise. In addition to the constant care to keep the vessel in top condition, the drills to insure the fighting readiness were frequent and unannounced).

September 28, 1943

0000 - Steaming as before. Course 255° True.
0850 - C/C to 253° True.
1030 - Steering gear and cable checked and greased.
1530 - Held small arms practice.
1800 - Set clocks back one hour.

September 29, 1943

0000 - Steaming as before base course 253° True.
1200 - Wound chronometer.
2305 - Taffrail log reading 1583.4 miles.

September 30, 1943

0000 - Steaming as before. Course 253° True.
1656 - Sounded GQ for drill purposes.
1707 - Secured from GQ drill.

October 1, 1943

0000 - Steaming on base course 253° True as third ship in four ship "Dog" formation en route to Bora Bora, Society Islands. AM 131 as guide ship; APc 96 as second ship and YMS 184 as fourth ship.
0250 - Taffrail log reading 1881.6 miles.
0652 - Taffrail log reading 1923.5 miles.

1130 - Taffrail log reading 1970.1 miles.(The three Taffrail log readings, taken at approximately four hour intervals show an average distance covered of about 43 miles in four hours, which translates to about 10 plus knots. The APc 96, which had a standard speed of 9 knots is probably having to strain a little to keep up).
1238 - C/S to 8 knots.
1247 - C/C to 170° True.
1424 - Coming alongside AM 131 to refuel.
1437 - Commenced taking on fuel.
1515 - Finished taking on 2300 gallons of fuel.
1519 - All lines cast off. Returning to position in formation.
1525 - In position on course 170° True.
1647 - C/S to 10 knots. C/C to 260° true.
2056 - Taffrail reading 2056.1 miles. No further remarks. (Signed: J.M. Dill, Lt.jg USNR Commanding).

October 2, 1943

0000 - Steaming as before on base course 260° True.
1730 - C/C to 255° True.
1755 - Set all clocks back one hour (now in Plus 9 time zone). (The Time Zone Chart of the World, H.O. Chart 5192, shows that the Tuamotu Archipelago, and the Society Islands, are included in the Plus 10 time zone. Tahiti and Bora Bora are in the Society Islands. At their latitude, approximately 20 degrees South, the Plus 10 time zone is skewed to the southeast and actually goes all the way to the boundary of the Plus 8 time zone, so that in this area a ship travels from Plus 8 to Plus 10 time zone. This keeps all of these groups in the same local time zone. This is important for commerce, communication and community. There is hardly any land out there except for these islands, so it makes no difference that they occupy the Plus 10 time zone and are not included in the Plus 9 time zone at all. The 183 will not be in the Plus 9 zone for very long, for when they get closer to the Tuamotu Archipelago they will enter the Plus 10 zone and be in it twice as long as they would have if the Archipelago lay in the Plus 9 and the Plus 10 zone. The two major islands of the Society Group are Tahiti, and Bora Bora. *(See End Note No.48)*.
2150 - APc 96 broke down. C/S to 1/3 rd.
2230 - APc 96 underway again. C/S to standard. Resumed station on AM 131.
2337 - Taffrail log reading 2310.5 miles. No further remarks.

October 3, 1943

0000 - Steaming as before on base course 255° True.
1700 - Sounded GQ.
1707 - Secured from GQ.
2345 - Taffrail log reading 2550.4. No further remarks.

October 4, 1943

0000 - Steaming as before on base course 255°. Visibility poor.
0310 - Taffrail reading 2590.1 miles.
0720 - C/C to 260° True.
1300 - Position of ship L. A. N. (local apparent noon by taking sextant sights of the sun) Lat. 11 degrees 43' South; Long. 135 degrees 16' West.

John Dixon Davis

1706 - Sounded GQ.
1710 - Secured from GQ.
2000 - Visibility very poor.
2105 - Slowed to 1/3 speed due to two red lights put up by AM 131.
2115 - Lost sight of APc 96. C/S to 1080 RPM.
2135 - Resumed position.
2312 - Taffrail log reading 2793.1 miles. No further remarks.

October 5, 1943

0000 - Steaming as before on base course 260° True.
1722 - C/C to 258° True.
2330 - Taffrail log reading 3035.5 miles. No further remarks.

October 6, 1943

0000 - Steaming as before on base course 258° True.
0915 - C/C to 165° True, reduced speed to 6 knots. C/C to 155° True in preparation to refuel from the AM 131.
1115 - Completed taking on 1200 gallons of fuel.
1140 - Resumed station.
1235 - LAN (local apparent noon) position: Lat 13° degrees 25' South; Long. 142° degrees 47' West.
1322 - C/C to 300° True. (Since October 4 the ship has been proceeding on its westward course on the northern side of the Tuamuto Archipelago in order to clear the western islands of the Archipelago and then turn south for a short time to arrive at Bora Bora which is 150 miles northwest of Tahiti. The noon position placed the ship a little farther south than they wanted to be and so the course was changed to take them a little farther north for four hours and then they resumed the base course).
1700 - 1706 GQ drill.
1730 - C/C to 258° True.
1800 - All clocks set back one hour (now in Plus 10 time zone).
2330 - Taffrail log reading 3270.4 miles. No further remarks.

October 7, 1943

0000 - Steaming as before on base course 258° True.
1300 - Position at L.A.N. Lat. 13° degrees 55' South; Long. 146° degrees 34' West.
1330 - Sounded GQ for gun practice.
1426 - AM 131 dropped target (probably an oil drum or buoy that would sink on its own after a time, unless the gun hit and destroyed it).
1450 - Commenced firing at target.
1458 - Ceased firing. Eight rounds expended. (We must assume that they did not destroy the target or they surely would have put it in the log).
1503 - Secured from GQ.
1544 - Steering engine broke down.
1553 - Steering engine working again.
2000 - C/C to 268° True.
2330 - Taffrail log reading 3441.6 miles. No further remarks.

October 8, 1943

0000 - Steaming as before on base course 268° True.

0925 - C/C 228° True. C/S to nine knots.

1300 - L.A.N. as follows: Lat.14° degrees 27' South; Long. 149° degrees 25' West. C/C to 218° True.

2340 - Taffrail log reading 3718.8 miles. (The L.A.N. position plot on Chart No. 1262a, 7th ed., Feb. 1941 shows the ships in the proper position to begin their gradual turn to the south toward their destination, Bora Bora).

October 9, 1943

0000 - Steaming as before on base course 218° True.

0445 - C/C 200° True.

0450 - C/S to five knots.

0458 - Form one eight (the ships line up in single file and maneuver slowly in a large circle off Bora Bora waiting for daylight and a pilot).

0535 - C/S to nine knots.

0610 - C/C to 323° True.

0720 - C/C to 290° True.

0727 - C/C to 215° True.

0758 - C/S to stop.

0810 - Lt.jg F.T. Haily came aboard as Pilot C/S to 1/3.

0825 - C/C to 200° True.

0828 - C/C to 190° True.

0831 - C/C to 106° True.

0835 - Switched engines to manual control. Proceeding to dock in Bora Bora.

0932 - All lines over. Ship tied to dock.

1045 - Captain's Mast: one man charged with being ashore without permission and having to be brought back under guard. Elected Deck Court. Above offense occurred in Balboa, Canal Zone on Sept 16, 1943.

1107 - Held Deck Court for the man cited above. Pleaded guilty to being absent from duty without permission from 1530 Sept. 16, 1943 to 1830 same date. Fined $75.

1400 - Taking aboard commissary stores.

2330 - Checked all lines half hourly. Single docking. No further remarks, (Signed: J.M. Dill, Lt.jg, USNR Commanding). (The first major leg of the voyage from the Canal Zone has been successfully concluded when reaching Bora Bora. The ship has traveled 3718.8 nautical miles since leaving the Canal Zone. The Taffrail log gives a reading of the total miles traveled, as well as the approximate speed of the vessel, at any given time. The distance traveled, as measured on the chart of her plotted course, is amazingly close to the Taffrail log reading. There were apparently no serious problems and no losses except for the pet monkey. Unlike today (the beginning of the 21st century) Bora Bora had a small population. Today it is about 4,225. Ensign Weltzien does not remember that anyone went ashore as there seemed to be little activity there. He does recall that it was a very beautiful island. Apparently there were some U.S. land forces based there as a deterrent to a possible Japanese invasion and various service vessels and warehouses to provision and refuel ships making landfall there going east and west across the Pacific).

October 10, 1943

0000 - Moored as before. All lines secure.

John Dixon Davis

0855 - Getting underway to take on fuel across the bay.
0909 - Tied up at fuel dock, port side to YMS 269 inboard.
0915 - Taking on fuel.
1342 - Getting underway. Returning to original berth.
1359 - Tied up starboard side to YMS 184 at Army pier Bora Bora.
1403 - APc 96 tied up outboard of us.
2330 - Lines checked half hourly while tied up. No further remarks.

October 11, 1943

0000 - Moored as before, starboard side to YMS 184, Bora Bora, Society Islands.
1530 - Four (4) drums fuel oil (probably these drums contained lubricating oil for the engines, fuel oil was diesel fuel for running the engines). Took aboard six (6) depth charges.
1810 - Executed colors.
2330 - Lines checked half-hourly; all secure.

October 12, 1943

0000 - Tied up as before.
0745 - Took aboard stores for the general mess.
0834 - Cast off all lines and got underway.
0930 - Took position on starboard quarter USS Zeal. Formation Dog - course 281° True.
1200 - Change to form Baker.
1404 - Began zig-zagging Plan # 10. (Ships at sea, especially when moving into areas where enemy submarines were likely to be encountered, did not keep a straight course for very long. This convoy did keep a straight course until leaving Bora Bora. By changing course at designated times to a designated course to be run for a certain length of time and then reversing the course, etc. the track on the ocean was like a saw's teeth - a zig-zag. This was designed to confuse the submarine captain, so that he did not know where to aim his torpedo. He only had a certain number to launch at the enemy and had to make every one count. The ships may have been on a zig when the torpedo was launched and by the time it got to the target ship it may have zagged and the torpedo missed completely and was wasted. Zig-zagging was used almost all the time and with great benefit. It also disguised the base course of the ship or convoy).
1510 - Ceased zig-zagging. On base course 281° True.
1633 - Began Zig-zagging Plan # 10.
1815 - Held GQ.
1900 - Secured from GQ.
1945 - APc broke down - reduced speed to 1/3.
2009 - APc taken in tow by AM 131 (USS Zeal).
2050 - Took position 1000 yards on starboard bow of AM 131 - base course 281° True.

October 13, 1943

0000 - Steering as before course 281° True.
0515 - Held GQ.
0550 - Secured from GQ.
0913 - C/C to 276° True.
1200 - Chronometer wound. Noon position 16° degrees 11' South, Long. 156° degrees 08' West, by celestial sights (This is just the plain old L.A.N. using the sun. But then the sun is a celestial body).

1830 - Sounded GQ.

1910 - Secured from GQ.

2307 - Taffrail log reading 445.6 miles (from Bora Bora). (Actually, the ships have moved only about 300 miles toward Samoa, the final destination. Remember the two periods of zig-zagging. All of these are a part of the Taffrail reading of 445.6. So the zig-zagging reduced the straight line travel toward Samoa by about 150 miles).

October 14, 1943

0000 - Steering as before course 276° True.

0505 - Sounded GQ.

0558 - Secured from GQ.

0818 - Commenced zig-zagging Plan # 10.

0820 - AM 131 left the formation.

1040 - AM 131 resumed guide position.

1230 - Noon position (L.A.N.) Lat 15° degrees 47' South; Long. 159° degrees 44' West. (The plot on the chart for the last 24 hours shows an advance of nearly 180 miles from the last position on 13 Oct. If there had been no zig-zagging the straight line advance would have been larger. The log does not say how long the zig-zagging continued).

1330 - Held all drills.

1352 - Secured from drills.

1852 - Sounded GQ.

1915 - Secured from GQ.

2330 - Taffrail log reading 670 miles. (Straight line distance approximately 480 miles from Bora Bora).

October 15, 1943

0000 - Steering as before course 276° True.

0510 - Sounded GQ.

0605 - Secured from GQ.

1300 - Position at L.A.N. Lat 15° degrees 37' South; Long. 163° degrees 40' West. (They must have had tail wind and no zig-zagging for the straight line distance from the L.A.N. position of 24 hours before is about 270 miles. This translates to a little better than 11 knots).

1908 - Sounded GQ.

1944 - Secured from GQ.

2340 - Taffrail log reading 880.2 miles. (This is approximately 210.2 miles from the Oct.14, 2330 Taffrail reading. There is a difference of about 50 miles between plot on the chart and the distance on the Taffrail log. Splitting the difference between the plot and the Taffrail reading may give the best answer as to the distance actually traveled in the last 24 hours).

October 16, 1943

0000 - Steaming as before on base course 276° True. Zig-zagging according to Plan #10.

0116 - Ceased zig-zagging. Came to formation 18.

0136 - Commenced zig-zagging in accordance with Plan # 10.

0540 - Sounded GQ.

0624 - Secured from GQ.

0959 - C/C 280° True.

1000 - Formation B.

1844 - Ceased zig-zagging. Came to formation 18.
1903 - Commenced zig-zagging.
1925 - Sounded GQ.
1930 - AM 131 left formation. APc 96 acting as guide.
1957 - Secured from GQ.
2050 - Ceased zig-zagging. C/S to 2/3 to avoid APc 96 which had stopped due to fuel line trouble. AM 131 broke formation to assist APc 96 if necessary. 2320 - AM 131 and APc 96 rejoined formation. C/S to standard.
2330 - C/C to 295° True. Commenced zig-zagging. Taffrail log reading 1095.6 miles.

October 17, 1943

0000 - Steaming on base course 295° True.
0610 - Sounded GQ.
0635 - Sighted land on starboard beam.
0649 - Secured from GQ.
0700 - Ceased zig-zagging.
0705 - Came to formation B.
0728 - Commenced zig-zagging.
0842 Ceased zig-zagging. Came to formation 18.
0930 - C/C to 281° True.
1043 - C/C to 026° True. Proceeding in channel to Pago Pago harbor.
1113 - Entering Pago Pago harbor, proceeding to dock at Governor's Landing.
1144 - All lines over. Tied up to Governor's Landing.
1410 - Taking on fresh water.
1420 Taking on 2200 gallons of diesel fuel.
1510 - Clocks set back one hour (now in Plus 11 time zone).
2330 - Checked lines half-hourly since docking. No further remarks. (Signed: J.M. Dill, Lt.jg, USNR Commanding). (The ultimate destination, American Samoa, has been reached without serious incident).

October 18, 1943

0000 - Moored as before.
1200 - Stores brought aboard.
2330 - Checked lines half-hourly throughout the day. No further remarks.

October 19, 1943

0000 - Moored as before.
1450 - Captain's Mast for man charged with being intoxicated on duty 9 October 1943. Restricted to ship for 15 liberties.
2345 - Checked lines half-hourly throughout the day. No further remarks.

October 20, 1943

0000 - Moored as before. 2330 - Checked lines half-hourly throughout the day. All secure. No further remarks.

October 21, 1943

0000 - Moored as before.

0835 - Tested acoustic hammer.

1030 - Took on 1150 gallons fresh water.

1635 - Took on 200 rounds armor piercing 30-30 cal shells. (They have about everything else ready for sweeping mines. These bullets will be fired at floating mines to pierce the steel shell so the mine will sink and be rendered harmless).

2330 - Checked lines half-hourly. All secure. (Why Samoa? More particularly, why the Island of Tutuila and its seaport capital Pago Pago? Arnold Lott tells the story briefly, but very clearly in his excellent work *Most Dangerous Seas*. He writes that the first mines planted by the US Navy in the Pacific during World War II, were laid around the south sea island of Tutuila in the Samoan group. "The Navy had maintained a small base there since 1899, noted chiefly for the fact that its name was "Pago Pago" but pronounced "Pango Pango". The old Bird-class minesweeper, *Kingfisher*, went to work late in December 1941 to plant 82 mines off Cape Fagauso and Taema Bank. In March 1942 *Gamble* (DM-15) and *Ramsey* (DM-16) [both World War I four stack destroyers converted to light minelayers] came down from Pearl to plant six more fields off Tutuila for a total of 400 mines. The war never reached Samoa. The mines lay undisturbed, even on that notable September 1942 day when the SS *Wisconsin*, perhaps carrying a load of rabbits' feet, sailed right through the middle of the field undamaged. From October 22, 1943 to January 8, 1944 Samoa's mines were cleared out by *YMS-183). (See End Note No.49).*

John Dixon Davis

Chapter 9

First Assignment - Tutuila

October 22, 1943

0000 - Moored as before.

0613 - Got underway for mine sweeping operations in company with YMS 86. Proceeding on various courses.

0917 - Streamed starboard "O" type gear with 30 foot pendant, 19 fathom depression wire, 250 fathoms sweep wire. (The 30 foot pendant hangs from the float or "pig". This means that the otter, or the multiplane water kite, which the pendant keeps from sinking, is 30 feet below the surface of the ocean. The otter pulls the sweep wire away from the ship at whatever distance is predetermined to be necessary. So any mines that are not laid deeper than 30 feet below the surface of the ocean will be swept by the cutters near the otter. When the mine cable is cut it floats to the surface where it is sunk by rifle fire).

1030 - Retrieved gear.

1142 - Dropped starboard anchor. 60 fathoms of chain out

1314 - Anchor's aweigh.

1340 - Streamed "O" type gear. 100 foot float pendant; 23 fathoms depressor wire; 250 fathoms sweep wire.

1413 - Steering various courses on field sweep of field "E", Fagauso Bay, (Tutuila) Samoa.

1839 - Executed colors.

2330 - Checked anchor bearings and anchor drift lead half-hourly. All secure. (The island of Tutuila is long and narrow, Ensign Weltzien remembers, and it took the better part of a day to reach Fagauso Bay on the north side of the island. Here we anchored overnight and began sweeping the following day in company with whichever ship, YMS 184 or YMS 86, was operating with us. We swept a number of mines at this location and were busy for several weeks).

Figure 18 - Flaoting mine with mine disposal officer. Courtesy of John J. Baker

October 23, 1943

0000 - Anchored as before.

0605 - Underway.

0635 - Streamed 250 fathoms sweep wire, 23 fathoms depressor wire and 100 foot float pendant.

0640 - Began sweep operations in company with YMS 86. On various courses and speeds.

1343 - retrieved gear.

1501 - Anchored Fagauso Bay in 15 fathoms of water, with 60 fathoms of chain out to starboard anchor.

2330 - Checked anchor, anchor bearings, drift lead half-hourly. All secure.

Figure 19 - Japanese mine case for further study

October 24, 1943

0000 - Anchored as before.

0600 - Anchor's aweigh.

0655 - Began first lap of day's operations on field "E". (The ships took two days to make a general exploratory sweep of the area where the mine field is supposed to have been laid. It is not clear, but the charts made by the mine layers may not have been available to the 183 and 86. Therefore they had to discover for themselves the area where there were no mines and start from that point sweeping one "strip" of ocean at a time [much like mowing grass] getting closer and closer to the shore with each pass. Dan buoys were placed to mark the edge of the swept area. When the next pass was made the dan buoys were moved to the new position so that the sweepers could always be in swept waters).

0816 - YMS 86 cut loose a mine.

1106 - YMS 183 cut loose 2 mines.

1200 - Secured for chow. (The layman might equate mine sweeping with a civilian job. A break for lunch? Really? Yes really. The crew had to eat, after the food was prepared, but regulations and common sense required that no one be below deck or under an overhead while sweeping, in case a mine went off under the ship. As described earlier, only the helmsman and the engine annunciator operator were supposed to be inside. All were supposed to have on life jackets and steel helmets. During chow break the ships just made lazy circles in cleared waters).

Figure 20 - Damaged float "pig" Courtesy of Stanley Klein collection Courtesy of Rhea Klein.

1254 - Resumed operations.

1320 - YMS 86 exploded one mine and seconds later 2 more mines exploded having been set off by the influence of the first explosion. (These mines were fairly close together).

1548 - Recovered gear after accounting for eight mines. (The log does not tell us what ships were in the operation for the purpose of placing the dan buoys (danners) and/or for sinking the floating mines with rifle fire. It may be that the 183 and 86 either placed the dan buoys themselves or relied on navigation alone to locate the edge of the mine field. This was more risky than using danbuoys. Also, with only a few mines being cut, it may be that the two sweepers took care of the sinking chores themselves).

1706 - Anchored Fagauso Bay. 14 fathoms water with 60 fathoms anchor chain out to starboard anchor.

2330 - Checked anchor bearings and anchor drift lead half-hourly. All secure.

Figure 21 - Repainting cutters. Courtesy of Stanley Klein collection

October 25, 1943

0000 - Anchored as before.

0740 - Anchor's aweigh.

0840 - Streamed gear. 250 fathoms sweep wire, 23 fathoms of depressor wire, 100 foot pendant.

0845 - Began sweeping operations in field "E" in company with YMS 86.

1635 - Retrieved gear and accounted for 2 (two) mines.

1704 - Anchored in Fagauso Bay. (Ensign Weltzien, the ship's navigator, gives a detailed account of the actual process of establishing the ship's position with reference to the mine field and the shore line of the island. He writes, "We were all feeling our way and tried to follow outlined procedures. On our flying bridge was a gyro compass repeater fitted with an alidade (a telescope with a single vertical cross hair somewhat similar to a telescopic sight on a rifle). This alidade could be turned in all 360 degree directions. We selected land marks on the shore which were indicated on the chart in the chartroom. We tried to select two objects (a mountain peak, church steeple or a fixed navigational marker like a beacon - no buoys, because they sometimes are not in the position marked on the chart) on the shore that were nearly 90 degrees apart as we looked at the shore. In the chart house the chart was tacked down on the chart table so that it could not slip or move. Fastened to the table, off to one side of the chart was a device used by architects and others who need an accurate and rapid way of drawing lines that are of a certain angle (0 degrees to 360 degrees). This device is called a Universal Drafting Machine. [When the chart is secured to the chart table, the drafting machine is oriented to the compass rose on the chart - when the drafting machine is set on 0 degrees, it lines up perfectly with 0 degrees on the compass rose on the chart]. When the angle is set, and this can be done in a second or two, no matter where the ruler of the drafting machine is placed on the chart, the edge is always the same angle until it is reset. The drafting machine was affectionately called a "One Armed Bandit". I suppose this was because it precluded the use of parallel rulers, which are slow and sometimes difficult to use). (After streaming gear far enough offshore where the danger of moored mines was not present we would start taking bearings on our landmarks. On the flying bridge, our Signalman 1/c, P.C. Smith and Quartermaster 1/c, A.J. Richard took 15 minute turns, taking the bearings and calling them down to the chart house. For example; they started by calling out the name of the object e.g. church steeple 163 degrees, mountain peak 247 degrees. After repeating these bearings several times, we eliminated naming the bearings and simply called out the bearing, i.e. 164°, 246°, etc. As the ship moved the bearings would change and we could fix our position very accurately every few seconds. We were often able to record accurately anywhere from 15 to 30 pair a minute. Ensign George Beck and I took turns recording the readings on the chart. I really enjoyed the work as I had been fascinated with maps ever since early childhood. They didn't hold a similar interest for George and since we needed an officer to oversee streaming of the gear on the fantail, he volunteered for that assignment. Once we had our gear streamed and landmarks established, we began to work our way inland, sailing parallel to the coast and the mines which were usually laid in lines parallel to the coast. Our sweep gear swept an area about 150 feet from our side. We began out beyond the 100 fathom line and worked our way in with our gear always between us and the island. After sweeping past the end of our designated area, we would turn away from the island and return to where we had started our original sweep, and work our way inland. This time we would chart our course about 100 to 125 feet in from our previous sweep line so that the ship would always be in swept water. We worked alone and in tandem with the 86 or the 184. In tandem, the lead ship would sail down the intended course and the tandem ship would follow the float or "pig" of the lead ship being careful to stay 25 to 50 feet inside the swept water area. Swept mines would be sunk by gun fire from whichever ship could accomplish it without endangering the other ship. We followed this procedure in most of the later operations as well).

October 26, 1943

0000 - Anchored as before.
0606 - Underway to sweep with YMS 86.
0645 - "O" type gear streamed using 90 foot float pendant.
0655 - Began making runs on Field "E" on course 045° True.
1549 - Recovering gear. Three mines accounted for by this ship this day.
1615 - All gear recovered, proceeding to Fagauso Bay anchorage.
2330 - Checked anchor bearings half-hourly. No further remarks.

October 27, 1943

0000 - Anchored as before.
0815 - Underway with YMS 86 streaming "O" type gear with 90 foot float pendant.
0922 - Started making runs on Field "E" on course 045° True. Made five runs.
1627 - All gear aboard and proceeding to Fagauso Bay anchorage.

October 28, 1943

0000 - Anchored as before.
0600 - Underway to sweep Field "E" with YMS 86.
0622 - Streaming starboard gear with 100 float pendant.
0645 - Started runs on course 090° True. Made five runs.
1023 - Recovering gear.
1050 - Streaming "O" type with 30 foot float pendant.
1125 - Starting runs along shore line. Made three runs.
1439 - Recovering gear.
1501 - Proceeding to Pago Pago by various courses and speeds.
1625 - Sighted a dan buoy drifting out to sea. Recovered dan buoy.
1834 - Tied up to Governor's Landing at Pago Pago.
2345 - Checked lines every half hour. No further remarks.

October 29, 1943

0000 - Tied up as before.
0607 - Underway to sweep with YMS 86 & YMS 272.
0614 - Proceeding out of harbor and by various courses to Afono Bay.
1104 - Anchored in Afono Bay.
2345 - Anchor bearings checked half hourly. No further remarks.

Figure 22 - Damaged multiplain water kite. Courtesy of Stanley Klein collection

October 30, 1943

0825 - Underway for sweeping operation with YMS 86 & YMS 272.
0853 - Port "O" type gear with 110' pendant.
0901 - Making peripheral Sweep of Field "F". Made 5 runs.
1617 - Recovering gear.
1715 - Anchored in Afono Bay. No further remarks.

October 31, 1943

0000 - Anchored as before.
0733 - Underway to sweep Field "F" with YMS 86 and 272.
0813 - Streaming port "O" type gear with 110' pendant..
0827 - Starting runs on course 000° True. Made 7 runs.
1546 - Recovering gear
1610 - Proceeding to Pago Pago harbor.
1758 - Tied up outboard YMS 184.

November 1, 1943

0000 - Tied up as before.
0530 - Linder, L.Y., SC 3/c transferred to Naval Hospital Mobile Unit No. 3.
0553 - Underway to sweep Field "F" with YMS 86 & YMS 272.
0735 - Having trouble with starboard engine. Returning to base.
0900 - Engine repaired, proceeding to Field "F".
1039 - Streaming port "O" type gear with 110' float pendant.
1105 - Starting run on Field "F" on course 045° degrees. Made 5 runs.
1546 - Cut two (2) mines during day.
1615 - Recovered gear, proceeded to Pago Pago.
1815 - Tied up outboard of YMS 184.

Figure 23 - Sinking floating mines with rifle fire. Courtesy of John J. Baker

November 2, 1943

0604 - Underway for sweep operation with YMS 272.
0755 - Port "O" type gear with 110' pendant.
0825 - Starting runs on Field "F" on course 050° degrees. Made three (3) runs.
1325 - Recovering gear, cut two (2) mines during day. Returning to base.
1420 - Captain's Mast for five men who missed reveille this date. Restricted to ship for four days.
1535 - Tied up at Governor's Landing.
1635 - Paymaster aboard. Officers and crew paid.
1655 - Paymaster left ship.
2345 - All lines checked half hourly. No further remarks.

November 3, 1943

0000 - Tied up as before.
0610 - Underway for sweep of Field "F" with YMS 86 and YMS 272.
0810 - Starboard gear streamed with 110' pendant.
0925 - Gear fouled on bottom.
1000 - Recovered gear. Evidence of having been caught on shoal. Position as follows: Lat. 14° degrees 13' 45". Long. 170° degrees 36' 55" West. (This shoal location is forwarded through Navy channels so that all ships everywhere can correct their charts and show the existence of this heretofore unknown shoal).
1005 - Streamed gear again. Starting run on course 135° degrees. Made 7 runs.
1515 - Recovering gear to remove a dan buoy caught in it.
1553 - Dan buoy removed, gear restreamed. Continued runs, Made 1 run.
1632 - Recovering gear. Proceeding to Afono Bay. Cut 2 mines during day.
1717 - Anchored in Afono Bay.

Figure 24 - Mine explosion Courtesy of the John J. Baker collection

November 4, 1943

0000 - Anchored as before.
0636 - Underway to continue sweep with YMS 272.
0710 - Starboard gear streamed with 110' pendant.
0750 - Starting runs of Field "F" on course 135° True. Made two runs.
0856 - Rain causing poor visibility.
1130 - Started sounding fog signals every two minutes.
1157 - Weather cleared. Secured from fog signals.
1318 - Starting runs on course 045° True. Made 3 runs.
1523 - Recovering gear. No mines cut. Returning to Pago Pago.
1945 - Tied up starboard side to YMS 272 at anchorage in Pago Pago Harbor.

November 5, 1943

0000 - Tied up as before.
0612 - Underway for Field "F" with YMS 272.
0844 - Streamed starboard gear with 110' pendant.
0857 - Starting runs on course 040° True. Made 10 runs.
1546 - Recovering gear. Cut two (2) mines during day.
1640 - Anchored in Afono Bay.

November 6, 1943

0824 - Underway for sweeping operations.

0835 - Starboard engine broke down.
0910 - Stopped all engines to repair same.
1140 - Proceeding to Base on port engine.
1445 - Tied up at Governor's Landing.
2345 - Checked lines half-hourly. No further remarks.

November 7, 1943

0000 - Tied up as before.
1115 - Taking aboard commissary stores.
2345 - Checked lines half-hourly throughout day. No further remarks.

November 8, 1943

1133 - Underway to lead three LST's out of the harbor through the swept channel.
1337 - LST's safely at sea. Returning to base.
1425 - Tied up at Governor's Landing.
1650 - Taking on commissary stores.
1827 - Colors.

November 9, 1943

1601 - Underway for sweep operations in Field "F".
0804 - Gear streamed with 110' float pendant. Made 6 runs on course 315° True.
1133 - Recovering gear.
1228 - All gear streamed with 60' float pendant.
1240 - Beginning runs alternating courses 135° True and 315° True. First run made on course 135° True. Made 7 runs.
1515 - Recovering gear and proceeding to Base.
1730 - Tied up at Governor's Landing.
1845 - Schwartz, H., SC 1/c, 706-85-55, USNR reported aboard for temporary duty.
2345 - Checked lines half-hourly. No further remarks.

November 10, 1943

0000 - Tied up as before.
1205 - Taking on 2500 gallons fuel.
1345 - Lt. Burger came aboard to inspect ship.
2345 - Checked lines half hourly. No further remarks.

November 11, 1943

0600 - Underway for sweep operations in field "A".
0754 - Gear out with 100' float pendant.
0940 - Beginning runs on course 285° True. Made 8 runs.
1511 - Recovering gear and returning to Base.
1637 - Tied up at Repair Base.. No further remarks.

Figure 25 - Exploding mine. Courtesy of Stanley Klein collection

November 12, 1943

0557 - Underway for sweep of Field "A".
0730 - Starboard gear streamed with 100' pendant.
0744 - Starting runs on course 285 True. Made four runs. Tied up at Repair Base.
2345 - Lines checked half-hourly. No further remarks.

November 13, 1943

0400 - Took on 800 gallons fresh water.
0600 - Underway for sweep operations in Field "C". Port gear streamed with 90' float pendant.
1020 - Making runs on course 135° True. Made 5 runs.
1450 - Recovered gear. Acting as mine disposal ship for YMS 86 and YMS 88. [This job required the sinking or destruction of floating mines].
1530 - Streaming magnetic gear.
1655 - Recovered magnetic gear. Returning to Base.
1659 - Sounded GQ.
1706 - Secured from GQ drill.
1754 - Tied up at Repair Base.
1840 - Captain's Mast: One man charged with jumping ship and attending movies. 11-12-43 while restricted to the ship. Awarded 15 hours extra duty.
2345 - No further remarks.

November 14, 1943

(Nothing worthy of note).

November 15, 1943

0600 - Underway for sweep operations.
0610 - Returning due to inclement weather.
0621 - Tied up at Repair Base.
0723 - Underway - weather clearing - Proceeding to Field "F".
0850 - Returning to Base.
1010 - Tied up at Repair Base. No further remarks.

November 16, 1943

Figure 26 - Broken cable cutter. Courtesy of Stanley Klein collection

0610 - Underway for sweep operation.
0717 - Streamed port gear with 100' float pendant.
0800 - Beginning runs of Field "A" on course 105° True.
1340 - Made 6 runs. Recovering gear.
1412 - Streamed port gear with 40' float pendant.
1436 - Making runs on course 105° True. Made 2 runs.
1606 - All gear recovered. Returning to Base.
1708 - Tied up at Repair Base.
2335 - Wright, W., StM 2/c treated for gash over right eye received when bunk chain broke.
2345 - No further remarks.

November 17, 1943

0559 - Underway for sweep operation.

0655 - Port gear streamed with 40' float pendant.
0729 - Beginning runs of Field "A" on course 105° True. Made 8 runs.
1301 - Gear fouled on a reef.
1335 - Gear free of reef. No damage done.
1545 - All gear recovered. Proceeding to Base. Cut one mine during day.
1636 - Tied up at Governor's Landing.
1805 - Taking on 1500 gallons of fuel.
2345 - No further remarks.

November 18, 1943

0603 - Underway for sweep of Field "A" with 100' float pendant.
0711 - Object on port bow resembling antenna float of mine. Object sunk by gun fire. Lat: 14° degrees 20' 20"; South; Long: 170° degrees 40' 16" West.
0713 - Maneuvering ship to sweep position where object was sunk.
0745 - Beginning runs on Field "A" on course 105° True. Made one run and cut loose one mine.
0900 - Gear fouled on bottom and broke loose.
0914 - Recovered gear.
0923 - Returning to Base.
1044 - Tied up at Governor's Landing.
2345 - No further remarks.

November 19, 1943

1605 - Underway for sweep of Field "A" with YMS 184.
0720 - Streaming gear with 70' float pendant.
0733 - Beginning runs on course 105° True. Made 6 runs.
1453 - Gear fouled on bottom. Paravane lost.
1530 - Gear recovered (less one paravane). Returning to Base. YMS 184 cut two mines during day.
1533 - C/C to 330° True. Proceeding to look for lost paravane.
1653 - Directed to lead ship in by Breaker Point.
1658 - Tanker passed us.
1713 - Returning to Base.
1749 - Tied up at Governor's Landing.
2345 - No further remarks.

November 20, 1943

0655 - Underway for sweep of Field "A".
0801 - Port gear streamed with 70' float pendant.
0843 - Beginning runs on course 070° True. Made four runs.
1500 - Gear recovered. Returning to Base. Cut one mine during day.
1548 Tied up to Repair Base.
1920 - Took on 1200 gallons of fresh water.

Figure 27 - Capt. Klein, Walter Weltzien and colleague planning mine field sweep Courtesy of Walter Weltzien

November 21, 1943

0910 - Captain's Mast: three men charged with disobeying ships order; left life jackets on deck. Restricted two days. (This seems to the layman to be "picky picky". Actually it may be the difference between life and death, or floating and drowning. If a sailor did not know where his life jacket was when he really needed it, he either had to steal someone else's or make do without it. If he was unconscious when he went into the water he would certainly drown. If he had his life jacket on he had the chance of staying afloat until his return to consciousness or rescue. It is strange that otherwise intelligent men would be so careless about these regulations designed for their own survival).

2345 - Checked lines half-hourly. No further remarks.

November 22, 1943

2230 - Took on 1400 gallons fresh water. 2345 - Checked lines half-hourly.

November 23, 1943

0625 - Underway to lead in ship. (Apparently the 183 is now on "station duty" which involves leading incoming or outgoing vessels through the swept channel. They also swept the entrance channel each morning to insure that it was clear of mines).

0720 - Sounded GQ.
0725 - Secured from GQ.
0748 - Gear streamed with 30' float pendant.
0838 - Recovered gear. Returning to Base.
0907 - Tied up at Repair Base.
1615 - Took on 600 gallons fresh water.
2345 - No further remarks.

November 24 1943

0530 - Underway to sweep channel.
0556 - Port gear streamed with 30' float pendant.
0810 - All gear recovered. Returning to Base.
0918 - Tied up at Governor's Landing.
1030 - Schwartz, H., S 2/c returned to duty from hospital.
1120 - Underway to lead ships in.
1202 - Met ships. Proceeding to lead them in.
1353 - Tied up at Repair Base. (It would be interesting to know what ships, how many and their destinations, entered or left Pago Pago each day. But apparently only the Port Director kept this information).

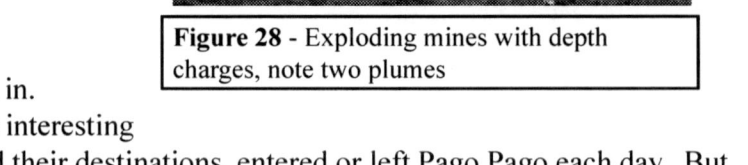

Figure 28 - Exploding mines with depth charges, note two plumes

November 25, 1943

0000 - Tied up as before. 1200 - Took on 1200 gallons of fresh water.

November 26, 1943

0628 - Underway for sweep operations in Field "A". Port "O" type gear streamed with 70' float pendant.
0819 - Beginning runs on course 250° True. Made 3 runs.
0954 - Began runs on course 135° True. Made 8 runs.

1353 - Retrieved gear. Returning to Base.

1417 - Fired K gun - Dropped charge on shoal. (In all probability, the shoal and its immediate surroundings could not be swept with the "O" type gear. The depth charge, fired from the K gun, would cause any mines close to the shoal to explode from the wave of detonation. There were apparently no mines in the vicinity of the shoal since no secondary explosions were reported).

1602 - Tied up at Repair Base.

November 27, 1943

0558 - Underway for sweep operation in Field "C" with YMS 86.

0740 - Port gear streamed with 70' pendant.

0755 - Beginning runs on Field "C" on course 135° True. Made 3 runs.

1150 - Recovered gear. Changed float pendant to 100' feet.

1232 - Beginning runs on course 135° True. Made 4 runs.

1530 - All gear recovered. Returning to Base. Cut 4 mines during day.

1656 - Tied up at Repair Base.

1843 - Took on 1500 gallons fresh water.

November 28, 1943

(Nothing of note to report).

Figure 29 - "Uncle Rafe", our mascot on smoke stack. Markings show mines swepted

November 29, 1943

0600 - Underway for sweep operations with YMS 86 in Field "C".

0748 - Port gear streamed with 100' float pendant.

0816 - Beginning runs on course 135° True. Made 4 runs.

1120 - Recovered gear to change length of float pendant.

1147 - Port gear streamed with 70' foot float pendant.

1217 - Beginning runs on course 135° True. Made 4 runs. - Recovered gear. Returning to Base. Cut 6 mines during day.

1624 - Tied up at Repair Base.

1845 - Took on 1200 gallons fresh water.

November 30, 1943

0605 - Underway for sweep operations in Field "C".

0718 - Gear streamed with 70' float pendant.

0730 - Beginning runs on course 135° True.

0746 - Mine reported on sweep wire on first run.

0750 - C/C to 180° True. Proceeding to deep water to maneuver ship to attempt to cut mine loose.

0817 - Retrieved depressor. Maneuvering ship still trying to shake object loose.

0827 - C/C to 215° True. Recovered rest of gear. Cutter showed evidence of mine having been caught between lip of cutter and sweep wire. (If it was indeed a mine, it sank when shaken loose or it remained anchored since the mooring cable was not completely cut. Otherwise it would have exploded or been brought up to the ship when the gear was recovered. Situations like this were very dangerous, for you really didn't know what the problem was until the mine came into view off the stern of the ship and this was too close for comfort).

0853 - Streamed Port gear with 100' float pendant. Beginning runs on course 135° True.

0910 - Securing due to rain. No runs made. (Some might wonder why rain would bother since the mines were already under water. The problem, of course, was that the sweeper had to know where she was located, literally every minute. Rain blocked the view of the various bearing points on shore which enabled the navigator to fix the position every minute or so. Thus it became too dangerous to continue).

0958 - Recovered gear. Returning to Base. No mines cut during day.

1124 - Tied up at Repair Base.

December 1, 1943

0000 - Tied up as before.

0645 - Underway for sweep operations in Field "C".

0810 - Streamed Port gear with 100' float pendant.

0817 - Beginning runs on course 135° True. Made 9 runs.

1513 - All gear recovered. Cut 4 mines during day.

1623 - Tied up at Repair Base.

December 2, 1943

0638 - Underway for sweep of Field "C".

0757 - Port gear streamed with 100' float pendant.

0802 - Beginning runs on course 135° True. Made 6 runs.

1328 - Gear recovered. Cut one mine during day. Returning to Base.

1500 - Tied up at Governor's Landing.

December 3, 1943

0000 - Tied up as before.

1000 - Took on 3000 gallons of fuel.

1605 - Took on food stores.

2345 - No further remarks.

December 4, 1943

0633 - Five men from YMS 98, including the CO came aboard. (This group came aboard to observe the techniques used by YMS 183 personnel when sweeping the Tutuila mine fields).

0635 - Underway for sweep of Field "C". 0745 - Returning due to inclement weather.

0803 - Tied up at Repair Base.

1101 - Changed berth to Customs Dock.

December 5, 1943

0603 - Underway for Field "C" with five men from YMS 98 aboard.

0730 - Gear streamed with 100' float pendant.

0735 - Beginning runs on course 260° True. Made 3 runs.

1125 - All gear recovered. Returning to Base.

1246 - Tied up at Customs Dock.

December 6, 1943

0610 - Underway for Field "C".

0740 - Gear streamed with 100' float pendant.

0745 - Beginning runs on course 260° True. Made 5 runs.
1127 - Beginning runs on course 090° True. Made 10 runs.
1520 - Recovered gear. Returning to Base.
1528 - Sounded GQ.
1531 - Secured from GQ drill.
1624 - Tied up at Governor's Landing.

December 7, 1943

0800 - Fumigating ship. (The layman would be amazed at the various vermin and varments that live on a ship along with the crew. For health and safety of the personnel periodic efforts at eradication have to be initiated. The average Naval vessel is infested with roaches, mice, rats, bugs and insects of various kinds. They come aboard in the commissary stores from the supply depots and ships, from the docks and piers to which ships are moored and from other vessels they tie up to. On the YMS all hatches leading to the outside are closed after all personnel are on deck. Inside, various spaces, aerosol bombs containing very strong insecticides and other noxious substances are set off. Usually, after two hours the job is done and the hatches are opened and the spaces aired out. The interesting part comes after the bombs first start releasing their gases. Roaches of all sizes, shapes and colors along with mice and rats come tumbling out on deck. The larger vermin sometimes make it to the side of the ship and fall into the water. The crew smash the bugs that don't die immediately and sweep everything over the side when the job is done. Of course, there is a good deal of cleaning to be done in the various spaces afterward as well. For a time after this fumigating the bugs and mice are hard to find. But in due time those that survived, now joined with new friends coming aboard after the fumigating, repopulate the vessel and at some point the fumigation takes place again).
1030 - Commissary stores being taken aboard. (The cycle begins again).
2345 - Checked lines half hourly. No further remarks. (There is no indication that any special note was taken of the second anniversary of the attack on Pearl Harbor and the beginning of the war).

December 8, 1943

0925 - Underway for Customs Dock.
0938 - Tied up at Customs Dock.
2345 - No further remarks.

December 9, 1943

0707 - Underway for sweep operations in Field "B".
0747 - Gear streamed with 70' float pendant.
0805 - Readjusting gear.
1040 - Beginning runs on course 090° True. Made one run.
1258 - Recovered gear. Returning to Base due to inclement weather.
1322 - Tied up at Governor's Landing.
1445 - Daniels, D.T., QM2/c, USN, 266-37-12; Schutt, C.E., MM 2/c, USN, 283-18-08; Rosbury, C.H., Cox, USN, 212-73-92; transferred to Naval Station 129.
1510 - Hankins, K.A., F 2/c, V-6 USNR, 564-97-29; Sharp, R.L., S 2/c, V-6 USNR, 866-26-28; Schones, R., S 2/c, V-6, USNR, 870-21-85; reported aboard for duty.
2345 - No further remarks.

December 10, 1943

0945 - Souza, J., S 1/c, USNR transferred to USN Mobile Hospital Unit # 3 at Naval Station # 129 for treatment.
1700 - Took on Commissary Stores.

December 11, 1943

0630 - Underway for sweep of Field "B".
0722 - Gear streamed with 60' float pendant.
0726 - Beginning runs on course 105° True. Made 5 runs. Gear struck bottom several times. No damage done.
1255 - Gear recovered. Proceeding to Base.
1325 - Tied up at Repair Base.
1500 - Took on 800 gallons fresh water.

December 12, 1943

1230 - Anderson, A.H., S 2/c 611-73-13 transferred to Base.
1245 - Stoker, R.A., S 2/c, 868-46-34, V-6 reported for duty.
1305 - Craft, W.J., GM 1/c, 257-78-28, F-4-C transferred to Base.
2345 - Checked lines half hourly. No further remarks.

December 13, 1943

1135 - Changed location to Dock # 9 at Repair Base.
2345 - No further remarks.

December 14, 1943

0803 - Underway for sweep of Field "B".
0829 - Returning to Base due to inclement weather.
0825 - Tied up at Repair Base.

December 15, 1943

0623 - Underway to sweep Field "B".
0713 - Streamed gear with 60' float pendant.
0720 - Starting runs on course 090° True. Made 2 runs.
0958 - Starting runs on course 065° True. Made 5 runs.
1525 - Recovered gear. Returning to Base.
1542 - Tied up at Repair Base.

December 16, 1943

0639 - Underway for sweep of Field "B".
0706 - Streaming gear with 60' float pendant.
0712 - Starting runs on course 065° True. Made five runs.
1010 - Gear fouled. Depressor broke loose.
1035 - Gear recovered and reassembled. Pendant shortened to 40', depressor to 9 ½ fathoms. 1105 - Starting runs on course 065° True. Made 2 runs.
1320 - Gear fouled. Depressor broke loose.
1350 - Gear recovered.
1357 - Looking for paravane lost on earlier sweep.

1416 - Returning to Base.
1442 - Tied up at Repair Base.
2045 - Took on 1400 gallons fresh water.

December 17, 1943

(Nothing of note to report).

December 18, 1943

0549 - Underway to sweep channel.
0615- Gear streamed with 40' float pendant.
0724 - Gear recovered. Returning to Base.
0831 - Tied up at Repair Base.
1030 - Launched Port Life Raft for test. Satisfactory.
2345 - No further remarks.

December 19, 1943

1045 - Smith, O.C., F 3/c Reported for duty.
1415 - Williams, S.G., EM 2/c, 656-10-89, V-6, USNR transferred to Naval Station #129.

December 20, 1943

(This page missing from the Log).

December 21, 1943

(Nothing of note to report).

December 22, 1943

2110 - Received storm warnings from Signal Tower.
2345 - Checked lines half hourly. No further remarks.

December 23, 1943

1053 - Took on 1300 gallons fresh water.
2345 - No further remarks.

December 24, 1943

1145 - Stocks, E.H., S 2/c, V-6; Gustafson, E.J. SC 3/c, V-6 reported aboard for duty.

December 25, 1943

0000 - Tied up as before.
0800 - Colors.
1851 - Colors.
2345 - Checked lines half hourly. No further remarks. (Signed: J.M. Dill, Lt.jg, USNR, Commanding).

December 26, 1943

0800 - Colors. Two men absent from muster.
0915 - Two men returned aboard.
1900 - Took on 1300 gallons fresh water.

John Dixon Davis

December 27, 1943

0636 - Underway to sweep Fields "C" & "D" with 40' float pendant.
0807 - Starting perimeter sweep of Field "C" & "D" on course 002° True; 100° True; 170° True; 267° True. Made 6 runs on each course
1500 - Gear recovered. Returning to Base.
1630 - Two men absent over leave returned to ship.
1645 - Captain's Mast. One man reprimanded and restricted to ship for 3 weeks. Three men absent over leave awarded 15 hours extra duty.

December 28, 1943

0631 - Underway to sweep Field "B". Gear streamed with 70' float pendant.
0812 - Began runs on course 065° True. Made 1 run. Gear struck bottom.
0841 - Recovered gear.
0910 - Streamed starboard gear with 60' float pendant.
0913 - Began runs on course 065° True. Made 2 laps.
1020 - Recovered gear having cut 3 mines.
1048 - Maneuvering ship to sink mines.
1300 - Streamed gear as before.
1315 - Began runs on course 065° True. Made 2 runs.
1515 - Recovered gear. Returning to Base.
1610 - Tied up at Repair Base.
1930 - Took on 1000 gallons fresh water.

December 29, 1943

0632 - Underway to sweep Field "B".
0703 - Starboard gear streamed with 60' float pendant.
0710 - Began runs on course 065 True. Made 3 runs.
0810 - Gear fouled.
0830 - Gear recovered. Knife (cutter) broken. Bridle smashed.
0835 - Sighted mine float beneath surface of the water.
0900 - Returning to Base for repairs. (The "O" type gear had to be rigged exactly right in order to be controlled and to function properly. In the case above the bridle, which keeps the paravane or otter at the proper angle has been ruined and the cutter broken. Replacements have to be made so that when a mine anchor cable is engaged by the sweep wire the mine mooring cable will slide down to the cutter and be cut. Rigging the bridle to the otter is an exacting job and is best done while the ship is moored in calm water. In all probability the gear was fouled and damaged by hitting a coral head).
0945 - Tied up at Customs Dock.

December 30, 1943

0635 - Underway to sweep Field "B".
0710 - Starboard gear streamed with 40' float pendant.
0720 - Gear fouled.
0740 - Gear recovered. No damage done.
1010 - Leading PC 596 into harbor.
1025 - C/C to 026° True.
1052 - Streamed gear as before.

1106 - Began runs on course 155° True. Made 4 runs.
1255 - Gear recovered. Returning to Base.
1353 - Tied up at Customs Dock.
1754 - Moved to Repair Base # 9 Dock.

December 31, 1943

0630 - Underway for sweep of Field "B".
0651 - Starboard gear streamed with 30' float pendant.
0740 - Recovering gear.
0904 - Returning to Base.
0922 - Tied up at Customs Dock.
2345 - Checked lines half hourly. No further remarks. (Signed: J.M. Dill, Lt.jg, USNR, Commanding).

January 1, 1944

0615 - Underway to sweep with YMS 98 in Field "B".
1310 - Gear secured, headed for harbor.
1730 - Robert W. Clayton, F 3/c, 347-15-77, USN reported for duty. (Robert (Bob) Clayton, as much as anyone and more than most is responsible for the publication of this history of the YMS 183. He started early gathering information, contacting former crew members and officers and provided the information he had gathered to the author. He with the author secured the ship's logs from the Department of Archives and History in College Park, Maryland. His narrative entitled "My Remembrance Of Duty On YMS 183" is used with his permission. Its various parts will be used at the proper time to give his memories of life aboard the ship. He writes, "After graduating from Electrical School in San Diego, I was made F 2/c at $54.00 per month, and was shipped by troop train to New Orleans, La., arriving about 11 PM. My name was called immediately, and I was loaded on board LST 267. The next morning upon awakening and going up on deck, I discovered we were heading down the Mississippi River. We went through the Panama Canal and eventually arrived at Pago Pago, Samoa. I was transferred to the receiving station where I stayed for a few days. Many times in the evenings I would see two little ships come in and tie up to the wharf. They were YMS 183 and 184. I admired these beautiful little ships, and thought it would be nice to serve on one of them, but it wasn't to be. My name was called and I was shipped to the receiving station in Noumea, New Caledonia. After about a week my name was called once again and I was placed on board the troop transport USS General John J. Pope, and away we went. She cruised at about 25 knots, which was very fast to me after being on an LST. We finally reached port and it was Pago Pago, Samoa. My name was called and I received my orders to report to

Figure 30 - Bob Clayton, EM 1/c, . Bob was instrumental in gathering materials for this history. He was an examplery sailor. Courtesy Bob Clayton

YMS 183 for duty. It was one of those little ships I had admired earlier. I reported aboard at 1730 on 1-1-44. I was an electrical striker and was placed under Cyrus D. Hall. EM 1/c. After about a month I was placed on messcook duty, peeling potatoes, serving food, washing dishes, and any other jobs required. Can you imagine, a big shot F 2/c being on messcook duty? I'll bet most of you can because it probably happened to you too.") *(See End Note No.50)*.

January 2, 1944

0000 - Moored alongside SC 1041, SC 702 at Pago Pago. (Nothing of note to report).

January 3 - 4, 1944

(Regular station duty and maintenance). (Sometime during this period Skipper Pete Dill received a V-Mail from his wife, Charlotte Dill, back home in Murfreesboro, Tennessee, announcing the arrival of their daughter Charlotte, (Jr.) on November 2, 1943. Of course there is nothing in the log about this, but Charlotte remembers that it took about 6 weeks for the V-Mail to make it from Murfreesboro to Samoa). Many people have heard about the V-Mail of World War II, but many have not. Called V, short for Victory, Mail, a special 8 1/2 x 11 paper form, with fold marks, and address side indicated, was available to service men and civilians alike for writing home or overseas. Its genius was that when the loved one of a serviceman mailed the V-Mail, properly folded and addressed, it went to a central military post office, one for the Pacific area and one for the European area. At this central post office the V-Mail, address side and message side were microfilmed on a roll of film. This roll of film was then sent to a central post office in the area designated where the film was used to print the V-Mail and send it on it's way to the addressee. Obviously, one roll of film could transport tens of thousands of letters across the oceans whereas the letters would have weighed perhaps hundreds of pounds if sent in their original state. This system saved a great deal of time and expense and was used extensively by service personnel and home folks alike. The most important factor in the morale of servicemen, and particularly those overseas, was mail. The various branches of the service did an excellent job in getting the mail to the serviceman, and getting his mail to his family back home. Charlotte's V-Mail announcing the birth of their daughter took six weeks. It may well have taken considerably longer than that if she had sent it by a regular airmail. The major shortcoming of this V-Mail was that you could only send one page of text per letter, and no photos or other enclosures could be sent this way). (Mail of any kind sent from the ship to any destination had to be inspected by the Captain or his designate. Letters had to be "censored" and the contents of packages approved. On the larger ships it took many officers to do this really arduous duty. On the YMS the CO designated the three other officers as censors. They had to make sure that crew members sent no information or artifacts that would reveal information that might be of use to the enemy. Most of the time nothing was revealed, but occasionally a clue might be inadvertently written. In this case the word or words were literally cut out of the page, before the censor stamped and initialed it as ok to send on. Crew members learned early on to write on only one side of a sheet of paper. Once in awhile a letter had so many deletions that the letter was returned to the author with the admonition to be more careful. In spite of what typical crew members may have thought, the censors detested this duty. There were several reasons for this. The officers instinctively didn't like the role of censor and it took time away from them that they might have used to catch up on sleep. Each officer censored his own mail).

January 5, 1944

0000 - Tied up with SC 1275, YMS 98 and YMS 184. (Nothing further to report).

January 6, 1944

0630 - Underway for sweep operations with YMS 98.
1400 - Returning to Base.
1405 - Received operational priority message from Base to assist plane bearing 215° True from airport at distance of 8 miles.

January 7 - 10, 1944

(Routine station duty, channel sweep, etc. On January 8, 1944 the mine fields around Pago Pago and Tutuila were considered swept. (See entry for October 21, 1943 on page above).

January 11, 1944

1125 - Capshaw, L.C., 295-23-96, MM (AA), reported for duty.

January 12 - 13, 1944

(Regular station duty etc.).

January 14, 1944

Moored with YP 237 and YMS 222 at Pago Pago. (Bob Clayton remembers going out every morning and every evening to sweep the main shipping channel into Pago Pago. He recalls a unique experience one day while sweeping a known field. "The YMS 272 was directly ahead of us and we were sweeping behind them much as you would plow a field. All at once mines started popping up from the 272's sweep. I think it was 22 mines that she cut in that one sweep. We would sink them with rifle or 50 cal. fire. Many times they would hit bottom and explode, sending a geyser of water into the air").

January 15 - 16, 1944

(Routine station duty).

January 17, 1944

Tied up at Governor's Landing with PC 1137, YMS 98 and 184. (Routine station duty).

January 18 - 20, 1944

(Routine station duty).

January 21, 1944

0701 - Underway for Apia, British Samoa. (Up until the end of WWI, British Samoa or Western Samoa was a possession of Germany. Germany came into possession by treaty with Britain many years earlier. However, New Zealand occupied the islands during WWI and afterward New Zealand was given a mandate by the League of Nations to administer the islands that make up Western or British Samoa. The two main islands are Savaii and Upolu. Apia is the capital city and located on Upolu. Western or British Samoa became an independent state on January 1, 1962 (from New Zealand-administered UN trusteeship). It is now a constitutional monarchy under a native chief. American Samoa, as previously indicated, has been and still is an American Territory, dating from the late nineteenth century. Today it is administered by the Office of Insular Affairs, US Department of the Interior. World War II brought both parts of Samoa into even closer association as they became potential targets for Japanese invasion. This is why the mine fields were laid around the Island of Tutuila by the US Navy soon after the attack on Pearl Harbor. It is not known if the British laid mines around Western Samoa. If they did they swept them up themselves. In any event there was a large pool of native labor, particularly in Western Samoa. These workers were hired by the military for work whereever needed and were transported to and from their home islands by the US Navy. One of the assignments the YMS 183, 184, and other minecraft had from time to time, when acting as station ships, was to transport these workers to the places where needed or back to their homes. American Samoa became an important hub of activity in the early days of the war because it was on the route of shipping, etc. from the Panama Canal on to Australia and the Southwest Pacific, and areas in between. Samoa played a large part in the staging of some of the early invasions by US Marines of the eastern most Mandated Islands of Japan like the Marshalls, Gilberts, and others. There was a repair base, SeaBee shops, barracks for Army and Marine troops, air fields, supply depots, hospital, etc. Even though, by late 1943, Samoa had become a "backwater" of the war in terms of offering direct resistance to the Japanese, it was still a vital facility for all Allied forces. In all probability, the trip to Apia, British Samoa, was to return and/or pick up native workers going to and from Pago Pago. *(See End Note No.51)*. (The voyage from Pago Pago to Apia probably took around 10 hours so that they arrived before dark on the 21st).

January 22 - 23, 1944

(Anchored at Apia.)
0000 - On the 23rd, SC 1041 anchored near us.

January 24, 1944

0808 - Anchor's aweigh, underway for Pago Pago.
1603 - Tied up at Pago Pago with YMS 184.

January 25 - 26, 1944

(Tied up Pago Pago with YMS 184 and 272. Continuing station duty).

January 27 -31, 1944

(Continuing station duty at Pago Pago).

February 1, 1944

(Continuing station duty at Pago Pago).

February 2, 1944

0640 - Five marines came aboard as passengers to Wallis Island.
0702 - Underway to escort LCT 168 to Wallis Island.
0820 - Set course 280° True, speed 6 knots. (The LCT, Landing Ship, Tank was a 286 ton, steel craft designed to carry tanks, trucks or other cargo up to 150 tons and to run its bow up on shore for unloading on the beach. The Mk 5 type, one of which the 168 was, was 117'6" long, beam 32', draft 2'10" forward, 4'2" aft. It had three Gray 225 hp diesels and triple screws. Speed: 8 knots; armament: 2 20mm cannons; complement: 1 officer, 12 enlisted men; capacity: 5 30-ton or 4 40-ton or 3 50-ton tanks or 150 tons general cargo. The 168 was built by Quency

Barge Builder, Quincy, Ill. Keel was laid Oct. 1, '42; launched Nov. 3, '42 and delivered Nov. 21, '42. The log gives no clue as to what the LCT 168 was carrying to Wallis Island. It could have been supplies for a military unit or it could have been going to Wallis Island empty to bring back equipment for repair at Pago Pago. Wallis Island was discovered by Samuel Wallis in 1767. French Missionaries became established on the island around 1837 and it became a French possession administered by New Caledonia after 1888. American troops were stationed there in June 1942. The LCT 168 was capable of making 8 knots, but this speed was rarely used except in the run to the beach in an invasion. In an ocean voyage of approximately 400 miles, the distance from Pago Pago to Wallis Island, in the open ocean and especially if it was loaded with 150 tons of cargo, the speed would have been less and if the seas were large, much less. It actually took about three days (24 hrs. x 3 = 72 hrs.). This is a speed of about 6 knots. It was not uncommon for YMS 183, when escorting landing craft of any type to have to reduce its speed from its standard speed of 10 plus knots to the best speed of the landing craft. Five to six knots seems a reasonable speed for the LCT).

February 3, 1944

(Escorting LCT 168 from Pago Pago to Wallis Island).
1535 - Crossed international date line. Date now

February 4, 1944.

February 5, 1944

(Maintaining base course 277° True, speed 6 knots).

February 6, 1944

1000 - Pilot came aboard to guide us into Wallis Island.
1033 - Anchored in 9 fathoms of water.

February 7, 1944

0000 - Anchored as before at Wallis Island.
1100 - Took aboard 1000 gallons of fresh water. (Ensign Weltzien remembers that there was a rumor that Wallis Island had been a leper colony and that no one had any interest in making liberty there. There is no mention of the marine passengers leaving the ship or what cargo the LCT 168 unloaded at Wallis Island).

February 8, 1944

1615 - Anchor's aweigh. Pilot aboard preparing to leave Wallis harbor.
1618 - Port engine reported overheating. Secured same.
1657 - Port engine repaired and working satisfactorily.
1715 - Left Wallis Island on base course 101° True. (Escorting LCT 168 from Wallis to Tutuila).

February 9, 1944

0830 - Making practice runs on LCT 168, instructing men in the use of underwater sound gear.
1816 - LCT 168 unable to continue due to engine trouble. Tow line passed to LCT.
1843 - Proceeding with LCT 168 in tow at 2/3 speed.
2200 - Crossed International Date line going east. (It is now **February 8, 1944**, once again).
2345 - No further remarks.

John Dixon Davis

February 9, 1944

2030 - Number one ship's service generator broke down.

February 10, 1944

0000 - Streaming as before on base course 101° True with LCT 168 in tow.
0610 - C/C to 080° True.
1523 - LCT 168 turned loose at entrance to anti-submarine nets at Pago Pago harbor.
1602 - Tied up outboard YMS 272 at Governor's Landing.

February 11, 1944

0840 - Voorhies, A.H., Jr., GM 3/c, 412-49-49 reported for duty. Underway for Repair Base.
1300 - Yard workmen came aboard to work on engines.

February 12, 1944

0715 - Three men came aboard to work on generator.
0920 - Took aboard 1200 gallons fresh water.
1315 - Souza, J., S 1/c transferred to Mobile Hospital #3 with old knee injury.

February 13, 1944

(Nothing of note to report).

February 14, 1944

1210 - Began fumigating ship.

February 15, 1944

(Nothing of note to report).

February 16, 1944

1440 - Bellvue, P.E., MoMM 1./c transferred to Mobile Hospital #3.
1530 - Took on stores for general mess.

February 17 - 18, 1944

(Nothing of note to report).

February 19, 1944

1000 - Inspection of ship by the Captain.
1515 - Took aboard commissary stores.

February 20, 21, 22, 23, 1944

(Nothing of note to report).

February 24. 1944

1013 - Underway to test engines and adjust sweep gear.
1117 - Gear streamed with 23' float pendant.
1518 - All gear recovered; returning to Base.

Figure 31 - From right to left A. J. Richard, Walter Weltzien and fellow crew members. Courtesy of Walter Weltzien

1612 - Moored at Customs Dock.

February 25, 1944

0550 - Hall, B.M., CBM left ship on leave. (Where would one go on leave for two or three days, in Samoa, during war-time? The log does not say, but there was undoubtedly a rest and recreation area for marines, soldiers, and sailors. Perhaps Chief Boatswain Hall just wanted to get off the ship for a few days for a change of scenery). 0608 - Underway to sweep channel.
0828 - Gear recovered, returning to Base.
0851 - Moored outboard YN 9 at Governor's Landing. (A YN was a net tender).
1412 - Took aboard commissary stores.

February 26, 1944

0605 - Underway to sweep channel.
1115 - Recovered gear, returning to Base.

February 27, 1944

0605 - Underway to sweep channel.
0622 - Gear streamed.
0832 - Recovered gear, returning to Base.
0852 - Tied up at Governor's Landing.
1042 - Took aboard 1100 gallons of fresh water.
1222 - Underway to lead in ships.
1232 - Ships not entering harbor; we are returning to Base.

February 28, 1944

0600 - Underway to sweep channel.
0618 - Gear streamed.
1000 - Recovered gear, returning to Base.
1450 - Hall, B.M., CBM returned after 72 hour leave.

February 29, 1944 (Leap year!).

(Routine channel sweep and typical day for a station ship).

March 1, 1944

(Routine station duty).

March 2, 1944

0554 - Underway to sweep channel.
0918 - Recovered gear and returned to Base.
1101 - Moored outboard of YMS 184 at Customs Dock.
1300 - Began fumigating ship. (This had to be done very frequently as the tropics fostered the rapid increase in vermin and varments).

March 3, 1944

1331 - Paymaster came aboard to pay crew.

March 4, 1944

1000 - Captain's inspection of ship. (Sometime during this period Captain Dill received a letter from his wife Charlotte. The most important news (according to Charlotte) was a progress report on the growth and development of little daughter, Charlotte, (Jr.). To make it as personal as possible, mother Charlotte saved the fingernail cuttings of their little daughter at about 6 weeks of age and enclosed them in the envelope with some photos and airmailed it all to Pete. He received it in due time. As often happened, when the mail arrived and the designated mailman from the crew handed out the bundles of letters that had accumulated over several weeks, and sometimes longer, the recipient hungrily grabbed his bundle, and, unless it happened to be raining, found a private place on deck and started reading his mail. Captain Dill did not wait to open his mail in his quarters, but on deck, and started reading. As he unfolded the sheets in the envelope, without ever noticing, the wind blew the precious little fingernail cuttings over the side. He didn't realize what had happened until he read a few minutes later in the letter that they were there. Thus, another of the problems of war. Perhaps, even more sad than this, was the countenance of that man or those several men, who at a given mail call received no mail at all. The letters were bundled together and tied with jute twine. Often it made a package with many letters and if mail was only now catching up with a person who had been in transit from somewhere else for duty on YMS 183, there might be several bundles with 100 letters or more. Many times the bundles had gotten wet, the ink was smeared, and there were all kinds of stains on some of the envelopes. But stained or not those letters were read over and over until they were almost memorized. Perhaps, 99% of the time that a person didn't get any mail, it was because no one had written to him. It took awhile, sometimes, for mail to catch up with a ship, but unless some very dire circumstance occurred, most of the mail posted from back in the States found its addressee. Receiving mail was the next best thing to getting orders to return to the States or the news that the war was over).

March 5, 6, 7, 1944

(Nothing of note to report).

March 8, 1944

0853 - Streaming gear to sweep Field "D".
1613 - Recovered gear, returned to Base.

March 9, 1944

0658 - Routine channel sweep.

March 10, 1944

(Nothing of note to report).

March 11, 1944

1005 - Captain's Inspection.

March 12, 1944

0556 - Underway for channel sweep. (Routine station ship day).

Figure 32 - Engine room personnel.

March 13, 1944

0551 - Underway for channel sweep.
1300 - Fumigating ship.

March 14, 1944

0630 - Underway to sweep channel.
0819 - Proceeding to Field "E" for operation with YMS 184.
1350 - Moored outboard of YMS 184 at Customs Dock.
1400 - Captain's Mast for man charged with drinking intoxicants while on duty 2-13-44. Pleaded guilty. Awarded restriction to ship for one week.

March 15, 1944

0620 - Routine channel sweep.

March 16, 1944

0628 - Underway to sweep channel. 0845 - Recovered gear; proceeding to Field "E".
1620 - Returned to Base. Took aboard commissary stores.

March 17, 1944

0545 - Underway for routine channel sweep.

March 18, 1944

1000 - Took on commissary stores.
1146 - Underway to swing ship and have gunnery practice.
1213 - Swinging ship. (This had to do with changing the ship's headings in order to calibrate the magnetic compass).
1413 - Held GQ drill.
1421 - Commenced firing 3" 50 cal.
1500 - Ceased firing 3" 50. Commenced firing 20 MM.
1524 - Ceased firing 20 MM; returning to Base.

March 19, 1944

0715 - Mr. Jacobs came aboard to check steering gear.
0802 - Underway to test steering apparatus.
0855 - Tests completed; returning to Base.
1025 - Tug came alongside and moved ship to Pier # 8.
1035 - Diver from Base came aboard to inspect rudder.
1301 - Shifted berth to fuel dock, Governor's Landing.
1842 - Executed Colors. (Signed: J.M. Dill, Lt.jg, USNR, Commanding.

March 20, 1944

(There were two pages of the log for this date, but the first one of them is missing, probably due to an error in reproducing them at the National Archives. The second page has one entry; 2330 - C/C to 270° True. By looking ahead in log we find that the destination of the ship is Espiritu Santo in the New Hebrides Islands and YMS 184 is accompanying YMS 183 on this voyage. For all practical purposes Espirito Santo is due west of American Samoa).

March 21, 1944

0000 - Steaming as before on base course 270° True.

1020 - Set clocks back one hour. (The international date line, which theoretically follows the 180th meridian and which is the line of demarcation where each new day begins, does not always follow the 180th meridian. This is especially true of a large area just west of Samoa from approximately 10 degrees south latitude to about 60 degrees south latitude. The international date line roughly follows the 176th meridian or longitude 176° degrees west, rather than 180° degrees. This change in location of the international date line is made by agreement between the various countries and island entities in that area so that they are operating on the same calendar. The reader may remember the puzzle leading up to the beginning of the 21st century. Everyone wanted to know on what island the new century and millennium would begin, or on which island the sunrise would first be seen. It began on one of the islands in this area, delineated above, as it was nearest to the arbitrary international date line and not meridian 180° degrees. When the writer of the log for March 21, 1944 wrote "1020 - set clocks back one hour" he should also have written, we have crossed the international date line and the date changes from March 21, 1944 to March 22, 1944. They crossed the arbitrary date line and the time zone line from + 11 to - 12 at the same moment. He probably should have written, in the interest of complete accuracy, that the local time is now, instantly, 0920 and the date, instantly March 22, 1944. Actually, as you will see below in the next log entry, he forgets this and doesn't change the date until the following day when he skips March 23, 1944 and goes to March 24, 1944). *(See End Note No.52)*.

March 22, 1944

(As noted above it became March 22 halfway through March 21, 1944 and this entry should be March 23, 1944). 2034 - Crossed 180th meridian. (The keeper of the log has forgotten that the ship has already crossed the international date line, so his log is one day late. He catches up, however for tomorrow's entry is dated March 24, 1944. Now he is back in synch).

March 24, 1944

0000 - Steaming as before on base course 270° True.

1300 - Began flag hoist drills with YMS 184.

1400 - Ceased drills. (There were a number of ways one ship could communicate with other ships or a shore base. They had radio, using voice or international Morse code, the blinker light using Morse code, semaphore flags or flag hoist. Each ship carried a rather large reference book with hundreds of combinations of signal flags and their meaning. Few if any, aboard the average ship knew very many of these from memory, so whenever a flag hoist was elected as the means of communication, someone had the book and told the signal man which flags and in what sequence from the top of the hoist they should be in, or what a certain sequence of flags from another ship meant. When the ship receiving the message had identified the flags and their sequence, they were snapped onto the halyard with a snaphook attached to each signal flag and raised about halfway to the yardarm. [The halyard was a small rope run through a pulley fastened to the cross piece (yardarm) near the top of the mast. The yardarm had a number of halyards, each reaching down to another pulley on the frame of the flag bag. In the flag bag were all of the signal flags that could possibly be needed]. This let the sending ship or base know that the flags had been identified and that the receiving ship was in process of determining what the hoist meant. When the meaning was understood the receiving ship "two blocked" or pulled the flags tight up to the yardarm. The sender now knew that the receiver had received and understood the message. If the message said that the ship should change course to a new heading, then the sender let the receiver know when to make the change by smartly pulling the flag hoist down. The command to "execute" meant that the hoist should come down and the message, whatever it was, should be carried out. When the signal to "execute" was seen by the receiver, he lowered his hoist to signal that he would carry out the command. The average YMS probably didn't use flag hoists very often. Some of them probably never had occasion to do so except when entering or leaving a harbor. At this time the ship's call sign was indicated by the flag hoist, two blocked to the yardarm. If the shore station needed to contact the ship it knew what call sign to use because it identified that particular ship. Each ship, from the battleship down to the SC, had its own call sign).

1700 - Held fire drill.
1724 - Held GQ drill.
2256 - C/C to 260° True

March 25, 1944

0000 - Steaming as before on base course 260° True.
0400 - Sighted unknown ship. Sounded General Quarters. (This was no drill, as they didn't know what was out there).
0412 - Challenged ship and received satisfactory reply.
0413 - Secured from GQ. (When the 183 challenged this ship they could barely see, since they had no radar, they probably used a special blinker light to signal the ship asking what ship it was. The other ship blinked back a special code that let the 183 know it was a friendly ship. Now if the other ship ignored the signal from the 183 or gave a wrong signal in return the 183 would have had no recourse but to fire on the other ship. Perhaps in this area at this time during the war, if it had been an unfriendly vessel it more than likely would have been a Japsubmarine on the surface recharging its batteries. If this was the case, then even the YMS would have had a chance. It could have raked the submarine's deck with 20MM and 30 cal machine gun fire, perhaps even with the 3" 50 cal cannon. This could have driven the submarine to dive where the YMS with its sonar could have depth charged it).
1315 - Set clocks back one hour (-11 time zone). (The -11 time zone begins at approximately the 173rd meridian east and this is where the 183 and 184 entered this time zone as they were voyaging from east to west).
1642 - Held fire drill and abandon ship drill.

March 26, 1944

0000 - Steaming as before on base course 260° True.
0900 - C/C/ to 296° True. Entering Selwyn Strait. (Sometimes called Selwyn Passage, between the islands named Pentecost and Ambrym these two islands along with a number of others form a north-south barrier on the eastern side of Espiritu Santo, the main island in the New Hebrides. There is only one other possible passage through these islands and it is doubtful the other could accommodate ships of any size. So as the ships enter Selwyn Passage they are approximately 60 miles away from the Naval Base at the Port of Santo and they now change course to the northwest for about 4 hours. This will bring them in line with the entrance to the harbor and then to the west to enter the harbor).
1316 - C/C to 300° True.
1350 - C/C to 270° True.
1410 - C/C to 280° True.

John Dixon Davis

1504 - Entering Espiritu Santo harbor.
1638 - Moored alongside YMS 184 at Berth # 1, Espiritu Santo.
1657 - Shifted berth to Pier # 1.
1735 - Took on 1200 gallons fresh water. [Fresh water was hard to come by. The YMS had an evaporator designed to make fresh water from salt. After one use, the evaporator had to be dismantled and cleaned before it could be used again. This was an intolerable situation, so the YMS had to beg fresh water from larger ships or a base. It was the only way to keep a supply of drinking and cooking water on hand. The crew never took a fresh water shower unless the ship was in port and then only when there was a guaranteed supply of fresh water At sea it was always a salt water shower]. (The New Hebrides Islands had been under some joint British-French governance for many years and still were in the WWII era. The many English and French names give testimony to this fact. In any event the British and Free French were our allies. They did not have the capacity to build a large Naval facility in that area so near to the Solomon Islands where the US Marines and Soldiers of the US Army were engaged in the bitter struggle for the Island of Guadalcanal. The US did have that capacity and the Naval Base was well underway on the southeast corner of the big island in late May, 1942. *(See End Note No.53)*. YMS 183 and 184 make their entrance on this scene nearly two years later).

March 27, 1944

0842 - Underway, shifting berth to fuel dock Pier # 7.
1015 - Took on 3500 gallons of fuel oil.
1028 - Shifted berth to Mine Depot Dock.
1145 - Minesweeping gear taken aboard.
1617 - Shifted berth to Pier # 1.
1800 - Executed Colors. (Signed: J.M. Dill, Lt.jg, USNR, Commanding).

March 28, 1944

0712 - Took on 1100 gallons of fresh water.
1020 - Took on commissary stores
1033 - Shifted berth to go alongside AM 64 in Berth # 1.
1122 - Stern line fouled in starboard screw.
1135 - Diver over the side working on fouled screw. (While this was not a frequent occurrence, it probably happened to every smaller ship from time to time. The lines used to tie the ship to a dock or another vessel would fall into the water. If the screws were turning the line would be drawn into the turning screws, sometimes wrapping the line very tightly around the propeller shaft and causing it to vibrate. The screw blades could become bent or the shaft rendered unable to turn, etc. Sometimes other debris in the water would be caught by a screw. The debris or lines, etc. had to be removed as soon as possible and the screw and propeller shaft inspected and tested before the ship could go on with its underway duties. In most cases a diver, with regular diving suit on with compressed air supplied had to be used to clear the screw. If the line was wrapped very tightly, it might take several hours to clear it. If there was damage to the symmetry of the screw or the shaft the vessel would have to go into drydock for repairs).

March 29, 1944

1503 - Took on 600 gallons of fresh water.
1515 - Underway for Noumea, New Caledonia with YMS 184 escorting the tanker Fort Donaldson and the Liberty ship Edwin Booth.

1608 - C/C to 110° True.

1747 - C/C to 142° True. (The ships have cleared the harbor and have turned to go down the channel between Malakula and Ambrym islands. After 4 hours on course 142° True the course is changed to 211° True. This course will take the ships out into the Coral Sea as they head for New Caledonia).

March 30, 1944

0000 - Steaming as before on course 142° True.

0007 - C/C to 211° True. (After 6 hours the course is changed to 167° True).

0638 - C/C to 167° True. (For the next 18 hours this course will take the ships parallel to the rather large island of New Caledonia which runs from northwest to southeast. The ships are off the east coast of the island and are headed in a southeastly direction).

March 31, 1944

0000 - Steaming as before on base course 167° True.

1440 - C/C to 142° True.

1837 - C/C 167° True.

2205 - C/C to 255° True (At 2205 the ships have cleared the southernmost island of those that lie east of New Caledonia. Its name is Mare`. The new course, 255° True, will take the ships toward the southern tip of New Caledonia where there is a passage through the coral reef. This passage is called Canal de Havannah. The sea port, Noumea, is situated on the southwest side of the island and can be reached through the Canal de Havannah. This passage saves ships from going some distance out to sea to avoid the extensive coral reef that encompasses the southern and southwestern areas of the island).

April 1, 1944

0000 - Steaming as before on base course 255° True.

0621 - C/C to 270° True.

0834 - Entering Havannah Passage, proceeding on various courses to Noumea.

1427 - Moored at Section Base, Port Noumea, New Caledonia.

1801 - Executed Colors. (Signed: J.M. Dill, Lt.jg, USNR, Commanding).

April 2, 1944

0825 - Shifted berth to outboard AM 62 at Repair Base.

0945 - Took on 1100 gallons fresh water.

1030 - Took aboard two boxes of engine parts.

1407 - Took aboard blower for engine.[This item provided an extra volume of air for the intake valves of the diesel engines].

1752 - Putnam, Lewis Franklin, S 2/c reported aboard for duty.

April 3, 1944

(Nothing of note to report).

April 4, 1944

1130 - Took aboard outboard motor for wherry. [Small lifeboat].

1420 - Tug alongside to tow us to drydock.

1504 Entering drydock.

John Dixon Davis

Figure 33 - Members of the crew. Courtesy of Walter Weltzien

1520 - Secured in ARD - 2, drydock.

April 5, 1944

0000 - Moored as before in ARD-2 drydock.

1750 - Deshler, F. A., Y 1/c transferred to USN Receiving Station, Noumea, New Caledonia. (When Deshler was transferred, it was a time of promise for Bob Clayton who had been a messcook since coming aboard in January, 1944. He remembers, "Since he (Deshler) was the only Yeoman on board, we were short a yeoman, so Captain Dill came around to the crew, and asked if anyone could type. Thank heaven, I had taken typing in high school, and my days as a messcook were over. I held the Yeoman's job for several months. It was a piece of cake compared to mess cooking.").

April 6 - 7, 1944

(Moored in drydock both days. Among other things, the bottom of the ship was scraped to remove all marine life including grasses, sea weed and barnacles. The landlubber would be amazed at the amount of growth of these items that were literally a part of the ship. Its actual weight in pounds, while considerable, was not the chief problem. The growth created a drag on the ship and could reduce its speed a knot or two, depending on how much had accumulated. The crew turned to to do the scraping and after a day or two the bottom had dried enough to inspect for worms and other signs of damage. Any damage was repaired and several new coats of copper paint, or some other type that also deterred worms, were applied. Perhaps the most memorable part of being drydocked was the stench. As soon as the ship was clear of the water, all of the marine life began to die. When marine life dies it begins to decay and smell. When all of this material was scraped off it fell to the deck of the drydock and putrefied. The smell had to be tolerated, for there was too much debris to try to remove by hand. When the drydock was flooded a few days later the debris washed away, and the cycle began again as other ships entered and were scraped.

April 8, 1944

0600 - Commenced flooding drydock.
0815 - Emerging from drydock. Tug alongside to tow us to Repair Base.
0830 - Moored alongside YMS 216 outboard AM 62 at Repair Base.

April 9, 1944

(Nothing of note to report).

April 10, 1944

0900 - Took aboard two sight (telescopic) replacements for 3" 50, Mark 7, Mod 1.
1113 - Tug alongside - shifting berth to inboard slip at Repair Base.
1400 - Paymaster came aboard and paid officers and crew.

April 11, 1944

1545 - Lt.jg, J.M. Dill, DV(G),USNR, 120378, was detached pursuant to BuPers SpdLtr 120378 Pers. 3161 - DL 5 dated 19, February 1944. Lt.jg E.R. Seaver, DEV(G), USNR, pursuant to above SpdLtr and to ComSoPac orders P16 - 4/00/(60) serial 8289p 119605 this date assumed command of YMS 183. (Signed: J.M. Dill, Lt.jg, USNR. (Of this time, now former skipper of YMS 183, Pete Dill has written, "Prior to leaving Samoa, I had requested orders to transfer into the Naval Air Corps. I had decided that I was rejected as several weeks had passed with no orders, but when the 183 arrived in Noumea, I found orders awaiting me to travel by NATS back to the States and to Hensley Airfield, Dallas, Texas for the beginning of Navy flight training. Hence, on April 11, 1944, I relinquished command of the 183 to Lt.jg, Robert Seaver as commanding officer). (Charlotte Dill, at the author's request, provided the following information regarding Lt.jg Pete Dill's Naval career following his detachment from the 183: he was awarded his Navy Wings on January 16, 1945, after just ten months. He served a tour in the Pacific as pilot of a PBM flying boat before the war ended and another after the war was over after which time he resigned from the Navy. The rapid completion of his flight training was the result of his already having more than 40 hours, etc. in the Piper Cub while a student at Middle Tennessee State University before the war). (Some time during the tenure of Pete Dill, as CO of the 183, someone painted the cartoon character Uncle Rafe, an infant boy with a muzzle loading rifle across his lap, on the smoke stack. The painting seemed almost professionally done and was as large as it could be given the dimensions of the stack. Underneath the figure of Uncle Rafe the tally of mines swept was kept. No one seemed to know who did the painting or when it was done. In a conversation with Pete Dill while gathering information for this book I asked him about it. He told me that he didn't know who did the painting and he was aware that it was a "dig" at him as a hillbilly from East Tennessee, but he rather liked it, so it stayed on the stack until the ship was decommissioned and probably for a good period of time after that).

John Dixon Davis

Chapter 10
The Third CO Takes Command

April 12, 1944

0000 - Moored as before at Repair Base, Noumea, New Caledonia.
1500 - Took aboard 1100 gallons of fresh water.
1748 - Executed Colors. (Signed: E.R. Seaver, Lt.jg, USNR, Commanding). (The 183 now has only three officers, since Dill was detached).

April 13, 14, 15, 16, 17, 1944

(Still moored at Repair Base. Nothing of note to report).

April 18, 1944

1145 - Took aboard commissary stores.
1250 - Kelly, D.P., BM 2/c transferred to Receiving Station, Noumea.
1400 - Hadley, J.A., RM 3/c, 342-56-67, and Schulte, A., GM 2/c, 648-32-95 reported aboard for duty.
1740 - Executed Colors. (Signed: E.R. Seaver, Lt.jg, USNR, Commanding).

April 19 - 20, 1944

(Nothing of note to report).

April 21, 1944

0815 - Underway for swinging ship and compass calibration.
1515 - Commenced streaming magnetic gear to repair it.
1600 - Recovered gear.
1657 - Moored alongside YMS 184 at Section Base.

April 22, 1944

0809 - Took on fuel oil from fuel dock.
1109 - Moored at Section Base.
1300 - Smith, O.C., F 2/c, transferred to Receiving Station, Noumea.

April 23, 1944

(Nothing of note to report).

Figure 34 - 3rd CO Robert Seaver Courtesy of Walter Weltzien

April 24, 1944

0550 - Underway for anti-aircraft firing drill.
1025 - Commenced firing 3" 50 and 20MM at sleeve [aerial target] towed by an airplane.
1045 - Commenced firing at surface target.
1525 - Returned to Base - moored at Section Base.

April 25, 1944

0551 - Underway for anti-submarine practice. (This involves finding and tracking a real submarine with the sonar gear and getting into position to depth bomb the submarine).
0848 - Commenced runs on sub.
1549 - Returning to Base. 1800 - Moored at Section Base. Took on commissary stores.

John Dixon Davis

April 26, 1944

0000 - Moored as before at Section Base Noumea, New Caledonia.

0534 - Underway for three day sweep operation.

0610 - All gear streamed.

1344 - Gear recovered. Day's sweep completed satisfactorily. Proceeding to Goro Bay to moor for the night.

1435 - Moored at Nickel Dock, Goro Bay, New Caledonia.

1735 - Executed Colors. (Signed: E.R. Seaver, Lt.jg, USNR, Commanding.) (New Caledonia, an overseas possession of France, was settled by both Britain and France in the first half of the 19th century. The Island was sighted by British navigator James Cook in 1774 and he gave it the Roman name for Scotland. It was annexed by France in 1853 and served as a penal colony for 40 years after 1864. At the beginning of WWII, France fell to the Germans, but the Free French kept the Island in the ranks of the Allies, and thus it also became the home of naval bases and early on was Admiral Halsey's headquarters. It is interesting to note that after the day's sweep the 183 moored at Nickel Dock in Goro. It is interesting because the mineral nickel had been found in large quantities in New Caledonia early on. Even today it produces 20% of the world's supply, exceeded only by Canada. I'm guessing that Nickel Dock was named for or had an historic connection to the production and shipping of nickel ore to customers around the world. Goro is a small seaport at the southeastern tip of the island near the entrance of Havannah Passage. *(See End Note No.54)*.

April 27, 1944

0000 - Moored as before at Nickel Dock, Goro Bay, New Caledonia.

1602 - Underway from Nickel Dock to start second day's operation of three day sweep.

0640 - All gear streamed.

1603 - Recovered gear, returning to Goro Bay to anchor.

1623 - Anchored in Goro Bay.

April 28, 1944

0605 - Underway for sweep operation.

0647 - All gear streamed.

1434 - All gear recovered. Three day sweep completed. Proceeding to berth B-14 to conduct listening watch in accordance with radio orders. (Berth B-14 in all probability was adjacent to the entrance to the harbor, and a vessel was positioned there at all times to listen for submarines using the sonar).

1540 - Relieved YP 421. Anchored in Berth B-14.

April 29, 1944

0000 - Anchored in Berth B-14 conducting listening watch.

1725 - Relieved by YP 421. Returning to Base.

1800 - Moored at fuel dock, Ducos Peninsula, New Caledonia.

1845 - Received 1800 gallons of fuel.

April 30, 1944

0000 - Anchored as before.

1715 - Underway for Section Base.

0759 - Moored at Section Base.

1200 - Received commissary stores aboard.
1300 - Voorhies, A. H., GM3/c, 412-49-49 transferred to Receiving Station. Freeman, M.D., PhM 2./c, 271-71-07 transferred to Receiving Station.
1355 - Worobey, Alex., 207-20-83, PhM 2/c, reported aboard for duty.
1900 - Took aboard cargo for delivery at Suva (Fiji) and Tonga (Tongatabu).

May 1, 1944

0534 - Lt. Butler reported aboard on temporary orders as passenger to Tongatabu.
0603 - Underway to escort SS Standard to designated point.
0818 - Took departure from Bulasi Pass, New Caledonia.
1755 - Held GQ drill. (The 183 left YMS 184 behind. They had been together since construction at Greenport in March 1942, a little over two years ago. Although the log makes no mention of it, it is believed that the 184 was to have gone to Guadalcanal on May 3rd and to destinations like Saipan, Tinian and Guam. YMS 184 was eventually turned over to the USSR 07-19-45. (See Appendix B).

May 2, 1944

0000 - Steaming as before on course 115° True in company with SS Standard.
0615 - C/C to 092° True.
1615 - Held GQ drill.

May 3, 1944

0000 - Steaming as before on Base Course 092° True in company with SS Standard.
1500 - Set all clocks ahead to - 12 time. (The - 12 time zone begins at approximately 173° degrees east longitude as the ship travels from west to east).
1820 - Held GQ drill.

May 4, 1944

0000 - Steaming as before on Base Course 092° True in company with SS Standard.
0400 - C/C/ to 026° True.
1810 - Held GQ drill.

May 5, 1044

0000 - Steaming as before on Base course 026° True. 1525 - C/C course to 058° True.
1805 - Held GQ drill.
2045 - Moored at King's Wharf, Suva, Fiji Islands.
2245 - Took aboard 1300 gallons of fresh water. ("As the crow flies" it is roughly 700 miles from Noumea to Suva. The course the ship had to take to avoid islands and reefs can be plotted from the information given beginning on May 1 above. The actual miles traveled was close to 1200). (Bob Clayton remembers Fiji as a "great place". He writes, "They even had a movie theater and the British Governor had a beautiful young daughter about 17 or 18 and she liked to go to the movies. It was a thrill just to see her after all those months at sea. This place also had a narrow gauge railroad that came right down to the docks. They had a little 4 man handcar that you had to pump. We would travel for miles on it at night, even found a farmer who sold us some fresh eggs. Brother, you talk about a treat."

John Dixon Davis

May 6, 1944

0900 - Took on fuel.

May 7, 1944

0605 - Underway for Tongatabu escorting S S Fort Moultrie.
0748 - C/C to 218° True.
1315 - C/C to 150° True.
1905 - Held GQ drill.

May 8, 1944

0000 - Steaming as before on base course 150° True escorting SS Fort Moultrie to designated point.
0653 - C/C to 080° True. Left SS Fort Moultrie.

May 9, 1944

0000 - Steaming as before on base course 080° True.
1510 - Moored to buoy in Nukulofa Harbor, Tongatabu Island.
1727 - Executed Colors. (Signed: E.R. Seaver, Lt.jg, USNR Commanding).

May 10, 1944

0814 - Moored to dock taking on fuel, water and provisions.

May 11, 1944

(Nothing of note to report).

May 12, 1944

0934 - Underway for sweeping operation.
1038 - Streamed all gear.
1345 - Recovered gear.
1400 - Streaming port gear.
1538 - Recovered gear. Returning to base.
1615 - Moored to buoy in harbor. (Bob Clayton remembers: "This place had a tea room where we could even buy a piece of cake. It really tasted good. We found one native man, his name was Johnny, who just delighted in showing us around the island. I suppose we gave him a tip. Every time we went on liberty, we would look for Johnny, and he was always there). (The Island Kingdom of Tonga, in the South Pacific, is located in Western Polynesia. Its nearest neighbor is Fiji to the northwest and the Samoas to the north-northeast. Western Polynesia includes the islands of Tonga, Samoa, Niue, Tuvala and Tokelau. Fiji is in the Melanesian area of the Pacific.

Tonga is one of the world's few remaining constitutional monarchies. It is the only South Pacific country never to have been colonized by a foreign power. Tonga is ruled by King Taufa'ahau Tupou IV. The reader will recall that the international dateline was moved, many years ago, east of the 180th meridian so as to include Wallis, Furtuna, Fiji, Tonga and Chatham islands. This change in the dateline makes the "far north" island of Tafahi, a volcanic island of the Tonga group, the first landmark in the world to greet each "new" day. So the saying goes, "Tonga is where time begins." The Kingdom of Tonga consists of 171 islands, (45 inhabited). The islands are divided into three main groups: Vava'u in the north, Ha'apai in the middle, and Tongatapu in the south. From south to north the islands of Tonga stretch more than 500 miles. The first European visitor came to Vava'u around 1750 when the Spanish commander

Francisco Mourelle came across Vava'u when sailing from the Philippines to Mexico. The Spanish navigator Malaspino followed 12 years later. The archipelago has been settled over 2000 years. Captain James Cook found Ha'api to be the perfect place of rest and relaxation. He made long stopovers at Nomuka in 1774 and 1777 and visited Lifuka in 1783. Captain Cook called them the "Friendly Islands". The Mutiny on the Bounty took place in Ha'api waters in 1789. It was here that Captain William Bligh and his loyal men were placed in a row boat and began their epic voyage of endurance to the island of Timor north of Australia. It was a voyage of over 4000 miles. The capital of Tonga is Nuka'alofa on the largest island, Tongatapu). *(See End Note No.55).*

May 13, 1944

0830 - Underway for sweep operation.
1607 - Recovered gear and returned to Base.
1715 -Moored outboard YMS 88 at Dock # 1.
2105 - Took on fuel.

May 14, 1944

(Nothing of note to report).

May 15, 1944

0850 - Underway for sweep operation.
0948 - Gear streamed. Beginning sweep.
1500 - Gear recovered. Returning to Base.
1625 - Moored to buoy in Nuka'alofa Harbor.
1840 - Paymaster came aboard to pay crew and officers.
1915 - Paymaster left ship.

May 16, 1944

(Routine sweep operation conducted. Nothing further to report).(The minefield which YMS 183 is now sweeping is what is left of the field of 551 planted by USS Montgomery DM-17 in June 1942. Soon after the field was laid mines began to explode. Whales which frequented that area of the waters around Tongatabu were running into the mines and setting them off. Of course, these explosions killed whales and soon the shores around the island "had an air of their own". In January, 1943, a hurricane wiped out a third of what was left of the field. It is now May 1944, and YMS 183 and others are cleaning up the rest of the field). *(See End Note No.56)*

May 17, 1944

(Nothing of note to report).

May 18,1944

0832 - Underway to lay dan buoys. (Walter Weltzien explains what was going on at this point. The main fields had been cleared, but there was one small field in water too shallow for the YMS. A mine disposal officer by the name of Dino Trainia had joined the crew to supervise the disposal of the swept mines. To sweep this last field they used motor launches and carried two native Tongans, for wages, to assist them. Weltzien writes, "Like Samoans, the Tongans were big, sturdy guys capable of hoisting a 100 pound dan buoy anchor from the bottom of the launch, but it took two of them to get it up and over the gunwale and into the water to anchor a dan buoy. We put-putted out to the minefield and searched the water until we spotted a mine. One of the natives immediately jumped in, tread water over the mine until we could place a dan buoy in line with it and repeat the operation at the other end of the line of mines. When we reached the end of the mine line, we summoned another launch and streamed a cable between both boats. We fed one end of the cable through a noose on the other end and pulled the cable taut. Then Dino swung into action. He dove in, followed the dan buoy cable down to the mine anchor cable, and fastened a dynamite cap to the mine anchor cable, and returned to the launch. We backed off a safe distance and he detonated the dynamite cap. There was a small explosion and the mine floated to the surface, its cable having been severed by the dynamite cap explosion. A third boat called a disposal boat then sank the floating mine with rifle fire. We did this for the rest of the mines except the last one. On the last one Dino fastened the dynamite cap to the mine casing. Dino returned to the launch and we backed off a very long distance from the mine. He detonated the dynamite cap and there was a huge explosion as the mine, still anchored under water, exploded resulting in hundreds of fish floating on the surface. The natives all jumped in with stringers in their mouths and collected the fish. This was their salary for the week. They received 50 cents per day and all the fish they could carry home".). (After a line of mines was disposed of, the dan buoys, their anchor cables and concrete anchors were recovered to be used again as needed).

May 19, 1944

(Nothing of note to report).

May 20, 1944

(Nothing of note to report).
(There is no record of the date of this event, but Weltzien remembers that "we were invited to the Queen's Palace to a roast pig dinner served on banana leaves, and were entertained by native singing and dancing." In all probability the three officers and 30 crew members were entertained in two shifts. Obviously, the ship could not be left unattended for a moment, even for the Queen).

May 21, 1944

1105 - Radio and minesweeping parts came aboard.

May 22, 1944

0000 - Moored as before to Dock # 1, Nuka'alofa, Tongatabu (sometimes spelled Tongatapu).
0800 - Executed Colors.
1150 - Underway, proceeding to Noumea, New Caledonia.
1105 - Set clocks back to -11 time.
1157 - Came to base course 245° True. (Bob Clayton writes, "In my humble opinion, when we left Tongatabu, we had just left paradise. It was one of the finest islands that we ever visited. Natives were very friendly, we got to know many of them.").

May 23, 1944

0000 - Steaming as before on base course 245° True.
1317 - C/C to 268° True. (As the crow flies, Noumea is approximately 1100 miles from Tongatabu and a little south of due west).

May 24, 1944

0000 - Steaming as before on base course 268° True.

May 25, 1944

0000 - Steaming as before 268° True.
0430 - Radar contact at 6 miles.
0431 - Sounded GQ alarm.
0543 - Challenged ship. Received satisfactory reply.
0550 - Secured from General Quarters. (There is some question about when the ship had her surface search radar installed. The log does not tell us. We know that is was after Pete Dill was detached. Weltzien seems to think that it was done at Noumea just before the ship left for Guadalcanal for the first time. But here we are, after extensive time in the repair base at Noumea in mid-April, and the ship has been to Tongatabu for extensive sweeping. In today's log, reference is made to a radar contact. It would appear that the radar was in use and was probably installed in mid-April in Noumea. Of all the YMSes with surface search radar, the 183, from all the evidence available, was the only one whose radar antenna was mounted on four legs that were secured to the deck of the flying bridge. This placed the sweep antenna just a few feet above the heads of anyone standing on the flying bridge. There probably wasn't any personal danger in being this close as long as one was not in the way of the microwave (radar) beam. All other YMSes seem to have had the radar installed just below the yardarm on the mast or on top of the mast. The higher the radar antenna the farther its beam could extend and pick up objects (land, other ships, etc.). There were two detriments to the placement of the radar on the 183: 1. Its range was materially reduced by being so low; and 2. The four legs were definitely in the way of the navigator using the alidade, and made accurate plotting of minesweeping courses very difficult. No one seems to know who ordered the placement of the radar on the flying bridge. It may have been the result of a notion of some Repair Base worker. Whoever it was, it was a mistake and later it would be relocated to the top of the mast. There may have been one positive element: being the only YMS with radar on the flying bridge made it easier to locate the 183 in a nest of ships or in Navy Photos of minesweepers in an anchorage. That four legged monster identified the 183 every time).

May 26, 1944

0000 - Steaming as before on base course 268° True.
0315 - C/C to 302° True.
0900 - C/C to 000° True.
1220 - Proceeding on various courses up channel at Noumea.
1358 - Moored alongside YMS 96 in Little Roads Anchorage.
1730 - Executed Colors. (Signed: E.R. Seaver, Lt.jg, USNR, Commanding).

May 27, 1944

(Nothing of note to report).

May 28, 1944

0000 - Moored at Section Base, Noumea, New Caledonia.
0835 - Bellvue, P.E., MoMM 1/c, 212-50-44 transferred to Mobile Hospital # 5.
0945 - Radio and Minesweeping gear transferred to Section Base.
1335 - Shifted berths to Ship Repair Base.

May 29, 1944

0000 - Moored as before at Ship Repair Base.

0820 - Schlechter, W.H., S 2/c 873-87-79; Zimmer, F.V., S 1/c, 872-87-21; and Schultz, A., S 2/c 887-89-84 reported aboard for duty.

1640 - Lt.jg Stanley C. Klein (120114) reported aboard for duty. (Lt.jg Klein was born in Detroit, Michigan in 1918. He was a graduate pharmacist. He received his commission after training at USNRMS Prairie State, New York, 5-12-42. He served on minecraft in the Atlantic Theater, graduated from the Naval Mine Warfare School at Yorktown, Va. and was attached to U.S.S Advanced LantPlt when ordered to the YMS 183. He was technically the relief for E.R. Seaver who had assumed command of the 183. Now the ship has its full complement of officers and Klein is the new Executive Officer).

1648 - Foley, Matthew O., SoM 3/c, 852-99-55 reported aboard for duty.

May 30, 1944

1230 - Washing machine and other gear taken aboard. (The addition of a washing machine on the small craft in WWII was a real luxury. No more scrubbing by hand. The wash still had to be hung on a clothes line for drying, but the washing machine really facilitated the laundry chore. The machinists and others whose dungarees became soaked with oil and caked with grease still had only one sure way to get them clean and that was to pull them through the salt water when the ship was underway. The work pants were tied to the stern of the ship with a line. After several hours of this treatment the grease and oil was washed out and the dungarees were clean. No soap in those days could do this. There was only one problem. This occurred once in a while when the knot used was not the correct one or the line was old or chafed and parted. The Pacific ocean floor was littered with dungarees lost in this way). May 31, 1944

0850 - Foley, M., SoM 3/c transferred to receiving station, Noumea.

1130 - Received commissary stores aboard.

June 1, 2, 1944

(Nothing of note to report).

June 3, 1944

1145 - Took aboard cargo for YMS 95.

June 4, 1944

0000 - Moored as before alongside Section Base Dock, Noumea.

0300 - Took on 1000 gallons fresh water.

0636 - Underway for Guadalcanal. Leaving harbor steering various courses.

0845 - Took departure from Bulari Pass, came to course 296° True. (This course takes the 183 away from the western side of New Caledonia and to the northwest toward The Solomon Islands, one of which is the famous Guadalcanal)

1630 - Held practice drills.

2149 - C/C to 319° True.

June 5, 1944

0000 - Steaming as before on base course 319° True.

1108 - C/C to 353° True.

1333 - C/C to 347° True.

1428 - Held GQ Drill.
1744 - C/C to 353° True.
1333 - C/C to 347° True.
1428 - Held GQ drill.
1744 - C/C to 353° True.

June 6, 1944

0000 - Steaming as before on base course 353° True.
0141 - C/C to 006° True.
0725 - Stopped port engine to repair trouble.
0735 - Started port engine.
Returned to speed.

June 7, 1944

0000 - Steaming as before on base course 006° True.
2200 - C/C to 307° True.

June 8, 1944

Steaming as before on base course 307° True.
0500 - C/C to 284° True.
0557 - C/C to 293° True.
0926 - C/C to 305° True.
1340 - C/C to 278° True.
1710 - C/C to 270° True.
1934 - Tied up alongside AG 50 at Lunga Point, Guadalcanal.
2030 - Taking on water. (An AG is an auxiliary for servicing naval vessels. In this case the AG 50 is a water barge).

June 9, 1944

0000 - Moored as before alongside AG 50 anchored off Guadalcanal.
0535 - Underway to anchorage.
0644 - Anchored in small craft anchorage, Lunga Pt., Guadalcanal.
1025 - Underway for Tulagi.
1233 - Moored to oiler at Tulagi.
1412 - Underway from Tulagi.
1606 - Picked up convoy (USS Stratford) on course 303° True. (The USS Stratford, AP 41, a 2632 ton transport. YMS 183 is escorting this vessel to Rendova Island). 1840 - C/C 263° True.
1940 - C/C to 238° True.
1947 - C/C to 290° True.
2219 - C/C to 284° True.

June 10, 1944

0000 - Steaming as before on base course 284° True.
0705 - C/C to 000° True.
1125 - Standing into Rendova Harbor.
1710 - Took on 600 gallons of fresh water. (Rendova Island, one of the New Georgia Group of the Solomon Islands, was embroiled in the offensive of the U.S. Marines to the north after the

capture of Guadalcanal. Rendova was secured by the Marines who then invaded New Georgia. The securing of these islands was necessary for there to be a secure base for the ultimate goal of establishing a base on Bougainville in the northern Solomons. These operations took place during the summer of 1943. The visit of YMS 183 to these parts came a year later after this area became a "back-water" of the war, having served as a stepping stone toward the conquest of all of the Solomon Islands).

1724 - Underway from Rendova harbor.

1920 - C/C to 210° True.

2225 - Radar contact. Sounded GQ. Challenged ships and received satisfactory reply.

2300 - C/C course to 313° True.

2320 - Secured from GQ.

June 11, 1944

0000 - Steaming as before on base course 313° True.

0646 - C/C to 010° True.

0742 - Entering Treasury Island harbor.

0825 - Anchored in Berth # 1 Treasury Island. (It is not clear which island of the Treasury Group was considered Treasury Island by the log writer. This little cluster of islands were secured by the Marines in October, 1943 and Mono island of the Treasury group may well have been the island where the 183 deposited its charge, USS Stratford AP-41. Mono Island may well be the one called Treasury Island in the log entry).

1027 - Underway for Guadalcanal.

1140 - C/C to 130° True.

1830 - C/C to 113° True.

June 12, 1944

0000 - Steaming as before on base course 113° True.

0100 - C/C to 090° True.

0727 - C/C to 093° True.

0926 - C/C to 117° True.

1445 - Anchored off Lunga Point, Guadalcanal.

1600 - Underway for Tulagi. (Tulagi is the main port in the Florida Islands across from and to the north of Guadalcanal. The body of water between the two islands was named Iron Bottom Sound after the famous battle during the night of Aug 8 - 9, 1942, when a Japanese cruiser force caught the American naval patrol off guard and sank four American Cruisers).

1800 - Moored alongside M 9 in Tulagi Harbor.

June 13, 1944

0000 - Moored as before, starboard side to USS Monadnock in Tulagi Harbor. (USS Monadnock CM 9, was a minelayer, converted from a coastal freighter, SS Cavalier capable of carrying railroad cars, and commissioned on 2 December 1941. At this period in 1944 she was involved in training exercises).

0714 - Shifted berth to alongside oiler.

1000 - Alongside water dock to take on fresh water.

1613 - Moored alongside USS Monadnock.

1900 Commissary stores and minesweeping gear taken aboard. *(See End Note No.57)*.

June 14, 1944

0759 - Underway to Guadalcanal.

1146 - Underway for Tulagi escorting USS Savo Island. (This is an extremely interesting entry, for USS Savo Island, CVE- 78 [baby flat top] of the Casablanca class, was commissioned 3 Februrary 1944, less than six months previously. This ship is named for the famous naval battle that took place just a few miles to the west of Tulagi on August 8-9, 1942, off Savo Island in the Solomons. According to The Dictionary of Naval Fighting Ships, USS Savo Island was probably on her way back to San Diego after acting as a delivery vessel for replacement aircraft in the Southwest Pacific. She may well have delivered some aircraft to Henderson Field on Guadalcanal and YMS 183 was escorting her to Tulagi. On July 6, 1944 Savo Island was back in San Diego where she received her own air squadron on board. She joined the 3rd Fleet at Pearl Harbor on August 4, 1944. The lowly YMS was unknown to and often ignored by the larger fleet types, but when their ability to sweep for mines and/or to search for enemy submarines was needed, the "big fellows" were only too happy to have the protection) *(See End Note No.58).*

1437 - Moored at Pier 6, Tulagi.

June 15, 1944

0633 - Underway for Guadalcanal. (It should be pointed out here that it was approximately 25 miles from Tulagi to Lunga Point. If the run was unencumbered by escorting or sweeping, etc. it was normally a two hour trip).

0830 - Standing into Lunga anchorage.

0840 - Detailed to screen duty. Proceeding to designated station.

0917 - On station screening on course 250° True and 070° True. (As noted before, screening designated areas was just another of the duties of a YMS in addition to sweeping mines. In this case, although the log does not give any coordinates, the screening line, 270° True and its reciprocal 070° True, was a straight line from designated point "A" to designated point "B" and back again, over and over until relieved by another screening vessel or ordered to secure by the SOP of the area. During a screening job like this the ship's sonar was active in seeking to locate enemy submarines and the surface search radar operating to pick up any activity on the surface. It is very likely that the screening line guarded the entrance to Sealark Channel where it connected to Indispensable Strait).

June 16, 1944

0000 - Steaming as before on courses 250° True and 070° True screening sector DD off Guadalcanal.

1015 - Ceased screening. Proceeding to Lunga Channel.

1040 - Lowered acoustic hammer. Commenced streaming gear.

1338 - All gear recovered. Returning to base.

1415 - Anchored off Lunga Point.

1600 - Underway for Kukum Dock.

1710 - Moored outboard PC 1590 at Kukum Dock.

2325 - Underway for Deep Bay, Malaita Island. (This Island in the Solomon Group is northeast of Guadalcanal. It is long and slender stretching from northwest to southeast and separated from Florida Islands and Guadalcanal by Indispensable Strait. It was widely rumored during this period of time that the natives of the Solomons and especially of Malaita continued to practice their long history of cannibalism. It was said that many soldiers of Nippon were served up for dinner by these natives. Historically, much of Micronesia and Melanesia had known the practice of cannibalism, but by WWII the influence of Christian missionaries through many years of service on these islands had led many of the people away from this practice. However, the practice did still continue in places).

June 17, 1944

0000 - Steaming on various courses to Deep Bay, Malaita Island in company with PC 1590.

1635 - Moored portside to PC 1590 in Deep Bay, Malaita Island. (The 183 has been sent to Deep Bay to check sweep a field that had been swept earlier, in case mines were missed then, or perhaps new mines laid. The PC 1590 was a steel hull submarine chaser which was originally laid down as a "180 foot" AM 86 named Constant (auxiliary minesweeper) but the plans were altered and she was launched and commissioned as a PC. Her actual length is 173'8", 295 tons, beam 23', draft 11'7', speed 18 knots. She was armed with 1 3"50 cal gun and undoubtedly other AA guns such as 20MM and 30 cal machine guns. She also would have depth charges on stern racks and K guns on either side midship. She could do everything a 180' AM could do except sweep mines. She is accompanying the 183 to act as a mine disposal vessel in case mines are cut). *(See End Note No.59).*

June 18, 19, 20, 21, 1944

(Engaged in sweep operation near Deep Bay, Malaita Island. One mine was cut on June 19. After the sweep operation on the 21st course was laid for return to Guadalcanal).

June 22, 1944

0000 - Streaming as before on course 307° True.
0350 - C/C to 270° True.
0811 Anchored off Lunga Point.
1327 - Taking on water at Kukum Dock.
1545 - Underway to screen sector BC.
1715 - On station screening on course 090° True and 170° True.

June 23, 1944

0841 - Ceased screening sector BC off Guadalcanal Island. (Continued rest of the day making station runs between Tulagi and Lunga Point, and taking on fuel from YOG 41).

June 24, 1944

1155 - Underway for Russell Islands. (This may have been a mail and/or light cargo delivery. The Russell Islands are approximately 50 miles west of Tulagi).
1735 - Moored starboard side to LCI 332 in Renerd Sound, Russell Islands.

June 25, 1944

1321 - Underway for Guadalcanal.
1920 - Anchored off Lunga Point.
1935 - Underway escorting USS Cygnus AF-23 [a provision ship] to Torokina, Bougainville, Island. (Bougainville Island, was named for the explorer Louis Antoine de Bougainville who explored the northernmost of the Solomon Islands in 1768. Germany took control of the northern Solomons in 1885, but transferred these islands, except Bougainville and Buka to the British in 1900. The Islands were occupied by the Japanese in 1939 and heavy fighting took place before they were forced to leave the Island in 1945. The sea port, Torokina, is located on the northern

shore of Empress Augusta Bay. It was, at the time of this visit by 183, a provisioning port for the Bougainville area. *(See End Note No.60)*. The USS Cygnus was a Provision Store Ship converted from a Munson liner, and commissioned in 1942. She was 355' long with a beam of 48' and a draft of 28'. Her economical cruising speed was 10.5 knots. She had two 3" 50 cal. dual purpose guns and two 20mm anti-aircraft guns. Her displacement fully loaded was 7,171 tons. *(See End Note No.61)*. 2200 - C/C to 260° True.

June 26, 1944

0000 - Steaming as before on base course 260° True escorting USS Cygnus to Cape Torokina, Bougainville, Island.
0113 - C/C to 285° True.
0628 - C/C to 292° True.
1615 - C/C to 309° True.
2210 -
2314 - Secured from GQ. C/C to 318° True. (Signed: E. R. Seaver, Lt.jg, USNR, Commanding).

June 27, 1944

0000 - Steaming as before on course 318° True.
0538 - C/C to 035° True.
0832 - C/C 075° True.
0905 - Anchored in Torokina Harbor, Bougainville Island.
1038 - Underway for screen duty.
1114 - On station screening on course 309° True and 129° True. (Empress Augusta Bay is a large open body of water on the western side of Bougainville. While Torokina harbor may have had anti-submarine nets encircling it, there was still a need for small ships with sonar to patrol the area for enemy submarines as an added protection for ships like USS Cygnus that would have been sitting "ducks" while at anchor. Actually the USS Cygnus, is named for the constellation Cygnus, which means The Swan and is often called The Northern Cross because the stars that make up the constellation make a fairly uniform cruciform cross. Four stars make the points at the head, which always points in a southerly direction, the tail 180° degrees from the head, and the two wing tips 90° degrees from an imaginary line from head to tail. Anyone who knows this constellation will attest to its resemblance to a swan, long neck and all, flying to the south. Deneb, the tail star of The Swan, is a first magnitude star and an excellent candidate for the ship's navigator to use when taking star sights with the sextant to fix the ship's position).

June 28, 1944

0000 - Steaming as before screening Torokina Harbor, Bougainville on course 309° and 129° True.
1250 - Ceased screening. Joining USS Cygnus as escort to Munda.
1523 - C/C to 138° True.
1945 - C/C to 129° True.

June 29, 1944

0000 - Steaming as before on base course 129° True.
0500 - C/C to 090° True.
0830 - C/C to 056° True.
0840 - C/C to 076° True.
1140 - Moored alongside USS Cygnus in Susavelle anchorage, New Georgia.

1155 - Underway to Munda pier.
1330 - Crossing Munda Bar.
1346 - Moored port side to pier at Munda.

June 30, 1944

0000 - Moored as before at pier Munda, New Georgia.
0934 - Underway from Munda to Susavelle Anchorage, New Georgia.
1115 - Moored alongside USS Cygnus in Susavelle Anchorage. (The log does not say at what time YMS 183 departed New Georgia for Guadalcanal).

July 1, 1944

0000 - Steaming as before on base course 090° True. Proceeding as before escorting AF 23, USS Cygnus to Guadalcanal.
0707 - Anchored off Lunga Point.
0952 - Underway for Tulagi Harbor. (The rest of the day was given to refueling)
1545 - Anchored in Swain Cove in Pervis Bay.

July 2, 3, 4, 1944

(Nothing of note to report).

July 5, 1944

1835 - Mulford, A.J. reported aboard from Hospital at Russell Island.

July 6, 1944

1555 - Underway for screening duties.

July 7, 1944

0000 - Screening as before on base course 090° True and 270° True. Screening Sector "Able" at Guadalcanal.

July 8, 1944

0000 - Screening as before Sector "Able" on same base courses 090° True and 270° True. Switching engines every four hours. (From time to time when the speed of the ship in an operation is required to be slow, 4 or 5 knots, for a long period of time one engine would be shut down and the other propelling the ship for several hours. This helped to reduce carbon buildup in the diesel engines. Diesels work best and keep themselves cleaner of carbon when they run at standard speed. One engine at standard speed was enough to drive the ship at the proper speed for screening).

July 9, 1944

0000 - Screening as before Sector "Able" on base courses 090° True and 270° True, using one engine and switching every four hours.

July 10, 1944

0000 - Screening as before Sector "Able" on base courses 090° True and 270° True at Guadalcanal.
1840 - Relieved of screening duties by PC 596, proceeding to Lunga Point anchorage.
1955 - Anchored at Lunga Point.

July 11, 1944

(The whole day engaged in refueling, taking on water, etc.)

July 12, 1944

0635 - Underway for sweeping operations.
1706 - Streamed both sides "O" type gear, with acoustic hammer to sweep Lunga Channel.
1223 - All gear aboard, proceeding to Lunga Point. (To anchorage).

July 13, 1944

0628 - Underway for sweep operations.
0705 - All magnetic gear streamed.
1313 - All gear aboard, returning to Lunga. (Signed: Walter Weltzien, Ens., USNR, Navigator)

July 14, 15, 16, 1944

(Sweeping operations all three days with both sides "O" type and acoustic).

July 17, 1944

0000 - Anchored as before in Lunga Harbor.
0629 - Underway for sweeping operations.
0720 - All gear streamed as follows, magnetic and acoustic gear. (The layman might wonder why minesweeping continued long after the fighting front had moved hundreds of miles beyond these backwater areas like the Solomons. These areas had been swept time and again during the fighting two years earlier and really the sweeping never stopped. There are two reasons for this: 1. Japanese submarines had the capacity to lay mines and that was a constant threat in the "backwater" areas, and there was always the possibility that a German submarine might have joined up with the Japnavy in the Pacific; 2. In addition to checking for mines day after day, the work was good practice for the sweepers and their crews and helped to keep them on their toes).
1334 - All gear aboard. Proceeding to base.

July 18, 1944

0601 - Underway for sweeping operations.
1130 - All gear aboard, proceeding to Tulagi. (The rest of the day spent in refueling and taking on fresh water).

July 19, 1944

0610 - Underway for sweeping operations.
1215 - All gear aboard. Proceeding to Lunga Point.

July 20, 21, 22, 23, 24, 25, 26, 27, 28, 29, 30, 1944

(Routine sweep operation conducted each of these days. During this period they were moored alongside PC 1130, PC 1137 one time each, DE 27 once and USS Monadnock once).

July 31, 1944

0735 - Donelly, A.W., Cox, transferred as of this date to Receiving Station at Navy # 152.

August 1, 1944 (Tuesday)

0615 - Underway from anchorage, proceeding under orders to Espiritu Santo.

August 2, 1944

0000 - Steaming as before on base course 128° True. Proceeding from Guadalcanal to Espiritu Santo.
0905 - C/C to 137° True.
2015 - C/C to 134° True.

August 3, 1944

0000 - Steaming as before on base course 134° True.
1542 - C/C to 295° True proceeding into harbor.
1651 - Moored to buoy in berth #1 in harbor.
1800 - Executed Sunset Colors. (Signed: Walter Weltzien, Ensign, USNR, Navigator).

August 4, 1944

(Took minesweeping gear aboard and took on fuel).

August 5, 1944

1212 - Underway for Suva, Fiji.

August 6, 1944

0000 - Steaming as before on base course 102° True.
2300 - Had generator trouble.

August 7, 1944

0000 - Steaming as before on base course 102° True.

August 8, 1944

0000 - Steaming as before on base course 102° True.
1616 - Moored South West side of King's Wharf. Alongside SC 1268.

August 9, 1944

0835 - Began unloading cargo.

August 10, 1944

1103 - Moored port side to Cargo Ship at PWD Dock.

August 11, 1944

0900 - One man returned aboard from Brig.
1005 - Same man transferred as of this date to Naval Dispensary for duty.

August 12, 1944

1015 - Captain held inspection of living quarters and top side.
1600 - Man reported aboard from Navy Dispensary for duty.

August 13, 1944

0000 - Moored as before port side to King's Wharf, Suva, Fiji with YMS 222, 265 and 271 moored outboard. Receiving power from YMS 222.

0540 - Switched to ship's generator.

1845 - Began taking power from YMS 265.

August 14, 1944

0715 - Underway, proceeding out of harbor for sweeping operations.

1618 - Gear recovered, proceeding to base.

August 15, 1944

0700 - Underway for day's sweeping operation. (There were several mine fields in the Fiji Islands. According to Arnold Lott, 26 fields containing 843 mines were laid in April of 1942. In January of 1943 more mines were laid bringing the total up to 1436. Lott writes, "The fields caught no known enemy ships, damaged no friendly ships, and were swept up August -October 1944.") *(See End Note No.62)*. (The Fiji Islands came under British control in the late 19th century and became a Crown Colony. The capitol city, Suva, was very European, with magnificent government buildings, streets and sidewalks, shops and facilities like any modern city of the WWII era. The British had brought in a large number of workers from India years before and had established a plantation economy. A middle class had developed from the descendants of these imported workers. They were the shopkeepers, taxi drivers, etc. Suva was an especially interesting place to see and the ship's company would have more time on this operation to take advantage of this opportunity).

August 16, 1944

(Nothing of note to report).

August 17, 1944

0620 - Underway for sweeping operations at Levuka, Fiji.

1235 - Moored to dock in Levuka Harbor. (Suva, the capital city is on the southeastern coast of the island of Viti Levu. Levuka is on the eastern coast of Viti Levu and has a large harbor. The log mentions three other YMSes on this operation, 222, 271, and 265. However, there may have been several more whose numbers we do not know. Walter Weltzien writes, "I also remember one operation in Fiji where the mines were laid in quite shallow water. We had about six sweepers on this maneuver and we were the lead ship. We sailed in a column parallel to the mine field and as close as we dared. Then on a given signal we all fired our port K-guns, turned 45 degrees to the right and at flank speed we hauled out as fast as we could. We counted nine or ten explosions: six depth charges and several mines. We repeated this maneuver several times until we felt that there were no more active mines in the area.").

August 18, 1944

0658 - Underway from dock (at Levuka) for sweeping operations.

1800 - Returned to port and moored alongside YMS 265.

1830 - Millet, Edward W., PhM 1/c, 663-04-45: Hill, John, (Sam), S 2/c, 839-00-02 reported aboard for duty this date.

John Dixon Davis

August 19, 20, 21, 22, 23, 24, 25, 1944

(Engaged in daily sweeping operations at Levuka. Nothing further to report).

August 26, 1944

1000 - Captain's Mast for one man. Awarded Deck Court.
1005 - Deck Court held for one man. Guilty by plea. Sentence - $25. Loss of pay for three (3) months, total loss of pay $75.00. Twenty (20) days confinement.

August 27, 28, 29, 1944

(Engaged in daily sweeping operations at Levuka. Nothing further to report).

August 30, 1944

0705 - Underway for daily sweeping operations.
0835 - All sweep gear inboard, returning to Suva, Fiji.

August 31, 1944

0830 - Zimmer, Frank, S 1/c, 872-87-21, reported back from sick bay for duty.

September 1, 1944

(Moored in Suva, Fiji. Nothing of note to report).

September 2, 1944

1232 - Woroby, Alexander, PhM 1/c, 207-20-83 transferred to Navy #130 for further transfer to Navy #140.
1235 - Change of command of USS YMS 183 from Lt. E.R. Seaver to Lt. S.C Klein.
1357 - Lt. E.R. Seaver detached as of this date.
1800 - Executed Sunset Colors. (Signed: Walter F. Weltzien, Ens., USNR, Navigator).

Chapter 11
The Fourth CO Takes Command

September 3, 1944

(Nothing of note to report).

September 4, 1944

0000 - Moored as before alongside King's Wharf Suva, Fiji Islands with YMS 271 moored outboard. Checking ship and lines regularly for safety.

1135 - Lilly, Albert W., Ensign DV(g) reported aboard for duty this date. (Little is known about Ens. Lilly. He was from Texas).

September 5, 1944

0647 - Underway from alongside dock, proceeding to new Sweeping operations.

1617 - Anchored at Vunda Point with 30 fathoms of chain out. (This is probably near the Nandi Bay area on the western side of Viti Levu).

September 6, 1944

0703 - Underway for sweeping operations.
1605 - All gear inboard, returning to base.
1700 - Moored to buoy at Vunda Point.
1730 - Transferred 1000 gallons of fuel from YMS 183 to YMS 271. (This seems a little strange and the question immediately arises, why the 271 needed the fuel right now? Did they not refuel when they should have, or did they have a leaky fuel tank? It may well have been that they received fuel heavily contaminated with water and they ran out of fuel because the tank was holding much more water than they knew. This sort of thing happened from time to time, especially when the vessel receiving fuel did not check it for water and other contaminates).

Figure 35 4th CO Lt. Stanley C Klein. Courtesy of Rhea Klein

September 7, 1944

0705 - Underway for day's sweeping operation.
0831 - Anchored in Momi beach in 8 fathoms of water.
1300 - Underway from anchorage for sweeping operations.
1630 - All gear inboard returning to base.
1734 - Moored to buoy at Vunda Point.

September 8, 1944

(Carried out routine sweeping operations).

September 9, 1944

(Carried out routine sweeping operations and proceeded afterward to Lautoka harbor).

September 10, 1944

(Nothing of note to report).

John Dixon Davis

September 11, 12, 13, 14, 15, 16, 1944

(Carried out daily sweep of Lautoka area).

September 17, 1944

(Nothing of note to report).

September 18, 1944

0000 - Moored as before at Lautoka alongside SC 1268 with YMSes 222, 265, 271, and SC 728.
0705 - Underway for day's sweeping operations.
1930 - Moored at Vunda Point.
0220 - One man came aboard AOL 2 hours and 50 minutes.

September 19, 20, 21, 22, 23, 1944

(Carried out daily sweep of mine fields in Lautoka area). (As noted earlier, there were a number of mine fields in the Fiji Islands and the total number of mines laid was 1436. It was an extensive sweeping operation and took the better part of two months. It seems that it was rather "humdrum" as one reads the log, but it was actually very dangerous work. The main positive factor was the absence of enemy guns and planes harassing the ships as they worked. Still one never knew when a mine might be exploded under one of the sweepers. Walter Weltzien writes, "I became well acquainted with the screws of the YMS in Fiji one day. We were sweeping with several other ships when our gear became fouled. We pulled out of formation and tried to retrieve our gear. The other ships continued sweeping. The depressor cable seemed to be fouled around a screw. Chief Boatswain Hall asked for a volunteer to dive down and assess the damage. No one volunteered (we must have had a crew of land lubbers that day) so I volunteered and dove down to inspect the problem. (Actually the screws were no more than 5 feet below the surface and under the stern of the ship). The depressor cable was caught on the port screw. I couldn't budge it, so I surfaced and said if they could give me a little time to get down to the screw again, and then give me a little slack on the cable, maybe I could pull it loose. Their timing was perfect because just as I reached the cable, it slacked off and I was able to pull it free. I came back aboard and went in to dry off. I was only there a few minutes when we felt a jar and heard a loud explosion. One of the other sweepers had detonated a mine. It didn't dawn on me until then that if I had been in the water then, I'd have been like a Tongatabu fish and somebody could have put me on a stringer.") (A Lt. Commander named Larsen was in charge of the Fiji sweep. He stayed on our ship and oversaw the entire operation and was very pleased with our efforts. At the end of the Fiji operation, Cmdr. Larsen recommended me for a citation. I never did know whether it was for the cable incident or my navigation work since I never got the citation.") *(See End Note No.63).*

September 24, 1944

(Nothing of note to report).

September 25, 26, 1944

(Continued sweeping operations in Lautoka area).

September 27, 1944

(Foul weather prevented sweeping operations).

September 28, 1944

(Nothing of note to report).

September 29, 30, 1944

(Continued sweeping operations in Lautoka area).

October 1, 2, 1944

(Nothing of note to report).

October 3, 1944

0701 - Underway for day's sweeping operations.
1335 - All sweep gear aboard, returning to base.
1725 - Armstrong, James E., F 2/c, 923-27-46, reported aboard.
1801 - Executed Sunset Colors. (Signed: Stanley C. Klein, Lt. DECV(G), USNR, Commanding).

Figure 36 - From left to right Weltzien, Beck, the "Skipper" Klein and Davis at Okinawa.

October 4, 1944

(Nothing of note to report).

October 5, 1944

0633 - Underway for day's sweeping operations.
1720 - All sweep gear inboard. Proceeding to Viatu. (Hum-drum day? Only 11 hours of sweeping a mine field).

October 6, 1944

0706 - Underway for day's sweeping operations.
1630 - All sweep gear inboard, proceeding to base.
1826 - Moored starboard side to YMS 271 at Ellington, Fiji Islands. (Do not know exactly where Ellington was, but was probably in the Lautoka area).

October 7, 1944

0724 - Underway for day's sweeping operations.
1544 - All sweep gear inboard, returning to base at Ellington,

October 8, 9, 1944

(Nothing of note to report).

October 10, 1944

1053 - Underway for day's sweeping operations.
1244 - All sweep gear inboard, returning to Ellington.

October 11, 1944

(Conducted daily sweeping operation).

John Dixon Davis

October 12, 13, 1944

(Nothing of note to report).

October 14, 1944

0010 - Four men reported aboard over leave.
1315 - Captain's Mast for four men AOL. All awarded warnings. Also one man given warning for sleeping in at reveille.

October 15, 1944

(Nothing of note to report).

October 16, 17, 18, 19, 1944

(Carried out day's sweeping operation at Lambasa).

October 20, 1944

1617 - Anchored at Lavenui Island.

October 21, 1944

1048 - Streaming gear to begin sweep on G #1.
1615 - All gear inboard, returning to base.
1638 - Moored port side to dock in Savu Savu Bay.

October 22, 23, 1944

(Carried out day's sweeping operation in Savu Savu Bay).

October 24, 25, 1944

(Nothing of note to report).

October 26, 1944

(Carried out day's sweep in Savu Savu Bay. Proceeded to Levuka Harbor).

October 27, 1944

(Nothing of note to report).

October 28, 1944

(Proceeded to Suva, Fiji).

October 29, 30, 31, 1944

(Nothing of note to report).

November 1, 1944

1845 - Flye, Horace N., StM 1/c, 854-86-28 reported aboard for duty as of this date. (Signed: Stanley C. Klein, Lt. USNR, Commanding).

November 2, 3, 4, 1944

(Nothing of note to report).

November 5, 1944

Sharp, R.L., SC 2/c, 866-26-28, transferred to Naval Dispensary for medical treatment.

November 6, 7, 8, 1944

(Nothing of note to report).

November 9, 1944

1407 - Hill, C., Stm 2/c, 722-19-83 reported aboard for duty.

November 10, 1944

0922 - Underway for embarking on Marine Railway.

November 11, 1944

0000 - As before on Marine Railway at PWD, Suva, Fiji.
1509 - Man transferred this date to Navy # 131 as prisoner.

November 12, 13, 14, 15, 1944

(Nothing of note to report).

November 16, 1944

1320 - Sharp, R. L. SC 2/c returned aboard from Naval Dispensary.
1535 - Left Railway and moored to pilings.
1759 - Moored port side to King's Wharf.

November 17, 1944

0611 - Underway, proceeding with PC 585 to Vunda Point.
1525 - Moored to buoy at Vunda Point.

November 18, 1944

1342 - Underway, proceeding to Lautoka.
1435 Moored port side to PC 585 at Lautoka.

November 19, 20, 1944

(Nothing of note to report).

November 21, 1944

0603 - Underway from Lautoka, proceeding to Ellington.
1120 - Moored outboard PC 585 at Ellington, Fiji.

November 22, 1944

0700 - Underway for day's sweeping operation.
1036 - Cut one mine on check sweeping of field.
1240 - Gear aboard returning to Ellington.

November 23, 1944

0608 - Underway, proceeding from Ellington to Levuka.
1215 - Moored alongside dock at Levuka, Fiji.

John Dixon Davis

November 24, 1944

0736 - Underway, proceeding to Suva.

1530 - Moored alongside Degei (a native ship) at PWD dock in Suva.

1540 - Running dock trials to test out port engine.

Figure 37 - YMS 183 anchored off port side of DM18 USS Breese, at Kerama Retto. U.S.Navy photograph.

November 25, 26, 1944

(Nothing of note to report).

November 27, 1944

1406 - Collins, S.R., SC 3/c, 641-78-10, V6, USNR reported aboard for duty as of this date. - Hadley, J.A. reported back aboard for duty.

November 28, 29, 30, 1944

(Nothing of note to report).

December 1, 1944

(Nothing of note to report).

December 2, 1944

1000 - Captain held inspection of ship. After inspection rest of the day spent taking on 2320 gallons of fuel.

December 3, 1944

1800 - Underway from alongside dock, proceeding to Tutuila, Samoa. (The Fiji mine fields' sweep is now officially completed).

December 4, 1944

0000 - Steaming as before on base course 081° True making standard speed, proceeding from Suva, Fiji Islands to Tutuila, Samoa Islands.

0900 - C/C/ to 054° True.

1320 - C/C/ to 071° True.

December 5, 1944

0000 - Steaming on base course 071° True.
1316 - C/C to 058° True.
1800 - Crossed International Date line going east. Date moved back to December 4, 1944.

December 5, 1944 (Second time)

0000 - Steaming as before on base course 058° True.
0800 - Standing into harbor at Tutuila.
0820 - Moored alongside Governor's Landing, Pago Pago, harbor, Samoa.
1010 - Took aboard 2540 gallons of fuel. (Signed: Stanley C. Klein, Lt., USNR, Commanding).

December 6, 1944

0636 - Underway to sweep channel.
0915 - Moored to Repair Base dock.

December 7, (three years since Pearl Harbor), 8, 9, 10, 1944

(Carried out the channel sweep each day).

December 11, 1944

0629 - Underway to sweep channel.
0947 - Hill, J.L. transferred to Naval Hospital. (Also entered in log on December 16, 1944 at 1545).

December 12, 13, 14, 15, 16, 1944

(Carried out channel sweep each day)

December 17, 18, 19, 1944

(Nothing of note to report).

December 20, 1944

0950 - Boday, S.J., MoMM 2/c returned from Sick Bay for duty.

December 21, 22, 23, 24, 25, 26, 27, 1944.

(Nothing of note to report).

December 28, 29, 30, 31, 1944

(Conducted regular channel sweep).

January 1, 2, 3, 4, 1945

(Conducted regular channel sweep).

January 5, 1945

(Conducted regular channel sweep). 1100 - Shurts, Carl E., MoMM 1/c transferred to sick bay as of this date.

January 6, 1945

(Conducted regular channel sweep).
1545 - Stocks, Eugene, S 1/c 753-15-35, returned aboard for duty as of this date.

John Dixon Davis

January 7, 8, 1945

(Conducted regular channel sweep).

January 9, 1945

(Conducted regular channel sweep).
0955 - Ayer, Myron E., QM 3/c returned aboard from dispensary for duty.

January 10, 11, 12, 13, 14, 15, 16, 17, 18, 19, 20, 21, 1945

(Conducted regular channel sweep each day).

January 22, 1945

(Conducted regular channel sweep).
1300 - Lail, H.J.,403-65-03, SoM 2/c, transferred as of this date to Navy # 129 for further transfer to Pre-Radio School in Chicago.

January 23, 24, 1945

(Conducted regular channel sweep).

January 25, 1945

(Conducted regular channel sweep).
1012 - Held GQ drill.
1055 - secured from GQ drill.
1130 - Entering AFD 20.
1325 - Secured in drydock.

January 26, 27, 28, 1945

(In drydock)

January 29, 1945

1320 - Cleared dry dock and proceeded to Repair Base Pier # 9.
1513 - Captain's Mast held for two men who failed to observe reveille.

January 30, 31, 1945

(Conducted regular channel sweep).

February 1, 2, 1945

(Conducted regular channel sweep).

February 3, 1945

0900 - Collins, S. R. SC 3/c reported aboard from sick bay for duty.
0945 - Stoker, R. A. reported aboard from sick bay for duty.
1700 - Underway for New Hebrides Islands.
1757 - C/C to 234° True on departure from Sail Rock.
2202 - C/C to 270° True. (As the 183 departs from Samoa for the last time this would be a good time to recount Walter Weltzien's tribute to the power and stability of the YMS. He writes, "The YMS vessels were all fitted with an overly large screw for the comparative size of the vessel. This gave them powerful pulling power but not great speed. It not only provided great towing

ability, as when mine sweeping, but it also kept them from yawing or being affected to any great extent by wind, sea or currents. We left either New Caledonia or Espiritu Santo for Samoa one day at the beginning of a storm that didn't quite reach hurricane force. [It is possible that voyage was from Samoa to one of the other places, but that is no matter]. We set our course for Samoa, which was 1500 miles distant, and for five days never saw the sun, moon or stars. We had no Loran or radio directional navigation aids. All we had was a strong, sturdy ship and excellent helmsmen. We estimated our speed at about 10.5 knots and kept sailing hoping to see some heavenly body to get some kind of navigational fix. We never got one celestial bearing, but after five days of dead reckoning sailing, we spotted Samoa and we were less than one mile off course. If we had drifted just one degree off course, we would have been at least 25 miles off course by the time we reached Samoa. The winds were gale force most of the way and at one point, Teboy, our lead Quartermaster, and I watched the inclinometer record a 55 degree roll. That's more than halfway over." *(See End Note No.64)*. (The center of gravity on the one stacker YMS was low enough to allow some radical rolls. A 55 degree roll is radical. Many ships could not come back from that far over. In addition to the design of the YMS, the careful stowage of many tons of concrete dan buoy anchors in the bilge added a great deal of stability in radical rolls).

Figure 38 - YMS 183 at King's Wharf, Suva Fiji. Courtesy of Bob Clayton.

February 4, 1945

0000 - Steaming as before on base course 270° True. Base speed 1000 RPM's. Proceeding from Tutuila, Samoa to Espiritu Santo, New Hebrides. Watch # 1 has the Watch.
1800 - Set all ship's clocks back one hour to +12 time zone.

February 5, 1945

Steaming as before on base course
0645 - C/C to 269° True.
1546 - Proceeding West in Latitude 14 degrees 45 seconds South. Crossed 180th meridian, changed date to February 6, 1945.

February 7, 1945

0000 - Steaming as before on base course 269° True, speed 1000 RPM.
1600 - C/C to 259° True.

February 8, 1945

0000 - Base course 259° True.
0545 - C/C to 258° True.
1317 - Slowed engines due to overheating.
1330 - Resumed speed.
1920 - C/C to 254° True.
2345 - Found pilot house and Flying Bridge repeaters to be 40 degrees from Master Gyro. Reset them and C/C to 230° True.

John Dixon Davis

February 9, 1945

0000 - Steaming as before on base course 254° True. Speed 2/3rds.
0740 - Standing into harbor at Espiritu Santo.
0850 - Moored port side to SC 231.
1000 - Frederick, John A. 906-66-72, F 2/c; Blosser, Elmer E., SoM 3/c, 663-39-72 reported aboard for duty as of this date.

February 10, 1945

0900 - Moored alongside Yard Garbage Scow at Pier "O".
1010 - Stoker, R.A., Cox 868-46-34, USNR transferred this date to Naval Hospital #140, Espiritu Santo.

February 11, 12, 13, 14, 15, 1945

(Nothing of note to report).

February 16, 1945

0000 - Moored as before alongside YR 47 at Pier #1. YMS 271 moored outboard to port.
1100 - Men from base brought refrigerator aboard.
1100 - Hall, Cyrus D. 360-02-27 CEM transferred this date to Receiving Station Navy #140 for further transfer to the U.S.A.
1330 - Roether, John L., 224-47-48, BM 1/c USN transferred as of this date to Naval Hospital Navy #140 for medical treatment.

February 17, 1945

1754 - Underway from pier #1 Espiritu Santo, proceeding to Guadalcanal.
1840 - Replaced pilot house (gyro compass) repeater.
1916 - C/C to 007° True.
2240 - C/C to 321° True.

February 18, 1945

0000 - Steaming as before on base course 321° True, speed standard, proceeding from New Hebrides to Guadalcanal in company with YMS 94 and YMS 271.
0110 - C/C to 294° True.
0524 - Port engine trouble. Secured engine and standing by to receive tow line from YMS 271.
0617 - Received towing line from YMS 271. Now being towed, making 1000 RPM on starboard engine.
0958 - C/C to 327° True.
1321 - Held GQ Drill.

February 19, 1945

0000 - Steaming as before on base course 327° True, being towed by YMS 271, proceeding from New Hebrides to Guadalcanal.
0850 - C/C to 306° True.
1543 - Held GQ drill.
2134 - C/C to 279° True.

February 20, 1945

(Proceeding on base course 279° True, being towed by YMS 271).

0142 - C/C to 308° True.
0214 - C/C to 303° True.
0245 - C/C to 295° True.
0720 - C/C to 270° True.
1115 - C/C to 355° True.
1235 - All anchor chain aboard proceeding on our own power to Tulagi.
1402 - Moored port side to YMS 271 at buoy #1 in Tulagi Harbor.

February 21, 22, 1945

(Nothing of note to report).

February 23, 1945

1045 - Underway for engine tests.
1106 - Moored port side to SC 1275.

February 24, 1945

0000 - Moored as before outboard YMS 1 in Purvis Bay. YMS 96 moored outboard to starboard.
1703 - Moored starboard side to PCS 1429, Gavana Inlet.

February 25, 1945

0912 - Moored outboard YMS 94 and YMS 271.
1121 - Underway for Guadalcanal carrying Guard Mail for USS Panamint. Passengers as follows: Lt. Comdr. Sonnerly, Lt.jg Miller, and four enlisted personnel. (Guard mail consisted of highly classified material which is received and delivered by the ship designated to carry Guard Mail. This was the most secure way to pass orders, operational plans, etc. from one ship to another, usually from the SOPA [Senior Officer Present] in an area to those under his command. Sometimes, the Guard Mail was actually physically carried by a Commissioned Officer, with a coterie of armed guards, both commissioned and enlisted. The USS Panamint, AGC 13, was a Mt. McKinley Class communications command ship converted in 1944 from the SS Panamint, a merchant marine vessel. The AGC vessels were fitted as flagships for Chiefs of Combined forces, with accomodations for Marine or Army units attached. Radio and radar equipment was particularly elaborate. Word was already getting around to the commanding officers of YMSes and many other ships that they would be a part of the soon to be initiated invasion of Okinawa. Thus the necessity of the literal tons of op plans, etc. that were delivered from the USS Panamint to all the ships to be involved). *(See End Note No.65).*
1305 - Passengers left ship, Guard Mail delivered.
1413 - Underway for Purvis Bay with Guard Mail and one passenger, John P. Ferguson S 1/c.
1515 - Laying to; Guard Mail being delivered. Passenger left ship.
1618 - Departing for USS Panamint with Guard Mail and passenger; McNanety, CRT.
1822 - Anchored in 13 fathoms of water.

February 26, 1945

0715 - Boat came alongside with two passengers. Ens. Rockafeller and a F 1/c. (There are three matters of interest in the log for this day. The first is that there was no Ens. Rockafeller, but Ens. John D. Davis, DVG, USNR reporting aboard for duty. Ens Davis was from Beaufort, NC, a senior at Wake Forest College when called into active duty. He received his commission from Northwestern University Midshipman School at Tower Hall in Chicago September 1944. After attending Naval Mine Warfare School at Yorktown, Va. he was ordered to the YMS 183 for duty. Apparently the writer of the log had John D. Rockefeller on his mind when he signed Ens. Davis aboard. Both the CO and ship's navigator signed the log and neither caught this error or the next, which is the second matter of interest for this day's log. The name of the F 1/c is not mentioned, nor who he was, a passenger or an enlisted man reporting aboard for duty. The third item of interest is what happened to Ens. Lilly and when? Ens. Davis came to fill the spot vacated by Ens. Lilly. There is no mention in the log of the date of Ens. Lilly's detachment).

(This rest of the day was spent taking on fresh water and voyaging to Purvis Bay).

February 27, 1945

(Nothing of note to report).

February 28, 1945

1215 - Underway for USS Panamint with Lt. Ryan as passenger.
1402 - Anchored abeam of USS Panamint.
1645 - Underway for Gavana Inlet
1837 - Moored port side to YMS 271 at repair buoy.

March 1, 2, 1945

(Nothing of note to report).

March 3, 1945

0702 - Underway for sweeping operations.
1226 - All sweep gear aboard, returning to base.

March 4, 1945

0706 - Underway for sweeping operations.
1040 - All magnetic gear streamed, beginning operations.
1324 - All gear aboard, returning to base.

March 5, 1945

0725 - Underway for sweeping operations.
0948 - All gear, "O" type streamed.
1244 - All gear inboard, returning to base.

March 6, 1945

0757 - Underway for Tulagi to run magnetic range.
0850 - Moored to buoy "A" Tulagi Harbor.
0915 - Paymaster came aboard to pay crew and officers.
0920 - Captain's Mast for one man, offense, Disrespect to an Officer, Conduct unbecoming a petty officer. Punishment, to be reduced to the next lower rating.
0950 - Paymaster left ship.
1355 - Underway from buoy to run magnetic degaussing range. (This will determine if the magnetic field of the ship is in a safe range).
1530 - Runs completed, returning to buoy in Tulagi.

March 7, 1945

(Nothing of note to report).

March 8, 1945

0000 - Moored as before port side to YMS 96, YMS 1 moored to starboard in nest with YMS 94, 86, SC 1275, at submarine buoy Gavana Inlet.
0851 - Laying to off USS Panamint awaiting Guard Mail.
0910 - Guard Mail, brought with four passengers, passengers as follows, Colonel Loomis, R.E. Healy, G.S Burch, T.P James, all USMC.
0930 - Proceeding to Lunga Point.
1120 - Passengers and Guard Mail left ship.
1140 - Received Guard mail for USS Panamint.
1330 - Standing off USS Panamint awaiting Guard Mail to return to Lunga Point.
1442 - Departing Lunga Point with Guard Mail and Colonel Babcock USA.
1600 - Standing in at Lunga Point, awaiting Guard Mail boat.
1605 - Boat came alongside, Colonel Babcock left ship.
1630 - Guard Mail and Officers came aboard, passengers as follows, Colonel Loomis, Corp. Burch, Corp. James, all USMC.
1633 - Underway for USS Panamint with Guard Mail and passengers.
1835 - Standing off USS Panamint awaiting boat for Guard Mail.
1840 - Boat came alongside, Guard Mail and passengers left ship.
1845 - Proceeding to Gavana Inlet.
1924 - Moored port side to YMS 271 at Gavana Inlet.

March 9, 10, 11, 12, 13, 14, 1945

(Continued Guard Mail Duty, routine replenishment of fresh water and fuel, receiving aboard commissary stores and ammunition and fumigating ship. Nothing else of note to report).

March 15, 1945

0017 - Underway from alongside YMS 271 proceeding out of harbor (Gavana Inlet, Florida Islands) on various courses and speeds.
0347 - All magnetic and acoustic sweep gear streamed.
0927 - All sweep gear inboard. Proceeding on various courses to fall in position with convoy.
1426 - Held GQ for firing practice at sleeve (towed by an airplane).
1545 - secured from GQ.

March 16, 1945

0000 - Steaming as before on base course 310° True, patrolling on starboard side of convoy as assigned, base speed 9.5 knots, proceeding from Solomon Islands to Ulithi Islands.
1530 - Reset all ships clocks back one hour for Minus #10 time zone.
2225 - C/C to 305° True. (From time to time comment has been made regarding the absence of items of interest and/or importance in the written log. For some reason these items were not recorded and except for the recollection by someone still living who was aboard at the time, the knowledge of that event, etc. would have been lost. Many of these items were not in the least trifling. I know of one incident of great importance for a ship that was present in Tokyo Bay for the surrender in September, 1945. That event and that ship's presence at the surrender is not mentioned in their log at all. Ens. Davis, new on board the 183, remembers an incident that taught him to

call the Captain to the bridge immediately when there was a problem. Davis had the Conn as officer of the deck as the convoy to Ulithi was forming up to make that long, slow voyage. The convoy had moved up through Indispensable Strait which separates the Florida Islands from Malaita Island and a course change was to be made. Radio silence was being observed so as not to call attention to the convoy. The convoy commander chose to signal the course change with signal flags. So as the ships in line of sight of the commander received the signal they bent the flags on the halyard and raised them up halfway to the yard arm. Each ship in line followed suit and raised the flags spelling out the course change and so on until all the ships had received the message. When the last ship in line had received and understood the message it two blocked or raised the flag hoist to the yardarm to let the ship next ahead know this. This went on until the commander had received confirmation that all ships had the message and understood it. The commander then two blocked his flag hoist. When the time came for the course change to be made, the commander notified the other ships by lowering his flag hoist smartly so that it was out of sight. The following ships, each watching the ship ahead then executed the command by smartly lowering their hoist. Whatever specifically was commanded by the signal hoist was then carried out. Alert lookouts, Signal Men and/or Quarter Masters were absolutely indispensable at all times and especially at a time like this. New officers were counseled by Skippers to rely on the senior enlisted men at all times for they knew "the ropes" as it were. All went well. "Smitty", the Chief Signal Man, who really knew his stuff, had the Signal Man's "bible" opened to the proper place as soon as he had finished writing down the flag hoist. He knew every flag in the flag bag, of course, but there were infinite combinations possible and so most of the time these had to be looked up. He had the answer located in just a matter of seconds. The command was to change course to "whatever" at the signal to execute. So far so good. The Skipper was notified of the flag hoist and he responded via the voice tube to the bridge to make the change when commanded. Then the "fun" began, as Davis recalls. It wasn't fun at all, for just as the 183 two blocked the hoist a sudden tropical rain squall engulfed the ship and for about 15 minutes 183 was traveling blind. Nothing could be seen, much less the flag hoist of the ship ahead. So for 15 minutes or so there was no way of knowing if the command had been executed. It seemed reasonable to suppose that it had not been executed, for no one could see anyone else to determine if it had or not. Davis did what seemed reasonable and maintained course and speed and finally the squall moved on, the sky was clear and there not one ship to be seen anywhere. Apparently, the command to execute had been given during the rain squall and the convoy had gone on its way and the 183 was all alone. This was a crushing development. Absolutely nothing left to do than to call down to the ward room and tell the Skipper, "I have lost the convoy." He came to the bridge immediately, got all the facts and ordered the radar (which was relatively new to the 183 and rarely used) turned on. It took awhile for the radar screen to heat up enough to evaporate the moisture that was keeping the screen from showing what was out there. (This also taught us that the more the radar was used, the better it functioned). Pretty soon the convoy appeared on the radar screen 20 odd miles to the northwest. "Just over the hill as it were". Stanley Klein was a good CO and also wanted his officers to be able to stand their watches with responsibility. He didn't give the command himself, but rather said to Ens. Davis, "Why don't you steer 300° degrees True and speed up to near flank and we'll catch up after awhile." Davis gave these commands and several hours later 183 caught up with the convoy and took her place in the screen. Nothing was ever said about losing the convoy and it was not entered in the log. "It was a great learning experience," Davis says, " and I never again failed to call the Captain immediately when there was even the suspicion of trouble."

March 17, 1945

0000 - Steaming as before on base course 305° True, base speed 9.5 knots, screening in position on starboard wing of convoy, proceeding from Solomon Islands to Ulithi Islands. 1000 - Commenced ZigZagging in accordance with plan # 3.

1356 - Ceased patrol ZigZagging per order of Screen Commander. Returned to station.

2036 - C/C to 288° True.

March 18, 1945

0000 - Steaming as before on base course 288° True, speed 9.5 knots. Screening on starboard wing of convoy (composed primarily of LST's loaded with Marines and their equipment and other screening-escort vessels).

0823 - C/C to 302° True.

March 19, 1945

0000 - Base course 302° True, speed 9.5 knots. Proceeding to Ulithi Islands.

1017 - C/C to 140° True preparing to go alongside LST 908 for fueling. (The 183 turned almost 180 degrees to head back toward the LST. Upon arriving near the LST, 183 turns back on the base course, 302° True, draws as close to the port quarter of the LST as is needed. The LST has dropped the fuel hose into the water and trailing from a boom to keep it away from the LST's screws; it is picked up by 183. The nozzle end is brought aboard the minesweeper, inserted into the fuel tank intake pipe and the LST starts pumping the diesel fuel into the 183's tanks. However, before the fuel is pumped, the engineers have checked the purity of the fuel. Otherwise they would not have taken the fuel aboard. In a moderate sea this operation is not too difficult, especially if one's helmsman is an expert. The receiving ship may move closer to the pumping ship and/or away from it momentarily to keep from hitting the pumping ship or moving away so far that the fuel hose is broken. The pumping ship maintains as exact a course as possible under the current conditions).

1230 - Completed taking fuel, returning to screening station.

2013 - USS Fair made underwater contact and fell out of position to drop depth charges. (The USS Fair DE-35 (Destroyer Escort) was the screen commander. This type vessel displaced 1,436 tons, length 289'5", beam 35'1", draft 11'10", speed 21 knots, armament, 3 3"/50, 1x2 40 mm, 9 20mm, 1 hedgehog, 2 depth charge tracks, 8 "K" gun projectors. She carried 15 officers and 183 enlisted. The Fair was named for Lt.(jg) Victor N. Fair, Jr. of Lincoln County, NC who died from wounds sustained when his ship, APD-3 was sunk by Japanese gunfire in the Solomons on Sept. 5, 1942. *(See End Note No.66)*.

March 20, 1945

0000 - Maintaining base course 302° True, speed 8.5 knots.

0906 -C/C/ to 298° True.

0920 - changed base speed to 7 knots.

1100 - Commenced ZigZagging.

1817 - Resumed previous station # 7 on starboard wing of convoy.

March 21, 1945

0000 - Maintaining base course 298° True, speed 9.5 knots.

1301 - Began ZigZagging per order of screen commander.

1347 - C/C to 308° True.

John Dixon Davis

March 22, 1945

0000 - Maintaining base course 308° True, speed 7 knots.
1005 - C/C to 325° True.
1147 - changed base speed to 8 knots.

March 23, 1945

0000 - Maintaining base course 325° True, speed 8 knots.
1345 - Increased speed to 10 knots.
1845 - YMS 86 dropped out of position. (We are) proceeding up to take over position # 5.
1900 - On screening station #5.
1959 - C/C to 358° True.

March 24, 1945

0000 - Steaming as before on base course 358° True, base speed 10 knots, screening on station #5 on starboard wing of convoy proceeding to Ulithi Islands.
0510 - Changing course to 313° True, to 265° True, to 316° True, to 358° True, to 359° True to 090° True in a 2 hour period. Base speed now 2 knots.
0800 - C/C to 135° True.
1205 - C/C to 315° True. Entering the harbor at Ulithi Atoll.
1405 - Moored alongside LST 908. (Ulithi Atoll, a member of the Caroline Islands, lies between Yap and Truk. Both Yap and Truk were fortified by the Japanese after being given a League of Nations Mandate for all the Caroline Islands after WWI. Ulithi, probably the remains of a huge volcanic crater had an anchorage area of 25 miles in diameter. The ring of small islands on the perimeter of the anchorage was formed over the centuries by the build-up of coral. The two main islands, though still quite small, are Mog Mog and Azor. Ulithi was invaded unopposed on September 25, 1944. The Japanese had moved out the month before, but they left their best defensive mine fields in the lagoon. Minesweepers, including (the old friend of YMS 183) YMS 184 went to work immediately. Soon Ulithi became a thriving fleet anchorage which some think helped to shorten the Pacific War by several months. Ulithi enabled the fleet to have a refuge for repair, refueling and rearming instead of having to go back to Pearl Harbor). *(See End Note No.67)*.

March 25, 1945

0848 - Underway from alongside LST 908.
1008 - Moored alongside YMS 96 at CM 12 (USS Weehawken, a Shawmut class mine layer, formerly SS Estrada Palma). *(See End Note No.68)*.
1457 - Underway from CM-12.
1550 - Moored port side to AO 71 to take on fuel. (AO 71, USS Neshanic, a Chiwawa class Fleet Oiler). *(See End Note No.69)*.
1721 - Completed taking on 1945 gallons of fuel.
1730 - Underway from alongside AO 71.
1756 - Moored port side to IX 162. (The IX 162, USS Lignite, was a B7-D1 Concrete Barge. It was commissioned in 1944. It had no engines but was towed to its place of service and anchored. It was a floating warehouse, 366'34" long, beam 54' and max. draft 26'. Except for fuel, fresh water and ammunition it carried commissary stores and other items needed by the average ship. *(See End Note No.70)*.
1835 - Underway from IX 162.

1854 - Moored starboard side to YMS 89 at CM 12, Ulithi Harbor.

March 26, 1945

0000 - Moored as before starboard side to YMS 89, outboard YMS 94 and CM 12 in Ulithi Harbor.

1245 - Underway from alongside.

1421 - Moored port side to YMS 1 in Northern Anchorage. (The log does not mention the fact that Ensign Davis had discovered that YMS 362, commanded by his brother, Lt. Tom I. Davis, was in the Ulithi anchorage. Davis of 362 had learned from a letter from their mother, sometime before, that Ens. Davis had been assigned to YMS 183. Lt. Davis had asked his bridge to be on the lookout for the 183, that his brother was aboard. Just a short time later the 362 spotted the 183 and sent over a blinker light signal of welcome to Ens. Davis. The 362 was underway at 1440 (according to the log of the 362) and heading for IX 151 for provisions. As 362 came into view, Ens. Davis, having already gotten permission from his CO, Stanley C. Klein, to visit his brother, if feasible, signaled over to 362 requesting permission to come aboard for a few minutes. 362 signaled back "permission granted". The 183's wherry, [life boat] with outboard motor, was quickly put over the side and Ens. Davis, with a Coxswain and two seamen navigated the short distance over to the 362. Ens. Davis recalls the pleasure of seeing his brother as they caught up on home news, and as he met his brother's officers, Burcal, Morris and Smith. Ens. Davis recalls, " I told my brother of hearing the BBC radio broadcast of the Iwo Jima invasion. I was sipping a cup of tea in the Grand Pacific Hotel in Suva, Fiji, while I was waiting for transportation to the 183. I didn't know for a fact that the 362 was at Iwo, but I felt that she was. I brought greetings from Stan Klein, as he and my brother had known each other briefly at the Section Base at Morehead City, NC early in the war. The 30 minutes were soon gone, and the wherry came alongside to pick me up. 362 was on her way to Peleliu and we were headed to Okinawa." Lt. Davis acknowledged in 1999 after reading the logs of the 362 that the brief reunion of the brothers was not recorded in the 362 logs either.)

1540 - Underway from alongside.

1620 - Anchored in 18 fathoms of water.

1830 - Sounded General Quarters, for air alert. (Although Ulithi was relatively safe, it was still close enough to Yap for an occasional suicide plane to pay a visit and there was always the possibility a Japanese submarine, regular and/or one man suicide type would try to breach the anti-submarine nets. Actually all of the mines, both Japanese and American were not yet swept up. There were still certain areas that would not be declared completely clear until sometime later).

1845 - Secured from GQ.

1900 - Underway for South anchorage to deliver Guard Mail.

2007 - Moored port side to IX 135 in South Anchorage. (IX 135, USS Arethusa was converted from the ex-SS Gargoyle).

2058 - Underway from alongside, returning to North Anchorage.

2230 - Went alongside LCFF 790 to return Officer messenger. (The LCFF was converted from Landing Craft, Infantry (Large) - LCI(L) to carry flag officers and crew. There were 30 or more of this type of conversions. *(See End Note No. 71).*

2235 - Standing by to anchor.

2240 - Anchored in 25 fathoms.

March 27, 1945

0601 - Underway from Ulithi Islands.

0700 - Standing outside of reefs awaiting convoy.
0840 - C/C to 037· True, base speed 6.5 knots.
1342 - C/C to 310° True.
1415 - C/C course to 326° True.
1800 - Set all ship's clocks back one hour for minus 9 Time Zone. (Signed: Stanley C. Klein, Lt. USNR, Commanding and W.F. Weltzien, Lt.jg, USNR, Navigator).

March 28, 1945

0000 - Steaming as before on base course 326° True, base speed 8 knots. Screening on starboard wing of convoy from Ulithi Islands to Nansei Islands (Okinawa).
0741 - C/C to 334° True.
0958 - C/C to 356° True.
1049 - C/C to 326° True.
1337 - C/C to 336° True, Speed 9 knots.

March 29, 1945

0000 - Maintaining base course 336° True, base speed 9 knots. Screening in station #5 on starboard wing of convoy proceeding to Nansei Islands. 0735 - C/C to 330° True. 1352 - changed base speed to 9.7 knots.
1706 - C/C to 332° True.
2026 - C/C to 325° True.

March 30, 1945

0000 - Steaming as before 325° True, speed 9.7 knots, screening station #5.
1345 - Came alongside IX 113 and began taking on fuel. (IX 113, USS Camel, was a Maritime Commission Z-ETI-S-C3 "Liberty Tanker" type; ex-SS William H Carruth. While taking fuel from USS Camel, Ensign Davis discovered that one of the officers on the Camel was a good friend from Midshipman School in Chicago. His name was Strandburg and he hailed from the upper mid-west. They carried on a conversation by hand semaphore signals (no flags) for at least 30 minutes. Both learned where some of the other midshipmen in their class had been assigned. Ensign Davis said, "It was almost like a visit from home".) *(See End Note No.72)*.
1455 - Secured taking on fuel.
1612 - Standing by to go alongside ARL 10 for water.
1635 - Began taking on fresh water. (ARL 10, USS Coronis was a Landing Craft repair ship and was commissioned in November 1944. She is practically brand new.) *(See End Note No.73)*.
1723 - Completed taking on fresh water.
1728 - Underway on various courses to get back in screening position.
2058 - Assigned station #8 on port wing of convoy. (The primary purposes of the screening vessels are to do a continuous sonar search of the area to the seaward of the convoy and a surface radar search for unidentified ships or objects within the range of their radar).

March 31, 1945

0000 - Maintaining base course 320° True, base speed 9.7 knots, screening in station #8 on port wing of convoy proceeding to Nansei Islands.
0535 - Made emergency turn to port, base course now 275° True.
0556 - Resumed base course of 320° True.
1330 - C./C to 326° True.

1640 - Changed base speed to 10 knots.
2038 - C/C to 324° True.

April 1, 1945

Steaming as before on course 324° True, base speed 10 knots, screening in station #7 on starboard wing of convoy.

0520 - Red Air Alert; sounded General Quarters. (The ship to ship radio was [TBS "talk between ships] now in constant use. The convoy was only 20 hours away from reaching the southwestern end of Okinawa, and already kamikazes, [suicide planes, called "divine wind" by Japanese] were reported in the area. The first wave of Marines and Army troops were landing on the lower western side of the island at about this time. After going inland a certain distance the Marines were to turn left and engage the Japanese forces on the northern part of the island. The Army troops were to turn south at the designated point and engage the Japanese on the southern end of the island. As it turned out there was little resistance to either group for a day or so. When air attack was imminent the words Flash Red were repeated several times on all the radio frequencies being guarded by the ships in the area. Flash Red required each ship to go to General Quarters and stay at GQ until the all clear was given by the announcement Flash Green on the radio. At General Quarters all guns are manned, each man wears his steel helmet and life jacket and each station is in sound powered telephone communication with the Commanding Officer on the Bridge. The sound powered telephone had no outside source of electricity. No even a battery. The sound of the talker's voice agitated a chemical compound which created a small electric current. The current going through a regular telephone wire to the recipient was modulated by the swender's voice and was heard by the recipient just as it was sent. Obviously these phones were used whether there was an outside source of current or not).

0538 - Secured from GQ.
1335 - C/C to 326° True and base speed to 8 knots.
2100 - C/C to 335° True and speed to 7 knots.
2340 - C/C to 291° True.

April 2, 1945

0000 - Maintaining base course 291° True, speed 7 knots, on starboard side screen.
0330 - C/C to 320° true.
0435 - Changed speed to 6.5 knots.
0515 - Changed speed to 8 knots. –
0540 - C/C to 290° True, speed to 10 knots.
0600 - Sounded General Quarters for possible air attack.
0628 - C/C to 320° True, now on air defense station. (Some of the crew remember two planes in the distance and one went into a steep dive from which it did not recover. Undoubtedly the first kamikaze, of hundreds we were to see in the next few months).
0753 - Secured from GQ. (The log does not say when, but it was about this time 183 and the other vessels of the screen were detached from convoy duty and directed to report to USS Terror, the flagship for minecraft under the command of Admiral Sharp, for assignment to other duties. [The LST's headed for the landing beach to unload the marines and their cargo]. The Terror was anchored in the anchorage at Kerama Retto. USS Terror, CM-5, was the only built-for-purpose large minelayer used in WWII). She was 5875 tons, 453'10" long, beam 60'2", draft 19'7", speed 20 knots, armament 4 5"/38 DP, 4x4 40mm, 14 20mm, 900 mines. She had a complement of 481 men, geared turbines, twin screws, and 11,000 h.p. During the Okinawa campaign Terror

was the "mother hen" for minecraft, supplier of technical equipment, temporary hospital for the injured and planner of tactics for minecraft in the area. She was also heavily engaged in anti-aircraft action against kamikazes). *(See End Note No. 74.).*

0853 - Flash Red, sounded GQ.

0858 - C/C to 295° True.

0917 - Secured form GQ.

1034 - Proceeding into harbor on various courses.

1135 - Lying to outside Kerama Retto anchorage awaiting instructions.

1515 - Set special sea detail; proceeding on various courses into harbor. [Special sea detail required the most experienced men to be ready to take the ship into port, or to sea or to moor or anchor. When whatever function was completed the special sea detail was dismissed]. 1540 - Moored starboard side to YMS 86 in Northwest Anchorage, Kerama Retto. (Kerama Retto was a group of islands about 20 miles west of the southern end of Okinawa. The several islands of the group were so situated that there was essentially a land-locked harbor with only the northern and southern ends open for entrance and egress. The ends were easily closed with steel anti-submarine nets and the anchorage created was approximately 6 miles long and two to three miles wide. It was an excellent anchorage for the many minesweepers and other small craft that were so essential in the anti-kamikaze campaign and for the quick repair of ships that were not too heavily damaged. Even ships as large as cruisers and CVE's could come in for taking on ammunition, fuel, etc. and then be out to sea again in a very short time. It was a refuge in every sense of the word except for the suicide planes that came over 24 hours a day every day and made anchoring in the harbor less than a place of certain safety).

1609 - Underway from alongside YMS 86, proceeding on various courses to anchor.

1758 - Dropped anchor in harbor off Aka Shima. [Jima and Shima both mean island or rock and Retto means "chain of islands"].

1835 - Underway to take screening station at north entrance of harbor.

1841 - Flash Red, sounded GQ.

1849 - On station, steering course 260° True.

1856 - Secured from GQ.

2000 - Screening on base course 080° True and its reciprocal 260° True at northern entrance of anchorage. (At the northern end of Kerama Retto are the two largest islands of the group, Zamami Jima on the western side and Tokashiki Jima on the eastern side. These islands are separated at their north ends by about 1 ½ miles of open and deep water. All of these islands seem to jut up from the ocean floor and the waters around them are fairly deep. The anti-submarine net was strung across from one island to the other except for an opening several hundred feet wide (which was kept closed except when vessels needed to come in or go out of the anchorage). A net tender was on duty at all times to open or close the entrance. Likewise, the southern end of the anchorage was sealed by an anti-submarine net extending for more than 3 miles from Hokaji Shima to a point on Tokashiki about 2 ½ miles from its southern end. The net entrance at the southern end, like the northern end was on the Tokashiki Jima side of the anchorage

Figure 39 - Ogan Rock, Kerama, Retto. From an oil painting, from memory, by the author.

and operated by a net tender. On this first night of screening duty by 183 (which we will refer to from here on as "the Ogan Patrol") the ship steamed back and forth between two points north of the anchorage and the anti-submarine nets. The western most point, which was designated "Able", was about ½ mile north of a conical rock, which was about ½ mile north of the eastern end of Zamami Jima. It jutted up from the ocean floor 50 to 90 feet below, and extended above sea level to a height of over 200 feet. It looked so much like the head of a whale poking up above the surface of the sea, that it was named by the ancient inhabitants whale rock or Ogan, which means whale in Japanese. It was a spectacular geologic formation and easy to spot from a great distance and the blip it made on the radar screen looked as big as one made by a battleship. The eastern most point of the screening course was designated "Baker". It was about ½ mile north of a small island, Gishibu Shima, which was at the northern end of Tokashiki Jima. The distance from point "Able" to "Baker" was about 3 miles. So beginning at point "Able" 183 steamed on course 080° True to point "Baker" where it made a 180° degree turn to course 260° True back to point "Able" and so on through the night. All the while the sonar was searching under water for submarines and the radar was searching the surface for anything floating. The Ogan Patrol was always interesting for when it began, usually just before sunset, bats, by the thousands came streaming out of the caves and crevasses for their nightly feeding forays. Then just before sunrise, they came streaming back for their daytime sleep. The time taken to move from point "Able" to point "Baker" was about 45 minutes to an hour. This meant that the 183 was steaming slowly, around 3 to 5 knots. This often necessitated the use of one engine only for a time and then the other. Steaming slowly on two engines was hard on the engines because of carbon buildup).

April 3, 1945

0000 - Screening as before on base courses 080° True and 260° True at 5 knots (Ogan Patrol). Ensign Davis, who stood the 0000 to 0400 watches and the 1200 to1600 watches remembers that it was cold when the 183 reached Okinawan waters on April 2. Although the latitude of Kerama Retto, around 25 degrees N, was about that of the Florida Keys, the men of the 183 and the other vessels had been down in the tropics for varying periods of time and did not need or have issued cold weather gear as they moved north. Crew member's Pea Jackets and officer's lined navy blue rain coats came out of storage.Some of the men, whose ears were especially sensitive, folded the brim of their white hats down so as to give their ears some cover. Also, coming out of the tropics into just moderately cooler temperatures was something of a shock).

0556 - Flash Red. Sounded GQ.
0614 - Secured from GQ.
0655 - Secured from screening station; proceeding into harbor.
0900 - Lying to in the harbor awaiting orders from USS Terror, CM-5.
0945 - Moored starboard side to USS Terror. (Although the log does not say, this was probably the time that cold weather gear for the crew and officers was brought aboard in boxes to be issued to the ship's personnel later that day).
1012- Underway from alongside Terror.
1030 - Moored alongside YMS 2.
1040 - Underway from alongside YMS 2.
1100 - Anchored in harbor at Kerama Retto.
1158 - Flash Red, sounded GQ.
1240 - Secured from GQ.
1725 - Flash Red, sounded GQ.

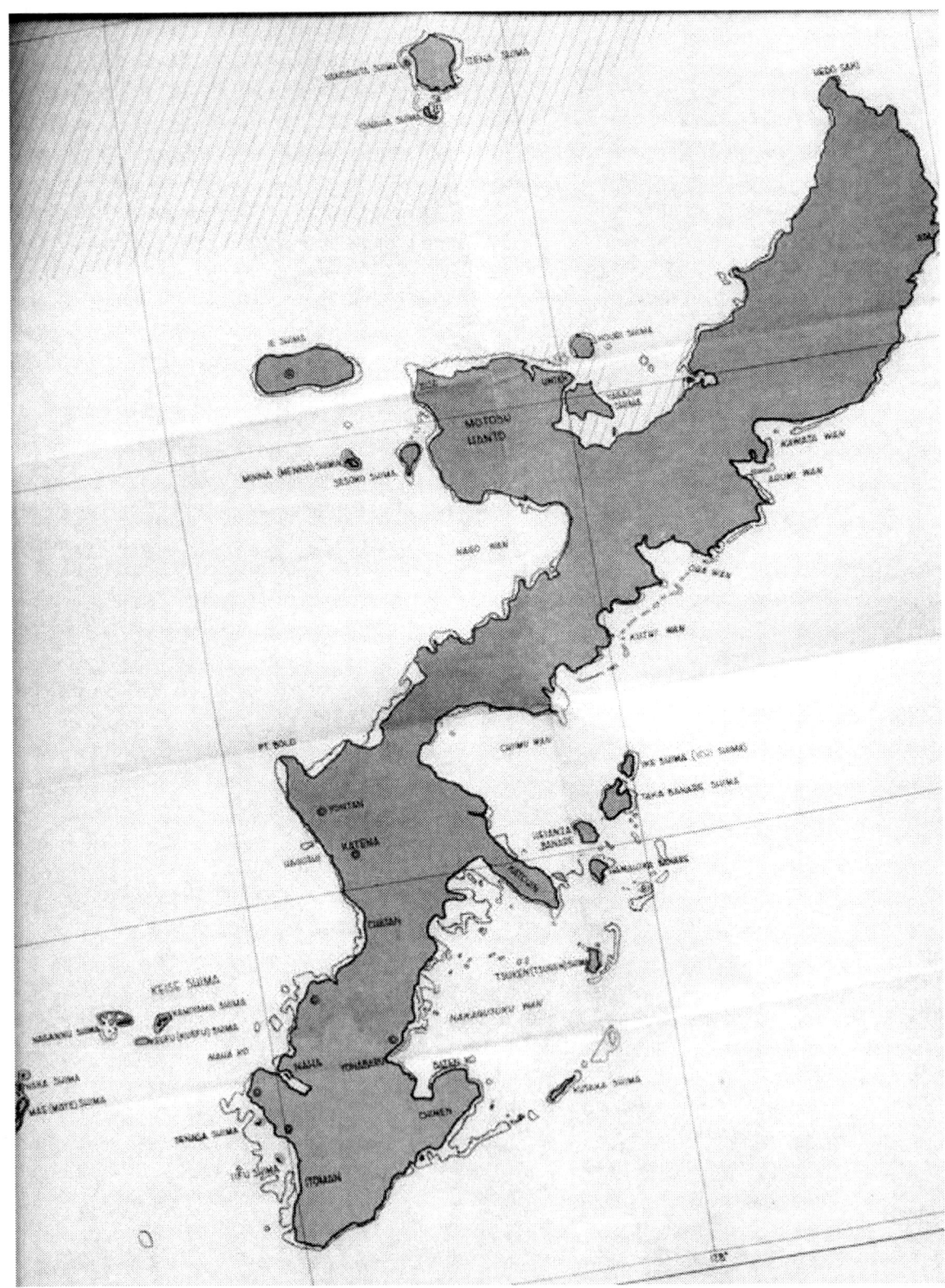

Map 1 Okinawa Gunto U.S. Navy Chart

1813 - Secured from GQ.

2000 - Standing radio and armed watches about the ship. (The height of the Japanese kamikaze effort to stall and perhaps defeat the Allied drive to defeat the Japanese was reached at Okinawa. It began much earlier as a sporadic effort here and there, and increased great momentum in the Philippines. Besides the airplane kamikazes there were suicide speedboats carrying hundreds of pounds of explosives to ram ships and sink them. Suicide swimmers were reported ready to swim out to a vessel in the darkness towing a floating mine or some other explosive device and upon reaching the side of a ship detonating the explosive. The swimmers would hide under floating debris, sometimes boxes and crates the Americans had thrown over the side into that great garbage receptacle known as "the deep six". On this first night at anchor in the great anchorage at Kerama Retto, all lookouts on duty were armed with carbines or rifles and the officers with their 45 cal. automatics. Any suspicious article in the water that came close to the ship was fired at many times "just in case". A chorus of rifle fire came from all parts of the anchorage throughout the night).

April 4, 1945

0820 - Anchor's aweigh; underway to search beaches for mines. (These would be mines swept earlier that were not sunk by the minesweepers in the initial sweeps of the campaign. In many cases these mines that were missed drifted up on the beaches. They had to be located and destroyed lest suicide swimmers use them on our anchored ships) 1001 -Sighted mine on northwest shore of Aka Shima

1110 - Sighted mine on north shore of Yakum Jima.

1135 - Sighted mine on east shore of Yakum Jima.

1248 - Sighted unidentified object on east shore of Koba Jima.

1301 - Completed search. (The locations of these beached mines were relayed to the Terror, which in turn notified the Army troops stationed on these islands who had them destroyed).

1509 - Entering harbor.

1524 - Moored starboard side to IX 113 to take on fuel. (This is our old friend USS Camel who refueled us at sea some days ago).

1607 - Underway from IX 113; steering various courses preparing to anchor.

1643 - Anchored off Fukashi Shima.

1700 - Underway for screening station at north entrance of harbor. (The "Ogan Patrol", 080° True to 260° True and back again through the night).

April 5, 1945

0615 - Secured from screening. Began streaming "O" type gear to sweep the channel into the northern entrance to the harbor.

0730 - All gear streamed - 200 fathoms of sweep wire, 9 fathoms of depressor wire; 50 foot float pendant.

0735 -(The three black balls are two blocked and the sweep of the channel is begun. The ship is already several miles north of the entrance on its "Ogan Patrol", so the time elapsed from that point to the entrance is not great. The distance beyond the entrance, where the net tender stood watch was probably only five or six miles).

0810 - All sweep gear aboard; proceeding into harbor.

0855 - Anchored in Kerama Retto harbor.

0915 - All ship's clocks wound & checked.

1130 - Flash Red; sounded GQ.

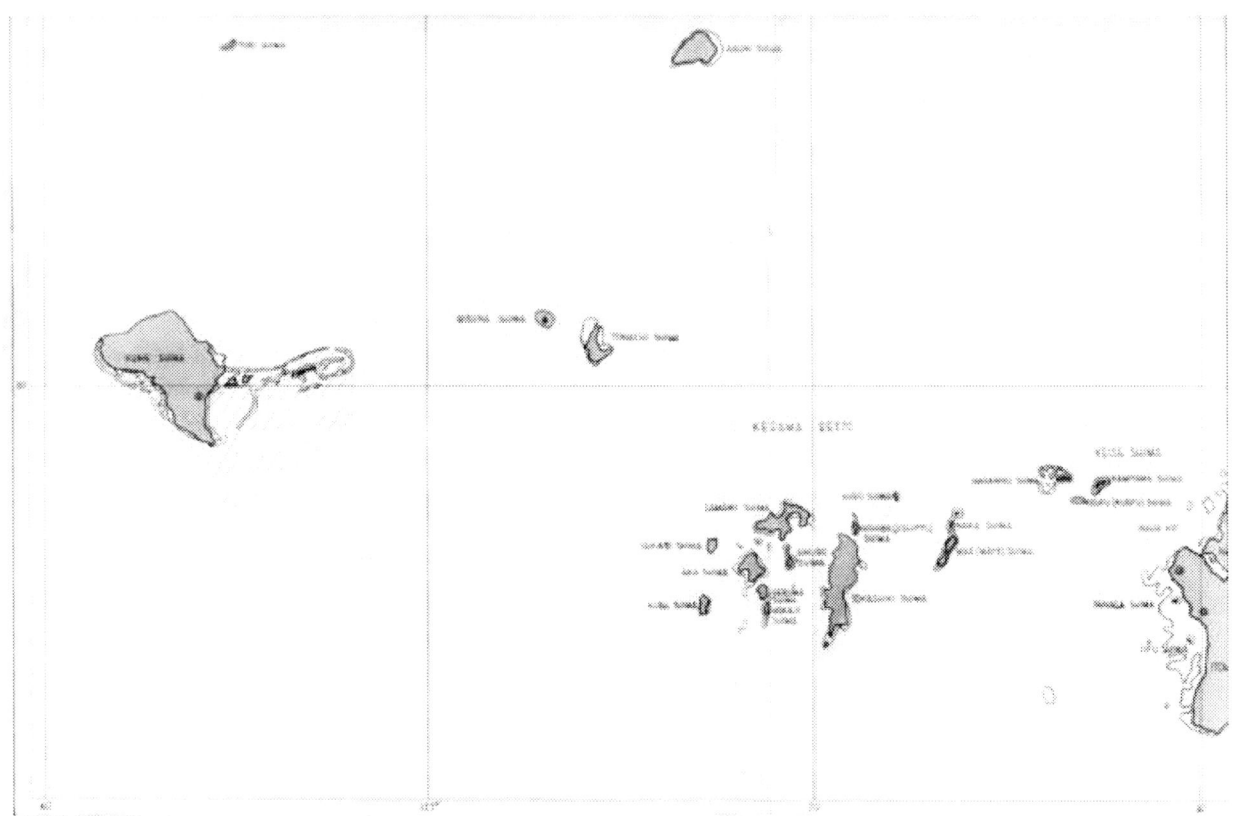

Map 2 - Kerama Retto and Kume Shima. U.S. Navy Chart

1150 - Secured from GQ.

1402 - Underway to shift berth; DM 18 (USS Breese) dragging anchor dangerously close. (The USS Breese was a WWI, four stack destroyer until converted to a light minelayer and commissioned as such in 1931. When the conversion took place one of her four stacks was removed in the interest of her new minelaying capability. The Breese took part in the laying of the many mine fields put down in the South Pacific in the early days of the war. YMS 183 helped to sweep up many of these fields in late 1943 and 1944. At Okinawa, Breese was a sort of command ship for a group of YMSes of which the 183 was a part. Consequently 183 anchored nearby the Breese when feasible. The Breese displaced 1700 tons, was 314' long. 32' at the beam and had a draft of 12'. Her speed was 30 knots, armament 3 3"/50 DP, 1x2 40mm, 6 20mm, 80 mines. Complement 149. Occasionally it was necessary to moor alongside Breese, but it was always done with trepidation, for Breese was an old rusting vessel and the steel guards for the screws on both sides of the stern were always broken, or bent, and while they may have kept us from bumping into her screws, the guards made "mince meat" of our wooden sides. We had to use every fender we possessed when alongside her. *(See End Note No.75)*. Another item which created mooring problems, especially in Kerama Retto was the rocky bottom. On average if 183 found good holding bottom [heavy sand/and or clay] in one out of four attempts, she was lucky. Sometimes when the "hook" was dropped and after giving plenty of time for it to lose its hold, if it was going to, and didn't, the engines were secured and the anchoring detail secured. Often when everyone had settled down to routine chores or catching a nap, if not on watch, (the first few weeks at Okinawa our crew, like everyone else's were walking "zombies" from lack of sleep from having to go to GQ so often), the anchor watch would call down to the skipper,

"Captain, we're dragging anchor." He really didn't need to call for when the anchor drags on a rocky bottom, you can feel the vibration all over the ship. The case on this day was not our dragging, but Breese dragging. Since it was easier for us to move, we moved to a new place and safer distance).

1805 - Captain left ship to attend conference aboard YMS 331.

1925 - Captain returned to ship.

1940 - Preparing to get underway for night screening assignment.

2000 - Underway; proceeding to night screening station.

2055 - On station steering 090° True and (its reciprocal) 270° True at the southern entrance to the harbor. (The anchorage at Kerama Retto was very crowded and it took some time to pick one's way through the many ships at anchor and get to the net entrance and then steam [term still used to mean proceeding by whatever mechanical means a ship had. In the old days it was steam engines. For the modern YMS it was diesel power. It was still referred to as steaming] to the screening position and begin the night's work).

April 6, 1945

0000 - Screening as before (using sonar and surface search radar) on courses 090° True and 270° True at southern entrance to Kerama Retto. (The screening stations afforded a view of the Island of Okinawa proper, for either was far enough north or south of Tokashiki Jima so that that island with its 700 foot plus ridge did not block out an open view of the battlefield 20 or so miles to the east. From that distance, no single tracers from whatever source were distinguishable. The whole eastern sky was a bright, slightly yellowish red, constant and unchanging the whole night through and until the daylight, brighter still, diluted it until it could not be seen).

0630 - Secured from screening station; returning to anchorage.

0655 - Lying to near USS Terror, awaiting permission to go alongside.

0725 - Permission not granted; standing by to anchor.

0730 - Anchored in Kerama Retto. (The anchorage chart we had been issued upon arrival was well laid out and clear for the different size ships, etc. The problem was that there were many more ships using the anchorage than had been anticipated, and the bottom in many places was not adequate for anchoring, so often, a ship had to anchor wherever it could, and hope the bottom was good and that another ship did not anchor too close to create a problem. Most difficult of all was the clutter of ships anchored in the areas designated as channels to the entrances, blocking safe, and quick access to the passageways through the nets)

1539 - Flash Red; sounded GQ.

1612 - Secured from GQ.

1650 - Anchor dragging; shifting berths.

1715 - Re-anchored with 45 fathoms of chain at A/S station # 5. (This station was located near the net tender and the entrance to the southern part of the anchorage. This anti-submarine station required that the screening ship use its sonar across the net entrance area all night long on the chance that a Japanese submarine, either one man or regular size might try to breach the net. Had one been detected, immediate use of depth charges would have come into play). (It is interesting to note that on April 6, 1945 the Japanese sent 355 suicide planes to Okinawa. They came from Kyushu and began arriving in the Kerama Retto-Okinawa area in the late afternoon. USS Terror sent out the Flash Red warning at 1539. Actually only a few Kamikazes reached the anchorage at Kerama Retto. All but 24 were shot down by fighter planes of the Navy and Marines on their Combat Air Patrol about 100 miles out from Okinawa, and the destroyer-minesweeper anti-aircraft picket line from 50 miles out back toward the island. The

24 getting through sank three destroyers and an LST and damaged 20 others including YMS 311 and 321. There wasn't a lot of activity in the anchorage itself, but every ship in there could hear the radio calls for assistance, the damage, casualty and sinking reports from many of the ships being attacked at various locations outside the harbor). *(See End Note No.76).* (Note: Even though there is no reference to it in the log, Ens. Davis remembers that a Liberty Ship, reportedly carrying a full load of ammunition, was sunk nearby during this time frame. Further research has confirmed that this freighter, SS Logan Victory, loaded with 7,000 tons of ammunition was hit by a kamikaze and immediately scuttled. Logan Victory was in process of anchoring in the West Anchorage, about 3 1/2 miles from the anti-submarine station where 183 was in position for the night's duty. It was in full view of 183 and thought by the crew to be a brand new ship since the paint job on the hull and superstructure was so bright. Everyone hoped that Logan Victory would be unloaded quickly. The memory of the explosion of USS Mt. Hood at Manus Island many months ago was still fresh. That explosion was an absolute disaster. Many of the crew of 183 gathered on the wing of the bridge and the flying bridge to get a better view. The anchor of the ammo carrier dropped into the water and the rattle of the chain through the hawse pipe could be faintly heard. Suddenly, out of nowhere a suicide plane crashed into the superstructure of the ammo carrier, hitting the port side (the side away from our view) and immediately the whole superstructure was engulfed in flames from the gasoline in the plane's tanks. We were transfixed by the scene. There was nothing we could do as two small islands connected by mud flats separated our anchorage from that of the ammo carrier. Her crew members ran down ladders where possible or jumped over the side into the water. It was impossible for us to get under way to seek shelter. If Logan Victory was going to blow up it would happen before we could get our anchor off the bottom. Almost immediately and almost imperceptibly we could see the ship was settling lower in the water. She must have had automatic sea cocks for she was sinking as the cargo holds filled with sea water flooding the ammunition and the bilges. It seemed to go very rapidly now. In almost no time the hull was under water, seemingly sitting upright as if resting on the bottom and only the two top levels of the superstructure, scarred by the intense fire, remained above the water. The fire was soon extinguished, the ammunition rendered harmless under the water and the superstructure slipped under the surface of the water. There was not going to be another Mt. Hood disaster. According to the official report of the loss of the Logan Victory, members of the crew were rescued by USS Strategy, AM308 and other small craft in the area. Of the 42 members of the armed guard 3 were killed. *(See End Note No. 77).*

April 7, 1945

0000 - Anchored as before on Anti-Submarine Station # 5 at Kerama Retto; all men on watch armed with rifles.

0416 - Ships in harbor and on screen firing at enemy plane; sounded GQ.

0443 - Secured from GQ.

0535 - Began bringing anchor up.

0550 - Underway to make sweep "Charlie" and "How". Flash Red; sounded GQ.

0610 - Secured from GQ.

0650 - All sweep gear streamed.

0725 - Channel sweep completed; recovering port gear.

0805 - Began sweeping anchorage with starboard gear.

1050 - All sweep gear aboard; sweep completed. (This was not an easy task with so many ships about. However, the channels had to be checked).

1124 - Moored starboard side to DM 18 (USS Breese).
1219 - Underway to sweep Northwest Ancorage.
1301 - All gear streamed; sweeping Northwest Anchorage for mines believed to have been dropped by Japanese plane during yesterday's raid. (All ships anchored in this area had to weigh anchor and move to another location for a time so a thorough sweep could be made).
1722 - Sweep completed after nine runs; Results negative.
1840 - Anchored in Anti-Submarine Station # 5.
2010 - Flash Red; sounded GQ.
2055 - Secured from GQ.

April 8, 1945

0000 - Anchored as before on A/S Station # 5.
0520 - Began bringing anchor in.
0545 - Underway for sweep operation.
0550 - Flash Red; sounded GQ.
0623 - All gear streamed; beginning sweep "Charlie".
0630 - Secured from GQ.
0900 - Completed sweep "Charlie". Recovering gear.
0915 - All gear aboard, returning to anchorage.
1030 - Moored starboard side of YMS 311 to take on provisions. (Probably while 183 was on sweep "Charlie" a provision lighter ["grocery delivery" service] with commissary stores for 183 had to leave them with YMS 311 for 183 to pick up. While alongside Ensign Davis recalls meeting the skipper of the 311. "Captain Klein of the 183 invited the Captain of the 311 over for coffee in the wardroom and to hear his account of the exploits of the 311 two days before when she shot down three suicide planes and was hit by a fourth. I can't remember the name of the skipper of 311, but he was still a little "jumpy" telling us about their close call. It seems 311 was in a sweeping formation somewhere between Ie Shima and Kerama Retto when five kamikazes appeared from nowhere. Four of them went for 311 and three were splashed by an alert gunner even before GQ could be sounded. The fourth kamikaze dived toward 311. There was no time for evasive action, only the 20mm guns had a chance to stop the plane, but they didn't. The fuselage of the plane sort of pancaked on the starboard side of the forecastle deck between the 3" gun and the pilot house. Its wings were sheared off, falling into the water and the fuselage skidded across the deck from starboard to port and into the water off the port side. Gasoline from the plane's tanks was splashed everywhere, but there was no fire. Unfortunately, three men were approaching their gun station on the 3" gun on the forecastle when the plane hit. One crew member was killed and two were injured. The 311, after a day or two of repair, the 3" gun was damaged, went back to Saipan for more extensive work. There is no question that if the fuselage had hit the pilot house or the 3" gun directly 311 may have been destroyed with a much larger loss of life").
1200 - Underway, proceeding to DM 18.
1400 - Flash Red; sounded GQ.
1420 - Secured from GQ.
1602 - Underway for screening station at Northern Entrance to harbor.
1650 - Relieved ship on station and began patrolling. (This is the "Ogan Patrol").

April 9, 1945

0000 - Screening as before on courses 090° True and 270° True. At Northern Entrance to Kerama Retto.

0400 - Secured starboard engine. (Didn't need both engines to maintain satisfactory speed for sonar screening so one engine could "rest" and not get the carbon build-up that always resulted from running slow for a long period).

0608 - Lit off starboard engine: preparing for sweep "Able". (The tradition bound Navy since the days of coal fired boilers to make steam, still used the term "to light off the boilers" (by actually starting the coal to burn by lighting a fire, to heat the water in the boilers for steam to run the steam engines). In the Navy of WWII you didn't start a diesel engine. You would "light off" the engine).

0650 - All gear streamed; beginning sweep.

0815 - Completed sweep. (This was channel leading to the Northern Entrance).

0850 - Anchored in small craft anchorage.

0910 - Underway to search beaches for mines. (This was a continuation of the search of the islands' beaches for mines that may have floated ashore after being swept).

1302 - Completed search; returning to anchorage.

1305 - Anchored in small craft anchorage.

1810 - Underway from anchorage, to A/S Station.

1850 - Anchored in A/S Station #2.

1910 - Anchor dragging; making preparations for getting underway (to re-anchor).

1915 - Anchor hooked securely; secured engines. [When the engines were closed down and made ready to start again at a moments notice, they were said to be secured].

April 10, 1945

0000 - Anchored as before on A/S Station #2, Kerama Retto.

0730 - Bring in anchor,

0739 - Underway for sweep "How".

0757 - All gear streamed; beginning sweep "How".

0845 - All gear aboard; returning to anchorage.

0908 - Anchored in small craft anchorage.

0950 - Anchor dragging; bringing it in in order to re-anchor.

1011 - Anchored in 15 fathoms of water with 60 fathoms of chain out.

1515 - LST 1033 anchored less than 50 yards to port fouling our anchorage. Lit off engines in preparation for getting underway.

1521 - Underway to shift berth.

1525 - Anchored in 18 fathoms of water with 60 fathoms of chain. (As mentioned earlier anchoring was a constant problem. LSTs like all landing craft anchored from the stern normally. They were used to running their bow up on the beach and the stern anchor kept them from broaching in the surf. They were usually very close together when on the beach for unloading whatever they were carrying. When they were ready to exit from the landing area they winched in the anchor cable (they did not use chains) plus the screws in reverse; was sufficient to pull them off in most cases. When it came time to anchor in deep water it was another matter. Being a large, shallow draft vessel with high freeboard (lots of sail, large areas of ship upon which the wind could act and offset efforts by the helmsman trying to steer his vessel successfully], getting in the right place where the anchor would hold and the wind didn't cause them to swing into other anchored vessels was a problem they never seemed to figure out. We were the little "guy" and if the LST anchored so near us that it was a threat to the safety of our ship it was our problem. So we moved to another location.

April 11, 1945

0000 - Anchored as before in Kerama Retto harbor.

1259 - Underway to IX 113 (our old friend USS Camel). 1325 - Moored port side to IX 113.

1355 - Completed taking on 1150 gallons of fuel. Underway to CM 12. (USS Weehawken, mine layer turned provision ship for minecraft).1418 - Moored starboard side to CM 12 for provisions.

1615 - Underway for DM 18 (USS Breese).

1640 - Moored starboard side to DM 18.

1735 - Underway for screening station.

1755 - Relieved SC 1004 on patrol station at Southern Entrance to harbor.

1837 - Flash Red; sounded GQ.

1931 - Secured from GQ.

April 12, 1945

0000 - Patrolling as before on courses 090° True and 270° True off Southern Entrance to Kerama Retto.

0558 - C/C to 310° True; proceeding to net entrance to commence channel sweep.

0635 - All gear streamed; commencing channel sweep.

0906 - Completed channel sweep; recovered gear; returning to anchorage.

0935 - Moored starboard side to DM 18.

0940 - Lt.jg Taylor and mine disposal party came aboard.

1001 - Underway for mine disposal mission. (The mission on this day was on the eastern side of Tokashiki, the large island of the Kerama Retto. The log does not mention it but 183 came up on the beached stern section of USS Halligan DD 584. She had been in the fire support group between Okinawa and Kerama Retto in the pre-invasion minesweeping operations beginning 25 March '45. Halligan continued her offshore patrols on March 26. At 1835 a tremendous explosion rocked the ship sending smoke and debris 200 feet in the air. The destroyer had hit a moored mine head on, exploding the forward magazines and blowing off the forward section of the ship including the bridge, back to the forward stack. Nearly 40% of the vessel was blown away, the remaining stern section drifted helplessly. She lost one half of her crew of 300 and only two of her 21 officers survived. On the 27th the remaining hulk went aground on the eastern side of Tokashiki. Seventeen days later 183 came as close as the water's depth would allow. It was a sickening and sad sight, and another reminder of what a naval mine can do. It certainly renewed the resolve of the minesweepers of 183 to do their best to rid the sea of these monsters). *(See End Note 78).*

1100 - Mine disposal party left ship for the shore where a mine had washed up. Their plan was to dispose of the mine by blowing it up. (The mine disposal party was taken to the shore in the ship's wherry with an outboard motor. In addition to Lt.jg Taylor and an associate to carry a canvas bag of tools, etc. 183 furnished a coxswain armed with a carbine, a signal man with semaphore flags, binoculars and a portable signal light. He was also armed. A third crewman from 183 was an armed guard. There were no walkie-talkies available to us so flags and blinker light had to do for communications. From the flying bridge the activities on shore could be seen reasonably well with binoculars. Lt.jg Taylor approached the mine, took a tool and un-bolted the access cover to the inside of the mine. While he was doing this, the signal man sent a message that this was a new type of mine which Mr. Taylor wanted to take back with him to

DM 18. He requested that the wherry tow the mine to the 183 for transport. In the meantime, Mr. Taylor removed the detonator and the explosive charge and placed it behind a large rock on the shore. The now empty mine case was rolled down to the water's edge. Mr. Taylor now placed a time fuse on the large amount of explosive, started it and he ran to a pre-selected location behind some rocks. The wherry had already moved off shore a safe distance. In a minute or two the fuse set off the mine's explosive. It made a lot of noise and blew a lot of sand into the air, but there was no damage to anyone. The wherry came back to shore took, the empty mine case in tow to the ship where it was hoisted aboard and secured to the deck).

1120 - Mine disposal officer reports mine to be a new type.
1310 - Launched wherry to retrieve mine.
1426 - Wherry returned to ship with mine in tow.
1433 - Hoisted mine (empty case) aboard.
1434 - Mine disposal party returned to ship.
1440 - Proceeding to next mine. (The locations of these mines had been plotted on the charts on a prior day of searching so that they could be found again quickly for disposal).
1555 - Mine disposal party left ship to dispose of another mine.
1556 - Anchored in 22 fathoms of water off east coast of Tokashiki.
1630 - Mine was detonated on beach by disposal party. (In order not to leave the empty mine case on shore for possible use again by the Japanese, Mr. Taylor blew it all up after taking the necessary precautions. Those on the 183 were startled by how close chunks of the mine case came to our anchored ship).
1722 - Mine disposal party returned aboard.
1802 - Underway to DM 18 to return disposal party.
1855 - Moored starboard side to DM 18.
1905 - Underway for night patrol station.
1915 - On station A/S #1 patrolling on courses 090° True and 270° True.

April 13, 1945

0000 - Patrolling as before on A/S #1 on courses 090° True and 270° True. (This is the Ogan Patrol at the northern entrance).
0620 - Began streaming double "O" type gear. (This means that "O" type gear for moored mines is streamed on the port and starboard side of the ship at the same time).
0626 - C/C course to 017° True.
0628 - All gear streamed; beginning sweep. (183 is sweeping from the northern entrance area to the north away from the anchorage for about 30 minutes, then turns almost 180° degrees and sweeps back toward the anchorage).
0700 - C/C to 192° True.
1740 - Recovered port gear; proceeding to harbor with starboard gear out to make sweep "How". (This is the channel sweep through to eastern side (the Tokashiki side) of the anchorage).
0910 - All gear recovered; proceeding to anchorage.
0945 - Moored starboard side to YMS 342.
1150 - Underway to PGM 20. (PGM 20, a Motor Gunboat, was converted from PC 1551 and commissioned December 2, 1944. She was practically brand new by the time she reached Okinawa. Steel hull, 500 tons displacement, length 173', beam 22', draft 8', speed 22 knots, armament 1 3"/23 DP, 1x2 40mm, 6 20mm, 1 60mm mortar, complement 28-65, diesel engines, twin screws. The PGM was an all purpose gun ship, designed to operate close in during an

invasion, and fast with anti-air craft weapons. A great support ship to have around). *(See End Note 79).*

1220 - Moored alongside PGM 20 to draw fog oil. (One of tasks of the small craft at night, if they did not have a special screening station, was to anchor on the windward side of the anchorage even when there was only a light breeze blowing. In this location a smoke or fog generator was started which turned a special blend of lubricating oil into dense, heavy white smoke or fog. The wind carried the smoke down on the ships in the anchorage and it effectively shrouded all but the vessels with the tallest masts. Screening vessels on the downwind side of the anchorage often had difficuly as the smoke drifted out over their patrol areas. Nevertheless, when the wind was right, the smoke protected the anchorage quite well. Many of the small craft were issued their smoke generators only after arriving at Kerama Retto-Okinawa. The generators were positioned on the fantail (stern) of the ship. Occasionally a generator would burst into flames, but they were usually extinguished without too much trouble. Of course, the generator was manned by a special group and they never left it unattended while in operation. Fire extinguishers and fire hoses were always on standby).

1237 - Underway from PGM 20 to retrieve drifting buoy on southern channel.

1258 - C/C to 197° True.

1305 - C/S to 1/3 , standing by to pick up buoy.

1325 - Survey boat came alongside.

1330 - Survey boat left ship.

1355 - Towing buoy to proper position.

1520 - Dropped buoy in proper position; returning to harbor. (The buoy was a marker buoy of some kind, perhaps for an obstruction, to mark a channel, etc. and it had apparently broken loose from its anchor. The survey boat could not handle the buoy that was now drifting and a hazard to navigation. 183 could handle the buoy, but did not know where it should go. The survey boat gave the proper location and 183 complied). 1605 - Anchored in Kerama Retto.

1755 - Underway for patrol station A/S #7.

1830 - On station.

1837 - The cruiser USS St. Louis, CL-45, exited the Southern Entrance of the anchorage right behind us about 300 yards off our port quarter (She was making her turn to the southeast when suddenly all of her 5"/38, twin mounted AA guns, on her starboard side (there seemed to be six or eight of them) began firing at something due south of the anchorage. After firing several rounds, we could see the splashes several miles away, there appeared a tiny black speck above the splashes and the next round or two produced a ball of fire where the speck had been seconds before. The St. Louis had knocked down a suicide plane with its radar controlled 5 inchers with only eight rounds, five to make him rise above the surface of the ocean and three to shoot him down. As the crew of the 183 cheered, they all agreed that this was an awesome sight. In all probability, most of those on the St. Louis were not aware of what had just happened, it was only a matter of a couple of minutes. Our signal man was instructed to send a blinker message to the St. Louis, "Glad you're on our side". The St. Louis blinker light came back with an acknowledgment of having received our message and then she was gone over the horizon to the southeast in the open sea.).

1838 - Sounded GQ as the St. Louis opened fire.

1846 - Secured from GQ.

John Dixon Davis

April 14, 1945

0000 - Patrolling as before on courses 070° True and 270° True on A/S Station #7 at southern end of Kerama Retto.

0515 - C/C to 015° True. (Preparing for morning channel sweep "Charlie").

0630 - All gear streamed; commencing sweep "Charlie".

0800 - Crew mustered on station; Colors lowered to half mast in mourning for President Franklin D. Roosevelt. (President Roosevelt died at his retreat in Warm Springs, Georgia, in the early afternoon (Eastern War Time) of April 12, 1945. On the western side of the International Date line, where we were, it was April 13 when he died. So less than 24 hours after his passing all military units in every theater had learned of the Nation's great loss and, as in our case, had lowered the Colors to half mast. Actually word of his death was spread over the radio, both civilian short wave, and military frequencies during the late night watches and in our case it was late April 13 and early April 14. As the log indicates, we were in the midst of the morning channel sweep "Charlie" when the Colors were lowered to half mast. Our sweep continued until completed, and all military activity continued unabated during this time in all theaters. Tokyo Rose, the infamous American defector, who was the spokesperson for the Japanese to American military personnel could be heard in the Okinawa area by anyone who wanted to listen. The log doesn't mention it, of course, but she predicted that The President's death would result in the failure of the war effort and that the US would now sue for peace. Her broadcasts were always followed by the playing of the Japanese national anthem by a symphony orchestra. It was an eerie piece of music. One of the bridge personnel said, "That music gives me the creeps").

0850 - All sweep gear aboard; returning to anchorage.

0925 - Anchored in Kerama Retto anchorage.

1100 - Anchor dragging. Preparing to get under way.

1105 - Underway to shift berths.

1120 - Anchored with 45 fathoms of chain. (Anchoring and staying anchored continued to be a problem. So much of the bottom in Kerama Retto was just rock).

1757 - Underway for A/S Station #1.

1840 - On station.

April 15, 1945

0000 - Patrolling as before on A/S Station #1 on courses 090° True and 270° True.

0625 - Streamed sweep gear; beginning sweep "Able".

0819 - All sweep gear aboard; proceeding to anchorage.

0950 - Moored starboard side to DM 18.

1321 - Lt.jg Eggleston and mine disposal crew came aboard.

1322 - Underway for mine disposal mission.

1405 - Anchored off north shore of Zamami Jima.

1415 - Mine disposal party left ship.

1455 - Mine disposal party returned to ship reporting the presence of Japanese soldiers ashore; mine was left untouched.

1502 - Anchor's aweigh; underway for next mine.

1555 - Anchored off east coast of Tokashiki.

1601 - Mine disposal party left ship to dispose of mine on beach.

1728 - Mine disposal party returned after disposing of mine.

1743 - Underway returning to anchorage.

1823 - Moored starboard side to DM 18 to transfer mine disposal party.
1826 - Underway for A/S Patrol #1.
1852 - On station steering courses 090° True and 270° True.
1923 - Flash Red; sounded GQ.
1944 - Secured from GQ.

April 16, 1945

0000 - Patrolling as before on A/S Station #1, Kerama Retto on courses 090° True and 270° True.
0556 - Relieved on screen by SC 686. (The SC, short for Subchaser or Submarine Chaser, was one of the smaller commissioned ships in the US Navy in WWII. Built of wood, they were affectionately referred to as the "splinter fleet". They were excellent screening vessels, mine disposal ships and because of their shallow draft excellent for close to shore control ships for invasions. The SC 686 displaced 98 tons, was 110'10" long, 17' beam, draft 6'6" and speed of 20 knots. Her armament consisted of 1 3"/50, 2x2 50 cal. mg. Her complement was 2 officers and 20 enlisted. Her engines were diesel and she had twin screws. The 686, like all of her sisters, went everywhere the rest of the Navy went). *(See End Note No.80)*.
0620 - Gear streamed. Commencing channel sweep.
0820 - Recovered port gear; continuing harbor sweep with starboard gear.
0849 - Cut anchor cable of LCI 643. (This of course was not intended. A group of LCI's with their bows nudging the shore line of Tokashiki and held there by their bow anchors had their stern anchors out beyond the edge of the channel. The 643's anchor was apparently farther out into the channel than it should have been and 183's sweep cable cut it and in a sense set it adrift, except that the bow anchor was still intact. Her stern swung toward the shore but she was so close to the LCI's on either side that all that happened was banging into them. No great harm was done. The LCI set another anchor in place and all was secure. The LCI was a landing craft for infantry, one of the many amphibious ships for landing troops in an invasion).
0900 - Fouled sweep wire in our own screw. Anchored to free cable.
0930 - Screw cleared; bringing in anchor.
1006 - All gear aboard; returning to anchorage.
1107 - Moored starboard side to YMS 342.
1811 - Underway for A/S Station #1. On station steering courses 090° True and 270° True.
2325 - Challenged ship standing into harbor.

April 17, 1945

0000 - Patrolling as before A/S Station #1.
0533 - Proceeding to harbor entrance to commence channel sweep.
0610 - Gear streamed; beginning sweep.
0755 - Recovered port sweep gear; continuing to sweep harbor with starboard gear.
0915 - All gear aboard; returning to anchorage.
0937 - Moored starboard side to YMS 243 in nest with DM 18 and PGM 20.
1105 - Completed taking 500 gallons of fresh water from DM 18.
1800 - Underway for A/S Station #5. Anchored on station.
1845 - Set security watch; all men on watch armed with rifles. (It was on an early evening like this one that a very interesting and funny event took place. Here again the log does not mention it but some of the crew witnessed it. Ensign Davis remembers, " 183 was anchored at the southern entrance of the nets, which was located near the southern tip of Tokashiki. The net tender was between 183 and the island in such a position as to quickly open or close the net

entrance as required. Lying offshore of the island, but inside the net was a huge rock. In the twilight it appeared to be twice as long as a football field and about 100 yards wide. It rose out of the water for perhaps 100 feet. In the near darkness it looked to us like another ship only much bigger than either the 183 or the net tender. It must have looked like that to the pilot of an aircraft flying over this area. We had been anchored for a short time and I was on the fantail enjoying the quiet and the beauty of the last glow of sunlight from the sun already below the horizon. In the lower latitudes there is very little time between the setting sun and the onset of night. Several of us noted the sound of an airplane engine, and as we followed its source which seemed to be coming toward us, we could make out the dark smudge with wings. It flew over us and over the net tender and the big rock described above. As it turned westward and away from us, somebody laughed and said that that pilot must be crazy, to be flying around slowly like that, for someone might shoot at him. As he passed over us he was close enough for the blue flame from his exhaust to be clearly visible. He went on to the west and the sound of his engine was almost gone when he comes back again. This time he is a little faster and a little higher. He passed to the south of us and over the net tender then over the big rock on which he drops a bomb. It must have been a large one, maybe 500 pounds, for the explosion was loud and the flash of light was like a large fireball. We were transfixed. It wasn't one of our planes but a Jap, but unlike his brothers, he didn't crash into the "USS rock", just dropped his bomb and hightailed it to the west. Within seconds after the explosion tracers from anti-aircraft guns from all over the southern part of the anchorage ripped into the twilight, but it was too late. He was gone. There was no doubt in our minds that the pilot thought there were three ships 'down there' and he wisely dropped his bomb on the largest of the three - the rock").

2218 - Flash Red; sounded GQ.
2305 - Secured from GQ.

April 18, 1945

0000 - Anchored in vicinity of southern net opening at A/S Station #5, Kerama Retto.
0328 - Anchor dragging; underway to shift berth.
0350 - Re-anchored in same vicinity.
0557 - Anchor's aweigh; underway for channel sweep.
0601 - Anchor brought aboard with stock broken from dragging during the night. (The stock on an anchor, like the Navy used, was a length of steel bar. The length of the stock varied, depending on the size of the anchor. At the mid-point of the stock it is fastened to the top of the shank just below a steel ring to which the anchor chain is shackled. The stock, extending on both sides of the shank, is parallel to the sea floor when the anchor is on the bottom. It keeps the flukes, which actually dig into the sea floor to hold the ship, from turning over so they, the flukes, can't dig into the bottom. Needless to say, when the bottom is rocky, the flukes cannot dig in even though the stock keeps them pointed downward ready to dig in when a proper bottom is found. When the stock is missing or half of it is broken off, as was the case above, the anchor can rarely hold the ship even when the bottom is good. A strain on the anchor would usually cause the flukes to turn over, losing their hold and the ship would drag anchor and drift. The damage to the stock was repaired by welders on a repair ship and now the anchor was as good as new. In all probability, one end of the stock was caught in a rock crevasse or crack and the strain on the anchor caused the stock to break off).
0620 - Gear streamed; commencing channel sweep.
0848 - All gear aboard; returning to anchorage.
1035 - Moored starboard side to USS Terror for sound gear repairs.

1100 - Completed taking aboard 1000 gallons of fresh water and 1200 gallons of fuel.
1545 - Routine watch; no remarks.
1927 - Flash red; sounded GQ.
1950 - Secured from GQ.

April 19, 1945

0000 - Moored as before to USS Terror. Checking lines regularly.
0030 - Lines broke loose from USS Terror. Adrift in the anchorage
0040 - Anchored off port quarter of USS Terror with 60 fathoms of chain.
0735 - Underway to USS Terror.
0807 - Moored starboard side to Terror.
0840 - Underway to anchor.
0848 - Anchored in vicinity of USS Terror with 60 fathoms of chain.
1757 - Underway for A/S station #5.
1823 - Anchored on station.
2140 - Sighted flashing white light on Aware Saki, a nearby island and reported same to CTG 51.15.3 (Commander Task Group).

April 20, 1945

0000 - Anchored as before on A/S Station #5 Kerama Retto. 0610 - Secured sonar and armed watch.
0812 - Underway for CM 5 (USS Terror).
0817 - Anchored in vicinity of CM 5.
1745 - Underway, proceeding alongside AOG 10 to take on fuel. (The AOG 10, USS Nemasket, was a Patapsco class Gasoline Tanker displacing 4,130 tons, 311' long, beam 49', draft 14'6", speed 15.5 knots (max); 8.8 (econ). She was armed with 4 3"/50 DP and 12 20 mm guns. She had a complement of 124 and was powered by diesel electric engines, twin screws and had 3,300 hp. She obviously carried diesel fuel also). *(See End Note No.81)*.
1827 - Completed taking on 2140 gallons of fuel.
1829 - Underway to transport area "Dog", Okinawa. ("Dog" was the area on the western side of the big island of Okinawa where transports anchored to unload their cargoes directly on the island and the soldiers and marines fighting the Japanese. However, while the log does not say why 183 was ordered to go to "Dog" about 30 minutes later the order was changed).
1853 - C/C to 314° True; returning to Northwest anchorage on radio orders.
1945 - Anchored in Northwest Anchorage.
1947 - Ship swinging close to LCI 651. Bringing in anchor.
2005 - Fouled our anchor in anchor cable of LCI 651. Anchor clear; preparing to re-anchor.
2020 - Anchored in Northwest Anchorage, Kerama Retto.
2203 - Flash Red; sounded GQ.
2224 - Secured from GQ.

April 21, 1945

0000 - Anchored as before in Northwest Anchorage, Kerama Retto.
0845 - Underway to DM 18 (USS Breese) in Southern Anchorage.
0945 - Moored starboard side to DM 18.
1036 - Underway to AV 10 to pick up mail. (AV 10, USS Chandeleur, was an aircraft tender. AV 10 was a Maritime Commission C3-S-B1 type ship. It was the home base for the PBMs, with mechanics and spare parts to keep them flying. The AVs were not a specific class but consisted

of many different hull types converted for sea-plane tender work. *(See End Note No.82)*. It was anchored near the buoy marking the landing and take-off area in Kerama Retto reserved for the Martin Mariners (PBM two engine flying boats) which were used primarily as night fighters. They also did scouting and transport of personnel and small cargo such as mail. A plane load of mail had probably come in on a plane from Guam and there was a sack for 183.)

1315 - Mail Orderly returned to ship; proceeding to Northwest Anchorage. (One of the delights for a sailor after being on his own vessel for weeks at a time is the opportunity to get off whenever possible for however short a time it might be. Many of the crew of 183 had been on the ship for several months without setting foot on land. Even the chance to go aboard another ship was coveted. The skipper or the Chief Boatswain could use designation as mail orderly as a reward for particularly good work performance by a crewman. The Mail Orderly was required to wear a clean work shirt (dungaree or denim) and wear a clean white hat. Of course, he carried the "badge" of his responsibility, the leather mail pouch. Most of the time the pouch was only a badge of responsibility, for the actual mail, accumulated over many weeks might fill several canvas mail bags).

1415 - Moored portside to DMS 13 in Northwest Anchorage to take on water. (DMS 13, USS Hopkins was converted from a Clemson Class Destroyer to a high-speed mine sweeper in the summer of 1940 and thus gave up her old designation and number DD-249. She had a distinguished career since launching as DD in 1921. This was another of the WW I type "4 pipers" (the U.S. transferred 50 of them to Britain as Lend-Lease in 1939-40). Hopkins gave up one stack when converted to high-speed minesweeper. She had already participated in a number of Pacific actions and invasions before the Okinawa campaign and had several Japanese planes to her credit. *(See End Note No.83)*. Ens. Davis remembers that while Hopkins was a good ship, 183 received the worse tasting water from her than from any other source during the war. The fresh water tanks on 183 were practically bone dry. Several other possible sources were contacted, but to no avail. Since Hopkins was nearby we blinked over to her with a request for several hundred gallons of fresh water. They gave us an "affirmative" and permission to come alongside. We did and took on 800 gallons. With profuse expressions of appreciation we got under way and headed for our anchorage. We had hardly gotten any way on when the engineering officer called the skipper and told him the water tasted awfully funny. Captain Klein tasted it and agreed. We blinked back to the Hopkins asking if the water was safe, that it tasted very odd. The reply, by blinker, was instantaneous. It was as if they were just waiting for our question, which they knew was coming. "Yes, it does taste funny, but it is safe. We had the inside of our fresh water tanks painted recently and the paint odor lingers on in the water. If you can drink it, do so, it won't do more than gag you. After all "beggars can't be choosers"." The water was used as quickly as possible, for everything possible, without wasting it. Very little was used for drinking).

1515 - Completed taking on 800 gallons of fresh water.
1542 - Underway to anchor.
1549 - Anchored in Northwest Anchorage.
1725 - Underway to Southern Anchorage.
1750 - Proceeding out Southern Entrance to Patrol Station Prep #3 at southern end of Kerama Retto.
1805 - On station steering courses 102° True and 282° True.

April 22, 1945

0000 - Patrolling as before on Prep #3 station.
0602 - Proceeding to southern net entrance to commence channel sweep.

Figure 40 - "Kamikaze" Suicide Plane crashes into the side of USS Pinkney, a close support hospital ship. This photo has appeared in many publications. U.S Navy Phtograph

0610 - Began streaming gear.
0622 - Gear streamed; commencing sweep.
0843 - Recovered gear; proceeding to anchorage.
0928 - Moored port side to YMS 271. 1710 - Underway for station Prep #3.
1735 - On station steering courses 102° True and 282° True.
1750 - Flash Red; sounded GQ.
1758 - Secured from GQ.
1858 - Flash Red; sounded GQ.
1925 - Secured from GQ. (The alert for imminent air attack was broadcast over the various radio frequencies the various ships in the area guarded 24 hours a day. There were two sources for these broadcasts, one was the SOP (Senior Officer Present) for the Okinawa area and his call was "Lionheart" and the other was Commander Minecraft in the Kerama Retto area whose radio call was "Wiseman". The warnings would sound something like this: "This is "Wiseman" (or "Lionheart") flash red, flash red. All ships in area go to general quarters. Kamikazes sighted (and he would give reported location) near Ie Shima headed south. I say again, this is "Wiseman", flash red, flash red. All ships go to general quarters." Frequently the kamikaze would be splashed by the ship or US Navy Combat Air Patrol reporting its presence. When this happened, the time spent at GQ was short. If there were several planes or one got through to the anchorage, the ships stayed at GQ and fired their AA guns at the plane if it could be done without endangering other ships. This was a constant danger. Usually called "friendly fire", with some frequency our own ships hit each other due to mechanical failure, but most often to human error. Sometimes when a small ship was surrounded by many others the danger of hitting your own neighbor was great. Often there was no clear shot at a kamikaze, but an enthusiastic gunner on 20mm or 50/cal would take one anyway and sometimes hit another US ship. 183 personnel learned very quickly not to even try to shoot unless we were on the fringe of, or outside of, the anchorage. Sandwiched in among so many others was just too risky. We came close to receiving "friendly fire" on a number of occasions. When the danger of an air attack was over, "Lionheart" or "Wiseman" would broadcast "Flash green, flash green, all ships secure from general quarters." Quite often, as was the case on April 22, ships would secure from GQ only to be called to GQ again a short time later).

Figure 41 - Making smoke to cover the anchorage in Kerama Retto. This was almost a nightly occurrence.

April 23, 1945

0000 - Patrolling as before on A/S Station Prep #3 on course 102° True and 282° True at southern end of Kerama Retto.

0620 - Streamed sweep gear; commenced southern channel sweep. (We streamed gear on port and starboard sides for the sweep of the channel from several miles south of the net entrance. When the net entrance was reached the port gear was recovered and the starboard gear remained streamed for the sweep of the channel in the anchorage. This was a slow and difficult process as other ships were reluctant to move out of the way and sometimes our paravane (otter) or float (pig) would become fouled in anchor chains or cables).

0755 - Recovered port gear; continuing sweep of harbor with starboard gear.

0826 - Proceeding to anchorage to make sweep "How" with starboard gear.

1003 - All gear recovered; proceeding to CM 9 (USS Monadnock).

1055 - Moored port side to CM 9.

1350 - Underway proceeding to anchorage.

1515 - Anchored in Kerama Retto anchorage.

1747 - Underway for A/S #7.

1830 - Relieved SC 1004 on station. (SC 1004 was one of a large number of wooden hull Submarine Chasers. They were commissioned ships, but had no names, only numbers. SC 1004 displaced 95 tons; length 110' 10 "; beam 17', draft 6'6"; speed 20 knots; armament 1 40mm; complement varied from 20 to 40 men; diesel engines, twin screws. The SC was an excellent anti-submarine vessel, support vessel for minesweepers and general utility. They went everywhere in the various war zones). *(See End Note No.84)*.

April 24, 1945

0000 - Continued patrol on A/S #7.

0600 - C/C to 000° True; proceeding to net entrance to begin channel sweep.

0828 - All gear recovered; proceeding to anchorage.

0918 - Anchored in Kerama Retto harbor.

1758 - Underway for A/S Station #5.

1815 - Anchored on A/S Station #5.

1900 - Set armed security watch. 2120 - Anchor dragging; beginning to weigh anchor.

2135 - Underway to re-anchor. 2150 - Anchored in same vicinity.

April 25, 1945

0000 - Anchored as before on A/S [anti-submarine] Station #5.

0550 - Underway for assigned channel sweep.
0618 - All gear streamed, commencing sweep.
0832 - All gear recovered; returning to anchorage.
0906 - Moored starboard side to YMS 243 (could be 293 - number illegible as log is written in longhand).
1430 - Took aboard sack of mail for YMS 408.
1756 - Underway for patrol station A/S Prep #2.
1834 - Came close aboard YMS 408 and delivered mail.
1945 - on station.

April 26, 1945

0000 - Patrolling on A/S Station Prep #2 (The Ogan Patrol) at Northern Entrance to Kerama Retto.
0555 - Relieved on station by PCS 1379; proceeding to entrance to commence sweep.
0618 - All gear streamed; commencing channel sweep.
0753 - Recovered all port gear; continuing to sweep harbor with starboard gear.
0924 - All gear recovered; returning to anchorage.
0944 - Moored port side to IX 113 (USS Camel) to take on fuel.
1020 - Completed taking on 1250 gallons of fuel.
1026 - Underway to DM 18 (USS Breese).
1052 - Moored starboard side to DM 18.
1257 - Underway to anchor.
1307 - Anchored in Kerama Retto harbor.
1757 - Underway to A/S station Prep #2.
1822 - On station. (Ogan Patrol)

April 27, 1945

0000 - Patrolling as before on A/S Station Prep #3.
0600 - Relieved on station by PCS 1379. (The PCS -- Submarine Chaser Sweepers seem to have the same hull dimensions as the YMS but no mine sweeping capability. It was armed with guns, rockets and depth charges. They were strictly an anti-submarine, escort type vessel). *(See End Note No.85)*.
0611 - Streamed sweep gear; commencing sweep of channel.
0727 - Recovered all port gear, leaving starboard gear to sweep anchorage.
0855 - all gear recovered; returning to anchorage.
0945 - Moored starboard side to CM 5 (USS Terror) to take on fresh water.
1048 - Completed watering; underway to anchor.
1105 - Anchored in small craft anchorage.
1752 - Underway for A/S Station #7.
1820 - On station.

April 28, 1945

0100 - Flash Red; sounded GQ.
0118 - Secured from GQ.
0605 to 0831 conducted routine channel sweep.
0917 - Moored port side to DM 18 (USS Breese).
1404 - Began showing educational movie in galley.
1610 - Completed movie in galley.

1750 - Underway to A/S Station Prep #3 at Southern Entrance to Kerama Retto.

1808 - On station.

1928 - Sighted enemy suicide plane 1500 yards off our starboard bow heading approximately 000° True, elevation 15 feet; opened fire with 30 cal., 50 cal. and 20mm guns.

1930 - Sounded GQ. (Walter Weltzien, Lt.jg and Navigator had the Conn as this was his regular watch. He was on the flying bridge and remembers while talking with Smitty (Signalman 1/c, C.P Smith) who was signalman of the watch, Smitty called to him from the other side of the bridge, "Mr. Weltzien, look at that plane." He pointed out over the water to a plane about ten feet off the surface heading right for us. "Can I shoot it?" I told him yes and hollered down to the bridge to sound GQ. Smitty's GQ station was right at that 50 caliber machine gun that was already firing, but shooting 50 caliber bullets at a Kamikaze plane is like throwing sand grains at an elephant. The plane came right at us, pulled up and over and dove on a troop transport in the harbor. I think we were the only ship in the harbor to get off a shot.") Ensign Davis also vividly remembers the incident. He recalls, "I was in the wardroom drinking coffee, when I heard several of the machine guns start firing. I could tell they were shooting at something on the starboard side of the ship and since I was by the port side wardroom hatch opening to the deck I went out to go to my GQ station on the fantail as I knew we would be called to GQ when I heard the shooting. I had just gotten on deck when I heard the sound of the plane's engine very close by and as I looked up it was diving back to water level, after just clearing our mast. It was heading due north into the harbor. Just seconds later it pulled up to about 50 feet, banked to the left and dove into the side of a large transport. About the time the fire from the exploding plane appeared, other ships in the anchorage began to shoot. I could see their tracers, but it was too late. We learned later that the plane hit the side of the steel hull of the ship, but did not penetrate it. However, the bomb the plane was carrying did penetrate the hull, exploding inside the galley killing 300 people. The ship was actually an Evacuation Transport, APH 2, USS Pinkney, a type of hospital ship which was designed to remain close to the place where troops were invading, fighting and being wounded USS Pinkney was a Maritime Commission C2-S1-A1 type; it was modified for tropic service, had C3 turbine machinery and a cruiser stern. Fully loaded it displaced 11,000 tons. Length 450' 2", beam 62', max draft 25'9"; 8,500 hp with a top speed of 16.5 knots. The Pinkney was commissioned in 1942. She was anchored near USS Terror when hit by the Kamikaze. *(See End Note No.86)*. She was not painted white, did not have a red cross on it, (probably would have made no difference) but was designed to blend in with the other vessels in its surroundings. Some Naval Photographer, probably on a ship nearer the harbor than we were got a picture of the explosion and the tracers. (Small Craft were not allowed to have cameras). This picture has appeared in many books and articles about the Okinawa campaign. I saw the same event. If I had had a camera I could have gotten the same picture. I suppose that the Japanese suicide pilot was planning to hit us, until he got closer and saw larger prey beyond us. He hopped over us and went for the anchorage. People on small craft didn't have it as good as larger vessels, but their small size was often protection from the Kamikaze if there were larger vessels in the area).

2111 - Secured from GQ.

2307 - Flash Red; sounded GQ.

2329 - Secured from GQ.

April 29, 1945

0000 to 0925 - Routine Patrol at A/S Station Prep #3; routine sweep of channel and anchorage and return to anchorage.

1044 - Moored port side to DM 18 (USS Breese). 1334 - Underway to anchor.
1341 - Anchored in Kerama Retto harbor.
1755 - Underway to A/S Station Prep #2.
1830 - Came close aboard YMS 408 and delivered mail.
1837 - Relieved SC 1012 on station.
1858 - Flash Red; sounded GQ.
1905 - Secured from GQ.
2150 - Flash Red; sounded GQ.
2225 - Secured from GQ.

April 30, 1945

0000 to 0929 - Routine Patrol at A/S Station Prep #2; relieved by SC 1012; conducted routine sweep of channel and anchorage and return to anchorage.
1022 - Moored port side to DM 18.
1305 - Movie party left ship for DM 18.
1408 - Movie party returned.
1410 - Underway to anchor.
1416 - Anchored in small craft anchorage.
1759 - Underway for A/S Station Prep #2.
1841 - Relieved SC 1012 on station. (These anti-submarine patrols and the routine sweeps seem in retrospect to be just repetitive "bla" duty. Far from that they were very necessary, as Japplanes in a Kamikaze attack could have one drop a few mines while the others diverted our attention. There was always the possibility that an enemy sub might be lurking near the channel waiting for a large ship. The sonar patrols were designed to detect their presence).

May 1, 1945

0000 to 0702 - Routine Patrol at A/S Station Prep #2 at Northern Entrance (Ogan Patrol); conducted routine sweep of channel and returned to anchorage.
0806 - Moored starboard side to AOG 10 to take on fuel.
0836 - Completed taking on 1370 gallons of fuel.
0840 - Underway to anchor.
1016 - Anchored in Kerama Retto. (I83 learned at this time that USS Terror had been hit by a Kamikaze at about 0400 this morning. We were on patrol outside the anchorage and while we were aware of activity in the area, there was activity every night, we did not get any specific information until mid-morning. The Kamikaze darted through a hole in the smoke screen off the port side of Terror and banked sharply around the stern and came in so rapidly only one of Terror's guns could open fire. As the plane crashed into the superstructure of the ship one of its bombs exploded, the other penetrated the main deck before exploding. The plane's engine tore through bulkheads before landing in the wardroom. The fire which resulted was put out in about two hours. The magazines were flooded preventing possible explosions there. Casualties included 41 dead, 7 missing and 123 wounded. Among the dead was Captain Clark, Admiral Sharp's chief of staff. Sharp was Commander, Minecraft Pacific Fleet. USS Terror had to return to the west coast for repairs. *(See End Note No.87)* Admiral Sharp moved his flag and the rest of his staff to WAGC-31, USS Bibb, a Coast Guard Cutter now a part of the Navy for the duration of the war. The Bibb, launched in 1937, displaced 2,750 tons and was 327' long. Her beam was 41', draft 15', speed 20 knots; range 8,000 miles at 12 knots; armament 2 5"/38, 6x2 40mm,

4 20mm. Her complement was 24 officers, 2 warrants, 226 enlisted. She had geared turbines, twin screws and 6,200 hp). *(See End Note No.88)*.

1753 - (Still May 1, 1945) Underway for A/S Station Prep #2.

1900 - On station.

2031 - Sideswiped by AM 232 while on Station Prep #2 on course 090° True.

2042 - Investigation revealed no serious damage.

2045 - AM 232 came close aboard to obtain information. (The three most feared events on a ship at sea in descending order are; 1. Uncontrollable fire; 2. Sinking from whatever cause; and 3. Collision with another ship which can cause fire and/or sinking. The incident with the AM 232 was not really a collision. The OD of 183, sensing that the AM was not alert to what was impending and changing his course (the AM's course) ordered the engines of 183 full astern, sounding the ship's horn with seven short blasts (collision warning) and using the helm to back away from but keep the bow of the ship toward the AM. offering the smallest target. This strategy worked, for the two ships "sideswiped" each other just aft of the bow of each ship, 183 starboard side, and AM starboard side. By the time they hit each other 183 was either dead in the water or actually backing away. It was an uneven match as the AM is made of steel plate and the YMS is wood. The AM only lost some paint. 183 cracked the upper part of frame no. 2 just below the forecastle deck flair. After assurance that each ship had suffered only minor or no damage, they backed away and resumed the patrol. There were two Anti-Submarine patrol stations at each end of the anchorage of Kerama Retto. One was a mile or so north of the net entrance and the second was four or five miles north of the net entrance. The opposite arrangement adhered at the southern entrance. Thus there were two ships on patrol on the same courses (090° True and 270° True) but their tracks were several miles apart. The surface search radar of each ship could tell where the other was at all times, how close they were to each other and in which direction each was traveling. On this night 183 had the outermost patrol and the AM 232 the inner patrol. Wind and current (tides) could cause a ship to be set toward or away from the nets and thus each other. What apparently had happened was that the current was moving the ships away from the nets and the northern entrance of the anchorage. With every reversal of course each of the ships was farther away from the nets, but since 183 was compensating for the set of the current, she was staying at the assigned distance from the nets. However, because the AM was not making a slight course change to keep their track the proper distance from the nets, they were getting closer and closer to the track of 183. The OD of 183 tried unsuccessfully to get the attention of the AM and had to take the drastic measures described above. (It was thought that the OD of the AM was not on the bridge for a period of time and the enlisted personnel were reluctant to take action on their own. By the time the OD of the AM returned to his post emergency measures were needed. Of course, the AM never admitted this and since the damage was very slight, no action was taken. 183 had some naval carpenters work on the cracked rib on several occasions, but there was always a slight leak when in heavy seas). (AM 232, USS Execute, was a 184' 6" Admirable Class Minesweeper, displacing 625 tons, beam of 33", draft of 10', Speed 15 knots, complement of 104, main armament 1 3"/50, diesel electric engines, twin screws, 1,800 hp. In size, weight, etc. 183 was no match for the AM). *(See End Note No.89)*.

Walter Weltzien remembers that night vividly. He writes, "John Davis, Stan Klein, the skipper and I were sitting in the wardroom about ready to turn in when we heard the seven blasts of the 183's horn along with the vibrations and noise of the main engines going in reverse at full speed. Stan shot out of the starboard hatch to the deck and to the bridge as if he had been shot out of a cannon. Stan had just cleared the hatch when we heard and felt a huge crunching along our starboard side and our ship listed to port. John and I rushed to the starboard hatch and he opened it and there was an AM we could reach out and touch. He said, very calmly, "Think we better go out the other side." The damage was not great but we needed some carpenters to repair our starboard bow. We had no carpenters aboard so we had to borrow a couple from a repair ship in the harbor. The only thing I remember about them is they both became seasick bobbing around on the bow while the ship was still at anchor. Another time we were patrolling along the north shore of Kerama Retto when someone spotted some figures moving on the shore. These islands were supposed to be free of Japanese. We put over an exploratory force armed with rifles to investigate. They encountered several Japanese, one of whom came out of a cave and tried to talk, but his lower jaw trembled so much no one could understand him. Our party returned to the ship without firing a shot and we reported the presence of Japanese on the island, and the Army took it from there.".

May 2, 1945

0000 to 0746 - Routine Patrol on A/S Station Prep #2; relieved by SC 1066; conducted routine channel sweep and returned to anchorage.

0842 - Moored port side to CM 9 (USS Monadnock).

0930 - Completed taking on 1600 gallons of fresh water.

1003 - Underway to go alongside PGM 10.

1019 - Moored port side to PGM 10 to transfer stores (The provision ship for small craft had left commissary stores, etc. for 183 on PGM 10. This is a good time to report on food, galley and ship's cooks, for the army is not alone in traveling on its stomach. A small craft like the YMS was not designed to spend more than a few days away from a shore base where fuel, water, food etc. could be replenished. In the Pacific our "shore base" was any ship which could give us food from their own supplies or from a transport of some kind which carried food stuffs of various sorts. Some of these required refrigeration, usually below freezing. Thus the YMS, with scarcely any freezer space, missed out on frozen food in an amount larger than could be eaten in one or two days. Consequently we ate mostly canned foods and bread made from "scratch" by the cook. Much of our food, especially the flour and fresh meat came from Australia or New Zealand. The flour was always full of weevils, and who knows what other varmints lived and died in those 100 pounds bags. We took the flour aboard and delivered it to the frustrated cook who declared that we might as well give it the "deep six" because no one would eat his bread. That was mostly true, for his loaves, golden brown and smelling pretty good were left on the galley table. Occasionally a brave soul dowsed a piece of bread with enough ketchup to be able to chew and swallow it. The cook asked for an audience with the captain and requested a transfer. The skipper assured the cook that he was doing the best he could with what he had and that when the crew got hungry enough they would eat cook's bread. This didn't help, and indeed, nothing did until a case of raisins was delivered on board. That night, fresh golden brown loaves were placed on the galley tables. Almost absentmindedly one sailor sliced off a piece, took a bite, chewed a few times and a smile crossed his face and he exclaimed out loud, "Say cook, this is the best raisin bread I've ever eaten. It sure beats that old stuff made from Australian flour." With that others tried it and soon the loaves were gone. When the watches changed, the hungry sailors besieged the galley wanting some of that new raisin bread. The cook promised to bake more loaves hereafter, and he kept his own counsel and the promise.

Most of the crew never knew that the chewy raisin masked the crunch and taste of the weevils. The same adulterated flour kept coming aboard and the cook's raisin bread was always in demand. Unfortunately there was no miraculous "cure" for the mutton. It came in sides (two sides made a whole sheep) weighing about fifty or sixty pounds. They had been in cold storage for who knows how long and when they came aboard the first time the gagging odor was evident, but everyone knew that cook could do wonders with it. He tried boiling, baking, frying, as a fricassee or smothered in onions, etc. But nothing could kill that smell and horrible taste. A fifty gallon drum of mint jelly was not enough to make it palatable. After that first try the routine was to deep six the side of mutton. It came aboard on the port side, with the other stores. The stores were placed on deck to be removed to the galley immediately. The side of mutton crossed over the deck to the starboard side and was sent to its watery grave. We pled with the provision ship's supply officer to let us leave it with him for someone else's use. We would even try to get it to the beleaguered troops ashore, but to no avail. It was a part of the plan for a ship our size and we had to take it. "Confidentially," he whispered to our commissary officer, "what you do with it after you sign for it is your business. If you can't eat it give it the deep six." That's exactly what we did. However, after the anchorage began to stink up with the rotting carcasses of sheep someone pulled some rank (we were told) and no ship was forced to accept mutton in its ration allotment. We wondered, but no one asked what they did with mutton after that. Some said that it made great bait for shark fishing, but we never did have time during this period to do any shark fishing. It might be of interest, at this point to mention the "egg bonanza".

Ensign Davis remembers that some large ship or other, had to empty its huge refrigerator due to a malfunction and any small craft was invited to come along side and get all the eggs they wanted. We rarely had fresh (cold storage) eggs, maybe a case on occasion, but we couldn't keep more than one in our refrigerator. This time we asked for and received 12 cases (12 dozen to a case times 12 = 144 dozen eggs.) The cases were lashed to the outside of the galley and the cook started a marathon of egg cuisine. He boiled, fried, scrambled them, made custard pies, cakes etc. and even took orders for special egg dishes that many had never heard of before. 144 dozen eggs is a lot of eggs. We couldn't eat them fast enough to catch up with the slow but inexorable spoilage factor. The last two cases were boiled and several cases of mustard, mayonnaise and ketchup were consumed to kill the taste of mostly rotten boiled eggs. "This experience did not," Ens. Davis recalls, "ruin our taste for eggs". Once in a while we managed to get a few dozen and cook fixed them and we ate them with appreciation. As far as I know we never did get any canned Australian butter, which I am told would not even melt in a hot frying pan).

1029 - Underway to anchor.
1044 - Anchored in Kerama Retto harbor.
1523 to 1618 - Paymaster came aboard to pay officers and crew and then left ship.
1756 - Underway to A/S Station Prep #2.
1856 - Relieved SC 1066 on station.

May 3, 1945

0000 to 0815 - Routine patrol and channel sweep and return to anchorage.
0903 - Anchored in Kerama Retto harbor.
1402 - Flash Red; sounded GQ.
1406 - Secured from GQ. (On a typical afternoon when there were a few hours to catch up on some sleep, do some personal chores, write a letter, do some laundry or whatever, for some of the crew it was a time for reflection, prayer and Bible study. The scenes of the night before, or the earlier morning hours when destroyers from the picket line entered the anchorage with their cargoes of dead and wounded, holes blown through their hulls, their bridges missing, their forecastles lined with blanket covered crewmen lined up in neat rows, were enough to give

one pause. It seemed that this scene was repeated almost everyday. It is said that there are no atheists in a fox hole. Well, there are none or few on a naval vessel either when it is in a war zone or anywhere when the weather turns sour. On a typical day like today a goodly number of 183 personnel gathered on the fantail, found a seat on the winch or the depth charges in their racks. Viewed from a distance no voices could be heard but the general scene spoke loudly of prayer and the reading of Psalms. The pages of the Bibles were turned in unison by the congregation to find the words of solace and assurance. Each man had a Bible, some were large, some were GI issues of the New Testament and Psalms. The faces of these men reflected their sense of utter helplessness. The fact that more of the crew were not gathered there didn't mean that those not present didn't share the fear and dread of another Kamikaze attack or the stupidity of a friendly fire incident. Except for one or two of the more hard bitten the whole complement shared something of the deep need these fantail petitioners exhibited. The fact that a few of these repentant people were often the tough talking, bully types was noted and forgiven, for we were all in the same "boat", and we would live and/or die together),

1751 - Underway for A/S Station Prep #2.
1839 - On station.

May 4, 1945

0000 to 0826 - Routine patrol and channel sweep and return to anchorage.

0945 - Flash Red; set condition II watch port section. (Since April 2, 183 and many other ships had been operating in the Kerama Retto area. A number of minecraft had been in the area since the middle of March. Almost daily Kamikazes would slip through the picket lines of destroyers and combat air patrols in the outlying areas and suddenly appear approaching the anchorage area where all of the big ship prizes were at anchor. This produced the "Flash Red" warnings of imminent attack and required all ships in the area to go to General Quarters. By early May, the crews of small craft were exhausted from lack of sleep. We had also learned that full GQ, manning the guns, depth charge racks, etc. was an exercise in futility while at anchor. We certainly weren't going to drop any depth charges and we were so sandwiched in by other ships, most of them much larger, that the chance of getting a shot at a Kamikaze was almost zero, plus there was a real risk that we might hit one of our own ships or be hit by one of them. Captain Klein and other skippers of small craft discussed this matter many times.. They decided that wearing out the men by going to General Quarters while at anchor was materially affecting the efficiency of the crews and produced no viable retaliatory threat to the enemy. Without any fanfare, 183, and other smallcraft decided to use only half the crew at GQ stations while in the anchorage. The halfsize sections would alternate (port and starboard) when GQ was sounded while at anchor. This materially boosted morale as well as the physical well being and efficiency of the crew. Of course, when at sea, on patrol, mine sweeping or any other underway activity outside the anchorage GQ was GQ and all battle stations were manned when it was sounded.

Ensign Davis remembers one incident relating to our effort to shoot at Kamikazes while in the middle of a hundred other ships at anchor. He says, "We were at GQ during midmorning, one day, while at anchor. The skipper warned all those manning guns to hold their fire until specifically ordered by himself (the CO was personally in phone connection with all areas of the ship) to fire. There was little or no chance that the smaller AA guns, the 20mm, 50/cal. or 30/cal could get a shot because the Kamikaze would have to be almost overhead for them to do so without shooting up our own ships. Friendly fire was always a real hazard. There was a fair chance that the 3" 50/cal "cannon" on the forecastle could get off a round if the suicider managed to survive the hail of fire that was being thrown at him by the ships on the perimeter of the anchorage. The gun crew of the 3" 50 was comprised of the pointer and trainer who, each, was sitting on a metal seat on each side of the base of the gun mount. The pointer elevated or depressed the barrel so that it was pointed at the target, and the trainer controlled the right or left movement. The two together kept the gun pointed at the target at all times. There were four other men plus the gunnery officer. One man was the fuse setter. He removed the shell - it was fixed ammunition - from the ready box, and set the fuse with a device at hand. By this time during the war a "so called" proximity fuse had been developed which did not have to be set, but was designed to explode when the projectile passed within a certain distance of the target. The fuse setter handed the shell to a handler near the gun, who in turn handed it to the loader. When the gun was ready to be loaded, the loader placed the nose of the projectile into the breech and with his right hand and arm slammed the whole shell into the breech which closed automatically. The gun was now ready to fire whenever the gunnery officer, on orders from the captain, gave the order to fire. The pointer and trainer each depressed the trigger on his double hand crank when he had the target in his sight. When both had the target in their cross hairs at the same time the gun would fire. A split second after firing the barrel recoiled and the breech opened automatically ejecting the empty shell case. The last man, called the hot shell man, who was well padded with asbestos gloves, hat and vest, caught the now superheated empty shell case and threw it over the side. If there was still a shot to be had the order was given to load and the process was repeated. On this morning," Ens. Davis continues, "the 'cannon' was manned and ready and the barrel was following the Kamikaze in its flight over the anchorage. The amount of AA fire at the plane was tremendous, but the plane kept coming, apparently not hit. A few seconds later the order was given to fire. Nothing happened. It was either a hangfire in which case the primer didn't have enough flame to ignite the powder in the shell and it was burning slowly, but could fire a few seconds later, or a misfire, in which case it was just a dud for some unknown reason. Our ammunition was "old" and this shell may have been damaged by moisture. In either case, regulations called for the elevation of the barrel to its highest point so that if the shell did fire it would go straight up. A few seconds passed before the frustrated gun crew realized what had happened and they watched the smoking and flaming Kamikaze begin to fall into the anchorage. Luckily, as we learned later, this one didn't hit a ship. After a wait of 30 minutes, the forecastle was cleared, the breech was opened ejecting the dud shell, and it was caught by the hot shell man who walked deliberately to the starboard rail and dropped it into the water. All were frustrated at our failure to fire at the enemy, but no one was hurt either. Incidentally, this was the last time we ever tried to fire the 'cannon'.")

1108 - Secured condition II watch; set condition III.
1750 - Underway for A'S Station Prep #2.
1830 - Relieved SC 1012 on station.
1926 - Flash Red; sounded GQ.
1952 - Secured from GQ. (The Ogan Patrol seemed to offer some sort of activity almost every time we had that patrol assignment. The log doesn't say much about what went on unless we were directly involved in firing our guns, which we never did at night as the suicide pilot could follow your tracers right down to your ship and crash into you. We heard that this had happened to a few other ships who fired through the smoke screen or out of the darkness at suicide planes. If we had dropped depth charges this would have been recorded, etc. It was on a night like this, on the Ogan Patrol, and we were at GQ. Ensign Davis, whose GQ station was on the fantail near the depth charges and who had a direct phone hookup with the bridge and the CO remembers that there were flashes of gunfire and explosions of what must have been bombs

dropped from Kamikazes off to the northwest of Ogan Rock. When the bridge talker's phone was open Davis could hear the excited chatter from several destroyers who were under attack by suicide planes. They were using their voice code names and we could have looked them up to see exactly which ships they were. While interesting, time did not allow for this and we were only "bystanders" anyway. Snatches of the conversations between these ships indicated that they were taking violent evasive action and firing all their guns at the attackers who were trying to bomb them before trying to crash their planes into the ships. Davis remembers one exchange between these ships that was really humorous while being deadly serious at the same time. "Barn Door, Barn Door, this is Sexmad, over". "Yea, Sexmad, this is Barn Door, over." "Yea, Barn Door, how about being a little more careful shooting so close to the water on your port side - uh, we're on your port beam and you're coming too close for comfort when you're shooting this way, uh -. Over". "Sexmad this is Barn Door, you must have us mixed up with Eight Ball, he's zig-zagging like crazy off our port bow and firing everything he has ammo for. He has a "kamicrazy" trying to get him from his port side. Uh - I'll see if I can raise him and tell him that you're on his port beam, uh - and to be more careful. Uh - out". Before Sexmad could try to get his call off to Eight Ball the following call in an absolutely ecstatic voice came over the speaker. "Barn Door, Barn Door, Sexmad, Sexmad, and any other of you poor guys in the area, we got that Japbastard who was trying to get us - uh this is Eight Ball, we got him, we got him - uh - splashed him as pretty as you please off our port bow. What a sight. - Uh - no more time for chit chat. That dead Jap's buddy is coming in for his turn. Wish us luck, this is Eight Ball, over and out." Our assignment was to patrol that stretch of water from Ogan Rock when it was bearing exactly 180° True from us and we were six miles away from it. At this point we changed course from 270° True to 090° True and headed back east to our turning point five or six miles northeast of Tokashiki Jima. We had our sonar going all the time and our surface search radar, and lookouts were watching for any thing on the surface or under it outside the northern entrance).

May 5, 1945

0000 to 0835 - Routine patrol and channel sweep and return to anchorage. At 0634 - DM 29 reported live Japanese pilot somewhere in water in our vicinity. A lookout was maintained for Japanese pilot while we continued our sweep. Did not locate him.

0900 - Anchored in Kerama Retto.

1744 - Underway for A/S Station Prep #2.

1830 - On station. Relieved SC 686. (DM-29 USS Henry A Wiley was a Robert H. Smith Class Minelayer,. Displacing 3,104 tons: length 376' 6", beam 40' 10", draft 14 '; speed 33 knots, armament 6 5"/38 DP, 2x4 49mm, 6 20mm, and 100+ mines; complement 363; geared turbine engines, twin screws, 60,000 shaft hp; she was commissioned in 1944. In addition to laying mines she was an excellent anti-aircraft ship. *(See End Note No.90)*.

May 6, 1945

0000 to 0809 Routine patrol and channel sweep and return to anchorage.

0545 - Relieved on station by SC 1012.

0836 - Moored port side to YMS 96.

0851 - Flash Red; sounded GQ.

1011 - Underway to anchor.

1129 - Anchored in Kerama Retto. (Undoubtedly, our Bible Study and Prayer group was once again on the fantail. The air raids, and the broken ships returning with their broken bodies to the anchorage seemed almost routine, but were never commonplace).
1632 - Underway to A/S Station #5.
1707 - Anchored on station. (Another night of pinging [sending sonar signals] across the net entrance and an armed watch on ship's deck. Suicide swimmers were still a threat).

May 7, 1945

0000 to 0831 - Routine patrol and channel sweep and return to anchorage.
0936 - Anchored in Kerama Retto harbor.
1300 - Captain's Mast held for one man. Offense, disrespect to an officer; failure to carry out orders; sentence - reduction in rate from 2/c to 3/c.
1753 - Underway for A/S Station Prep #4.
1836 - Relieved PC 800 on station.
2225 - Electric steering engine failed: switched to manual steering.
2330 - Found cause to be burned out fuse; replaced fuse; gear back in operation.

May 8, 1945

0000 to 0832 - Routine Patrol, relieved on station by PC 1179, channel sweep and return to anchorage.
0950 - Moored port side to AOG 10 to fuel.
1015 - Fueling completed; underway to CM 9.
1037 - Moored port side to CM 9.
1235 - Underway to anchor.
1306 - Anchored in Kerama Retto harbor.
1749 - Underway to A/S Station #3.
1830 - Relieved SC 1012 on station.

May 9, 1945

0000 to 0845 - Routine patrol, relieved on station, channel sweep and return to anchorage.
1651 - Underway for A/S Station #5.
1726 - Anchored in vicinity of A/S Station #5.
1805 - Underway to take Station A/S #7 on orders of CTG 51.15.3.
1822 - Relieved PC 800 on station.
1924 - Flash Red; sounded GQ.
2003 - Secured from GQ.

May 10, 1945

0000 to 0745 - Routine Patrol, relieved on station, channel sweep, visibility very poor and return to anchorage.
0918 - Moored starboard side to YMS 271 alongside CM 12 (USS Weehawken).
1220 - Underway to anchor in Kerama Retto harbor.
1246 - Anchored.
1925 - Started making smoke. (When anchored inside the nets at night, a circumstance that did not happen very frequently, 183 anchored on the windward side of the anchorage along with other small craft. When an air alert was sounded these vessels were ordered to make smoke with a smoke generator on the stern. This time of year the prevailing wind was from south to north

and the smoke drifted from the smoke makers and covered the anchorage and the ships in it. Only the mast tops protruded above the smoke from time to time. The only vessels to be seen were the smoke makers, and apparently they were not considered worthy targets by the Kamikazes).

1935 - Smoke generator flared up, smoke discharge pipe caught fire. Secured generator and extinguished flames. No damage done. (The smoke was produced by heating a heavy oil, like lubricating oil and when it was hot enough to boil, a heavy white smoke was produced and it poured out into the air through a discharge pipe. Being about the weight of air, the smoke remained close to the water and covered the ships in the harbor. The smoke was flammable when hot and occasionally if the flames heating the oil were turned up too high the oil would catch fire. For this reason fire extinguishers and water hoses were always nearby when making smoke)

1943 - Resumed making smoke.

2235 - Stopped making smoke.

May 11, 1945

0000 - Anchored as before in Kerama Retto Harbor.

1115 - Carpenter from USS Mona Island to work on bow damaged in sideswiping incident with AM 232. (ARG 9 was a repair ship for ships with internal combustion engines. This would include practically all small craft. She was a Maritime Commission EC2-S-C1 type. She displaced 8,700 tons; 442' long; beam 57'; draft 20'6"; speed 12.5 knots; armament 1 5"/38 DP. 3 3"/50 DP, 2x2 40mm, 12 20mm; complement 574; reciprocating engines, single screw, 1950 hp; commissioned in 1944). *(See End Note No.91)*.

1530 - Carpenter left ship.

1731 - Underway for A/S Station #5.

1751 - Anchored in vicinity of A/S Station #5.

May 12, 1945

0000 to 0845 - Routine sonar watch at Southern Entrance of nets, conducted channel sweep, and returned to anchorage.

1755 - Underway for A/S Station Prep #4. Relieved PC 800 on station.

1920 - Flash Red; sounded GQ.

1950 - Secured from GQ.

May 13, 1945

0000 to 0543 - Routine patrol, relieved on station and returning to anchorage.

0740 - Moored port side to YMS 89 in nest with ARG 9 (USS Mona Island). (Carpenters from Mona Island continue to work on damage on starboard bow of 183).

1726 - Underway to A/S Station #5.

1830 - Anchored on A/S Station #5.

1901 - Flash Red; sounded GQ.

2043 - Secured from GQ.

May 14, 1945

0000 to 0650 - Conducted sonar watch and got underway to USS Mona Island.

0732 - Moored port side to YMS 293 in nest with ARG 9.

0743 - YMS 89 moored outboard..

0912 -Underway to anchor.

0918 - Anchored in Kerama Retto harbor.
1805 - Underway for A/S Station #5.
1837 - Anchored on A/S Station #5.
1939 - Flash Red; sounded GQ. (This was a very poplar time for the Kamikazes to come calling. It was sort of twilight, all was peaceful and quiet and a suicide plane would slip into the area. Sometimes they hit a ship, sometimes they didn't).
1944 - Secured from GQ.
1948 - Flash Red; sounded GQ. 2002 - Secured from GQ.

May 15, 1945

0000 to 0655 - Routine sonar watch and then underway for USS Mona Island.
0734 - Anchored in vicinity of USS Mona Island.
1108 - Underway to go alongside ARG 9.
1134 - Moored port side to YMS 408 in nest with ARG 9.
1153 - YMS 176 moored outboard of us.
1811 - Underway for A/S Station #5.
1840 - Anchored on station.

May 16, 1945

0000 to 0645 - Conducted sonar watch and then underway to USS Mona Island.
0733 - Moored port side to YMS 279 in nest with USS Mona Island.
1749 - Underway to A/S Station #5.
1824 - Anchored in vicinity of A/S Station #5.
2010 - Flash Red; sounded GQ.
2055 - Secured from GQ.

May 17, 1945

0000 to 0645 - Conducted sonar watch and then underway for ARG 9.
0900 - Moored port side to ARG 9.
1753 - Underway for A/S Station #5.
1823 - Anchored on station.
1938 - Flash Red; sounded GQ.
2047 - Secured from GQ.

May 18, 1945

0000 to 0646 - Conducted sonar watch and then underway for ARG 9.
0745 - Moored port side to ARG 9.
1751 - Underway for A/S Station #5.
1821 - Anchored on station.

May 19, 1945

0000 to 0640 - Conducted sonar watch and then underway to USS Mona Island.
0806 - Anchored in vicinity of USS Mona Island in Kerama Retto harbor.
1652 - Underway to draw fog oil (oil used to make smoke screen).
1735 - Moored port side to LST 617 to draw fog oil.
1741 - Fog oil aboard; underway for A/S Station #2.
1810 - Anchored on A/S Station #2.

May 20, 1945

0000 to 0626 - Conducted sonar watch and underway to sweep channel.
0644 - All gear streamed; commencing sweep.
0815 - Recovered port gear; sweeping harbor with starboard gear.
0945 - Recovered all gear; returning to anchorage. 1016 - Moored starboard side to PGM 20.
1215 - Underway for CM 9.
1311 - Moored port side to CM 9.
1729 - Underway for A/S Station Prep # 3.
1750 - Relieved SC 632 on station.
1918 - Flash Red; sounded GQ.
2006 - Secured from GQ.

May 21, 1945

0000 to 0605 - Continued routine patrol, relieved on station by SC 732 (?) and commenced channel sweep.
0733 - Sweep gear fouled on bottom and parted.
0814 - Recovered remaining gear.
0825 - Recovered lost gear.
0855 - All gear streamed on starboard side; proceeding with harbor sweep.
0950 - Recovered all gear; returning to anchorage.
1051 - Anchored in Kerama Retto.
1750 - Underway for A/S Station Prep #3.
1815 - Relieved the ship on station (the ship's number illegible).

May 22, 23, and 24, 1945 –

(Logs for these three days are missing).

May 25, 1945

0000 to 1747 - Routine sonar watch on A/S Station #2.
1748 - Underway for A/S Station Prep #3.
1834 - Relieved SC 632 on station.

May 26, 1945

0000 to 0536 - Continued routine patrol and relieved on station by SC 632.
0610 - Streamed gear; commencing channel sweep.
0755 - Recovered all gear; returning to anchorage.
0928 - Anchored in Kerama Retto.
1748 - Underway for A/S Station Prep #2.
1825 - Relieved PC 800 on station.

May 27, 1945

0000 to 0523 - Continued routine patrol, then relieved on station by PC 800.
0603 - All gear streamed.
0609 - Port float (the pig) broke loose.
0644 - All gear recovered.
0700 - Recovered drifting float.
0726 - Streamed gear; commencing channel sweep.

0853 - Recovered gear; returning to anchorage.

1022 - Moored starboard side to DD 779. (The log often doesn't say why 183 went along side another ship. Even so, there are times when the purpose is apparent from something written in the log earlier. However, on this day there was a special reason why 183 went along side DD 779 and there is no hint in the log as to why. 779 was getting ready to head back to the states for major repair to severe damage to her superstructure, bridge and flying bridge. She had been hit by a Kamikaze a day or two before out on the picket line, with some casualties, killed and injured. She was brand new, having been commissioned in 1944 and Okinawa was a major action. She was USS Douglas H Fox, Sumner Class Destroyer with a displacement of 2200 tons; length, 376' 6"; beam 40' 10"; draft 15' 8"; speed 35 knots; armament 6 5"/38 DP, 2x5 21" torpedo tubes; complement of 345; geared turbines with twin screws, 60,000 hp. *(See End Note No.92)*. Ensign Davis remembers this "visit" very well. "The crew of 183 had seen many other ships battered to pieces by Kamikazes, but this was the first one they had ever seen up close, along side. The dead and wounded had been removed two days earlier and as much of the wreckage as possible had been removed, but she was still a mess. No bridge or flying bridge, a jury rigged mast held in place by guy wires so that radio antennae could be used. Davis recalls that 183's skipper, Stan Klein, was a good friend of the navigator of the Fox and the navigator had invited the 183 over to receive any supplies and equipment that the Fox would not need on its trip back to the states and to give his friend a chance for a visit, since they had not had one before. It was a moving experience to see these people who had just lost many shipmates and had a close call with being sunk and killed").

1710 - Underway, steaming on various courses for DM 18.

1728 - Came close aboard DM 18 to pick up mail.

1730 - Mail aboard; proceeding to A/S Station Prep #2.

2140 - AM on our port quarter hit by bomb.

2147 - Sounded GQ.

2204 - Secured from GQ.

May 28, 1945

0000 to 0504 - Continued patrol and then relieved on station by PC 800.

0550 - Streamed gear; commencing channel sweep.

0723 - Recovered gear; returning to anchorage.

0815 - Anchored in Kerama Retto harbor.

1755 - Underway for A/S Station #5.

1817 - Anchored on station.

May 29, 1945

0000 to 0745 - Continued routine sonar watch and relieved on station, and returned to anchorage.

1755 - Underway for A/S Station #2.

1832 - Anchored on A/S Station #2.

May 30, 1945

0000 to 0745 - Continued routine sonar watch, relieved on station and returned to anchorage.

1658 - Underway for A/S Station #2.

1807 - Relieved PC 1179 on station.

May 31, 1945

0000 to 0611 - Continued sonar watch, relieved on station by PC 1179 and returned to anchorage.
0715 - Moored to Starboard side of AO 4. (This ship, USS Brazos was a Kanawha/Cuyama class Fleet Oiler built and commissioned in October 1919. Displacement; 14,500 tons; Length 476', beam 56', draft 28'; speed 12 knots (max); 9 knots (economy). Armament 2 5"/38 DP, 4x2 40mm, 4x2 20mm; complement 475; capacity 55,700 barrels; reciprocating engines, twin screws, 10,400 hp). *(See End Note No.93)*.
0745 - Underway for CM 12.
0805 - Moored starboard side to CM 12.
1013 - Underway to anchor.
1035 - Anchored in Kerama Retto harbor.
1455 - Flash Red; sounded GQ.
1531 - Secured from GQ.
1537 - Flash Red; sounded GQ.
1551 - Secured from GQ.
1754 - Underway for A/S Station Prep #3.
1815 - On station. (Signed: Stanley C. Klein, Lt. USNR, Commanding; Walter Weltzien, Lt. jg. USNR, Navigator).

June 1, 1945

0000 to 0520 - Continued patrol, relieved on station by PC 800.
0544 - Anchored in Kerama Retto.
1556 - Underway to go alongside DM 18.
1610 - Moored starboard side to DM 18.
1718 - Underway for A/S Station #5.
1735 - Anchored on station.

June 2, 1945

0000 to 0945 - Continued routine sonar watch and underway for Small Craft Anchorage.
0958 - Anchored in Kerama Retto.
1758 - Underway to A/S Station #2.
1838 - Anchored on station.

June 3, 1945

0000 to 0756 - Continued routine sonar watch, then underway to a new anchorage.
0837 - Moored starboard side to YMS 427 in nest with DM 18.
1040 - Underway to allow DM 18 to shift berths.
1110 - Moored starboard side to DM 18.
1340 - Underway while DM 18 shifts berths. (All the berth shifting by DM 18 could have been caused by her anchor dragging or the wind had shifted causing her to swing too close to another ship, etc.)
1342 - Flash Red; sounded GQ.
1412 - Secured from GQ.
1430 - Moored starboard side to DM 18.
1809 - Underway for A/SD Station Prep #4.
1834 - Relieved SC 632 on station.

John Dixon Davis

June 4, 1945

0000 to 0530 - Continued patrol, relieved on station by PC 800 and returning to anchorage.

0640 - Moored starboard side to DM 18.

0643 - Underway from DM 18 to anchor.

0745 - Anchored in Kerama Retto harbor.

0845 - Underway for Typhoon anchorage at Unten Ko, Okinawa. (We did not know it at the time, but the typhoon we were seeking shelter from came to be known "affectionately" as Halsey's Typhoon. It apparently passed between Guam and Okinawa on the 5th of June. When its presence was reported on June 4th it was southeast of Okinawa and its course could have brought it very near to or across Okinawa. Small Craft in the Okinawa area were ordered to Unten Ko. This shelter was being developed for small craft at the mouth of a small channel on the northeast side of the main island's Motobu Peninsula. (The island Ie Shima, where Ernie Pyle, the famous and beloved news reporter was killed earlier, lies just to the west of the peninsula). The anchorage area was protected from the wind on all sides except from the northwest. Admiral Halsey's name will be forever attached to this storm for they encountered it on June 5th while enroute to Kyushu for operations against Japanese airfield there. Instead of slowing down or taking evasive action, it is said that the Admiral ordered Task Groups 30.8 and 38.1 to plow on through it. It was a near disaster as seven ships suffered severe damage, including heavy cruiser USS Pittsburgh (CA-72) which lost approximately a 100 foot section of her bow. In addition there was heavy damage to four carriers and the loss of 76 aircraft; however, only six men were killed. All personnel on 183 later saw that bow section of Pittsburgh, which did not sink, but was towed back to Guam where it remained anchored in the harbor for quite a long time. *(See End Note No.94)*.

0917 - Leaving Kerama Retto harbor. C/C to 041° True.

1152 - C/C to 037° True.

1227 - C/C to 014° True.

1240 - C/C to 103° True.

1320 - Entering Unten Ko.

1345 - Pilot came aboard.

1402 - Pilot left ship.

1420 - Anchored in Katena Wan, Okinawa.

1557 - Underway to shift berths.

1600 - Re-anchored in Katena Wan [Bay].

June 5, 1945

0000 - Anchored as before for the next 24 hours.

1140 - Flash Red; sounded GQ.

1151 - Secured from GQ.

1940 - Flash Red; sounded GQ.

1957 - Secured from GQ.

June 6, 1945

0000 - Anchored as before.

Figure 42 – Captain Mitchell flanked by Dudley and Davis

0937 – Getting underway for Kerama Retto. (Obviously the typhoon has not hit the Okinawa area, but small craft nevertheless discovered a safe haven in case of need).
1043 - Departing Unten Ko; C/C to 285° True.
1052 - C/C to 278° True.
1110 - C/C to 268° True.
1126 - C/C to 194° True.
1147 - C/C to 263° True.
1159 - C/C to 221° True.
1607 - Moored starboard side to DM 18 in Kerama Retto anchorage.
1637 - Flash Red; sounded GQ.
1703 - Secured from GQ.
1902 - Underway to anchor.
1908 - Anchored in vicinity of DM 18.
1923 - Underway to shift berth.
1932 - Anchored in vicinity of K-85, Kerama Retto.

June 7, 1945

0000 - Anchored in vicinity of berth K-85 until 1755 when underway for A/S Station Prep #3.
1805 - Relieved PC 1179 on station.

June 8, 1945

0000 - Patrolling as before on A/S Station Prep # 3, Kerama Retto.
0323 - Hit anti-submarine net buoy.
0335 - Clear of nets, no apparent damage. (The currents around Kerama Retto were sometimes very swift and often unpredictable. The nets at either end of the anchorage were anchored at intervals and the buoys at the anchor site did not move, but the buoys in between the buoy anchors curved in or out depending on the current's direction. Of course, at night, the buoys could not be seen and the distance from the nets had to be ascertained by using the radar on distant fixed objects. For some reason the ship was swept into the nets, but quick action putting the engines in reverse enabled us to get away from the nets, and re-establish our proper distance from the nets, and change our heading to compensate for the power of the current sweeping us toward the nets).
0545 - Relieved on station by SC 632.
0605 - All gear streamed; commencing channel sweep.
0745 - All gear recovered; returning to anchorage.
0818 - Anchored in Kerama Retto harbor.
1803 - Underway for A/S Station #5.
1820 - Anchored on station.

June 9, 1945

0000 to 0800 - Continued sonar watch and underway for USS Weehawken.
0828 - Moored starboard side to USS Weehawken.
0938 - Underway for LST 617.
0945 - Lying to in vicinity of LST 617 waiting for permission to go alongside.
1416 - Moored port side to LST 617.
1440 - Flash Red; sounded GQ.
1454 - Secured from GQ.

1555 - Underway for anchorage.
1602 - Anchored in Kerama Retto harbor.
1803 - Underway for A/S Station Prep #2.
1840 - Relieved PC 584 on station.
1943 - Flash Red; sounded GQ.
2014 - Secured from GQ.

June 10, 1945

0000 to 0530 - Continued routine patrol, relieved on station by PC 800 and returned to anchorage.
0625 - Anchored in Kerama Retto harbor.
1751 -Underway for A/S Station #5.
1809 - Anchored on station.

June 11, 1945

0000 to 0750 - Continued sonar watch and then underway to shift berth.
0810 - Anchored in Kerama Retto.
1757 - Underway for A/S Station #2.
1845 - Anchored on station.

June 12, 1945

0000 to 0546 - Continued sonar watch until ordered underway for typhoon anchorage at Katena Wan, Okinawa.
0558 - Leaving harbor; C/C to 035° True.
0755 - C/C to 216° True. Storm danger over; returning to Kerama Retto. 1154 - Moored starboard side to IX 113, USS Camel.
1253 - Underway to DM 18.
1543 - Underway to anchor.
1615 - Anchored in Kerama Retto harbor.
1757 - Underway for A/S Station Prep #2.
1939 - Relieved PC 800 on station.

June 13, 1945

0000 to 0525 - Continued routine patrol until relieved on station by PC 800.
0545 - Streamed gear; commencing channel sweep. (The log does not record the following incident which happened on the sweep of the channel from the northern entrance of Kerama Retto to the north (000° True) for about 10 miles. The course was then reversed and the channel swept back to the entrance where the gear was recovered. Ensign Davis recalls that he was now standing the 0400 to 0800 and 1600 to 2000 watches to become accustomed to the navigator's responsibility. Lt.jg Weltzien was awaiting his relief after 22 months on 183 and he was making certain that Davis knew what he was supposed to do and how to do it. The sunrise and sunset watches were necessary for the navigator to take star sights when at sea and to do the navigating. It was on a morning like this one when the first leg of the sweep was done, the course had been reversed, and the three black balls at the yardarm and mast head designating minesweeper at work were swaying with the motion of the ship that it happened. Suddenly on the northern horizon a light that seemed brighter than the rising sun in the eastern sky flashed toward 183. It was a blinker light sending a message. Whatever ship it was was hull down [far enough away so that the curvature of the earth was higher then the hull of the approaching ship and only

the top of the mast could be seen] and invisible to 183. The message was read out loud by the signal man to Ens. Davis, who had the con. The message: "What ship are you?" Our reply: "We are USS YMS 183 sweeping the channel to Kerama Retto. Please stand clear. What ship are you?" The unknown ship replied: "We are the battleship USS Texas and we will follow you in." Ens. Davis remembers how pleased the whole bridge crew was at this reply. After the repeated ignoring of the minesweeper by most ships including cruisers, CVE's, and destroyers day after day, having a capital ship acknowledge our importance was a real lift).

0732 - All gear recovered; returning to anchorage.
0930 - Anchored in Kerama Retto harbor.
1748 - Underway for A./S Station #2.
1830 - Anchored on station.

June 14, 1945

0000 to 1753 - Continued sonar watch followed by routine day in Kerama Retto anchorage, then underway for A/S Station #2.
1831 - Anchored on station.

June 15, 1945

0000 to 0743 - Continued sonar watch then underway to shift berths.
0819 - Anchored in Kerama Retto anchorage.
0853 - Churchill, James W., S 2/c, 728-06-36; Cornish, Billie L., S 2/c, 974-58-19; Coons, Homer D., F 2/c, 343-38-85, reported for duty.
1750 - Underway for A/S Station #2.
1820 - Moored starboard side to AO 93 to take on water.
1840 - Underway for A/S Station #2.
1909 - Anchored on station.

June 16, 1945

0000 to 0745 - Continued sonar watch then underway to shift berth.
0820 - Anchored in Kerama Retto anchorage.
1805 - Underway for A/S Station #2.
1829 - Anchored on station.

June 17, 1945

0000 to 0757 - Continued sonar watch then underway to shift berth.
0825 - Anchored in Kerama Retto anchorage.
1753 - Underway for A/S Station #2.
1828 - Anchored on station.

June 18, 1945

0000 to 0755 - Continued sonar watch then underway to shift berth.
0821 - Anchored in Kerama Retto anchorage.
1630 - Ens, Gerald G. Dudley, (D)L, USNR, 411396 reported aboard for duty. (Dudley hailed from Tarrytown, NY. Records indicating the college from which he graduated and the midshipman's school he attended could not be found). He started out like the rest of the officers had started with responsibility for minesweeping, engineering, commissary, etc).
1759 - Underway for A/S Station #2.

1838 - Moored starboard side to AO 86 to take on water.
1908 - Completed taking on water.
1950 - Underway for A/S Station #2.
2014 - Anchored on station. (Signed: Stanley C. Klein, Lt. USNR, Commanding; and Walter Weltzien, Lt.jg, USNR, Navigator).

June 19, 1945

0000 to 0800 - Continued sonar watch, then underway to berth K-100.
0830 - Anchored in vicinity of berth K-100. 1600 - Lt.jg. Walter Weltzien detached from duty. (Lt. Weltzien has some clear memories of this day. He writes, "It was early in June 1945 at Kerama Retto. An incoming PBY brought our usual supply of mail and in it was orders for me to be relieved of duties and returned to the US for 30 days leave upon arrival and reporting of Gerald Dudley, Ens., USNR. I had waited 22 months for this and couldn't stop smiling for a week. I was the happiest guy on the ship. The war was practically over and they didn't need me anymore. I was tickled pink and couldn't wait for Dudley to arrive. He finally did arrive, and I packed my gear. The next day a motor launch came to take me to the troop transport for my trip back to the States. I stood on the starboard rail, still smiling, faced aft and saluted the ensign and dropped into the launch. Fred Campagnoli, the exec from one of the YMSes, (Verplanck's boat) we had worked with was already in the launch. He greeted me warmly as I looked back at the 183 and my shipmates for the last time. I couldn't answer him; I had a lump in my throat the size of a football and tears dimmed my vision. I was finally leaving the 183, a moment I had looked forward to for almost two years, and yet it had turned into one of the saddest days of my life. Fred said to me, 'I know just how you feel; it isn't easy, is it?' And it wasn't but turned out to be one of the moments I look back on with the most nostalgia").
1800 - Underway for A/S Station #2.
1840 - Anchored on A/S Station #2. (Signed: Stanley C. Klein, Lt. USNR, Commanding; and John D. Davis, Ensign, USNR, Navigator).

June 20, 1945

0000 to 1600 - Continued sonar watch, changed berth to K-100, and spent day with regular routine in port.
1756 - Underway to A/S Station #2.
1830 - Anchored on station.

June 21, 1945

0000 to 1810 - Continued sonar watch, changed anchorage to K-100 at 0800 and carried out routine in-port activities. Underway for A/S Station #2.
1841 - Flash Red; sounded GQ.
1846 - Anchored on station.
1935 - Secured from GQ.
2005 - Began making smoke as ordered.

June 22, 1945

0000 to 0755 - Continued sonar watch, stopped making smoke at 0120, and underway for new anchorage at berth K-100.
1200 - YMS 271 moored along port side.
1757 - Underway for A/S Station #2.

1820 - Moored port side AO 86. Taking on water.
1851 - Underway for A/S Station #2.
1906 - Flash Red; sounded GQ.
1918 - Anchored on station #2.
1902 - Secured from GQ. Began making smoke.
2000 - Stopped making smoke.

June 23, 1945

0000 to 0800 - Continued sonar watch. Prepared to get underway.
0801 - Underway to LST 284.
0828 - Moored port side to LST 284. Began taking VT ammunition aboard.
0856 - Completed taking 52 rounds VT "ammo". (Ensign Davis recalls this day and the receiving of the VT ammunition. It was to be the answer to poor anti-aircraft gunnery for small craft. The larger ships like destroyers, cruisers, etc. had radar control for their AA guns, particularly the 5"38. The smaller vessels like the YMSes had one 3"50 gun on the forecastle and it was directed by two men turning cranks to move the barrel from right to left and up and down so as to bring the enemy aircraft into the gun sight where it was ready to be fired when the order was given. Just prior to loading the 3"50 shell into the breech of the gun, the Gunner's Mate made the last range adjustment on the projectile. The order to fire was given by the gunnery officer and if everything went well the projectile had a good chance of hitting the aircraft. This of course rarely happened, for time was the crucial factor. By the time the gun was fired the plane was already out of range and the projectile exploded harmlessly. If there were, say, 50 ships firing at the same target the odds of one of them getting a hit on the enemy plane were materially enhanced. But on this day, ships like YMS 183 became remarkably better at hitting enemy aircraft. The new VT ammunition now made it possible to hit or damage the enemy plane without having to set a range because the projectile had built into it what was called a "proximity fuse". This VT projectile would explode when it came within a certain distance of the aircraft and the shrapnel could damage or cripple the plane. You didn't have to have the exact range and the time to get set up with VT ammo was materially reduced. In the event that the VT projectile did not come close enough to the plane to explode, it simply continued on for several seconds and then exploded harmlessly. "Man, oh, man," one of the gun crew was heard to say, "these babies will make us top gun in the fleet." Ensign Davis remarks, "This might well have been a good prophecy except for the fact that 183, and many others, never got to fire their VT ammo. The small craft did not fire any guns at this stage because the danger of hitting our own ships was too great in the anchorage, and when in a situation where the guns could be fired, 183 never was approached close enough by an enemy plane. Add to this the fact that the Okinawa Campaign was winding down and you have the story.") Underway for AOG 10.
0953 - Anchored in small craft anchorage after taking on fuel from AOG 10.
1935 - Underway for berth K-90, Kerama Retto.
1945 - Anchored in berth K-90.
2000 - Anchored as before in berth K-90, 245° degrees true from WAGC-31, USS Bibb (Coast Guard Cutter, now Adm. Sharpe's flagship). (Note: Berth K-90 is on the western side of the anchorage and very close to the southeastern tip of Geruma Shima. The island gives protection to the Bibb from the west. The ships anchored in the rest of the anchorage to the east provide protection on the eastern side. YMS 183 is anchored in such a position so that if called on to make smoke during the night, the smoke would drift over Bibb and other larger vessels, blown by the normally south to southwest winds at this time of the year. Add 100 or more other small

craft to the smoke making detail and the whole anchorage could be enveloped by white smoke in a few minutes. If the wind was not blowing too hard the smoke settled in among the ships effectively hiding them from view from above. However, if the wind was blowing too hard smoke was not effective).

June 24, 1945

0000 - Anchored as before, bearing 245° True from WAGC-31, USS Bibb.
0225 - Started making smoke. 0400 - Stopped making smoke.
0600 - Underway for new anchorage in vicinity of berth K-100, Kerama Retto.
1330 - Brown, J.D., S1/c injured on LCVP moored from the stern. (Note: This man was in a working party from another vessel, and not a member of the crew of YMS 183).
1544 - Underway for Northwest Anchorage.
1703 - Anchored in Northwest Anchorage.
1820 - Underway for smoke station in Kerama Retto.
2000 - Anchored in vicinity of USS Bibb.

June 25, 1945

0000 to 1642 - Anchored in vicinity of USS Bibb and then underway for Northwest Anchorage.
1805 - Anchored in Northwest Anchorage. (Note: the Northwest Anchorage lay between the western tips of Aka Shima and Zamami Shima. Although outside the inner anchorage of the Kerama Retto, it nevertheless afforded a good anchorage. In the case of the frequent visits of the 183 to the Northwest Anchorage for the last several days, a number of other escort vessels gathered there as well. Unfortunately the log of 183 only mentions PGM 32, PGM 30, YMS 81 and YMS 371. There were others, including an Under Water Demolition Team representative and CO's of two LSTs and several smaller landing craft. The CO's of these vessels and other units, gathered there for planning sessions with the Commander of a small force of mine sweepers and other escort vessels which would lead an assault on and occupation of Kume Shima by several hundred marines. Kume Shima is an island roughly 10 miles long and 8 miles wide with coral reefs extending out from the eastern side of the island for several miles. It is about 35 miles slightly north of due west from Kerama Retto. There is one almost circular harbor about 3 1/2 miles in diameter on the southeastern side of the island. The harbor is fairly shallow with 8 to 10 fathoms of water in the deepest part. The island had a dirt airstrip and was fairly heavily wooded. Aerial reconnaissance did not show any evidence of a resident population of civilians or troops. It was, however, widely thought that suicide planes from Formosa or Kyushu or China landed on the airstrip in the early evening and took off at dawn with little fear of being detected by the CAP or Navy picket vessels early enough to prevent a successful attack on our ships. So there were three good reasons to take the island which had been mostly ignored since the beginning of the Okinawa Campaign. In American hands the island could no longer harbor suicide planes, nor could any Japanese troops sequestered there be of any danger to our forces. It afforded Navy radar units an excellent location for early warning radar receivers. The die was cast, Kume Shima must be assaulted and captured. The first part of the operation required that the little harbor be cleared of mines as well as the rest of the approaches to the shoreline. There was room for only one minesweeper to tackle this job. YMS 183, with Stanley C. Klein, Lt. USNR, who was the senior YMS skipper in the group, was chosen to make the initial sweep of the harbor just prior to the landing of the Marines from the LSTs).
2000 - Anchored as before in Northwest Anchorage.
2225 - Underway for Kume Shima.

June 26, 1945

0000 - Steaming as before on course 257° True. Following PGM 32.

0250 - Started streaming "O" type gear on starboard side. (Note: The little armada had been underway for about 4 1/2 hours before arriving at "Point Buick" which was the starting point, south of the island, for the assault and troop landing).

0304 - All gear streamed

0317 - Steering course 000° True. (Note: 183 is preparing to enter the atoll-like harbor, bounded on the western side by the island itself and on the north, east and south by the coral reef. The only entrance to the harbor was a gap in the reef at the southern end. This was the first hurdle for 183, to enter the entrance with gear already streamed and to do it without getting it snagged on the reef).

0420 - Steering course 025° True. [Note: 183 has now cleared the entrance and is slowly turning to the right (starboard) to follow a course parallel (as possible) to the reef. This is all being done in the middle of the night, no artificial light, only the stars and a low moon. There are no charts of the harbor, so the location of any inside reefs and shoals are unknown. We could only watch carefully for the behavior of the sweep gear and the surface of the water to give us clues about these possible hazards].

0428 - Steering course 045° True. [Note: The CO, who has the conn, is trying to place the otter and mine cable cutters, both of which hang on the pendant from the float, (or "the pig") as close to the beach as possible, so that any mines in the more shallow water will be swept. The under water demolition people will take care of the waters from the beach outward to about a depth of 25 plus feet. They might expect mines in this shallow water, or underwater obstructions designed to rip the bottoms of landing craft approaching the shore. The log does not state how long the pendent on 183's gear is, but probably around 25 or 30 feet. Mines under the surface at this depth would be swept and leave a safe depth free of mines for the LSTs as they approached the shallow water near the beach which is being cleared by the under water demolition people].

0429 - Steering course 025° True.

0432 - Steering course 205° True.

0436 - Steering course 180° True. Sweep gear started dragging bottom. [Ensign Davis, whose mine sweeping station was on the fantail of 183, and responsible with the Chief Boatswain for the proper activity of the sweep gear may have been the first one to see the otter broach (come clear out of the water) after hitting bottom on what was probably a sand shoal. About five minutes earlier, the dynamometer, which measures the pull of the sweep gear, had shown a sharp increase in the pull which indicates dragging bottom or picking up some obstruction and dragging it along. At that point the CO started a sharp turn to port to pull the sweep gear farther away from the shore, or the shoal, or whatever it was. 183 was now, at 0436 (see above) steering back directly toward the entrance to the harbor. Two minutes later the sweep gear had settled down and was no longer dragging bottom. In the next ten minutes the CO made another sharp turn to port and reversed the course from 180° True to 000° True. He is actually starting over again on the sweep of the harbor, only this time the otter and float are sweeping some distance to the west of where they were with the beginning pass. Fortunately, for the timing of the operation, 183's gear seemed to be working properly. It would have taken some time to stream new gear or even to bring in a back-up sweeper to replace 183 had this been necessary].

0438 - Sweep gear clear of bottom.

0455 - Steering course 000° True.

0512 - Steering course 313° True.

0518 - Steering course 294° True. (Note: It was at this point, with our sweep gear past the section of beach where the LST's would put their bows on the shore to unload their cargo of Marines and equipment, the Underwater Demolition Teams in 4 LCVP type small landing craft passed astern of 183 and headed for the shallow water where their work would now begin).

0521 - Steering course 315° True.

0522 - Steering course 317° True.

0525 - Steering course 323° True.

0527 - Steering course 325° True.

0529 - Steering course 165° True. (Note: This is a sharp turn to port which will take 183 across the entrance of the lagoon in preparation for exiting the harbor and then recovering the gear southwest of the harbor entrance)

0529 - Steering course 165° True.

0530 - Steering course 125° True.

0532 - Steering course 155° True.

0536 - Steering course 165° True.

0538 - Steering course 140° True.

0540 - Steering course 180° True. (Note: This is a 40 degree turn to starboard which will line up 183 with the entrance to the lagoon and take her back out to sea south of the island. After exiting the entrance 183 reports to the Senior Officer Present that no mines were found in the harbor. Later we learned that the under water demolition people found no obstructions or demolition charges or mines in the shallow water. It was a relief to discover that there were no impediments to an uneventful landing on Kume Shima. But the only way to determine this was to actually go in and find out).

0607 - Steering course 240° True. (Note: After 183 had cleared the harbor entrance the two LSTs, in single file, silently slide by astern of us, into the harbor and put their bows on the shore).

0619 - Started recovering sweep gear.

0722 - All gear aboard. Proceeding to Point Buick.

0730 - Steaming on course 235° True astern of YMS 81.

0745 - Following YMS 81. Acting as mine disposal vessel.

1200 - Following astern of YMS 371. Acting as mine disposal vessel. (Note: After Kume Shima was invaded the several YMSes involved in the total operation formed an echelon sweep operation south and southwest of the island. This area had not been swept before. However, no mines were found and the operation was terminated at 1257).

1257 - Falling in astern of PGM 30.

1500 - Following PGM 30 in column formation.

1600 - Steaming as before on course 077° True, proceeding to Kerama Retto.

1730 - Standing into Kerama Retto anchorage.

1857 - Started taking water from AO-86.

1917 - Completed taking on water and proceeding to anchorage.

1945 - Anchored vicinity USSCG Bibb. [Note: it was on a night such as this one, but earlier in the campaign that Ensign Davis remembers with great appreciation the excellent talent and training of several Motor Machinists and the Electrician, Bob Clayton. During that day one of the two ship's service generators had stopped running. The back-up generator started up automatically, but it soon developed a "knock". Fortunately, we were in the anchorage area and requested permission to come alongside another YMS (can't remember which one) and permission was granted. When the CO of the other YMS learned of our plight, he offered to furnish us power while our machinists took both generators apart to replace rings and whatever else was needed.

After several hours of work the repaired parts were all laid out to be reinstalled. However, the machinists were literally exhausted, even more than the rest of the crew after a day of continuous General Quarters and several days with little sleep. The CO of the host YMS told our skipper that he would stand our watches and continue to furnish power so that our crew could get some sleep. This offer was gratefully accepted. Lines to the other YMS were inspected to assure that they were secure and the power connection was all right. Everybody turned in. The other YMS would assure our safety by checking the mooring lines, etc. every fifteen minutes. The literal heart of our ship was the redundant generator system. It provided power to run all internal systems, raise and lower the anchor, fill the compressed air tanks to start the main engines, etc. Without the generators, or power from an outside source, we could not function at all. We slept without a worry, knowing that our friends were looking out for us. At about 0200, one of our crew awoke to visit the head and became aware that we did not have any lights in the compartment. He looked outside and discovered that all of our mooring lines had parted as well as the power lines and we were literally adrift and not too far from the rocky shore. This crew member ran through the crew's quarters and then through the wardroom yelling at the top of his lungs that we were adrift. (Our friends had failed us. We never did find out what had happened, but surmised that the gangway watch on the other YMS had simply failed to check the mooring lines as promised, they chafed through and parted. The skipper immediately ordered the anchor let go to stop our drifting any closer to the shore. It was impossible to start the main engines without compressed air. If the anchor did not hold, we were literally in shallow water. The bottom was rocky. The anchor could not get a hold on anything, and simply slipped over one rock after another. You could feel the bumping all through the ship. When the skipper ordered the anchor let go, he also had a several of the crew members bring heavy battery powered lanterns into the generator room to give light to the machinists as they set to work feverishly to put one of the generators together. The anchor was still sliding over the rocks and we were getting closer to the beach. It seems incredible that in about 15 minutes the generator coughed to life. We had power but little time. It took a few minutes to fill the compressed air tanks and get a main engine started and then the second one. We were now under way, the winch had power to raise the anchor and we were not going to pile up on the rocks after all. If any one of these factors had not fallen into place it might have been a different story. Most of all our survival depended on the expertise of the machinists and the electrician. They knew what to do and they did it. Unfortunately, as was true of many incidents, there is no mention of this close call in the ship's log.

All of the episodes were not life threatening, though some definitely were. Some were just plain humorous after the event, though at the time they were fraught with great danger. Others are just interesting as, for example, the first and only liberty while operating in the Okinawa area. Ensign Davis remembers that by late May or early June of 1945 the crew of 183 had not been on shore since early March. There was only one stop on the way to Okinawa where liberty ashore was even a remote possibility and that was at Ulithi. You guessed it. Very few of the ships stopping at Ulithi to refuel, re-provision, etc. were able to get on the "shore liberty schedule" for one of the small islands ringing the atoll. Almost everyone who stopped at Ulithi, going or coming, had heard of Mog Mog the main liberty island at Ulithi. However, few ever had liberty there. It was just a physical impossibility. Someone speculated that if all liberty parties stepped ashore on Mog Mog at the same time the island would have sunk below the surface of the lagoon. Probably few, if any, crew members of small craft ever got ashore there. So by early May (the dates are not certain as they were not logged) the crew of 183 and other YMSes attached to the mine squadron whose commander and staff rode USS Breese, DM 18, got their only liberty in the Okinawa campaign. The commander of our mine squadron was a man with a big heart. He sent official messages to the skipper of 183 and the others in his squadron, that the fantail of Breese was officially "land" and a place for liberty for one third of the YMS crew at such and such hour on such and such date. While it is true that a US Navy vessel could carry on board cases of beer for use on shore, the said beer could not be consumed aboard ship Therefore, the squadron CO, by declaring the fantail of Breese to be "land" made it possible at the designated times, under the proper supervision, for the liberty starved crews to enjoy a "cool one" for up to 30 minutes. The liberty period ended after 30 minutes. Each YMS in the squadron came alongside DM - 18 for an hour and one half, while one third of the crew "went ashore" for a beer. Each ship provided its own beer, Shore Patrol, canned peanuts, etc. Of course, if there were enemy planes or other dangers possible at the scheduled times, they were postponed until another day. This liberty plan was exercised several times and then as conditions changed it was terminated. However, there were many appreciative sailors on the several YMSes in that squadron).

June 27, 1945

0000 - 0345 Anchored as before vicinity of USSCG Bibb. Routine watch, no remarks.

0400 - 0602 Anchored as before. [Note: Ens. Davis remembers that for several weeks, going back into late May, the commissioned officer of the watch while at anchor was required to be present on the bridge at all times, and that only he could transmit or receive radio messages addressed to 183. On the face of it, this is not an unusual requirement except for the change in radio protocol, which heretofore, designated the senior Quartermaster or Signalman as well as the Officer of the Watch as voice radio operators. The reason this new requirement was instituted stemmed from the improper use of the inter-ship radio frequencies by erstwhile "country and western singers" accompanied mostly with guitars, but sometimes with a "mouth organ", mandolin or a "Jew's harp". Occasionally a duet or even a quartet could be heard. Some talented crews probably could have made the "country" hit parade. It appeared that on some of the ships (probably mostly small craft for no one really knew for sure) even crew members not on watch waited in line for their "chance" on the radio. It seems like an innocent thing that was going on here. What can be wrong with relieving the interminable boredom of these night time watches? If the ship had an underway patrol station, etc. it was a different matter (plus there was always an Officer on the bridge while underway). The night sky, every night, in the east over Okinawa was as brilliant as a sunrise. The small arms fire from various ships pumped into the flotsam and jetsam drifting around their anchored hulls and the suffocating white oil smoke had long ago ceased to be new or interesting. The long hours of practically nothing going on was just too much silence. No one knows how it started. Someone probably took his musical instrument up on the bridge to an inconspicuous place to practice. Unbeknown to the musician someone near the radio lifted the microphone off its hook, depressed the transmit button and without any announcement the musician was on the air without even knowing it. After a time the transmitter button was released and the radio was again in receive mode. Immediately, someone, among the hundreds who were guarding this particular frequency, began transmitting accolades to the unknown ballad singer and perhaps volunteered one of his own buddies for the next performance. Through it all, each person had the "good" sense not to give any personal names or radio call signs. Therefore, because of the large number of ships on this particular frequency, it was virtually impossible to know who was abusing the radio frequency. When one ship was transmitting, no matter what the subject matter, no other ship could transmit, but only listen. It is difficult to believe that any officers were present when their own radio was transmitting the country music. It tied up the frequency so that no one else could transmit the necessary information or orders for the proper conduct of the war. Some of the "performers" went on and on for long periods of time. Lionheart and Wiseman, the call signs for the two senior commanders tried to intimidate the performers, but to little avail. Half the night was a country music "concert". Lionheart and Wiseman called a conference with all COs of the vessel types abusing the radio frequency. They laid the law down. Each of these vessels (there may have been more than 100 of them) would have its CO on the bridge from 2000 hours until 0600 the following day, or an officer or officers designated by the CO for the various 4 hour watches. Only the CO and these designated officers could use the radio. Those who were found to be guilty of this frivolous use of the ship's radio would be Court Martialed. Needless to say, this pretty much ended the "Major Bowes" amateur hour. No CO was about to spend the whole night on the bridge unless it was at GQ or some other emergency. Therefore on each ship the officer watch list was sent over to Lionheart and Wiseman. A roving small craft with radio direction finders plied the waters of the anchorage pinpointing the source of illegal transmissions. In a couple of weeks no more "country music wannabees" were heard. This is why, when Ens. Davis relieved Ens. Dudley, Ens Dudley had to affirm that no radio transmissions were made during his watch, or that if one was made, he, Ens. Dudley made it and described the subject matter in detail. Of course, incoming messages were recorded in the radio log].

0602 - 0620 Underway to new anchorage in vicinity of CM-12, USS Weehawken.

2000 - Anchored as before in Kerama Retto.

2240 - Started making smoke.

2300 - Stopped making smoke. (Note: Most of the time when the order to make smoke came down, the small craft with the smoke generators were already positioned so that the smoke drifted from their sterns across the anchorage. The smoke making ship was pretty much out in the open. This was not a big problem because these ships were small and usually not of interest to the suicide pilot who was more interested in the larger vessels. Usually the smoke makers didn't get too much smoke over themselves unless the wind suddenly shifted. Ens. Davis remembers an evening when he was "thrust" into a situation where he experienced being enshrouded in the smoke in an open boat. He recalls that his skipper, Stan Klein, was in a meeting of minecraft group commanders along with a number of YMS COs. They were making plans for one of the operations involving YMSes. As the meeting, which was being held on a 220' AM, was breaking up the Commander of the squadron mentioned that he sure did miss getting to play Chess. He said nobody on the AM played and he didn't know where to find an occasional opponent. Stan was aware that Davis had said that he enjoyed playing chess, so he, Klein volunteered Davis as a worthy opponent at the first opportunity. Davis protested, when apprised of the situation and the invitation, that he was merely a rank amateur and beginner and that the Commander would probably beat him in 6 moves. Well the date was set and the next evening around 2100 the Commander sent his personal LCVP, Coxswain, armed guard and all to YMS 183 to fetch Davis for the night's game. As it happened, the smoke station for 183 was a mile or two from where the AM was anchored. It took awhile for the Coxswain to pick his way between the anchored ships, all enshrouded in white smoke. Finally, he found the AM, Davis climbed the gangway and was escorted to the wardroom of the AM where the Commander was waiting for the game to begin. The board was set up and after a few minutes of "getting to know you" banter the Commander thanked Davis for coming over to play a game or two. He then invited the Ensign to sit. Davis again expressed his fear that he was no expert at the game and apologized in advance for what he felt would be a boring game for the Commander. The game began, and sure enough Davis was check-mated in 6 moves. The board was reset and another game began and after 7 or 8 moves Davis was checkmated again. The Commander, a very pleasant fellow, called for his Steward to bring coffee and pie alamode'. During this refreshment period the Commander opined that Davis, while still inexperienced, should play every chance he could get, that his game would continue to improve. After what seemed to be only a few minutes, the Commander, looking at his watch, said that an hour and one half is long enough to keep you away from 183. He called his orderly, gave instructions to escort Davis to the gangway where the LCVP was waiting to return him to 183. He extended his hand in farewell and thanked Davis again for coming over to play a game or two of Chess. Davis remembers his reaction to this "command performance". He says he didn't like it when it happened, but recalls that "rank has its privileges" so he couldn't refuse the "invitation" nor did he want his CO to lose face. The matter of not being a good chess player was really not the issue. The matter of the time and the circumstances was. It was a war zone, it was in the dark of night, in an open boat and the whole anchorage was full of choking smoke. As the LCVP picked its way between the anchored ships the sounds of small arms fire emanating from them were alarmingly close. The armed lookouts on each of the ships were patrolling the guard rails, peering down into the dark water for any sign of movement, debris, etc. that might be hiding a suicide swimmer. These patrols fired many rounds of rifle ammo at real or imagined danger. The whine of ricocheting 30 and 45 caliber bullets could be heard all around and an occasional splash when one plowed into the water nearby. The Japs be-damned, our danger was friendly fire. The fact that we made it without injury was a miracle).

June 28, 1945

0000 - 0800 Anchored as before.
0835 - Underway to AM 240.
0903 - Moored on port side of AM 240.
1426 - Underway for new anchorage.
1449 - Anchored in vicinity of USS Mona Island (ARG-9, a repair ship). (There was nothing to report for the rest of the day ending at 2400).

June 29, 1945

0000 - 0658 Anchored as before and then underway for LST 617.
1025 - Moored starboard side of YMS 176 outboard of LST 617. (Note: LST 617 was probably a supply ship of some sort for minesweeping gear, or provisions, etc. Word had come down that we would be involved in the East China Sea sweep soon to be undertaken by a large fleet of minesweepers of all types. We were gradually picking up gear and other supplies in preparation for this undertaking).
1225 - Underway for anchorage.
1234 - Anchored in Kerama Retto.
2345 - Anchored as before. (No activities of note to report).

June 30, 1945

0000 - Anchored as before.
0040 - Started making smoke.
0130 - Stopped making smoke.
0430 - Started making smoke.
0441 - Stopped making smoke.

0811 - Underway and proceeding to area assigned for sweeping maneuvers. (Note: this was a practice session in preparation for the East China Sea Sweep).
1220 - Received orders to return to the anchorage.
1445 - Anchored in Kerama Retto.
1646 - Underway to AM 361.
1746 - Received dan buoys from AM 361. (Note: our principal task on the East China Sea sweep was to mark the areas that had been swept by the AMs and the DMSs. See Appendix C).
1815 - Anchored in small craft anchorage Kerama Retto.
2052 - Started making smoke.
2105 - Stopped making smoke.

July 1, 1945

0034 - Started making smoke.
0039 - Stopped making smoke. (Note: Creating a smoke screen for the anchorage was rarely the same each time it was done. There were many variables such as the direction of the wind and its strength, or if there was no wind at all. Sometimes after laying down a good thick layer of smoke and the wind was very light or non-existent, it would take a periodic injection of new smoke to fill in the gaps and cover the ships in the anchorage. When the danger of attack was possible as reported on radar or from night fighters in the area new smoke would be started and when the danger had ceased, we stopped making smoke).
0423 - Started making smoke.
0427 - Stopped making smoke.
0748 - Under way for USS (Weehawken) CM-12.
0816 - Anchored vicinity CM-12 Kerama Retto anchorage.
0817 - Pac 71a, Reg. No. 10237 placed on bridge. (Note: This was probably a new edition of the radio call names of all the Navy ships).
1226 - Under way for small craft anchorage.
1304 - Moored to starboard side of YMS 271.
2000 - Moored as before to starboard side of YMS 271 in small craft anchorage Kerama Retto. [Note: the log makes no mention of our ship getting access to a movie projector and a film to show on the forecastle before darkness set in when no lights could be shown. It wasn't the best set up for a movie, but it was better than none at all. Of course, if there was danger of a suicide plane in the area, the film would be stopped and we would go to GQ. On this evening, this did not happen. The forecastles of 183 and 271 were filled with off duty crew from both ships. The movie was almost over when a loud bang was heard in the generator room. The power was off momentarily until the second ship's service generator started automatically. The engineering officer, Ens. Dudley, rushed to the hatch to the generator room and was met there by the motor machinist's mate who had the duty when the generator stopped. He reported that it looked like a piston rod had broken and had been thrust through the engine block. On closer inspection this proved to be the case. The skipper joined in the discussion in the generator room, and when apprised of the situation said that he would check with the USS Mona Island about the problem and possible availability (a time to assess and repair the problem). He said it had to be soon, for the East China Sea sweep, which included YMS 183 was due to begin July 5th. However, he felt that even if the generator could not be fixed in the next day or so, he would not report it and 183 would just take her chances on one generator. The other three officers disagreed, saying they didn't think this was a good idea. If the remaining generator should fail another vessel would have to be detached from the sweep formation to tow 183 back to Kerama

Retto. The skipper said that he would check it out the next day. For most of the crew a non-functioning generator was nothing new. They broke down frequently and the "motor macs" always got them going again. It had been a good movie, no kamikazes showed up, so maybe this night might be a good one for some uninterrupted sack time. Several of the crew realized immediately that if the generator could not be repaired or replaced by July 5 183 would have to miss the East China Sea sweep. Some of this group also realized that being "providentially" hindered from going on an assignment might not be hard to live down].

July 3, 1945

0000 - Anchored as before in small craft anchorage Kerama Retto with YMS 271 moored on port side.

0340 - Started making smoke.

0425 - Stopped making smoke.

1215 - Underway for USS Mona Island.

1230 - Moored on starboard side of PGM 10, outboard of Mona Island for availability.

1338 - Held General Quarters.

1400 - Secured from GQ.

1634 - PGM 10 underway.

1641 - Moored starboard side of AM 119. (Note: While alongside Mona Island the skipper conferred with the engineers on the repair ship and learned that Mona Island did not carry spare generators, and even if they had one it would take a week or more to install it. The generator was beyond repair and 183 would have to go back to Guam to get a new one. The skipper reported to Admiral Sharp our unfitness to take part in the East China sweep and 183 was scratched from the list of 49 YMSes scheduled to take part. All of us had mixed feelings about this. We wanted to go and take part in this operation and yet we were secretly relieved that we didn't have to. Okinawa was essentially secured, but the really tough one, the invasion of Japan, was yet to come).

July 4, 1945

0000 - Moored as before on starboard side of AM 119.

1002 - Underway for anchorage.

1028 - Anchored in small craft anchorage vicinity USS Mona Island.

1400 - Lt.(jg) D.W. Mitchell, Jr., 224415, reported aboard for duty. (Note: Lt. (jg) Douglas Mitchell had come as relief for our Executive Officer, George Beck who had been on 183 since Miami, Florida in August 1943. Beck was now headed back to the states and 30 days leave. Mitchell was from Dalton, Georgia, a graduate of the University of Georgia and he had completed one year of law school before enlisting in the Navy and being commissioned an Ensign. No information is available on his family, his midshipman school or his duty prior to coming to 183).

2000 - Anchored as before in small craft anchorage vicinity of Mona Island.

July 5, 1945

0000 - Anchored as before.

1220 - Captain left the ship.

1600 - Anchored as before. Captain returned to ship.

2345 - Watch relieved. Routine watch; no further remarks. (Note: there is one further remark - George Beck signed the log at the end of his last watch, the 2000 to 2345. He apparently departed from 183 the next day. The log does not mention his leaving). [Note: According to The Official Chronology of the U.S. Navy in World War II -1945, TF (Task Force) 39 (Rear Admiral Alexander Sharp) composed of 7 light mineslayers (DM), 52 minesweepers (AM), 6 high speed minesweepers (DMS), 49 motor minesweepers (YMS) and 7 net layers, begins minesweeping operations in the East Chins Sea. But for our broken generator we would have been with them]. *(See End Note No.95).*

July 6, 1945

0000 - Anchored as before.
1332 - Underway for YW 88.
1403 - Moored port side to YW 88 taking on fresh water.
1423 - Underway for small craft anchorage.
1444 - Anchored in small craft anchorage Kerama Retto.
1538 - Captain left ship.
1728 - Captain returned to ship. (Note: Mention has been made of "friendly fire" and the ever present danger of it. On an afternoon much like this one, on July 6, Ens. Davis remembers an incident, the likes of which always made those who witnessed it sick to their stomachs. 183 was anchored near the nets on the eastern side of Hojaki Shima. All was quiet and peaceful. There were several CVEs, "baby flattops", in various places in the anchorage. They often came in to refuel and replenish ammunition. One of them was anchored on the western side of Hojaki Shima. A radio message for all ships came from Wiseman saying that two F6F Hellcats would be catapulted off this particular CVE in about 5 minutes. All ships should be certain that their anti-aircraft gunners had this message and that they hold their fire. The ships nearest this CVE were asked to acknowledge this message. Many ships did. It was presumed that all had "gotten the word". Shortly, we could see the two F6Fs taking off almost simultaneously. They were hardly airborne off the bow of the carrier when a stream of 20mm tracers from the closest ship, which appeared to be an LCI, reached up to the two planes. Smoke and flames burst from their engines and as they fell only one parachute opened. Even though we were a good half mile away, our crew was yelling, "Don't shoot, they are ours. Don't shoot, they are ours." Word came later that one pilot survived and one was killed. There was always somebody who didn't get the word. Ens. Davis remembers hearing, on the night the announcement that the battle for Okinawa was over and the island secured that in the joy and celebration expressed by the firing of various weapons by troops and naval personnel in the Buckner Bay area 25 Americans were killed and many others wounded by falling shrapnel). (Note: An interesting event took place one morning in May or June as we were about to terminate our A/S Patrol below the southern entrance to the anchorage at Kerama Retto. This was the back and forth sonar patrol that we used radar for positioning, etc. It was daylight, but the smoke from the anchorage was being blown out over and around us as the wind had shifted to the north. This was really no bother,

Figure 43 – Nest of YMSes waiting for assigmnet

for the radar was our eyes. The fellow on the radar screen sent up a report to the bridge that there was a surface contact bearing 180° True. He said that it had just suddenly appeared. He had hardly gotten this information out when the radar beam completed another sweep and he yelled, "It's still there but a mile closer. Could it be a suicide speed boat?" The radar beam made another sweep and the crewman was on the bridge saying, "Its going to hit us." Just at that moment through a break in the smoke we could see a PBM night fighter at a couple of hundred feet altitude heading into the anchorage at Kerama Retto where he would make his approach for landing in the seaplane "runway" and anchorage. Ens. Davis opines that this is probably the only time that surface search radar picked up a flying aircraft).

July 7, 1945

0000 - Anchored as before in small craft anchorage at Kerama Retto.

0730 - Underway, Watch relieved (Note: for the last several days the skipper had been meeting with Admiral Sharp's staff in preparation for escorting the various ships involved with minecraft from Kerama Retto to Buckner Bay. Today is the day for the move. Buckner Bay now becomes the main anchorage for all ships at Okinawa, now that the island is secure).

0806 - Steering course 170° True. (The convoy will leave Kerama Retto from the southern entrance, make a left turn, pass the southern tip of Okinawa to port and after a fifteen mile run up the east coast of Okinawa enter Buckner Bay).

0840 - Lighted off sound gear (sonar to screen for possible Japsubmarines).

0935 - Taking screening station 1000 yards ahead of DM 33 (USS Gwin) as ordered. Escorting CG 31 (Bibb), CM 12 (Weehawken) and ARG 9 (Mona Island). From Kerama Retto to Buckner Bay.

0950 - Steering course 120° True.

1045 - Steering course 090° True.

1213 - Steering course 060° True.

1600 - Preparing to enter Buckner Bay.

1745 - Anchored in Buckner Bay vicinity of ARG 9.

July 8, 1945

0000 - Anchored as before in Buckner Bay.

0953 - Underway for ARG 9.

1004 - Moored on starboard of YMS 415.

1805 - Underway for anchorage.

1824 - Anchored in Buckner Bay vicinity berth B-210.

2017 - Started making smoke.

2023 - Sounded General Quarters.

2041 - Stopped making smoke.

2056 - Secured from GQ. (Note: Moving to Buckner Bay did not end the war for us. Even though Okinawa was now secured, suicide planes were still coming from Formosa, Mainland China and Japan seeking to sink ships and kill Americans. The smoke screen over the anchorage was still very effective, however).

July 9, 1945

0000 - Anchored as before vicinity berth B - 210 (Buckner Bay).

1125 - Underway for YMS 360.

1241 - Moored on port side of YMS 360 in Buckner Bay.

1505 - Electrician repaired recognition lights.
1515 - Radio technicians come aboard to test radio gear.
1554 - Radio technicians leave ship.
1804 - Underway for anchorage.
1818 - Anchored in Buckner Bay vicinity berth B - 210.

July 10, 1945

0000 - Anchored as before in Buckner Bay berth B - 210.
0800 - Anchored as before. Captain left ship.
0930 - Millet, Phm 1/c, left ship.
0935 - Millet, Phm 1/c, returned to ship.
1000 - Captain returned to ship.

July 11, 1945

0000 to 2400 - (Nothing of note to report).

July 12, 1945

0000 - Anchored as before in Buckner Bay vicinity berth B - 209.
0332 - Started making smoke.
0421 - Stopped making smoke.
1110 - Underway for LST 617.
1124 - Moored port side of LST 617. Taking on fuel and water in preparation for rendezvous with AKA 101 as per orders of 1025 Item this date.
1200 - Moored as before.
1215 - YMS 324 came alongside.
1225 - YMS 324 left from alongside. (Note: Although the log has not said so yet, 183 is preparing to leave Buckner Bay, Okinawa for Guam for replacement of the ship's service generator. Any excess gear not needed in a rear area is transferred to the ships remaining in the forward area).
1239 - Underway from the LST 617 for YMS 390.
1255 - Moored port side to YMS 390 to transfer 50 rounds of VT ammo to them. (Note: These are the 3" 50 cal proximity rounds 183 had received a few days earlier. These were of great use to the ships remaining in the forward area).
1814 - Underway standing out of Buckner Bay.
2015 - Cleared anti-submarine nets.
2025 - Steering course 220° True. YMS 360 taking station behind.
2145 - Steering course 225° True.
2249 - Steering course 336° True.

July 13, 1945

0000 - Steaming as before on course 336° True in company with YMS 360 to rendezvous with DD 349 and AKA 101. Changed course to 357° True. Speed one third.
0115 - Steering course 176° True.
0255 - Steering course 356° True. (Note: after clearing the anti-submarine nets it is apparent from the course changes since 2025 that 183 and 360 are merely going back and forth off the southeastern end of Okinawa while waiting to rendezvous with DD 349 (USS Dewey) and AKA 101 (USS Ottawa II). The log does not state, nor does memory of living crew members shed any light on

this maneuver. If the rendezvous was made we do not know why and if not, why not. In any event we do know that DD 349 and AKA 101 did not head for Guam, which was the destination of YMS 183 and 360. We know USS Ottawa II went to Ulithi. USS Dewey may have stayed in the Okinawa area. It may have just been feinting maneuver to confuse Japanese submarines. Whatever was going on here, 183 and 360 begin their heading for Guam very soon. *(See End Note No.96)*.

0415 - Steering course 176° True.

0426 - Steering course 155° True, steaming at standard speed.

0522 - Steering course 147° True. (Note: a straight line course from Buckner Bay to Apra Harbor, Guam would be approximately 130° True. However, there is a northward flowing current, 2 to 3 knots, flowing between the Marianas Islands and Okinawa referred to as the Japan Stream. It is analogous to the Gulf Stream in the Atlantic Ocean. Therefore, to have steered a course of 130° True, 183 would have ended up far north of Guam. To compensate for the sweep of the current to the north over several days steaming a general course around 10 to 15 degrees to the right of 130° True, or approximately 140° True seemed to be a good starting course. Although 183 and 360 were traveling alone, covering a distance that was about their fuel limit, they checked their position with celestial navigation (star sights with the sextant) every dawn and post sunset. As they moved along over the 1500 miles there were only minor course changes that had to be made. This may have been only the second time for 183 that this distance was covered without another vessel to refuel her. *(See End Note No.97)*.

0800 - Steaming as before on course 147° True in company with YMS 360.

1137 - Secured starboard engine to repair oil leak.

1209 - Starboard engine repaired and in use again.

1630 - Steering course 136° True.

2000 - Steaming as before on course 136° True.

2200 - Steering course 139° True. (Note: Davis recalls that he, as navigator did all of the celestial navigation, and that this course change is the result of the evening celestial fix which suggested that we needed to change course to the right by a small amount. He still does not know why he did not record the lat. and long. coordinates in the log. It should have been done).

July 14, 1945

0000 - Steaming as before on course 139° True.

1050 - All clocks wound and reset. (Note: 183 has moved from time zone -9 east into -10 east. The clocks have been set ahead one hour).

1600 - Steaming as before on course 139° True.

1615 - Steering course 125° True.

1915 - Secured starboard engine for repairs.

1933 - Sighted convoy dead ahead. Changed course to 105° True.

1935 - Changed course to 080° True to avoid convoy. 1937 - Starboard engine in use again.

1947 - Changed course to 180° True.

2008 - Changed course to 125° True.

2315 - Checked pilot house repeater with master gyro and found that the pilot house repeater read 15 minutes lower than the master gyro. (Note: The repeater in the pilot house is the compass dial the helmsman uses to keep the ship's heading on the correct course. The master gyro has to be assumed to always be correct unless there is obvious failure. This can be roughly checked by comparison with the reading of the magnetic compass. Therefore when the pilot house repeater is not showing what the master gyro is actually "saying", the dial on the repeater must be aligned with the master gyro so that what the helmsman steers is what the gyro says is the true course).

July 15, 1945

0000 - Steaming as before on course 125° True. Proceeding from Okinawa Shima to Guam Island.
0350 - Checked pilot house repeater with master gyro and found repeater to be one degree low.
0400 - Steaming on course 125° True.
0415 - Checked pilot house repeater with master gyro and found that both read the same; 125° True.
1615 - Wound and set all clocks. (Continued on course 125° True)

July 16, 1945

0000 - Steaming as before on course 125° True. Proceeding from Okinawa Shima to Guam Island, followed by YMS 360. (This course was maintained until 2045 when course is changed to 116° True).

July 17, 1945

0000 - Steaming as before on course 116° True.
0650 - Steering course 115° True.
1215 - All clocks wound and set.
1745 - Reduced speed to one third. Standing by to take YMS 360 in tow. [Shortly before this entry a message from 360 stated that both engines had stopped and the probable cause was there was too much water in the fuel tanks which meant that there was less fuel than there was supposed to be and they had literally run out of "gas" (diesel fuel). This was a very common problem especially for small craft that had to refuel from barges, other vessels and tanks that had been contaminated with water. If the Engineering Officer and the head Motor Machinists checked the quality of the fuel before taking it into their tanks this problem could have been reduced considerably. Sometimes, however, this was not a very good option depending on weather conditions, etc.)
1823 - Heaving line passed to YMS 360.
1827 - Towing line secured to YMS 360.
1848 - Increased speed gradually to 940 RPMs. 200 fathoms of tow line out.
2000 - Steaming as before on course 115° True with YMS 360 in tow.
2200 - Steering 114° True.
2207 - Steering 113° True. (Note: When 183 was taking 360 in tow 183 sent an urgent short wave message to the Port Director at Apra Guam giving their position and requesting that a sea going tug come out to meet them and take 360 into the harbor. This was urgent as 183 was low on fuel and did not have the capability of taking 360 into the harbor. The Port Director acknowledged receipt of message and said the tug would be underway at first light. When 183 finally had 360 in tow they were probably less than 100 miles from Guam. One could begin to smell the green vegetation blowing off the island by the southeast wind. The best safe speed was about 3 knots, or less. Sea conditions were moderate and there was no need to take the chance of parting the tow line and having to do all of that over again. So everyone settled down to a "slow tow" through the night. Ens. Davis remembers these details very well and again says that all of this should have been in the log, but wasn't).

John Dixon Davis

July 18, 1945

0000 - Steaming as before on course 113° True. Proceeding from Okinawa Shima to Guam Island, with YMS 360 in tow.
0800 - Steaming as before on course 113° True.
1035 - Steering course 110° True.
1155 - Steering course 111° True. (Note: by now the sea going tug was in sight heading toward them with a "bone in her mouth").
1248 - Steering course 120° True. (Note: The towing line has been cast off 360, 183 speed very slow as the tow line is taken in).
1345 - Reduced speed and completed taking in tow line. (Note: After this 183 makes her best speed to the harbor).
1430 - Moored on starboard side of Y.O. 39 to take on fuel.
1450 - Clocks set ahead one hour.
1656 - Underway for anchorage.
1730 - Moored port side to ACM 8 in Apra harbor, Guam.
1740 - YMS moored to starboard.
1852 - Executed colors. (Note: USS Picket, ACM 8, was an auxiliary minelayer. The ACM's now coming on the scene are becoming the flagships of various minesweeping squadrons. While in Guam our squadron commander and his staff, who are responsible for 183, 360 and a number of other YMSes ride the USS Picket. We get our orders through them and they are "our big brother" when it comes to all of our needs, technical as well as recreational. *(See End Note No.98)*.

July 19, 1945

0000 - Moored as before in Apra Harbor on starboard side of ACM 8 with YMS 360 moored to port. (Note: Most of the day was spent assessing our needs for provisions, engine repair, consultations on replacement of ship's service generator, and information on recreational facilities. The most interesting item we were immediately concerned with was the operation plan for the invasion of Japan. It was delivered personally to our skipper by registered Guard Mail. There it was, what we knew was coming sooner or later. The skipper took it into his stateroom where he spent some time looking through it alone. When he came out, he went over to the safe in the wardroom where all confidential materials were stored and spun the combination. He turned the handle, opened the safe door, placed the very thick book inside, shut the door, spun the combination, tried the handle. When satisfied it was locked he turned to the other three officers and said, "When we get a chance tonight we'll all look at it together").
1745 - Began taking power from ACM 8.

Chapter 12

Preparation For The Invasion Of Japan

July 20, 1945

0000 - Moored as before in Apra Harbor, Guam.

1806 - Underway for ATR 81.

1813 - Moored port side to ATR 81 in berth 303. (ATRs were wooden-hulled Rescue Tugs, built to patrol convoy lanes. Displacement: 852 tons; length 165'6"; Beam 33'4"; Draft 15'6"; Speed 12 knots; Armament 1 3"; complement 35; Triple-expansion reciprocating steam engines, single screw, 1600 hp. They were not named. *(See End Note No.99)*.

2000 - Moored as before to ATR 81 with YMS 360 on starboard side.

July 21, 1945

0000 - Moored as before to ATR 81 with YMS 360 on starboard side.

1030 - Inspection held by executive officer (Lt.jg Douglas Mitchell).

1125 - YMS 360 took signal duty.

1303 - YMS 360 underway from alongside.

1304 - SMITH, C.P., Jr., C.S.M.(AA)(T), USN(274-38-34); SHURTS,C.E., MoMM1/c, USNR(410-25-64); SHARP, R.L., SC2/c, USN(866-26-28); LEVESQUE,L.L., GM 3/c, USNR(806-75-90); transferred to Receiving Ship for transportation to the United States.

1337 - Moored starboard side to YMS 441 in berth 301.

1352 - YMS 360 moored to port side.

1502 - YMS 441 underway from starboard side. YMS 345 now on starboard side.

July 22, 1945

0000 - Moored as before with YMS 345 on starboard side and YMS 360 on port side.

1148 - YMS 345 underway from alongside. LCI 603 now on starboard side. (Note: During the average day in Guam, various crew members visited the warehouses on the beach with work orders or chits for machinery and engine parts. These items were essential for the repair of the engines, etc. Officers and men alike had great difficulty in getting these parts and supplies unless they "crossed the palm" of the supply personnel with a suitable trophy from the forward area. For example, a gold tooth knocked from the jaw of a dead Japwould bring the highest reward from supply. This of course was government property, we were trying to get our ships ready to invade Japan, but our "comrades in arms" on the beach refused to fill our orders unless we bribed them. If we couldn't produce a Japear, tooth, etc. the part we needed was not in stock and would have to be ordered from the states. This was a constant problem and until we alerted higher authority to the problem our maintenance and repair languished. The supply people could not believe that since we had been in the Okinawa area for 3 ½ months we did not have these gruesome trophies by the bucket-full. The truth is that our feet never set foot on terra firma for nearly 5 months. Even if we had possessed a tooth, we wouldn't have traded it for a fuel injector that would hasten our voyage into the maws of Kyushu. Another problem stemmed from the fact that we would be among hundreds of minecraft in that invasion fleet on November 1, 1945. There were items for safety and comfort for the crew that were not obtainable since our ship's life expectancy was only 30 minutes once the invasion began. Therefore an 8 square foot piece of floor linoleum for the wardroom, to replace the original worn through to the wooden deck underneath, was not available to us. Why, the reasoning went, put in a new floor covering when we would be sinking within 30 minutes after the invasion began? Gratefully, they did not deny us bullets).

1910 - Movie party left ship.

2155 - Movie party returned.

July 23, 1945

0000 - Moored as before to buoy in berth 301 with YMS 360 on port side and LCI 603 on starboard side in Apra Harbor, Guam Island.

1000 - LCI 603 underway from alongside. YMS 477 moored to starboard side. (Note: There were many interesting things to see in Apra Harbor. It was like a bustling city. On the northwest side of the harbor giant earth movers were trundling their multi ton loads to the end of an ever lengthening coral sea wall. Eventually this breakwater would almost enclose the whole harbor making it virtually landlocked and protected from the sometimes vicious weather from that quarter. If anyone had time to kill, which wasn't often, the flying bridge made a great viewing stand as we watched these ant like creatures, several miles away from our anchorage, hastily dumping their loads and then returning for more and more. This went on for 24 hours a day, day after day. The Sea Bees did some great work all over the Pacific area and they were still working on this project when we left Guam some weeks later. We do not know when it was finished).

2000 - Moored as before.

July 24, 1945

0000 - Moored as before to buoy in berth 301 Apra Harbor, Guam, with YMS 360 on port side and YMS 477 moored on starboard side. 0820 - YMS 360 underway from alongside.

1040 - YMS 360 moored to port side.

1206 - FERRIS, George Elmer (620-90-86), MoMM 1/c, V-6, USNR; and WIELEBA, Casmir (n), (622-86-94), GM 2/c, V-6, USNR; reported aboard for duty. (Note: There were many advantages to being in a rear area like Guam. Not only were there facilities for emergency repairs for even the big ships like cruisers and battleships there were also recreational facilities and frequent visits by USO entertainment groups. The crew of 183 had hardly ever seen one of the big new battleships even in the distance. But in Guam a big new one came in for one reason or another every now and then while we were there. On an afternoon like this one Ens. Davis remembers a work party he was on coming back to 183 from the supply depot. They were traveling in the 9' wherry (a round bottom lap strake row boat with small outboard motor on the stern). The small outboard motor was the prized possession of the crew of any YMS. When we went ashore and had to wait for the work party to return to the dock or barge or a supply ship, a guard was always stationed in the wherry to guard the outboard motor to insure that it was not stolen by our "comrades in arms from another ship". While they were doing their assigned work, the battleship USS New Jersey II, BB 62, had entered Apra Harbor and had moored to a huge mooring buoy with her anchor chain. This mooring buoy was right in our path as we returned to 183. There this huge vessel, of the Iowa Class (Missouri was also a sister) blocked our path. We decided to go around the mooring buoy, but as we began this course change we decided to go between the buoy and the New Jersey and under the mooring chain. It was an awesome experience. We cut the motor while we were under the overhang of the bow and looked up at the bull nose (through which the mooring chain went from the ship to the buoy). We learned later this was seven stories above the water-line. We must have looked like a bunch of country bumpkins staring up at a skyscraper in Manhattan. This was the closest we ever came to a battleship). (Remembering battleships brought to mind the visit of HMS King George V. She was a neat looking ship, though she was not as large as the New Jersey II. It was a few days before Chief Signal Man C.P. Smith was transferred back to the States. Ens. Davis remembers that several of the ship's company were watching as this British man-of-war was shepherded into the harbor by several tugs. Several were on the flying bridge of 183 including Chief Smith and Davis. The large, very bright signal light on the starboard wing of the Britisher's highest bridge was carrying on, blinking rapidly without letup. It might have been just a means of getting attention. Ens. Davis asked Chief Smith, "Is he (the King George V) saying anything? He's too fast for me." Chief Smith said, "Oh yes, he's saying something, but you may not want to know what it is." Davis replied, "Yeh, read it for me." Smith replied, "Well, he's making the same statement over and over again and here he goes again. The limey says, 'All Yanks eat sh..'. Just about that time, Davis recalls, there was a chorus of horns and whistles from all classes of US Navy ships and many blinkers were signaling to the "limey". "We were not in a favorable position to read what our "comrades in arms" were saying to him, we could only imagine. In the interest of Allied solidarity, we chose to ignore the "limey" altogether").

July 25, 1945

0000 - Moored as before to buoy in berth 301, Apra Harbor, Guam, with YMS 360 on port side and YMS 477 on starboard side. (Note: For the rest of this day routine maintenance and repair was carried on and preparations were continued for the removal of the useless ship's service generator and the installation of a new one. Almost every day from the vantage point of 183's location the bow of the cruiser USS Pittsburgh could be seen tethered to a buoy on one side of the harbor. This section of the bow was said to be 100 feet long and was torn off in a typhoon on June 4, 1945. No personnel were lost and after shoring up the bulkhead she slowly made her way to Guam, arriving on June 10. The bow which did not sink was later retrieved and towed into Apra Harbor where it was moored to a buoy. It floated vertically and the many feet of the bow sticking out of the water looked like a giant narwhale breaking the surface to breathe. Naval personnel facetiously referred to the storm in which the Pittsburgh lost her bow as "Halsey's typhoon" as the Admiral was commander of the task force buffeted by the storm. *(See End Note No.100).*

July 26, 1945

0000 - Moored as before to buoy in berth 301, Apra Harbor, Guam, with YMS 360 on port side and YMS 477 on starboard side. (Note: The rest of the day was spent on repair, etc. Now that 183 was fairly well repaired except for the installation of the new generator there was more time for rest and recreation. The crew took turns going ashore for "fun" and the officers took turns visiting the "officers club". The officers' club was on a rather high hill and good walking distance from the dock area. This in itself made it difficult for any but the most dedicated to get "a drink". The landlubber does not realize that it took many days ashore, and a good deal of walking to get one's land legs back. Going up that hill was a real obstacle course. Davis remembers, while he and a buddy sat on a bench of some kind to rest, observing a score of other officers as they trudged up that hill to the club. The club did not open until 3 PM and if you were early a line formed so that there was some order in going to the bar for a beer or whatever. The club closed at 5 PM so that many of the officers tried to do in two hours what they might have taken several hours to do as a civilian. They were hot, sweaty, tired from the hill climb and really thirsty for something other than water. It didn't take long for some of them to get a little woozey. Those who used some control did OK. Those who did not exercise any control found it difficult to "navigate". In any event, when 5 PM came, the bar was closed down and those still on their feet

John Dixon Davis

were pushed out the door. Those not on their feet were assisted or carried out by their buddies. It was some sight to see this crowd, many of whom were in good shape, come running down the hill in about one quarter of the time it took to climb it 2 hours before. So much for rest and recreation at Guam).

July 27, 1945

0000 - Moored as before to buoy in berth 301, Apra Harbor, Guam, with YMS 360 on port and YMS 477 on starboard. (Note: The rest of this day was spent in normal, port routines. We saw various ships come and go from the harbor. The really big ships would draw an audience from the 183 crew who happened to be on deck, but the comings and goings of the many ships soon became commonplace and drew little attention. An interesting ship arrival on July 27, 1945, we learned much later, was that of USS Indianapolis (CA-35). Some of us were bound to have seen her, but without taking any special note of the fact, it was just another cruiser. She had made a stop, the day before, on July 26, at Tinian Island which is about 80 miles north of Apra Harbor and just a few miles southwest of Saipan. Only a handful of military personnel knew why she stopped at Tinian. We learned much later that the stop was to deliver essentials of what was to become known as the Hiroshima atomic bomb. After this delivery, Indianapolis came to Apra Harbor. The next day, July 28, 1945, she departed Guam for Leyte. Surely we saw her leave the harbor, but this historic moment did not register for we didn't know what we might have seen until much later. As the world came to know later, Indianapolis was torpedoed and sunk in the early morning hours of July 30, 1945. *(See End Note No.101)*.

July 28, 1945

0000 - Moored as before to buoy in berth 301, Apra Harbor, Guam, with YMS 360 on port side and YMS 477 on starboard side. (Note: we were all three scheduled to go into dry dock and were waiting for that time to be assigned. Meanwhile, we were engaged in the regular, daily routine. There was nothing of note to report for this date).

July 29, 1945

(Nothing of note to report for this date).

July 30, 1945

(Nothing of note to report for this date). [From time to time the skipper and his three officers gathered around the wardroom table. The safe was opened and they studied the operation plan for the invasion of Japan. There was our number, YMS 183, along with a couple of hundred other YMSes. We were scheduled along with many of the others to become involved about two weeks before the troops came ashore on November 1, 1945. The life expectancy of 183 and many of the others was estimated to be about 30 minutes. That didn't mean that all of us would likely be destroyed in the first 30 minutes, but that a lot of us would be. The catch was which ones? Somewhere in this tome we saw that in the first three days of the invasion there was likely to be one hundred thousand casualties].

July 31, 1945

(Nothing of note to report this date).

August 1, 1945

0000 - Moored as before to buoy in berth 301, Apra Harbor, Guam with YMS 360 moored to port and YMS 477 to starboard.

1137 - YMS 477 underway from alongside starboard side.

1141 - YMS 345 moored to starboard side. (Note: It would seem to the civilian reader that these ships came and went with no reason stated. Actually, a buoy or berth was like a parking lot for automobiles. When there was no need to go anywhere, staying in the nest of ships was like parking. The ships had to refuel, restock provisions, etc. and at the appointed time assigned by the oiler, or water barge, etc. the YMS had to leave the nest and go to wherever these providers happened to be located. Sometimes they were nearby and at other times in distant locations. When provisioning was completed the YMS returned to the nest to which it was assigned. In this way the Port Director knew where any vessel was at all times).

1141 - YMS 345 moored to starboard side.

1520 - Tug alongside to take YMS 360 in tow. (Note: As a result of the water in the fuel of YMS 360, her main engines had to undergo a complete overhaul. That is why she had to be towed. Her ship's service generators were still working, however).

1609 - Underway steaming on various courses to go alongside YMS 360.

1621 - Moored to starboard side of YMS 360 at buoy Charlie 3.

August 2, 1945

0000 - Moored as before port side to YMS 360 (same as being moored to starboard side of YMS 360) at buoy Charlie 3, Apra Harbor, Guam.

0703 - YMS 357 Moored on starboard side.

1425 - Mooring chain secured to buoy Charlie 3.

1615 - Wound and set all ship's clocks.

August 3, 1945

0000 - Moored as before to buoy Charlie 3 with YMS 360 on port side and YMS 357 on starboard, Apra Harbor, Guam.

0735 - YMS 357 underway from starboard side. SC 671 moored to starboard side.

0736 - SC 671 underway from starboard side. [Note: SC 671 had the Guard Mail (official Navy mail) and regular mail delivery duty. She only stopped long enough to drop off what was addressed to YMS 183 and 360 and to pick up our out-going mail].

0740 - SC 1040 moored to starboard side.

1220 - Captain left ship.

1620 - YMS 357 moored to starboard.

1640 - Captain returned to ship. (Note: When moored to a buoy and/or a pier and the Captain had a meeting with whomever, usually an LCVP or something similar was sent to pick him up and deliver him to the vessel, etc. where the meeting was being held. When this assignment was completed the Captain was returned to the ship).

August 4, 1945

0000 - Moored as before at buoy Charlie 3, Apra Harbor, Guam with YMS 360 on port side and YMS 357 on starboard.

0630 - YMS 357 underway from starboard side.

1000 - Captain's inspection started.

1030 - SC 1311 moored to starboard side. Captain's inspection completed.

1310 - Started taking water from NOB barge 245.
1350 - Completed taking on fresh water. 1000 gallons received.
1515 - SC 1311 underway from starboard side.
1640 - Received stores aboard.
1733 - YMS 357 moored to starboard side.
1746 - Started taking power from YMS 360.

August 5, 1945

0000 - Moored as before to buoy C-3, Apra Harbor, Guam with YMS 360 to port and YMS 357 to starboard.
0600 - Stopped taking power from YMS 360.
0615 - YMS 357 underway from starboard side.
1511 - Underway to go alongside of ATR 73 (a wooden hull rescue tug).
1600 - Moored as before to port side of ATR 73 in berth 306.

August 6, 1945

0000 - Moored as before, starboard side to ATR 73 with YMS 357 on port side, berth 306, Apra Harbor, Guam. (Note: At 0245, a B-29, "Enola Gay", took off from Tinian Island carrying the bomb that USS Indianapolis had delivered on July 26. Tinian Island was about 80 miles north of Apra Harbor, Guam. At
0915, the atomic bomb was dropped on the city of Hiroshima. Of course, the only people who knew this were a handful of military at Tinian and the crew of "Enola Gay". It would be more than a week before we, and most of the rest of the world would know about it and the second bomb dropped on Nagasaki on August 9). *(See End Note No.102)*.
0615 - YMS 357 underway from port side.
0617 - PGM 28 moored to port side.
1815 - USO Party left ship. (Note: Half of the crew went ashore to see an entertainment by a USO Troupe.)
2215 - USO Party returned to ship.

August 7, 1945

0000 - Moored as before on port side of ATR 73 with PGM 28 on port side in berth 306, Apra Harbor, Guam.
0815 - PGM underway from alongside.
0955 - Captain left ship.
1800 - USO Party left for beach.
2150 - USO Party returned to ship.

August 8, 1945

0000 - Moored as before to port side of ATR 73 with YMS 357 on port side in berth 306, Apra Harbo, Guam.
0630 - YMS 357 underway from alongside. PC 813 moored to port side.
1100 - Received 1000 gallons of fresh water.
1615 - Passed mooring chain to buoy.
1630 - ART 73 underway from starboard side.
1635 - YMS 140 moored to starboard side.

August 9, 1945

0000 - Moored as before to buoy in berth 306, Apra Harbor, Guam, with YMS 140 on starboard side and PC 813 on port side. (Note: Sometime in the early morning hours a second atomic bomb was dropped on Japan, this time on the city of Nagasaki. As with the bomb on the 6th, no one knew about this one either, except for the principals involved).
1230 - Working party left ship.
1605 - Working party returned to ship.

August 10, 1945

0000 - Moored as before to buoy in berth 306, Apra Harbor, Guam, with YMS 140 on starboard side and PC 813 on port side.
0914 - Technicians came aboard.
1045 - Technicians left ship.
1245 - PC 813 underway from alongside. YMS 429 moored to port side.
1925 - YMS 429 standing radio watch..

August 11, 1945

0000 - Moored as before to buoy in berth 306, Apra Harbor, Guam, with YMS 140 on starboard side and YMS 429 on port side.
1000 - Garbage barge came along side to pick up our garbage. Following the departure of the barge an inspection of the ship by the Captain was held. 1619 - Captain left ship. (Note: Planning for the invasion of Japan continues, as well as preparation for dry docking of 183 and the installation of a new ship's service generator).
2200 - Captain returned to ship.

August 12, 1945

0000 - Moored as before to buoy in berth 306, Apra Harbor, Guam, with YMS 140 on starboard side and YMS 429 on port side.
0815 - Technicians came aboard.
1500 - Technicians left ship.
1840 - GOLLADAY, Marvin E., PhM 1/c, (603-09-57) reported aboard for duty.

August 13, 1945

0000 - Moored as before to buoy in berth 306, Apra Harbor, Guam with YMS 140 on starboard side and YMS 429 on port.
0810 - Technicians came aboard.
1245 - Technicians came aboard to install fathometer. (Note: With the fathometer the crew could be reasonably certain what the depth of the water was at any given time. This device would add immeasurably to the accuracy of navigation in shallow water adding to safety).
1540 - Captain left ship.
1615 - Technicians left ship. (Note: The gangway watch failed to log the Captain back aboard).

August 14, 1945

0000 - Moored as before to buoy in berth 306, Apra Harbor, Guam, with YMS 140 on starboard side and YMS 429 on port.
0008 - YMS 429 taking power from us.

0545 - YMS 429 now giving up power. (Note: Apparently YMS 429 had a generator failure and 183 gave them power until they could get their problem fixed and make their own power).

0950 - Pay Master came aboard to pay Ship's Company.

1045 - Pay Master left ship.

1231 - Working party left for beach.

1710 - Working party came aboard with Ship's Service supplies. (Note: These supplies were comprised of many different items that the average crew member needed from time to time such as pencils, paper, envelopes for mailing letters, shaving cream, tobacco products, toilet articles, certain items of clothing, candy, etc., etc. These items were sold to the individual at the Ship's Service Store. The profit from their sale was returned to the general fund for the purchase of items that could benefit the whole crew. One of the commissioned officers was assigned by the Captain to administer this service and keep accurate records for auditing. Enlisted men could volunteer to run the store for wages under the supervision of the officer administrator. Of course, as with everything on a Naval vessel, the Captain had full responsibility for the proper operation of the Ship's Service Store. On a small vessel like 183 this did not involve a very large sum of money, but on a large ship it created an account of many thousands of dollars very quickly).
2000 - Moored as before. YMS 429 receiving power from us. [Note: In the last day or so rumors were circulating that the U. S. had dropped some sort of new bomb on Japan. We did not know any details or even if it was true and if so, what the outcome might be. But sometime in the late afternoon of this day, civilian short wave radio broadcasts were carrying news that Japan had agreed to surrender. There was still no official word from the Navy. But the prospect of the war coming to an end was almost too good to be true. Actually it was 1449 at Tokyo, August 14 (East Longitude date, where we were it was two hours later because of the different time zones) that Radio Tokyo sent the news around the world that the surrender terms had been accepted. President Truman received the official notification 1550 August 14 (West Longitude date) and announced it from the White House at 1900 the same day. Where we were at Guam it was the next day (August 15) since we were west of the international date line, but in the East Longitude area. The President declared a two-day holiday of jubilation. *(See End Note No.103)*].

August 15, 1945

0000 - Moored as before to buoy in berth 306, Apra Harbor, Guam with YMS 140 on starboard side and YMS 429 to port side.

0600 - Taking power from YMS 429.

1030 - YMS 429 underway from alongside. YMS 360 moved to port side.

1110 - Completed taking water from NOB (Naval Operating Base) fresh water barge 245. Received 1300 gallons.

1515 - Wound and set all ship's clocks.

1635 - Captain left ship. (Note: Again the gangway watch failed to log the skipper back on board later).

August 16, 1945

0000 - Moored as before to buoy in berth 306, Apra Harbor, Guam, with YMS 360 on port side and YMS 140 on starboard side.

0400 - Diver inspected bottom. (Note: This may have had something to do with preparation for dry docking, or to determine if the bottom was fouled enough to be scraped and painted when in dry dock).

0800 - Technicians came aboard.
1515 - Technicians left ship.
1821 - Commissary stores came aboard.

August 17, 1945

0000 - Moored as before to buoy in berth 306 Apra Harbor, Guam, with YMS 360 on port side and YMS 140 on starboard side.
0830 - Technicians came aboard.
1230 - Captain left ship. (Note: Again the skipper was not logged back aboard by the watch, nor were the technicians logged off the ship. The euphoria created by the war coming to an end was possibly too much for the gangway watch to handle).

August 18, 1945

0000 - Moored as before to buoy in berth 306 Apra Harbor, Guam with YMS 140 on starboard side and YMS 360 on port side.
1440 - Received 7 drums of lube oil.
1520 - Technicians came aboard.
1545 - Technicians left ship.
1755 - G S K Supplies came aboard.

August 19, 1945

0000 - Moored to buoy in berth 306 with YMS 360 on port side and YMS 140 on starboard side in Apra Harbor, Guam. 0827 - Underway steaming on various courses for Dry Dock ABSD-6.
0856 - YT 446 (Yard Tug) came alongside to assist in docking.
1015 - Moored starboard side to PCS 1402 standing by to enter Dry Dock.
1035 - Lines passed from Dry Dock. Secured engines. Entering Dry Dock.
1200 - In Dry Dock ABSD-6.
1428 - Secured generator, taking power from dry dock. (Note: Something needs to be said about the experience of being dry docked in one of the huge Advanced Base Section Docks. It is really a floating dry dock. Composed of steel pontoons, with very high steel sections on the fore and aft ends of the pontoon, which are joined together by their sides until eight or ten pontoons are one unit like the hull of a ship. The high steel section at each end of each pontoon is also joined firmly to its neighbor so that the whole series is one unit. Each pontoon, with its high steel sections was towed from the States to whatever location it was assigned to, in this case, Apra Harbor, Guam. The dry dock is flooded by sinking the pontoons with sea water to whatever depth is required to admit the ships that will be lifted out of the water to expose their hulls. When the proper depth of water in the inner part of the dry dock is reached, the pumps filling and sinking the pontoons are stopped. The high sections at the end of each pontoon remain above the water line giving stability and positive buoyancy to the whole unit. The position of each ship being dry docked is predetermined by engineers and supports for the keel are properly placed so that the ship, no matter its size, will be adequately supported when it is out of the water. When all of the ships being dry docked are in the proper place, as determined by civil engineers using transits, they are secured in that place with mooring lines. When all is ready, the pumps begin removing the water from the ballast tanks and the dry dock begins to float higher and higher, lifting all of the ships out of the water at the same time. When the deck of the dry dock is above water the pumps are stopped and the vessels inside the dry dock are ready for whatever work needs to be done. The chocks, which keep the hull upright after being lifted out of the water,

are checked for snug fit against the hull as the ship(s) are raised out of the water. At this point, the vessel looks like it did when being built, the keel resting on the ways and chocks or other types of bracing from the deck to each side of the ship keeping it upright. The pipe(s) through the hull carrying the ship's sewage into the sea when afloat are connected to a pipe line in the dry dock to carry it to a sewage treatment plant within the dry dock. After the sewage line is hooked up, the crews of each ship begin to scrape the marine growth off the bottom. Some of the ships have more than others, but all have some and it contributes to slowing the speed of the vessel and increased fuel consumption. Anyone who has never worked around boats in salt water and especially in the tropics would be amazed at the variety of marine life growing on a ship's bottom. Ships that remain at anchor for long periods of time are usually worse than those that are underway more. This growth includes sea weed of many varieties, barnacles, certain types of coral, oysters, mussels, etc. and all of the types of crabs, and small fish that feed off the sea weed. It is a sight to behold, but it must come off and that right away while it is still wet and relatively soft. Marine paints that help protect and preserve steel and wooden bottoms cannot be applied unless the bottom is smooth. Proper inspection of the bottom cannot be made until the bottom is scraped. On wooden vessels, the paint is especially important for killing the many varieties of wood boring worms and protecting from new infestations. Sometimes, the planking on a wooden hull ship has to be replaced because worms have weakened it by boring so many holes. Scraping the bottom vies with cleaning the bilges as the "nastiest" chore on a ship. It is hard work, most of it over head, with the scraped material falling on the scrapper. It requires a good deal of physical force, especially on the barnacles and other shell fish attached. All of this falls to the deck of the dry dock and almost immediately it all begins to putrefy and the stench is horrendous. Hosing the deck down with salt water can never be started soon enough to stop the stench and it never goes away until the dry dock is flooded when the ships leave. Sometimes a poorly connected sewer pipe will spill a good deal of its refuse on the dry dock deck. Add this to the rotting marine material and it is no wonder that the average sailor was wont to say, "I didn't join the Navy for this").

1600 - (Note: By this time all hands had begun the odious task of scraping the bottom. The plan was to work around the clock to get it done so that there would the maximum drying time of the wooden bottom before the anti-fouling, anti-worm paint is applied. Even though we now know that Japan has surrendered and ostensibly there is no more rush to get the dry docking done and the ship back in the water, this is not the case. The dry dock has a schedule and unless there is a dire emergency, like a hole in the bottom of one of the ships, the dock will be flooded on schedule and the newly repaired ships will be expelled and a new "batch" brought in. There are many, many ships that need dry docking, war or no war. It is also just beginning to sink into our minds, that while the Japanese will soon stop shooting at us, there are still thousands of mines, theirs and ours, that must be destroyed or rendered safe. Who will do this job? You guessed it. We are still at war while everyone else is now preparing to go home).

August 20, 1945

0000 - In Dry Dock ABSD-6, in Apra Harbor, Guam. Receiving shore power (from the Dry Dock). (Note: The Dry Dock was a self contained machine shop, repair ship, power source, sewage treatment plant, etc. all in one. There was little that we required at this time that ABSD-6 could not supply).

0400 - (Note: Sometime during this period the scrapping of the bottom and wash down was completed. Twenty four hours of drying time should have the bottom ready for painting, which the ship's crew would also do).

0805 - Technicians came aboard. (Note: Among our urgent needs was the replacement of the ship's service generator and the relocation of the radar antenna. These technicians were preparing for these two jobs. The skipper climbed down one of the ladders from the deck of 183 to the deck of the Dry Dock. He wanted to check on the condition of the bottom and to check the "zincs". Even on a wooden ship static electricity is created when the hull moves through the water and is dissipated into the water by way of any metal which is a part of the ship, such as the screws and the drive shaft. These items are made of brass and as the static electricity bleeds off it takes a little brass with it. In time the screws can be dissolved to the point where they will easily bend or break. In order to slow this process down, or even prevent it, a small block of zinc is attached to each brass strut which holds one of the drive shafts from an engine. The static electricity now bleeds through the block of zinc, since it is softer, taking particles of zinc instead of brass. Therefore the brass is "saved" as long as there is some zinc left on the strut. Ens. Davis recalls that the skipper remarked that about one half of each zinc block still remained and should last for sometime yet).

1600 - Technicians left ship.

August 21. 1945

0000 - In Dry Dock ABSD-6 Apra Harbor, Guam. Receiving shore power.

1030 - Started painting bottom of ship. (Note: The rest of the day was spent painting the bottom, preparing for new ship's service generator and relocating the radar antenna.

2000 - In dry dock as before.

August 22, 1945

0000 - In Dry Dock ABSD-6 Apra Harbor, Guam. Receiving shore power.

0811 - Technicians came aboard. (Note: These technicians dismantled the radar support tower from the flying bridge. The radar sweep antenna would be mounted on the mast later. For some unknown reason, when the surface search antenna was installed at Noumea, the previous fall, the technicians built a four legged steel tower about ten feet high and mounted the antenna on top of that. The legs of the tower were bolted into the deck of the flying bridge which was the overhead of the pilot house. It worked well in this location, but had two serious flaws. The four legs made the detailed plotting while minesweeping very difficult as they seemed to always be in the line of sight when taking bearings. The second flaw, while not as serious as the first, nevertheless, made our radar less efficient than the mast mounted antenna because it was 15 feet lower. This reduced the range of our radar because the line-of-sight radar waves hit the horizon sooner than if the antenna had been higher. Therefore we could not pick up surface objects that were more distant. Perhaps the only redeeming feature of the flying bridge mounting was the fact that no other YMS was ever seen with a mount like this. When 183 was in a nest or anywhere within visual range that four legged tower on the flying bridge announced her presence. Ens. Davis recalls that he may have personally seen 100 to 150 different YMSes at one time or another during his 16 months in the Pacific theater. He never saw another with the antenna mounted on the flying bridge. The assumption seems reasonable that 183 was the only one with the radar mounted on the flying bridge). (Note: The rest of the day was spent in repair and maintenance).

John Dixon Davis

August 23, 1945

0000 - In Dry Dock ABSD-6 Apra Harbor, Guam. Receiving power (shore). Working party came aboard to work on hull. (Note: The Dry Dock was lighted as if it were noon time. This made 24 hours work possible in the dry dock).

0345 - Working party left ship. (Note: There were two places on the hull that were probably worked on during the night. One was the cracked frames at the bow on the starboard side right under the forecastle decking. The planking fastened to this frame would admit sea water when our bow buried her stem into a high wave. Really didn't take in a lot of water, but it made the forward part of the main deck messy on the starboard side around the Gunner's Armory and storage compartment. Some water also got into the chain locker, but that was of no consequence. These cracked frames resulted from being sideswiped by USS Execute AM 232 on May 1, 1945. The other hull work had to do with replacing some oakum caulking above the water line, about amidships, which had come out probably from pounding against another ship while moored alongside during a moderate sea. We often had to leave a nest of ships when this happened and we anchored by ourselves to save the hull from damage).

0810 - Technicians came aboard. (Note: They came to prepare for the transfer of the radar antenna from the flying bridge to the top of the mast).

1510 - Moved Radar Antenna from flying bridge to top of mast. (Note: Insulated steel cable stays which were rigged before to give the mast added support were now tightened so that the mast could not sway fore and aft or from side to side. A crane attached to the Dry Dock had lifted the antenna from the 4 legged frame on the flying bridge to a shelf on top of the mast to which the antenna was bolted. Ens. Davis remembers that the absence of the radar on the flying bridge made the lookout crews and others feel "naked". They also had to find new "grab bars" to hold to in stormy seas now that the 4 legs of the radar were removed).

1545 - Technicians left ship.

August 24, 1945

0000 - In Dry Dock ABSD-6 Apra Harbor, Guam. Receiving shore power.

0905 - Moved generator from generator room. (Note: all was in readiness. The old generator had been completely disconnected from the electric circuits, and the engine itself was unbolted from its bed and was just sitting there. The overhead of the generator room directly above the old generator had a large square cut out so that the crane could drop its hook into the generator room and lift out the old generator. When this was completed the engine bed was ready for the new generator).

0925 - The new generator is brought aboard. (Note: It is lowered into the generator room and set on its bed by the crane and bolted down. As soon as the circuitry was attached, the engine was started and the generator began making electricity. As soon as this test was successfully completed carpenters from the dry dock rebuilt the overhead (roof), covered it with heavy canvas and painted it with several coats of heavy gray paint to seal it from leaking).

1300 - Held quarters on the forecastle. Life jackets and helmets checked.

August 25, 1945

0000 - In Dry Dock ABSD-6 Apra Harbor, Guam. Receiving shore power. (Note: The sewage pipe from the ship to the dry dock is removed, and all debris, tools, etc. are removed and stowed in the proper place on the dry dock).

0851 - Started flooding dry dock.

0940 - Ship now water borne.

0955 - Stopped taking shore power.
1035 - All lines clear - being towed to berth 307 by ITV 455.
1055 - Moored starboard side to YMS 402 in berth 306. (Note: The log never recorded how many or what types of ships were in the dry dock at the same time we were. We kept no record, but it seems there were half a dozen YMSes, two or three destroyers, a cruiser, and many other types of small craft. These dry docks were capable of lifting a battleship out of the water).
1200 - Moored as before. YMS 345 moored to port side.

August 26, 1945

0000 - Moored as before to YMS 402 in berth 306 Apra Harbor, Guam - with YMS 345 on port side.
0830 - Removed depth charges and smoke pots. (Note: The removal of these items confirmed the news that the war was over).
1230 - MILLET, Edward August, 663 04 45, PhM1/c, and FERRIS, George Elmer, 620 90 86, MoMM 1/c transferred to Receiving Station at Navy # 926 for transfer to United States.

August 27, 1945

0000 - Moored as before starboard side to YMS 402 with YMS 345 on port side in berth 306 Apra Harbor, Guam.
0945 - YMS 345 underway from alongside. (Note: the rest of the day was spent in securing loose gear and in general preparing for going back to sea).

August 28, 1945

0000 - Moored as before starboard side to YMS 402 in berth 306 Apra Harbor, Guam.
0815 - Technicians came aboard.
1020 - Received four (4) drums of lube oil and one drum of gasoline on board.
1215 - Received 800 gallons of fresh water from NOB water barge #245.
1500 - Technicians left ship

Figure 44 - Beck, Weltzien, Captain Klein, Davis in battle gear

August 29, 1945

0000 - Moored as before starboard side to YMS 402 in berth 306 Apra Harbor, Guam.
1040 - HARRIS, C.L., BM 1/c; MALLOY, F. (n), QM 1/c; and MURPHY, J.F., F 1/c(EM) reported aboard for duty.
1255 - Technicians came aboard.
1615 - Technicians left ship.

August 30, 1945

0000 - Moored as before starboard side to YMS 402 in berth 306 Apra Harbor, Guam.
0805 - YMS 402 underway from alongside. Moored to port side of YMS 360.
1700 - GSK supplies came aboard.

August 31, 1945

0000 - Moored as before starboard side to YMS 360 in berth 306 Apra Harbor, Guam.
0801 - Technicians came aboard.

1028 - Captain left ship.

1535 - Received fresh and dry provisions aboard.

2230 - Captain returned to ship.

September 1, 1945

0000 - Moored as before starboard side to YMS 360 in berth 306 Apra Harbor, Guam.

0836 - Wound and set all ship's clocks.

0953 - Received minesweeping gear aboard. (Note: This would be our main activity for the next several months).

1205 - Received 1700 gallons of fresh water.

1225 - YMS 163 moored to port side.

1615 - Received GSK stores aboard.

September 2, 1945

0000 - Moored as before starboard side to YMS 360 with YMS 163 on port side in berth 306 Apra Harbor, Guam.

0845 - YMS 360 underway from alongside. Moored starboard side to PC 1223.

1305 - BEATY, QUINCE EDWARD, 300 94 65, BM 1/c; RICHARD, ALFRED JOSEPH, 666 07 28, QM 1/c; and AYER, MYRON ELMER, 329 16 64, QM 3/c, transferred to Receiving Station at Navy # 926 (for transfer to the United States).

1350 - Captain left ship. 1620 - Captain returned to ship.

1647 - Underway from alongside YMS 193. (Note: This may be an error in transcription. It probably should be YMS 163).

1704 - Moored port side to YOG 39. Started taking on fuel.

1745 - Underway from alongside YOG 39. Steering on various courses starting out of Apra Harbor, Guam, proceeding to Saipan.

1804 - Steering base course 018° True, speed 700 RPMs.

1810 - C/S 760 RPMs.

1845 - C/C to 019° True.

2340 - C/C to 042° True. Speed 760 RPMs. (Note: Earlier this day in Tokyo Bay, Japan the formal surrender ceremonies took place. The war was indeed over. It is of interest to note, that among the really big and famous ships from many nations present at the surrender, there were 12 wooden hull YMSes. They were YMS 177, 268, 276, 343, 362, 371, 390, 415, 426, 441, 461, and 467). *(See End Note No.104)*.

September 3, 1945

0000 - Steering as before on base course 042° True. Speed 760 RPMs.

0005 - YMS 345 reports steering cable broken.

0040 - YMS 445 ordered to take YMS 325 in tow.

0418 - C/C to 040° True.

0610 - C/C to 030° True.

0630 - C/C to 028° True.

0819 - C/C to 045° True.

0821 - C/C to 050° True.

0825 - Entered Saipan Harbor.

0827 - Passed through net entrance.

0847 - Anchored in Saipan Harbor, Saipan in berth L-39.

0900 - YMS 176 moored on port side.
0915 - YMS 222 moored on starboard side.
1315 - Captain left ship.
1835 - Wound and set all ship's clocks. (Note: The Captain was not logged back aboard ship).

September 4, 1945

0000 - Anchored as before in berth L-39, Saipan Harbor with YMS 222 on starboard side and YMS 176 on port side..
0658 - YMS 222 underway from alongside.
0700 - YMS 176 underway from alongside.
0706 - Underway steering various courses for another berth.
0738 - Moored port side to YMS 222 in berth L-24.
0810 - Captain left ship.
1215 - Underway steering various courses for Tanapag Harbor.
1308 - Moored starboard side to PC 779 alongside ARG-2. (USS Luzon).
1312 - SC 1319 Moored on port side.
1810 - Captain returned to ship.

September 5, 1945

0000 - Moored as before starboard side to PC 779 with SC 1319 on port side alongside ARG-2 in Tanapag Harbor, Saipan.
0705 - Underway steering various courses for anchorage.
0733 - Moored port side to YMS 222.
0925 - Degaussing officer came aboard.
0945 - Underway steaming on various courses for degaussing range.
0955 - Started running range.
1114 - Completed run. (Note: A ship's inherent magnetic field can change over time and must be checked so that the degaussing coil around the inside of the ship's hull reduces the ship's field to the minimum. We recently changed a ship's service generator, moved the radar antenna to the top of the mast, removed the old 4 legged stand that held the radar antenna, removed depth charges, etc. All of these things caused the ship's field to change and running the range told us what was needed to minimize the field). 1235 - Degaussing officer left ship.

September 6, 1945

0000 - Anchored as before vicinity berth L-24 Saipan Harbor, Saipan.
1310 - Captain left ship.
1330 - Underway steaming on various courses for berth H-10.
1406 - Moored starboard side to YW 69. Taking on water.
1449 - Underway steaming on various courses for anchorage.
1530 - Anchored vicinity L-24. (Note: Captain not logged back aboard).

September 7, 1945

(Nothing of note to report for this day).

September 8, 1945

0000 - Anchored vicinity berth L-24 Saipan Harbor, Saipan.
0900 - Wound and set all ship's clocks.

John Dixon Davis

1000 - Captain's inspection held.

1845 - Man injured when water taxi came alongside is brought aboard for treatment. Name; Rudy Minster, 306 67 05, from LSM 377. Badly lacerated toes on right foot. Given first aid. (Note: Ens. Davis remembers this incident. The water taxi, an LCT, or something similar, was assigned to make regular runs between shore and the far reaches of the anchorage. It usually ran a regular schedule picking up those who wished to go ashore and returning to their ships those who had finished their business and/or recreation on the beach. The taxi had come alongside to allow some YMS 183 personnel to come aboard. She was on the starboard quarter and as the small waves raised and lowered the LCT bobbed up and down. She was held off by personnel pushing and keeping her off the quarter of 183, but close enough for our people to jump aboard 183 at the opportune time. There were a number of other men from other ships sitting on the gunwale of the LCT with their feet on the edge of the LCT's narrow deck. A particularly strong wave pushed the LCT against the quarter of 183 and when the LCT came up and the 183 went down the unfortunate man from LSM 377 had his right foot caught in the scissor like action and the toes on that foot were crushed between the two vessels. The man screamed in pain and passed out. Fortunately some of his shipmates were able to keep him from falling between the vessels. He was brought aboard 183 where our PhM tended to his wounds. It was determined after examination by the PhM that the injured man needed a doctor's care in a hospital. The Port Director was called by radio to send a small boat ambulance to pick the man up).

2000 - Injured man transferred to Port Surgeon's boat to be taken to hospital.

September 9, 1945

(Nothing of note to report for this day).

Chapter 13

On To The Mine Fields of Japan

(The War Is Over, But Not for Mine Craft)

September 10, 1945

0000 - Anchored as before in berth L-24 Saipan Harbor, Saipan.
0910 - Captain left ship.
0944 - Underway steaming various courses to take on fresh water.
1035 - Moored starboard side to YMS 341 alongside YW-69.
1040 - YMS 193 moored to port side.
1055 - Received 1100 gals. of fresh water.
1106 - Underway steaming on various courses for YOG-72 for fuel.
1130 - Moored port side to YOG-72.
1210 - Completed taking on fuel.
1215 - Wound and set ship's clocks.
1245 - Underway for anchorage.
1300 - Anchored in berth L-23.
1305 - Captain returned to ship.
1424 - Underway steaming on various courses standing out of Saipan Harbor.
1450 - Steering course 320° True, speed 400 RPMs proceeding from Saipan to Okinawa.
1520 - C/C to 290° True. Speed 700 RPMs.
1543 - C/S to 800 RPMs.
1556 - C/C to 320° True. C/S to 400 RPMs.
1708 - C/S to 700 RPMs. Formed in convoy on station.
1721 - Base course 307° True. C/S to 800 RPMs.
1830 - Lighted off navigational lights. (Note: This was the first time that anyone aboard YMS 183 had ever seen navigational lights turned on. Even though the surrender was signed over a week ago, the Navy brass didn't want to take any chances on a rogue Jap submarine trying to continue the war. Therefore, all naval vessels observed "darkened ship" until September 10. It was Ens. Davis' watch and he remembers the absolute confusion these lights created. Red and green lights, white masthead and range lights, some lights down near the water (small craft in the navy screen) some way up high (the several Liberty and Victory ships which were being escorted. It was impossible to tell who was what or where.
The only sure thing was that everybody seemed to be going in the same direction. Distances and relative positions were impossible to determine by sight. The radar was lighted off and suddenly all was well, as relative positions, distances, etc. were all right there on the radar screen. No sweat. The regular lookouts were at their stations, but they didn't know what they were seeing. That was ok, as the radar was our trusted lookout).
1900 - C/C to 307° True.
2012 - C/S to 700 RPM.
2029 - C/S to 600 RPM.
2043 - C/S to 700 RPM.
2127 - C/S to 760 RPM.
2235 - C/S to 720 RPM.
2247 - C/S to 700 RPM.

2318 - C/S to 760 RPM.

2329 - C/S to 800 RPM. (Note: When in a convoy as a member of the screen or escorts it always took some time to adjust your speed to all of the other ships in the screen and to the escortees. They were different sizes in this case and some could adjust their speeds to a finer point than others, so in order to stay in your proper position frequent speed adjustments were necessary).

September 11, 1945

0000 - Steaming as before on course 307° True. Speed 9 knots. Port screen vessel position # 4 (USF10-B) (Note: The log does not list the names or numbers of the ships of the screen or of those large freighters being escorted. We can glean the names and/or numbers of some of the screening ships because they are mentioned at one time or another in the log for the next several days of activity. A partial list of the YMSes includes 176, (183), 193, 222, 319, and 341. There may have been a few more, but they are not known to us. DE 640, USS Fieberling, was screen commander).

Figure 45 - It's a big ocean

0607 - Secured navigational lights.

0735 - C/S to 760 RPMs.

1755 - Changed TCP frequency from 2716 to 3000 by order of screen Commander.

1843 - Lighted off navigational lights.

2210 - C/S to 760 RPMs.

September 12, 1945

0000 - Steaming as before on base course 307° True. Speed 9 knots.

0625 - Secured navigational lights.

1600 - Steaming as before. (Note: The weather and the seas had been ideal since leaving Saipan. There was no chop on the water, almost oily smooth, but underlying the surface were rather large "rollers" running from east to west. Since they were running in the same direction we were going it was very pleasant. Up one "hill" and down the other. The frequency of the waves was wide and slow but over the last several hours the troughs were getting deeper. Still no wind to speak of and the surface of the sea was hardly rippled. Hardly any roll, just the up and down one wave and then another. Ens. Davis remembers talking to the skipper about these conditions. They both knew that a storm at sea could generate swells thousands of miles away. There had been no reports of bad weather anywhere as far as skipper knew; however he agreed we ought to ask the screen commander about this and weather predictions for the next several days)

1750 - Set clocks back one hour to conform with Minus 9 (Item time - east longitude). Turned on navigational lights.

2330 - Stopped starboard engine for repairs. Port engine 900 RPMs.

2345 - Both engines 760 RPMs.

September 13, 1945

0000 - Steaming as before on base course 307° True, speed 9 knots. Proceeding from Saipan to Okinawa.

0100 - Shifted screen position by order of screen Commander. Relative bearing from guide 307° degrees, distance 3 miles.
0530 - Turned off navigational lights.
0617 - C/S to 720 RPMs. C/C to 303° True.
0820 - YMS 176 reported floating mine. DE 640 left position. Guiding on YMS 176.
1117 - Proceeding to former position.
1812 - Turned on navigational lights.

September 14, 1945

0000 - Steaming as before on base course 303° True. Speed 9 knots, proceeding from Saipan to Okinawa in convoy in port screen position #4 USF10-B.
0600 - C/C to 306° True.
0637 - Turned off navigational lights.
1825 - Turned on navigational lights.
1835 - Wound and set ship's clocks.

Figure 46 - Nest in Fukuoka

September 15, 1945

0000 - Steaming as before on base course 306° True. Speed 9 knots. Port screen vessel in convoy proceeding from Saipan to Okinawa.
0545 - Turned off navigational lights.
0630 - C/C to 282° True.
1138 - C/C to 278° True.
1835 - Turned on navigational lights. (Note: No messages of warning about a possible typhoon received as yet. However, we were all beginning to feel that something was on the way, but we did not know where or when or if our paths would cross. All we could get was that no serious weather was expected in the Okinawa area. The wind from the east was moderate and the waves high and their frequency faster, but still not too bad and since we had been assured that it would not get any worse we could manage this type of weather all right).

September 16, 1945

0000 - Steaming as before on base course 278° True. Speed 9 knots. Proceeding from Saipan to Okinawa in convoy screen position #4.
0038 - Electric steering out. Now steering manual control. Steering various courses while convoy reforms for run into Buckner Bay. (Note: The wind was picking up rapidly now. And it was adding a knot or two to the speed of the convoy which was due to make landfall at Buckner Bay around 0800).
0400 - Steaming on course 335° True. (Note: Steering under manual control was difficult and cumbersome at best, but in these seas that were building higher and higher the helmsman was

unable to check the swing of the ship as quickly as with the electric steering motor and the course was zig-zaggy at best. At times it seemed that we would broach before the rudder took hold and the bow would swing back the other way. This type of exercise would be repeated over and over through the night and the helmsmen had to be relieved for rest much more frequently than usual).

0530 - C/C to 345° True. Speed 6 knots. (Note: We were close to making landfall at Okinawa but needed to go a little farther north.

0630 - Turned off navigational lights. (Note: The wind, now howling, was blowing the tops off the waves and salt water spray was beginning to pelt us when on the crest of a wave. When the Liberty ship on our starboard beam, 5 or 6 hundred yards away, was in the trough, you couldn't see the top of his mast. When we were on the crest (the waves were coming in on our starboard quarter) you could look down on the Liberty ship and when it was on the crest it looked like it might fall over onto us. While standing on the starboard wing of the pilot house, the ship rising abruptly on a wave coming under us, one felt as if he could reach out and stick his finger into the side of the wave. Sometime during this period we were released from our escort duty along with other YMSes. The log does not say so, but we were told that the Liberty and Victory ships were going to stay at sea to ride out the typhoon. This was the first official word we had had that we were in a typhoon, but it was really no surprise to be told this).

0700 - C/C to 005° True. (Note: this course change would enable us to get into position to turn west toward the entrance to Buckner Bay. When trying to make this course change, the ship would not respond to the helm. The engines had to be used as well as the helm to make this change and it took a little while to do it. We were proceeding independently now and presumably the other YMSes were happy to follow us).

0730 - Proceeding independently to Buckner Bay.

0800 - Steaming on various courses for Buckner Bay. (Note: For the next several minutes it became apparent that we could not get into Buckner Bay because the waves were too big and the wind too strong, and there was a jam up of ships trying to get out of Buckner Bay. We couldn't have gotten by them even if we had wanted to. Someone sent a radio message that all YMSes at sea in the Okinawa area should go up the eastern side of the island, round the northern tip of the island and go to the Unten Ko small craft shelter on the western side of the island. Neither the skipper nor the other three officers thought there was any wisdom in this suggestion (order?). To have followed this advice would have put us head on into the teeth of the typhoon winds. We were not sure where the center of the storm was, but we knew it had to be south of the island.

Figure 47 - Refueling at sea

The outer winds were coming from the east-northeast. We were not going to deliberately go head first into those monster seas. If we had any chance at all to survive this storm we had to put the island between ourselves and the oncoming seas. We had to go south, with the wind and waves, until we could turn west and get on the lee side of Okinawa. The skipper chose this course, ignored the advice (order?) from whomever it had come and notified our little band of YMSes what we were going to do. They all responded that they would follow our lead).

0825 - Unable to enter Buckner Bay due to typhoon. Proceeding to Unten Ko with YMSes following. C/C to 240° True. (Note: This course would take us a few miles south of the southern tip of Okinawa and then a course change to the north-northwest and then north would put the island between us and the typhoon whipped ocean. For the next 90 minutes we had quite a ride and we were lifted and almost engulfed by the huge seas coming on us from almost dead astern. The sky was still bright and sunny with few clouds, but the wind velocity continued to increase. In retrospect we were still in the outer bands of the storm. The waves were going faster than we could go and they lifted us to their crests as they passed under us. As we were picked up by the stern the ship raced "downhill" as the bow plowed into the next wave causing green water to flood the forecastle before rising up out of the water. The main danger here was in keeping the ship 90 degrees to the waves so that we didn't turn side to them and capsize. Fortunately our electric steering motor was back in use about this time).

0903 - Using electric steering.

0921 - C/C 270° True. (Note: We were now south of an east-west line running through the southern tip of Okinawa. We stayed on this course for about 30 minutes then turned northwest).

0953 - C/C to 316° True. (Note: we kept this course for about 25 minutes clearing the bulge of the southern end of the island. We are now on the lee side of the island and it protects us from the terrible waves. The wind is just as strong but the waves on this side of the island are small because there has not been enough distance from the shore on the lee side to build up more than moderate seas. The sunny sky is gone and dark cloud bands, very thick and low, plus the increasing rain and salt spray have made it quite dark and visibility decreases by the minute. The radar still functions well enough to show us the coastline and any other ships nearby. The noise of the wind through the rigging and around the pilot house and fixtures on the deck is loud enough to require more volume in one's speaking voice to be heard even inside. The ship is rolling and pitching enough to require standing and holding on to a stanchion or something attached to a bulkhead when trying to eat. Thick soup was the easiest to handle. Mug of soup in one hand and the other holding on to something. Rolling was not too bad, but the wind hitting the starboard side with full force kept us heeled over about 10 degrees to port most of the time and more with periodic stronger gusts).

Figure 48 - At Pearl Harbor on the way back to the States

1017 - C/C to 350° True. (Note: We are now coming up to the point of clearing the hump on the west side of the island near the town of Naha. We hold this course for about an hour).

1113 - C/C to 015° True. (Note: We now have a straight shot at the western end of Ie Shima about 30 miles, "as the crow flies" north of Naha).

1117 - Turned on stern light. (Note: We wanted to be seen by who ever might be following us).

1118 - Stopped long enough to pick up two men in LCVP who were lost in the typhoon. SMILEY, Henderson, Jr., S 1/c, 976-63-91; and OLSEN, William E., S 1/c, 314-25-38. LCVP sank. (Note: we tried to tow the LCVP but it broke apart. These men were lucky. If we had not come along when we did they would surely have been lost. They were stationed in the Naha area.).

1200 - C/C to 000° True.

1215 - C/C to 005° True.

1225 - Turned on all navigational lights. (Note: It was now like night time and anything we could do to help others see us was called for).

1302 - C/C to 010° True. [Note: As we head north toward the western end of Ie Shima (the island where Ernie Pyle, the famous news reporter and a favorite of the G.I.'s was killed) a course some 10° degrees or so to the east of true north would accomplish our purpose from our present location. However, the wind while not being able to build up large seas because of our proximity to Okinawa, was constantly blowing us to the west. We had to change course several times in order to counteract the problem and arrive off the western tip of Ie Shima in sight of this offshore island].

1445 - C/C to 020° True.

1500 - C/S to 900 RPMs.

1505 - C/C 025° True.

1516 - C/C to 040° True.

1535 - C/C to 045° True.

1541 - C/C to 050° True.

1605 - C/C to 090° True. Rounding Ie Shima.

(Note: We had gone some distance northwest of Ie Shima so this course, 090° True would take us toward Okinawa and the entrance area to Unten Ko.

1701 - C/C to 093° True. (Note: We are now in the vicinity of Kouri Shima which is a small island on the north side of the channel to Unten Ko. It is 5 P.M. (civilian time) and it is getting even darker than before. We are looking for channel markers and debating whether or not we should try to go in and take our chances on going aground or going back into more open water and anchoring. We couldn't see any channel markers, but we could see an AMc lodged on a coral reef to the south of us. A study of the US Navy chart for this area suggested that we

Figure 49 - Preparing to come along side

may be a little too far to the south of the channel to Unten Ko. We changed course to 080 True, speed dead slow. It wasn't long before the first channel marker was spotted. Relief, but then as we approached the first one we could not see the next one, so we didn't know whether to go right or left or straight ahead. Ens. Davis recalls, "I was OD. It was my watch, plus I didn't have any stomach for ending up like the AMc across the way. I suggested to the Captain that I take the Navy chart, a good flash light and a hand held search light and one of the quartermasters to use the hand held search light and someone to man the voice powered phone and go up to the acoustic hammer on the bow. While the ship was moving ahead as slowly as possible, the bridge would give me our heading, and with this orientation I could look at the chart, using my flashlight, and tell the quartermaster where to shine his search light in the hope of picking up the next channel marker. It worked! When a marker was recognized, (they were long poles driven into the coral reef and the tops were painted white) I relayed, through the phone talker the change in heading, if necessary. The quartermaster held his hand searchlight on the marker, moving the beam back and forth across it, until the signal man on the flying bridge could see it and shine the big search light on the marker. The skipper was able, in this way, to bring us into

Figure 50 - Leaving the nest

the channel and then into the creek of Unten Ko. The channel was not straight and it was narrow. It took us about an hour from the time we found the first marker until we entered the creek. I assume the YMSes following us did the same thing we did, and as I recall they all got into the haven safely. Fortunately for all, being this close to the semi mountainous coast gave excellent protection from the wind and the rain was only light and sporadic at this time.

1840 - Standing into Unten Ko channel. (Note: Unten Ko was on the banks of a small creek, or stream or strait that separated the small island of Yagachi Shima from the northeastern side of the Motobu Hanto peninsula. It was enclosed by relatively high ground on all sides and gave excellent protection for small craft. It was selected by Admiral Sharp to be fashioned into just such a place of refuge during the planning for the Okinawa invasion. This area was secured along with the rest of the northern two thirds of Okinawa within a few weeks of the invasion. Adm. Sharp never hesitated to send his YMSes to this place if there was even a remote chance that a typhoon might come across the area. He sent us there several times when an impending typhoon later veered away. He never apologized for this and his minecraft people loved him for it. Regrettably, when the war ended and Adm. Sharp retired, his replacement seemed not to know minecraft or care for them personally).

1930 - Moored starboard side to YMS 470. (Note: "YMS 470 was already here. Don't know how long she had been here or where she came from," Ens. Davis recalls; "we just ran our bow into the muddy bank, tied up, and received the 319 to moor on our port side. We made a deal with 470 and/or 319 to share power during the night and hit the sack, exhausted. One other item that was of concern the first time we came to Unten Ko was a note on the chart which said there was a leper colony at this place. After the events of this day no one cared about lepers, just a ship that could still operate and no casualties.").

1940 - YMS 319 moored to port side.

2000 - Moored as before at Dolphin 4 (a mooring spar) in Unten Ko.

September 17, 1945

0000 - Moored starboard side to YMS 470 with YMS 319 moored to port side at Dolphin # 4 in Unten Ko. (Note: The typhoon, which was still very much alive and proceeding north-northeast, was still buffeting the east coast of Okinawa, but we were secure. Conditions improved during the day but there was no place for us to go so we took in as much sack time as possible).

2340 - Received 300 gals. fresh water from YMS 222. (Note: The log does not mention the loss of four of our sisters in this typhoon: 98, 341, 421, and 472, or when we got the word on their sinkings).

September 18, 1945

0000 - Moored to YMS 470 with YMS 319 on port side at Dolphin #4, Unten Ko.

0550 - YMS 319 underway from port side. Turned on navigational lights.

0556 - Underway steaming on various courses for Buckner Bay.
0845 - Base course 035 True. Speed 5 knots.
0900 - C/C to 080 True.
0920 - C/C to 125 True.
1007 - C/C to 070 True.
1010 - C/C to 080 True.
1014 - C/C to 75 True.
1017 - C/C to 080 True. (Note: All of these course changes in the short period of time had to do with rounding the northern end of Okinawa and dodging debris in the water. The day was bright and clear with very little wind. The terrible condition of the ocean just 36 hours before was only a memory and except for having to go slowly and our concern for possible survivors from the lost ships it was a good day. The water was full of telephone poles. Probably lost over the side from a freighter in the storm. We had to be very careful not to hit one, or run over one and have our screws damaged. Had to dodge quite a few of them. There were, also, several flights of P51 fighters patrolling close to the water and not far off shore. They were probably looking for survivors, etc.).
1025 - C/C to 125° True.
1145 - C/C to 210° True. (Note: The northern end of the island has now been cleared and we are on a southwest course for Buckner Bay. Care still had to be taken not to collide with debris of all kinds. The farther south we proceed the less debris there is and we can increase speed).
1530 - C/C to 230° True.
1600 - Proceeding to Buckner Bay.
1605 - Speed 11 knots.
1809 - Anchored in Buckner Bay, berth B-208.
1850 - YMS 222 moored to port.

September 19, 1945

0000 - Anchored as before in berth B-208 in Buckner Bay, Okinawa with YMS 222 moored on port side. (Nothing of note to report for this day).

September 20, 1945

0000 - Anchored as before in berth B-208 in Buckner Bay, Okinawa, with YMS 222 moored on port side.
1100 - Gyro (Compass) secured for repairs.
1435 - Lighted off gyro.
1610 - Captain left ship.
1627 - Captain returned to ship.

September 21, 1945

0000 - Anchored as before in berth B-208 Buckner Bay, Okinawa, with YMS 222 moored to port side.
1505 - DEL ROSSO, JOSEPH N. 320-64-19 MoMM 2/c; HAMPTON, MALCOM M. 832-70-39 MoMM 2/c; SMITH, DONALD E., Sr. 945-23-66 S 1/c; and SMOOT, THOMAS E., Jr., 920-77-18, S 1/c reported aboard for duty.

September 22, 1945

0000 - Anchored as before in berth B-208 Buckner Bay, Okinawa with YMS 222 Moored on port side.

0845 - YMS 222 underway from alongside.

1705 - YMS 222 moored to port side.

1710 - Received dry stores aboard.

September 23, 1945

0000 - Anchored as before in berth B-208 Buckner Bay, Okinawa with YMS 222 moored to port side. (Nothing of note to report for this day).

September 24, 1945

0000 - Anchored as before in Buckner Bay, Okinawa. YMS 222 moored to port side.

0740 - Standing by to get under way.

0800 - Underway steering various courses for ARG-9 (USS Mona Island).

1100 - Moored port side YMS 325 alongside ARG-9 for availability.

1200 - Moored as before. SC 1314 moored to starboard side.

1400 - Received 700 gallons fresh water from ARG-9.

September 25, 1945

0000 - Moored as before on starboard side of YMS 325 with SC 1314 on our starboard side ARG-9.

0708 - YMS 325 underway. YMS 386 on port side.

0718 - YMS 386 underway. Moored port side to ARG-9.

1015 - SC 1314 under way from starboard side.

1025 - YMS 265 moored to starboard side.

1316 - YMS 365 - underway from starboard side. Captain left ship. YMS 243 moored to starboard side.

1715 - KLIVANS, JAMES MONROE, 949-60-84, SM 3/c; and CLARK, HOWARD BRUCE 927-37-36 RT 3/c (T), reported aboard for duty.

1735 - Wound and set all ships clocks. Captain returned to ship.

1820 - Captain left ship. (Note: Captain was not logged back aboard).

September 26, 1945

0000 - Moored as before on starboard side of ARG-9 with YMS 243 moored to starboard side.

0843 - Underway steering on various courses for minesweeping depot.

0931 - Moored starboard side to dock at Minesweeping Depot, Buckner Bay, Okinawa.

0957 - YMS 243 moored to port side.

1315 - Started removing topside weight as ordered by CTF 52 in radio message dated 230916. Following items were removed:

  1 Ready Locker 3"/50

  1 Ready Locker 20 M

  2 Depth Charge Release Track Mk VII

  2 20 MM Magazines - left hand

  8 20 MM Magazines – right hand

  20 Depth Charge Mk VI

100 Rds Ammunition V-T Mk 58-0

700 Rds Ammunition 50 Cal A.P.I.

700 Rds Ammunition 50 Cal Tracer

1050 Rds Ammunition 50 Cal Incendiary.

720 Rds Ammunition 20 MM H.E.T.

840 Rds Ammunition 20 MM H.E.I.

3000 Metallic Belt Links 50 Cal.

1 Mark I Acoustic Hammer, box & Y frame

1 Ingersoll Rand Hammer, size 5(a)

W E A – 1 Sound gear

Recorder Can - 55100   Serial   1734

Driver Amplifier   Serial 1-556

Receiver Ind. Oscillator Serial 1-397

Remote Training Control Serial 1-404

Motor Generator Unit - Navy type No.

C.G. 21742, Mfg. Type No. M1-8994

Relative bearing unit, Complete with accessories. complete set of spares for motor generator unit.

Complete set of spares for WEA - 1 Sound Gear. Various parts and tubes and complete set of Spares for Recorder Can (one).

1510 - Completed removal of topside weights.
1531 - Underway steering various courses for ARG-9.
1646 - Moored port side to YMS 325 alongside ARG-9.

September 27, 1945

0000 - Moored as before port side to YMS 325 alongside ARG-9, Buckner Bay, Okinawa.
0910 - YMS 325 underway alongside. Now moored to SC 1314.
0945 - YMS 243 - moored to starboard side.
1200 - Moored as before. Completed taking fuel from ARG-9.
1510 - Set and wound all clocks.
1734 - Underway steaming on various courses standing out of Buckner Bay for Unten Ko. (Note: The log does not tell us, but there was only one reason to go to Unten Ko and that was for shelter from an impending typhoon. Ens. Davis has a vague memory of a storm reported down south between Guam and the Philippines and after the disaster on Sept. 16 when a storm that was not supposed to come near to Okinawa came through like a "freight train". There was obviously "scrambled egg on some faces" as well as on the visors of their hats after flubbing that one. Somebody high up did not want to take another chance. So we headed out for Unten Ko).
1825 - Standing into Buckner Bay to take 193 in tow.
1900 - Standing out of Buckner Bay with YMS 193 following astern. (Note: YMS 193 had engine breakdown and needed to be in Unten Ko).

2000 - Proceeding from Buckner Bay to Unten Ko with YMS 193. Base course 040° True; speed 640 RPMs.

2015 - C/S to 600 RPMs.

2100 - C/S to 500 RPMs.

2120 - C/S to 400 RPMs.

2243 - Stopped port engine. Starboard ahead 560 RPMs.

2331 - C/S to 640 RPMs starboard. Port stopped. (Note: Towing YMS 193 required a very slow speed so as not to break the towing cable while at the same time making some forward progress. We had to stop one engine from time to time and only run the other. When a diesel engine runs at a slow speed for too long a time the carbon built up in the cylinders begins to damage the engine).

2340 - C/S speed to 500 RPMs on both engines.

September 28, 1945

0000 - Steaming as before on course 040° True, speed 6 knots proceeding from Buckner Bay to Unten Ko. YMS 193 following astern. (Note: Apparently YMS 193 is now able to operate under her own power and able to make 6 knots).

2355- C/C to 025° True. (Note: This little convoy is steaming up the eastern side of Okinawa and is poised to begin the turn to the left around the northern end of the island. The weather is obviously good as the speed being recorded is just below standard).

0154 - C/C to 000° True.

0330 - C/C to 303° True.

0347 - C/S to 7 knots.

0355 - C/C to 298° True.

0400 - C/S to 8 knots.

0435 - C/C to 270° True.

0450 - C/C to 227° True.

0620 - Secured navigational lights.

0655 - Proceeding on various courses and speeds standing in to Unten Ko.

0800 - Proceeding as before, standing in to Unten Ko.

0817 - Moored to dolphin 3 with sweep wire secured to mooring buoy.

0930 - YMS 178 moored to port side.

0943 - YMS 222 moored to starboard side.

1500 - Received dry provisions aboard.

September 29, 1945

0000 - Moored as before to dolphin 3 in Unten Ko with YMS 176 on port side and YMS 222 on starboard side. (Nothing of note to report for the rest of the day).

September 30, 1945

0000 - Moored as before to dolphin 3 in Unten Ko with YMS 176 to port side and YMS 222 to starboard. (Nothing of note to report for the rest of the day).

October 1, 1945

0000 - Moored as before to dolphin 3 Unten Ko, with YMS 176 on port side and YMS 222 to starboard.

1300 - Captain left ship.

1630 - Captain returned to ship. (Nothing of note to report for the rest of the day.

October 2, 1945

0000 - Moored as before to dolphin 3, Unten Ko, with YMS 176 on port side and YMS 222 on starboard side. (Nothing of note to report for the rest of the day).

October 3, 1945

0000 - Moored as before to dolphin 3 at Unten Ko, Okinawa with YMS 176 on port side and YMS 222 on starboard side. (Nothing of note to report for the rest of the day).

October 4, 1945

0000 - Moored as before. (Nothing of note to report for the rest of the day).

October 5, 1945

0000 - Moored as before to dolphin 3 in Unten Ko with YMS 176 on port side and YMS 222 on starboard side.
0805 - Held quarters on forecastle.
0810 - HADLEY, Jack A., 342-56-67 RdM 3/c suffered first degree burns on first, second and third fingers of left hand and first and second fingers of right hand when striking a match and igniting match box. First aid applied by PhM.
0845 - Captain left ship.
1130 - Captain returned to ship.

October 6, 1945

0000 - Moored as before to dolphin 3 at Unten Ko with YMS 176 on port side and YMS 222 on starboard.
0825 - CLENDRGIN, L. D., MoMM 3/c, 928-52-57; BORDEN, F. R., GM 2/c, 614-31-95; and POPE, H.A., EM 3/c 385-71-14, came aboard as passengers to Buckner Bay.
0844 - Underway steaming on various courses for Buckner Bay.
0925 - Following YMS 90 to Buckner Bay. Speed 11 knots, course 051° True.
1113 - C/C to 108 True.
1135 - C/C to 150° True.
1235 - C/C to 205° True.
1507 - C/C to 230° True.
1540 - Maneuvering on various courses and speeds to give berth to ships standing out of Buckner Bay.
1715 - Standing into Buckner Bay.
1752 - Moored starboard side to LST-804.
1802 - YMS 389 moored to port side.
1900 - Finished taking fresh water (from LST-804).
1917 - Anchored in Buckner Bay.

October 7, 1945

0000 - Anchored as before in Buckner Bay vicinity berth B-217.
0830 - Three passengers brought from Unten Ko left ship.
1026 - Captain left ship.
1312 - Underway for ARG-9.

1500 - Captain returned to ship. (Note: The skipper was attending a meeting relative to our soon proceeding to Japan with others to clear several harbors on Kyushu. The skipper requested permission for YMS 183 and others to return to Unten Ko immediately as there was a typhoon not too far away between Okinawa and Formosa. Even though the predicted course of this storm, dubbed "Louise", would take it into the East China Sea and away from Okinawa on the 8th of October [the next day] our skipper reminded the Commander that experience had shown that predicted courses for typhoons rarely were achieved. Also he reminded the powers that be that Unten Ko was only 8 hours away and these YMSes would be protected there if Louise didn't follow her predicted course. Ens. Davis recalls, "Our hearts sank when the skipper told us the Commander said emphatically, something like 'permission denied', you will stay in Buckner Bay. This typhoon will miss Okinawa by a wide berth and we can get on with getting you people ready to go to Japan. We've lost enough time already.'" [Not a direct quote, but the gist of the conversation]. We were less than 3 1/2 weeks after the September 16 typhoon (which we didn't know anything about) and lost 4 of our sisters in that one. We all agreed that Admiral Sharp would have already sent us to Unten Ko. We wouldn't have had to ask").

1656 - Anchored vicinity ARG-9.

2000 - Wound and set ship's clocks.

October 8, 1945

0000 - Anchored as before in Buckner Bay in vicinity of ARG-9.

1105 - Underway for ARG-9.

1132 - Moored port side to YMS 151 alongside ARG-9.

1406 - YMS 383 underway from alongside.

1704 - Underway steaming on various courses for anchorage.

1713 - Anchored in Buckner Bay vicinity ARG-9. (Note: It appears that our gut feeling of yesterday, Oct. 7, that we ought to be headed for Unten Ko just in case "Louise" changed course was going to prove to be valid. The mid afternoon advisories on the 8th reported that "Louise" had begun to veer away from the East China Sea and to the north toward Okinawa. All ships in Buckner Bay were alerted to expect 60 knot winds late in the evening of the 8th with gusts of 90 knots early in the morning of the 9th. On this new course "Louise's" "eye" would pass Okinawa around 1030 on the 9th. We could have made it to Unten Ko with plenty of time to spare if we'd been given permission yesterday. But it was too late now. Already the wind was freshening and we knew it would be tough, but a maximum of 90 knots with the wind coming off the land could be handled with luck. We secured everything topside as well as below deck. We paid out some more anchor chain to our 500 pound anchor. This plus using the engines, if necessary, ought to get us through. "Louise", however, failed to conform to pattern, and during the evening of the 8th as it reached 25 degrees North and directly south of Okinawa it slowed to six knots and greatly increased in intensity. As a result, the storm became the most violent at Okinawa since the invasion in April. *(See End Note No.105)*.

October 9, 1945

0000 - Anchored as before in Buckner Bay vicinity ARG-9.

0625 - Started main engines. Wind velocity increasing.

1000 - Using engines to relieve strain on anchor chain. (Note: The strain of the anchor chain in the 40 knot plus wind had the chain stretched out like a violin string. The engines were making standard speed and the chain was still taut. At about this time, ARG-9 (USS Mona Island) which, because of the wind direction now from the east was anchored ahead of us. Her blinker light suddenly started sending us a message. "YMS 183 we have lost our anchor and are underway with no way on and are drifting down on you. Get under way and move immediately. We have no control.").

1135 - Set special sea detail. Started bringing anchor in.

1152 - Starboard chain parted. Lost 500# anchor and approximately 15 fathoms of chain. Underway for new anchorage. (Note: When the anchor chain was "straight up and down" a wave raised the 183 up several feet, the anchor was, without doubt, caught under a ledge of rock on the bottom and could not move. Something had to give and the weakest link in the chain parted and we too were adrift, but we did have our engines running already and were able to move out of Mona Island's way. This time we anchored in a place on the eastern side of the Bay where no one could anchor in front of us as long as the wind came from the east. This lessened the chance of someone else drifting down on us for the time being. However, in order to anchor with the only anchor we now had , a 300 pounder, and have the best chance for it to hold us we needed to have a lot of chain out. We still had 30 odd fathoms of chain left in the starboard chain locker and about 45 fathoms with the 300# port anchor. We had to fasten or bend the two chains together so that we could have the maximum out with the smaller anchor).

1200 - Steaming in Buckner Bay while two anchor chains are bent together. (Note: By this time, according to the Naval record, visibility was zero, and the wind from east and northeast was at 60 knots and rising. The radio was jammed with cries for help from ships of all sizes reporting lost anchors, collisions, and groundings. The process of bending the two chains together is a back breaking job under the best of circumstances but under way with the wind blowing at 60 knots and the ship pitching and rolling it was horrendous. The Boatswain and his crew took the starboard chain, or what was left of it and flaked it down on the port side of the forecastle deck. The front end of the chain was shackled to the anchor after being run through the port side chock at the bow. The bitter end of the starboard anchor chain is shackled to the forward end of the chain in the port chain locker after it is run through the chain stop on the port side. Now we can anchor with 75 or 80 fathoms of chain out. This will give us a great deal more holding power and with the engines going full ahead riding up on the taut chain it would help insure that it was less likely to break.

We maneuvered 183 to the spot where we wanted to drop the anchor. We let the anchor go and it went down to the bottom, about 10 fathoms deep. All the while we were letting the wind push us backward as the chain paid out. We tried to keep it going out as slowly as possible by using the brake on the winch until we came to the shackle fastened to the port side chain. Once this shackle had passed through the chock the chain was free to pay out and the brake on the winch could not stop it. Only the chain stop could stop the chain now. We were now backing down slowly so the chain would pay out and lie on the bottom before taking the strain of the ship. As the chain ran through the chock it picked up speed and passed through the chock like the proverbial freight train. Only an experienced Boatswain could read the painted markings on the links as they sped by. These markings indicated how much chain was already out and by simple math how much was left in the chain locker. The chain was not fastened to the ship in the chain locker. This made it possible for the ship to slip the anchor in an emergency and to get underway immediately. The chain was fastened to the ship by the chain stop and then with the use of a pelican hook. If the chain was not stopped in time all of the chain would run out of the chain locker and end up in the water. This meant that 183 would not be anchored, all chain would be at the bottom of the bay along with our only anchor and the ship relegated to wandering around Buckner Bay in the dark trying to avoid collisions   and/or running aground. This was indeed the "moment of truth". The chain had to be stopped in the next few seconds or it was all over. Our Boatswain 1/c, a new man and our leading Boatswain, had come aboard for duty a few days before we left Guam in early September. I understood that he had served on a cruiser before coming to us after the war ended. You could tell that he knew what he was doing when he was bending the two chains together. As the chain was racing through the port side bow chock you could see him as he read the markings in the light of his flashlight which to anyone else was just a blur of color. He took hold of the pipe railing on the side of the forecastle, and with his right foot flipped the chain stop over on to the chain. The stop merely bounced on the links as they passed underneath it. The chain was moving too fast for the stop to fall between two links and stop the chain. Without a moment's hesitation, our Boatswain, jumped into the air and came down with all his weight and might on his right foot on top of the bouncing stop. This forced the metal stop down between two links and the chain stopped. We all held our breaths. The chain did not break from the sudden stop and it began immediately to grow taut out beyond where we could see it as the anchor held and the chain became like a "violin string". Immediately, the engines were revved up to flank speed to take as much strain as possible off the anchor and chain and keep our bow into the wind. We still had a chance, whereas before we had little or none and it was all due to our Boatswain's Mate 1/c, Charles L. Harris, (560-21-76) of Charleston, West Va. Those of us who were in a position to see what he did also knew that he had saved the ship, and possibly our lives, at the risk of his own. If the chain had snapped, the loose end could have whipped around and literally cut him in two pieces, or his legs, or thrown him into the boiling cauldron of Buckner Bay. Without a word of direction, he immediately secured a pelican hook to the chain and fastened it to the chain pad eye by the winch. If the anchor held on the bottom and the chain did not break, the pelican hook would keep the ship tethered and we had a chance).

1312 - Anchored in Buckner Bay. Using engines to relieve strain on anchor chain. (Note: By 1400, according to the Navy account of typhoon "Louise", the wind was at 80 knots with gusts of greater intensity. The bay was now in almost total darkness and was the scene of utter confusion as ships appeared from nowhere in the darkened bay and collided with or almost collided with other ships. Even if the anchor held we could still be stove in by another ship and we would be just as sunk as if we piled onto the rocks. The skipper directed Ens. Dudley and Ens. Davis to go up on the flying bridge and stand by the big search-blinker lights in case another ship seemed to be heading for us. We could beam the lights on our hull so the approaching ship could see exactly where we were located and possibly avoid hitting us. We almost didn't make it to the flying bridge. The short ladder from the wing of the pilot house to the flag bag deck was completely exposed to the full force of the wind. It almost blew us away as we could just barely, in turn, hold on. We did make it).

1545 - Turned on anchor lights.

1615 - Barometer rising. Winds still typhoon velocity. (Note: By 1600, according to the Navy records, *(See End Note No.106)* the typhoon reached its peak, with steady winds of 100 knots and frequent gusts of 120 knots. Even though the barometer reached its lowest point about this time (968.5 millibars) and began to rise the maximum winds continued unabated for another two hours. Ens. Davis recalls a general radio message from a larger ship during this time stating that their anemometer had been carried away and that the last reading of wind velocity was a gust of 150 knots.

When Davis and Dudley reached the flying bridge earlier, they noticed immediately that the whip radio antennas mounted on a frame above the back of the flying bridge, some made of spring steel as big around as a man's thumb and about 8 feet tall, were bent over by the wind 90 degrees from vertical. They didn't move and only several hours later, as the wind abated, did they rise gradually from the 90 degree position until they were completely vertical again. The sound of the wind was deafening. The rain and salt spray was horizontal and when one was exposed to it, it felt like being peppered by pea gravel. One result of wind and spray which wasn't noticed until the next day was the large areas on the windward side of the mast which had lost their paint (several coats) as if it had been sand blasted and de-barked. Sometime around 1600 and before the wind started its shift to the north, as the center of the typhoon (the eye) moved off to the north-northeast, the presence of Dudley and Davis on the flying bridge became crucial. They had been on the flying bridge for two hours or more, (couldn't have come down safely if they tried) taking shelter behind the wind deflecting bulkhead enclosing the front and two sides of the flying bridge. They could not converse with each other without putting mouth to ear and yelling. They were drenched and had been for hours, although it was not cold. For the tropical low pressure winds around the eye, and thus the water and spray accompanying it was quite mild. The two lookouts saw the running lights of a vessel at about the same time as the pilot house signaled the same sighting through the voice tube. The red light on the right and the green light on the left of the blob, a little darker than the surrounding area, spelled clearly only one message - a ship was heading directly for us.

At this point we could not tell what sort of ship she was, but that really didn't matter, for any sort of vessel hitting us bow on into our side could stove us in seriously enough to sink us and himself too. The lookouts lit off the searchlights, Dudley manned our port search light and Davis the starboard. Our starboard light was beamed down to illuminate the hull and the stern so the approaching ship could see what he had to miss. He might not be able to control the direction of his own vessel, but he could at least tell where he needed to go whether or not he could go there. The port light was played on the bow and the chain and down on the deck so that our own people could see better as they prepared fenders and bumpers to cushion the shock of a possible collision. Now it was just a matter of waiting. We could not go anywhere. We could not get out of his way. Our chain was still holding and the engines going ahead at flank speed relieved the chain of a good deal of pressure. Fortunately we were anchored at the eastern side of the bay so that no other vessel was tempted to pass our bow, in which case he might break our anchor chain. Our bow was still headed to the east, as the wind was still blowing from east to west.

At this time we were able to identify the ship on a collision course with us. It was an LCI (Landing Craft Infantry). An amphibious ship, bigger and heavier than a YMS and made of steel plate. She was capable of dealing a fatal blow to us. We had been in her sight for sometime and we could tell from the slight movement of her bow to the west that her skipper was doing all he could to change direction enough to pass by our stern. The LCI was starboard side to the heavy wind, which had her heeled over to port most of the time, and she was rolling in the huge waves inside the bay. The LCI must have been backing down on one engine, if not both, for as she pitched and rolled there was not much forward motion discernible. Her skipper seemed to be trying to slow his ship down enough so that the wind and waves would blow them beyond our stern since it appeared that he could not turn his bow enough to head behind us. If this wasn't his plan whatever he had in mind worked. With most of our crew, except for the engineers and the bridge personnel on the fantail, holding onto lifelines and prepared with all kinds of cushioning gear at the ready, we watched the LCI, as if in slow motion, glide past our stern. She was on an angle which put her a little nearer to our starboard quarter than the port. She came no closer than 12 inches to us. Our whole crew could have stepped aboard the LCI without mishap during the minute that it took for her to pass us by. There was no touching, only cheering from our people and theirs as a catastrophe was avoided by the proverbial "gnat's eyebrow". In just a few minutes the LCI disappeared into the darkness. We regretted not getting her number. If she survived the night we would have thanked her people the next day. Soon, the wind began to shift to the north and we tended to follow this change as we headed more to the north and we were starboard side to the eastern side of the bay. Even when the wind went more to the northwest and we headed into it in that direction, luckily, we were still far enough off shore to have plenty of depth not to go aground.

2052 - Stopped engines. (Note: By 2000 the wind had begun to abate materially as the center of the storm had moved 60 odd miles to the northeast of Buckner Bay and was now blowing across the bay from the northwest which reduced the seas in the bay greatly. We stopped our engines but left them idling in case they were needed again very quickly. The wind continued to blow in gale force gusts, but 183 was able to hold its anchored position through the night).

October 10, 1945

0000 - Anchored as before in Buckner Bay vicinity berth B-212. (Note: All through the early morning hours the wind and rain continued. Davis and Dudley had come down from the flying bridge and regular lookouts of the watch took their places. The whip antennas were gradually returning to near their normal vertical position. The engines remained at idle. There was still danger of drifting or out-of-control ships hitting us or our anchor chain. We still maintained a sharp watch, but fortunately no other vessel came close to our position although there were still many of all sizes milling around in the harbor. Some had been aground but when the wind shifted to the north and then the northwest they were blown back into the bay and to its southeastern side. Our bow was heading north and then northwest as the ship swung on the anchor. Of the few ships which had managed to remain anchored none was very close to us although at first light we could make out the shapes of several which were obviously aground or piled on rock outcrops in the bay. *(See End Note No.107)*.

0740 - Secured the engines. (Note: By this time the wind had abated enough for us to feel confident that the anchor and chain would hold us against it. We could also see reasonably well in the distance, and the radar was still working well and even better since the rain had slackened although it continued to rain in squalls. The skipper, Boatswain's Mate and others made a thorough inspection of the outside of the hull, the deck, forecastle deck, mast, radio antennas and other areas that had been exposed to the extreme typhoon winds. One of the notable discoveries was that the chain stop, which Boatswain's Mate Harris had jumped on with his foot and the weight of his body to cause the stop to engage the space between two links, and indeed, did stop the chain, had been damaged. We did not know until now that the chain stop, bolted through the forecastle deck with four 5/8" bolts to the cross members below the deck, had been jerked at least 4 inches forward when the chain came to its sudden stop. It was still securely bolted to the deck and the pelican hook that Harris had attached immediately after the chain had been stopped had taken all of the strain of the chain. Failure of the chain stop was now highly unlikely as long as the pelican hook was in place. Just as alarming was the discovery that there was only six or eight feet of chain left in the chain locker. We had been that close to losing it all and having to face almost certain disaster).

0800 - For the rest of the day the crew continued inspection and maintenance of equipment and machinery. All reports from the various departments indicated that we were ready to get under way for whatever assignment we might get. We were operational. We reported this to the Commander of Minecraft aboard USS Terror. We later learned that of all the YMSes in Buckner Bay at this time only YMS 183 and perhaps one other could operate as soon as the typhoon had passed the area. For several days after, 183 was a "taxi" service, delivery ship, personnel carrier and sightseeing "bus" throughout the bay for the Commander Minecraft's Staff who needed to see the destruction up close).

October 11, 1945

0000 - Anchored as before in Buckner Bay vicinity berth B-212.
0932 - Captain left ship.
1042 - Captain returned to ship. (The rest of the day was spent tidying up the ship and resting. Twenty-four hours plus of typhoon was really debilitating).

October 12, 1945

0000 - Anchored in Buckner Bay as before vicinity berth B-212.
0910 - Underway for LST-804.
0933 - Moored starboard side to LST-804.
1020 - Completed taking fuel and fresh water.
1041 - Underway for anchorage.
1048 - Anchored in Buckner Bay.
1400 - Captain left ship.
1845 - Captain returned to ship.

October 13, 1945

0000 - Anchored as before in Buckner Bay.
0755 - Underway steaming on various courses for LST-617.
0832 - Received Pay Accounts from LST-617.
0900 - Anchored vicinity ARG-9.
1000 - Held Captain's inspection.
1050 - Underway steaming on various courses for Baten Ko.
1335 - Moored starboard side to AM-299.
1606 - Underway for Lignite for fresh provisions. (Lignite, IX-162, was a concrete barge for storage and dispensing of food, fresh provisions, etc. It was towed to its assigned harbor, anchored there and served the vessels in that area. This vessel was grounded in the typhoon and presumably had been refloated and reanchored).
1730 - Moored starboard side to YO-49 alongside Lignite.
1836 - Completed taking on fresh provisions.
1840 - Underway for anchorage.
1845 - Anchored in Buckner Bay in berth L-145.

October 14, 1945

0000 - Anchored as before in Buckner Bay in berth L-148.
0533 - Underway to pick up working parties for LST 617.
0634 - Six man working party came aboard from AM 381.
0700 - Seven man working party came aboard from AM 104.
0700 - Six man working party came aboard from AM 382.
0714 - Six man working party came aboard from AM 340.
0718 - Six man working party came aboard from AM 380.
0804 - Moored port side to AM 102 to receive six man working party.
0812 - Underway steaming on various courses for LST 617.

0902 - Delivered all working parties to LST 617. (Note: there is no record of the LST 617 suffering any particular damage during the typhoon. Our log does not say what the occasion was for all of these working parties to be delivered to LST 617. However, there was some reason why they needed extra man power at this time. Perhaps to clean up after taking on water, etc.).

0955 - Anchored Buckner Bay vicinity CM-5 (USS Terror).

1025 - Underway to take Chief of Staff of MinePac aboard.

1105 - Chief of Staff and party came aboard. Steaming on various courses for AD-20. (AD-20 USS Hamul was a destroyer tender. As we cruised over to AD-20 and later on the way back to CM-5, at the direction of the Chief of Staff, 183 made a circuitous route in order for him to see the various wrecked, grounded and abandoned ships. They were, of course most interested in the destroyed YMSes. Ens. Davis remembers overhearing conversations between two of the officers with "scrambled eggs" on the visors of their hats. The Chief of Staff was on the flying bridge with the skipper. When 183 passed a large outcropping of rock in the middle of the bay there was a YMS, (number forgotten) perched on top, a good 15 feet above the water level of the bay. It was, of course completely abandoned. It was a queer sight. The keel was broken just about midships. The bow half was tilted down toward the water and the stern half was tilted down toward the water. There was a gaping space in cross section of the hull where it had snapped in two when the high water of the typhoon had receded and left the YMS hanging on the rock pinnacle and no water to support the bow and stern. One of the officers on the Chief of Staff's staff said to the other, as they viewed this sad sight, "be sure to remind me when we get back to Terror to send a motor whale boat and some men over to this YMS to see if they have any black shoe polish in small stores." Davis recalls the queasy feeling he had as he turned away from these officers, whose khaki uniforms were starched, ironed, and spotless. The thought that these characters literally held his fate in their hands made him almost do something he had never done before or since - get seasick and retch over the side.

1155 - Anchored vicinity of AD-20. Chief of Staff and party left ship.

1223 - Chief of Staff and party came aboard.

1227- Underway steaming on various courses for CM-5.

1305 - Chief of Staff and party left ship.

1318 - Anchored in Buckner Bay vicinity CM-5.

October 15, 1945

0000 - Anchored as before in Buckner Bay vicinity CM-5.

1245 - Captain left ship.

1545 - Captain returned to ship.

1900 - Wound and set ship's clocks.

October 16, 1945

0000 - Anchored as before in Buckner Bay vicinity CM-5.

1052 - Underway.

1110 - Anchored in vicinity CM-5.

1250 - Captain left ship.

1525 - Captain returned to ship.

1702 - Underway for AO-82 to deliver sweep gear.

1808 - Moored starboard side to AO-82. (Note: AO-82 was a fleet oiler, USS Cahaba. The sweep gear was probably destined for the Japanese area and the AO-82 was going to deliver the gear).

1819 - Transferred sweep gear. Underway for anchorage.

1827 - Anchored in Buckner Bay near Baten Ko. (Note: Baten Ko was at the south end of Buckner Bay).

October 17, 1945

0000 - Anchored as before in Buckner Bay vicinity of berth B-53.

0547 - Underway steaming on various courses for CM-5.

0617 - CTG 52.9 came aboard. (This was Commander of Task Group 52.9. Don't have a name, but he was probably going to take over the Minecraft leadership in Buckner Bay. All signs pointed to Terror preparing to leave for Japan soon).

0730 - Anchored vicinity AD-20. CTG 52.9 left ship.

0935 - CTG.9 returned to ship.

0938 - Underway proceeding to CGC-31 (WAGC-31, Coast Guard Cutter Bibb. CTG 52.9 will take up residence on Bibb).

1030 - CTG 52.9 left ship.

1110 - Moored to port side of LST-617.

1345 - Completed taking on fresh water and dry provisions. Took stores aboard for delivery to AM-317 and AM-299.

1352 - Underway from alongside of LST-617.

1410 - Moored on starboard side AM-317 to transfer stores.

1427 - Underway to AM-299.

1440 - Moored on port side AM-299 to transfer stores.

1603 - Underway for anchorage.

1608 - Anchored vicinity berth B-216.

1759 - Wound and set ship's clocks.

October 18, 1945

0000 - Anchored as before in Buckner Bay in vicinity berth B-216.

0930 - Captain left ship.

1100 - Received one drum gasoline aboard.

1108 - Captain returned to ship.

1545 - Captain left ship.

1620 - Captain returned to ship.

October 19, 1945

0000 - Anchored as before in berth B-216 Buckner Bay, Okinawa.

0755 - Underway for ARG-6 (USS Cebu).

0852 - Moored on starboard side of ARG-6 for availability.

1405 - Disbursing Officer and Storekeeper came aboard to pay ship's company.

1442 - Disbursing Officer and Storekeeper left ship.

1610 - BLATT, SEYMOUR, BM2/c, 818-09-60; PREIS, GEORGE J., RdM2/c, 869-62-69; FELTEN, HAROLD, PhM2/c, 721-24-70; and ELLIOTT, C.P., F2/c(EM), 953-46-24 reported aboard for duty.

October 20, 1945

0000 - Moored as before, to ARG-6.

0915 - VERITY, H.W., MoMM1/c, 642-72-30; MULFORD, A.J., Jr., MoMM2/c, 647-23-29; BODAY, S., MoMM2/c, 205-21-23; HARRIS, C.L., BM1/c, 560-41-76; SCHULTE, A.W., GM2/c,

648-32-95; and BLOSSER, E.E., SoM3/c, 663-39-72; were transferred to Receiving Station for further transfer to U.S. 1015 - Received 1200 gallons fresh water from ARG-6.

October 21, 1945

0000 - Moored as before to ARG-6. 0855 - Received GSK stores aboard.

1405 - SC 716 moored to starboard side.

1812 - Wound and set all ship's clocks.

October 22, 1945

0000 - Moored as before on starboard side of ARG-6 with SC 716 on our starboard side.

1341 - Underway to moor alongside ARG-6 aft.

1349 - Moored to YMS 286 alongside ARG-6.

October 23, 1945

0000 - Moored as before on starboard side of ARG-6.

0950 - Captain left ship.

1105 - Captain returned to ship.

1225 - Underway steaming on various courses for anchorage.

1234 - Anchored in vicinity berth B-214.

1835 - Wound and set all ship's clocks.

October 24, 1945

0000 - Anchored as before in vicinity berth B-214.

1330 - Working party left ship.

1600 - Anchored as before. Working party returned. Received GSK supplies aboard.

October 25, 1945

0000 - Anchored as before in vicinity berth B-214.

0824 - Captain left ship.

0837 - Captain returned to ship.

1345 - Captain left ship.

1535 - Captain returned to ship.

1715 - Received gear aboard for CM-5. (CM-5, USS Terror, departed Buckner Bay for Sasebo, Japan on October 17 or early October 18).

1725 - Captain left ship.

1800 - Captain returned to ship.

October 26, 1945

0000 - Anchored as before in berth B-214.

1052 - Underway steaming on various courses for Baten Ko.

1334 - Moored alongside IX-133 (USS Antona).

1347 - Received 50 gallons lube oil. Underway.

1413 - Moored port side to IX-113 (USS Camel) for fuel.

1458 - Completed taking on fuel. Underway steaming on various courses.

1711 - Moored port side to YMS 222.

1751 - Received fresh provisions aboard.

1810 - Received dry stores aboard.

1908 - Underway from alongside YMS 222.
1920 - Anchored in Buckner Bay vicinity berth L-148.

October 27, 1945

0000 - Anchored as before in berth L-148.
0805 - Underway for LST 804.
0905 - Moored starboard side to LST 804.
0911 - YMS 387 moored to starboard.
0945 - Stopped taking fresh water (from LST 804).
1010 - Underway for minecraft dock.
1054 - Moored port side to YMS 90 at minecraft dock. (Note: YMS 90 had been grounded in typhoon Louise and was refloated October 24th. Sometime later she was returned to a rear area for decommissioning. Apparently she was being repaired for this return. *(See End Note No.108)*.
1435 - Received minesweeping gear aboard.
1640 - Received Ship's Service Stores aboard.
1815 - Wound and set all ship's clocks.

October 28, 1945

0000 - Moored as before to YMS 90.
1113 - Underway steaming on various courses for harbor entrance.
1200 - Steaming as before standing out of Buckner Bay. Base course 034° True, speed 10 knots. Following LSM 271 in company with AM 371 and SC 716.
1345 - C/C to 045° True. (Note: The little convoy is steaming up the eastern side of Okinawa on its way to Japan).
1714 - C/C to 345° True. (Note: The convoy has cleared the northern tip of Okinawa and has made a course change to carry it northwestward to clear the islands south of Kyushu, Japan).
1750 - Turned on all navigational lights.

October 29, 1945

0000 - Steaming as before on base course 345° True, speed 10 knots enroute from Buckner Bay, Okinawa to Sasebo, Japan.
0106 - C/BC (base course) to 016° True. (Note: the convoy has gone far enough to the west to clear the islands below Japan. The new course will take them up the west side of Kyushu toward Sasebo)
0620 - Secured navigational lights.
1000 - C/C to 023° True.
1700 - Wound and set all ship's clocks.
1745 - Turned on all navigational lights.
1901 - C/C to 017° True.
2333 - C/BC to 021° True.

October 30, 1945

Steaming as before on course 021° True, speed 10 knots, proceeding from Okinawa to Sasebo, Japan in company with AM 371, LSM 271 and SC716.
0643 - Turned off navigational lights.
0705 - C/C to 005° True.
1030 - C/C to 042° True. Following LSM 271 into Sasebo Harbor.

1125 - Received Harbor Charts from entrance boat. Standing into Sasebo Ko.
1330 - Moored to port side of LCS-13 alongside CM-5 to transfer freight.
1355 - Completed transfer of freight.
1450 - LCS 13 underway. Moored to port side of CM-5.
1600 - Received 1000 gal. Water.
1630 - Received 2000 gal. Fuel.
1640 - Underway from alongside CM-5.
1655 - Moored starboard side to YMS 357.

October 31, 1945

0000 - Moored as before in Sasebo Ko, Japan, starboard side to YMS 357.
0930 - Captain left ship.
1115 - Captain returned to ship.
1420 - Captain left ship.
1655 - YMS 357 underway from alongside, YMS 441 moored to starboard side.
1735 - Wound and set all ship's clocks
1750 - Captain returned to ship.

November 1, 1945

0000 - Moored as before to YMS 441 in Sasebo Ko, Japan. (Note: Sasebo Ko was a very large harbor with a very narrow entrance. It was almost landlocked. It was between Fukuoka to the north and Nagasaki to the south. Ens. Davis recalls the absolute destruction of everything on the shore line and inland as far as one could see. There were all kinds of vessels being built near the water, some of them looked like the one man suicide submarines. Others were larger, but all were destroyed where they lay in the various stages of construction. Already the harbor was filled with all types of Allied vessels, doing various jobs regarding the clearing of wrecked and sunken Japanese vessels of all kinds. It was a monumental task, but in a few short weeks it was done and Allied supply ships started pouring supplies into the occupation forces. It appeared that all the Japanese had left was manpower. There were still several million troops in China, Manchuria, Korea and the home islands combined. There were several thousand aircraft hidden in small groups near grass airfields from which they could take off to crash our invasion forces. There were also hundreds, maybe even thousands of artillery pieces out of sight in caves facing the sea. These guns were already zeroed in on certain areas of the landing beaches and we knew they were there because they were required by the Allied occupation

Figure 51 The city of Fukuoka at wars end - Courtesy Tom Marshall

John Dixon Davis

forces to be spiked and the cave entrances to have large white flags to mark their location. Needless to say there were many, many white flags to be seen on the southwestern and western sides of Kyushu. This, we were told by those who went in to sweep other areas in and around Japan, was the case everywhere. *(See End Note No.109)*.

0905 - Captain left ship.
1217 - Underway for YMS 449.
1247 - Moored to YMS 449 in dock area B.
1305 - Captain returned to ship.
1330 - Liberty party left ship.
1340 - Captain left ship.
1450 - Captain returned to ship.
1545 - YMS 429 moored on starboard side.
1624 - Captain left ship.
1730 - Received fresh provisions aboard.
1825 - Liberty party returned to ship.
1830 - Captain returned to ship. (Note: The liberty area at this stage of the occupation was little more than a clearing on the beach, a cold beer for each man and a field for a softball game. This was the first time ashore since leaving Guam in late September).

November 2, 1945

0000 - Moored as before to YMS 449 with YMS 429 moored to starboard side.
1520 - GOLLADAY, MARVIN E., PhM 1/c, 603-09-57 detached from duty and transferred to Receiving Ship.
1610 - YMS 429 underway from alongside YMS 432 on starboard side.
1647 - Wound and set all ship's clocks.
1651 - Underway steaming on various courses for entrance to Sasebo Harbor.
1923 - Standing out of Sasebo Ko proceeding to Fukuoka. Speed 7 knots, course 265° True in company with 6 YMSes -C/BC to 012° True. 2204 - C/BC to 025° True. (Note: The six YMSes were not noted in the log. However, we worked with the following while sweeping in Fukuoka: 93, 291, 293, 297, 299, 300, 319, 325, 357, 362, 372, 374, 388, 389, 398, 429, 432, 441, 444, 446, 449, 468, 473 and the six were certainly in this group. The others were already in Fukuoka or came after we arrived).

November 3, 1945

0000 - Steaming as before on base course 025 True. Speed 7 knots in company with YMSes proceeding from Sasebo Ko to Fukuoka, Japan.
0634 - Turned off navigational lights.
0635 - C/C to 148° True.
0650 - Commenced streaming magnetic sweep gear.
0725 - Gear streamed.
0750 - Commenced pulsing. (Note: An explanation is needed here. In January 1945, the planning, production and deploying of aerial mines in a joint operation of the Navy and the Air Force was finally begun. The operation named STARVATION, was designed to choke off the delivery of oil, coal, minerals, foodstuffs, etc. to the home islands of Japan. From January through mid-August all types of mines, magnetic, acoustic, pressure and combinations of these four triggering devices were built into the mines for the particular place they were to be laid. All had ship's counters, various delaying devices and a disarming switch that would render them

harmless by the middle of October 1945. After all, if we were going to invade the home islands we did not need to have to worry about the mines we had laid for their ships that had not been detonated. In all, during the five phases of Operation STARVATION there were several thousand mines of all types laid. During this period Japan's ability to get the raw materials to continue the war was irreparably crippled and her merchant marine lay on the bottom all around the home islands, in her ports, her straits and waterways. *(See End Note No110)*. This is where YMS 183 comes into the picture. While there were still many fields of Japan's moored mines still in place and in process of being swept, the urgent sweeping now was clearing ports, straits and waterways which had been the targets for the influence mines which were laid by the B-29's. Fukuoka was one of the important ports on the northwestern side of Kyushu which had been vigorously mined, on a number of occasions. It had to be swept for the various types of influence mines which were "unsweepable", insofar as this might be possible. Allied shipping which had to use this port, among others, to supply the Allied Occupation forces, had to be carefully checked. When 183 streamed magnetic gear on this day, November 3, 1945, even as she and the other six were doing this as they entered the main shipping channel the magnetic pulsing began. This magnetic sweep was continued until the ship was almost to the outer harbor entrance at which time the pulsing ceased, so that the ship could reverse course and begin pulsing again to the point where they began earlier. They could not make a 180° change in course while the pulsing was in progress because this would put the minesweeper in the magnetic field for a short time. If a mine was detonated at this point the minesweeper would be blown up).

0940 - Stopped pulsing. C/C to 330° True.

0950 - Commenced pulsing.

1216 - (Stopped pulsing). Started recovering gear.

1245 - All gear aboard. (Note: Course reversed to 148° True to Point Laura near Fukuoka where course was changed to 073°True).

1600 - Steaming on course 073°True. (Headed toward point Kitty at the entrance to the inner mole or harbor protected by a concrete breakwater). (Note: At point Laura we were able to see the outer harbor and it was filled with ships of all kinds and sizes. From this distance they looked to have been untouched by the war as they lay at anchor. What was all this talk about decimating the Japanese merchant marine? Within 15 minutes we knew the answer. These ships were sunk. The water in the harbor was not deep enough to cover them as they sat on the bottom. The average depth in this area was 4 to 6 fathoms. If it had been deep enough probably all that we could have seen would have been mast or funnel tops.

1620 - C/C to 125° True standing into inner harbor, Fukuoka.

1636 - Moored starboard side to YMS 374.

1700 - YMS 432 moored to port side.

November 4, 1945

0000 - Moored as before to port side of YMS 374 with YMS 432 on port side in inner harbor Fukuoka, Japan.

0634 - Underway standing out of harbor.

0700 - Commenced streaming magnetic sweep gear.

0740 - Gear streamed.

1016 - Started pulsing.

1200 - Steaming on course 180° True.

1431 - Stopped pulsing. Started recovering gear.

1540 - Gear recovered.
1600 - Steaming on various courses for harbor.
1709 - Moored alongside YMS 374 in Fukuoka harbor.
1900 - Captain left ship.
2300 - Captain returned to ship.

November 5, 1945

0000 - Moored as before to YMS 374 in Fukuoka Ko, Japan.
0630 - Underway for outer harbor.
0705 - Commenced streaming gear.
0732 - Completed streaming gear.
0740 - Started pulsing.
0800 - Steaming on base course 330° True.
0925 - Stopped pulsing.
1114 - C/C to 140° True. Started pulsing.
1245 - Stopped pulsing, started recovering gear.
1340 - Gear recovered. Steaming on various courses for inner harbor.
1410 - Moored to YMS 374 in Fukuoka Ko.
1440 - Liberty party left ship.
1505 - Captain left ship. (Note: The city of Fukuoka was within a 20 minute walk from the docks along the waterfront. The Senior Officer Present of the Navy had several small personnel boats to ferry people from the various ships to the shore. At this time, this service was used primarily for liberty parties going into what was left of the city. The Occupation troops were in charge of the land and some of them considered naval personnel as guests. Except for a few moderate sized brick and/or concrete buildings there was absolutely nothing standing for block after city block. All of this area was burned out by the fire bomb raids of the B-29's. Where the buildings made of wood, housing small businesses and homes, had once stood there were now literally thousands of vegetable garden plots. Allied personnel were constantly warned against eating anything that had not been thoroughly cooked. All kinds of intestinal ailments could result by doing so, because the populace used their own feces to fertilize the gardens. What cultural shock we experienced when we first saw the mother of a small child hold the kid over the flower pot or garden plot so the bowel movement could be readily mixed in with the soil. This, of course, explained the pervasive stench of human waste that was, at that time, first noticed many miles at sea almost before one was in sight of land.
On the fringes of what used to be the business district were many small businesses and homes that somehow escaped the destruction by fire. It was in these small shops and restaurants that sailors might find souvenirs to send home, or maybe sample the Japanese food if it was really well done. Also, Japanese beer was in good supply and was said by many Americans to be quite tasty. Among the very few items for sale in the shops were small wooden items like buckets, baskets, etc. Every sailor bought a few of these and carried them back to their ships. After taking them aboard, many had second thoughts and tossed them over the side. Of course, they floated and at first light for several days the water adjacent to the nests of YMSes was clogged with small wooden craft items that would never make it to the States. Little money was expended for these items anyway, the thinking went. One pack of Camels would buy most of them and at 5 cents a pack, the American was wealthy. It was widely reported that some of the Ship's Service Stores on many of the YMSes had run out of tobacco items for sale as they had been bought and were used for barter on the beach. Many sailors had to replenish their supply

for personal use by buying them back from Japanese kids and vendors of the beach. It took some time to restock the Ship's Service Stores with tobacco products, especially cigarettes).

1800 - Liberty party returned to ship.

1810 - Captain returned to ship.

November 6, 1945

0000 - Moored port side to YMS 374 with YMS 432 on starboard side in Fukuoka Ko, Japan.

0605 - Underway from Fukuoka proceeding on various courses to Iki Shima.

0736 - Base course 335° True. Speed 10 knots. (Note: Iki Shima was 35 miles slightly north of due west of Fukuoka. It was the closest of the two Japanese islands, in the Tsushima Straits, between Fukuoka and Pusan, Korea. It was in an area that B-29 planted influence mines were not dropped and it had been swept of moored mine fields. Therefore it was safe for metal hull ships to anchor in the harbor there. YMS 183 needed to replace its worn out magnetic sweep cable and Iki Shima was the closest safe place for the ACM-5, USS Barbican, a light mine layer, to anchor and make the transfer. Otherwise 183 would have had to go back to Sasebo to make this exchange).

0850 - C/BC to 270° True.

1055 - C/BC to 190° True.

1134 - C/BC to 135° True. Standing into Hansei Ura, Iki Shima.

1200 - Moored to ACM-5. (Note: YMS 183 had gone around the northern side of the island and down the western side to the little harbor called Hansei Ura. It was a very small but well protected bay. There were not many native people in this area. A number of other metal hull ships were anchored here also, waiting for the ship channels into Fukuoka to be declared safe from our own influence mines. Ens. Davis remembers that there were on this island and gliding on the sea breeze nearby many Great Asian Owls, the largest species of Owl in the world. They appeared to be at least as big as Pelicans, if not larger, and they paid us no mind and continued their gliding and searching for food).

1526 - Captain left ship.

1615 - Captain returned to ship. Completed transfer of damaged magnetic cable to ACM-5 and new magnetic cable from ACM-5. [Note: Most of the magnetic sweeping since coming to Fukuoka was done using a new technique called the "Jig Sweep". In this method the electrode of the single magnetic cable (around this single cable was where the magnetic field was created which could cause the detonation of the magnetic mine if all conditions were right) was shackled to the otter of the "O" type sweep gear. When the "O" type gear and magnetic cable were paid out from the stern together, the "O" type gear pulled the end of the magnetic cable with it so that the single magnetic cable (the magnetic field producer) took the shape of a large letter "J". This significantly changed the magnetic field from that produced in the regular mode (with the cable following straight astern of the minesweeper). It was dubbed the "Jig Sweep". It put new types of strain on the old magnetic cable we had been using and it finally had to be replaced. One of the interesting responses, by Japanese fishermen, to our sweeping the approaches to Fukuoka with the regular "O" type or "Jig Sweep" was to get their relatively small boats right in the danger zone of the sweep gear. This was the area where they would most likely be killed if a mine was detonated. The fishermen thought we were fishing for their fish and they were not going to take that in addition to military defeat. For several days we had to shoot near them with our submachine gun to shoo them away. They seemed to finally get the message].

1801 - Underway for AM 381.

1814 - Moored to port side of AM 381.

1820 - Wound all ship's clocks,
1900 - Completed taking 2500 gals. of fuel from AM 381.
2140 - Underway to anchor.
2159 - Anchored in Hansei Ura.

November 7, 1945

0000 - Anchored as before in Hansei Ura, Iki Shima, Japan.
0605 - Ledger, S/2c 751-11-26 came aboard as passenger to Fukuoka.
0625 - Underway proceeding from Hansei Ura to Fukuoka.
0637 - Course 310° True. Speed 10 knots.
0640 - C/C to 330° True.
0645 - C/C to 000° True.
0650 - C/C to 010° True.
0707 - C/C to 040° True.
0713 - C/C to 000° True.
0723 - C/C to 020° True.
0725 - C/C to 035° True.
0730 - C/C to 088° True.
0800 - Steaming as before on various courses for point Victor. (Note: Victor was the beginning point for the shipping channel, to be swept, into Fukuoka Harbor).
1206 - C/S to 400 RPM's preparatory to streaming gear at point Victor.
1210 - Commenced streaming gear. Course 150 True°.
1347 - Gear streamed. Commenced pulsing.
1619 - Stopped pulsing. Started recovering gear.
1704 - All gear recovered.
1722 - Shut off navigational lights. Standing in inner harbor at Fukuoka Ko.
1802 - Moored to YMS 449.
1810 - Ledger, S2/c, 751-11-26 left ship.
2245 - Transferred 1000 gallons fuel to YMS 449. (Note: Until the shipping channel could be declared safe and larger provision ships could come into Fukuoka, the YMSes had to pretty much provide for their own provisioning).

November 8, 1945

0000 - Moored as before to YMS 449 in Fukuoka Ko, Japan.
0812 - Underway from alongside YMS 449.
0815 - Steaming on various courses to sweeping area.
0904 - Commenced streaming gear.
1010 - Gear streamed, commenced pulsing. Base course 330° True.
1213 - Stopped pulsing.
1215 - C/C to 153° True.
1220 - Commenced pulsing.
1415 - Stopped pulsing.
1510 - All gear recovered. Proceeding to harbor.
1603 - Moored to YMS 449 in Fukuoka Harbor.
1605 - Captain left ship.
1830 - Wound and set all ship's clocks. (Captain returned to ship).

November 9, 1945

0000 - Moored as before to YMS 449 in Fukuoka Harbor, Japan.
0812 - Underway steaming on various courses for sweeping area.
0855 - Commenced streaming gear.
0925 - Gear streamed. Course 330° True.
1010 - Commenced pulsing.
1200 - Ceased pulsing.
1215 - C/C 150° True.
1224 - Commenced pulsing.
1430 - Stopped pulsing. Recovering gear.
1517 - Gear recovered. Proceeding to Fukuoka Harbor.
1600 - Standing into inner harbor. (Note: these days in early November were ideal weather wise. It was just like "Indian Summer" in these latitudes back in the States. There was little or no wind, and the sea was oily smooth with only the slightest swells. The sun's reflection off the mirror like surface began to take its toll. Many who had never felt the need to wear sunglasses before now began to experience severe headaches and terrific eye strain. The Pharmacist's Mate recommended sunglasses and hats that shaded the face. This seemed to do the trick. But for some the need to wear sunglasses persisted through the years).
1609 - Moored to YMS 449.
1618 - Captain left ship.
1635 - YMS 291 moored to port side.
1815 - Captain returned to ship.

November 10, 1945

0000 - Moored to YMS 449 with YMS 291 on port side in Fukuoka, Japan.
0753 - Liberty party left ship.
0805 - Underway for sweeping area.
0856 - Commenced streaming gear.
0921 - Gear streamed.
1055 - Commenced pulsing. Course 330° True. [Note: As is true of almost all minesweeping, especially of influence mines, the channels where the mines are suspected of being located have to be swept, time after time, and day after day. The U.S. mines which had been laid by the B-29s were known to be in a general area. We had charts showing where the bombardiers thought they had dropped the parachute rigged 2000 lb. ground mines. There were so many variables that the best the plane's crew could do, as Ens. Davis recalls, was to write on the charts, as they actually did, "this stick of mines shown on the chart are, by radar, within plus or minus 1 mile in deflection and plus or minus 2 miles in range and by navigation only 40% were thought to be within a radius of 1 mile of the position indicated on the chart. At best, these are not the most desirable directions. Add to this the following factors: most of the mines had ship's counters so that an infinite number of ships had to pass over a mine before it would explode. Say there were five mines in a "stick". Each one would require a different number of activations before exploding. For example, mine no. 1 had 2 ship's counters; mine no. 2, had 4 ship's counters; mine number 3 had 5 ship's counters; mine no. 4 had 7 ship's counters; and mine no. 5 had 20 ship's counters. Long after the first four mines had been activated and sunk or damaged four Japanese ships, there was still one more waiting. But in the thinking of the Japanese defenders all of the mines in that area were gone. This, of course, was an erroneous conclusion. The second variable built into a mine had to do with what influence or combination of influences

created by a passing ship (enemy or friendly) would set it off. As noted earlier there was just the magnetic mine which was activated by the magnetic field of a ship. The magnetic mine could be configured to have an acoustic activator also, so that it had to be a metal ship that made a certain amount of noise at the same time as a proper magnetic field was present. The same mine could require 2 passes of a magnetic field and 4 of an acoustic source before it would explode on the last activation of either influence. Add to these the pressure principle (the oyster mine) and we ended up trying to sweep the unsweepable mine. As a final factor, all the mines laid were timed, by one means or another, to disarm themselves in the middle of October. Now we are sweeping the unsweepable mine well into November. Did we not trust our mine builders? We did not, for here again so many things could happen to keep the disarming device from working. There could well be a mine out there just waiting to sink an American ship. We could not take the chance].

1200 - Stopped pulsing.
1205 - C/C to 150° True.
1209 - Started pulsing. Magnetic cable began smoking from excess heat. Apparently no damage done to cable. (Note: We were, as normally, generating 3000 amps at 100 volts. This is a tremendously powerful direct current and the heat generated is normally very high. All of the cable that is in the water stays cool, and all of the cable is in the water except for a few feet from the junction box to the water at the stern. In this case it seemed that one of the electrodes at the junction box was not tightly attached and there was some arcing which caused the heat to build up. As soon as this was noted the cable was taken off line, and the electrodes checked and tightened. A wet rag was tied around the cable that was heating up to cool it and in a few minutes the pulsing began again and there was no problem).
1435 - Started recovering gear.
1501 - Gear recovered.
1552 - Moored to YMS 432.
1603 - YMS 449 moored to starboard side.
1605 - Two men on liberty party did not return. Being held in Brig. Captain left ship.
1830 - Wound and set all ship's clocks.

November 11, 1945

0000 - Moored as before to port side of YMS 432 with YMS 449 on starboard side in Fukuoka, Japan.
0812 - Underway for sweeping area.
0845 - Commenced streaming gear.
0930 - Gear streamed.
0953 - Commenced pulsing. Course 330° True.
1155 - Ceased pulsing.
1205 - C/C to 160° True.
1209 - Started pulsing.
1404 - Stopped pulsing.
1425 - Started recovering gear.
1451 - Gear recovered. Proceeding to inner harbor.
1540 - Moored to YMS 432.
1548 - YMS 449 moored to port.

Chapter 14
Fifth CO Takes Command

November 12, 1945

0000 - Moored to YMS 432 in Fukuoka Harbor.

1300 - LT. Stanley C. Klein, DE, 120124, USNR, relieved of command by LT. DOUGLAS W. MITCHELL, JR., D(L) 224415, USNR, in accordance with U.S. Navy Regulations Article 824. Authority for relieving: AdCominPac dispatch #042257.

1505 - Underway.

1530 - Moored to YMS 449 alongside YMS 362.

1612 - Underway from YMS 449.

1620 - Moored to starboard side of ACM-5. (Note: At this point Lt. Klein, former skipper of YMS 183 stepped aboard USS Barbican and took up residence there as Commander of the Minesweeping Squadron at Fukuoka).

1755 - Wound and set all ship's clocks. The log for this day was signed by D. W. Mitchell, Lt., USNR, Commanding and by John D. Davis, Ens., USNR, Navigator.

Figure 53 - The fifth CO LT. Douglas W. Mitchell, Jr.

November 13, 1945

0000 - Moored to ACM-5 with YMS 449 on starboard side in Fukuoka Harbor. (Nothing further to report for the rest of this day).

November 14, 1945

0000 - Moored as before to ACM-5 with YMS 449 on starboard side in Fukuoka Harbor.

0930 - Received fresh provisions for YMS 449. (Nothing else of note to report).

November 15, 1945

0000 - Moored to ACM-5 in Fukuoka Harbor.

0905 - Underway to fuel from AM 381.

1015 - Moored on starboard side of AM 381 for fuel and provisions.

1145 - Received 4300 gallons of fuel and dry provisions.

1150 - Underway for ACM-5.

1155 - Moored port side to YMS 449 alongside ACM-5.

John Dixon Davis

November 16, 1945

0000 - Moored to YMS 449 with YMS 429 moored to starboard side in Fukuoka Harbor.
0605 - YMS 429 underway. YMS 374 on starboard side.
1455 - Captain left ship.
1515 - Moored to port side of ACM-5.
1730 - Wound and set all ship's clocks.
1735 - Captain returned to ship.

November 17, 1945

0000 - Moored portside to ACM-5 with YMS 429 on starboard side in Fukuoka, Japan. (Nothing further to report for this day).

November 18, 1945

0000 - Moored port side to ACM-5 with YMS 429 moored to starboard in Fukuoka, Japan.
0625 - Underway for sweeping area.
0725 - Started streaming magnetic sweep gear.
0855 - Started pulsing. Base course 330° True.
1025 - Stopped pulsing.
1122 - C/C to 150° True.
1230 - Started pulsing.
1415 - Stopped pulsing.
1455 - Started recovering gear. All gear aboard. Proceeding to harbor.
1622 - Moored to starboard side to YMS 449 in Fukuoka, Japan.

November19, 1945

(Conducted sweeping assignment which was exactly the same as Nov. 18, 1945, same courses, same speeds, etc. Returned to Harbor and moored to port side of YMS 429).

November 20, 1945

(Conducted sweeping assignment which was exactly the same as Nov. 18 and 19, 1945, same courses, same speeds, etc. Returned to harbor and moored port side to ACM-5).

November 21, 1945

0000 - Moored on port side of ACM-5 with YMS 429 on (our) port side in Fukuoka Harbor.
1443 - Underway for AM 217 to take on provisions.
1505 - Moored port side to AM 217.
1528 - Completed taking on fresh provisions. Underway for berth.
1546 - Moored port side YMS 441.
1600 - Moored as before. Wound and set all ship's clocks.
1825 - YMS 374 to port side.

November 22, 1945

0000 - Moored on port side of YMS 441 with YMS 374 on port side in Fukuoka, Japan.
0643 - YMS 374 underway.

Figure 54 Enson Gerald Dudley

0637 - Underway for sweeping area.
0730 - Commenced streaming gear.
0755 - Gear streamed.
0830 - Keeping station on YMS 372.
0945 - Started pulsing.
1038 - Stopped pulsing.
1109 - C/C to 150° True. Commenced pulsing.
1238 - Stopped pulsing. Started recovering gear.
1310 - All gear aboard. Proceeding to harbor.
1320 - Moored to YMS 429 in Fukuoka Harbor.
1430 - YMS 449 moored on port side. Captain left ship.
1915 - Captain returned to ship.

November 23, 1945

0000 - Moored port side of YMS 429 with YMS 449 on port side in Fukuoka.
0635 - YMS 449 underway.
0636 - Underway for sweeping area.
0740 - Started streaming gear.
0812 - Gear streamed.
0840 - Commenced pulsing. Base course 330° True.
0855 - Ceased pulsing.
0912 - Started pulsing.
1012 - Ceased pulsing. C/C 150° True.
1118 - Commenced pulsing.
1230 - Stopped pulsing.
1344 - Commenced pulsing.
1449 - Ceased pulsing.
1503 - Started recovering gear.
1518 - All gear aboard. Proceeding to harbor.
1710 - Moored on port side of ACM-5.
1721 - YMS 429 moored to port.
1850 - Wound and set all ship's clocks.

Figure 55 - Ensign Ken Storey and Japanese Dog

November 24, 1945

0000 - Moored starboard side to ACM-5 with YMS 429 on port (side) in Fukuoka.
0635 - YMS 429 underway.
0643 - Underway for sweeping area.
0845 - Commenced streaming gear.
0910 - Gear streamed. Started pulsing on cross sweep of channel. Base course 060° True and (its reciprocal) 240° True. (Note: Essentially we are now sweeping back and forth across the channel we have been sweeping all this time and roughly 090° degrees to the original direction of the channel. This is to vary the direction of the magnetic field across any mines that may still be on the bottom and are still armed. If there should be one, perhaps we might "lift" it (detonate it). Theoretically, there should be none. But nobody really knows).
1505 - Ceased pulsing. Started recovering gear.
1535 - Gear aboard. Proceeding to harbor.

1700 - Moored to YMS 293 in Fukuoka.

1714 - YMS 429 moored to port.

November 25, 1945

0000 - Moored to YMS 293 with YMS 429 to port in Fukuoka, Japan.

0635 - Underway for sweeping area.

0830 - Started streaming gear.

0845 - Gear streamed. Started pulsing on cross sweep of channel. Base course 060° True and 240° True.

1438 - Ceased pulsing. Commenced recovering gear.

1515 - Proceeding to harbor.

1635 - Moored to YP 644 for fresh provisions.

1645 - Completed taking fresh provisions.

1659 - Underway from YP 644.

1715 - Moored to port side YMS 297.

1720 - YMS 429 moored to port.

1759 - ENSIGN KENNETH A. STORY, D(L), USNR 457297, reported aboard for duty. (Note: Ens. Story was a graduate of The University of Washington NROTC. His home was Bremerton, Washington).

1815 - Captain left ship.

2000 - Wound and set all ship's clocks.

2200 - Outboard motor stolen from wherry. (Note: This was a big loss for the ship. It was probably stolen by crew from one of the other YMSes. At this point in the occupation of Japan no Japanese was ever observed anywhere near the U.S. ships in the harbor. Stealing items from one ship by a crew member(s) of another was a common practice. Also, one ship rarely, if ever, lent an item of equipment to another except in the direst of circumstances. The item on loan was rarely ever returned. Each ship's crew was responsible for itself. There is no recollection that we ever recovered the stolen outboard motor).

2255 - Captain returned to ship. (Note: The only time a Japanese ever came aboard the 183 happened as follows. One evening, about this time in November, two of the crew missed the last liberty boat (taxi) bringing American crews back to their ships. They were stranded on shore and it could have put them into some serious trouble. They were lucky, however, in that a couple of Japanese men with a row boat on the shore near the dock agreed to take the 183 sailors back to the ship out in the harbor, for a fee. The sailors had no cash left on them but convinced the Japanese men they would get the money when they got back to the ship. In a short while the row boat pulled up to the stern of 183. The sailors said they would be back with the money in a few minutes. The sailors had one of the Japanese men come aboard 183 to hold the bow line of the row boat. The sailors went forward to their quarters. Moments after the sailors reached their quarters, the gangway watch on his patrol of the deck spotted the Japanese man on the stern and could see part of the row boat with another person in it. Undoubtedly the watch remembered the earlier warnings that there might be attempts by suicide teams to blow up U.S. ships in the harbor. Without hesitation the gangway watch unholstered his loaded 38 cal revolver and started blasting away at the Japanese men. The one on the stern of 183 dived over the side and the oars in the oarlocks of the row boat could be heard getting fainter having already disappeared into the darkness. The two sailors and others were startled by the gun fire and the watch explained what had happened. They were troubled at first, for they really intended to pay the Japanese men. However, as they thought about it, it became funny and they realized that there was nothing they could do to pay the men for their water taxi service).

November 26, 1945

0000 - Moored to YMS 297 with YMS 429 on port side in Fukuoka, Japan.
0645 - Underway to sweeping area.
0825 - Commenced streaming gear.
0840 - Gear streamed.
0842 - Started pulsing on cross sweep of channel. Base course 240° - True and 060° True.
1432 - Stopped pulsing.
1437 - Started recovering gear.
1454 - All gear recovered. Proceeding to Fukuoka.
1625 - Moored to YMS 449 in Fukuoka.
1714 - YMS 374 moored alongside to port.

Figure 56 - Ensign Storey and Dudley

November 27, 1945

0000 - Moored to YMS 449 with YMS 374 on port side in Fukuoka.
0620 - YMS 374 underway.
1100 - YMS 449 underway. Moored to port side of YMS 429.
1526 - Underway for AM 381.
1537 - Moored to starboard side of AM 381. Started taking on fuel.
1644 - Underway for anchorage having completed taking on fuel.
1649 - Moored to port side of YMS 293. (Note: Bob Clayton, our No. 1 Electrician, remembers liberties in what was left of the city of Fukuoka. He recalls that the street cars still in operation would stop for an American serviceman at any time the serviceman raised his hand to indicate that he wanted to get on board. Being a good electrician, he noted that the electrical controls were made by General Electric Co. in New York. Clayton writes, "I went into a large department store one day and the Japanese clerk came to wait on me, and I would point to an item and ask, 'How much is this?' She finally said to me, in perfect English, 'Sailor, just tell me what you want and I will try to help you find it.' He learned that she had been educated in San Francisco).

November 28, 1945

0000 - Moored port side to YMS 293, Fukuoka harbor, Japan.
0640 - Underway for sweeping area.
0720 - Anchored in Fukuoka 800 yards from beach at Saito Zaki.
1020 - Sent shore party in boat to take (magnetic) tail ashore. (Note: Ens. Davis recalls that Saito Zaki was a moderate size community or small town about 3 miles north west of the entrance through the mole (a break water) at the inner harbor of Fukuoka. On the chart prepared by the air force, which we were using, it was indicated that two sticks of B-29 laid mines may have fallen very near to the town and in the shallow waters between it and the shipping channel from Fukuoka to the Sea of Japan beyond Iki Shima. The area between the shipping channel and the shore at Saito Zaki was too shallow to be sweep by a YMS. Therefore, to insure that there were no "live" magnetic mines in these shallows we anchored off shore in water that was deep enough for 183 not to hit bottom. The army had provided a bulldozer which met us on the beach. The

LCVP which brought the shore party from the ship also towed the long section of the magnetic cable, by its electrode end to the shore. We would be sweeping the shallow waters almost up on the beach, but instead of the ship pulling it, the bulldozer pulled the cable along the shore line, so that the shallow area was covered by the magnetic field. When all was ready, the ship cranked up the magnetic generator and began pulsing. The magnetic field created "penetrated" the muddy bottom and any mine that may have been there. If it was still armed (though it wasn't supposed to be) it would be detonated and rendered safe for the Japanese as well as the Allies. A stout line had been secured to the single cable near the electrode and was fastened to the bulldozer. The electrode was allowed to remain in the water near the shore. In this way the water completed the circuit to the electrode of the shorter cable. When the pulsing began, just as if the ship was pulling it through the water, we were sweeping. When the pulsing for a given area was completed (according to a predetermined time period), the pulsing was stopped, the bulldozer towed the end of the cable up the beach to a predetermined point. At this time the signal man in the shore party blinked to the ship that we were ready to begin pulsing again and the Electrician's Mate (probably Bob Clayton) threw the switch which sent the current down the long tail, through the water to the short tail and the circuit was completed and the magnetic field created).

1130 - Commenced pulsing on static sweep.

1200 - Pulsing as before. (Note: During the afternoon on this first day of static pulsing off Saito Zaki our routine was interrupted in a pleasant way when a dozen or so of Japanese School children came running down the shore toward the bulldozer and the small cluster of crew in the shore party. The children, who looked to be maybe 2nd or 3rd graders, kept a quiet and respectful distance but showed great interest in what we were doing. They had their cloth school bags with their books and slates. Several of them were eating something they had in their pockets. It appeared that they might be eating candy or something similar. Ens. Davis recalls asking one of them what he was eating. The little boy shook his head and shrugged his shoulders in the universal sign language which meant I don't understand you. At that moment, Davis noticed that the title on one of the school books was written in English, something like "Cherry Blossom Time In Nippon". That was the key. These children were learning to read English but could not yet speak it or understand it when spoken. However, they did know "cigaretto" and B-29, boom. Davis picked up a stick laying on the beach and wrote in the wet sand "what is it that you are eating?" The eyes of the first ones to see the question in the sand brightened and several exhaled what sounded like the stereotyped "Ah, so". They drew closer and one of the boys stuck his hand in his pocket and showed the Americans what they were eating. He extended his closed hand, opened it as if offering a portion to Davis. It was a dried sardine about 3 inches long and big around as a lead pencil. No sugar, but excellent protein. Davis had already learned that aragato meant "thank you". He took the small fish examined it closely and returned it to the little fellow with a "no aragato". The boy seemed to understand. There was some time before the next change in the operation with the static sweep was to take place and so the Americans had a look at the school books, wrote questions in the sand and got answers written in the sand by the kids. This was a refreshing change of pace and sailors and kids seemed to enjoy it. Almost as suddenly as the children had appeared they ran and skipped on up the beach to their homes laughing and talking all the way. Probably talking about those strange Americans. Davis said that the odor of the dried sardine reminded him of the sun dried shad fish roe, heated in the oven at home on a typical October Sunday afternoon just a few years before).

1628 - Stopped pulsing. Commenced recovering gear.

1648 - Shore party returned to ship

1650 - All gear aboard.
1707 - Underway for inner harbor.
1727 - Moored on port side of YMS 473
1743 - YMS 429 moored to port.
2028 - BOBIN, JOSEPH Anthony, BM 2/c(T) USN, 300-61-34, reported for duty.
2145 - YMS 473 underway. Now moored to YMS 293.

November 29, 1945

0000 - Moored to port side of YMS 293 with YMS 429 on port side.
0649 - YMS 429 underway from alongside.
0656 - Underway for Saito Zaki.
0735 - Anchored 800 yards from beach at Saito Zaki.
1023 - Tail (magnetic) secured to beach. Commenced pulsing on static sweep.
1200 - Pulsing as before. (Note: Around 1400 the sweep shore party began watching the eastern end of the beach where the static sweep was being conducted in the hope that the school children might stop by again today. Sure enough, it wasn't long before they appeared and gathered near the crew. Ens. Davis was prepared for them. He had brought 6 fresh oranges with him from the ward room. After some greetings and questions and answers in the sand, Davis produced one of the oranges from his coat pocket. When the kids saw the orange their eyes widened in astonishment. It was probably a rare thing to see an orange. Some of these children may never have seen one. In any event Davis had them line up in a semi-circle and they held their hands together to make a cup. They were orderly, quiet, no pushing or shoving as they waited. Davis cut each orange into the proper number of sections so that all would have a taste. As he placed a section in each pair of hands, each child bowed from the waist and said either "aragato" or "zank you". No one started to eat their piece of orange until the signal was given. They didn't gobble it down, but took their time, savoring each bite. Soon the children started up the beach toward their home laughing and talking as they ran along. Someone in the shore party was overheard saying that this duty on the beach today was better than a liberty).
1606 - Stopped pulsing. Commenced recovering gear.
1640 - All gear aboard.
1656 - Underway for inner harbor.
1725 - Moored to YMS 300.

November 30, 1945

0000 - Moored to port side of YMS 300.
0815 - YMS 389 moored to port side.
1725 - Underway from alongside YMS 300, proceeding to Buoy #1.
1734 - Moored on port side of YMS 398.
1810 - Wound and set all ship's clocks.

December 1, 1945

0000 - Moored port side to YMS 398 at Buoy #1 in Fukuoka Harbor, Kyushu, Japan.
0638 - Underway from Buoy #1.
0730 - Following Guinea Pig LST's (possibly LST 553 and 768) as survivor ship. (Note: Our job was to follow the "Guinea Pigs" to pick up survivors in case of a mining. This is one of the more interesting activities of the sweeping operation in Japan. As noted earlier, the U.S. mines we were trying to sweep were considered "unsweepable" from the very beginning. We had swept

the ship channels into Fukuoka many, many times with regular magnetic sweeps. These were modified with the use of "O" type gear pulling the magnetic tail in a large "J" configuration call a Jig Sweep. None of these techniques "lifted" any mines. This was good news and bad news. Presumably there were no live mines to be swept. In all probability, the thinking went, all the mines had either been detonated (the large number of sunken Japanese ships attested to the fact that many mines did their job), or had automatically disarmed in mid October as they had been pre-set to do. However, perhaps a few had been damaged in some way when being dropped from the B-29s and the disarming device rendered inoperable. This could mean that there might be a mine or mines still waiting for just the right combination of circumstances to set it off. Some of the mines laid in these waters contained the pressure trigger (the Oyster Mine). The only way to check for the presence of this type of mine was to actually run a ship of sufficient tonnage up and down the channel deliberately trying to detonate a mine and, of course, sacrificing the large ship to destruction - thus the name "Guinea Pig". A skeleton crew manned these ships with no one inside except the helmsman and engine control operator. As an added measure of protection for these two volunteers, the overhead and deck in the pilot house were padded with several layers of hammock mattresses. If these men were blown upward by an exploding mine, their steel helmets and the mattresses might prevent them from incurring severe injuries to the head and neck and the legs. According to Arnold Lott, 306 influence mines were laid in the Fukuoka area. As noted from the log of 183 no mines were lifted sweeping from October 13 to 27. Also, throughout November no mines were found. The channel was declared to be clear for LST traffic in early December. Captain F.F. Sima headed up the Guinea Pig operation for larger vessels from early December to the 27th. No mines were lifted during the entire Fukuoka sweep, but a total of 1,445 sweep days were spent to prove that Fukuoka was clear. *(See End Note No.111).*

1200 - Steaming as before behind LST's.
1600 - Steaming as before. (Guinea Pig operation ceased for the day)
1605 - Entering inner harbor.
1610 - Moored to YMS 468.
1755 - YMS 357 moored to port.
1806 - Underway to shift berths.
1828 - Moored alongside YMS 93.
1825 - YMS 398 moored on port side.

December 2, 1945

0000 - Moored on port side of YMS 93 with YMS 398 on port side in Fukuoka Harbor, Kyushu, Japan.
0655 - Underway for sweeping area.
0845 - Gear streamed.
1015 - Commenced pulsing.
1130 - Ceased pulsing.
1140 - Started recovering gear.
1209 - All gear recovered.
1311 - Moored to YMS 300.
1350 - YMS 299 moored to starboard.
1722 - Underway from alongside YMS 300.
1735 - Moored to YMS 319.

1830 - SCHONES, ROBERT (n), GM 3/c, 870-21-85 and HAMPTON, MAlCOLM McKENLEY, MoMM 2/c, 832-70-39, transferred to AN 69 for transportation to Continental United States for discharge in accordance with ALNAV 252. (Note: Increasingly, the number of Naval personnel eligible for discharge from the service is leaving many vessels short handed. To help keep ships in operation, dischargees are transferred to ships returning to the states as crew members. In this way personnel not ready for discharge can be used on the vessels still needed for operating in the western Pacific).

1908 - HARDMAN, ERVIN R., S 1/c, 756-39-42, reported aboard for duty.

December 3, 1945

0000 - Moored to YMS 319 in Fukuoka, Kyushu, Japan.

Figure 57 - YMS 183 crew in an informal pose

0652 - Underway for sweeping area.
0905 - Started streaming gear.
0932 - All gear streamed.
1049 - Started pulsing.
1225 - Stopped pulsing and commenced recovery of gear.
1253 - All gear aboard. Proceeding to Fukuoka.
1315 - Moored on port side of YMS 388 in Fukuoka Harbor.
1335 - YMS 319 moored to port.
1414 - Captain left ship.
2220 - Captain returned to ship.

December 4, 1945

0000 - Moored to YMS 388 with YMS 319 on port side in Fukuoka, Japan.
0740 - YMS 319 underway from port side.
0745 - Underway for sweeping area.
0935 - Commenced streaming gear.

0950 - All gear streamed.
1030 - Started pulsing.
1115 - Stopped pulsing.
1243 - Started pulsing.
1343 - Stopped pulsing.
1350 - Started recovering gear.
1417 - Gear aboard; proceeding to harbor.
1446 - Moored to YMS 398 in Fukuoka harbor.
1600 - YMS 93 moored to port side.
2330 - MORGAN, ARTHUR WILLIAM, RdM 3/c, 756-71-95, reported aboard for duty.

December 5, 1945

0000 - Moored to YMS 398 with YMS 93 on port side in Fukuoka harbor.
1330 - Underway for YMS 362.
1348 - Moored port side to YMS 362. (Note: YMS 362 was one of the YMSes present in Tokyo Bay for the surrender of Japan on Sunday, September 2, 1945.
1530 - Captain left ship.
2322 - Captain returned to ship. (Note: Unfortunately, the log rarely notes the many liberties the crew enjoyed while at Fukuoka. At every opportunity, after the ship was moored at the end of a typical day's operations, liberty was declared for a portion of the crew. Many times it was early enough in the day for the crew to get a chance to see whatever there was to see in this destroyed city. They explored the stores, the alleys, the restaurants and bars and places of entertainment. They came back with souvenirs of all kinds. One day several of the crew found a warehouse on the outskirts of the city which was filled with thousands of army rifles and bayonets of various types and what seemed to be tons of small caliber ammunition. It was, of course, under guard by troops of the army of occupation. It seems that the army realized that the Navy had little time to garner souvenir weapons so they had the warehouse open for Navy crews to take rifles back to their ships so that every crew member could take a rifle back home. No one seems to know how they did it, but several of our men brought back 300 rounds of 30 cal. ammunition that fitted the standard Japanese army rifle which was comparable to the U.S. Army's Springfield rifle of WWI. The rifles and ammunition were brought aboard and under the direction of the Gunner's Mate the 30 cal. rounds were impounded and the rifles checked to be sure that they were not loaded. A few of them were in pretty good shape, but most were pretty well worn or damaged. But a souvenir is a souvenir and an evidence that one has been in battle. It was too bad that those supply warehouse characters back in Guam couldn't have been in on this operation).

December 6, 1945

0000 - Moored port side to YMS 362 in Fukuoka Harbor.
1247 - YMS 362 underway from port side.
1255 - Moored port side to YMS 429.
1425 - Captain left ship.
1432 - YMS 362 moored to starboard side.
1435 - Received dry provisions aboard.
1625 - BLATT, SEYMOUR (n), BM 2/c, 818-09-60 and ARMSTRONG, JAMES Simler, EM 3/c, 923-27-46, transferred for transportation to United States for discharge.
1930 - Captain returned to ship.

2025 - WELSH, JAMES, S 2/c, 609-89-39, reported aboard for duty.

December 7, 1945

0000 - Moored to YMS 429 with YMS 362 on starboard side in Fukuoka Harbor.
0903 - Underway for YMS 389.
0918 - Moored to port side of YMS 389.
1040 - YMS 325 moored to port side.
1325 - YMS 389 underway from starboard side.
1330 - Moored to port side of ACM 5.
1455 - YMS 325 underway from port side.
1530 - Captain left ship.
1753 - Wound and set all ship's clocks.
2008 - Captain returned to ship.
2015 - Underway for YMS 362.
2025 - Moored port side to YMS 362.

December 8, 1945

0000 - Moored starboard side of YMS 362 in Fukuoka Harbor.
1000 - Captain inspected the ship.
1030 - Captain's inspection completed.
1640 - Underway for YMS 319.
1650 - Moored to YMS 319. (Note: Bob Clayton, our Electrician's Mate, recalls an interesting procedure relative to Japanese flag vessels when we arrived in Japan some weeks earlier. Every time an American ship met or passed a Japanese ship, the Japanese ship would dip his colors and hold them at half mast until the American ship acknowledged the Japanese salute by dipping the Stars and Stripes and immediately returning to its normal position. When this was done the Japanese ship returned its flag to the normal position. On several occasions there were a number of Japanese ships coming and going and this required that we have a Seaman standing by for some time in order to take care of this saluting by the vanquished Japanese).

December 9, 1945

0000 - Moored to YMS 319 in Fukuoka Harbor.
0707 - Captain F.F. Sima, CTG 52.16 came aboard.
0800 - Underway for rendezvous with guinea pig ships.
1100 - Met guinea pig ships and relayed information to them.
1300 - Close aboard USS Scoter, AM 381.
1312 - Captain F.F. Sima left ship. (Note: Captain Sima had just taken charge of the large ship guinea pigs and probably was making contact with them in preparation for their part in the operation to clear the shipping channels. The log of 183 does not record any details about the large guinea pig ships. Captain Sima's flag was apparently on the AM 381, a 220' AM. *(See End Note 112).*
1334 - Moored to YMS 429.
1645 - Underway for YMS 93.
1945 - Moored on port side of YMS 93.

December 10, 1945

0000 - Moored in Fukuoka Harbor on port side of YMS 93.

1138 - Captain left ship.
1430 - Captain returned to ship.
1840 - Received stores aboard.
1930 - Put anchor chain on YMS 93. Wind velocity increasing. (Note: The weather since coming to Japan from Okinawa in late October had been idyllic. Warm, almost windless days and cool fall-like nights were a welcome relief after the typhoons of mid-October and earlier. Since late November the early morning temperatures were often in the 20's only to warm up into the 60's by early afternoon. These temperatures were not unlike those of the same latitude in the U.S. During the day, Dec. 10, the wind shifted to the northwest and the temperature began to drop. Fortunately, since we were moored inside the breakwater of the inner harbor, the chop of the water was not too bad. It was apparent that our old hawsers could not stand much strain so our anchor chain was put over to the YMS 93 as insurance against being cast adrift if the "hemp" lines parted. As the wind increased, the low clouds began to spit snow. Word of severe weather with gale force winds had been received earlier. This was a Siberian cold front sweeping across Korea, the Sea of Japan and now hitting the west coast of Japan. The YMSes in nests (moored together to a common buoy) were beginning to suffer damage to their sides, and gunwales. The ships were now bobbing up and down in the wind and waves. They were not on the same sequence. One ship would be raised up, while those on either side were down. As they changed positions in a matter of seconds, the side of each ship scraped the side of the adjacent ship. Of course fenders were in place on the sides of each vessel and they helped to cushion the bumping and grinding of wooden hull against wooden hull. We were on the port side of YMS 93 so our starboard side and his port side were doing battle. We lost several fenders as the lines holding them parted from the weight of the two ships grinding against each other. We considered getting underway from 93 and anchoring by ourselves. We didn't try this, however, because we had already had experience with this bottom with a layer of mud so thick that the anchor could not hold, and the harbor was so small that we might have dragged anchor and been beached. We had one large fender with a steel rod through the center which we fastened amidships with steel sweep wire. The 93 had several fenders that seemed to be holding up for them. The temperature was below freezing and snow and sleet were slanting in almost horizontally. All hands were standing by the fenders, adjusting them as needed for most of the night. It was almost like being in a typhoon. By early morning the wind had abated to just a stiff breeze so that the wave action in the inner harbor was inconsequential. There had been superficial damage to our hull, however. The bumper on the starboard side had been chewed up in several places and the gunwale scraped and scarred from the steel wire holding the large fender. None of this was life threatening however, just a sad sight to see the hull all chewed up).

December 11, 1945

0000 - Moored on port side of YMS 93 in Fukuoka harbor.
0840 - Underway for YMS 446 for fuel.
0908 - Moored to YMS 446.
1103 - Completed taking on fuel.
1114 - Underway for YMS 93.
1130 - Moored port side to YMS 93.
1535 - Captain left ship.
2000 - Captain returned to ship.

December 12, 1945

0000 - Moored as before on port side of YMS 93 in Fukuoka Harbor.
1520 - Wound and set all ship's clocks.
1640 - YMS 319 moored to port side.. (Note: No further remarks for this day).

December 13, 1945

0000 - Moored to YMS 93 with YMS 319 on port side in Fukuoka Harbor.
0915 - Captain left ship.
1245 - Captain returned to ship.
1938 - Captain left ship.
2330 - Captain returned to ship.

December 14, 1945

0000 - Moored to YMS 93 with YMS 319 moored to port in Fukuoka Harbor.
1003 - Put chain on to buoy #1.
1015 - YMS 319 underway from port side.
1016 - YMS 93 underway from starboard side.
1224 - Underway for sweep of Fukuoka Inner Harbor.
1353 - Gear streamed (magnetic).
1400 - Started pulsing. (Note: In order to sweep the inner harbor all the other vessels, mostly YMSes, had to vacate the area to give us as much ease as possible in this relatively confined area. Although we felt it was unlikely, there was also the possibility that a magnetic mine might be lifted, and if near a YMS it could have been devastating).
1549 - Stopped pulsing.
1600 - Started recovering gear.
1629 - All gear aboard.
1730 - Moored to buoy #1.
1745 - YMS 319 moored to port side.
1750 - YMS 468 moored to starboard side.

December 15, 1945

0000 - Moored as before to buoy #1 with YMS 319 on port side and YMS 468 on starboard side in Fukuoka Harbor.
0645 - YMS 468 underway from alongside.
0650 - YMS 319 underway from port side.
0730 - Underway for sweep of inner harbor.
0800 - Started streaming magnetic gear.
0824 - Gear streamed.
0840 - Started pulsing.
1634 - Stopped pulsing. (Note: For 8 hours we had been steaming around and across the inner harbor, dodging mooring buoys, while trying to give every square foot of the inner harbor a "good dose" of magnetic field).
1638 - Started recovering gear.
1657 - All gear aboard.
1715 - Moored to buoy #1. YMS 388 moored to port side.
1805 - YMS 444 moored to starboard side.

December 16, 1945

0000 - Moored to buoy #1 in Fukuoka Harbor with YMS 444 on starboard and YMS 319 on port side.

0745 - Underway for magnetic sweep of inner harbor. 0808 - Started streaming gear.

0835 - Gear streamed.

0849 - Started pulsing.

1122 - Stopped pulsing.

1145 - All gear aboard.

1215 - Moored to buoy #1.

1255 - O'DELL, E. R., SM 1/c, 628-32-64 and MURRAY, THOMAS JAMES, S 1/c, 715-09-22 reported aboard for duty.

1405 - PREIS, GEORGE JOHN, RdM 2/c, 869-62-69; SMITH, DONALD EDWARD, S 1/c, 945-23-66; WIELEBA, CASIMIR (n), GM 2/c 622-86-94; FLYE, HORACE NATHANIEL, StM 1/c, 854-86-28 detached from duty and transferred FFT to the United States.

1435 - Captain left ship. CRANFORD, M.H., S.2/c, 264-17-42 reported aboard for duty.

1521 - Underway for YMS 388.

1535 - Moored to YMS 388.

1630 - YMS 468 moored to port side.

2030 - Captain returned to ship.

December 17, 1945

0000 - Moored as before to buoy in Fukuoka Harbor with YMS 388 on starboard and YMS 468 on port. (Note: Nothing worthy of note to report for this day).

December 18, 1945

0000 - Moored to buoy in Fukuoka Harbor with YMS 388 on starboard and YMS 468 on port side. (Note: Nothing worthy of note to report for this day).

December 19, 1945

0000 - Moored as before to buoy in Fukuoka Harbor with YMS 388 on starboard and YMS 468 on port.

1350 - YMS 388 underway from alongside. YMS 319 now moored to starboard side.

1400 - Wound and set all ship's clocks. (No further remarks for this day).

December 20, 1945

0000 - Moored as before to buoy in Fukuoka Harbor with YMS 319 on starboard and YMS 468 moored to port side.

0955 - Underway to rendezvous with LST 828 and escort to LST anchorage.

1220 - Completed escorting LST 828; proceeding back to harbor.

1240 - Moored to YMS 429.

1430 - YMS 429 underway.

1610 - ATA 203 (auxiliary tug) moored along port side. (Note: The coming of the LST 828 to Fukuoka signals that the harbor and shipping channels leading to it are declared clear of mines. Fukuoka now becomes an important port in western Kyushu for supplying the occupation forces in that area of Japan. There were, in Fukuoka, a number of large docks for loading and unloading ocean going ships. When we first entered this seaport there was heavy traffic by medium size Japanese vessels transporting former Korean slave laborers back to Korea. The Koreans were brought to these docks from their various places of labor by whatever land transportation was available. They were assembled on the docks and waited their turn to get on board a ship that would take them back to Korea. It had been reported that there may have been more than a million of these people from all over Japan to be repatriated. Often, the hundreds of people waiting on our dock included entire families, father, mother and children. They had personal belongings and that was about all. There was no shelter for them if the weather was bad and once they were in their places waiting for their transportation. They had to stay put. We had the opportunity to get close to these docks from the land side on one occasion. It wasn't far from the path we took from the liberty boat landing when we came ashore on liberty. As noted earlier, the disposal of human waste in Japan before the occupation forces came was absolutely primitive. You could smell the country while still far out to sea. We noted that these Korean refugees, through no fault of their own, contributed to this stench. On the dock, that we were able to see up close, was the evidence that there were whole families who had been slaves. In little clusters, four or five feet in diameter, were the individual piles of dung deposited there by a typical family. Reminiscent of the story of the three bears, there was a larger deposit, obviously made by the father, one not as large made by the mother, and one or more smaller deposits made by each child. We saw this sort of evidence all over the surface of the dock. The piles of dung were all neatly arranged and still there even after the slave laborers had been loaded onto the ships. I don't know who was responsible for cleaning the dock before the next batch of slaves marched onto the dock. Maybe, the next group cleaned the area or just found a spot that was not recently used and thus afforded some space for this important function. In all probability, many of these laborers had been enslaved in Japan for many years. By early December, it appeared that most of the Koreans slated to leave Japan from Fukuoka had been accommodated. The traffic of these repatriating ships was reduced to practically zero).

December 21, 1945

0000 - Moored as before to buoy in Fukuoka harbor with YMS 444 on starboard and ATA 203 on port side.
0820 - YMS 444 underway from alongside. Now moored starboard side to YMS 362.
1000 - Inspection party came aboard.
1140 - Inspection party left ship. (Note: The log does not state from whence the inspection party came, but it was clear that this bunch of junior officers had not been at sea for very long. They had the gall to ask over and over again why the hull and deck were needing paint and in such bad shape. One of the Ensigns was really troubled that the seat for the hatches on deck did not seem to fit properly thus compromising out watertight integrity. Somehow we saw the picture. These were regular Navy, not long out of Annapolis and doing their best to "knock" the reserves who were winning the war while these smug "aristocrats" were still in school. Somebody didn't have anything for them to do so they set them on us. We gave thanks to Neptune when they left).
1345 - ROSS, DONALD, MoMM2/c, 311-40-79, USN came aboard for transportation to Sasebo.
1600 - Underway for entrance to Fukuoka Wan.
1628 - Standing out of Fukuoka proceeding to Sasebo, Japan in company with YMS 362.
1715 - Turned on navigational lights.
1826 - C/C to 270 True°.
2030 - C/C to 280° True.
2110 - C/C to 208° True. Base speed 8 knots.

December 22, 1945

0000 - Steaming as before on base course 208° True, speed 7 knots, proceeding from Fukuoka to Sasebo, Kyushu, Japan in company with YMS 362.

0150 - C/C/ to 193° True. 0401 - C/C to 090° True.

0535 - C/C to 270° True. (Note: At 0401, we had reached the point where we were due west of the entrance of Sasebo. So our course was changed to due east. However, it became apparent that we were proceeding much faster than 7 knots because of a very swift current. There was very little wind so it had to be the current that was pushing us toward Sasebo so that at this rate we would arrive at the entrance before daylight. This was not good. That little entrance channel was tricky enough in daylight, in the dark even with radar it was to be avoided. Ens. Davis had the 4 to 8 watch and recalls that all signs indicated that we had to stay at sea until daylight. There was only one way to do this safely and that was to reverse course for a period long enough to take us away from Sasebo to a point where we could again head due east to the entrance in daylight. There were two of us, 183 and 362. Since we were the lead ship, with the senior Captain, it was our responsibility to notify 362 what was about to take place. Davis removed the MN radio transmitter phone from its hook, depressed the transmit button and said, "Primecut 2, Primecut 2 this is Donnicker 3, Over." "Donnicker 3, this is Primecut 2, over". "Primecut 2, we are approaching Sasebo entrance too fast. The current is pushing us so that we must be making 14 knots, at least. At this rate we will be at the entrance long before daylight. On my signal, in a few minutes, Donnicker 3 will make a course change to starboard and steady on 270° True. This will reverse course and this will slow us down considerably. You are to follow in our wake and make your turn to starboard in our water coming to course 270° True. Please acknowledge. Over". "Donnicker 3, this is Primecut 2, we acknowledge and are standing by to execute course change." "Primecut 2, this is Donnicker 3, we now execute turn to starboard and will steady on course 270° True. Over." Davis speaks to the helmsman, "Hard right rudder, steady on course 270° True." Helmsman to OD, "Hard right rudder, sir, steady on course 270° True." OD to helmsman, "Very well." In a few minutes radar reports to the bridge that YMS 183 is passing YMS 362 with 300 yards to spare. "Donnicker 3, Donnicker 3, this is Primecut 2, over." Primecut 2, this is Donnicker 3, over." "Donnicker 3, this is Primecut 2, we are now making turn to starboard and are steady on course 270° True." "Primecut 2, this is Donnicker 3 your course change is acknowledged. This is Donnicker 3, out").

0634 - C/C to 090° True. (Note: After an hour of going west, 270° True, 183 and 362 reversed course again to due east, 090° True and are now in such a position as to reach the entrance of Sasebo harbor after sunrise with plenty of daylight).

0830 - Standing into Sasebo Ko on course 095° True, speed 5 knots.

0925 - Medical officer came aboard from harbor entrance boat. Received harbor charts. (Note: Among other pieces of information that we needed for a successful stay was the news that the whole harbor of Sasebo was dangerously polluted with several types of bacteria. In fact a number of ships, some of them larger types, had so many personnel in sick bay that they could not operate. In order to protect our crew we were to place a large container of fresh water, 30 gallons or so, on deck. We were to empty the contents of a large bottle of strong disinfectant into the container, and mix thoroughly. All personnel were to carefully wash their hands in this mixture every time they touched anything that had touched the water of the harbor. In this way our people could keep from being infected. Diarrhea and other intestinal problems could be prevented in this way. Our water supply for drinking, cooking and washing was in our own tanks. Our task was to keep from bringing the germs aboard in the first place through contact with water in the harbor. As mentioned earlier, Sasebo harbor was almost completely landlocked and the natural flushing of the harbor waters was slow and with as many U.S. ships as there were in the harbor it had become a cesspool).

0927 - Medical officer left ship.
0950 - Standing into harbor.
1135 - Moored to YMS 362 in Cove "A" in Sasebo Ko, Kyushu, Japan.
1410 - Captain left ship. (Note: Gangway watch failed to log Captain back aboard later).

December 23, 1945

0000 - Moored as before to YMS 362 in Cove "A", Sasebo Ko, Japan.
0819 - Underway for ACM-1 (USS CHIMO).
0900 - Moored to port side to YMS 362 alongside of ACM-1.
1415 - YMS 362 underway from ACM-1.
1418 - Moored to port side of ACM-1. Captain left ship.
1712 - Captain returned to ship.

December 24, 1945

0000 - Moored to port side of ACM-1 in Sasebo Ko.
0734 - Underway on various courses in Sasebo Ko.
0920 - Moored port side to YMS 318 at salvage dock.
0930 - Received two fifteen man life rafts aboard from YMS 318. (Note: During the passage of the Siberian Cold front earlier in December while at Fukuoka, both our 15 man life rafts were damaged rather severely by the vessels on either side. YMS 318 was being cannibalized as it was not feasible to spend the money to get it back in operation now that the war was over).
1009 - Underway in Sasebo Ko.
1048 - Moored to starboard side to YOG 78 to take on fuel.
1205 - Underway in Sasebo Ko.
1250 - Moored alongside YMS 390 - port side to.
1345 - LCVP came alongside with working party and provisions.
1425 - Medical officer came aboard. (Note: We already knew that we would soon be returning to the States. The Medical officer came aboard to check on the health of the crew to be sure they were healthy).
1445 - Medical officer left ship.

December 25, 1945

0000 - Moored as before to starboard side of YMS 390 in Sasebo Ko.
0922 - Church party went ashore.
1300 - Church party returned to ship. (No further remarks on Christmas Day).

December 26, 1945

0000 - Moored as before along starboard side of YMS 390, Sasebo Ko.
1310 - Underway in Sasebo Ko.
1407 - Moored alongside LST 494 in Sasebo Harbor.
1613 - Completed taking on provisions, dry and fresh.
1620 - Underway in Sasebo Ko.
1650 - Moored to port side of AM 127 to take on lube oil.
1736 - Underway in Sasebo Ko.

1800 - Moored alongside ACM-1, lines to starboard in Sasebo Ko.
1804 - WOOTAN, THEO CARL, Cox(T), 975-63-72, reported for duty.
2056 - HANBEY, JAMES R., Qm 1/c(T), USNR V-6, 386-58-38, reported aboard for duty.
2117 - Following men transferred as indicated: MALLOY, FRANCIS (n), Qm 1/c, 720-58-22 to YMS 342; MURRY, THOMAS JAMES, S 1/c, 915-09-22 to YMS 271; FREDERICK, JOHN ANTHONY, MoMM 3/c, 906-66-86 to U.S.S. Chimo, (ACM-1).

December 27, 1945

0000 - Moored as before starboard side to ACM-1, in Sasebo Ko.
0725 - LCVP from ACM-1 taking on fuel.
0738 - O'DELL, E.R., SM1/c, 628-32-04, transferred to U.S.S. Chimo, ACM-1 for duty.
0740 - LCVP completed fueling - 100 gallons. (Note: This was a switch for 183. Only rarely did another vessel refuel from a YMS. Generally these were cases of emergency need by another YMS or other small craft and a very small vessel like an LCVP which also used diesel fuel).
0820 - Underway in Sasebo Ko.
0857 - Moored to port side USS YP 634.
0910 - Men came aboard from the USS Yosemite (AD 19) to effect repairs on hull and forecastle deck. (Note: The cracked ribs at the bow under the forecastle deck on the starboard side continue to bug us since we were sideswiped by the AM on Ogan Patrol at Okinawa. Damage to the hull bumpers was caused by the Siberian Cold Front a few weeks before at Fukuoka. The AD 19 was a destroyer tender. It was a nice looking vessel 530 feet long).
1603 - KEECH, THOMAS WOODROW, QM 3/c(T), 928-03-30, USNR V-6, reported aboard for duty.
1645 - Underway in Sasebo Ko.
1710 - Moored to starboard side IX 118 in Sasebo Ko. (Note: IX 118, USS Giraffe was a Liberty type tanker from which we are topping off our fuel tanks).
1818 - Underway in Sasebo Ko.
1840 - Moored starboard side to USS YMS 248 in Sasebo Ko.

Chapter 15
Break Out The Homeward Bound Pennant

December 28, 1945

0000 - Moored starboard side to YMS 248 in Sasebo Ko, Kyushu, Japan.

0802 - YMS 361 in coming alongside port side, punched a hole in gunwale.

0805 - YMS 361 moored to port side.

1025 - Captain left ship.

1135 - Captain returned to ship. (Note: The log does not record it, but the Captain ordered the Homeward Bound Pennant two blocked to the top of the mast in place of the commissioning pennant. This was an old Navy tradition requiring ships that were homeward bound to add more bunting to the Commissioning Pennant so that it was many feet longer and easily visible from afar. Upon reaching the first U.S. port, the pennant was taken down and divided among the crew, with the captain receiving the blue upper end portion).

1150 - Underway in Sasebo Ko standing out of harbor on various courses and at various speeds.

1357 - Cleared Sasebo Harbor entrance enroute for Saipan, Marianas Islands in Task Group 53.2.11. Steaming at various speeds and courses conforming to the swept channels.

1500 - Base course 180° True. Base speed 8 knots.

1600 - Steaming as before. Average speed 8 knots.

1722 - Turned on Navigational lights.

1835 - C/C 185° True.

1935 - C/C 200° True.

2335 - Radar out of operation. (Note: Unfortunately the log of 183 does not contain a list of the ships in Task Group 53.2.11. There were a number of YMSes, several AM's for refueling of the small craft, and several other types. It was a rag-tag group. Most were battle worn and scarred, with all kinds of mechanical and electronic problems. This included 183. Log does not mention when the Radar became operable, but it probably wasn't out for very long. Late in the afternoon a light snow began to fall. It covered the decks and all horizontal surfaces with a thin white shroud. It was a nice touch. Sort of a farewell gesture from Japan).

December 29, 1945

0000 - Steaming as before on course 200° True, speed 8 knots in task Unit 53.2.11 enroute from Sasebo, Kyushu, Japan to Saipan, Marianas Islands.

0029 - C/C to 193° True.

0435 - C/C to 140° True.

1725 - Turned on Navigational lights.

1933 - C/C to 146° True.

December 30, 1945

0000 - Steaming as before on base course 146° True, speed 8 knots in Task Unit 53.2.11 enroute from Sasebo, Japan to Saipan, Marianas Islands.

0050 - Radar in operation. (Note: The log does not indicate when the radar failed).

0132 - C/C to 127° True.

0707 - Secured all Navigational lights.

1200 - Steaming as before.

1430 - Electrical steering out of order. Changed to manual.

1519 - Electrical steering in use again.

1547 - Exercised crew at emergency drills.
1617 - Secured from all emergency drills.
1725 - Turned on Navigational lights.
2100 - Port tachometer out (gauge showing shaft RPMs for port screw).
2220 - Radar out of operation.
2233 - Radar back in operation.

December 31, 1945

0000 - Steaming as before on base course 127° True, base speed 8 knots. Enroute from Sasebo, Japan to Saipan, Marianas Islands in Task Unit 53.2.11.
0653 Turned off all Navigational lights.
1045 - Changed from electrical to manual steering.
1052 - Changed from manual to electrical steering.
1400 - C/C to 123° True.
1615 - Commenced emergency drill exercises.
1645 - Secured from emergency drills.
1720 - Turned on Navigational lights. (Note: On this day, December 31, 1945. World War II officially ended. However, the work of American mine craft still continued in Japan, Korea, China (on the coast and up the big rivers for as far as 100 miles). As the battered mine craft were ordered back to the states many still were sweeping mines and in danger. More and more Japanese mine craft were doing the actual sweeping, which was as it should be. The last ship lost in WWII was AM 371, USS Minivet. It is ironic that she was named for a type of cuckoo shrike of Asiatic origin. She sank in minutes, after hitting a mine, with the loss of 31 killed or missing while placing dan buoy markers for the Japanese sweepers clearing the Tsushima Straits between Japan and Korea. Records show that Minivet was the first American minesweeper lost in these operations which had cleared and destroyed 20,000 mines since the end of the fighting war. *(See End Note No. 113)*

January 1, 1946

0000 - Steaming as before on course 123° True, speed 8 knots proceeding from Sasebo, Japan to Saipan with Task Group 53.2.11.
0625 - Secured Radar.
0649 - Secured Navigational lights. (Note: Maintained course 123° True all day).
1711 - Turned on all Navigational lights.
1712 - Lit off Radar.

January 2, 1946

0000 - Steaming as before, course 123° True, Speed 8 knots, proceeding from Sasebo, Japan to Saipan with Task Group 53.3.11.
0300 - Changed course to 151° True.
0620 - Secured Radar.
0630 - Secured all Navigational lights.
1302 - Changed course to 146° True, changed speed to 9 knots.
1709 - Turned on all Navigational lights.
1715 - Lit off Radar.
1725 - Radar out of commission.
1850 - Radar back in operation.

1916 - Radar out of operation.
1930 - Radar back in operation.
1958 - Changed course to 135° True.
2020 - Secured Radar.

January 3, 1946

0000 - Steaming as before on course 135° True, speed 9 knots, proceeding from Sasebo, Japan to Saipan with Task Group 53.2.11.
0622 - Secured all Navigational lights.
0830 - Changed speed to 8 knots.
1020 - Changed speed to 9 knots.
1710 - Turned on all Navigational lights.
1915 - Changed speed to 7 knots.
2035 - Changed speed to 8 knots.

January 4, 1946

0000 - Steaming as before on course 135° True, speed 8 knots, proceeding from Sasebo, Japan with Task Group 53.2.11.
0600 - Secured Navigational lights.
0900 - Set all ship's clocks ahead one hour to conform with time zone (-10).
1805 - Turned on all Navigational lights.
2202 - Lit off Radar.

January 5, 1946

0000 - Steaming as before on course 135° True, speed 8 knots. Proceeding from Sasebo, Japan to Saipan with Task Group 53.2.11.
0003 - Changed course to 145° True.
0401 - Electrical steering in operation.
0624 - Changed course to 126° True.
0645 - Secured all Navigational lights.
0815 - Proceeding into Saipan Harbor on various courses and speeds.
0922 - Moored starboard side to YMS 176 outboard of AM 224 in Saipan Harbor.

January 6, 1946

0000 - Moored as before starboard side to YMS 176 outboard of AM 224 in Saipan Harbor.
0837 - Underway from YMS 176 proceeding to Tanapag Harbor on various courses and speeds to take on water.
1116 - Moored starboard side to YMS 41 outboard of YW-69.
1200 - Moored as before, YMS 176 alongside port side.
1507 - Underway from YMS 41 proceeding into Saipan Harbor on various courses and speeds.
1548 - Anchored in Saipan Harbor in vicinity Berth Love 35.
1600 - Anchored as before. YMS 176 moored to starboard side. (Note: At about this time an urgent message to all ships, from YMS 362, came over the inter-ship radio. "Primecut 2" was appealing for the loan of a handybilly, as she was taking on water and the electric bilge pumps had been shorted out and they could not be used. The only thing 362 could do was borrow a handybilly (portable gasoline powered water pump) or bail the bilge by hand with buckets. No one responded to their plea. One or two specific YMSes were called for help but they denied

having a handy billy. No one believed 362 and thought they might have been using this as a ruse to get a handybilly for themselves at someone else's expense. This is what the watch on 183 thought. However, Ens. Davis looked over at 362, which was anchored some distance away, through the binoculars, and sure enough, he could see all hands turned to literally bailing out 362 with buckets and small G.I. cans. At about this time, the station Coast Guard emergency utility vessel radioed 362 that she was on her way to pump out 362. This was done and 362 lived to sail another day.

January 7, 1946

0000 - Anchored as before in vicinity Berth Love 35 in Saipan Harbor, with YMS 176 moored to starboard side.
0940 - YMS 176 underway from alongside.
1415 - YMS 193 moored port side to deliver lube oil.
1420 - YMS 193 underway from alongside.
1508 - Underway proceeding on various courses and speeds to Pier C to take on provisions.
1610 - Moored port side to YMS 311 at Pier C.
1650 - Underway proceeding on various courses and speeds to outer harbor.
1733 - Moored starboard side to YMS 319 to transfer stores.
1752 - Underway for YMS 176.
1813 - Moored portside to YMS 176 to transfer stores.
1836 - Underway to anchor in outer harbor.
1914 - Anchored in vicinity Berth Love 23 Saipan Harbor. (Note: The various YMSes in our Task Group were moving about the harbor rather quickly so that all fuel is topped off, the water tanks filled and all the provisions needed for the next leg of the voyage home. We are eleven days out of Sasebo, Japan, including the last three days in Saipan. There are many more to go but we are ready).

January 8, 1946

0000 - Anchored as before in vicinity Berth Love 23 in Saipan Harbor.
0815 - Underway to clear Saipan Harbor.
0829 - Standing out of Saipan Harbor.
0850 - Cleared Saipan Harbor enroute to Eniwetok with Task Group 53.2.11. Course 025° True.
1015 - Changed course to 104° True.
1745 - Turned on all Navigational lights.
1830 - Lit off Radar.

January 9, 1946

0000 - Steaming as before on base course 104° True. Base speed 7 knots, enroute from Saipan to Eniwetok with Task Group 53.2.11.
0640 - Turned off all Navigational Lights.
0950 - Base speed changed to 8 knots.
1044 - Base speed changed to 6 knots.
1750 - Turned on all Navigational Lights.

January 10, 1946

0000 - Steaming as before on base course 104° True, base speed 7 knots enroute from Saipan to Eniwetok with Task Group 53.2.11.

0647 - Turned off all Navigational Lights.
1017 - Left formation to go alongside AM 224 (USS Eager) to trade movie.
1040 - Completed trading, resuming position in formation. (Note: "Going alongside" while underway at sea meant getting as close to the other ship as possible without any danger of hitting the other. We then rigged a type of "breeches buoy" line to the AM and passed our movie over to them and they returned the container to us with their movie inside. The seas were moderate and it all went off very easily. Movies were obviously very important entertainment. Sometimes when a trade for a movie we had not seen was impossible there were always a number of the crew who wanted to see the old one over again).
2000 - Changed course to 103° True.

January 11, 1946

0000 - Steaming as before on base course 103° True, base speed 7 knots, enroute from Saipan to Eniwetok with Task Group 53.2.11.
0620 - Turned off all Navigational Lights.
1730 Turned on all Navigational Lights.
1750 - Changed base speed 11 knots.
1834 - Changed base speed to 9 knots.

January 12, 1946

0000 - Steaming as before on base course 103° True, base speed 9 knots, enroute from Saipan to Eniwetok with Task Group 53.2.11.
0606 - Turned off all Navigational Lights.
1723 - Turned on all Navigational Lights.
2005 - Changed base course to 100° True.

January 13, 1946

0000 - Steaming as before on base course 100° True, base speed 9 knots, enroute from Saipan to Eniwetok, Marshall Islands in company with Task Group 53.2.11. Set all ships clocks ahead one hour from King time to Love time (from minus ten to minus 11 time zone). (Nothing further to note on this day).

January 14, 1946

(Note: Regrettably the log page for this date was not included in the material from Archives and History purchased for this history. We know, of course, that on this day Task Group 53.2.11 entered the protected waters of Eniwetok Atoll. The estimated 1000 mile cruise from Saipan took 6 days. It has been 16 days since leaving Japan in the snow).

January 15, 1946

Moored as before to AM 224 in Eniwetok Harbor. Set clocks ahead to minus 12 time. (Note: In a few days we will cross the international date line and lose 24 hours).
1140 - YMS 362 moored to port side.
1143- YMS 362 underway from alongside.
1234 - Captain left ship.
1700 - YMS 176 moored to starboard side. Received fresh and dry provisions.
1710 - YMS 176 underway from alongside.

1820 - Captain returned to ship. (Note: there were recreational facilities on the Island of Eniwetok, the main one of the many comprising Eniwetok Atoll. It had an air strip that only ran in one direction because the island was too narrow to accommodate a strip that was at an angle to the central one. The Atoll was so large that one could not see the many small islands directly across the lagoon. It was really hot here at this time of year for very little wind was blowing. Eniwetok Atoll became famous in the post war era when various nuclear devices were tested there as did one of the smaller islands named Bikini).

January 16, 1946

0000 - Moored as before port side to AM 224 in Eniwetok Harbor.
0815 - YMS 176 moored to starboard.
1243 - YMS 176 underway from alongside followed by YMS 183 from alongside AM 224.
1254 - Anchored in Eniwetok Harbor with YMS 176 moored to starboard side.
1440 - Captain left ship.
1824 - Captain returned to ship.
2247 - YMS 176 underway from starboard side. (Note: Ship's crew enjoyed a few liberties at the recreational area for soft ball and other games. There was also a refreshment bar and a ship's service store).

January 17, 1946

0000 - Anchored as before in Eniwetok Harbor, Marshall Islands with 55 fathoms of chain in 22 fathoms of water.
0814 - Underway enroute to Pearl Harbor in company with Task Unit 53.2.11.
0844 - Proceeding out of Eniwetok in single column, speed 8 knots, course 118° True.
0948 - Changed course to 071° True. (Note: The Task Group left the Atoll the same way it came in three days earlier, in single file, as the two entrances were very narrow).
1601 - Increased speed to 9 knots.
1900 - Turned on Navigational Lights.
1905- Commenced using Radar for search and position keeping.

January 18, 1964

0000 - Steaming as before on base course 071° True, base speed 9.5 knots, enroute from Eniwetok, Marshall Islands, to Pearl Harbor, Oahu, T.H. in company with Task Unit 53.2.11.
0732 - Turned off all Navigational lights.
1846 - Turned on all Navigational lights.

January 19, 1946

0000 - Steaming as before on base course 071° True, base speed 9.5 knots, enroute from Eniwetok, Marshall Islands to Pearl Harbor, Oahu, T.H. in company with Task Unit 53.2.11.
0615 - Radar out of operation.
0632 - Radar back in operation.
0715 - Turned off all Navigational lights.
1830 - Turned on all Navigational lights.

January 20, 1946

0000 - Steaming as before on base course 071° True, base speed 9.5 knots, enroute from Eniwetok, Marshall Islands to Pearl Harbor, Oahu, T.H. in company with Task Unit 53.2.11.

0711 - Navigational Lights all turned off.
1819 - Turned on all Navigational Lights.

January 21, 1946

0000 - Steaming as before on base course 071° True, base speed 9.5 knots, enroute from Eniwetok, Marshall Islands to Pearl Harbor, Oahu, T.H. in company with Task Unit 53.2.11.
0655 - Turned off all Navigational Lights.
1802 - Turned on all Navigational Lights.
2001 - Changed base course to 074° True. (Note: When making long voyages at sea, 1200 or more miles, the shortest route is not what appears as a straight line on a regular Mercator chart. Because of the curvature of the earth what is called a "great circle" course must be plotted and this requires small changes of course every few hundred miles. In a typical Task Unit the Senior Officer Present is responsible for setting and maintaining the proper course. This does not absolve the Captain of each vessel in the Task Unit from having his Navigator keep his own course by celestial navigation when the sun, planets and stars are not blotted out by clouds. In this case, dead reckoning is used. While not as accurate as celestial navigation, dead reckoning (using course, speed, wind and wave action on the ship) is better than nothing. Often, the Task Unit leader will ask for the position each ship's navigator has plotted on his chart at a given time each day, say at 12 noon local time or 2200. This enables all ships to gauge the accuracy of their positions as they are compared with each other's. These positions are rarely exactly the same, but most are near enough to each other to be considered fairly accurate. During the war communications of this sort while at sea were made via flag hoist, semaphore, or blinker light. Radio at sea might be picked up by the enemy. Now however, since the war is over, the easy way, by using "talk between ships" radio, is used for these reports. Ens. Davis, the Navigator since Lt.jg Weltzien was detached in June, recalls the satisfaction of taking star sights every sunrise and sunset and having the "fixes" on the chart agree with those of some of the other vessels. He also recalls that he didn't use the sun or the moon or the planets, because they required too much "figuring". He and his Quarter Master did use the full moon's light to get a perfect star fix at midnight on one occasion. The moonlight was bright enough to give a true horizon so that the angles of three different stars could be accurately measured with the sextant).

January 22, 1946

0000 - Steaming as before on base course 074° True, base speed 9.5 knots, enroute from Eniwetok, Marshall Islands to Pearl Harbor, Oahu, T.H. in company with Task Unit 53.2.11.
0001 - Electric steering out of order.
0023 - Electric steering back in operation.
0634 - Turned off all Navigational Lights.
0840 - Shifted to manual steering. Took steaming position alongside of USS AM 224 with lines number 2 and number 4 over from starboard side, preparatory to taking on fuel.
0842 - Fuel line taken aboard.
0847 - Cast off all lines and fuel line from AM 224. No fuel received. (Note: The rolling of both ships made this positioning too dangerous. It could have caused the vessels to roll into each other. Another way had to be tried).
0910 - Went alongside USS AM 224. Secured bow line and received fuel line aboard. Commenced taking on fuel.

1040 - Completed taking on fuel, released fuel and bow lines and resumed position in steaming formation.

(Note: The bow line of 183 was secured to the stern of the AM and the fuel line was passed down this line from the AM and secured to the 183. The nozzle was then inserted into the fuel tank. When the pumping was complete both the fuel line and the bow line were disconnected and 183 now had enough fuel to get to Pearl Harbor. This arrangement obviated the possibility of collision and gave 183 room to maneuver so as to stay as nearly as possible right off the stern of the AM).

1200 - Set ship's clocks back 24 hours to Zebra Time Zone. Crossed the 180th Meridian. (This is the International Date Line. We are heading east so there are two Tuesdays, and each is January 22, 1946. We gained a day whereas when the ship crossed the line going west it lost one day completely).

1747 - Turned on all Navigational Lights.

2200 - Changed speed to 8 knots.

2255 - Changed base speed to 7 knots.

2335 - Changed base speed to 9.5 knots.

January 22, 1946 (The extra day)

0000 - Steaming as before on base course 074° True, base speed 9.5 knots, enroute from Eniwetok, Marshall Islands to Pearl Harbor, Oahu, T.H. in company with Task Unit 53.2.11.

0600 - Stopped all engines to remedy overheated condition.

0615 - Engines resumed base speed.

0636 - Turned off all Navigational Lights.

1125 - Slowed speed to one-third so that anchor could be more easily secured.

1130 - Resumed base speed of 9.5 knots. (Note: Next to very stormy weather with high winds and high seas in the order of sea conditions that make for very unpleasant cruising is a moderate sea coming on the beam of a vessel hour after hour and sometimes day after day. The course cannot be changed for obvious reasons. Such was the case, which began, a couple of days after departing Eniwetok. Our heading was roughly east-north-east and the moderate seas were rolling in from a little west of north so that we rolled from port to starboard, back and forth, back and forth, sometimes as much as 35 degrees on the inclinometer. These seas were coming on our port beam. Very unpleasant for many reasons, not the least of which, was being able to have anything stay where it was put unless secured in some way. All the pots and pans in the galley were in their metal fences in storage areas and there was just enough space between pot and fence so that with every roll of the ship the pot slammed into the metal fence making a sound like someone hitting the pot with a hammer. The noise could be heard from stem to stern, through the day and through the night. Dish towels were stuffed between pots and fences to muffle the noise, but not for long. Somehow the cushioning gear would work loose and the banging began again, or because the stove near these storage areas was often very hot flammable cushions could not be used. Among other things that worked loose, having not been secured too well, was one of the anchors. It began to shift around and had to be re-secured. That was the reason speed was reduced. Working at the bow while rolling as we were, was a dangerous job. By reducing speed we were able to reduce the violence of the rolling).

1733 - Turned on all Navigational lights.

2220 - Electric steering our of order, steering manual.

2235 - Electric steering back in operation.

January 23, 1946

0000 - Steaming as before on base course 074 True, base speed 9.5 knots, enroute from Eniwetok, Marshall Islands to Pearl Harbor, Oahu, T.H. in company with Task Unit 53.2.11.
0611 - Turned off Navigational Lights.
1720 - Turned on all Navigational lights.
2000 - Changed course to 079° True. (To continue our Great Circle course).

January 24, 1946

0000 - Steaming as before on base course 078° True, base speed 9.5 knots, enroute from Eniwetok, Marshall Islands to Pearl Harbor, Oahu, T.H. in company with Task Unit 53.2.11. Set all ship's clocks ahead one hour to Zone Xray.
0700 - Turned off Navigational Lights.
0800 - Electrical steering out of order. Steering manual.
1055 - Electrical steering back in operation.
1800 - Turned on all Navigational lights.

January 25, 1946

0000 - Steaming as before on base course 078° True, base speed 9.5 knots, enroute from Eniwetok, Marshall Islands to Pearl Harbor, T.H. in company with Task Unit 53.2.11.
0041 - Radar inoperative.
0058 - Radar back in operation.
0210 - Electrical steering inoperative.
0226 - Electrical steering back in operation.
0400 - Stopped starboard engine for repairs, proceeding on port engine.
0415 - Changed speed to 7.5 knots.
0458 - Secured port engine for minor repairs, laying to independent of Task Unit. (Note: One cannot imagine how quiet it is with both engines silent, the other ships moving on without you and nothing but water all around).
0520 - Port engine back in operation.
0649 - Turned out Navigational Lights.
0725 - Resumed steaming position in Task Unit Formation.
1055 - Starboard engine back in operation.
1136 - Changed base speed to 9.5 knots.
1741 - Turned on Navigational Lights.
2120 - Stopped starboard engine for minor adjustments. Changed speed to 6 knots. Left steaming formation.
2130 - Changed speed to 7 knots.
2137 - Starboard engine back in operation. Resumed base speed of 9.5 knots. (Note: As mentioned earlier this was really a rag-tag bunch of worn out ships. 183 was not the only one breaking down every day or so. Many of the others did as well. The fact that we got most of them back to the states was a testament to the quality of the Navy's training of the enlisted men. They loved those engines and motors and the wooden hull that carried the whole thing).

January 26, 1946

0000 - Steaming as before on base course 078° True, base speed 9.5 knots, enroute from Eniwetok, Marshall Islands to Pearl Harbor, Oahu, T.H. in company with Task Unit 53.2.11. Radar inoperative.

0150 - Resumed position in Task Unit formation.
0400 - Stopped starboard engine for minor repairs.
0423 - Starboard engine back in operation.
0642 - Turned off all Navigational Lights.
1315 - Changed base course to 074° True.
1727 - Left position in formation to go alongside USS YMS 176 to transfer engine parts.
1750 - Completed transfer of engine parts.
1756 - Resumed position in Task Unit steaming formation.
1801 - Turned on all Navigational Lights.
2335 - Secured engines to transfer suction to forward fuel tank.
2343 - Resumed base speed.

January 27, 1946

0000 - Steaming as before on base course 074° True, base speed 9.5 knots, enroute from Eniwetok, Marshall Islands to Pearl Harbor, Oahu in company with Task Unit 53.2.11.
0400 - Lights of Oahu Island, T.H. visible on port bow, range 15 miles.
0448 - Changed speed to 6 knots.
0510 - Changed course to 357° True.
0530 - Changed speed to 9.5 knots.
0543 - Engines stopped. Task Unit lying off Pearl Harbor entrance.
0547 - Task Unit standing into Pearl Harbor in column formation at various speeds and courses.
0617 - Turned off all Navigational lights.
0708 - Stopped starboard engine, proceeding on port engine.
0811 - Starboard engine back in operation.
0826 - Moored starboard side to USS AM 224 at D.E. Docks (Destroyer Escort), Pearl Harbor, T.H.
0830 - Commenced taking on fuel oil.
1000 - Set all ship's clocks ahead ½ hour to conform with time zone.
1018 - Completed taking on 2,000 gallons of diesel fuel and 800 gallons of fresh water.
1028 - Underway from alongside USS AM 224.
1103 - Moored port side to USS YMS 193 at Victor Docks, Pearl Harbor, T.H.
1223 - USS YMS 81 moored to starboard side.
1314 - Mail Orderlies sent ashore.
1430 - Mail Orderlies returned to ship. (Note: Moving about now for 30 days since leaving Sasebo, Japan, no mail had had time to catch up with us. This plus the confusion created by the war's end and personnel and ships moving toward the west coast in droves had really fouled up the mails. 183 hadn't had any mail in quite some time. From 1430 until time for taps it was sack time and mail reading time for practically everyone on board. It takes a while to read 50 or more letters at one sitting and some of the crew had that many to devour. Bob Clayton recalls that he had been on board 183 since Jan. 1944, 2 years. Ens. Davis recalls that he departed Pearl Harbor just a little more than one year ago with orders to report to the YMS 183. It took him more than a month to find her at Guadalcanal where she was preparing to help invade Okinawa).

January 28, 1946

0000 - Moored as before port side to YMS 193 with YMS 81 moored to our starboard at Berth 5, Victor Docks, Pearl Harbor.
0650 - Underway to permit inboard AOG to leave berth.

0825 - Moored port side to YMS 193, Berth 5 Victor Docks, Pearl Harbor.

0850 - YMS 81 moored to our starboard side.

1540 - Received fresh provisions aboard. (Note: Liberty schedules were already prepared and they began earlier this day. This was the first time in over a year that many of the crew of 183 had a chance of any good Liberty. The Skipper wanted everybody to get as much Liberty time as possible as the next leg of the journey to the States was at least as long as the one just completed. Of course, a good deal of time would be spent in the next several days doing some overhaul to the engines, steering motor, generators, etc. as well as provisioning).

January 29, 1946

0000 - Moored as before port side to YMS 193 with YMS 81 on our starboard at Berth #5 Victor Docks, Pearl Harbor, T.H.

0950 - WELCH, James, S 2/c, 604 89 39, was transferred to USN Hospital Aiea Heights for treatment not due to misconduct.

January 30, 1946

0000 - Moored as before port side to YMS 193 with YMS 81 moored to starboard at Berth 5 Victor Docks, Pearl Harbor, T.H.

0738 - Underway to allow YMS 193 to leave nest.

0755 - Moored port side to YMS 176 Berth 5 Victor Docks, Pearl Harbor.

1005 - Received fresh provisions aboard.

1045 - Captain's material inspection of ship.

1110 - Inspection completed.

1403 - Underway.

1410 - Laying to, to allow inboard ship to leave nest.

1452 - Moored port side YMS 306 Victor Docks, Pearl Harbor.

January 31, 1946

0000 - Moored port side to YMS 306, Victor Docks, Berth #5, Pearl Harbor.

1010 - Captain's material inspection of ship.

1040 - Inspection completed.

1100 - Received dry provisions aboard.

1440 - YMS 390 moored to our starboard side.

February 1, 1946

0000 - Moored port side to YMS 306 with YMS 390 on our starboard side at Berth 5, Victor Docks, Pearl Harbor, T.H.

1200 - Moored port side to YMS 306, with PGM 15 on starboard side.

1400 - Received fresh stores. (Note: Routine maintenance continues and Liberty Parties ashore as scheduled).

February 2, 1946

0000 - Moored as before to port side of YMS 306 starboard side PGM 15 at Berth 5, Victor Docks, Pearl Harbor, T.H. (Note: No further activity of note to report for this day).

February 3, 1946

0000 - Moored port side to YMS 306, starboard side to PGM 15 at Berth 5, Victor Docks, Pearl Harbor, T.H. (Note: No further activity of note to report for this day).

February 4, 1946

0000 - Moored port side to YMS 306, starboard side to PGM 15 at Berth 5, Victor Docks, Pearl Harbor, T.H.

0926 - YMS 306 underway from Port side.

0931 - YMS 81 came along port side.

1030 - Pay Master paid ship. (Note: Undoubtedly a good portion of this money was destined for the shops, restaurants, etc. of Honolulu. No further activity of note to report for this day).

February 5, 1946

0000 - Moored port side to YMS 81, starboard side to PGM 15 in Berth 5, Victor Docks, Pearl Harbor, T.H.

1403 - Received fresh provisions aboard. (Note: No further activity of note to report for this day).

Chapter 16
California Here We come

February 6, 1946

0000 - Moored as before port side to YMS 81, starboard side to PGM 15 at Victor Docks, berth 5, Pearl Harbor, Oahu, T.H.
0025 - Captain returned to ship.
0915 - Provisions brought aboard.
1015 - USS PGM 15 underway from Starboard side.
1022 - Underway in Pearl Harbor at various courses and speeds. Captain at the conn. Special sea detail set.
1234 - Moored starboard side to USS YOG 18 at D.E. Docks, Pearl Harbor.
1243 - USS YMS 81 moored to port side.
1259 - Commenced taking on diesel fuel.
1400 - Completed taking on fuel - 5370 gallons.
1405 - USS YMS 81 underway from alongside.
1409 - Underway in Pearl Harbor at various courses and speeds. Proceeding to rendezvous with Task Unit E8.2.2.
1441 - Cleared Pearl Harbor entrance.
1510 - Set sea watch.
1600 - Steaming as before on base course 150° True, base speed 10 knots, enroute from Pearl Harbor, Oahu, T.H. to San Pedro, California, USA, in company with Task Unit E8.2.2. This ship number 2 in port column of double column formation.
1747 - Turned on all Navigational Lights.
1815 - Changed course to 030° True.
1815 - Changed base course to 017° True.
2000 - Changed course to 025° True.
2117 - Changed speed to 7 knots. Port running light out; emergency light mounted.
2150 - Changed speed to 10 knots.
2210 - Changed base course to 001° True.

February 7, 1946

0000 - Steaming as before on base course 061° True, base speed 10 knots enroute from Pearl Harbor, Oahu, T.H. to San Pedro, California, USA in company with Task Unit E8.2.2.
0130 - Changed speed to 6 knots. (Note: Anyone familiar with the ship channels from Pearl Harbor through the islands and then toward California will recognize the foregoing courses and speeds as leading the Task Unit through the Kiawi Channel between the islands of Oahu and Molokai and into the open Pacific Ocean on a north easterly course).
0635 - Turned off all Navigational Lights.
0930 - Set all ship's clocks ahead 1 hour to Zone William time.
0955 - Hauled down colors in accordance with orders of CTU. (Note: There is no explanation for this order. It could have been, and probably was done so that all ships could fly a new ensign. Some of the colors were old, weather and battle worn, and frankly quite tattered).
1118 - Changed base speed to 10 knots.
1345 - Changed base course to 068° True.
1810 - Turned on all Navigational Lights.

February 8, 1946

0000 - Steaming as before on base course 068° True, base speed 10 knots, enroute from Pearl Harbor to San Pedro, California, in company with Task Unit E8.2.2.
0655 - Turned out all Navigational Lights.
0826 - Changed to base speed 7 knots.
1345 - Changed to base speed 11 knots.
1350 - Changed course to 075° True.
1429 - Changed base speed to 9 knots.
1615 - Electrical steering inoperative. Steering manual.
1624 - Electric steering back in operation.
1746 - Turned on all Navigational Lights.

February 9, 1946

0000 - Steaming as before on base course 075° True, base speed 9 knots, enroute from Pearl Harbor, T.H. to San Pedro, California in company with Task Unit E8.2.2.
0645 - Turned off all Navigational Lights.
0840 - Changed course to 070° True.
0925 - Changed base course to 066° True, base speed 8 knots.
1252 - Changed base speed to 10 knots. (Nothing of note to report for the rest of this day).

February 10, 1946

0000 - Steaming as before on base course 066° True, base speed 10 knots, enroute Pearl Harbor, T.H., to San Pedro, California in company with Task Unit E8.2.2.
0628 - Turned out all Navigational Lights.
0632 - Changed course to 067° True.
1725 - Turned on all Navigational Lights.
1800 - Lit off Radar.

February 11, 1946

0000 - Steaming as before on base course 067° True, base speed 10 knots, enroute Pearl Harbor, T.H. to San Pedro, California in company with Task Unit E8.2.2.
0100 - Set all clocks ahead one hour to Zone Victor Time.
0655 - Changed base speed to 8 knots.
0714 - Turned off all Navigational Lights.
0730 - Changed base course to 069° True.
1055 - Changed base speed to 10 knots.
1435 - Changed base speed to 9 knots.
1808 - Turned on all Navigational Lights.
1820 - Changed base speed to 8 knots. (Note: The changes of base speed were necessitated by wind and sea conditions which at some periods of time acted to push the ship ahead a little faster or caused it to move more slowly through the water. The prime effort was, of course, to keep the same distance behind the ship ahead, be it the CTU (lead ship) or the ship just ahead in the line of ships. At times the distances increased or shortened. In order to keep up but not run into the ship ahead required the frequent adjustment of speed).

February 12, 1946

0000 - Steaming as before on base course 069° True, base speed 8 knots. Enroute from Pearl Harbor, T.H. to San Pedro, California in company with Task Unit E8.2.2.
0150 - Changed base speed to 10 knots.
0701 - Turned off all Navigational Lights.
0725 - Changed base course to 071° True.
0830 - Left position in formation to go along starboard side of USS Improve (AM 247) (to receive diesel fuel). No lines over. (Note: We had learned that when refueling from an AM we did not need to be tethered by a rope. The refueling ship merely allowed the fueling hose to trail behind his stern, the ship to be refueled simply picked up the hose, placed the nozzle in the fuel tank pipe after checking the fuel for water or trash and filled the tank. When this was completed, the hose was dropped into the water, and was reeled in aboard the refueling ship).
0940 - Completed fueling, Resuming position in the formation.
1245 - Changed base speed to 7 knots.
1505 - Left position in formation to come along starboard side of USS Inflict (AM 251) to take on water. Commenced taking on water. No line over.
1525 - Completed taking on 800 gallons of water.
1734 - Changed speed to 10 knots. Turned on all Navigational Lights.
1803 - Lit off Radar.

February 13, 1946

0000 - Steaming as before on base course 071° True, base speed 10 knots, enroute from Pearl Harbor, T.H. to San Pedro, California, in company with Task Unit E8.2.2.
0633 - Secured Radar.
0645 - Turned off all Navigational Lights.
0715 - Changed base course to 073° True.
1737 - Turned on Navigational Lights and lit off Radar. (Nothing further of note to report for this day).

February 14, 1946

0000 - Steaming as before on base course 073° True, base speed 10 knots, enroute from Pearl Harbor, T.H. to San Pedro, California in company with Task Unit E8.2.2.
0629 - Turned off all Navigational Lights.
0817 - Changed base course to 078° True.
1540 - Changed base speed to 11 knots.
1545 - Changed base speed to 10.5 knots.
1720 - Turned on all Navigational Lights.
1746 - Lit off Radar.

February 15, 1946

0000 - Steaming as before on base course 078° True, base speed 10.5 knots enroute from Pearl Harbor, T.H. to San Pedro, California in company with Task Unit E8.2.2.
0607 - Turned off all Navigational Lights.
0610 - Secured Radar.
1700 - Turned on all Navigational Lights.
1720 - Lit off Radar.

1915 - Received orders from C.O. USS AM 247 designating this ship as guide and O.T.C. (Officer in Tactical Command) of Unit. Base course and speed same as before.

February 16, 1946

0000 - Steaming as before on base course 078° True, base speed 10.5 knots enroute from Pearl Harfbor, T.H. to San Pedro, California acting as O.T.C and guide of Task Unit E8.2.2.

0100 - Advanced ship's clocks one hour to conform with Zone Uncle Time.

0945 - Hoisted colors. (Note: The Task Unit was nearing the Catalina Islands and around mid-day a lookout on the flying bridge called out, "Floating mine dead ahead". The OD and others on the bridge picked up binoculars and looked at the object and all agreed it was a floater. We alerted the crew and had the Gunner's Mate issue rifles to his mine sinking cadre. We also notified the other ships that a mine had been spotted and that we were going to sink it, so stand clear. As we approached the mine so as to pass it on our starboard side about 50 yards and to shoot at it from that position. The Captain was on the bridge viewing the mine through his binoculars when he said, "That's a new type of mine. It has flippers." By this time it was apparent that this "mine" was really a large elephant seal. It had been napping and was startled by the sound of the ship approaching. Rifles were turned in to the Gunner, the other ships apprised of the new development and we settled back into the routine as we approached the mainland at San Pedro).

1230 - Lit off Radar.

1328 - Changed base course to 070° True.

1637 - Turned on Navigational Lights.

1815 - Changed base course to 085° True.

2000 - Formed unit into single column formation, standing into San Pedro Harbor, California, U.S.A.. Changed course to 080° True.

2110 - Changed course to 060° True.

2135 - Decreased speed to 1/3 ahead. (Note: The log does not record it, but at some point during this time a California Department of Agriculture Inspector came aboard from a launch while we were still underway. He was authorized to seize and dispose of any vegetables, fruits, etc. from outside of California. This comprised of "deep sixing" (throwing over the side) all of our Irish potatoes, citrus fruits, lettuce, celery and anything else of this nature. Obviously, this was designed to keep foreign diseases out of California. So here we were, entering the good ole U.S. of A, throwing several hundred pounds of potatoes and other eatables into the ocean just outside of San Pedro. After our crew had carried out the Inspector's directive, he gave the Skipper a chit (receipt), hailed his launch, jumped in and went to another YMS in the group).

2140 - Increased speed to 8 knots.

2142 - Proceeding into San Pedro Harbor at various courses and speeds.

2241 - F.A.W Jorgensen, Pilot, came aboard from launch.

2242 - Changed to manual engine control.

2244 - Entered San Pedro Harbor.

2355 - Moored Cerritos Channel Docks, Terminal Island, California, starboard to YMS 294. (Note: 51 days after leaving Sasebo, Japan in a light snow storm, we have arrived in San Pedro. We had no undue delays along the way and had no casualties of any kind. We had two passengers from Japan who completed the voyage in good fashion. One was a little dog, of unknown ancestry, who quickly became a member of the ship's company, sea legs and all. The other passenger was a sailor returning to the States to be discharged. His name is not remembered, but his proclivity for sea sickness is. When we started to leave a port, he would retire to the starboard side lazaret on the fantail with several quarts of water, a loaf of bread and several raw onions. He had a cot and blankets. The crew checked on him faithfully several times a day but he didn't come up on deck except when we returned to a port. He emerged looking like death itself, pale, underweight, gaunt and weak but thankful to have made it. It took him several days to regain his strength after we hit San Pedro and he left the ship to be discharged).

February 17, 1946

0000 - Moored starboard side to YMS 294 at Cerritos Docks at Berth 5 U.S. Naval Base, San Pedro, California.

0051 - Received 1700 gallons water.

1200 - YMS 361 moored to port side.

1235 - Ross, Donald (n) MoMM3/c, 311-40-79, USN, transferred to Separation Center Shoemaker, California. (Note: Beginning with our arrival at San Pedro a waiting game began. There must have been at least fifty (50) YMSes at Navy Base, Terminal Island, San Pedro when we arrived, and they were coming in from the Pacific daily. There were nests moored to the dock with at least 4 and sometimes 6 YMSes alongside each other. At places there was hardly room for another one to pass up or down the channel. All were waiting for official word of their disposition. A few would be kept in commission. These were the ones with the least need of repair and interestingly enough they were not always the youngest ships (the last built). Some of the older YMSes had had better luck in getting routine maintanance on their hulls, more frequent overhauls on the engines, better luck dodging typhoons, etc. In any event, "the word" began to drift down to the ships that a certain one would be going to the east coast for overhaul and retention in the active fleet. The rest of us waited for assignment to west coast bases (San Francisco or Seattle) for decommissioning and then put on the market for sale. After all, these vessels were built for the war, there were hundreds still in commission in the U.S. Navy and there was no way in the world that more than a few could be saved. Even knowing all of this, the YMS crewman who had come to love his wooden "dreadnaught" could not visualize with anything but displeasure the sight of one no longer flying the "stars and stripes" and the Commissioning Pennant). (Nothing else of note to report for this day).

February 18, 1946

0000 - Moored starboard side to YMS 294 with YMS 361 on port side in berth 5 Cerritos Channel, San Pedro, California. (There is nothing of note to report for this day).

February 19, 1946

0000 - Moored starboard side to YMS 294 with YMS 361 on port side in Berth 5, Cerritos Channel, San Pedro, California.

1505 - KLIVANS, J.K., SM 2/c, 949-60-84; WOOTEN, T.C., Cox., 975-63-72; ARMSTRONG, E.C., StM 3/c, 831-01-33; SCHLECTHER, W.H., SM 3/c, 873-87-79; HAWKINS, K.A., MoMM 2/c; HADLEY, J.A., RdM 3/c, 343-56-67; CORNISH, W. (n), MoMM 1/c, 921-35-98 were detached to USN Receiving Station, San Pedro, California pending discharge from Naval Service in accordance with ALNAV 252.

(Nothing else of note to report for this day).

February 20, 1946

0000 - Moored starboard side to YMS 294 with YMS 361 on port side in Berth 5, Cerritos Channel, San Pedro, California. (Nothing of note to report for this day).

John Dixon Davis

February 21, 1946

0000 - Moored starboard side to YMS 294 with YMS 361 on port side in Berth 5, Cerritos Channel, San Pedro, California. (Nothing of note to report for this day).

February 22, 1946

0000 - Moored starboard side to YMS 294 with YMS 361 on port side in Berth 5, Cerritos Channel, San Pedro, California.
1315 - YMS 361 underway from along our port side.
1322 - Underway from alongside YMS 294.
1350 - Moored starboard side to YMS 331.
1358 - YMS 361 came along our port side. (Nothing else of note to report for this day).

February 23, 1946

0000 - Moored starboard side to YMS 331 with YMS 361 on port side in Berth 5, Cerritos Channel, San Pedro, California.
1725 - Received dry provisions. (Nothing else of note to report for this day).

February 24, 1946

0000 - Moored starboard side to YMS 331 with YMS 361 on our port side in Berth 5, Cerritos Channel, San Pedro, California. (Nothing of note to report for this day). (Note: During these days of waiting the regular ship's routine is carried out, repairs, etc. have been made, the crew takes turns on Liberty and boredom is all pervading).

February 25, 1946

0000 - Moored starboard side to YMS 331 with YMS 361 on our port side in Berth 5, Cerritos Channel, San Pedro, California. (Nothing of note to report for this day).

February 26, 1946

0000 - Moored starboard side to YMS 331 with YMS 328 on our port side at Berth 5, Cerritos Channel, San Pedro, California.
1125 - HURWITZ, M.L., ETM 3/c, 945-70-05; BERG, A.H., PhM 2/c, 867-06-65; SAMON, J.J., Y 3/c, 841-55-30; REILLY, R.J., QM 2/c, 879-99-54, reported on board for duty.
1345 - Received G.S.K. Stores.
1435 - BURNETTE, J.D., SC 3/c, 246-02-89 reported on board for duty. (Nothing else of note to report for this day).

February 27, 1946

Moored starboard side to YMS 331 with YMS 328 on our port side at Berth 5, Cerritos Channel, San Pedro, California. (Nothing of note to report for this day).

February 28, 1946

0000 - Moored starboard side to YMS 331 with YMS 328 on our port side in Berth 5, Cerritos Channel, San Pedro, California.
1530 - FELTON, HAROLD (n), PhM 2/c, 721-24-70; STOCKS, EUGENE (n), Cox, 753-15-35; CLARK, N. B., RT 3/c, 927-37-36, transferred to Receiving station, Terminal Island. (Nothing else of note to report for this day).

March 1, 1946

0000 - Moored starboard side to YMS 331 with YMS 328 moored to our port side in Berth 5 Cerritos Channel, San Pedro, California.
1500 - BARKLEY, EARL L., Y 2/c, 866-69-82, reported aboard for duty. (Nothing else of note to report for this day).

March 2, 1946

0000 - Moored as before. (Nothing of note to report for this day).

March 3, 1946

0000 - Moored as before. (Nothing of note to report for this day).

March 4, 1946

0000 - Moored as before.
1430 - KEECH, T.W., QM 3/c, 928-03-30 transferred to R/S Terminal Island for discharge.
1450 - Received fresh and dry provisions. (Nothing else of note to report for this day).

March 5, 1946

0000 - Moored as before.
1600 - CORNISH, BILLIE L., GM 3/c, 974-58-19; DEL ROSO, JOE, MoMM 1/c, 420-64-19; SMOOT, THOMAS E., S 1/c, 920-77-18; PUTNAM, LEWIS F., S 2/c, 892-87-31; ZIMMER, FRANK V., MoMM 3/c, 872-87-21; transferred to R/S Terminal Island. (Nothing else of note to report for this day).

March 6, 1946

0000 - Moored as before.
0825 - Underway from alongside YMS 331 proceeding on various courses and speeds to Fueling Docks, San Pedro, California.
0837 - Passed through Pontoon Bridge, Cerritos Channel.
0849 - Passed through inner breakwater.
0951 - Moored port side to Fueling Docks in Berth 88, Basin Channel, San Pedro.
1015 - Started receiving fuel.
1130 - Received 4100 gallons of fuel.
1217 - Underway from Fueling Docks, Basin Channel, San Pedro proceeding on various courses and speeds to Berth 5, Cerritos Channel, San Pedro.
1306 - Passed through entrance of inner harbor breakwater.
1318 - Passed through Pontoon Bridge entering Cerritos Channel.
1344 - Moored starboard side to YMS 401 in Berth 3, Cerritos Channel, San Pedro.
1410 - SMITH, J. D., S 2/c, (Serial number not entered) reported aboard for duty. (Nothing else of note to report for this day).

March 7, 1946

0000 - Moored starboard side to YMS 401 with YMS 270 on port side in Berth 3, Cerritos Channel, San Pedro.
0207 - Captain returned to ship.
1445 - Captain left ship. (Nothing else of note to report for this day).

John Dixon Davis

March 8, 1946

0000 - Moored as before.
0550 - Captain returned to ship.
1040 - Captain left ship.
1223 - Captain returned to ship.
1245 - Received stores aboard.
1417 - Underway from Cerritos Dock. 1432 - Passed through Pontoon Bridge.
1445 - Anchored in Inner Mole, San Pedro.
1630 - YMS 331 moored to port side. (Nothing else of note to report for this day).

March 9, 1946

0000 - Anchored as before.
1320 - Captain left ship. (Nothing else of note to report for this day).

March 10, 1946

0000 - Anchored as before. (Nothing else of note to report for this day).

March 11, 1946

0000 - Anchored as before.
1405 - LCP #63222 reported for duty. PERRY, A.A., Cox, 964-53-53; OWENS, C.E., F 1/c, 358-74-73; SMITH, J.C., S 1/c and WIDMER, R.E. F 1/c, 784-77-97.
1700 - Fuller & Co. representative came aboard.
1715 - Fuller & Co. representative left ship. (No record of the business of Fuller & Co. Rep.). (Nothing else of note to report for this day).

March 12, 1946

0000 - Anchored as before. (Nothing of note to report for this day).

March 13, 1946

0000 - Anchored as before in Inner Mole, San Pedro, California with YMS 331 on port side.
1045 - Received stores aboard.
1625 - HACHENBERG, C.D., 671-87-70, Sm 3/c; ANDRUS, D.D., 891-04-64, F 1/c; WOLF, L.A., 753-49-51, MoMM 3/c; BUIE, IVY, 831-39-86, S 2/c and GRAHAM, W.R., 831-29-20, S 2/c reported for duty.
1710 - Port anchor dragged. Nest drifted and stern of ships hit the stern of ARG 5 (USS Oahu, a sister ship of USS Mona Island, ARG 9, which we had a lot of contact with at Okinawa).
1805 - Anchored in Inner Mole. 1815 - Underway for new berth.
1835 - Moored on port side of YMS 394 alongside pipe line dock in Inner Mole, San Pedro.
1845 - Damage from collision slight. Aft life raft and rack pushed out of position and port after davit bent slightly.
1945 - YMS 331 moored to port side.
2300 - Captain returned to ship.

March 14, 1946

0000 - Moored starboard side to YMS 394 with YMS 331 moored on port side at pipe line dock in Inner Mole, San Pedro. (Nothing of note to report for this day).

March 15, 1946

0000 - Moored as before.
0810 - Pilot came aboard.
0852 - LCP #63222 and boat crew, PERRY, AA, Cox, 964-53-53; OWENS, C.E., F 1/c, 358-74-73; SMITH. J.C., S 1/c; and WIDMER, R.E., F 1/c 784-77-97 transferred to NOB Terminal Island. (Note: when YMS 183 was assigned to an anchorage in the Inner Mole, a small boat, LCP and crew were temporarily assigned to the ship because of the great distance from the anchorage to the various docks, etc. crew members needed to access. Now that 183 was changing berths to the Cerritos Channel docks, access to the shore was only a few feet away so the LCP was returned to its base).
0855 - Underway.
0917 - Moored port side to YMS 306 in Cerritos Channel. Pilot left ship.
1210 - YMS 317 moored to starboard side.
1300 - Workmen from Navy Yard, Terminal Island, came aboard to clean fresh water tanks.
1357 - BUIE, I., S 2/c, 331-39-86, transferred to Receiving Station, Terminal Island.
1630 - Workmen from Navy Yard left ship.

March 16, 1946

0000 - Moored as before.
0940 - Disbursing Officer came aboard to pay ship.
1000 - Disbursing Officer left ship. (Nothing else of note to report for this day).

March 17, 1946

0000 - Moored as before. (Nothing else of note to report for this day).

March 18, 1946

0000 - Moored as before.
0915 - Mr. Jacobs, AIM representative, came aboard.
1050 - Mr. Jacobs left ship.
2027 - GSK stores were brought aboard. (Nothing else of note to report for this day).

March 19, 1946

0000 - Moored as before.
1015 - CO2 fire extinguishers taken ashore for recharging.
1615 - CO2 fire extinguishers brought aboard recharged. (Nothing else of note to report for this day).

March 20, 1946

0000 - Moored as before.
1500 - Underway.
1552 - Moored starboard side to YMS 326 at pipe line dock, Inner Mole, San Pedro. (Nothing else of note to report for this day).

March 21, 1946

0000 - Moored as before.
0942 - YMS 60 moored to port side.
1135 - Underway for fuel docks.
1210 - Stopped starboard engine. Believe starboard screw fouled.

1310 - Moored port side to berth 215, Fueling Docks, East Basin Channel, San Pedro.
1355 - Underway. Testing starboard engine at various speeds.
1446 - Moored port side to Berth 215 Fueling Docks, San Pedro.
1453 - Commenced taking on fuel.
1500 - Diver from Navy Yard, Terminal Island, went down to inspect screws.
1527 - Completed taking on fuel.
1540 - Diver completed work on screws. Removed rope fender and line from starboard screw.
1550 - Underway. Steaming on various courses and speeds to join convoy bound for San Francisco.
1622 - Cleared Long Beach harbor entrance.
1639 - Set course 279° True, speed 9 knots. Steaming in company with 4 YMS vessels enroute from San Pedro, California to San Francisco, California.

March 22, 1946

0000 - Steaming on course 270° True, speed 9 knots in company with 4 YMS vessels enroute from San Pedro, to San Fransisco.
0425 - Changed course to 329° True.
0555 - Secured Radar.
0610 - Secured all Navigational Lights.
0852 - Changed course to 337° True.
1359 - Changed course to 330° True.
1650 - Changed course to 320° True.
1820 - Turned on all Navigational Lights.
1825 - Lit off Radar.
2115 - Changed course to 336° True.

March 23, 1946

0000 - Steaming on course 336° True, speed 9 knots in company with 4 YMS vessels enroute from San Pedro to San Francisco.
0300 - Changed course to 344° True.
0410 - Changed course to 338° True.
0423 - Changed course to 328° True.
0534 - Changed course to 348° True.
0554 - Changed course to 350° True.
0600 - Reduced speed to 8 knots.
0622 - Secured all Navigational lights. 0645 - Changed course to 003° True.
0646 - Secured Radar.
0735 - Pilot came aboard. (Note: At about 0600 the large navigational light on the S.E Island of the Farallon Islands came into view. It was not a light house, but a large lighthouse like light mounted on a steel tower. These islands, a National Wildlife Reserve, and mostly rocks, are almost due west of the Golden Gate Bridge and the entrance to San Francisco Bay. The light is probably 30 miles from The Bridge. All ships, entering and exiting the entrance to the Bay must pause somewhere in the vicinity of the light to either embark or disembark a licensed Pilot who actually has the responsibility for conning the ship into or out of the Bay. A sailing vessel, usually a moderate size two masted schooner sails back and forth 24 hours a day with a cadre of Pilots waiting for the arrival of a ship. When a ship arrives, it lays to and the Pilot Ship sends a pilot to that ship (and this includes Naval vessels). He comes aboard and proceeds to the bridge with the Captain and now at the direction of the pilot the ship (in our case, YMS 183)

proceeds eastward up the entrance channel into San Francisco Bay. This was a very interesting time, especially passing under the Golden Gate Bridge and into San Francisco Bay. Ens. Davis recalls that no one on board was aware that YMS 183 had passed under the Brooklyn Bridge at 1613 on January 15, 1943, three years, two months and eight days before. This was learned later while reading a copy of the Log Book. Another interesting factor was the effect of the direction of the ocean tide. Upon entering when the tide is coming in, the ship's speed is augmented to a considerable degree and the time of passage reduced greatly. However, if a ship enters when the tide is going out just the reverse holds. The voyage is lengthened and forward speed reduced no matter what the engines are set on. It was exactly the experience of a ship going up or down a river).

0745 - Proceeding on various courses and speeds into San Francisco Bay.
0908 - Passed under Golden Gate Bridge, entered San Francisco Bay.
1010 - Anchored in Berth 78, Anchorage 6C in San Francisco Bay.
1025 - YMS 2 moored to starboard side.
1038 - YMS 119, moored to port side.
1050 - Pilot left ship.
1655 - YMS 119 underway from port side. (Note: This anchorage area, referred to as the mud flats, as we learned later, was not suitable for vessels with deeper drafts, but just right for small craft. This anchorage was off shore a short distance west of the City of Berkeley where the University of California is located and, in fact, the Bell Tower on that campus was one of our reference points for determining that our anchor had not dragged. While proceeding to our anchorage after passing under Golden Gate Bridge we also passed the infamous Alcatraz Island).

March 24, 1946

0000 - Anchored in Berth 78, Anchorage 6C in San Francisco Bay with YMS 2 moored to starboard side. (Nothing else of note to report for this day).

March 25, 1946

0000 - Anchored as before.
1447 - YMS 193 moored to port side. (Nothing else of note to report for this day).

March 26, 1946

0000 - Anchored as before.
0940 - YMS 193 underway from port side.
0945 - YMS 2 underway from starboard side.
1000 - Underway for water barge.
1115 - Moored port side to YW 112 in Berth 2, Anchorage 6B in San Francisco Bay.
1120 - Commenced taking on fresh water.
1130 - YMS 407 moored to starboard side.
1140 - Completed taking on water.
1205 - YMS 407 underway from starboard side.
1210 - Underway for anchorage.
1230 - Anchored in Berth 78, Anchorage 6C in San Francisco Bay.
1241 - YMS 2 moored to starboard side. (Nothing else of note to report for this day).

March 27, 1946

0000 - Anchored as before. (Nothing else of note to report for this day).

March 28, 1946

0000 - Anchored as before.

1145 - Dry provisions came aboard. (Nothing else of note to report for this day). (Note: 183 is gradually preparing for the final leg of its journey toward decommissioning. Word had already come down that her last days as a Commissioned Ship of the United States Navy would be spent in Seattle, Washington. After a brief respite in San Francisco we would be making that last journey).

March 29, 1946

0000 - Anchored as before.
1010 - YMS 2 underway from alongside.
1028 - Underway for water barge.
1122 - Moored starboard side to YW 117 in Berth 2, Anchorage 6B in San Francisco Bay.
1126 - Commenced taking on water.
1130 - Fresh provisions came aboard.
1135 - YMS 407 moored to port side.
1145 - Completed taking on water.
1215 - YMS 407 underway from port side. 1226 - Underway for anchorage.
1236 - Anchored in Berth 14, Anchorage 6C in San Francisco Bay.
1245 - YMS 2 moored to starboard side.
1345 - YMS 2 underway from starboard side. (Nothing else of note to report for this day).

March 30, 1946

0000 - Anchored as before. (Nothing else of note to report for this day).

March 31, 1946

0000 - Anchored as before. (Nothing else of note to report for this day).

April 1, 1946

0000 - Anchored as before.
1113 - Underway for pier 17, Treasure Island.
1444 - Moored on port side of YMS 119 in Berth D-1, pier 17, Treasure Island, California.
1500 - Completed taking on 840 gallons diesel and 1000 gallons of water. (Nothing else of note to report for this day).

April 2, 1946

0000 - Moored to pier 17, Berth D-1 at Treasure Island, on port side of YMS 119.
0720 - Underway for anchorage.
0745 - Anchored in Anchorage 6C. (Nothing else of note to report for this day).

April 3, 1946

0000 - Anchored as before. (Nothing else of note to report for this day).

April 4, 1946

0000 - Anchored as before.
1015 - Underway for water barge.
1117 - Moored to port side of YMS 399 alongside YW 117.

1145 - YMS 274 moored to port side.
1230 - Completed taking on water.
1249 - YMS 274 underway from YW 117.
1300 - Underway from YW 117 and anchored in Anchorage 6C. (Nothing else of note to report for this day).

April 5, 1946

0000 - Anchored as before. (Nothing of note to report for this day).

April 6, 1946

0000 - Anchored as before. (Nothing of note to report for this day).

April 7, 1946

0000 - Anchored as before. (Nothing of note to report for this day). (Note: One day during the stay in San Francisco Bay a Tidal Wave, originating somewhere in the Aleutian Islands of Alaska, made its way across the Pacific Ocean. It devastated the city of Hilo on the big Island of Hawaii. Ships in and around San Francisco Bay were warned to be ready for a rapid rise of water, even in the Bay. Fortunately, the wave was insignificant by the time it reached the coast of California and the 12 inch rise in the Bay was hardly noticed).

April 8, 1946

0000 - Anchored as before.
0948 - Underway for water barge.
1004 - Moored on starboard side of YMS 119 alongside YW 112.
1134 - Underway from YMS 119 after taking 1600 gallons water.
1140 - Anchored in Anchorage 6C, San Francisco Bay.
1345 - YMS 420 moored to port side.
1450 - YMS 420 underway from alongside.
1503 - Underway on various courses and speeds for San Francisco Light Ship. (Note: This is an error and should have been entered as S.E. Farallon Lighthouse).
1558 - Passed under Golden Gate Bridge.
1600 - Steaming as before on course 270° True at various speeds.
1725 - Rendezvous accomplished with T.U. (Task Unit) 99.12.2, OTC (Officer in Tactical Command) in this vessel (Lt, D.W. Mitchell, Captain of YMS 183), enroute from San Francisco for Seattle.
1753 - Changed course to 290° True.
1800 - Changed course to 306° True.
1848 - Turned on all Navigation Lights.
1950 - Increased speed to 8 knots.
2013 - Changed course to 327° True.

April 9, 1946

0000 - Steaming on course 327° True, speed 8 knots in company with T.U 99.12.2, OTC in this vessel, enroute from San Francisco to Seattle.
0401 - Changed course to 340° True.
0558 - Secured all Navigational Lights.
0635 - Decreased speed to 7 knots.
0636 - Changed course to 342° True.

0645 - Changed course to 340° True.
0922 - Increased speed to 7.5 knots.
1145 - Secured Radar.
1400 - Lit off radar. (Note: Use of the Radar while running parallel to the coast line was a great aid to navigation. The Radar could give accurate information on the distance from the shore, which was not visible to the eyes of the lookouts. Also, the fathometer was useful in confirming the general location of the ship because in these waters the depth of the water, as indicated on the charts, was relatively uniform).
1430 - Changed course to 357° True.
1850 - Turned on all Navigational lights.

April 10, 1946

0000 - Steaming on course 357° True, Speed 7.5 knots, in company with T.U. 99.12.2, OTC in this vessel, enroute from San Francisco to Seattle.
0207 - Changed course to 005° True.
0555 - Secured all Navigational Lights.
0753 - Changed course to 000° True.
1259 - Changed course to 005° True.

Figure 58 – Return to the States at San Pedro, California

1712 - Changed course to 010° True.
1745 - Turned on all Navigational Lights.
1840 - Increased speed to 8 knots.

2058 - Changed course to 015° True.

April 11, 1946

0000 - Steaming on course 015° True, Speed 3 knots in company with T.U. 99.12.2, OTS in this vessel, enroute from San Francisco to Seattle.
0120 - Changed course to 005° True.
0431 - Changed course to 000° True.
0437 - Changed course to 355° True.
0445 - Changed course to 005° True.
0553 - Secured all Navigational Lights.
0558 - Changed course to 347° True.
1218 - Changed course to 000° True.
1222 - Changed course to 347° True.
1225 - Changed course to 000° True.
1235 - Changed course to 347° True.
1530 - Changed course to 353° True.
1720 - Changed course to 000° True.
1752 - Turned on all Navigational Lights.
1819 - Changed course to 010° True.
1828 - Changed course to 340° True.
1835 - Changed course to 015° True.
1906 - Changed course to 040° True.
1919 - Reduced speed to 7 knots.
2035 - Changed course to 105° True.
2108 - Passed Cape Flattery abeam to starboard, entered the Strait of Juan de Fuca.
2215 - Changed course to 107° True.

April 12, 1946

0000 - Steaming on course 107° True, Speed 7 knots in company with T.U. 99.12.2, OTC in this vessel, proceeding through the Strait of Juan de Fuca, enroute from San Francisco to Seattle.
0125 - Decreased speed to 5.5 knots.
0235 - Changed course to 090° True.
0237 - Increased speed to 6 knots.
0340 - Stopped port engine, proceeding at 4 knots on starboard engine alone. (Note: We are now in unfamiliar, relatively confined waters with some traffic from other ships negotiating the Strait and it is the middle of the night Also, there are tricky tides and currents in the Strait. It seemed wise to slow down so as to stay in the Strait in the darkness and wait until daylight to start the complicated passage down to Seattle).
0512 - Changed course to 100° True.
0545 - Changed course to 105° True.
0603 - Changed course to 110° True.
0635 - Increased speed to 5 knots on starboard engine.
0701 - Changed course to 115° True.

Figure 59 – Return to Fukuoka after day sweep.

0731 - Changed course to 122° True.
0737 - Changed course to 125° True.
0738 - Decreased speed to 3 knots on starboard engine.
0838 - Started port engine, stopped starboard engine, proceeding at 4 knots on port engine.
0841 - Changed course to 135° True, started starboard engine, increased speed to 10 knots.
0845 - Changed course to 152° True.
0850 - Changed course to 154° True.
0918 - Changed course to 156° True.
0954 - Changed course to 135° True.
1013 - Decreased speed to 6 knots.
1035 - Increased speed to 7 knots.
1118 - Increased speed to 8 knots.
1130 - Changed course to 180° True.
1134 - Increased speed to 8.5 knots.
1137 - Changed course to 175° True.
1200 - Changed course to 190° True.
1220 - Increased speed to 10 knots.
1237 - Changed course to 085° True.
1239 - Decreased speed to 8 knots.
1244 - Changed course to 090° True.
1256 - Decreased speed to 5 knots.
1315 - Stopped all engines, laying off Pier 91, Seattle, awaiting berth.
1326 - Started all engines, proceeding on various courses and speeds to Manchester.
1430 - Stopped all engines, laying to off Manchester Pier awaiting berth.
1455 - Started all engines, proceeding to pier.
1501 - Moored starboard side to Berth B, Manchester Pier.
1525 - Took on 800 gallons of fresh water.
1530 - YMS 326 moored to port side.
1605 - YMS 326 underway from port side.
1900 - YMS 333 - moored to port side.
2012 - YMS 333 underway from port side.

April 13, 1946

0000 - Moored starboard side to Berth B, Manchester Pier, Puget Sound, Washington.
0811 - Underway, proceeding on various courses and speeds for anchorage in Yukon Harbor.
0900 - Anchored in Yukon Harbor.
0925 - YMS 119 - moored to starboard side. (nothing else of note to report for this day).

April 14, 1946

0000 - Anchored in Yukon Harbor, Seattle, Washington, with YMS 119 on starboard side. (Nothing else of note to report for this day).

April 15, 1946

0000 - Anchored as before.
1210 - YF 887 moored to stern to take ammunition.
1310 - YF 887 underway. (Nothing else of note to report for this day).

April 16, 1946

0000 - Anchored as before.
1427 - Underway for water barge.
1531 - Anchored in Yukon Harbor.
1623 - Underway for water barge.
1640 - Moored on port side of YW 130 to take on water.
1658 - Received 1750 gallons of water.
1705 - Underway from YW 130.
1725 - Moored to starboard side of YMS 117.
1800 - YMS 119 moored to port side.

April 17, 1946

0000 - Moored as before. (Nothing else of note to report for this day).

April 18, 1946

0000 - Moored as before.
0830 - YMS 117 underway.
0945 - YMS 199 underway from port side. Dropped anchor.
1030 - YMS 117 moored to starboard side. (Nothing else of note to report for this day).

April 19, 1946

0000 - Anchored as before.
0810 - YMS 117 underway.
0940 - Underway from Yukon Harbor on various courses and speeds for Pier 42, Seattle, Washington.
1110 - Moored port side to Pier 42.
1115 - YMS 331 - moored to starboard side. (Nothing else of note to be reported this day).

April 20, 1946

0000 - Moored as before. (Nothing else of note to be reported for this day).

April 21, 1946

0000 - Moored as before. (Nothing else of note to be reported for this day).

April 22, 1946

0000 - Moored as before.
0945 - BOHRER, J.H., RM 3/c, 317-23-47, USNR, reported for duty.
1200 - Decommissioning started this date. (Note: Except for personnel changes and a few changes in the berthing location of YMS 183 at Pier 42 there is little recorded in the log about the process of decommissioning. These details are remembered by several of the crew who were present during this period and the use of photographs made by these men and others serve to give a good record of this process. The Decommissioning Group of the Thirteenth Naval District, located in the Exchange Building in Seattle became our "headquarters" and the director of all that we did to get the ship ready to become a non-Naval vessel and suitable for sale to civilian interests. The Commandant, Thirteenth Naval District (Officer-in-Charge, Demobilized Shipping) would have the responsibility for the ship after decommissioning and until sold.
The sequence of events that follows is not necessarily exact, but is the description of a generalized process that removed and stored any and all materials, equipment, arms and ammunition, etc.

that the Navy needed to keep out of civilian hands, while at the same time leaving the materials, equipment, etc. that would make the vessel desirable and useful to a potential buyer. Among the first items removed to Navy storage was the "deep six" weighted canvas bag for the emergency destruction of secret communications and any secret communications still in the combination safe in the ward room. These items, and all others removed from the ship in the days to come were receipted for by the Office of Demobilized Shipping. The safe was removed. Top side weight was next to go as the stability of the ship would be increasingly compromised if the center of gravity was changed upward by removing heavy items in the lower part of the hull first. These heavy items included all radios on the bridge except the TBS which would be needed until the decommissioned ship was finally laid up. The radar antenna on top of the mast was a heavy item made "heavier" by its distance above the water line of the ship. The magnetic sweep gear timers, etc. fastened to the bulkhead in the chart room, were removed more for the secret nature of their construction than their weight.

The two heaviest items topside were the 3"/50 "cannon" on the forecastle, probably weighing ½ ton and the magnetic cable and its reel, on the fantail. This gear probably weighed several tons. Depth charges, and launching tracks had already been removed along with Ready Lockers, ammunition for 3"/50, 20mm AA guns, Acoustic Hammer, etc. [See log entry for September 26, 1945 above]. Anchors and chains remained on board. The "O" Type sweep gear, steel wire, paravanes, floats [or pigs], depressors, etc. were removed. After removal of this topside weight the hull came up out of the water several inches.

Of particular interest was the materiel and equipment in the lower part of the hull and in the bilges. It was a surprise to see many sets of parallel steel rods which were used in early days to make underwater noise for acoustic sweeping. The acoustic hammer was added soon after and the parallel rods were no longer used. Each set weighed 100 pounds or more and there were many of them. Also stored in the bilges were the dan buoy anchors which were round cakes of concrete, each weighing at least 100 pounds. There must have been 30 or more removed. This weight in the lowest part of the hull had added significantly to the stability of the ship and the "good ride" she always was. This weight also may have been part of the reason we were able to ride out two very disastrous typhoons. When the bulk of these heavy items were removed the hull drew at least 12 inches less than when ready for minesweeping, etc. Even moored to the pier, she bobbed about like a cork. Every little passing wave made her rock and pitch).

April 23, 1946

0000 - Moored port side to pier 42, Seattle, Washington with YMS 331 on starboard side. Stopped weather observations this date. (Decommissioning process continues. Nothing of note to report).

April 24, 1946

0000 - Moored as before.
1200 - Moored as before.
1420 WILLIAMS, E., StM 1/c, 377-68-59, USNR; LESTER, H.L., S 1/c, 756-13-69, USNR; GUDAKUNST, P. (n), MoMM 3/c, 313-75-62, USNR; SWARTZ, R.D., MoMM 3/c, 285-64-64, USNR; MERCER, A.D., S 1/c, 377-68-59, USNR; ARTERBURN, K.L., RdM 3/c, 877-49-13, USNR, reported aboard for duty.

April 25, 1946

0000 - Moored port side to pier 42, Seattle, Washington with YMS 331 on starboard side.

1000 - YMS 331 underway.

1200 - YMS 326 moored to starboard side. (Nothing else of note to report).

April 26, 1946

0000 - Moored to pier 42, Seattle, Washington with YMS 326 on starboard side.

1510 - FITZGERALD, RICHARD O., 579-94-28, Cox, USN reported for duty. (Nothing else of note to report).

April 27, 1946

0000 - Moored as before to pier 42, Seattle, with YMS 326 on starboard side.

1440 - BORKSTROM, M. C., SC 1/c, 381-41-56, USN reported aboard for duty. (Note: Increasingly, the rates coming aboard for duty are "regular Navy" (USN) as they are obligated to serve out their enlistment for a specific length of time established when they joined. The great majority of enlistments during the war were for the "duration of the war". These people were classified as Naval Reserves (USNR) and were demobilized according to a point system. Length of time served, married, children, etc. were factors in determining how many points a reservist had accumulated when the war ended, thus determining when the Navy was required to demobilize the sailor. In general, this was a good system but it did not allow for timely implementation, especially for personnel serving on ships which were located far from the continental U.S. and/or large bases where the supply of replacements was adequate. In the early weeks after VE Day, many ships were rendered inoperable for varying periods of time because they did not have replacements for those personnel given orders back to the states. They could not safely function until their crew was made adequate with replacements. These replacements had to come from new enlistments or from transfers from other ships returning to the states. It took some time for the system to function properly. Many ships returned to the states with crews made up of men with orders to the states to demobilize and they were required to serve on those ships transporting them. This wasn't a bad idea, but it did lengthen the time between a sailor's receiving his orders to a Demobilization Center and his arrival there. It generally took much more time than being a passenger on a fast transport. Some of the ships, like YMSes, which needed passengers to be crew members, in order to safely transit the Pacific Ocean, were slow and plagued by frequent stops for repairs. Even so, they were headed east and home. Better to be on course 090° True at a slow speed than riding the anchor in Fukuoka or Sasebo. Nothing else of note to report).

April 28, 29, 30, 1946

(Moored port side to pier 42, Seattle. Routine of preparing the ship for decommissioning continues).

May 1, 1946

0000 - Moored as before. 1400 - BURNETT, J.C., SC 3/c, 246-07-89, USNR; BOHRER, J.H., RM 3/c, 317-23-47, USNR; ARTERBURN, K.L., RdM 3/c, 877-49-13, USNR; transferred to Receiving Station, Pier 91, Seattle, Washington.

May 2, 1946

0000 - Moored as before. 1320 - BOBIN, J.A., BM 2/c, 300-61-34, USN; and CRANFORD, M.H., S 2/c, 264-27-42, USNR, transferred to Receiving Station, Pier 91, Seattle, Washington.

1540 - Underway to shift berth at pier 42. (Note: YMS 326 which had been moored on our starboard needed to go alongside the pier for the removal of some very heavy equipment that required the use of a crane. We moved to give 326 our berth).

1601 - Moored port side to YMS 326 at pier 42 (south), Seattle, Washington. (Nothing else of note to report for this day).

May 3, 1946

0000 - Moored port side to YMS 326 at pier 42 (south), Seattle, Washington.

1035 - YMS 199 moored to starboard side.

1125 - YMS 199 underway from Starboard side.

1245 - BARKELEY, E. L., Y /2c, 866-69-82, USNR; SWARTZ, R.D., MoMM 3/c, 285-64-64, USNR; SAMON, J. J., Y 3/c, 841-55-30, USNR; GUDAKUNST, P. (n), MoMM 3/c, 313-75-62, USNR; REILLY, R. J., QM 2/c, 879-99-54, USNR, transferred to Receiving Station, Pier 91, Seattle, Washington (Nothing else of note to report for this day).

May 4, 1946

0000 - Moored as before.

0850 - G.S.K. stores came aboard.

1705 - Mr. and Mrs. Arthur V. Story came aboard. (Note: Mr. and Mrs. Story are the parents of Ens. K.A. Story, our fourth officer. Their home is in Bremerton, Washington). 1855 - Mr. and Mrs. Story left ship.

May 5, 6, 7, 8, 9, 10, 11, 12, 1946

(Nothing of note to report for any of these days).

Chapter 17

Sixth CO Takes Command and Decommissioning

May 13, 1946

Figure 60 -.The Sixth CO John D. Davis, Ensign

0000 - Moored port side to YMS 326 at pier 42 (south), Seattle, Washington.

1445 - LT. D.W. MITCHELL, (D), 224415, USNR, relieved of the command of the USS YMS 183 this date by ENSIGN JOHN D. DAVIS, (D) 384175, USNR in accordance with Commander Western Sea Frontier dispatch 071740 April 1946 quoted below:

"D-A- GLOY 061740 - NYYO -W- KATY STAR GR 34 BT

Attention Bupers Personnel 3137 X Ensign John D. Davis D (L), 384175, USNR DIRDET USS YMS 183 X Respise as CO USS YMS 183 and as relief of Lieut. Douglas W. MITCHELL D (L), 224415 BT

(Note: No ceremony involved. No secret codes, etc. to be signed for, etc. A hand shake and the traditional "I relieve you, sir" by the new CO. Former CO Mitchell saluted the quarter deck, climbed over the gunwales of 183 and 326, up the gangway of 326 to pier 42. He picked up his Navy luggage, carried there by the gangway watch of 183, and disappeared among the workmen and machines as he headed for the foot of the pier where he could hail a taxi. What little work that remained to be done to get ready for the final inspection just prior to decommissioning continued. The log was signed at the end of this day by John D. Davis, Ensign, USNR, Commanding and by John D. Davis, Ensign, USNR, Navigator).

May 14, 1946

0000 - Moored port side to USS YMS 326 at pier 42 (south), Seattle, Washington. (Nothing of note to report for this day).

May 15, 1946

0000 - Moored as before.
1000 - Set special sea detail.
1014 - YMS 326 underway from our port side.
1024 - YMS 270 underway from our port side. (The log does not say when the YMS 270 moored between 183 and pier 42. There were a number of YMSes, like 183, preparing for decommissioning and they were changing berths with some frequency as was necessary for getting alongside of pier 42).
1030 - Moored port side to YMS 91. Secured special sea detail.
1400 - Inspection party came aboard.
1515 -USS YMS 297 came along starboard side.

1553 - Inspection party left ship. (Nothing else of note to report for this day).

May 16, 1946

0000 - Moored port side to USS YMS 91 with USS YMS 297 moored to starboard side at pier 42 (south), Seattle, Washington.

Figure 61 - Decommissioning ceremony for the YMS 183

0930 - Captain Lillard came aboard. (The skeleton crew remaining on 183 were in dress blues and assembled on the quarterdeck, at attention, as Captain Lillard came aboard).

0933 - Captain read decommissioning orders quoted herewith for information:

From: Puget Sound Naval Shipyard

To: Commanding Officer, USS YMS 183

Subject: USS YMS 183 - Decommissioning of

References: (a) CNO desp. 141930 of Feb. 1946 Article 1510, U.S. Navy Regulations 1920 Comdt PSNS ltr. A4-1 (200) Ser. 6684 of Mar. 1946

Reference (a) directed Commandant, Thirteenth Naval District to decommission subject vessel.

Subject vessel will be decommissioned this date and when ready for disposalwill be turned over to Commandant, Thirteenth Naval District (Officer-in-Charge, Demobilized Shipping).

Subject Vessel is in satisfactory condition and is receipted for in accordnce with reference (b) and (c).

W.M. THOMPSON

J.S. LILLARD

Captain, USN

By direction

Executed colors; ship is hereby decommissioned.

(Note: The Bosun called out the order, "Hand, Salute". We were facing the colors aft and as the stars and stripes were lowered, on the bow the Union Jack was lowered simultaneously with the commissioning pennant from its permanent place at the very top of the mast. At the completion of this observance, the colors were folded and presented to Captain Davis of the former USS YMS 183 along with the Jack and pennant. At this point Captain Lillard and his party exited the 183).

No one on board knew any details of the building and launching of the 183. Some believed, what most thought

Figure 62 Another view of Decommissioning ceremony for the YMS 183

Figure 63 YMS 183 waiting to be sold to civilians

was just scuttlebutt, that the renowned Kate Smith had christened the ship. As we know now, sixty odd years after the fact, this was not only true, but Kate offered a prayer that would have been fitting to recall at this ceremony. But we did not know. She prayed, "I christen you YMS 183 and pray to God that you may always float, that you have a good crew and that you will always bring your crew back to shore safely". (See the beginning of Chapter 2 above). Kate's prayer had been answered. YMS 183 had weathered all storms, been missed by or dodged several Jap suicide planes, swept 200 plus American laid defensive mines and a number of Jap mines, never ran aground, but was involved in a collision which, however, did not prove to be serious. The work for which USS YMS 183 was built to do has been done and she is now just YMS 183 or ex-USS YMS 183. She is an ex-*Wooden Dreadnaught* and in the careful hands of her remaining crew she will be laid up and made ready for disposition to some non Navy entity for a useful life after the war.

The skipper called to the OD just outside the wardroom door, "Dudley, (Ens. Gerald Dudley) "light off the main engines, set the special sea detail and stand by to get underway in 20 minutes." The CO signed the typed ship's log for this day, May 16, 1946 and put it in the official envelope for sending the final logs to the Bureau of Naval Personnel. Turning to Ens. Ken Story the CO said, " Ken is there anything else we need to do?" Story replied, " I don't know of anything else, but we do have several days after we get to Kennydale to take up any slack."

OK, Ken, see if you can get these logs to the Guard Mail courier at the Dock Master's office before we get underway. I don't suppose we will be coming back this way again."

At this moment the hiss of the compressed air entering a cylinder of the port engine could be heard and immediately the reciprocating pistons came to life as the superheated air from the compression ignited the diesel fuel being injected as a fine mist into each cylinder in turn. The engine roared and was slowed down to idle by the "black gang". In a few moments the same sounds came from the starboard engine and they both had a muffled throb as they warmed up for more efficient power. Ens. Davis remembered the countless times this routine was carried out. It was comforting to hear and feel those big engines warming up, and the continuing sound from the ships sevice generator. He almost dozed off as he sat in the wardroom. "I'll miss this place", he was thinking when Ens. Story entered the wardroom.

"The ship's logs are in the mail, Captain," Ens. Story announced, "the special sea detail is set, the main engines warmed up, and we are prepared to get underway when you are ready."

"Very well," the CO responded, as he rose from the wardroom chair which was a great deal the worse for wear, with the upholstery worn through to the padding. "I'm on my way to the flying bridge."

While climbing the ladders to the flying bridge, the CO was aware that several ex-YMSes were already backing into the harbor channel beyond the pier. No one had thought to count the number of YMSes decommissioned on this day. In retrospect there seem to have been at least 10 or 12. Many were moored alongside another, three or four deep from the pier itself. As each one cast off and was underway, the mandatory long blast from the ship's whistle (horn) signifying the intent of the vessel to back into the main stream beyond the pier was sounded. The lookouts on the bridge were intent on the moves of the other vessels to be able to give the skipper advanced warning of possible problems.

183 was now free to get underway as ex-YMS 297 had already gotten underway from the starboard side of 183. The skipper, leaning over the port side of the flying bridge ordered, "Let go one, three and four." Then into the voice tube into the pilot house, "Starboard engine ahead one." As soon as the ship responded to the starboard engine, beginning to inch forward, the CO commanded into the voice tube "All stop." The ship moving forward ever so slowly put a strain on line no. two (which tended from the forward quarter toward the after part of the ship, but secured to a cleat on the Ex-YMS 91. The effect of this forward movement of 183 while moored by line no. two, had what was called a spring effect causing the stern to move away from the 91. When forward motion was stopped and the stern began to move away, the CO called down to the pilot house, "All back one." The two engines went into reverse together relieving the strain on line no. two, at which time the command was given to "Let go two". Now all lines were on board and the ship is underway. However, now that she is no longer a commissioned ship, there is no Union Jack to be taken in at the bow or Colors to be transferred from stern to the main mast. She is just another ship backing into the main channel of Seattle harbor.

Figure 64 – Removal of the 3 inch gun

"One long blast," the skipper called out. The horn sounds, 183 slowly backs into the channel. "Right 15 degrees rudder. All stop." The stern swings toward the starboard. "All ahead one, rudder midships. Steer 330° degrees True. Secure special detail."

183 begins to move forward up the harbor channel. The string of ex-YMSes can be seen extending up ahead and in a few minutes those following 183 come into view as this armada of wooden dreadnaughts proceeds to its civilian destination. These vessels are salt water ships, but they will be laid up in the fresh water of beautiful Lake Washington until sold or otherwise disposed of. This stint in fresh water was to be the death knell for the various species of Teredo worms boring their tunnels in the wooden hulls of the YMSes. Being salt water creatures, the Teredo, apparently could not survive in fresh water.

By various courses and speeds, to stay behind the ex-YMS immediately ahead, but not too close, 183 makes her way around West Pt. in the Discovery Park area and into Shilshole Bay into which the Ship Channel draining Lake Washington empties. It is interesting to note that this is an important exit and egress channel for the various species of salmon which go up into Lake Washington to spawn and the young return to the sea to mature.

After entering the Ship Channel the ships ahead of 183 were virtually stopped as they came closer to the Ballard Locks, officially known as the Hiram M. Chittenden Locks. The locks had been built by the U.S Army Corps of Engineers many years before. My memory does not serve me well at this point, but I think the locks could accommodate two YMSes at the same time. Therefore, when it came our turn to enter the locks, that would lift us twenty some odd feet above Puget Sound level, I seem to recall that another YMS came in sort of alongside, but with her bow adjacent to our quarter. We moved very slowly forward toward the eastern gate of the lock which was closed. When we had reached the desired position we were stopped and the western gate was closed behind us. When it was securely closed, the valve on a large pipe connected to the Lake Union (fresh water) side of the lock was opened. Slowly the two YMSes rose higher and higher as the fresh water poured into the Lock chamber from below. In due time the level of the water in the Lock chamber was the same height as the Ship Channel on the eastern side of the locks. Now the eastern gates are opened and the vessels move into the waters of Lake Union, through the Montlake Cut which runs by the campus of The University of Washington just before entering into Union Bay of Lake Washington. Mileage wise this was not a long voyage, but the number of YMSes involved, the twists and turns at very slow speed, going through the locks, etc. consumed several hours from the time we left pier 42 in Seattle Harbor to our entrance into Lake Washington proper. As we slowly made our way by the University campus, the memory of many students lounging on the meadow adjacent to the Montlake Cut on this Spring day stands out. It is such a beautiful area.

After entering Lake Washington we turned to starboard, and increased speed. We were heading south now, on our way to the south end of Mercer Island. However, we had hardly increased our forward motion when we were forced to make a hard left turn and back the engines, for there was a "glut" of YMSes ahead of us. The problem was the Evergreen Point Floating Bridge which carries Highway 520 across the Lake. The concrete pontoons were the highway. Two of the pontoons were rigged to be pulled aside to allow vessels to come through, but only three or four could come through during a single opening so that vehicular traffic would not back up too much. Therefore, we were once again required to bide our time and await our turn to go through. Finally, our turn came and after passing through the relatively narrow opening in the pontoon bridge we pushed our speed up to standard and headed in a generally southern direction toward the northwesteern side of Mercer Island. There were several YMSes ahead of us and several following. We were all trying to get around the south end of the island where each, in turn, would change course to the northeast and head for the eastern shore of Lake Washington to the town of Kennydale. It was getting late in the afternoon and we all wanted to make our last port of call before it got dark.

Finally, Kennydale came into view and a small boat with several naval personnel came alongside to give us a mimeographed chart of the harbor facilities. It showed a number of large mooring buoys out in the harbor and a series of short, narrow docks leading to the shore in front of Kennydale. Some of the YMSes were already moored to buoys. Their crews would be taken ashore in smallboats. Others of us were assigned to certain docks where we would moor. Our assigned dock was number such-and-such. The lookouts located it and I made the turn to starboard into the slip between the two docks.

It was a perfect day and a perfect location for the perfect landing. No wind was blowing, no seas were running, there was no current to contend with. I was standing on the port wing of the bridge (pilot house). 183 was dead in the water but lined up with the starboard side of the dock and about three feet from the dock and the ship's length from where the bow should be located when we were moored.

"Rudder amidship, port back, one, starboard ahead one. All stop." Just like that the bow swung ever so slightly toward the dock.

Immediately, I ordered, "Starboard, back one; starboard stop." This little kick from the backing of the starboard engine for just a few seconds was enough to stop the swing of the bow toward the dock and started the stern to swing toward the dock ever so slowly. I ordered, "Port ahead, one; Port stop." Our port side was now about one foot away from the dock, but we needed to be about a ship's length nearer the shore end of the dock. We were essentially dead in the water with no wind setting us on or off the dock, and no current to contend with. I ordered, "Rudder amidship; all ahead one; all stop." This little kick from a few seconds of both screws turning started the ship forward, but just barely moving. In a very short time the ship, still only a foot or so from the dock was almost where she needed to be for mooring. I ordered, "Rudder amidship; all back one; all stop." As any landlubber would say, "She stopped on a dime." I ordered, "Pass lines one, two, three and four to the dock and secure. Also, double all lines and use chafing gear." No heaving lines were needed, the line handlers simply handed the lines to the men on the dock who secured them to the mooring cleats.

Figure 65 YMS 183 at Union Oil dock in Coos Bay, Oregon

My last order as skipper of 183 was, "Secure main engines and generators; dog and lock all hatches. Mr. Dudley and Mr. Story will take charge of the final cleanup and security crew. Good luck to you all. It was good to have served with you."

It was all over and done in just a few minutes. I went below to the wardroom picked up my uniform bag and official orders folder and walked down the port side to the gangway which had been placed from the after gunwale to the dock There was really no sound anywhere. Nothing was running and my footfalls on the wooden deck had a hollow sound. I paused a moment, looked fore and aft one more time and although it was definitely not required, I saluted the quarter deck one last time. Once on the dock, I headed for the bus which was to take us to the 13th Naval District headquarters for sleeping quarters and orders to the separation center on the east coast. I couldn't look back.

Bob Clayton, our very dependable Electrician's Mate, was in the party from the crew that had a few more days of service on 183. They finished up, secured, battened down, in general put the ship in condition to remain in Lake Washington for some period of time with only cursory inspections from time to time. Bob joined the crew of 183 on January 1, 1944 and had served on her continuously and very responsibly since that date and was the crew member with the most longevity still on board It was decided before hand that when the final crew left the ship, Bob would have the honor of being the last Navy man to leave her. He remembers that the last several days of securing the ship took place while she was moored to a buoy with five other YMSes at Kennydale. When the time came for all to depart, Bob was the last one to go over the gunwale into the small boat which would carry them to the beach. I have no doubt that these stalwarts all saluted the quarter deck as they disembarked.

Figure 66 – Ready to depart from YMS 183

John Dixon Davis

Chapter 18
Epilog

In the early 1950's, the date is not certain, Arthur J. McCourt, a former officer attached to YMS 184, and his wife, were traveling from their home in Seattle, Washington to San Francisco on a vacation trip. This was, of course, many years before The Interstate Highway System was begun and they were traveling down scenic Highway 101 which parallels every twist and turn in the coast line. As they were passing through Coos Bay, Oregon they saw a sight which surprised them both. There, tied up to a dock of the Union Oil Co., was the YMS 183. (Incidentally, YMS 184 was transferred to the Soviet Navy in 1944). They stopped, took pictures and found that the now empty hull was the home of George and Bernice Williamson and also their business location i.e. an outboard motor and fisherman's bait shop. (A copy of the picture that Art and his wife took appears in this book). They sent snapshots to Pete and Charlotte Dill in Murfeeesboro, Tennessee. This was the first contact the outside world had with 183 since she was decommissioned in 1946.

Art McCourt was an officer on the YMS 184 when she and the 183, with Pete Dill aboard, were under construction at the Greenport Basin and Construction Co. in Greenport, NY, in 1942. The McCourts and the Dills became close friends and each couple had their first child at about the same time in early 1943. Although Art was transferred to an AM before the two sister YMSes departed for the Pacific, the two families remained close friends through the rest of the war and for many many years after. The McCourts are now deceased, as is Pete Dill.

Some years later when the Naval Mine Warfare Association was organized, Pete Dill and Bob Clayton became re-acquainted and at the urging of Richard Hanson, Historian for the group, they began to search their memories and provided Hanson with pictures, written memories, etc. for his use in writing a history of YMS 183. Unfortunately, Hanson's health failed and about all he was able to complete was the story of the last days of 183 in Coos Bay, Oregon. This monograph by Hanson was circulated by Dill and Clayton among the living members of the crew they could locate. It was later published by the Turner Publishing Co. of Paducah, Ky. for NMWA. The monograph is entitled "Ultimate Fate of YMS 183" and is included in the book Naval Mine Warfare published in 1995.

As noted in the Foreword, I began preparations for writing the history of the YMS 183 during the 50th anniversary years of World War II. At that time I was unaware of the existence of the Naval Mine Warfare Association, nor was I aware that Pete Dill, whom I did not know, and Bob Clayton whom I did, were seeking to do the same thing through Richard Hanson. I was able to get information on the building of the ship from printed materials the other two did not know about and from several builders of 183 still alive and active. Pete Dill, the first officer assigned to 183, did not really come on the scene until after the hull was launched and much of the gross construction was finished. During this period in the middle 90's our paths crossed and the arrangement was made for me to write the history with permission to use whatever pictures, memorabilia, personal experiences, etc. they would contribute. So we have now come full circle. We have the story of her construction, testimonies of several of the crew from commissioning to decommissioning, including personal experiences, the movement of the ship and her exemplary service during 40 months (3 years and 4 months) and the immediate period after decommissioning. The deck logs of YMS 183, were secured from the National Archives and they are the official thread that runs though the whole story. There is an entry from the log in this book for each day 183 was in commission. In a few cases, where required, corrections of fact, typos, etc. have been made by the author/editor.

Between the time 183 was decommissioned in May 1946 and destroyed by burning in 1970 she had four owners and called several locations her home port. The first owner, according to Richard Hanson, author of the Monograph Ultimate Fate of YMS 183, was the Imperial Tugboat Co. which paid $8000. for her on February 14, 1948. Actually, according to Emery Hanson, who later became the last owner, The Imperial Tugboat company was owned by The Coos Bay Pilots. The Pilots provided pilotage for ships crossing the bar. Emery was involved in this endeavour by actually providing transportation for the pilots for about 30 years (1952-1982). He picked up the pilots and took them to the ship waiting offshore and took the pilots from the outgoing ships back to shore.

Imperial Tugboat, also, provided tug service in and around the Coos Bay area. A gentleman, named Dale Holden, senior pilot in Coos Bay during the 1950's, was the person who went to the Seattle area (possibly Kilisut Harbor) to pick up the YMS 183 and tow it to Coos Bay for Harbor Tug & Barge. By this time the 183 was prettry well stripped. The Harbor Pilots bought the engines for their Pilot Boats. The Company bought and sold Navy surplus from a variety of decommissioned vessels. (See End Note No. 19). [Note: Pilot Boats are vessels that lay off harbor entrances with a crew of licensed mariners who are certified for piloting an ocean going vessel into a specific port. The Master of a ship cannot do this for a given port unless licnsed for that specific port. The owner of the ship paid the fee to the licensed pilot. The Pilots kept the engines and other machinery but sold off most of what they could not use for the maintanance and repair of their pilot boats and thus many items like port holes, smoke stack, compasses, steering wheel, etc., etc. were soon to be found on other vessels of the area.] The 183 was soon emptied of everything and was indeed an empty hull. She was bought by George and Bernice Williamson and tied up at the dock across from the Union Oil Co.

The Williamsons lived aboard the 183 and modified the pilot house and deck houses and added a deck house from mid-ships aft. This housed their store from which they sold outboard motors, bait and fishing gear. For about 10 years the Williamsons maintained this commercial venture. It was during this period that the McCourts discovered the 183, took pictures and notified the Dills of their discovery. I am certain that the McCourts and Dills were pleased that 183 was engaged in fishing pursuits, outboard motors, fishing baits of various kinds and advice on the best fishing locations for the angler. She was not engaged in catching great schools of commercial fish and carrying them in the hold which was formally the magnetic generator room. Really nothing wrong with this use of an ex- YMS except that after the first catch of pogies, menhaden, or shad the ship immediately stank of rotting fish and was never to lose that smell. (Note: John Davis remembers that two former YMSes, bought by a fish meal company in his home town of Beaufort, NC. in the 1950's or 60's tied up at the town docks

Figure 67 - YMS 183 now a sales outlet for outboard motors and bait shop at Coos Bay, Oregon

every night. These former YMSes were named Lynn Anne and Pauline. When visiting family at the old home town in the 60's Davis climbed aboard these ships just to look around. A number of modifications had been made. They were still YMSes, but the stench of dead fish permeated the whole hull. And he couldn't wait to get onto the dock. He wondered, at the time if 183 had ended up like this. " Heaven forbid," he thought. "Of all the uses to which a decommissioned hull could be put," a former crew member like Davis imagined, "becoming a pogy boat was the absolute worst.") Across the next few years various crew members learned that 183 had a genuinely happier fate. Friendly people, adults and children, were always about. Her battered hull was painted and caulked where needed, the deck house was enlarged and her owners lived aboard. She was still afloat and moored to a real dock across from the Union Oil Co. rising and falling with the incoming and ebbing tide. This wasn't too shabby, considering the use to which other YMSes were put, on the east and west coasts.

In 1959 Emery Hanson and his wife Louise bought the empty hull of 183 and moved it to a parcel of shore land they had leased near the bridge to Charleston in the Coos Bay area. Their plan was to use the ship much as the Williamson's had, but in a more stable setting. Emery's idea was to bury the hull in the sand, upright and leveled fore and aft and athwart ships. At the proper height above the high tide mark, with lines from the ship to the dock he constructed, she looked like she was in the water, but was not, and was as stable as if on dry land - no pitch nor roll. Of particular interest is the way that Emery positioned the ship as he did and where she remained for another decade.

His main idea was to float the hull into the position he wanted and then fill the pond he had created with sand which would hold the ship upright and level. To accomplish this, he had to first determine if the shore sand would hold enough water to float the ship without it seeping into the sand. He had a bulldozer dig out a trench big enough to hold the 136'x24' hull, stopped up the open end with sand and waited over night to see what would happen to the water level. The pond he had created seemed not to have lost any water to seepage so he knew his idea would work. The bulldozer then opened up the end of the pond facing the open water. The hull was worked into position; hawsers fastened to the cleats and the bulldozer then pulled 183 into the pond. The water was deep enough so that the hull floated in with little more that the keel touching the sand bottom. The open end of the pond was closed by the bulldozer pushing sand into the opening. Now 183 was floating in the pond. Sand was pushed into the pond from all sides, causing the water to rise and in turn causing the hull to rise. Emery had secured a couple of water pumps to supplement the water in the pond if needed, but they were not needed. As the sand pushed into the pond from all sides raised the hull, care was taken to level the ship fore and aft and athwart ships, with the mast 90 degrees to the leveled deck. When the hull was exactly positioned and stablized, the excess water was let out and the sand leveled around the water line. The hull was now as firm as if built on land. It was indeed on land, her water line well above the high tide mark.

Emery Hanson was the 4th owner of 183 and when the hull was situated properly, he and his wife moved into the topside spaces over the main deck and set up house keeping. City water and sewer were connected. A dock-like ramp from the roadway alongside the port side of the ship provided access to the main deck. Mr. and Mrs. Cutting [John and Charlene] rented the large cabin which had been constructed from midships aft for use as a restaurant. Entrance to the restaurant was gained from the port side of the main deck. The Hansons gained access to their living quarters by use of a ladder on the starboard side of the hull. Their store selling bait, fishing tackle, etc. was below the main deck.

During the next ten years, as the business grew, the Hansens built a larger building across the street and gradually it housed the bait and tackle inventory and also provided space for the salvage

Figure 68 - Her "finest hour" before being burned by owner Emery Hanson

yard of parts from YMS 183 as well as other vessels that Emery bought for salvage.

In 1969, Hanson decided he should give up the lease on the land occupied by 183 as he no longer wanted to pay the rent. What to do with the 183, why cut it up into manageable pieces and burn them on the shore. Although Hansen says now that if he had it to do over again he would not have burned 183, but moved it to another location, where it might possibly still be intact. But he cut the hull apart after the cabins had been removed and salvaged various parts as he came to them cutting with his chain saw. (Note: His saw ran into flat pieces of bronze that were fastened to the frames in a criss-cross or x pattern. These bronze pieces were on both sides of the ship between the water line and the deck. Hansen removed them and sold them for scrap. He said he figured they were a part of the degaussing coil which aided in the reduction of the ship's magnetic field. Actually he was in error about the degaussing coil. The bronze frames were for lateral support of the oak frames much like the diagonal supports in the sides of a house. They were bronze for the absence of magnetic qualities and for anti-rust qualities. The degaussing coil was formed by a single well insulated copper wire which was secured to the inside of the hull just below the deck and running the inside perimeter of the hull. It was connected to a direct current source in the generator room from which currents of various strengths were introduced to alter the ship's magnetic field. Presumably the actual coil was cut up by the chain saw and sold for scrap also).

In 1970 (according to Emery Hanson's taped interview) the ship was reduced to pieces small enough to be dragged down the shore, pilled up and burned. Of course, any items that had salvage resale value were put into the inventory of the new store across the road. (Note: Richard Hanson's Monograph gives the date of the burning as 1978 which is in error. It was 1970 as stated above).

Richard Hanson quotes several old timers as saying "she burned in a blaze of glory and was the best fire they had seen around Charleston, Oregon in many a year." Richard Hanson continues, "The coals remaining were washed to sea by the next tide; so in the end, YMS 183 returned to the sea where she had served so gallantly during World War II. An incredible end to a gallant lady."

Appendix A

"Newspaper Articles from The Suffolk Times, of Mattituck, NY"

(The following articles are reprinted with the permission of *The Suffolk Times* of Mattituck, (Long Island) NY 11295).

The misplaced minesweeper - Search under way for warboats built at Greenport

Basin - By Tim Wacker (June 24, 1999) GREENPORT—Since Caleb Horton built the Van Buren back in 1834, the first vessel ever constructed here, there've been a lot of ships erected on the village waterfront, some notable, some not so. Former Lieutenant j.g. John Davis is interested in one of the latter. Specifically, a U.S. Navy yard minesweeper, YMS 183, that Mr. Davis spent 14 months aboard. Now he wants to document its demise or, more hopefully, its new home port for a book he is writing on the role of minesweepers in World War II.

It's doubtful that it's still afloat, but I'm going to try and find out," said Mr. Davis by phone this week from his home in Black Mountain, NC. "A well-maintained and well-built wooden vessel can last a long time."

Mr. Davis's ambitions may seem questionable. At 136 feet long and 300 tons the minesweepers weren't much to look at. But they had the vital task of clearing the waters of magnetic mines so troopships and battleships could do their jobs unfettered. Hollywood has spent millions documenting the exploits of the Army and the Marine Corps in places like Omaha Beach and Okinawa. Now Mr. Davis wants to make sure the YMS gets its place in history.

"Nobody in the general public knows what minesweepers were," he said. "If it weren't for them, not a single invasion in Europe or the Pacific could have taken place. They cleared the mines close to shore so the troops could go in. Without them the soldiers would have had to swim to shore."

Research leads to village

Mr. Davis's mission is not to revive fond memories but to document facts. All told, 36 of over 450 minesweepers constructed during the war were launched from the Greenport Basin and Construction Co. That's more than from any other shipyard in the country. So if you want to write a book about these ships, Greenport's the place to start looking.

Here's part of what Mr. Davis has so far. The wooden hull of the YMS was less susceptible to detonating the magnetic mines strewn by both sides through the waters of the Atlantic and Pacific oceans. But the YMS also spent plenty of time as an escort, protecting slower-moving troop landing craft against possible submarine attack.

In the 14 months Mr. Davis was aboard the YMS 183, she escorted marines to Okinawa and immediately after the war helped clear the waters in and around Japan of mines.

From there it was back to the states, where the 183 was decommissioned in Washington state, where she was sold and where the ship's trail grows cold. Mr. Davis is hoping anybody who knows anything of her fate will help fill in the gaps.

"I'd like to find out who bought her and what they are doing with her," he said. "Who knows, the hull may still be hauling fish somewhere in Alaska."

There were minesweepers that had more notable fates than that, though. The original Calypso, owned by Jacques Cousteau, was a YMS, and John Wayne was reported to have converted a minesweeper for cruising.

Kate Smith launched it

Mr. Davis also wants to research the birth of the YMS 183, and that's where Greenport comes in. A small clipping from The Suffolk Times says the ship was christened by the singer and radio personality Kate Smith when it was launched from the Greenport Basin and Construction Co. on June 25, 1942.

Greenport Basin eventually became Greenport Yatch and Shipbuilding, but present owner Steve Clark told Mr. Davis that fires in 1947 left few records behind. Now Mr. Davis is hoping that anyone who helped build the minesweepers, and the 183 in particular, can help him with his research.

He can be contacted at (828) 669-7690 or by mail at P.O. Box 55, Black Mountain, NC 28711. Email may be sent to jdavis6169@aol.com. "If nobody in the present generation writes something about it, nobody in the forthcoming generation will know anything about it," Mr. Davis said of the motivation behind his research. "That little vessel you all built in Greenport swept a lot of mines."

Minesweeper search hits paydirt (by Tim Wacker - *The Suffolk Times,* July 1, 1999)

GREENPORT – It's hard to imagine that once there were almost as many boat builders working in this one-square-mile municipality as there are now residents living here.

But World War II was a busy time and the country was working around the clock, with Greenport in the thick of it. It's just that most people these days don't realize it. A story in last week's Suffolk Times helped jog a few memories.

"There were 1700 men working there," said Donald Frederick a former carpenter at Greenport Basin and Construction Company, now home to Greenport Yacht and Ship Building on Carpenter Street. "We were working 11 hour shifts, both day and night. There were a lot of minesweepers that went out of there."

Minesweepers are what North Carolina Navy veteran John Davis is all about. He's been researching one specific sweeper, the yard minesweeper, for a book he's writing and his efforts took him to Greenport and The Suffolk Times, which wrote about him last week.

The response to that article suggests Greenport was a much different place a half-century ago. Around 1941 an unknown named Marshal Pollack drifted into town and he soon after owned a large chunk of Greenport Basin and Construction Co. and held contracts for building minesweepers for the U.S. Navy, according to Mr. Frederick. Suddenly there was work for everyone at the shipyard.

"It was a big place," he said. "People came from Patchogue, Moriches and as far away as East Hampton."

Mr. Frederick, a Greenport native now living in Southold, says he was 27 when he started working at Greenport Basin. The wood-hulled boats he helped build were in high demand for dislodging the magnetic mines that the Germans and Japanese were dropping all around the globe.

Mr. Frederick worked there from 1941 to 1945. Hourly wages were 72 cents, 92 cents or $1.02, depending on your skills. Fresh-cut oak and fir was fashioned into hulls for yard minesweepers being built three-a-month. Better pay than most for work that was, at times, highly skilled.

"You had all kinds of broad ax and adz work; we didn't have much machinery." Mr. Frederick said. "There was a lot of hand work. It brought out a lot of boatbuilders and shipbuilders. Many of the old fellows, they broke in us young fellows."

Greenport Basin started out making 96-foot minesweepers but those were quickly replaced by the 136 yard minesweepers, so called because they were too small for open-ocean duty and were supposed to be deployed from shipyards.

Radio personality Kate Smith was on hand for the christening for the first (see note below) YMS, numbered 183, but her contract didn't allow her to sing, Mr. Frederick recalls. After that, lesser notables christened subsequent ships as another 35 yard minesweepers were eventually launched into Greenport Harbor. Despite the mass production, Mr. Frederick says, the ships were ready to take on the mines they were charged with eradicating.

"They were top-notch, almost yacht-style," he said. "They were sound."

Mr. Frederick worked at the shipyard until the war's end slackened demand in 1945 and the layoffs started. Around that time Mr. Davis was commanding the YMS 183 toward her decommissioning in Washington State.

Fifty-four years later, Mr. Davis wants to document the birth, life and death of the YMS and he's combing the country for clues. The first to surface here were crisp pictures of minesweepers in various stages of production provided by Stewart Dewar of Southold, whose father worked at Greenport Basin. Next came Mr. Frederick's recollections, which are as sharp as Mr. Dewar's photos. Both are a big help in Mr. Davis's research.

"It's kind of slow going and then all of a sudden something happens, like at your place with these pictures and these individuals," he said.

Mr. Frederick knows of three others who worked the shipyard with him who might be able to help Mr. Davis. But he warns that the author better move quickly. WWII is fading farther into history, and so are Greenport's memories of it.

"I can tell you that there aren't many fellows left that worked there," he said. "If he wants to get that info, he'd better get in touch."

(Note: The YMS 183 was the first to be built of the new class of YMSes characterized by having only one smoke stack. The first 134 YMSes all had two stacks).

(The following story appeared on the front page of *The Suffolk Times,* June 18, 1942)

Kate Smith To Sponsor Minesweeper At Gpt. Basin & Const. Co.

Greenport Plans Welcome to Star; June 25th Broadcast to Tell Work Done by Company

The Songbird of the South, better known to many radio listeners as Kate Smith, will personally sponsor the first of the new group of the YMS motor minesweepers, the YMS 183, at the Greenport Basin & Construction Company's plant on Thursday, June 25.

It has always been known that Kate Smith and her manager, Ted Collins were very much interested in war work and shipyards. However, the officials of the Greenport Basin consider themselves extremely fortunate in having Miss Smith consent to sponsor one of their vessels.

It was originally planned to have Kate Smith's regular noonday broadcast, "Kate Smith Speaks," made from the shipyard. In this broadcast, which is made over a nationwide hookup of ninety-three stations, Miss Smith planned to tell some of the history of the Greenport Basin and Construction

Company as well as giving a resume of the work being done here at the yard. Circumstances beyond the control of Miss Smith, the Greenport Basin and Construction Company and the Columbia Broadcasting System make this broadcast impossible. However, the broadcast on the 25th, which will be made from New York City, will be devoted to telling of the work done at the Greenport Basin and Construction Company.

    A rousing welcome to Greenport is being planned for the arrival of Miss Smith. She will be met at the entrance to the village by the Greenport Basin and Construction Company Band, company officials, and a "guard of honor" from the Yard Police. She will be escorted the length of Front Street, up Main Street to Bay Avenue, down Bay Avenue to Carpenter Street and directly to the entrance of the plant. There she will be officially greeted by Theodore W. Brigham, president of the Greenport Basin and Construction Company.

    It is hoped that many radio fans from this vicinity will listen to Miss Smith's broadcast of the 25th.

Appendix B

"YMSes, Their Builders and Their Post War Dispositions"

Builders of YMSes in WWII (Alphabetical Order)

1. Associated Shipbuilders, Seattle, Washington (10 Units)
2. Astoria Marine Construction, Astoria, Oregon (16 Units)
3. Ballard Marine Railway Co. Inc., Seattle, Washington (8 units)
4. Bellingham Marine Railway & Boat Builders, Bellingham, Wash. (18 units)
5. Burger Boat Co., Manitowoc, Wisconsin (14 units)
6. Campbell Machine Co., San Diego, California (4 units)
7. Colberg Boat Works & Stephen Bros., Stockton,. California (12 units)
8. Dachel-Carter SB Corp., Benton Harbor, Michigan (8 units)
9. Gibbs Gas Engine Co., Jacksonville, Florida (33 units)
10. Greenport Basin & Construction Co., Greenport, L.I., New York (39 units)
11. Henry C. Grebe & Co., Chicago, Illinois (25 units)
12. Harbor Boat Co., Terminal Island, California (14 units)
13. Herreshoff Mfg. Co., Bristol, R.I. (2 units)
14. C. Hiltebrant DD Co., Kingston, New York (25 units)
15. Hubbards South Coast Co., Newport Beach, Cal. (6 units)
16. Robert Jacob Inc., City Island, New York (24 units)
17. Kruse & Banks SB Co., North Bend, Oregon (8 units)
18. Al Larson Boat Shop, Terminal Island, Long Beach, Cal. (8 units)
19. J.H. Martinac SB Corp., Tacoma, Washington (16 units)
20. Mojean & Erickson, Tacoma, Washington (9 units)
21. Henry B. Nevins, Inc., City Island, New York (24 units)
22. Northwestern SB Co., South Bellingham, Washington (2 units)
23. Rice Brothers Corporation, East Boothbay, Maine (11 units)
24. Seattle SB & DD Co., Seattle, Washington (8 units)
25. Frank L. Sample, Jr., Boothbay Harbor, Maine (12 units)
26. San Diego Marine Construction Co., San Diego, California (13 units)
27. South Coast Co., Newport Beach, California (13 units)
28. Stadium Yatch Basin Co., Cleveland, Ohio (24 units)
29. Tacoma Boat Bldg., Tocama, Washington (18 Units
30. Wm. Stone & Son, (city?) (4 units)
31. Weaver Shipyards, Orange, Texas (26 units)

32. Western Bost Building Co., Tacoma, Washington (6 units)

33. Wheeler SB Corp, Brooklyn, New York (20 units)

Note: The following pages of Appendix B will list the YMS hull numbers, in sequence, beginning with # 1. Each hull number will be followed by a number which refers to the number of the builder in the list above. (In this example YMS # 1 was built by Henry B. Nevins, no. 21 in list above). Three dates follow the builder's number: the first is date keel was laid; second is date hull was launched; third is the date completed. In most cases the ship was commissioned at this time or very soon after. A remarks column follows for any information specific to this ship: for example when struck from Naval register, or when sold, sunk or other wise disposed of, etc.

Hull No	Builder No	Keel Laid	Launch Date	Date Completed	Remarks
1	21	3/4/41	1/10/41	3/25/42	Struck Nav Reg 04-17-46
2	21	3/7/41	1/28/42	4/9/42	Struck Nav Reg 02-07-47
3	21	3/18/41	4/13/42	4/25/42	Transf France 10-02-44 re-named Heliotrope D-334-sold to France 03-21-49
4	21	8/20/41	3/14/42	5/1/42	Struck Nav Reg 06-19-46
5	21	8/14/44	4/13/42	5/19/42	Struck Nav Reg 04-17-46
6	21	8/8/41	5/19/42	0618-42	Struck Nav Reg 06-18-42
7	21	10/31/41	5/11/42	6/4/42	Struck Nav Reg 06-10-47
8	21	1/23/42	6/2/42	6/27/42	Struck Nav Reg 06-19-46
9	21	2/4/42	6/15/42	7/11/42	Struck Nav Reg 06-19-46
10	21	3/7/42	6/30/42	7/24/42	Struck Nav Reg 05-19-46
11	21	4/18/42	7/20/42	8/6/42	Struck Nav Reg 06-19-46
12	23	4/21/41	03/14/42	7/1/42	Struck Nav Reg 04-17-46
13	23	4/21/41	5/2/42	8/13/42	Transf to France as Basilic D-317 on 10-09-44 sold to France 03-21-49
14	23	7/1/41	6/13/42	10/7/42	Sunk in collision, Boston Harbor on 01-11-45 with DD-638, North Channel
15	23	7/5/41	7/16/42	12/5/42	Transf to France as Myosotis D-338 10-01-44 sold to France 03-31-49. Mined Port of Saigon 8 Jul. 49
16	23	3/14/42	9/7/42	2/15/43	Transf France asa Capucine D-338 10-18-44 Sold to France 03-21-49 in reserve 1955, scraped 1957
17	23	5/2/42	10/24/42	4/26/43	Struck Nav Reg 06-19-46
18	13	6/6/41	12/8/41	5/9/42	Transf France 10-01-44 as Glycine D-332 sold to France 03-21-49
19	13	6/27/41	12/8/41	6/20/42	Sunk by mine 09-24-44 at 06 53 N, 134 10 E, in Palau Islands, Caroline Islands
20	10	6/27/41	11/1/41	4/18/42	Transf to France as Gentiane -20-44 sold to France 03-21-49

Hull No	Builder No	Keel Laid	Launch Date	Date Completed	Remarks
21	10	6/28/41	11/25/41	4/18/42	Sunk by mine 43 06 N 05 54 E on 09-01-44 Southern France. Salvaged & sold to Thailand in 1956 as Ta Dindeng
22	10	7/8/41	12/31/41	5/14/42	Struck Nav Reg 07-19-46
23	10	7/23/41	12/13/41	5/7/42	Transf to France as Perce Neige, D-201 03-06-44. Sold to France 03-21-49
24	10	11/6/41	1/10/42	5/25/42	Sunk by mine 43 25 N 06 4 E. on 08-16-44 Southern France
25	10	11/28/41	1/28/42	6/5/42	Struck Nav Reg 07-17-47. Sold to Peru, name changed to Bondy (listed 1956 Janes)
26	10	12/15/41	2/28/42	6/16/42	Transf to France 03-10-44 as Pimpernelle D-211. Sold to France 04-28-49
27	10	12/24/41	3/7/42	6/30/42	Transf to France 10-09-44 as Hortensia D-333. Sold to France 03-21-49
28	10	1/13/42	3/31/42	7/17/42	Transf to France 10-14-44 as Auberpine D-315. Sold to France 03-21-49. Transf Vietnam as HamTo
29	10	1/30/42	4/11/42	7/29/42	Transf to France 10-02-44 as Jasmin D-335. Sold to France 03-21-49
30	10	3/3/42	5/9/42	8/11/42	Sunk by mine 41 23 N, 12 45 E off Anzio
31	10	3/16/42	5/23/42	8/18/42	Transf to France 03-10-44 as Primevere D-21. Sold to France 03-21-49
32	14	5/7/41	10/1/41	5/14/42	Struck 06-19-46
33	14	5/8/41	10/8/41	6/10/42	Transf to Russia 08-17-45 Struck Nav Reg 10-29-56
34	3414	5/13/41	10/21/41	6/27/42	Transf France 10-05-44 as Anemone D-311 Sold to France 03-21-49
35	14	5/17/41	11/7/41	7/13/42	Struck Nav Reg 07-17-47 Sold to Peru named San Martin (listed 1956 in Janes)
36	14	10/6/41	1/21/42	7/31/42	Transf France 10-24-44 as Campanule D-321 Sold France 03-21-49
37	14	10/13/41	1/28/42	8/21/41	Transf France 10-14-44 as Balsamine D-316
38	16	5/2/41	1/24/24	4/3/42	Transf to USSR 07-19-45
39	16	5/23/41	12/23/41	3/7/42	Sunk by mine 06-26-45 at 01 19 S 116 49 E Balikpapan, Borneo
40	16	6/19/41	3/14/42	4/23/42	Struck Nav Reg 05-01-46
41	16	6/28/41	4/14/42	5/12/42	Struck Nav Reg 06-19-46
42	33	6/6/41	3/17/42	4/25/42	Transf to USSR 07-19-45

John Dixon Davis

Hull No	Builder No	Keel Laid	Launch Date	Date Completed	Remarks
43	33	6/12/41	3/30/42	5/11/42	Transf France 10-20-44 as Lotus D-324 Sold to France 03-21-49
44	33	6/18/41	4/10/42	5/25/42	Struck Nav Reg 06-19-46
45	33	6/20/41	4/20/42	6/5/42	Re-named Barbet AMS-41 on 09-01-47
46	33	6/24/41	4/30/42	6/20/42	Struck Nav Reg 06-10-47
47	33	6/26/41	5/7/42	7/2/42	Struck Nav Reg 10-24-45
48	33	6/27/41	5/15/42	7/14/42	Sunk 02-14-45 by USS Fletcher, DD-445 after damaged by shore batteries at Corregidor
49	33	6/30/41	5/22/42	7/24/42	Struck Nav Reg 07-03-46
50	33	7/16/41	6/6/42	8/3/42	Damaged by mine, sunk same day by Allied forces 06-18-45 at 01 18 S 116 49 E Balikpapan, Borneo
51	33	7/16/41	6/22/42	8/12/42	Struck Nav Reg 06-10-47
52	33	8/5/41	7/15/42	8/21/42	Struck Nav Reg 06-19-46
53	33	8/25/41	7/24/42	8/31/42	Struck Nav Reg 07-03-46
54	9	5/20/41	11/1/41	2/9/42	Struck Nav Reg 06-19-46
55	9	5/26/41	11/22/41	3/3/42	Transf France 09-30-44 as Geranium D-331 Sold to France 03-21-49
56	9	5/30/41	12/6/41	3/18/42	(no info available)
57	9	6/5/41	12/15/41	3/19/42	Struck Nav Reg 06-19-46
58	9	6/19/41	12/22/41	4/16/42	Transf France 10-20-44 as Armoise D-313 sold to France 03-21-49
59	9	7/14/41	12/30/41	4/24/42	Tranf USSR 06-06-45
60	9	9/19/41	1/19/42	5/2/42	Struck Nav Reg 06-10-47
61	9	9/23/41	2/3/42	6/6/42	Struck Nav Reg 06-19-46
62	9	11/12/41	2/25/42	5/23/42	Transf France 10-24-44 as Clematite D-323 sold to France 03-21-49
63	9	11/26/41	3/6/42	6/2/42	Transf France 10-02-44 as Tiare D-353 sold to France 03-21-49
64	9	1/4/42	3/25/42	6/24/42	Transf France 10-18-44 as Jonquille D-336 sold to France 03-21-49
65	9	1/7/42	3/30/42	7/5/42	StruckNav Reg 06-10-47
66	31	7/22/41	09/31/41	6/30/42	Struck Nav Reg 05-01-46
67	31	7/22/41	2/17/42	7/15/42	Struck and sold 05-27-46
68	31	7/22/41	2/24/42	8/1/42	Struck Nav Reg 07-03-48
69	31	7/22/41	5/5/42	8/15/42	Transf France 09-30-44 as Marjolaine D-337 sold to France 03-21-49. 1961 sold to Madagascar, new name, Tanamasoandro.
70	31	7/22/41	3/12/42	9/7/42	Sunk by typhoon off Leyte 10-17-44, 1056 N 125 12 E.

Hull No	Builder No	Keel Laid	Launch Date	Date Completed	Remarks
71	31	7/22/41	3/26/42	9/23/42	Sunk by mine off Borneo 04 59 N 119 47 E
72	31	7/22/41	4/9/42	1/15/43	Struck Nav Reg 03-28-46
73	31	7/22/41	4/23/42	1/22/43	Struck Nav Reg 06-10-47
74	31	7/22/41	4/30/42	2/8/43	Struck Nav Reg 06-19-46
75	31	7/22/41	5/26/42	2/22/43	Struck Nav Reg 10-29-56
76	28	4/25/41	11/8/41	6/4/42	Struck Nav Reg 05-01-46
77	28	5/2/41	10/11/41	5/15/42	Transf France 03-06-44 as D-202, sunk by mine off Marseilles 10-25-44.
78	28	5/16/41	12/11/41	6/17/42	Transf France 10-05-44 as Belladone D-318. Sold to France 1949. 1954 Bach Dang of S. Vietnam
79	28	6/12/41	12/27/41	6/26/42	Struck Nav Reg 02-19-48 Transf to Turkey as Kas, 1956
80	28	6/27/41	5/5/42	7/15/42	Named Albatross AMS-1 02-18-47, chg to MSC(0) 12-07-55 Struck 03-20-58
81	28	7/16/41	5/30/41	7/28/42	Struck Nav Reg 06-10-47
82	28	10/24/41	6/13/42	8/10/42	Transf France 10-05-44 as Dahlia D-325 sold to France 03-21-49
83	28	11/24/41	6/27/42	6/30/42	Transf France 10-20-44 as Digitale D-236 sold to France 03-21-49
84	11	6/2/41	3/3/42	5/23/42	Sunk by mine 07-09-45 at 01 19 S 116 48 E Balikpapan, Borneo
85	11	6/2/41	3/19/42	6/30/42	Transf to USSR 08-17-45
86	18	6/26/41	1/31/42	5/12/42	Struck Nav Reg 04-17-46
87	18	7/18/41	1/31/42	8/15/42	Struck Nav Reg 04-17-46
88	15	6/20/41	10/18/41	5/5/42	Transf USSR 08-27-45
89	15	7/11/41	11/22/41	6/11/42	Struck Nav Reg 05-01-46
90	15	7/24/41	12/19/41	7/24/42	Struck Nav Reg 06-05-46
91	15	10/18/41	3/7/42	8/21/42	(no info available)
92	15	11/21/41	5/14/42	9/24/42	Struck Nav Reg 10-24-45
93	15	12/19/42	5/16/42	10/21/42	sold 02-19-47 (to whom)
94	7	6/7/41	12/15/41	3/11/42	Struck Nav Reg 06-10-47
95	7	6/6/41	12/16/41	3/12/42	Struck Nav Reg 06-19-46
96	7	6/11/41	2/10/42	4/11/42	Struck Nav Reg 01-03-46
97	7	6/6/41	2/16/42	4/11/42	Struck Nav Reg 02-07-47
98	7	6/12/41	12/13/41	4/23/42	Lost in Typhoon 09-16-45 Okinawa
99	7	6/6/41	12/11/41	4/27/42	Struck Nav Reg 01-03-46
100	2	7/15/41	4/12/42	6/20/42	Transf USSR 08-17-45
101	2	7/22/41	6/20/42	7/17/42	Struck Nav Reg 06-19-46
102	2	6/26/41	8/1/42	8/22/42	Struck Nav Reg 06-10-47

John Dixon Davis

Hull No	Builder No	Keel Laid	Launch Date	Date Completed	Remarks
103	2	7/22/41	8/29/42	9/19/42	Damaged by mine and beached 04-07-45, Okinawa
104	25	5/21/41	2/17/42	5/29/42	Struck Nav Reg 07-03-46
105	25	5/13/41	3/10/42	7/17/42	Struck Nav Reg 05-01-46
106	25	5/21/41	4/19/42	8/18/42	Struck Nav Reg 06-10-47
107	5	5/13/41	3/28/42	8/3/42	Struck Nav Reg 04-17-46
108	5	5/15/41	4/18/42	8/24/42	Struck Nav Reg 07-03-46
109	5	5/21/41	5/16/42	9/4/42	Renamed Brambling AMS- 42 09-01-47. Chg to MSC(0)-42 Struck Nav Reg 11-01-59
110	5	8/25/41	07/16/42	10/10/42	Struck Nav Reg 04-17-46
111	5	8/27/41	7/25/42	10/28/42	Struck Nav Reg 07-17-46
112	5	8/27/41	7/25/42	10/28/42	Struck Nav Reg 04-17-46
113	0.05	6/4/41	2/13/42	8/12/42	Renamed Brant AMS-43 09-01-47 chg MSC(0)-43 02-07-55 Struck 11-01-59
114	114.26	6/26/41	3/13/42	8/12/42	Renamed Courlan AMS-44 09-01-47, chg MSC(0)-44 02-07-55 Struck Nav Reg 11-01-59
115	26	6/26/41	4/3/42	9/21/42	Struck Nav Reg 07-19-46
116	26	6/26/41	4/20/42	10/31/42	Struck Nav Reg 08-15-46
117	12	5/8/41	8/23/41	4/11/42	Struck Nav Reg 06-10-47
118	12	5/14/41	10/27/41	5/7/42	Struck Nav Reg 04-17-47
119	119.12	7/15/41	3/2/42	6/11/42	Struck Nav Reg 06-10-47
120	12	8/23/41	4/4/42	8/1/42	Renamed Crossbill AMS-45 09-01-47 chg MSC(0)-45 02-07-55 Struck Nav Reg 11-01-59
121	17	5/15/41	3/14/42	7/22/42	Struck 07-03-46
122	17	5/15/41	6/2/42	9/24/42	Struck 04-17-46
123	17	7/2/42	3/14/42	8/24/42	Struck 04-17-46
124	17	12/4/41	6/6/42	10/23/42	Struck 04-17-46
125	19	6/2/41	12/18/41	7/25/42	Struck 05-01-46
126	19	7/3/41	3/3/42	9/11/42	Struck 04-17-46
127	19	10/10/41	5/2/42	10/30/42	Gnd. Sunk, Aleutians 1-10-44
128	19	5/17/41	12/18/41	7/17/42	Struck 05-01-46
129	29	5/27/41	12/18/41	7/17/42	Struck 05-01-46
130	29	6/20/41	12/18/41	8/27/42	Struck 04-17-46
131	29	7/12/41	3/4/42	10/1/42	Struck 04-17-46
132	29	7/12/41	5/2/42	11/10/42	Struck 04-17-46
133	32	7/14/41	12/18/41	7/21/42	Foundered Coos Bay, Oregon, 02-20-43
134	32	8/13/41	3/16/42	9/8/42	Struck 04-17-46
135	2	5/20/42	12/26/42	2/20/43	Transf USSR 09-06-45

Hull No	Builder No	Keel Laid	Launch Date	Date Completed	Remarks
136	2	7/16/42	2/8/43	3/19/43	Renamed Egret AMS-46 09-01-47, chg MSC(0)-46 02-07-55 Struck 11-01-59
137	2	8/8/42	3/19/43	4/17/43	Transf England 04-17-43 returned 12-10-45, struck 10-15-46
138	2	8/29/42	4/17/43	6/7/43	Struck 06-19-46 Sold to Thailand as Laoya (1956)
139	2	1/4/43	5/19/43	6/24/43	Transf USSR 07-19-45
140	2	2/12/43	6/19/43	8/12/43	Struck 06-10-47
141	2	3/24/43	7/19/43	8/28/43	Transf Engand 08-28-43 Returned 05-23-47, Struck 06-10-47
142	2	4/22/43	6/16/43	9/30/43	Transf England 09-30-43 Struck 10-28-47
143	26	4/20/42	6/30/42	2/16/43	Transf USSR 05-17-45
144	26	4/20/42	7/30/42	3/17/43	Transf USSR 05-17-45
145	26	5/8/42	9/7/42	04-21-434	Transf USSR 05-22-45 Struck 10-29-56
146	26	6/19/42	9/30/42	6/23/43	Sunk in typhoon 10-09-45 Okinawa
147	32	5/11/42	10/24/42	2/26/43	Struck 02-07-47
148	32	6/8/42	11/29/42	5/15/43	Transf England 05-15-43 Returned 11-10-46, Struck 12-13-46
149	32	10/26/42	4/5/43	8/14/43	Transf England 07-03-43 Returned 06-06-47, Struck 08-28-47
150	32	12/6/42	4/5/43	8/14/43	Transf England 08-14-43 Struck 08-28-47
151	6	6/15/42	3/31/43	10/5/43	Grounded in typhoon at Okinawa 10-09-45, hulk destroyed 12-26-45
152	6	8/3/42	4/17/43	11/26/43	Transf England 11-26-43 Struck 08-28-47
153	6	8/7/42	7/31/43	11/23/43	Transf England 11-23-43 Struck 07-17-47
154	6	8/14/42	9/4/43	1/1/44	Transf England 01-01-44 Struck 05-19-45
155	5	6/29/42	10/27/42	2/11/43	Transf England 03-04-43 Returned 05-24-46, loan to Netherlands as Vliestroom MV-40 Ret. 07-27-47 Struck 09-16-47
156	5	7/10/42	11/12/42	3/13/43	Transf England 03-26-43 Returned 04-10-46. Loan to Netherlands 04-10-46 as Texelstroom MV-39 Returned 07-27-47 Struck 09-16-47
157	5	7/18/42	12/1/42	4/15/43	Transf England 04-28-43 Struck 08-28-47
158	5	8/8/42	12/26/42	5/28/43	Struck 06-19-46
159	5	8/15/42	1/16/43	6/17/43	Struck 08-15-46
160	5	8/25/42	1/30/43	7/9/43	Struck 09-16-47
161	5	12/1/42	4/3/43	7/27/43	Transf England 09-02-43 Returned 11-12-46, Struck 12-13-46
162	5	12/10/42	4/24/43	8/20/43	Transf England 09-02-43 Returned 11-12-46, Struck 12-13-46

John Dixon Davis

Hull No	Builder No	Keel Laid	Launch Date	Date Completed	Remarks
163	8	4/23/42	10/27/42	3/8/43	Struck 02-07-47
164	8	4/24/42	11/28/42	3/27/43	Renamed Bobolink AMS-2 02-18-47, chg to MHC-44, 02-07-55, converted at Charleston NSY begin 03-01-55 completed 09-30-55, Struck 01-01-60
165	8	5/25/42	1/16/43	4/3/43	Struck 08-28-46
166	8	5/25/42	1/16/43	5/27/43	Struck 07-19-46
167	8	8/5/42	6/12/43	7/31/43	Transf England 08-10-43 Struck 08-28-47
168	8	9/14/42	7/4/43	8/29/43	Transf England 09-07-43 Returned 09-03-46, Struck 12-13-46
169	8	9/22/42	4/24/43	6/19/43	Transf France 08-26-44 Amarante D-301, sold to France 03-21-49
170	8	10/1/42	5/29/42	7/10/43	Renamed Bunting AMS-3 02-18-47, chg MHC-45 02-07-55, converted at Charleston NSY begin 03-22-55 completed 08-23-55, Struck 06-01-60
171	11	5/22/42	11/21/42	3/29/43	Transf England 04-08-43 Returned 04-27-26, Transf Greece 04-27-46 as Kefallinia M207
172	11	5/22/42	11/26/42	4/17/43	Transf England 04-28-43 Returned 04-15-49 Transf to Greece as Kerkyra M-208 Struck 09-08-52
173	11	5/28/42	12/7/42	5/1/43	Transf England 05-13-43 Struck 08-28-47
174	11	6/23/42	12/19/42	5/22/43	Transf England 06-07-43 Struck 06-10-47
175	11	6/27/42	1/9/43	6/5/43	Transf England 06-15-43 Returned 06-06-47, Struck 06-10-47
176	11	7/4/42	1/23/43	7/10/43	Struck 09-25-46
177	11	9/7/42	3/20/43	7/18/43	Struck 09-25-46
178	11	9/7/42	4/24/43	7/31/43	Transf USSR 07-19-45 Struck 10-29-56
179	11	10/27/42	5/8/43	8/14/43	Renamed Cardinal AMS-4 02-18-47 Chg MSC(0)-4 02-07-55 Struck 11-01-59
180	11	10/27/42	6/5/43	8/28/43	Transf USSR 08-27-45
181	11	1/21/43	6/24/43	9/12/43	Transf England 09-24-43 Returned 09-03-46 Struck 12-13-46
182	11	1/22/43	7/15/43	9/25/43	Transf England 10-07-43 Struck 08-28-47
183	10	3/28/42	6/25/42	1/14/43	Struck 06-10-47 ((Launched by Kate Smith; 1st "one stacker" to be completed 06-25-42))
184	10	4/15/42	7/18/42	1/25/43	Transf USSR 07-19-45
185	10	5/29/42	8/8/42	2/9/43	

Hull No	Builder No	Keel Laid	Launch Date	Date Completed	Remarks
186	10	5/12/42	8/22/42	2/20/43	Transf England 02-20-43, Rtn 12-15-43. Loan to Greece 12-15-43 as Letos M-210. Given outright to Greece 07-22-52
187	10	6/27/42	9/7/42	3/12/43	Transf England 03-12-43 Rtn 07-10-47. Struck 07-10-47
188	10	7/22/42	9/26/42	3/30/43	Transf England 03-30-43 Rtn 01-01-47, Struck 12-14-46
189	10	8/25/42	10/14/42	5/10/43	Transf England 05-01-43 Rtn 08-29-47. Struck 08-29-47
190	10	8/22/42	10/31/42	5/10/43	Transf Engkand 05-10-43 Rtn 12-15-43. Loan to Greece 12-15-43 as Kos. Sunk by mine 04-15-44 37 43 N 23 34 E, Cape Turbo
191	10	9/7/42	11/14/42	6/1/43	Transf England 06-01-43
192	10	9/30/42	12/5/42	6/1/43	Renamed Condor AMS-5 02-18-47, chg MSC(0)-5 02-07-55. Transf Japan 03-18-55 as Ujishima MCS-655. Rtn and struck 03-31-67
193	10	10/31/42	1/2/43	6/28/43	Renamed Fulmar AMS-47 09-01-47, Chg MSC(0)-47 02-07-55. Struck & sold 10-01-68
194	10	11/18/42	1/30/43	7/11/43	Transf England 07-12-43 Rtn 12-29-47. Struck 12-29-47
195	14	4/3/42	8/10/42	3/20/43	Chg to Chauvenet AGS-11 on 03-20-45. Struck 07-03-46
196	14	4/6/42	8/14/42	4/14/42	Struck 06-19-46
197	14	4/24/42	8/24/42	5/6/43	Struck 06-19-46
198	14	5/6/42	9/7/42	5/29/43	Struck 08-15-46
199	14	8/11/42	10/10/42	6/9/43	Struck 02-07-47
200	14	8/19/42	10/26/42	7/5/43	Struck 06-19-46
201	14	8/28/42	11/19/42	7/24/43	Renamed Courser AMS-6 02-18-47, Chg to MSC(0)-6 02-07-55. Struck 11-01-59
202	14	9/14/42	12/9/42	8/11/43	Transf England 08-11-43 Rtn 02-12-48. Struck 02-28-47
203	14	10/15/42	1/15/43	8/31/43	Transf England 08-31-43 Rtn 11-12-46. Struck 11-12-46
204	14	11/2/42	3/2/43	9/14/43	Transf England 09-14-43 Rtn 09-03-46. Struck 12-13-46
205	14	11/30/42	3/31/43	9/29/43	Transf England 09-29-43 Rtn 09-03-46. Struck 06-10-47

John Dixon Davis

Hull No	Builder No	Keel Laid	Launch Date	Date Completed	Remarks
206	14	12/18/42	4/29/43	10/16/43	Transf England 10-16-43 Rtn 05-23-47. Struck 06-10-47
207	16	4/16/42	8/1/42	1/18/43	Trans France 03-16-44 as Petunia D-355. Sold to France 03-21-49
208	16	4/16/42	8/8/42	2/20/43	Transf France 03-27-44 as Genet D-355. Sold to France 03-21-49
209	16	4/30/42	8/15/42	3/24/43	Transf England 03-24-43 Rtn 04-15-46. Loan to Greece 04-15-46 as Zakynthos M-212. Given to Greece 07-22-52
210	16	5/4/42	9/7/42	4/19/43	Transf England 04-19-42 Rtn 04-10-46. Struck 09-16-47
211	16	5/18/42	10/10/42	5/17/43	Transf England 05-07-43 Rtn 08-29-47. Struck 08-28-47
212	16	5/21/42	10/16/42	5/29/43	Transf England 05-29-43 Rtn 06-06-47. Struck 06-10-47
213	16	6/13/42	11/13/43	6/17/43	Transf England 06-17-43 Rtn 05-14-68. Struck 08-28-68 (Last two dates may not be accurate)
214	16	8/24/42	2/26/43	7/2/43	Transf England 07-02-43 Rtn 12-10-46. Struck 10-15-46
215	16	8/18/42	2/22/43	7/22/43	Renamed Crow AMS-7 02-18-47. Chg to MSC(0)-7 on 02-07-55 Struck 11-01-59
216	19	6/16/42	10/17/42	2/26/43	Transf USSR 07-19-45
217	19	6/20/42	11/21/42	4/29/43	Transf England 02-29-43 Rtn 05-28-46. Struck 07-17-47
218	19	7/18/42	12/23/42	6/23/43	Renamed Curlew AMS-8 02-18-47. Chg MSC(0)-8 on 02-07-55. Transf Korea 01-06-56 Kum Hwa MSC(0)-519
219	19	10/23/42	1/23/43	7/20/43	Renamed Flicker AMS-9 02-18-47. Chg MSC(0)-9 on 02-07-55. Struck 01-01-60
220	19	11/25/42	3/6/43	8/30/43	Struck 06-19-46
221	19	12/31/42	4/22/43	9/16/43	Transf England 09-16-43 Rtn 02-12-47. Struck 02-12-47
222	20	5/10/42	11/11/42	4/24/43	Struck 05-01-46
223	2	6/10/42	12/27/42	4/29/43	Transf England 06-28-43 Rtn 11-12-46. Struck 12-13-46
224	20	11/23/42	2/28/43	8/19/43	Struck 06-19-46
225	20	1/9/43	4/25/43	10/10/43	Transf England 10-14-43 Rtn 11-12-46. Struck 12-13-46
226	25	3/16/42	8/31/42	1/16/43	Transf France 10-02-44 as Asphodere D-314. Sold to France 03-21-49

Hull No	Builder No	Keel Laid	Launch Date	Date Completed	Remarks
227	25	4/4/42	9/7/42	3/20/43	Transf France 03-20-44 as Zinnia D-273. Sold to France 03-21-49
228	25	4/21/42	10/2/42	5/5/43	Struck 02-19-48. Transf & sold to Turkey as Kemer (1956)
229	25	9/7/42	1/11/43	6/5/43	Transf England 06-05-43 Rtn 12-15-43. Loan to Greece 12-15-43 as Patmos M-2229. Struck 09-08-52 and transf to Greece
230	25	9/7/42	2/20/43	7/6/43	Transf England 07-07-43 Rtn 01-01-47 & struck. Sold to Netherlands 01-02-47
231	25	10/5/42	4/3/43	8/6/43	Renamed Firecrest AMS-10 02-18-47. Transf Japan 03-15-55 as Etajima MSC-656. Rtn & struck 03-31-67
232	25	1/12/43	4/26/43	9/7/43	Transf England 09-08-43 Rtn 11-10-46. Struck 12-13-46
233	25	2/27/43	7/22/43	10/8/43	Transf England 10-08-43
234	25	4/27/43	9/4/43	11/1/43	Transf England 11-02-43 Rtn 01-12-47. Struck 08-20-47
235	28	7/4/42	2/15/43	7/20/43	Struck 08-28-46
236	28	6/24/42	1/16/43	6/23/43	Transf England 06-26-43 Rtn 09-03-46. Struck 02-25-47
237	28	6/6/42	9/7/42	11/20/42	Transf USSR 07-19-45
238	28	5/11/42	9/12/42	11/23/42	Renamed Flamingo AMS-11 02-18-47. Chg MSO(O) 11-02-55. Struck 11-01-59
239	28	5/6/42	10/27/42	4/16/43	Struck 02-19-48. Sold to Turkey as Kerempe (1956)
240	28	4/11/42	10/31/42	5/25/43	Transf England 05-25-43 Rtn 05-07-46. Transf Greece 05-07-46 as Ithaki M-214
241	29	5/20/42	9/7/42	2/18/43	Transf USSR Struck 10-28-56
242	29	6/1/42	10/10/42	3/27/43	Chg to Harkness, AMCU-12
243	29	6/1/42	11/10/42	5/19/43	Struck 01-21-46
244	29	10/5/42	12/18/42	7/3/43	Transf England 07-07-43 Rtn 11-14-47 & struck
245	29	10/20/42	2/6/43	7/26/43	Struck 06-19-46
246	29	11/24/42	3/11/43	8/26/43	Transf England 08-27-43 Rtn 07-31-46. Struck 10-29-46
247	31	5/27/42	10/14/42	5/13/43	Transf Norway-Vinstra M-317
248	31	5/30/42	10/24/42	6/2/43	Struck 06-19-46
249	31	5/30/42	11/17/42	6/26/43	Struck 07-03-46
250	31	5/30/42	12/9/42	7/30/43	Struck 06-10-47
251	31	5/30/42	12/24/42	8/30/43	Struck 07-03-46

John Dixon Davis

Hull No	Builder No	Keel Laid	Launch Date	Date Completed	Remarks
252	31	5/30/42	6/24/43	9/29/43	Transf England 09-29-43 Struck 08-28-47
253	31	5/30/42	7/3/43	10/21/43	Transf England 10-21-43 Struck 08-28-47
254	31	5/30/42	1/31/43	11/11/43	Transf England 11-12-43 Rtn 01-01-47. Struck 09-16-47
255	31	5/30/42	5/22/43	11/29/43	Transf England 11-30-43 Sunk by mine off Boulogne, France 05-10-44
256	31	6/3/42	8/28/43	12/20/43	Transf. England 12-20-43
257	31	10/15/42	9/30/43	1/19/44	Transf England 10-20-44 Rtn 08-29-47. Struck 08-28-47
258	31	10/31/42	10/28/43	2/8/44	Transf England 02-08-44 Rtn 08-29-47. Struck 12-23-47
259	27	5/16/42	8/21/42	3/5/43	Struck 09-16-47
260	27	5/20/42	9/6/42	4/9/43	Transf USSR 08092045
261	27	6/9/42	9/25/42	7/8/43	Transf England 07-09-43. Struck 8/28/1947
262	27	8/21/42	11/2/42	8/11/43	Chg to Gillis AMCU-13
263	27	9/6/42	12/24/42	9/10/43	Chg Simon Newcomb AGS-14 03-20-45. Chg to AGSc-14 07-29-46. Ground3ed 08-49. Struck 01-31-50
264	27	9/24/42	1/18/43	10/26/43	Transf England 10-26-43 Rtn 11-10-46. Struck 12-13-46
265	17	5/4/42	11/25/42	3/6/43	Struck 06-10-47
266	17	5/16/42	12/24/42	4/8/43	Transf USSR 08-17-45
267	17	7/2/42	3/6/43	6/21/43	Struck 06-10-47
268	17	10/31/42	1/2/43	6/28/43	Renamed Lapwing AMS-48 09-01-47. Chg to MSC(0)-48 02-07-55. Struck 11-01-59
269	4	4/15/42	9/7/42	2/23/43	Struck 06-10-47
270	4	5/11/42	9/7/42	3/25/43	Struck 06-10-47
271	4	7/3/42	10/17/42	4/21/43	Renamed Lorikeet AMS-49 09-01-47. Chg MSC(0)-49 02-07-55. Struck 10-01-68
272	4	7/20/42	11/14/42	5/28/42	Transf USSR 07-19-45 Struck 10-29-56
273	4	9/7/42	12/26/42	7/7/43	Transf USSR 07-19-45
274	4	9/7/42	1/9/43	7/29/43	Struck 06-10-47
275	4	11/6/42	2/4/43	8/20/43	Sunk typhoon Okinawa 10-09-45
276	4	11/21/42	3/5/43	9/22/43	Struck 02-07-47
277	19	2/5/43	6/19/43	10/18/43	Transf England 10-19-43 Struck 08-28-47
278	19	3/11/43	7/17/43	11/12/43	Transf England 11-12-43 Struck 08-28-47
279	11	1/23/43	7/29/43	10/2/43	Transf England 10-15-43 Struck 08-28-47
280	11	1/25/43	8/12/43	10/16/43	Transf England 10-30-43 Struck 08-28-47

Hull No	Builder No	Keel Laid	Launch Date	Date Completed	Remarks
281	26	7/30/42	10/30/42	7/28/43	Transf England, 08-26-43 Struck 08-28-47
282	26	8/15/42	11/30/42	8/26/43	Transf England 08-26-43 Struck 06-28-47
283	26	9/30/42	12/30/42	9/21/43	Struck 07-07-47
284	26	10/30/42	2/17/43	10/29/43	Transf England 11-02-43 Rtn 07-31-46. Struck 07-17-47
285	22	6/16/42	3/20/43	6/26/43	Transf USSR 09-06-45
286	22	6/16/42	3/20/43	7/27/43	Struck 09-25-46
287	1	7/16/42	10/27/42	3/15/43	Transf USSR 09-02-45
288	1	8/12/42	11/28/42	3/19/43	Transf USSR 08-17-45
289	1	10/29/42	1/26/43	6/14/43	Struck 02-19-48
290	1	11/30/42	2/27/43	7/17/43	Renamed Nightingale AMS-50 09-01-47, Chg MSCV(0)-50 02-07-55. Struck 11-01-59
291	1	1/29/43	4/20/43	8/9/43	Renamed Reedbird AMS-51 09-01-47. Chg MSC(0)-51 02-07-55. Struck 10-01-68
292	1	3/3/43	6/8/43	10/9/43	Struck 02-07-47
293	1	4/22/43	7/7/43	10/12/43	Struck 09-25-46
294	1	6/10/43	8/11/43	11/9/43	Renamed Redpoll AMS-57 09-01-47. Chg MSC(0)-57 02-07-55. Struck 07-01-59
295	1	7/10/43	8/11/43	11/9/43	Transf SU 07-19-45, Struck 10-29-56
296	1	8/19/43	11/3/43	12/31/43	Struck 06-10-47
297	29	1/7/43	4/24/43	9/20/43	Struck 10-08-46
298	29	2/10/43	6/16/43	10/22/43	Struck 07-03-46
299	30	6/5/42	11/14/42	4/7/43	Renamed Rhea AMS-52 09001-47. Chg MSC(0)-52, 02-07-55. Struck 11-01-59
300	30	6/15/42	12/7/42	7/3/43	Struck 02-07-47
301	30	11/14/42	5/1/43	9/11/43	Transf USSR 08-17-45
302	30	12/7/42	6/12/43	11/5/43	Struck 01-22-48
303	23	5/13/42	7/21/43	8/11/43	Struck 07-19-46(Sold 1949, re-named Wolf III)
304	23	6/15/42	8/10/43	10/1/43	Sunk by mine. St Vaast, Normandy 49 33 N 01 14 W on 07-30-44
305	23	7/18/42	9/30/43	11/17/43	Transf Norway as Gaula M-318 on 05-18-45. Rtn & sold to Norway 06-07-48. Struck 08-12-48

John Dixon Davis

Hull No	Builder No	Keel Laid	Launch Date	Date Completed	Remarks
306	23	9/7/42	9/30/43	11/17/43	Renamed Goldfinch AMS-12 02-18-47. Chg MSC(0)-12 02-07-55. Sold to MVTI, Portland, Me. 11-01-59 & struck. Renamed Aqualab. Sold to Peter Christensen 1973
307	23	10/26/42	12/31/43	2/25/44	Struck 02-19-48. Sold to Turkey as Kirie (1956
308	21	2/25/43	7/21/43	8/27/43	Struck 01-08-46
309	21	4/5/43	8/17/43	9/13/43	Struck 11-13-46
310	21	4/17/43	9/11/43	9/13/43	Struck 06-05-46
311	21	5/7/43	10/6/43	11/4/43	Renamed Robin AMS-53 on 09-01-47. Chg to MSC(0)-53 on 02-07-55. Struck 08-01-61
312	21	6/7/43	11/9/43	12/4/43	Renamed Grackle AMS-13 on 02-18-47. Chg MSC(0)-13 on 02-07-55. Struck 03-01-63
313	12	5/30/42	2/13/43	6/12/43	Struck 06-10-47
314	12	6/6/42	3/17/43	7/15/43	Struck 06-10-47
315	12	6/13/42	4/14/43	8/16/43	Struck 06-19-46
316	12	6/19/42	5/1/43	8/25/43	Struck 06-10-47 Sold 12-29-47 317.
317	27	10/30/42	2/27/43	11/18/43	Renamed Grosbeak AMS-14 Chg MSC(0)-14, 02-07-55. Struck 11-01-59
318	27	12/23/42	5/1/43	12/30/43	Struck 03-12-46, destroyed 02-27-46
319	27	1/19/43	6/5/43	2/4/44	Tranf Maritime Commission 08-48 and sold
320	18	7/20/42	1/9/43	8/18/43	Struck 06-19-46. Sold 12-29-47
321	18	8/29/42	2/20/43	10/25/43	Renamed Grouse AMS-15 Chg MSC(0)-15 02-07-55. Grounded off Rockport, Mass. 09-21-63. Destroyed 09-28-63
322	18	1/11/43	5/31/43	11/19/43	Struck 04-17-46. Sold 02-05-47
323	18	2/26/43	7/15/43	12/27/43	Struck 06-19-46. Sold to Korea 04-47
324	18	6/3/43	10/14/43	2/28/44	Renamed Gull AMS-16 02-18-47 Chg AMCU-46 08-01-54. Chg to MHC-46 02-07-55. Struck 1959
325	18	7/22/43	1/11/44	4/7/44	Struck 03-05-47. Sold 01-16-48
326	3	6/2/42	11/17/42	3/15/43	Struck 06-10-47. Sold 04-08-47
327	3	6/2/42	12/5/42	4/19/43	Renamed Ruff AMS-54 09-01-47. Chg MSC(0)-54 02-07-55. Struck 11-14-69
328	3	7/6/42	12/19/42	5/26/43	Struck 01-16-48
329	3	11/20/42	2/23/43	7/3/43	Struck 02-06-48

Wooden Dreadnaught

Hull No	Builder No	Keel Laid	Launch Date	Date Completed	Remarks
330	3	12/8/42	3/27/43	8/6/43	Transf Korea as Kang Kyong YMS 510 04-47. Struck 06-19-46
331	3	12/19/42	4/24/43	9/10/43	Struck 10-29-46 Sold 02-18-48
332	3	3/3/43	6/5/43	10/12/43	Transf USSR 09-06-45
333	3	6/11/43	9/4/43	12/2/43	Struck 10-29-46 Sold 01-24-47
334	24	6/9/42	10/24/42	3/1/43	Struck 06-19-46. Sold to Thailand 11-26-47 & named Bangkeo (1956)
335	24	7/8/42	11/21/42	4/9/43	Transf Philippines 05-26-48 Struck 09-16-47
336	24	10/27/42	12/19/42	5/24/43	Struck 10-21-46 sold 10-21-47
337	24	11/27/42	2/20/43	7/9/43	Struck 08-15-56 sold 02-28-56
338	24	1/2/43	3/20/43	8/12/43	Struck 06-19-46 sold 10-21-47
339	24	3/8/43	5/8/43	9/25/43	Transf Nationalist China 06-30-48. Struck 07-13-48. Seized by Red China 1949
340	24	3/24/43	6/26/43	10/30/43	Struck 06-10-47. Sold 12-29-47
341	24	5/14/43	8/21/43	12/11/43	Foundered typhoon 09-16-45 Okinawa
342	4	1/11/43	4/5/43	10/16/43	Struck 08-15-46 destroyed 03-04-48
343	4	2/10/43	5/1/43	11/11/43	Struck 03-14-47, Sold 07-17-47
344	4	3/8/43	6/14/43		Chg and completed as YDG-6, 08-12-43
345	4	4/6/43	8/14/43	12/11/43	Struck 07-03-46, sold 05-27-46
346	9	8/24/42	1/5/43	8/16/43	Transf Nationalist China 10-27-48
347	9	9/1/42	1/7/43	8/24/43	Struck 02-14-48
348	9	9/15/42	2/9/43	9/8/43	Transf Turkey 05-10-48 as Kulluk M-516. Struck 02-19-48
349	9	09-17042	3/5/43	9/16/43	Struck 02-07-47, sold 03-09-48
350	9	10/12/42	1/29/43	9/27/43	Sunk by mine off Cherbourg, France, 07-02-44. This place and date from the ship's log. Other sources erroneously report the sinking off Utah Beach, Normandy.
351	9	10/16/42	2/21/43	10/9/43	Struck 06-19-46. Sold 04-47
352	9	1/12/43	5/14/42	10-21043	Struck 07-03-46. Sold 08-02-47
353	9	1/15/43	5/20/43	11/9/43	Sold to Thailand 10-15-47 as Ta Dindeng
354	9	1/13/43	5/29/43	11/15/43	Transf Korea 04-06-47 as Kanjim YMS-501
355	9	1/11/43	6/8/43	11/27/43	Struck 05-01-46, Sold 12-10-47
356	9	2/26/43	9/6/43	12/10/43	Transf Korea 11-12-46, Struck 06-19-46
357	9	3/3/43	09/16/43	12/27/43	Struck 08-15-46. Sold 02-20-47
358	16	9/9/42	3/22/43	8/6/43	Transf to Korea as Kyong Chu YMS-502
359	16	9/12/42	4/9/43	8/20/43	Struck 02-07-47. Sold 01-06-48
360	16	10/21/42	6/16/43	9/3/43	Struck 04-17-46. Sold 01-06-48

John Dixon Davis

Hull No	Builder No	Keel Laid	Launch Date	Date Completed	Remarks
361	16	10/31/42	6/11/43	9/17/43	Struck 05-01-46. Sold 02-06-47
362	16	11/24/42	5/2/43	9/30/43	Renamed Hawk AMS-17 on 02-18-47. Chg to MSC(0)-17 02-07-55. Struck 10-17-57. Sold
363	33	11/13/42	6/8/43	8/12/43	Struck 06-19-46. Sold 10-21-47
364	33	11/24/42	6/2/43	8/21/43	Struck 03-12-48. Sold 06-03-48
365	33	12/2/42	6/26/43	8/28/43	Damaged by mine 06-26-45 Balikpapan, Borneo. Sunk by U.S. Forces. Struck 07-25-45
366	33	12/10/42	7/5/43	9/7/43	Damaged beyond repair by hurricane. Destroyed by burning 12-29-47
367	33	12/16/42	7/15/43	9/20/43	Struck 10-21-48. Sold 10-27-48
368	33	12/31/42	7/17/43	9/27/43	Struck 06-10-47. Sold 10-22-47
369	33	1/13/43	7/24/43	9/9/43	Renamed Heron AMS-18 on 02-18-47. Chg to MSC(0)-18 02-07-55. Transf to Japan 03-21-55 as Nuwajima MSC-657. Rtn 03-21-55. Struck 03-31-67. Used as a target.
370	33	1/23/43	8/7/43		10-19-43 Struck 06-19-46. Destroyed 04-07-48
371	31	11/17/42	11/27/43	2/29/44	Renamed Hornbill AMS-19 on 02-18-47. Chg to MSC(0)-19 02-07-55 Struck 11-01-59. Sold
372	31	12/11/42	12/23/43	3/28/44	Renamed Hummer AMS-20 on 02-18-47. Chg to MSC(0)-20 02-07-55. Transf Japan 03-16-59 as Ninoshima, MSC-662
373	31	12/1/42	1/29/44	4/28/44	Renamed Jackdaw AMS-21 on 02-18-47. Chg to MSC(0)-21 on 02-07-55.Transf to Brazil on 01-18-63 as Jurva M13
374	31	1/31/43	2/17/44	5/31/44	Renamed Kite AMS-22 on 02-18-47. Chg to MSC(0)-22 on 02-07-55. Transf to Korea 01-06-56 as Kim Po MSC(0)-520
375	10	12/8/42	2/27/43	7/26/43	Sold to Turkey 05-10-48 as Kozlu M-513. Struck 02-19-48.
376	10	1/5/43	3/13/43	8/9/43	Renamed Lark AMS-23 on 02-18-47. Chg to MSC(0)-23 02-07-55. Transf to Japan 03-16-59 as Moroshima
377	10	2/3/43	4/3/43	8/23/43	Transf to Norway 05-18-45 as NYMS-377. Renamed Driva M319, sold to Norway 06-07-48. Struck 08-12-48

Hull No	Builder No	Keel Laid	Launch Date	Date Completed	Remarks
378	10	3/3/43	4/27/43	9/7/43	Damaged by mine, Normandy 07-30-44. Struck 09-16-44, Sold 08-01-47
379	10	3/15/43	5/29/43	9/27/43	Transf to Norway 03-22-45 as NYMS-379, later renamed Alta (M320). Rtn 06-07-48 & sold to Norway Struck 08-12-48
380	10	4/6/43	6/26/43	10/11/43	Transf to Norway 03-22-45 as NYMS-380, later renamed Vorma (M321). Rtn & sold to Norway 06-06-48. Struck 08-12-48
381	10	5/21/43	7/17/43	10/30/43	Transf to Norway 03-22-45 as NYMS-381, later renamed Begna. Rtn 06-07-48 & sold to Norway. Struck 08-12-48
382	10	6/29/43	8/21/43	11/18/43	Transf to Norway 03-22-45 as NYMS-382. Sunk off Cherbourg by submarine torpedo 05-07-45. Struck 02-07-46
383	7	4/29/42	9/29/42	2/24/43	Foundered in typhoon 10-09-45 off Okinawa. Struck 10-24-45
384	7	4/30/42	10/17/42	4/9/43	Struck 01-12-46, destroyed 01-12-46
385	7	6/18/42	10/27/42	4/30/43	Sunk by mine, Caroline Islands 10-01-44. Struck 10-14-44
386	7	10/6/42	3/23/43	7/23/43	Struck 07-03-46. Sold 05-27-46
387	7	10/23/42	4/16/43	8/17/43	Struck 07-03-46. Sold 05-27-46
388	7	11/5/42	5/10/43	9/24/43	Struck 06-19-46. Sold 11-05-47
389	28	11/4/42	3/6/43	8/15/43	Struck 07-17-47. Sold 08-21-47
390	28	11/6/42	4/3/43	8/30/43	Struck 06-10-47. Sold 02-05-47
391	28	11/9/42	5/8/43	9/19/43	Struck 06-10-47. Sold 11-13-47
392	28	11/14/42	06/12/43	10/11/43	Struck 06-19-46. Transf to Korea 04-47
393	12	6/27/42	5/25/43	9/14/43	Struck 06-10-47. Sold 10-21-47
394	12	7/3/42	6/24/43	10/22/43	Struck 09-25-46. Sold 11-28-47
395	12	7/11/42	7/15/43	11/19/43	Renamed Linnet (AMS-24) on 02-18-47. Chg to MSC(0)-24 on 02-07-55. Struck 10-01-68. On sale
396	12	7/18/42	8/9/43	1/11/44	Struck 06-10-47. Sold 10-21-47
397	21	6/9/42	12/5/42	1/25/43	Struck 03-14-47. Sold 07-10-47
398	21	6/16/42	1/4/43	3/13/43	Struck 06-10-47. Sold 12-01-47
399	21	6/27/42	2/8/43	4/9/43	Sold 01-22-47. Struck 06-10-47
400	21	7/3/42	3/24/43	4/14/43	Renamed Magpie (AMS-25) on 02-18-47. Sunk by mine near Chusan Fo, Korea 10-01-50 Struck 10-20-50
401	0.21	7/17/42	4/1/43	6/4/43	Struck 02-07-47. Sold 10-29-47

John Dixon Davis

Hull No	Builder No	Keel Laid	Launch Date	Date Completed	Remarks
402	21	7/24/42	4/17/43	6/25/43	Remaned Seagull (AMS-55) on 09-01-47. Chg to MSC(0)-55 02-07-55. Struck 11-01-99. Sold
403	21	8/1/42	5/22/43	7/20/43	Struck 06-10-47. Sold 05-19-47
404	21	8/10/42	5/26/43	8/6/43	Struck 02-25-47. Sold 12-03-47
405	11	1/25/43	8/24/43	11/8/43	Struck 02-25-47. Sold 02-14-47
406	11	1/28/43	9/6/43	11/20/43	Transf Norway 0o5-18-45 as NYMS-406, later renamed Rana(M-330). Rtn 06-07-48. Sold to Norway 06-07-48. Struck 08-12-48
407	11	4/21/43	9/16/43	12/8/43	Struck 07-31-46. Sold 02-19-47
408	11	4/21/43	10/9/43	12-18-43.	Struck 07-17-47. Sold 06-18-47
409	11	5/12/43	10/27/43	1/1/44	Foundered in hurricane off Atlantic coast, 09-12-44. Struck 10-14-44
410	4	8/2/43	2/22/44	9/18/44	Struck 11-21-46. Sold 11-04-46
411	4	10/10/43	4/22/44	8/9/44	Struck 08-28-46. Sold 12-29-47 to Philippines
412	4	11/30/43	5/3/44	9/16/44	Sold 05-13-47
413	4	1/14/44	7/4/44	10/26/44	Struck 01-28-47. Transf to Korea 04-06-47 as Kwang Chu (YMS-503)
414	28	9/14/43	3/11/44	9/6/44	Struck 02-25-47. Sold 11-14-47
415	28	10/5/43	4/14/44	10/1/44	Renamed Chatterer (AMS-40) on 03-11-47. Chg to MSC(0)-40 on 02-07-55. Transf to Japan 04-16-55 as Yurishima (MSC-661). Struck 05-01-68
416	0.28	1/9/44	5/28/44	10/21/44	Struck 02-07-47. Sold 12-06-47
417	28	1/9/44	6/29/44	11/10/44	Renamed Merganser (AMS-26) 02-18-47. Chg to AMCU-47 10-01-54. Chg to MHC-47 02-07-55 Struck 05-01-59
418	11	9/16/43	2/22/44	9/21/44	Struck 02-07-47. Sold 12-17-47
419	11	9/17/43	3/11/44	10/28/44	Renamed Mockingbird (AMS-27) 02-18-47. Chg to MSC(0)-27 02-07-55. Trnsf to Korea 01-06-56 as Kochang (MSCO-521)
420	11	9/18/43	4/8/44	2/5/45	Struck 01-31-50. Sold to Canada 12-03-51 as Cordova (MCA-158)
421	11	9/20/43	4/15/44	3/3/45	Foundered in typhoon off Okinawa 09-16-45. Struck 10-24-45
422	2	10/9/43	6/1/44	9/27/44	Renamed Osprey (AMS-28) 02-18-47. Chg to MSC(0)-28 on 02-07-55. Transf to Japan 03-22-55 as Yakushima (MSC-658)
423	2	12/27/43	8/5/55	10/25/44	Struck 02-25-47. Sold 12-26-47

Hull No	Builder No	Keel Laid	Launch Date	Date Completed	Remarks
424	2	1/1/44	8/12/24	11/24/44	Grounded and damaged in typhoon at Okinawa 10-09-45. Destroyed 12-18-45. Struck 01-03-46
425	2	6/6/44	9/30/44	12-21-44.	Renamed Siskin (AMS-58) 09-01-47. Chg to MSC(O)-58 on 02-07-55. Struck 10-01-68. Sold
426	20	9/30/43	2/9/44	9/25/44	Struck 06-10-47. Sold 06-17-44
427	20	11/4/43	3/25/44	11/28/44	Struck 02-25-47. Sold 12-09-47
428	20	2/10/44	6/5/44	1/24/45	Transf USSR 05-17-45. No record of ultimate fate
429	20	3/27/44	9/30/44	3/16/45	Struck 02-25-47. Sold 01-23-48
430	29	11/10/43	3/23/44	10/10/44	Renamed Ostrich (AMS-29) 02 18-47. Chg to MSC(O)-29 on 02-07-55. Struck 11-01-59
431	29	1/10/44	5/20/44	11/13/44	Struck 08-14-46. Sold 04-01-47
432	29	3/24/44	7/8/44	12/30/44	Struck 02-25-47. Sold 01-22-48
433	29	6/7/44	9/30/44	2/13/45	Struck 08-28-46. Sold 04-47
434	19	10/30/43	5/10/44	11/15/44	Renamed Parrakeet AMS-30 02-18-47. Struck 06-23-47. Sold 10-09-47
435	19	5/11/44	9/30/44	3/5/45	Transf USSR 05-17-45 Destroyed 07-53-56. Struck 10-29-56
436	19	6/15/44	3/14/45	5/31/45	Struck 03-05-47. Sold 05-13-47
437	19	10/3/44	4/22/45	7/25/45	Renamed Partridge (AMS-31) 02-18-47. Sunk by mine off Korea 02-02-51. Struck 02-27-51
438	16	11/1/43	7/7/44	10/25/44	Struck 03-05-47. Sold 05-27-47
439	16	10/21/43	7/14/44	11/18/44	Struck 07-19-46. Sold 03-17-47
440	16	10/24/43	10/28/44	12/29/44	Struck 08-28-46. Sold 10-21-47
441	16	11/27/43	11/13/44	2/20/45	Renamed Pelican (AMS-32) 02-18-47. Chg to MSC(O)-32 on 02-07-55. Transf to Japan 04-16-55 as Ogishima (MSC-659). Struck 05-01-68
442	14	10/12/43	4/20/44	10-13-44.	Renamed Plover (AMS-33) on 02-18-47. Chg to MSC(O)-33 on 02-07-55. Struck 10-01-68
443	14	10/21/43	5/5/44	11-14-44.	Renamed Redhead (AMS-34) on 02-18-47. Chg to AMCU-48 on 09-01-45. Chg to MHC-48 on 02-07-55 Struck 11-01-59
444	14	11/16/43	7/20/44	12/21/44	Renamed Turkey (AMS-56) on 09-01-47. Chg to MSC(O)-56 on 02-07-55. Struck 10-01-68. Sold

John Dixon Davis

Hull No	Builder No	Keel Laid	Launch Date	Date Completed	Remarks
445	14	3/25/44	9/28/44	03-20-45.	Struck 03-05-47. Sold 05-13-47
446	14	5/22/43	02/26/44	06/08/44	As PCS-1393. Chg to YMS 446 on 09-27-43, Renamed Sanderling (AMS-35) on 02-18-47, Chg to AMCU-49 02-01-55.Chg toMHC-49 on 02-07-55. Struck11-01-59
447	16	6/17/43	3/18/44	06/28/44	As CS-1394. Chg to YMS-447 on 09-27-43.Transf USSR 03-27-45. No record of ultimate fate
448	16	6/22/43	03/27/44	07/25/44	As PCS-1395. Chg to YMS 448 on 09-27-43, Transf USSR 04-24-45. No record of ultimate fate
449	27	6/5/43	2/29/44	07/07/44	As PCS1398. Chg to YMS-449 09-27-43Struck 07-19-46. Sold 02-06-47
450	27	8/7/43	4/15/44	11/25/44	as PCS1399, chg toYMS-450 10-07-43Transf to Philippines 01-22-48 as Tarlac (P-11).
451	27	9/22/43	05/20/44	12/26/44	as PCS-1400. Chg to YMS-451 on 10-07-43. Chg from YMS 451 to PSC-1400 06-23-44, Chg from PCS-1400 to AMS-59 (unamed) 09-27-47. Struck 09-16-47. Loaned commercially 09-17-47. Rtn 04-14-52. Reinstated on Navy List 11-04-53 as PCS-1400. Named Coquille (Pcs-1400) 02-15-56. Struck -7-02-56. Sold 03-14-57
452	27	3/3/44		07/22/44	Chg to PCS-1401 06-23-44, 02-13-45, Named McMinnville (PCS-1401) 02-15-56 Struck 08-01-62 Sold 05-28-63
453	10	7/20/43	10/02/43	06/27/44	As PCS-1406. Chg to YMS-453 on 09-27-43, Transf USSR 05-24-45. No record of ultimate fate.
454	10	08/24/43	10/23/43	06/30/44	As PCS-1407. Chg to YMS-454 on 09-27- Grounded in typhoon on Tsuken Shima, off Okinawa, 10-09-45. Hulk destroyed 12-20-45. Struck 01-03-46.
455	10	8/21/43	11/13/43	07/21/44	As PCS-1408. Chg to YMS-455 on 09-27-43.Transf USSR 05-30-45. No record of ultimate fate.
456	10	10/4/43	12/11/43	8/21/44	Transf USSR 05-16-45. No record of ultimate fate
457	10	11/17/43	1/8/44	9/13/44	Transf USSR. 03-31-45 No record of ultimate fate

Hull No	Builder No	Keel Laid	Launch Date	Date Completed	Remarks
458	10	12/3/43	2/12/44	10/9/44	Struck 02-25-47. Sold 09-26-47
459	10	1/12/44	4/8/44	10/30/44	Destroyed 01-12-46 YMS-456 through 459 were the former PCS-1409 through 1412, redesignated YMS 09-26-43 before being laid down.
460	28	6/8/43	12/04/43	05/27/44	as PCS-1415. Chg to YMS-460 on 09-27-43 Transf USSR 04-05-45. No record of ultimate fate.
461	28	6/8/43	01/08/44	06/21/44	as PCS-1416. Chg to YMS-461 on 09-27-43. Renamed Swallow (AMS-36) 02-18-47. Chg to MSC(O)-36 on 02-07-55. Transf to Japan 04-16-55 as Yugeshima (MSC-660). Struck 05-01-68.
462	14	4/4/43	10/11/43	6/9/44	as PCS-1427. Chg to YMS-462 09-27-43. Transf USSR 04-12-45. No record of ultimate fate.
463	14	5/5/43	03/21/44	07/15/44.	Transf Korea 05-10-47 as Kang Nung (YMS-507). Struck 12-23-47
464	0.09	5/14/43	12/09/45	06/13/44.	as PCS-1432. Chg to YMS-464 on 09-27-43. Transf USSR 05-15-45. No record of ultimate fate.
465	9	6/21/43	01/04/44	06/17/44	as PCS-1433. Chg to YMS-465 on 09-27-43. Transf USSR 05-08-45. No record of ultimte fate.
466	9	6/24/43	01/22/44	07/04/44	as PCS-1434. Chg to YMS-466 on 09-27-43. Transf USSR 05-31-45. No record of ultimate fate.
467	9	6/14/43	02/22/44	09/04/44	as PCS-1435. Chg to YMS-467 on 09-27-43. Struck 02-07-47. Sold 11-07-47.
468	9	6/12/43	03/23/44	08/31/44	as PCS-1436. Chg to YMS-468 on 09-27-43. Struck 01-19-48. Sold to Turkey 05-10-48 as Kusadashi (M 514)
469	9	7/30/43	03/17/44		as PCS-1437. Chg to YMS-469 on 09-27-43.
470	9	8/12/43	04/05/44	10/14/44	as PCS-1438. Chg to YMS-470 on 09-27-43. Renamed Swan (AMS-37) 02-18-47. Chg to MSC(0)-37 on 02-07-55. Struck 11-01-59. Sold 1961.
471	9	9/15/43	05/23/44	10/27/44	as PCS-1439. Chg to YMS-471 on 09-27-43. (AMS-38) 02-18-47. Chg to MSC(0)-38 on 02-07-55. Struck 11-01-59.

John Dixon Davis

Hull No	Builder No	Keel Laid	Launch Date	Date Completed	Remarks
472	9	9/17/43	06/21/44	11/10/44	as PCS-1440. Chg to YMS-472 on 09-27-43. Lost in typhoon off Okinawa 09-16-45. Struck 10-24-45.
473	12	5/10/43	04/22/44	08/22/44	as PCS-1443. Chg to YMS-473 on 09-27-43. Struck 06-19-46. Sold to Korea 07-24-47
474	12	5/14/43	05/23/44		as PSC-1444. Chg to YMS-474 on 10-07-43. Chg back to PSC-1444 on 06-23-44. Named Conneaut (PSC-1444) 02-15-56. Struck 09-05-57. Sold 1957.
475	26	4/30/43	06/01/44	08/16/44	Struck 10-29-46. Sold 01-21-47
476	26	4/30/43	06/14/44	11/21/44	as PSC-1448. Chg to YMS-476 on 10-07-43. Chg back to PSC-1448 on 06-23-44. Transf Korea 06-09-52 as Hwaseong (PCS-205).
477	29	7/12/43	11/06/43	07/10/44	as PCS-1453. Chg to YMS-477 on 09-27-43. Struck 08-28-46. Sold 04-47
478	29	9/2/43	01/08/44	08/21/44	as PSC-1454. Chg to YMS-478 on 09-27-43. Grounded at Waknoura, Japan 10-08-45. Hulk destroyed 10-24-45. Struck 03-20-46.
479	20	4/28/43	19/30/43	07/20/44	as PSC-1456. Chg to YMS-479 on 09-27-43. Renamed Waxbill (AMS-39) 02-18-47. Chg to AMCU-50 on 02-01-55. Chg to MHC-50 on 02-07-55. Struck 11-01-59.
480	4	5/25/43	11/20/43	03/15/44	as PCS-1463, Chg to YMS-481 on 09-27-43. Chg to Degaussing Vessel, YDG-7, 12-23-43. Struck 04-12-46. Sold 08-27-47
481	4	05/25/43	11/20/43	03/15/44	as PCS-1463, Chg to YMS-481 on 09-27-43. Sunk by shore batteries off Tarakan, Borneo 05-02-45. Struck 06-02-45.

In addition to the 481 YMSes listed above and the 33 shipyards that constructed them, there were 80 more YMS types built specifically for Lend Lease to Britain. These were contracted for separately and received from the builders by British crews. They were designated BYMS to distinguish them from those built for the US Navy.

Many of the shipbuilders of the US Navy YMSes also were contracted to build some of the 80 BYMSes. There were, however, three shipyards that built BYMSes, but did not participate in the building of US Navy YMSes. These three builders were: American Car & Foundry Co., Wilmington, Del.; Barbour Boat Works, New Bern, NC; and Westergard Boat Works, Inc., Biloxi, Miss. (See

Griffiths, Patrick. "History of the BYMS Part 1 & 2". *Warship International.* (Toledo, Ohio: The International Naval Research Organization, Inc., Vol. XXXIV, No. 1 & 2, 1997).

A total of (481 + 80) 561 YMSes were completed between early 1942 and mid 1945. Of this number 234 were transferred to other navies.

(Note: The information above on the 481 YMSes comes primarily from *Dictionary of American Naval Fighting Ships, Vol. V* (Washington, D.C.: Navy Department, History Division,1970) pp. 498-516. See also Elliott, Peter. *Allied Minesweeping in World War 2.* (Letchworth, Hertfordshire: The Garden City Press, 1979). Pp. 74-79.)

I am also indebted to Allie Ryan, George Schneider and Fred Scripture for suggestions and advice in the use of this information.

War Losses of US YMSes

Note: (In numerical sequence and based on the information contained in the list above)

(In some cases the Latitude and Longitude coordinates are given in the list above)

By enemy action

Ship #	Cause of Loss	Day of Loss	Location
YMS 19	Sunk by mine	9/24/1944	Caroline Islands
YMS 21	Sunk by mine	9/1/1944	Southern France
YMS 24	Sunk by mine	8/16/1944	Southern France
YMS 30	Sunk by mine	1/25/1944	Off Anzio, Italy
YMS 39	Sunk by mine	6/26/1945	Balikpapan, Borneo area
YMS 48	Shore batteries	2/14/1945	Corregidor
YMS 50	Shore batteries	6/18/1945	Balikpapan, Borneo area
YMS 71	Sunk by mine	4/3/1945	Off Borneo
YMS 84	Sunk by mine	7/9/1945	Balikpapan area
YMS 103	Beached after mining	4/7/1945	Okinawa
YMS 304	Sunk by mine	6/30/1944	Normandy
YMS 350	Sunk by mine	7/2/1944	Cherbourg, France
YMS 365	Sunk by mine	6/26/1945	Balikpapan area
YMS 378	Written off after mining	7/30/1944	Normandy
YMS 385	Sunk by mine	10/1/1944	Carolina Islands
YMS 481	Shore batteries	5/2/1945	Tarakan, Borneo

John Dixon Davis

By storm, grounding or collision

Ship	Cause of Loss	Day of Loss	Location
YMS 14	Sunk by collision	01/11/1945	Boston Harbour
YMS 70	Sunk in storm	10/17/1944	Off Leyte
YMS 98	Sunk in typhoon	09/16/1945	Okinawa
YMS 127	Lost by grounding	01/16/1944	Aleutian Islands
YMS 133	Foundered	02/20/1943	Off Coos Bay, Oregon
YMS 146	Sunk in typhoon	10/9/1945	Okinawa
YMS 151	Sunk in typhoon	10/9/1945	Okinawa
YMS 275	Sunk in typhoon	10/9/1945	Okinawa
YMS 341	Sunk in typhoon	9/16/1945	Okinawa
YMS 383	Sunk in typhoon	10/9/1945	Okinawa
YMS 409	Foundered in hurricane	9/12/1944	Eastern seaboard of U.S.
YMS 421	Sunk in typhoon	9/16/1945	Okinawa
YMS 424	Sunk in typhoon	10/9/1945	Okinawa
YMS 454	Sunk in typhoon	10/9/1945	Okinawa
YMS 472	Sunk in typhoon	9/16/1945	Okinawa
YMS 478	Lost by grounding	10/8/1945	Japan

YMSes lost while serving with the Royal Navy in WWII

Ship Number	Cause of Loss	Day of Loss	Location
BYMS 2019	Sunk by mine	9/9/1943	Catrune, Italy
BYMS 2022	Sunk by mine	8/16/1944	Frejus, Southern France
BYMS 2030	Sunk by mine	10/8/1944	Le Harve, France
BYMS 2077	Sunk by mine	10/24/1944	Corinth, Greece
BYMS 2255	Sunk by mine	10/5/1944	Boulogne, France

YMSes lost while serving with other Allied Navies in WWII

Ship Name	Ship Number	Cause of Loss	Day of Loss	Location
Magpie	AMS-25 (ex YMS 400)	sunk by mine	10/1/1950	Chusan Po, Korea
Partridge	AMS-31 (ex YMS 437)	sunk by mine	2/2/1951	off Korea

YMSes lost in the Korean War in 1950-51

Ship Number	Country	Cause of Loss	Day of Loss	Location
YMS 77	French	Sunk by mine	10/25/1944	Marseilles
YMS 190	Greece	Sunk by mine	4/15/1944	Cape Turbo
YMS 382	Norway	Sunk by B-boat	5/7/1945	Cherbourg
GYMS 2191	Greece	(Ex-RN BYMS 2191)	6/5/1945	Aegean Sea
GYMS 2074	Greece	(Ex-RN BYMS 2074	Date not dentified	Aegean Sea

John Dixon Davis

Appendix C

Primer on WWII era Mines and Minesweeping

There were four types of naval mines used by the various combatants in WWII. They are:

1. The moored (or anchored) mine;
2. The magnetic mine;
3. The acoustic mine; and
4. The pressure mine.

(Note: While much of this material was secret during WWII, it has for a long time been available to the public in many written works).

The moored mine is essentially a watertight container, usually a ball shape, made of steel, which is full of air and buoyant material, and will float if allowed to. The steel ball contains, in addition to the material above, the explosive charge and the devices which will cause the charge to explode. When the mine explodes, the ship which set off the mine is subject to great damage from the force of the explosion. When the mine is "laid" or "sown" (put in the water, usually in a predetermined place) it floats on the surface for a few minutes while its anchor (an empty metal container open to the water) fills and causes the anchor and the mine attached to it by a cable to sink to the bottom. When the anchor (with mine attached) comes to rest on the bottom of the sea it releases the mine and allows it to float to the surface. Usually, however, the combatant laying the mine prefers that the mine not be visible to his enemy. So he fixes a device to the anchor which will let out only enough cable to keep the mine at a predetermined depth under water. Now the mine is anchored by a cable (moored), at a depth predetermined (say 10, 15 or 20 feet etc.) below the surface. It cannot be seen by the enemy, and usually cannot be moved from its location [except when there are very strong currents or some other unusual phenomenon occurs, or perhaps a minesweeper comes along and cuts the cable and the mine "pops" to the surface and is sunk by rifle fire from the minesweeper].

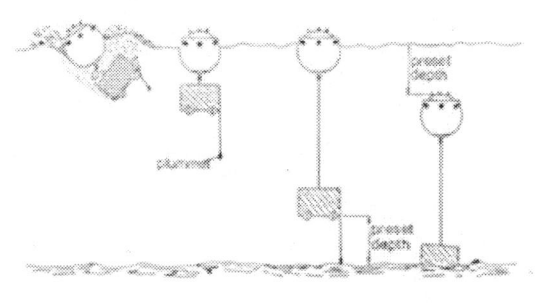

Laying The Moored Mine

Diagram 1 – Laying the Moored Mine

The moored mine is usually detonated when a ship or submarine strikes the mine and bends one of its "horns" so that the charge explodes. The "horns" protrude from the mine case at several points on its circumference. Because the mine has to be hit by a ship it is often referred to as a contact mine. (Note: Arnold Lott reports that the minelayer *Montgomery* laid 551 contact mines around Tongatabu in the Tonga Islands on

June 10, 1942). This field was designed to keep Japanese vessels, of whatever kind, from entering this area, or to sink them if they did. [Actually, a friendly vessel ran the same risk if it tried to cross the minefield, for a mine does not know who is friend or foe]. For some time after the *Montgomery* finished this job, explosions were heard coming from the mine field and no ships were in the area. It seems that whales (variety unknown) were accustomed to using this area, possibly for mating, or feeding, and were, with some frequency, hitting these mines, resulting in the whales' maiming or death. The carcasses drifted to the beaches and harbor of Tongatabu, "giving it an air all its own." Late in the year a hurricane hit Tonga and the wind and waves "decimated" the mine field. [Lott, Arnold S., Lt. Commander, U.S. Navy. *Most Dangerous Sea.* (Annapolis, MD: U.S. Naval Institute, 1959), p. 135].

Perhaps most people who have any knowledge of Naval mines think of a black, steel ball with several spike-like things sticking out from the upper part of the ball as described above. There are two types of horns, both of which were used on mines in WWII. The first type was invented by a German scientist in 1868 by the name of Dr. Otto Herz. It was still in use in WWII by the Japanese, and others. Technically called the Herz Chemical horn, it was simply a hollow, watertight lead tube threaded at the bottom end so that it could be screwed into the steel ball (the mine case). Inside the lead horn is a glass vial containing a bichromate solution. When a ship struck a lead horn, being soft, it was easily bent so that the glass vial inside was broken and the bichromate solution spilled into the lower half of the lead horn. At the bottom of the horn are two electric wires (neither touching the other). When the solution, almost immediately, covers these two wires, a simple battery is created, making enough electricity to activate the detonator which sets off the charge. Ship hits horn of mine, horn bends, and glass vial is crushed, bichromate solution creates battery with electric wires taking the current to the detonator. That's it. In a matter of seconds the ship is damaged and possibly sunk. (See diagram of the Herz horn). [See, Griffiths, Maurice. *The Hidden Menace.* (Greenwich, England: Conway Maritime Press, 1981), pp. 44-45]. The Japanese used the Herz horn mine almost exclusively in WWII.

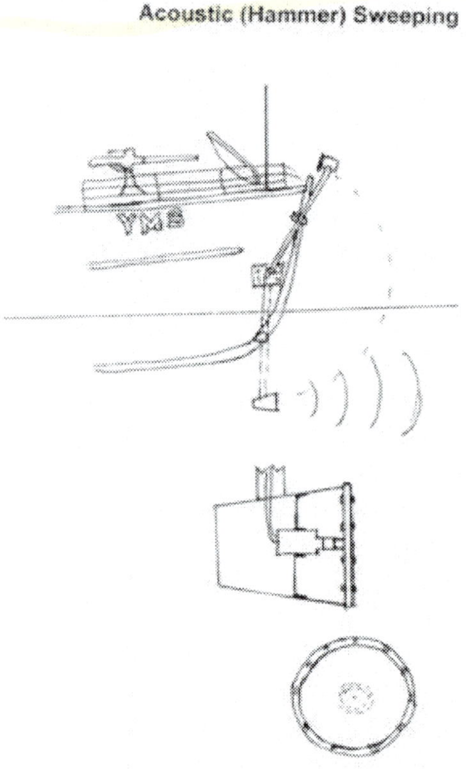

Diagram 2 Details of the Acoustic Hammer

The second type of contact mine is essentially the same as the Herz horn except that the horn is made of a dissimilar metal from the steel mine case, usually copper. The copper horn is insulated from the mine case so that it does not touch until a ship hits and bends the copper horn against the mine case. Being in salt water, when the dissimilar metals touch, a battery is created, an electric current is generated which sets in motion the firing of the detonator exploding the mine. The U. S Navy used this type, the Mk 6, in the

WWII era. In either case the laying of both types is roughly the same. Ships and submarines were used to lay these types.

The moored contact mine is made in various sizes, carrying various weights of explosive, some obviously more powerful than others. The different sizes are used in different depths of water. Also, some contact mines have a flotation device attached to the top of the mine case, so that if only this device (called an antenna) is hit the mine will explode. There are many variations of contact mines, but essentially they are as described above.

The procedure for removing and/or rendering the contact mine harmless is called mine sweeping. There were two basic techniques for sweeping the moored contact mine in WWII. The most frequently used and most effective is called the *Oropesa* sweep. The name comes from the name of the British trawler in WWI on which this technique was developed. It was so effective in all regards that it became the standard method for contact sweeping in WWI, WWII and afterward.

Dan Buoy

The *Oropesa* sweep (often referred to as "O" type) consisted of twisted steel cable of high strength but moderate flexibility, usually one half inch to five eighths inches in diameter. The twist or "lay" of the wire is crucial in this technique. If the sweep gear is streamed off the port (left) side of the minesweeper, the sweep wire must be "right hand lay". That is, the twist of the wire is to the right. The lay can be determined by placing one's right hand on a strand of wire as if shaking hands with it and if the twist goes around as the fingers do, it is right hand lay and must be used only on the port (left) side. If the twist is to the left, as in shaking hands with the left hand, then this is left hand lay and this wire must be used on the starboard (right) side only. The layman might think this to be a little "picky". But the fact is that the wire, while being pulled through the water at speeds up to ten knots, is placed under tremendous stress. If the wrong lay is used, the resistance of the wire to the flow of water can cause the steel sweep wire to unravel and upset the sweeping effort; if not indeed cause its failure. (See diagrams of "O" type components that follow).

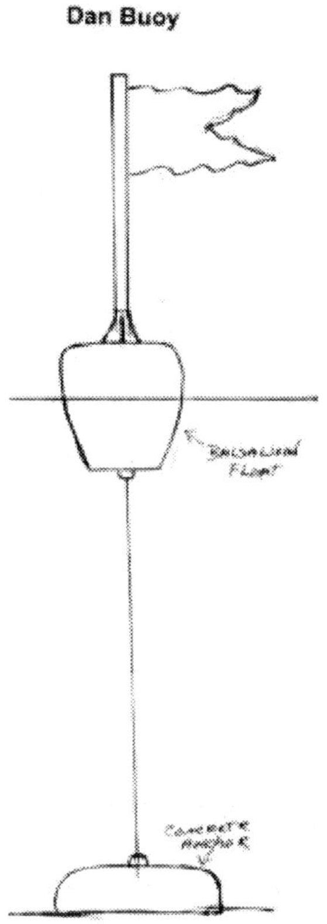

When the "O" type sweep begins, a torpedo shaped steel float (called the "pig" by the ship's crew) has a length of sweep wire shackled to the bridle underneath it, (this is called the pendent) and the other end of the wire (pendent) is shackled to a steel multiplane water kite called the "otter". The otter has a chain sling which is prefigured to make the otter pull away from the minesweeper and at the same time pull down on the wire fastened to the float. The length of the wire from float to otter determines the depth of the sweep, the float keeping the otter, sweep wire, etc. from sinking. The pig has a receptacle on its top side which holds a six or eight foot bamboo or steel

Diagram 3 Details of Dan Buoy

pole with a small flag on it (so it can be seen at all times from the minesweeper). The pig is lifted by davit into the water beside the ships after quarter at the stern. The float, or pig, is allowed to drift away as the otter is lowered into the water, by davit, off the stern of the ship. As the ship goes forward very slowly, the otter, connected to the ship by the sweep wire on a reel at the winch, "bites" into the water and pulls the sweep wire, unwinding the wire on the winch. The pig and the otter pull away from the stern of the ship on an approximate 45 degree angle and several hundred feet from the ship. When the desired length of sweep wire is paid out the winch is stopped.

At this point another multiplane water kite, with a sling configured to pull the kite straight down, is secured to the sweep wire. This kite is called the depressor and it pulls the sweep wire down to the desired depth just aft of the ship's stern by means of a length of wire equal to the length of wire from the pig to the otter. This wire is fastened to the depressor and engages the sweep wire by means of a snatch block. The depressor is also connected by wire to another reel on the winch so that its distance from the stern of the ship can be adjusted while at the same time pulling the sweep wire to the proper depth, matching the depth at the pig.

After the full length of sweep wire is reeled off the winch drum, the float (pig) and otter are pulled away from the ship for a considerable distance. The wire tends back toward the minesweeper and the total configuration resembles a large letter J with the top of the letter J at the stern of the sweeper. The area from the ship's stern to the otter is the area that is being swept. Any moored mines in this area will have their anchor cables engaged by the sweep wire and cut.

Depending on the actual sweeping situation, size and location of the field, the type of mines expected, etc., cutters capable of severing the mine's anchor cable can be placed in various locations on the sweep wire. When the sweep wire engages the mine cable it slides along the sweep cable toward the otter. When it comes to a cutter the mine cable is severed and the mine "pops" up to the surface.

At this point a mine disposal vessel locates the floating mine and sinks it with rifle fire. Sometimes the bullet that pierces the steel mine case hits a horn, or the detonator inside, and the mine explodes. If the disposal vessel is at a safe distance there is little likelihood of damage or injury. Actually, by international agreement, the moored contact mine is to be equipped with a device which disarms the mine when it is cut and comes to the surface. However, after a mine has been in the water for a period of time, marine life such as oysters, barnacles, seaweed, etc. grow around this device and very often keep it from functioning. Therefore, when the mine pops to the surface it is still armed and liable to explode when disturbed.

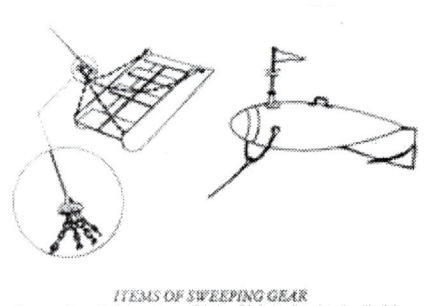

ITEMS OF SWEEPING GEAR
Oropesa float (right) and otter (left), with inset showing detail of the link coupling between towing wire and otter chain

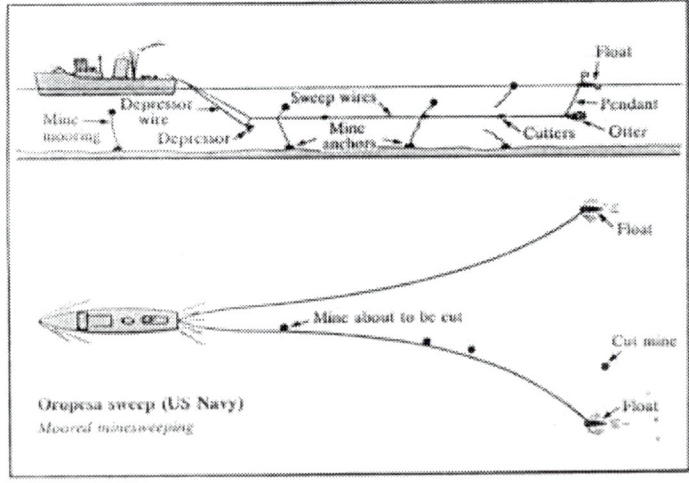

Diagram 4 – Oropesa sweep (US Navy)

Usually several minesweepers sweep together in echelon. The first sweeper is in water that is known to be clear, or expected to be (or hoped to be). It sweeps a broad width with the second sweeper inside the area swept by the first one. The third sweeper stays within the swept area of the second and so on, depending on how many are involved. If you will picture several grass mowers, each following the one in front with its left wheels in the area mowed by the mower just ahead (the swept area, or the safe area), you can see how it works in minesweeping. Often, the edge of the area just swept is marked by placing dan buoys (small balsa wood buoys with a flag pole and an anchor to hold them in place). The next ship in line guides on these buoys to stay in the swept (safe) area. After the sweep is done, the buoys are gathered up by a vessel called a "danner" (which placed the dan buoys to mark the cleared areas in the first place) for use again and again. (See the diagrams below).

When a minesweeper begins to stream its sweep gear (of whatever type) it raises three black balls, one on each end of the signal yard arm and one at the top of the mast. There are halyards at all three locations especially for the black balls. These three black balls announce to all ships within sight that the minesweeper is engaged in mine sweeping and they must stand clear.

There are two reasons they should stand clear. One is obvious: there may be mines in the vicinity and they can sink a friendly ship as well as an enemy. The second, not so obvious to the layman (and actually not so obvious to other naval vessels, for they sometimes did not observe the black ball warning and cut across our path), is that the mine sweeper is towing at least a quarter mile of gear, either wire for moored mines or flotation cables for magnetic mines.

If another ship cuts across this gear streaming out from our stern, several things could happen. The offending ship might destroy very, very expensive equipment which could nullify the usefulness of the minesweeper until new gear could be installed, and/or the offending ship could ride over the sweep gear and then have it foul its own screws and possibly put it out of action for an extended period of time. Perhaps of greatest importance, as mentioned above, is the possibility that there are mines in that area that the minesweeper will sweep, but the offending ship will get to them first and perhaps be damaged or sunk.

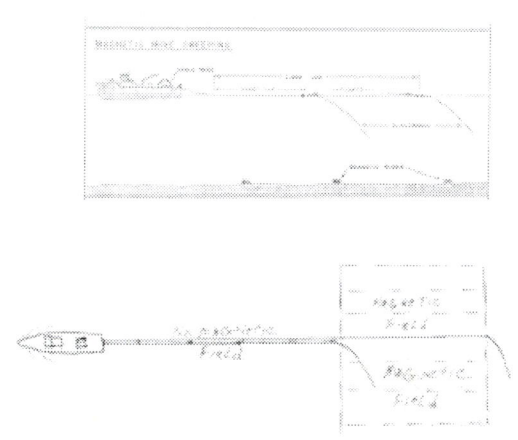

Diagram 5 Detail of Magnetic Mine Sweeping

The black balls were made on a wire frame about three feet in diameter which was covered with heavy, black wool, flag bunting. The frame could be folded back on itself making a flat "half moon" for easy storage in the flag bag when not in use. It was easily unfolded to make the round ball when needed. When the sweeper recovered its gear and it was all back on board the black balls were lowered and stowed in the flag bag.

The **magnetic** mine, while invented during the latter stages of WWI, was rarely used by anyone until WWII and then first by the Germans against Britain in 1939. [See Levie, Howard S. *Mine Warfare At Sea*. (Boston: Martinus Nijhoff Publishers, 1992), pp. 104-108].

The magnetic mine is almost always a ground mine. That is, when laid, it rests on the bottom until activated by a target vessel. It does not have to be touched or "bumped", but rather relies exclusively on the influence of the magnetic field of the target vessel. Usually, the more steel there is in a ship the larger and stronger its inherent magnetic field becomes. When a ship passes over the magnetic mine, if the ship's magnetic field is strong enough, a very sensitive needle (not unlike that in a Boy Scout's compass, which is activated by the earth's magnetic field) is caused to move. When the moving "needle" touches a terminal, an electric current from a battery is caused to flow to the detonator, which then sets off the explosive charge. Since weight is no great problem for a ground mine (as it would be for a buoyant moored mine) it can be packed with a ton or more of explosive and thus can be used in deeper water with devastating effect.

The countermeasure for the magnetic mine is to create a magnetic field of great strength at a safe distance from the minesweeper and thus "fool" the magnetic mine and cause it to explode without harming anyone.

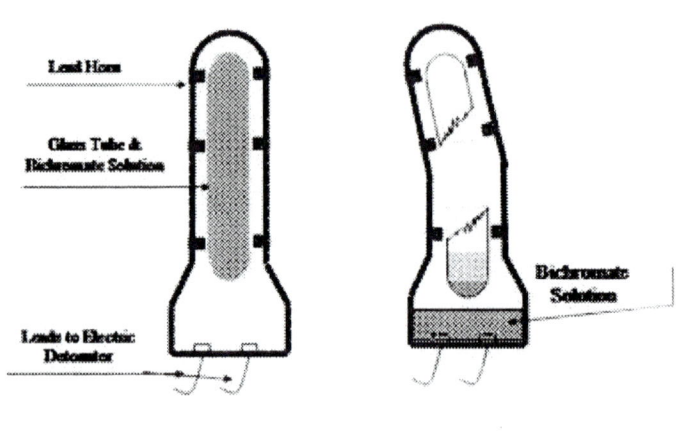

Diagram 6 – The Herz chemical horn (detail)

After months of experimentation the British developed equipment and techniques that became the standard for magnetic minesweeping for the U.S Navy as well as for themselves. We learned what we know from them.

On the fantail of the YMS, just aft of the main propulsion engine room's after bulkhead, a well was cut into the deck that extended four or five feet into the hull. It was sealed from the interior of the hull and the bilge, although there was drain pipe to allow any water that collected in the well to drain into the sea.

Inside this well was a large spool, turned by an electric motor. The magnetic sweep gear, referred to by the crew as the "tail," was wound on the spool when not in use and covered by a heavy tarpaulin. When the sweeper was ready to start a magnetic sweep, the black balls were hoisted to the yardarm and the masthead, and the magnetic spool or winch was placed in reverse and the magnetic tail paid out slowly as the sweeper moved forward at a moderate speed. The forward speed kept the magnetic tail trailing directly aft of the sweeper.

The great breakthrough made by the British in magnetic sweeping was as follows.

As anyone with a rudimentary knowledge of physics knows, passing a direct current of electricity through a single wire causes a magnetic field to be created. The size and strength of the field created is proportional to the amperage of the current. Therefore, if a single wire could be trailed behind the minesweeper at a safe distance, and a current passed through it, the resulting magnetic field created could cause a magnetic mine to explode. The problem is how to create the field at a predetermined distance aft of the ship and not have the magnetic field beginning at the stern of the sweeper in such a way as to endanger the ship. The answer is actually a simple one, although it took quite a bit of effort to come up with it.

The magnetic sweep tail was composed of two wires, completely insulated from each other and the sea, and encased in a flexible rubber hose, six to eight inches in diameter, filled with buoyant material so that each one floated on its own. The two were bound together with flexible canvas belts about every ten feet. The belts keep the two floating cables together, but allow them to move slightly independently of each other as when the ship is making a turn in its sweep path and when the tail is being wound on the spool.

These wires (floating cables) ran together for approximately 160 yards (in which space the opposite flow of current in the two wires canceled the magnetic field made by the other). At the 160 yard point, one of the wires terminated in a bare electrode several feet long which hung down into the sea. The second wire, now without its partner, continues on for approximately 500 yards where it too, terminates in a bare electrode hanging down into the sea. When a direct current is passed through one wire of the cable, it goes to the electrode and into the sea (which is a conductor of electricity) and back to the other electrode and back to the generator, thus completing the circuit. With this arrangement, the only place where a magnetic field is created is in the last 500 yards of the tail where it is a single floating wire, thus making a magnetic field around it. This places the magnetic field at a safe distance behind the sweeper. (See Griffiths, *Op. Cit.*, pp. 93-94).

To generate an electric current of sufficient amperage to create a magnetic field capable of setting off a magnetic mine resting on the bottom many feet below the surface, the YMS used a 500 horsepower diesel engine with a 2 ton flywheel connected to an electric generator. This generating system was capable of producing a current of 3000

amperes at 100 volts in pulses of several seconds' duration. This created a very strong magnetic field.

Two sweepers were capable of pulsing together as they covered the areas to be swept for magnetic mines. This created a larger area of coverage. However, depending on the particular area to be swept, one sweeper was capable of covering a smaller area suspected of having magnetic mines. When a magnetic mine was set off it simply exploded with no damage to the sweeper and little or no damage to the magnetic tail. (See the diagrams below of magnetic sweeping).

All ships have an inherent magnetic field of their own. It is the ship's magnetic field that may set off the magnetic mine. Therefore, any effort to reduce the inherent magnetic field of a ship can pay rich dividends by making the ship less likely to set off a magnetic mine. The process whereby a ship's own magnetic field is reduced or nearly nullified is called degaussing. When a ship is degaussed, an electric wire coil is attached to the inside of the hull, and the proper amount of current (determined by testing) is applied continuously to counter the ship's inherent field. The YMS had a degaussing coil and was also made of wood. Wood has no magnetic field; therefore the YMS was an excellent ship for magnetic sweeping, especially in shallow waters.

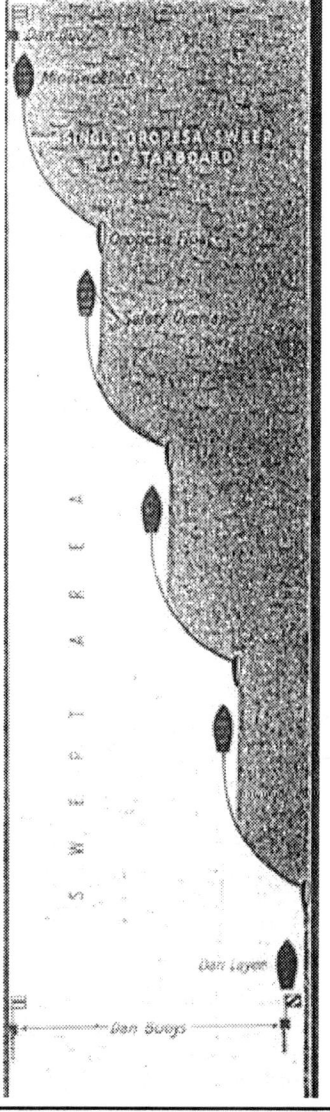

Diagram 7 Details of Oropesa Mine Sweeping process

The third type of mine that minesweepers were involved with in WWII was the **acoustic** mine. This was usually a ground mine (resting on the bottom) that was activated by the typical sounds made by the engines of certain ships traveling at moderate speeds. There was a hydrophone (underwater microphone) in the detonator circuit of the mine and when the proper frequencies and volume were picked up by the microphone it activated the detonator which was set off by current from a battery in the mine.

The acoustic mine was very similar to the magnetic mine in most details except for the means of activating the mine, i.e., magnetic field or sound vibrations.

Although the British Admiralty had been working on a design for an acoustic mine long before WWII it was first used by the Germans in the war. When the British recovered one of the German acoustic mines in 1940, it was immediately apparent what the new mine was. After much trial and error a technique for successfully sweeping the acoustic mine was developed. It turned out that the commonplace riveting hammer (used in ship building and steel building construction) was the answer.

It was encased in a metal container sealed from sea water and the riveting hammer placed so that it beat on a steel diaphragm. It was driven by compressed air and the container lowered into the water and secured to the bow of the sweeper when sweeping for acoustic mines. The diaphragm was three feet in diameter and the continuous, rapid pounding of the riveting hammer gave out just the right frequency and volume to activate the acoustic mine. It was so effective that it was detonating acoustic mines as much as a mile away. The hammer was raised out of the water when not in use. (See Levie, *Op. Cit.*, pp. 108-109. Also. Griffiths, *Op. Cit.*, pp. 100-101). (See diagram below).

The acoustic hammer technique was, of course, used by the U.S. Navy, also.

It should be noted here that influence mines were not only used as a single means of sinking a ship, as for example a magnetic mine, or an acoustic mine (and later as we shall see) as a pressure mine. In order to confuse the enemy, two (and sometimes three) of these capabilities were built into the same mine. It was not uncommon for a single mine to require activation by a ship's magnetic field and its underwater sounds at the same time to explode. Just the magnetic field was not enough. Just the underwater sounds were not enough. Both influences had to be present at the same time to activate the mine. Thus a minesweeper could sweep all day with its magnetic tail and not produce a detonation. But when magnetic sweeping occurred at the same time as running the acoustic hammer, an influence mine so configured would be set off.

Nor was this the end of the problem. Often the builder of the mine would include what was called a"ships counter". This device could be preset to count the activations by whatever means, and only after reaching this number would the mine explode. For example, a magnetic mine might be set to receive ten activations by a ship or a mine sweeper. The eleventh activation (or ship or sweeper) would detonate the mine. There were many variations of this technique. In the early days it sometimes made the mine sweeper people think that there were no mines present after, say, seven passes. They go home for the day and a few hours later a ship comes in and is blown up. "How could this happen?" they would ask. The answer, of course, was "ships counters". Therefore, minesweeping people never reported that there were no mines in the area, but rather that to this point none have been found, and they keep right on sweeping, especially if influence mines are suspected to be in the area.

The fourth type of mine used late in WWII was the **pressure** mine. Called an "oyster" by the British, who developed it before the beginning of WWII, it was not used by them until after the Germans started using them immediately after the Allied invasion of France in June of 1944. The British did not initiate their use because they were unable to "sweep" them. The Hague Convention forbade the use of a mine that could not be swept. The Germans developed a pressure mine in the early years of the war, but they were afraid to use it for fear the British would recover one (as they did early on) and use it against the Germans. So Hitler saved his"super secret weapon" for use immediately after the Allied invasion of France. The U.S. Navy developed a pressure mine but withheld its use until very late in the war when it was laid by B-29 aircraft throughout the harbors and shipping lanes of Japan beginning in mid -1945.

The pressure mine was based on the simplest way to detect the momentary water pressure drop under a ship as it passes over the bottom. It was a ground mine, laid by aircraft or submarine, and when a ship passed over it a simple diaphragm was activated and the detonator exploded the mine. One problem with the pressure mine, which too often caused it to explode prematurely, was that it was sensitive to pressure changes caused by heavy wave action of the ocean. It was as if a ship was passing over it. This problem was corrected by including with the pressure diaphragm, a magnetic and/or acoustic component. This required that a magnetic field and/or the noise of a ship's screws be present at the same time the pressure drop was detected. Used in this combination the mine was "unsweepable" unless an actual ship was used. And this was exactly how these mines were "swept".

A stripped down freighter, with a skeleton crew, was actually sailed up and down the shipping lanes and channels in the attempt to detonate any of these mines that still lay unexploded before they were programmed to neutralize themselves by various means (a clock, water soluble plugs that eventually melted, allowing water to fill the mine, etc.). These ships were called "guinea pig" ships for obvious reasons. It was only after many passes by the "guinea pigs" that the channels were declared safe. [See Hartmann, Gregory K. *Weapons That Wait, Mine Warfare in The U.S. Navy.* (Annapolis, MD: Naval Institute Press, 1979), pp. 67-68. Also, Levie, *Op. Cit.*, pp. 110-111. Also, Lott, *Op. Cit.*,. pp. 73-74; p. 253].

Minelaying and mine clearance were very important functions in WWII. According to Samuel Loring Morison, "So total was the havoc wreaked by mines that during World War II, on average, one ship was sunk for every 35 mines laid." He goes on to report that more than 700,000 mines were laid in the European theater alone.

He also reports the use of influence mines, by the U. S., in March - August 1945, in Japanese shipping routes and harbor approaches (11,000 were laid by aircraft). This was called Operation Starvation designed to cut Japan off from any imports for its war machine. Because of the estimated 670 Japanese merchant ships damaged or sunk, including 65 Japanese warships, Japan's ability to continue the manufacture of war equipment collapsed. [Morison, Samuel Loring. *Guide To Naval Mine Warfare.* (Arlington, Virginia: Pasha Publications, Inc., 1995), p. 6].

John Dixon Davis

Appendix D
Misc. Items Not In Text of the Book

Donald Frederick tape notes:

I mentioned two planking crews. When they got the planks ready the less experienced men hung them and bolted them, so it was a continuous thing going all the time. Once things got going it was almost an assembly line. We think of Henry Ford and his assembly line.

I know of no one living today who did any planking or caulking on the YMSes. The yard caulkers were unable to keep up with demand on the boats so outside caulkers were brought in from around the country to help.

With regard to picture it was Marshal Tullock standing next to Theodore Brigham. I can't identify any of the others. No pictures of planking or framing taken at night. Didn't know what went on day shift.

The hulls were gotten overboard as soon as they could be floated and much of the finish work was done over board this so the next ones could be started.

The roller chucks may have been an after thought but several of the hulls had to be hauled to put them on (bilge keel). Later they were put on before launching.

Boats were hauled several times during construction for finishing, etc.and final painting before they left for delivery. They were delivered to the Brooklyn Navy Yard. I was never fortunate enough to get to go on a a delivery trip.

Night crew was small only about 70, consisted of carpenters, machinists, black smiths, welders, support staff for the yard compared to 1000 + or - a few on the day crew.

Sometime, probably about 1944 they bought another yard adjacent to the Brigham yard and built many steel tank lighters which employed several hundred more people: steel workers, welders, machinists. These boats were all finished there and about every week or two a tug would arrive and tow a string of them, 8 or 10, out for delivery.

In our conversation recently you asked about women working in the yard. Besides the women in the office there were women security who worked in the so-called guard house, the entrance we came through, as we were required to wear a badge with our identification. Other women did clean-up work both on the boats and in the buildings. These were known as the "hurricane gang". Also, a nurse and several girls in a "so-called" cafeteria, really a coffee shop where we could get coffee, soda, bullion, rolls, etc. on our breaks there. We were allowed two breaks, one in each half of the shift. Another bit of trivia: when I said the rudder ports were installed before launching, on one hull, I remember, my partner and I worked `in the lazerettes and he brought fish line and bait and actually caught fish through the open rudder ports.

I'll give you the names of the only two, that I know, who still are around who worked in the yard whom you may contact if you wish, One is Dick Gattis and I'll give you their addresses, etc. on the paper. Dick worked in the joyner shop and probably had more to do with the (pilot) houses and finish work around and Henry A. Clarke, Jr. was the son of Henry, Sr. who was the foreman of the night crew. Henry worked in the drafting room but only in the early part of it because he left to go in the service sometime in 1942.

On the first YMSes, we knew nothing about any sonar gear except that a bunch of wires were left hanging, bundled together. Later on what looked like a small bathtub was brought in from the welding shop were it was built. The hull was hauled out and was cut through and the bathtub like container was fastened into place. Then plywood covers were bolted temporarily at both top and bottom, so that the boat could be put overboard again and the sonar gear could be installed from the inside. Once that was all done, the boats could be launched again and a diver could remove the bottom plywood cover or it could be removed while the hull was still on the ways. (Ed. Note: This enabled the sonar gear to operate as it could now be lowered below the bottom of the hull and used to send sound waves through the water to detect submarines that might be in range. When the sonar was not being used for this purpose it was pulled up inside the hull in the bathtub like container, for protective storage).

My Recollections of US Navy Minesweepers
Built at the Greenport Basin & Construction Company
in Greenport, New York during 1940 to 1945

By Edward A. Lademann, Jr., Southhold, NY

My father, Edward A. Lademann, was a Marine Electrical Engineer for the Smith Meeker Engineering Company of New York City, NY. He did all types of Marine electrical work on all types of vessels from the mid 1920's to the early 1950's, traveling as far away as Texas for his company in the late 1930's. In early

1940 he had to go to Greenport, L.I., NY to do work on a large yacht taken over by the US Navy, and at the same time his company received a contract for the new 96 foot AMS (AMc) Class Minsweepers to be built at the Greenport Basin & Construction Co. in Greenport.

At the time we were living on the western end of Long Island. My father knew he would be in Greenport for an extended time, so we moved to a nice home overlooking Greenport Harbor and the shipyard where the ships were being built. This was in April of 1941, prior to US involvement in World War 2. This was a beautiful place and you could see all the activities going on where the minesweepers were being built and tested in the harbor. He also bought us a small rowboat which I used daily to see what was going on in the shipyard.

Soon after we were settled there the GB&C Co. received a contract for the first of more than thirty to forty 136 foot YMS Class Minesweepers. I was in my very early teens and I remember my father bringing me to the shipyard and letting me be on the ships, many times, while they were being launched. I also had the fun of being on them several times while on the sea trials getting ready to be taken by the Navy.

My biggest thrill was when the YMS 183 was sponsored by our most famous singer, Kate Smith, and I was on it when it was launched and rode the railway into the water. After the launching I was brought up to see Kate Smith and received her autograph and she sang a few lines of "God Bless America" for me. There was never or will there ever be a singer who can sing that song like she did. This was a special occasion which I have never forgotten and will always remember. I was also on another ship that was sponsored by the late opera star Lily Pons when it was launched.

I really enjoyed the years while the minesweepers were being built and tested at GB&C Co. as it was a small part of the war effort done in a small village like Greenport. People came from all over to work on the minesweepers and the small landing craft which were built in Section 2 of the shipyard.

The Coast Guard Reserve also had many converted yachts stationed in Greenport at another shipyard close by and should be remembered for their important patrol duty. I got to know many of the crews as we ran errands for them while in port.

I really feel proud in writing about my experience of being on and around these minsweepers which did a very valuable service in the Navy in keeping our harbors free of any possible mines and also while being deployed overseas during combat operations to keep the combat ships safe from mines.

I will also note that in the early 1950's the Navy built a larger wooden hulled AM or AS Class Minesweeper at the Luders Marine Construction Co. in Stamford, Conn. and my father was in charge of the electrical work for his old company there also.

It is my hope that someday we can find a shipshape YMS and bring it to Greenport to use as a memorial to all the men and women who played a part in the construction of these ships at GH&C Co. It would be a nice tourist attraction for this small community as well as the preservation of a piece of history.

I appreciate very much being asked to write this for former Lt.jg John D. Davis and wish him the best of luck in getting his book out so that the story of what the minesweepers did will be told.

Good Luck to you John and "God Bless America".

Sincerely, Edward A Lademann, Jr. February 11, 2001

[Author's Note: Instructions for keeping the ship's log].

The narrative history of a U.S. Navy ship is written in the log book. Each day's events involving receiving or detacting of personnel, ship movement, courses, speeds, operations, health of crew, receiving stores, fuel, ammunition, etc. are to be recorded in the log. In the directions for keeping the log it is required that the log be kept by civil time (local as opposed to Greenwich). Entries shall be most carefully made in the remarks of every injury, accident, or casualty, however slight, to any member of the personnel giving particulars. When ships pass they will be noted in the remarks: if they make signals, note in the remarks. It is also required that the log be forwarded to the Commandant of the Naval District for approval at the end of the quarter and forwarded by him to the Bureau of Naval Personnel, Navy Department. The copy of the log forwarded to the Bureau of Naval Personnel shall be written in ink. (See End Note No. 38, p. 2).

The Commanding officers of all Naval vessels shall carefully attend to the keeping of the log, especially when the ship is newly commissioned.. Lt.jg King Upton certainly did in those first few months when the training of the crew to become a smoothly operating team was of paramount importance. His logs tell this story very well, and they were written in ink.

(Copy of Navy Press Release)

HEADQUARTERS OF THE
COMMANDANT THIRD NAVAL DISTRICT
FEDERAL OFFICE BUILDING, 90 CHURCH STREET
NEW YORK, NY

PUBLIC RELATIONS BUREAU

Immediate: 062342
Release: Public Relations Officer
Tel. Rector 2-9100
Extensions 743-747

NOTE TO EDITORS; Reporters & photographers may cover the launching of the YMS 183 upon presntation

of the usual credentials. The time of the launching will
be 6:00 P.M., EWT. The time of the launching is NOT
to be given out in advance of the event.

Kate Smith, radio star, will christen and sponsor the YMS 183, another minesweeper for the United States Navy, at the Greenport Basin & Construction Company in Greenport, L.I., N.Y, on Thursday, June 25, 1942.

Miss Smith will send the vessel down the ways to join the Navy's fleet of fighting ships in the Greenport yards before workers of the yard and Navy officials to begin a special double ceremony, which will also include the launching of the C4596, a tank lighter, sponsored by Louisa Corrozzo, Front street, Greenport, the wife of Angelo Corrozzo, a carpenter in the shipyard.

(30)

TMH:ce (10-1-2, 20, 30, 60, 80-5D.)
(This is a copy of a Leter of Commendation
received by the USS YMS 183)
CdS63/P20-1
Serial No. 101   COMMANDER DESTROYER SQUADRON 63   C/O Fleet
Post Office
San Francisco,
California
July 9, 1945
From:Commander Destroyer Squadron SIXTY-THREE.
To:Commander Minecraft, U.S. Pacific Fleet.

Subject:Performance of duty of Lieut. Comdr. M.T. Lambert, USNR,
Commander Mine Squadron 105, 20-27 June 1945.

> 1. Commander Destroyer Squadron SIXTY-THREE served as Task Group Commander for the KUME SHIMA Attack Group (Task Group 31.24) during the capture of that island on 26 June, 1945.

2. Although not under the command of Commander of Task Group 31.24, Lt. Comdr. Lambert, as Commander Task Unit 32.6.5, was assigned a minesweeping task by Commander Task Force 31 which required the closest cooperation between the Minesweeping Unit and the Attack   Group.
Lt. Comdr. Lambert was of the greatest assistance to Commander Task
> Group 31.24 in the planning of the operation by advising as to the best methods of minesweeping, and in shaping his plans to fit those of the Attack Group Commander. During the approach to the objective, Lt. Comdr. Lambert so skillfully navigated and maneuvered his Task Unit that the Attack Group was able to make its approach close behind the Sweeping Unit (YMS 183) and deploy into swept water at the objective exactly on schedule.

The YMS 183, of Lt. Comdr. Lambert's Task Unit, performed an out- standing mission by entering Shimajiri Wan through a narrow channel in the reef ahead of the vessels of the Attack Group, and conducting an exploratory sweep of the LST Area inside the Wan. The promptness and efficiency with which the YMS 183 carried out her assignment made possible the early entry of the LST's into Shimajiri Wan, the meeting of HOW hour at 0700 (high water) and contributed greatly to the success of the operation.

CHARLES A. BUCHANAN

Copy to: LT. Comdr. Lambert.
C.O. YMS-183

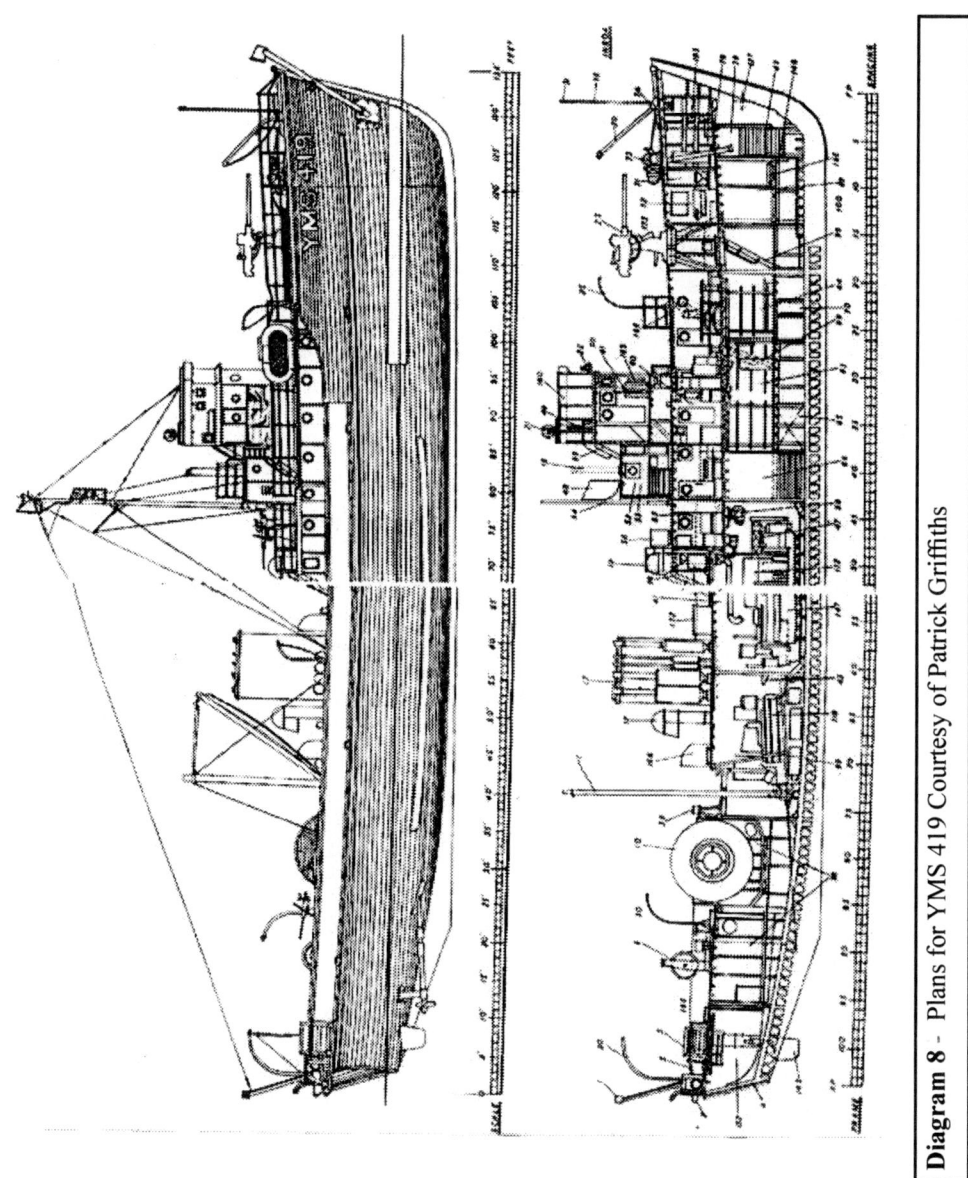

Diagram 8 - Plans for YMS 419 Courtesy of Patrick Griffiths

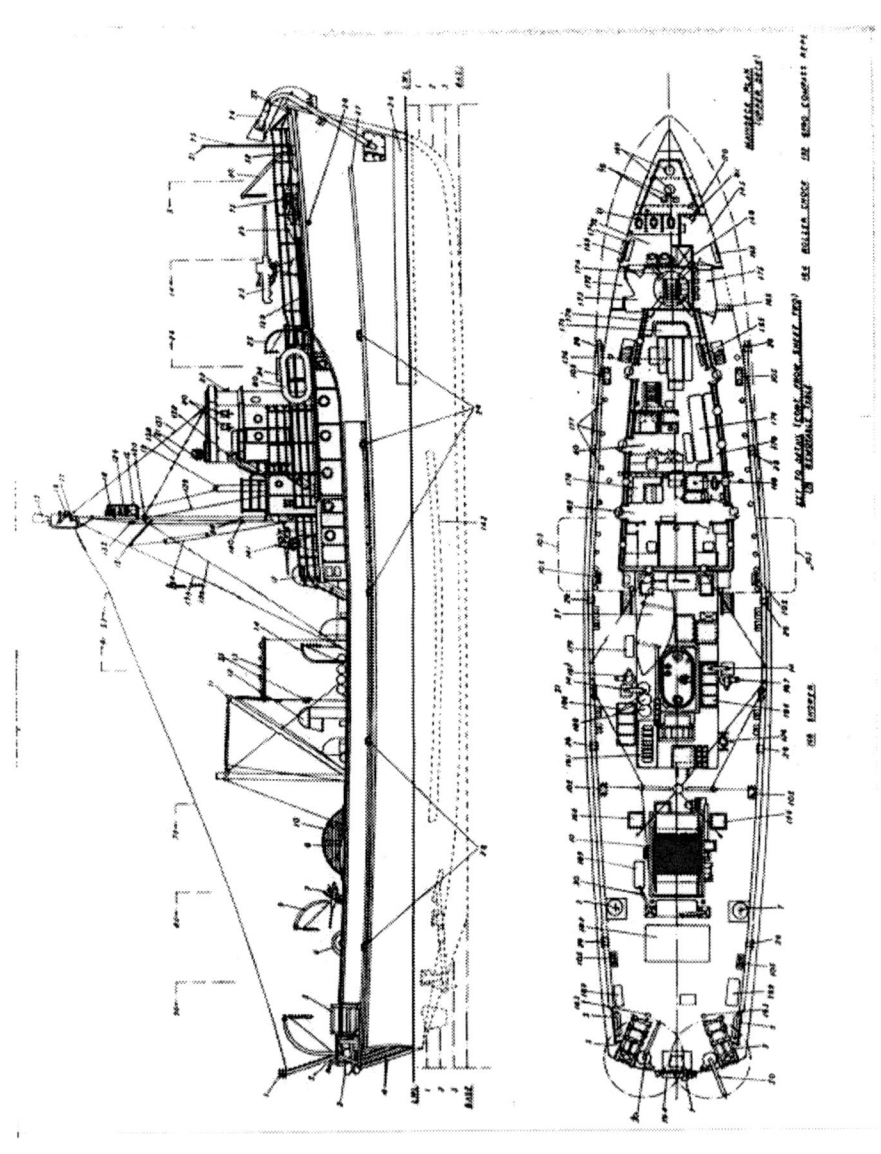

Diagram 9 - Plans for YMS 419 Courtesy of Patrick Griffiths

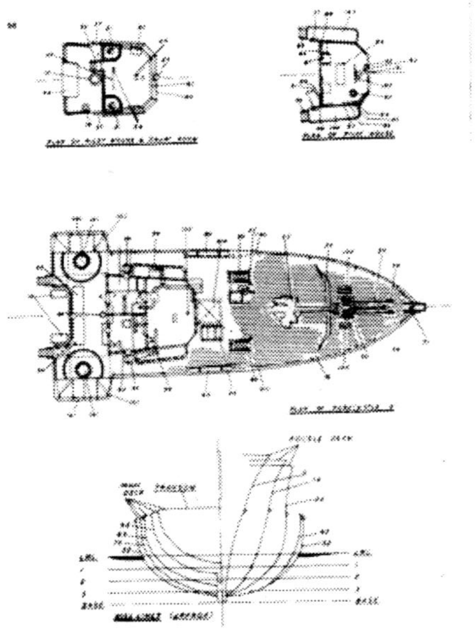

Diagram 10 Plans for YMS 419 Courtesy of Patrick Griffiths

No. 1, 1997

87

Key to Detail

1. Stern Light
2. M/S Rollers
3. Depth Charge Racks
4. Wooden Fenders
5. Otter & Depressor
6. Wire Winch
7. Twin .50 M.G. (Not R.N.)
8. Oropesa Float
9. Hatch Davit
10. LL Cable Reel
11. Boom
12. Vent Trunk
13. Diesel Exhaust
14. D.C. Davits
15. Radar Antenna
16. Station-Keeping Light
17. Upper Mast Band
18. Minesweeping Light
19. Antenna Trunk
20. Polarity Light
21. 12" Searchlight
22. Range Light
23. 3"/50 Cal. Gun
24. Ready-Use 3" Ammo.
25. 3" Ammo. Davit
26. Sheathing
27. Rubbing Strake
28. Fairlead
29. Breakwater
30. Davit
31. Anchor Light
32. Mooring Chock
33. Bow Chock
34. Acoustic Hammer
35. 500-Watt Floodlights
36. Steering Gear
37. Vertical Ladder
38. M/S Gear Stowage
39. LL Sweep Terminal Box
40. Engine Room
41. Generator Room
42. Access Door
43. Log Desk
44. Lube Oil Sump Tank
45. Lube Oil Clarifier
46. Ship's Svc. Switchboard
47. Starting Batteries
48. Flag Locker
49. Bulwark
50. Pilot House
51. Engine Controls
52. Chart House
53. Radio Room
54. Mast
55. C.O.'s Cabin
56. 20mm Ready-Use Locker
57. 12-Foot Dinghy
58. Steering Engine
59. Master Gyro Compass Rm.
60. Galley
61. Steering Stand & Wheel
62. Magnetic Compass
63. Seamen's Mess (18 men)
64. Seamen's Mess (11 men)
65. Fuel Tanks
66. Sound Room
67. Fresh Water Tank
68. 3" Gun Support
69. For'd Magazine
70. After Magazine
71. Crew's Head
72. Crew's Washroom
73. Electric Windlass
74. Chain Stopper
75. Jackstaff
76. Forecastle Deck
77. Main Deck
78. Chain Pipe
79. Chain Locker
80. Life Raft
81. W/T Door
82. Collapsible Shelf
83. Plywood Bulkhead
84. Voice-Pipe
85. Echo-Ranging Bridge Unit
86. Sparred Platform
87. Gyro Alarm Unit
88. Remote Control Unit
89. General Alarm
90. Sliding Panel
91. Radiophone Remote Control
92. Whistle Valve
93. Engine Room Telegraph
94. V.P. to C.O.'s Cabin
95. V.P. to Wardroom
96. V.P. to Gyro Room
97. V.P. Return
98. Axial Flow Fan
99. Inclined Ladder
100. Store Room
101. Chart Table
102. Steering Wheel Shaft
103. Hinged Gun Platform
104. Removable Deck Section
105. 6" Bitt
106. 3 Pipe Berths
107. 2 Pipe Berths
108. Master Gyro Room
109. Refrigerator
110. Refrig. & Dry Storeroom
111. Ship's Svc. Generator
112. Ship's Svc. Switchboard
113. CO_2 Cylinders
114. Distiller
115. Distiller Pump
116. Engineer's Store
117. Fire & Flushing Pump
118. Main Engine
119. Heating Boiler
120. Lube Oil Storage Tank
121. Hose Reel
122. Gauge Board
123. Special Svc. Air Compressor
124. Starting Air Tanks
125. Lube Oil Transfer Pump
126. Hand Pump
127. Acoustic Hammer Hinge
128. Masthead Light
129. Catch Net
130. Lower Mast Band
131. Gaff
132. Sidelight
133. Blinker Lights (P. & S.)
134. Recog. Light Fittings
135. Upper Aft Stay (P. & S.)
136. Lower Aft Stay (P. & S.)
137. Upper Forestay (P. & S.)
138. Lower Forestay (P. & S.)
139. Lower Shroud (P. & S.)
140. Lower Diamond Shroud
141. Single 20mm Oerlikon
142. Bilge Keel
143. Twin Rudders
144. Platform
145. Drying Room
146. Tank Space
147. LL Sweep Generator
148. Platform Deck
149. M/S Reel Well
150. Rudder Stop
151. Steering Quadrant
152. Steering Gear Compartment
153. Depth Charge Stowage
154. Space for M/S Winch & LL Reel Controllers
155. Shelves
156. Work Bench
157. Communication Booth
158. Diesel Transfer Pump
159. Foam Containers
160. Starting Air Compressors
161. Echo-Ranging Unit
162. Distiller Test Tank
163. Special Svc. Generator Switchboard
164. Lockers
165. Radiator
166. Hatch
167. W/T Bulkhead
168. Shower
169. Manhole
170. Windlass Controller Space
171. Urinal
172. Locker for Deck Gear
173. Vestibule
174. Gun Foundation
175. Ammo. Clip Storage
176. Removable Table
177. Stanchions
178. Seat
179. Stowage for "T" Cutters
180. Windscreen
181. 10-Man Liferaft
182. Wire Winch Seating
183. Emergency Tiller Deck Plate
184. Roller Chock
185. Wardroom
186. D/C Reload Rack for 4 D/Cs
187. D/C Thrower
188. Marker Buoy Stowage
189. 3" Ready-Use Ammo. Locker
190. Anchor Cable
191. Hinged Guardrail
192. Gyro Compass Repeater
193. Bosn's Store

Diagram 11 Key to detail for YMS 419 Courtesy of Patrick Griffiths

Mine Sweeper YMS-183

Mf. 24 enlisted men. 1/18/43

horized in accord. Max. War Effort Program. Keel laid March 28, 1942 at
enport Basin & Const. Co., Greenport, L. I. Date comp. per building yd.
/42. Fitting out yd. - New York. Launched June 25 at Greenport, N.Y.,
hips N.Y. 272030 of June '42. CNO Ser. 142338 Aug.4,1942, Com3 authorized to
ept, fit out and place in full commission, upon comp. fitting out and when
dy for sea report Cominch U.S. Fleet and ComEastSeaFron for shakedown and
erd routing. Acceptance trials successfully completed Jan. 4, Sub-BD Insurv
. mailgram 5 Jan. 1943. Accepted 14 Jan., Nyd. New York 142102 Jan. 1943.
ced in commission 15 Jan., Nyd. N.Y. 152048 Jan., 1943. Minesweeping Trials
mpleted, Com3 251932 Mar.'43. To report Eastseafron for temp. duty, Cominch 251645 Mar.'43.
orting for shakedown 4/2, YMS-183 021730 Apr.'43. Directed report CTG 02.3 for temp. duty,
~~EastSeaFron 022128 Apr.'43. Reported for temp.duty 4/5, YMS-183 041600 Apr.'43.~~
orted Com 3 for duty 4/14, Com3 141331 Apr.'43. Temporary duty completed 23 July
. To proceed to assigned station 3rd Fleet. CominCh conf. 231822 July.
parted N.D3 on 27 July 43 to assigned station 3rd Fleet. Com 3 conf.
2042 July.//On arr., Com 13 auth. decom., trans. MC or recc. I&S action.
NO Pl 141930 Feb 46.//Reporting to CWSF 17 Feb 46. YMS-183 Pl 172045 Feb 46.
Decommissioned 16 May 46, 13ND Pl 161934 ~~May 46.~~ Stricken 10 JUN 1947 Naval Regist[er]

[illegible] (NAME) — YMS 183 (NO) — Motor Minesweeper (CLASSIFICATION) — 3rd Fleet (ASSIGNMENT)

BUILT BY Greenport Basin & Construction Co ACQUIRED FROM
Greenport, L.I., New York, 1942-43 NObs511

ITEM	DATA	SOURCE
Material of Hull	Wood	
Length	136'	
Breadth	24' 6"	
Draft		
Displacement		
Capacity		
Propulsion	Diesel Reduction	
Contract No	NObs 511	
Contract Date	3-14-42	
Keel Laid	March 28, 1942 (YMS 183ser. 437221)	
Launched	June 25, 1942	(C-YS/A4-1)
Completed	1-14-43	
Delivered	1-14-43	
~~Commission~~ In service	Jan 15 1943	(YMS183)

ITEM	DATA	SOURCE
15. From Com 3 -- departed for assigned station 27 July 1943		3rd Fleet C-YMS 183 (11579)
16.		
17.		
18. Commissioned	Jan. 15, 1943	(YMS183)
19.		
20.		
21.		
22.		
23.		
24. Stricken	6-10-47	
25. Di Sur	2-20-48	13ND DR 2-29-48
26. Purchaser -	Imperial Tugboat Co.	
27.		
28.		

YMS 183

SHIPS INFORMATION
BUREAU OF SHIPS, PUBLICATION SEC.

Diagram 12 Status report regarding YMS 183 from beginning to end

Appendix E

Muster Roll of The Crew of YMS 183"

Name	Serial No.	Rate	Reported	Detached	Rate	Place Enlisted
Anderson, Alfred H.	611-73-13	S2/c	1/15/43	12/11/43	S/1c	Chicago, Ill.
Ayer, Myron E.	329-16-64	A.S.	1/15/43	3/9/45	QM3/c	Minneapolis, Minn.
Baker, Lonnie	279-62-26	PhM2/c	1/15/43	7/19/43	PhM1/c	Cincinnati, Ohio
Beaty, Quince E.	300-94-65	A.S.	1/15/43	9/2/45	BM1/c	Chicago, Ill.
Craft, William J.	257-78-28	GM2/c	1/15/43	12/11/43	GM 1/c	Baltimore, Md.
Daniels, Durwood T.	266-37-12	QM3/c	1/15/43	7/27/43	QM 2/c	Norfolk, Va.
Deshler, Finley A.	620-19-12	Y2/c	1/15/43			Des Moines, Iowa
Dickinson, Dwight S.	212-37-04	MM1/c	1/15/43			Springfield, Mass.
Donelly, Arthur W.	201-77-89	S2/c	1/15/43	7/31/44	Cox	Boston, Mass.
Enochs, Cooler	274-32-94	MM1/c	1/15/43	3/27/43	MM1/c	New Orelans, La.
Fenick, Harvey H.	638-84-71	S2/c	1/15/43			Minneapolis, Minn.
Hall, Bruce M.	267-86-33	BM1/c	1/15/43			Key West, Florida
Hall, Cyrus D.	360-02-27	EM1/c	1/15/43	2/16/45	CEM	Houston, Texas
McDaniel, Clarence E.	632-82-11	MM2/c	1/15/43	1/23/43	MM2/c	Los Angeles, Calif.
McFarland, Walter E.	207-33-93	GM3/c	1/15/43			New Haven, Conn.
Miller, Kenneth N.	238-81-14	S2/c	1/15/43	3/20/43	S1/c	Albany, New York
Morgan, Elmer Lee	375-94-68	MM2/c	1/15/43	9/14/43	MM2/c	San Francisco, Calif.
Mulford, Alexander, Jr.	647-23-29	F1/c	1/15/43	10/20/45	Mo2/c	New York, NY
Richard, A.J.	666-07-28	S1/c	1/15/43	9/2/45	QM 1/c	Springfield, Mass.
Roether, John T.	224-47-48	S1/c	1/15/43	2/16/45	BM1/c	New York, NY
Rosbury, Cecil H.	212-73-92	S1/c	1/15/43	12/09/43	COX	Springfield, Mass.
Schurts, Carl E.	410-25-64	MOM2/c	1/15/43	7/21/45	MM1/c	Cincinnati, Ohio
Schutt, Charles Earl	283-18-08	F1/c	1/15/43	12/09/43	MM2/c	Washington, DC
Smith, Charles P., Jr	274-38-34	SM2/c	1/15/43	7/21/45	C.S.M.	New Orleans, La.
Souza, Joseph (n)	204-73-37	A.S.	1/15/43	12/10/43	S1/c	Providence, R.I.
Styckiewicz, Joseph P.	212-62-02	SC3/c	1/15/43	6/29/43	SC 3/c	Springfield, Mass.
Welch, J.L.	201-62-67	S2/c	1/15/43	4/26/43	S1/c	Boston, Mass.
Williams, Samuel G.	656-10-89	EM3/c	1/15/43	12/18/43	EM 2/c	Raleigh, NC
Smith, Ralph R.	201-08-87	S1/c	1/16/43	1/23/43	S1/c	Portland, Maine
Verity, Harold W.,Jr.	642-72-30	S2/c	1/16/43	10/20/45	Mo1/c	New Haven, Conn.
Bula, Sigmund S.	707-94-45	F1/c	2/11/43			New York, NY
Kelly, Daniel P.	212-44-94	Cox	3/26/43	4/18/44	BM 2/c	Boston, Mass.
Baron, R.R.	706-97-25	S2/c	4/2/43	8/18/43	S 2/c	New York, NY
Gouge, Edward C.	244-60-11	F 1/c	4/6/43	4/19/43	F1/c	Temporary Duty
Shepherd, J.H.	656-29-41	S 1/c	4/12/43	4/19/43	S1/c	Temporary Duty
Blumenthal, Albert	709-50-33	F 1/c	4/14/43	12/9/43	F1/c	New York, NY

John Dixon Davis

Name	Serial No.	Rate	Reported	Detached	Rate	Place Enlisted
Boday, Sigmund S.	205-21-23	F 2/c	4/14/43	10/20/45	Mo2/c	Pawtucket, R.I.
Welch, J.L.	201-62-67	S 1/c	6/19/43	6/25/43	S1/c	Boston, Mass.
Krier, Jack		SC 3/c	6/25/43	07/9/43		
Freeman, M.D.	271-71-07	PH M2/c	7/18/43	30/4/44	Phm2/c	Birmingham, Ala.
Levesque, Lionel J.	202-31-75	SC 3/c	7/18/43	12/9/43	S3/c	Boston, Mass.
Hanson, Charles	810-09-60	S 2/c	7/27/43	8/05/43	S2/c	New York, NY
Daniels, Durwood	266-37-12	QM 2/c	8/05/43	12/09/43	QM 2/c	Norfolk, Va.
Linder, LY	634-45-43	SC 3/c	8/27/43			Louisville, Ky.
Flye, Horace N.	854-86-28	StM2/c	10/07/43	12/16/45	Stm1/c	Chicago, Ill.
Hankins, K.A.	564-97-29	F 2/c	12/09/43			Los Angles, Cal.
Schones, Robert	870-21-85	S 2/c	12/09/43	12/2/45	GM3/c	Minneapolis, Minn.
Sharp. Robert L.	866-26-28	S 2/c	12/09/43	7/21/45	SC2/c	Kansas City, Mo.
Stoker, Robert	868-46-34	S 2/c	12/12/43			Milwaukee, Wis.
Armstrong, E.C.	831-01-33	StM3/c	12/15/43	2/19/46	StM3/c	Jacksonville, Fla.
Stocks, Eugene	753-15-35	S 2/c	12/24/43	2/28/46	Cox	Springfield, Ill.
Clayton, Robert	347-15-77	F 2/c	1/01/44			Little Rock, Ark.
Voorhies, A.H., Jr.	412-49-49	GM 3/c	2/11/44	4/30/	GM 3/c	San Diego, Cal.
Putnam, Lewis	892-87-31	S 2/c	4/02/44	3/5/46	S 2/c	Spartanburg, S.C.
Hadley, J.A.	342-56-67	RM 3/c	4/18/44	2/19/46	RM3/c	Kansas City, Mo.
Schulte, Arthur W.	648-32-95	GM 2/c	4/18/44	10/20/45	GM2/c	Omaha, Nebr.
Worobey, Alexander	207-20-83	PH M2/c	4/30/44	9/02/44	PhM1/c	Bremerton, Wash.
Frederick, John A.	606-66-86	F1/cMo	5/25/44	12/26/45	Mo3/c	Camden, NJ
Foley, M.O.	853-99-55	SoM3/c	5/29/44	5/31/44	SoM3/c	Chicago, Ill.
Schlechter, W.H.	873-87-79	S 2/c	5/29/44	2/19/46	SM3/c	St. Louis, Mo.
Schultz, A. L.	887-89-84	S 2/c	5/29/44			San Francisco, Cal.
Zimmer, F.V.	872-87-21	S 1/c	5/29/44	3/5/46	Mo3/c	St.Louis, Mo.
Hill, John (Sam)	839-00-02	S 2/c	8/18/44			Birmingham, Ala.
Millet, Edward A.	663-04-45	PhM 1/c	8/18/44	8/26/45	PhM1/c	San Francisco, Cal.
Armstrong, James E.	923-27-46	F 2/c	10/03/44			(Illegible)
Blosser* E.E.	663-39-72	SoM3/c	2/09/45	10/20/45	SoM3/c	San Francisco, Cal.
Churchill, James W.	728-06-36	S 2/c	6/15/45			
Cornish, Billie L.	921-35-98	S 2/c	6/15/45	2/19/46	Mo1/c	Philadelphia, Pa.
Ferris, George E.	620-90-86	MoM1/c	7/24/45	8/26/45	Mo1/c	
Wieleba, Casmir (n)	622-86-94	GM2/c	7/24/45	12/16/45	GM2/c	Detroit, Michigan
Harris, C.L.	560-21-76	BM1/c	8/29/45	10/20/45	BM1/c	Charleston, W. Va.
Malloy, F. (n)	720-34-22	QM1/c	8/29/45	12/26/45	QM1/c	Philadelphia, Pa.
Murphy, J.F.	872-81-74	F1/cEM	8/29/45			St. Louis, Mo.
Del Rosso, Joseph N.	420-64-19	MoM2/c	9/21/45	3/5/46	Mo1/c	
Hampton, Malcom M.	832-70-39	MoM2/c	9/21/45	12/2/45	Mo2/c	Chattanooga, Tenn.
Smith, Donald E.	945-23-66	S1/c	9/21/45	12/16/45	S1/c	Rockford, Ill.

Name	Serial No.	Rate	Reported	Detached	Rate	Place Enlisted
Smoot, Thomas, E., Jr.	920-77-18	S1/c	9/21/45	3/5/46	S 1/c	
Borden, F.R.	614-31-95	GM2/c	10/06/45			
Clendrgin, L.D.	928-52-57	MoM3/c	10/06/45			
Pope, H.A.	385-71-14	EM3/c	10/06/45			
Blatt, Seymour	818-09-60	BM2/c	10/19/45	12/6/45	BM2/c	Philadelphia, Pa.
Elliott, C.P.	953-46-24	F2/c(EM)	10/19/45			Detroit, Michigan
Felten, Harold	721-24-70	PhM2/c	10/19/45	2/28/46	PhM2/c	Reno. Nevada
Preis, George J.	869-62-69	RdM2/c	10/19/45	12/16/45	RdM2/c	Milwaukee, Wis
Bobbin, Joseph Anthony	300-61-34	BM2/c T	28-Nov-45	5/2/46	BM2/c	Chicago, Ill.
Hardman, Ervin R.	756-39-42	S1/c	12/02/45			Charleston, W. Va
Morgan, Arthur William	756-71-95	RdM3/c	12/04/45			St. Louis, Mo.
Welsh, James S.	609-89-39	S 2/c	12/06/45			Buffalo, NY
Cranford, M.H.	264-47-12	S2/c	12/16/45	5/2/46	S2/c	Raleigh, NC
Hanbey, James R.	386-58-38	QM1/cT	12/16/45			Seattle, Wash.
Murray, Thomas James	715-09-22	S1/cQM	12/16/45	12/26/45	S1/cQM	Newark, NJ
O'Dell, E.R.	628-32-04	SM1/c	12/16/45	12/26/45	SM1.c	Chicago, Ill.
Wootan, Theo Carl	975-63-72	Cox (T)	12/26/45	2/19/46	Cox	Birmingham, Ala.
Keech, Thomas W.	928-03-30	QM3/cT	12/27/45	3/4/46	QM3/c	Baltimore, MD
Berg, A.H.	867-06-65	PhM2/c	2/26/46			
Burnette, J.C.	246-02-89	SC 3/c	2/26/46	5/1/46	SC3/c	
Hurwitz, M.L.	945-70-05	ETM3/c	2/26/46			
Reilly, R.J.	879-99-54	QM 2/c	2/26/46	5/3/46	QM2/c	
Samon, J.J.	841-55-30	Y 3/c	2/26/46	5/3/46	Y3/c	
Barkley, Earl L.	866-69-82	Y 2/c	3/01/46	5/3/46	Y2/c	
Smith, J.D.		S 2/c	3/06/46			
Owens, C.E.	358-74-73	F1/c	3/11/46	3/15/46	F 1/c	
Perry, A.A	964-53-53	Cox	3/11/46	3/15/46	Cox	
Smith, J.C.		S 1/c	3/11/46	3/15/46	S 1/c	
Widmer, R.E.	784-77-97	F1/c	3/11/46	3/15/46	F 1/c	
Andrus, D.D.	891-04-54	F 1/c	3/13/46			
Buie, Ivy	831-39-86	S 2/c	3/13/46			
Graham, W. R.	831-29-20	S 2/c	3/13/46			
Hachenberg, C.D.	671-87-70	Sm 3/c	3/13/46			
Wolf, L.A.	753-49-51	MoM3/c	3/13/46			
Bohrer, J.H.	317-23-47	RM3/c	4/22/46	5/1/46	RM3e/c	
Arterburn, K.L.	877-49-13	RdM 3/c	4/24/46	5/1/46	RdM3/c	
Gudakunst, P. (n)	313-75-62	MoM3/c	4/24/46	5/3/46	Mo3/c	
Lester, H.L.	756-13-69	S 1/c	4/24/46			
Mercer, A. D.	377-68-59	S 1/c	4/24/46			

John Dixon Davis

Name	Serial No.	Rate	Reported	Detached	Rate	Place Enlisted
Swartz, R.D.	285-64-64	MoM3/c	4/24/46	5/3/46	Mo3/c	
Williams, E.	377-68-59	StM1/c	4/24/46			
Fitzgerald, Richard O.	579-94-28	Cox	4/26/46			
Borkstrom, M.C.	381-41-56	SC 1/c	4/27/46			
Bellevue, P.E.	212-50-44	MoMM1/c	9/14/43	5/28/44	MoMM1	Springfield, Mass.
Coons, Homer D.	343-38-85	F 2/c	6/15/45			
Levesque, Laurent L.	806-75-90	S 2/c	6/25/43	7/21/45	GM3/c	Manchester, N.H.
Wright, Willie (n)	636-88-89	Matt3/c	1/15/43			Macon, Georgia
Gustafson, Frederick J.	607-37-61	S 3/c	12/24/43	12/31/43	S 3/c	Boston, Mass.
Clark, Howard Bruce	927-37-36	RT3/c(T)	9/25/45	2/28/46	RT3/c	
Klivans, James Monroe	949-60-84	SM3/c	9/25/45	2/19/46	SM2/c	Cleveland Ohio
Armstrong, James Simler	923-27-46	EM3/c		12/6/45	EM3/c	Johnstown, Pa.
Golladay, Marvin E.	603-09-57	PhM2/c		10/20/45	Phm1/c	Washington, DC
Hawkins, K.A.		Mo2/c		2/19/46	Mo2/c	
Ross, Donald	311-40-79	Mo3/c		2/17/46	Mo2/c	Detroit, Mich.

End Notes

1 *Webster's Collegiate Dictionary*, Fifth Edition(Springfield,Mass.S.A:G. & C. Merriam Co., Publishers), 1941, page 305.

2 Lott, Arnold S., Lt. Commander, U.S. Navy, *Most Dangerous Sea. A History of Mine Warfare and an Account of U.S. Navy Mine Warfare Operations in World War II and Korea.* (Annapolis, Maryland: U.S. Naval Institute, 1959). page vii.

3 Smith, Avery W., Editor, " Kate Smith Launching Big Success". *The Bowline* (Greenport, Long Island, N.Y. published by The Greenport Basin and Construction Company, Vol. 2, No. 11, July 3, 1942).

4 Still, William N., Jr., "Wooden Ship Construction in North Carolina in World War II." *The North Carolina Historical Review.* (Raleigh: North Carolina Division of Archives and History, Volume LXXVII, No. 1, January, 2000), page 37.

> (Note: It should be noted here for those not familiar with President Roosevelt's background and experience in government, he was also especially knowledgeable in matters concerning the armed forces and particularly the Navy. He came by this experience (which served him well when he became President) as a result of his own natural love for the water, for boats and ships. Even more importantly he was Assistant Secretary of the Navy in the administration of Woodrow Wilson. Josephus Daniels, of Raleigh, NC, was Secretary of the Navy and Roosevelt's boss during that period, 1913-1921). See: Taylor, Blaine, "Rehearsal For Glory, FDR As Assistant Secretary of the U.S Navy". *Sea Classics*. (Canoga Park, CA: Challenge Publications, Inc., Volume 3 Number 7, July 2000).

5 Goodwin, Doris Kearns, No Ordinary Time, Franklin and Eleanor Roosevelt: *The Home Front In World War II.* (New York: Simon & Schuster 1994) 9 - 39.

6 Stone, Herbert L., "Building The "Sweeps", *YACHTING*. (Concord, NH, Yachting Publishing Corporation, Vol. LXXII, No. IV, October, 1942) page 21.

7 Zinn, Franklyn K., "YMS versus AMC". *U.S. Naval Institute Proceedings.* (Annapolis, Maryland: U. S. Naval Institute, Volume 125, October 1999) p. 65.

8 Sutton, George W., Jr., "Here Come The YMS Sweepers", *Motor Boating*. (New York: Hearst Magazines, Inc., Vol.70, No. 4, October, 1942) p. 30.

9 *Ibid.*

10 One often sees the terms "boat" and "ship" used interchangeably. Technically a "boat" is any vessel that is not too heavy for a larger vessel to hoist aboard itself. If the vessel is too heavy for another vessel to hoist aboard, it is a "ship". The YMS at 300 plus tons was too heavy and thus was and always is a "ship."

11 Scripture, Fred, "YMS History And Specifications", *The Silent Defenders*. (New Holland, PA: Naval Mine Warfare Association, Summer 1999) p. 11.

12 See Appendix B

13 *Ibid.*

14 Scripture, Fred. *Loc. Cit.*

15 Sutton, *Op. Cit.* p. 85.

16 Sutton, *Op. Cit.* p.30

17 Lott, David N. "Canoe Club Navy". *Motor Boating.* (New York: Hearst Magazines, Inc. Vol. 73, No.4, April 1944). p.36.

18 Webb, Barry. Audio Tape Interviews with Monroe Burt and Sherrill Pemberton of Greenport. Long Island, NY.

19 Yost, Don. Audio Tape Interview with Emery Hanson of Coos Bay, Oregon, August, 2000.

20 Elliott, Peter. *Allied Minesweeping In WW2.* (Annapolis, Md: Naval Institute Press, 1979). pp. 77-78.

21 Hoyt, C. Sherman, Lt. Cmdr., USN. "Great Lakes Yards Humming!" *Yachting.* (Concord, N.H.: Yachting Publishing Corporation, Vol. LXXI, No. VI, June 1942). p. 23.

22 Sutton, *Op. Cit.* p.33.

23 Sutton, *Op. Cit.* p.31.

24 *Ibid*

25 Smith, Avery W. "Ships To Sweep The Sea Lanes". *Motor Boating.* (New York: Hearst Magazines, Inc., Vol. 70, No.4, October, 1942). p. 40.

26 Webb, Barry. *Op. Cit.* (Sherrill Pemberton interview)

27 Smith, Avery W., Editor, "Kate Smith Launching Big Success." *The Bowline.* (Greenport, Long Island, N.Y.: Published by The Greenport Basin and Construction Company,. Vol. 2, No. 11, July 3, 1942). p.1.

28 Smith. "Kate Smith Launching…", *Op. Cit.,* p. 6.

29 Smith. "Kate Smith Launching…", *Op. Cit.,* p. 1

30 Webb, Ida. Letters To The Author in 1999-2000.

31 Smith. "Kate Smith Launching…", *Op. Cit.,* p. 2.

32 Smith. "Kate Smith Launching…", *Op. Cit.,* p. 3.

33 Smith. "Kate Smith Launching…", *Op. Cit.,* p. 1.

34 Smith, Avery. "Ships To Sweep…", *Op. Cit.,* p. 39.

35 Webb, Barry. *Op. Cit.* (Monroe Burt interview).

36 *Ibid.* (Sherrill Pemberton interview).

37 Dill, J. Madison and Charlotte Ezell. Letters, Narratives, Emails and Telephone Conversations with the author, 1999, 2000, 2001.

38 *Navy Log Form* 16-29674-1

39 Cope, Harley F., Captain, USN. *Command At Sea.* (New York: W.W. Norton & Company, Inc. 1943). pp. 51 - 52.

40 *The Bluejackets Manual, United States Navy.* (Annapolis, Maryland: U.S. Naval Institute, Eleventh Edition, 1943). p. 67.

41 Cope. *Op. Cit.*, pp. 230-231.

42 Ibid, pp. 23 - 31.

43 Dill, *Op. Cit.*

44 *Op. Cit.*, pp. 93 - 94.

45 Bowditch, Nathanial, *American Practical Navigator* (Washington, DC: U.S. Government Printing Office, 1943) pp. 22 - 24.

46 Weltzien, Walter. Letters and conversations with the author.

47 Bowditch, *Op. Cit.* p. 173.

48 *Ibid*, pp. 140 - 141.

49 Lott, Arnold. *Op. Cit.* p. 135.

50 Clayton, Robert. Letters and conversation with the author.

51 CIA - *The World Factbook* - 2000. Articles on "Samoa" and "American Samoa".

52 Bowditch, *Op. Cit.* pp. 140 - 141.

53 Lott, Arnold. *Op. Cit.* p. 77.

54 "New Caledonia and Dependencies," Microsoft ® Encarta ®, Online Encyclodedia 2001. http://encarta.msn.com © 1997 -2001 Microsoft Corporation, All rights reserved. (page 128) CIA - The World Factbook - 2000. Article on New Caledonia.

55 "Tonga" http://www.vacations.tvb.gov.to/totapu.html

56 Lott, Arnold. *Op. Cit.* pp. 135-136.

> [Note: Certain of the following End Note References are to http://www.Ibiblio.org/hyperwar (Formated by Patrick Clancy). For those readers who use the internet these sources, marked with an (*), can be accessed by the following procedure:
>
> Write google in the internet or web address box – then click on Go;
>
> Write hyperwar in the google search box - then click on google search;
>
> Hyperwar, U.S. Navy in World War II, appears in the menu - Click on it;
>
> Ships of the U.S. Navy, 1940 - 1945 appears on the menu - click on it.
>
> Scroll down to the type, name and number of the ship (some have links for more information)].

57 CM 9, USS Monadnock (minelayer) (*)

58 CVE 78, USS Savo Island (*)

59 PC 1596 (Patrol craft) (*)

60 http://www.solomonsislands.com/?t=solomon/categories/history.txt Copyright 2000 World News.com

61 AF 23, USS Cygnus (provision store ship) (*)

62 Lott, Arnold. *Op. Cit.* p. 135 (page 145) Weltzien. Op. Cit.

63 Weltzien, *Op. Cit*,

64 *Ibid*

65 AGC 13, USS Panamint (Communications Command Ship) (*)

66 DE 35, USS Fair (*)

67 Lott, Arnold. *Op. Cit*. pp. 179-180.

68 12, USS Weehawken (minelayer) (*)

69 AO 71, USS Neshanic (fleet oiler) (*)

70 IX162, USS Lignite (provision ship) (*)

71 USS LCFF 790 (landing craft command ship) (*)

72 IX 113, USS Camel (oil tanker) (*)

73 ARL 10, USS Coronis (landing craft repair ship) (*)

74 CM 5, USS Terror.(minelayer) (*)

75 DM 18, USS Breese (minelayer) (*)

76 Lott, Arnold. *Op. Cit* . pp.233-234

77 SS Logan Victory, a commercial ammunition carrier, not a Navy ship)

78 DD 584, USS Halligan (*)

79 PGM 20 (motor gunboat) (*)

80 SC 686 (submarine chaser) (*)

81 AOG 10, USS Nemasket. (gasoline tanker) (*)

82 AV 10, USS Chandeleur (aircraft tender) (*)

83 DMS13, USS Hopkins (fast mine sweeper) (*)

84 SC 1004 (submarine chaser) (*)

85 PCS 1379 (submarine chaser on YMS hull, but not a minesweeper (*)

86 APH 2, USS Pinkney (an evacuation transport) (*)

87 See Also CM 5, USS Terror (*)

88 WPG 31, USS Bibb (Coast Guard command ship) (*)

89 AM 232, USS Execute (minesweeper) (*)

90 DM 29, HenryA.Wiley.(mine layer) (*)

91 ARG 9, USS Mona Island (repair ship) (*)

92 DD 779, USS Douglas H. Fox (*)

93 AO 4, USS Brazos (fleet oiler) (*)

94 http://www.history.Navy.Mil/faqs/faq102-1.htm

95 http://www.lbiblio.org/hyperwar/USN/USN-Chron/USN-1945.html (Scroll down to July 5, 1945 - East China Sea Sweep)

96 AKA 101, USS Ottawa; DD 349, USS Dewey. (*)

97 Bowditch, *Op. Cit* ., p.263. (*)

98 ACM 8, USS Picket (auxiliary minelayer) (*)

99 ATR 81 (rescue tug) (*)

100 CA 72, USS Pittsburg's bow in Apra Harbor (*)

101 CA 35, USS Indianapolis (*)

102 Morison, S.E., *Op. Cit.*, p.520

103 *Ibid*, p.571

104 www.history.Navy.mil/faqs/faq69-2.htm

105 *Op. Cit.,* 102-6.htm (Typhoon Louise)

106 *Ibid*

107 *Ibid*

108 *Ibid*. (YMS 90)

109 Morison, S.E., *Op. Cit.,* p. 472.

110 Lott, *Op Cit.*, pp. 224-228.

111 *Op. Cit.,* p. 258.

112 *Op. Cit.,* p. 258.

113 *Cit.*, p. 257. (See also: AM 371, USS Minevet. (*))

John Dixon Davis

Bibliography

Allen, Thomas B. and Polmar, Norman. *Code-Name Downfall, The Secret Plan To Invade Japan-And Why Truman Dropped The Bomb.* (New York: Simon & Schuster. 1995).

The Bluejackets Manual, United States Navy. (Annapolis, Maryland: Eleventh Ed.U.S Naval Institute, 1943).

Bovbjerg, Richard V. *Steaming As Before.* (Bethesda, MD: International Scholars Publications. 1994).

Bowditch, Nathaniel, LLD. *American Practical Navigator, An Epitome Of Navigation And Nautical Astronomy.* (Washington: United States Printing Office. 1943).

Clayton, Robert. Letters, Emails and Telephone Conversations with author concerning YMS 183.

Cope, Harley F., Captain, U.S.N. *Command At Sea.* (New York: W.W. Norton & Company, Inc. 1943).

Deck Log of USS YMS 183, January 15, 1943 – May 16, 1946

Dictionary of American Naval Fighting Ships, Vol. V (Washington, D.C.: Navy Department, History Division, 1970.)

Dill, J. Madison and Charlotte Ezell Dill. Letters, Narratives, Emails and Telephone Conversations with the author, 1999, 2000, 2001.

Elliott, Peter. *Allied Minesweeping in World War 2.* (Annapolis, Md.: Naval Institute Press, 1979).

Frederick, Donald. Audio Tape, Letters and Telephone Conversations with the author 2000 and 2001. (Mr. Frederick, of Southold, NY, was a carpentry expert at the Greenport Basin & Construction Co. during WWII).

Gerken, Louis C., *Mine Warfare Technology,* (Chula Vista, CA: American Scientific Corp. 1989).

Goodwin, Doris Kearns. *No Ordinary Time, Franklin and Eleanor Roosevelt: The Home Front In World War II.* (New York: Simon & Schuster 1994).

Griffiths, Maurice. *The Hidden Menace.* (Greenwich, England: Conway Maritime Press 1981).

Griffiths, Patrick. "History of the BYMS Part 1". *Warship International.* (Toledo, Ohio: The International Naval Research Organization, Inc., Vol. XXXIV, No. 1, 1997).

Griffiths, Patrick "History of the BYMS Part 2". *Warship International.* (Toledo, Ohio: The International Naval Research Organization, Inc., Vol. XXXIV, No. 2, 1997)

Hanson, Richard, Monograph *The Ultimate Fate of YMS. 183.* (Mailed to J. Madison Dill in 1992 by Richard Hanson).

Hartmann, Gregory K., *Weapons That Wait, Mine Warfare in The U. S. Navy.* (Annapolis, MD: Naval Institute Press, 1979).

Hoyt, C. Sherman, Lt. Cmdr., USN. "Great Lakes Yards Humming!" *Yachting.* (Concord, N.H.: Yachting Publishing Corporation, Vol. LXXI, No. VI, June 1942).

Jane's Fighting Ships. (1944/45 Edition).

Levie, Howard S. *Mine Warfare At Sea.* (Boston: Martinus Nijhoff Publishers, 1992).

Lott, Arnold S., Lt Commander, U.S. Navy. *Most Dangerous Sea.* A History of Mine Warfare and an Account of U.S. Navy Mine Warfare Operations in World War II and Korea. (Annapolis, MD: U.S. Naval Institute, 1959).

Lott, David N. "Canoe Club Navy". *Motor Boating.* (New York: Hearst Magazines, Inc. Vol. 73, No. 4, April 1944).

Morison, Samuel Eliot. *History Of United States Naval Operations In World War II, Volume XIV, Victory in the Pacific 1945.* (Boston: Little, Brown and Company. 1960).

Morison, Samuel Eliot. *History Of United States Naval Operations In World War II, Volume XV, Supplement and General Index.* (Boston: Little, Brown and Company, 1962).

Morison, Samuel Loring, *Guide To Naval Mine Warfare.* (Arlington, Virginia: Pasha Publications, Inc., 1995).

Navy Log Form 16-29674-1.

Scripture, Fred, "YMS History And Specifications", *The Silent Defenders.* (New Holland, PA: Naval Mine Warfare Association, Summer 1999).

Smith, Avery W., Editor, "Kate Smith Launching Big Success." *The Bowline.* (Greenport, Long Island, N.Y.: Published by The Greenport Basin and Construction Company,. Vol. 2, No. 11, July 3, 1942).

Smith, Avery W., Editor, "Admiral's Wife Sponsors YMS 184." *The Bowline.* (Greenport, Long Island, N.Y.: Published by The Greenport Basin and Construction Company, Vol 2, No. 13, July 30, 1942).

Smith, Avery W. "Ships To Sweep The Sea Lanes." *Motor Boating.* (New York: Hearst Magazines, Inc., Vol. 70, No. 4, October, 1942).

Still, William N., Jr., "Wooden Ship Construction in North Carolina in World War II." *The North Carolina Historical Review.* (Raleigh: North Carolina Division of Archives and History, Volume LXXXVII. No. 1, January, 2000).

Stone, Herbert L., "Building The Sweeps." *YACHTING.* (Concord, NH: Yachting Publishing Corporation, Vol. LXXII, No. IV, October, 1942).

Sutton, George W., Jr. "Here Come The YMS Sweepers." *Motor Boating.* (New York: Hearst Magazines, Inc. Vol. 70, No.4, October, 1942).

Webb, Barry. Audio Tape Interviews with Monroe Burt and Sherrill Pemberton of Greenport, Long Island, NY.

Webb, Ida. Letters To The Author

Yost, Don. Audio Tape Interview with Emery Hanson of Coos Bay, Oregon.

Zinn, Franklin K. "YMS Versus AMC" *US Naval Institute Proceedings* (Annapolis, Maryland. U.S. Naval Institute, Volume 125 October, 1942)

About the Author

Author Davis was a crewmember of USS YMS 183 and served aboard her for 14 months. He joined the Navy V7 program and attended Naval mine warfare school. After growing up in the town of Beaufort, North Carolina, and being near the ocean; it was a natural thing for him to join the Navy. It should also be noted that his brother was serving simultaneously on board YMS 362. A fascinating point in their lives was when they rendezvoused at Ulithi Anchorage.

CPSIA information can be obtained at www.ICGtesting.com
Printed in the USA
LVOW110218300413

331538LV00001B/6/A